GEOGRAPHICAL ATLAS
OF THE WORLD

Designed and produced by Engineering Surveys Reproduction Ltd

Cartographic Design and Production Manager
Keith Brook

Senior Cartographic Editor
Zoë Goodwin

Cartographic Editor
Lindsay Evans

Cartographers
Nicky Chapman
Mike Larby
Gill Dalton
David Handley-Clarke
Chris Major

Cartographic Consultant
Allan Marles

Cartographic Illustrator
Janos Marffy

Illustrator
Tom McArthur

The publishers wish to thank all those involved in the production of
this atlas, and in particular the photo technicians at ESR Ltd, Richard
Ross, John Gill, Michael Hodson Designs, Apollo Colour Repro Ltd,
E.S. Computing Ltd, Typogram Ltd, and Link-Line Ltd.

This 1992 edition published by Tiger Books International PLC, London
Copyright ©1989 Colour Library Books Ltd, Godalming, Surrey
First revision 1991
Second revision 1992
Printed and bound in Spain by Graficromo, S.A.

ISBN 1-85501-219-7

GEOGRAPHICAL ATLAS OF THE WORLD

Foreword by WILLIAM R. MEAD

Professor Emeritus of Geography at
University College London

TIGER BOOKS INTERNATIONAL
LONDON

FOREWORD

In 1636 a bound collection of maps was published by Gerard Mercator and John Hondt with a frontispiece illustrating the titan Atlas bearing the world on his shoulders. As a result, the word 'atlas' entered the vocabulary as a synonym for a book of maps. In the seventeenth century only the very rich could afford the luxury of an atlas. Cartographic masterpieces by Dutch map engravers offered their patrons the first view of a world the horizons of which were being swiftly broadened by maritime discovery.

Today, most households can afford an atlas even if they do not own one. Certainly, the need for and the attraction of the atlas have never been greater. Never have so many people been on the move around the world. Never have so many been concerned with the impact of world events. 'Atlas-eaters', Dylan Thomas called those who were hungry for world news. The atlas, through its co-ordinates of latitude and longitude, can answer the question 'Where?'. Or, perhaps, more precisely, the index to the atlas provides the answer – hence the importance of the extended index to the Atlas of the World.

In an atlas, the science of map-making is married to the art of map presentation. Techniques of production are increasingly refined; sources of information are increasingly precise. Satellite imagery, photogrammetry and computerisation have transformed map production. Most of the Atlas of the the World consists of topographical maps, with our own respective home areas receiving generous treatment. The thematic maps of the introductory section, necessarily selective in the topics that they treat, offer perspectives on the world distribution of a number of critically important phenomena.

An atlas is no substitute for a globe. The two are complementary, for not even the larger globes can include a fraction of the information that is packed into an atlas. The task of projecting the globe onto a flat surface has taxed the ingenuity of mathematicians since the Greeks first attempted to measure the circumference of the Earth. The variety of formidably-named projections employed in the Atlas of the World illustrates the extended range of options available to present-day cartographers.

Atlases have a romantic appeal as well as a utilitarian value. The novelist Alan Sillitoe, in a memorable essay on maps, recalls the flights of fancy set in motion by his 'first cheap layer-tinted atlas'. To turn the pages of the Atlas of the World – to contemplate the controlling features of land and sea, to reflect upon the boundaries that define the outlines and shape the destinies of countries and to respond to the magic of the infinity of place-names – is to experience a stimulus to the imagination as well as to the intellect.

William R. Mead
PROFESSOR EMERITUS OF GEOGRAPHY, UNIVERSITY COLLEGE LONDON.

CONTENTS

Foreword   5

Contents   6-7

Continents and Nations of the   8-9
World

AN INSIGHT TO OUR WORLD

The Solar System   10-11

Earth and Moon   12-13

Moving Continents   14-15

The Earth's Landscape   16-17

The Atmosphere   18-19

Evolution of Life   20-21

Exploration and Discovery   22-23

Organisations and Affiliations   24-25

Population   26-27

Health   28-29

Education and Work   30-31

Land Use   32-33

Food   34-35

Energy and Minerals   36-37

Trade   38-39

Wealth and Debt   40-41

THE WORLD IN MAPS

Map Legend   42

Regional Map Coverage   43-47

The World (Atlantic centred)   48-49
1:85,000,000

EUROPE

Europe   50-51
1:12,500,000

Southern England and Wales   52-53
1:1,175,000

Northern England and Northern   54-55
Ireland
1:1,175,000

Scotland   56-57
1:1,175,000

Ireland   58-59
1:1,000,000

British Isles and Central Europe   60-61
1:5,000,000

Scandinavia and the Baltic   62-63
1:4,500,000

Benelux and France   64-65
1:3,000,000

The Iberian Peninsula   66-67
1:3,000,000

Italy, Switzerland and Austria   68-69
1:3,000,000

Germany, Poland and   70-71
Czechoslovakia
1:3,000,000

Yugoslavia, Hungary, Romania   72-73
and Bulgaria
1:3,000,000

Greece and the Aegean   74-75
1:3,000,000

Turkey   76-77
1:3,500,000

Eastern Europe   78-79
1:8,000,000

ASIA

Northern Asia 80-81
1:17,000,000

Southern Asia 82-83
1:25,000,000

Russia 84-85
1:11,500,000

China, Mongolia, North and 86-87
South Korea
1:11,500,000

Japan 88-89
1:4,500,000

South-east Asia 90-91
1:12,000,000

Indian Subcontinent 92-93
1:10,500,000

Middle East 94-95
1:6,000,000

Arabian Peninsula 96-97
1:6,000,000

AFRICA

Africa 98-99
1:23,000,000

North Africa 100-101
1:9,000,000

North-east Africa 102-103
1:9,000,000

West Africa 104-105
1:9,000,000

Equatorial Africa 106-107
1:9,000,000

Southern Africa 108-109
1:9,000,000

AUSTRALASIA

Australasia 110-111
1:19,000,000

Australia 112-113
1:10,500,000

New Guinea and Pacific Isles 114
1:5,000,000 and 1:11,500,000

New Zealand 115
1:4,500,000

THE AMERICAS

North America 116-117
1:20,000,000

Alaska and Western Canada 118-119
1:9,000,000

Eastern Canada 120-121
1:9,000,000

North-west U.S.A. 122-123
1:5,000,000

North-east U.S.A. 124-125
1:5,000,000

South-west U.S.A. 126-127
1:5,000,000

South-east U.S.A. 128-129
1:5,000,000

Mexico 130-131
1:6,500,000

Central America and the 132-133
Caribbean
1:7,000,000

South America 134-135
1:16,000,000

Northern South America 136-137
1:11,000,000

Southern South America 138-139
1:11,000,000

POLAR REGIONS

The Arctic 140
1:30,000,000

The Antarctic 141
1:30,000,000

The World (Pacific centred) 142-143
1:85,000,000

INDEX

Glossary and Abbreviations 144-145

Index 146-272

CONTINENTS AND NATIONS OF THE WORLD

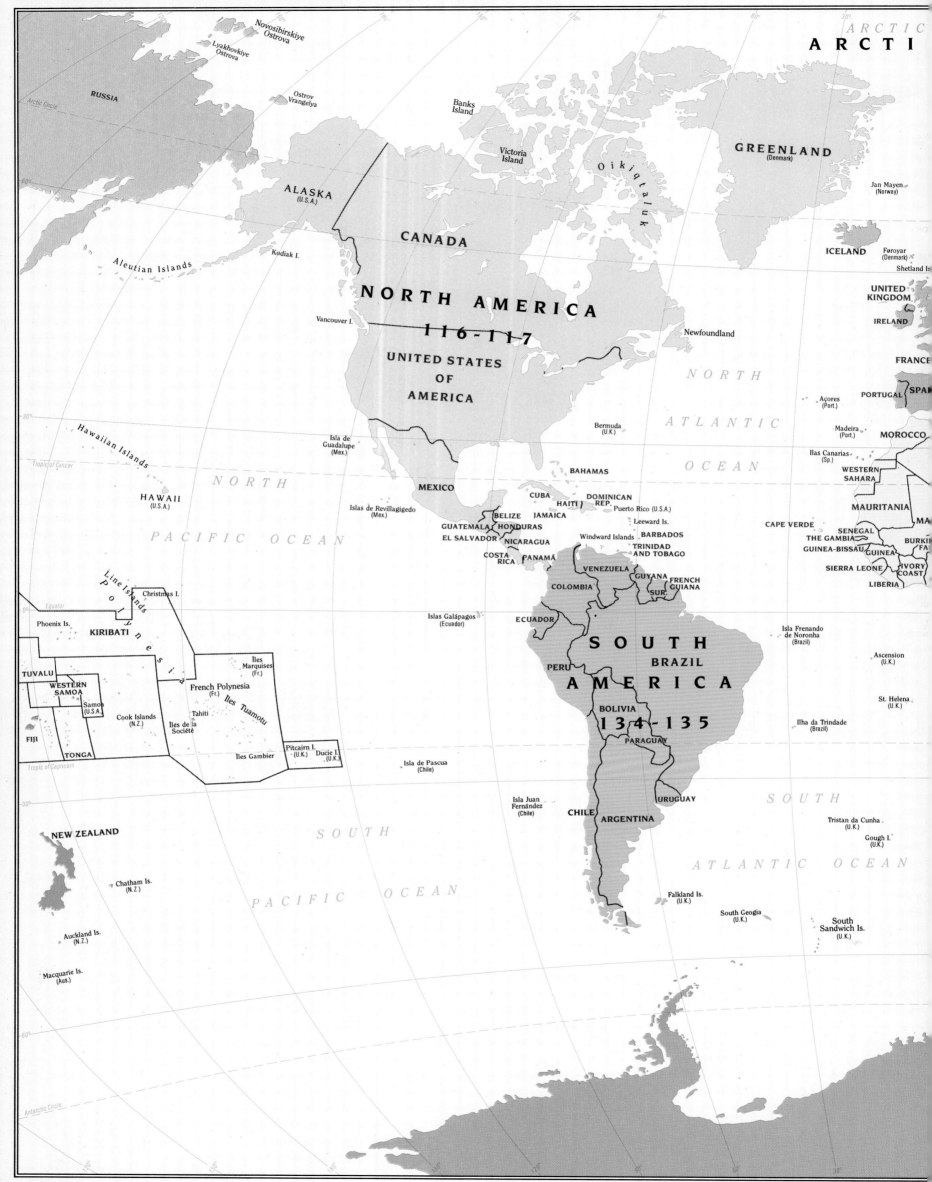

ARCTIC

RUSSIA

Novosibirskiye Ostrova

Lyakhovkiye Ostrova

Ostrov Vrangelya

Banks Island

GREENLAND
(Denmark)

Jan Mayen
(Norway)

ALASKA
(U.S.A.)

Victoria Island

Oikiqtaluk

ICELAND

Føroyar
(Denmark)

Shetland Is.

Arctic Circle

Aleutian Islands

Kodiak I.

CANADA

UNITED
KINGDOM

IRELAND

Vancouver I.

NORTH AMERICA
116-117

UNITED STATES
OF
AMERICA

Newfoundland

NORTH

ATLANTIC

OCEAN

FRANCE

PORTUGAL

SPAIN

Açores
(Port.)

Isla de
Guadalupe
(Mex.)

Bermuda
(U.K.)

Madeira
(Port.)

MOROCCO

Tropic of Cancer

HAWAII
(U.S.A.)

NORTH

Hawaiian Islands

PACIFIC OCEAN

MEXICO

Islas de Revillagigedo
(Mex.)

BAHAMAS

CUBA
HAITI

DOMINICAN
REP.

Puerto Rico (U.S.A.)

JAMAICA

Leeward Is.

Ilas Canarias
(Sp.)

WESTERN
SAHARA

MAURITANIA

CAPE VERDE

MA

GUATEMALA
EL SALVADOR

BELIZE
HONDURAS

NICARAGUA

Windward Islands

BARBADOS

SENEGAL
THE GAMBIA

BURKINA
FA

COSTA
RICA

PANAMA

TRINIDAD
AND TOBAGO

GUINEA-BISSAU

GUINEA

VENEZUELA

GUYANA

FRENCH
GUIANA

SIERRA LEONE

IVORY
COAST

LIBERIA

COLOMBIA

SUR.

Line Islands

Christmas I.

Polynesia

Islas Galápagos
(Ecuador)

ECUADOR

Isla Frenando
de Noronha
(Brazil)

Equator

Phoenix Is.

KIRIBATI

PERU

SOUTH

BRAZIL

Ascension
(U.K.)

Iles
Marquises
(Fr.)

TUVALU

WESTERN
SAMOA

Samoa
(U.S.A.)

French Polynesia
(Fr.)

Iles Tuamotu

AMERICA
134-135

BOLIVIA

St. Helena
(U.K.)

FIJI

Cook Islands
(N.Z.)

Tahiti

Iles de la
Société

PARAGUAY

Ilha da Trindade
(Brazil)

TONGA

Iles Gambier

Pitcairn I.
(U.K.)

Ducie I.
(U.K.)

Isla de Pascua
(Chile)

URUGUAY

SOUTH

Tropic of Capricorn

Isla Juan
Fernández
(Chile)

CHILE

ARGENTINA

Tristan da Cunha
(U.K.)

Gough I.
(U.K.)

NEW ZEALAND

ATLANTIC OCEAN

Chatham Is.
(N.Z.)

SOUTH

Falkland Is.
(U.K.)

South Geogia
(U.K.)

South
Sandwich Is.
(U.K.)

Auckland Is.
(N.Z.)

PACIFIC OCEAN

Macquarie Is.
(Aus.)

Antarctic Circle

West of Greenwich

1:73,000,000 (Scale at the Equator)

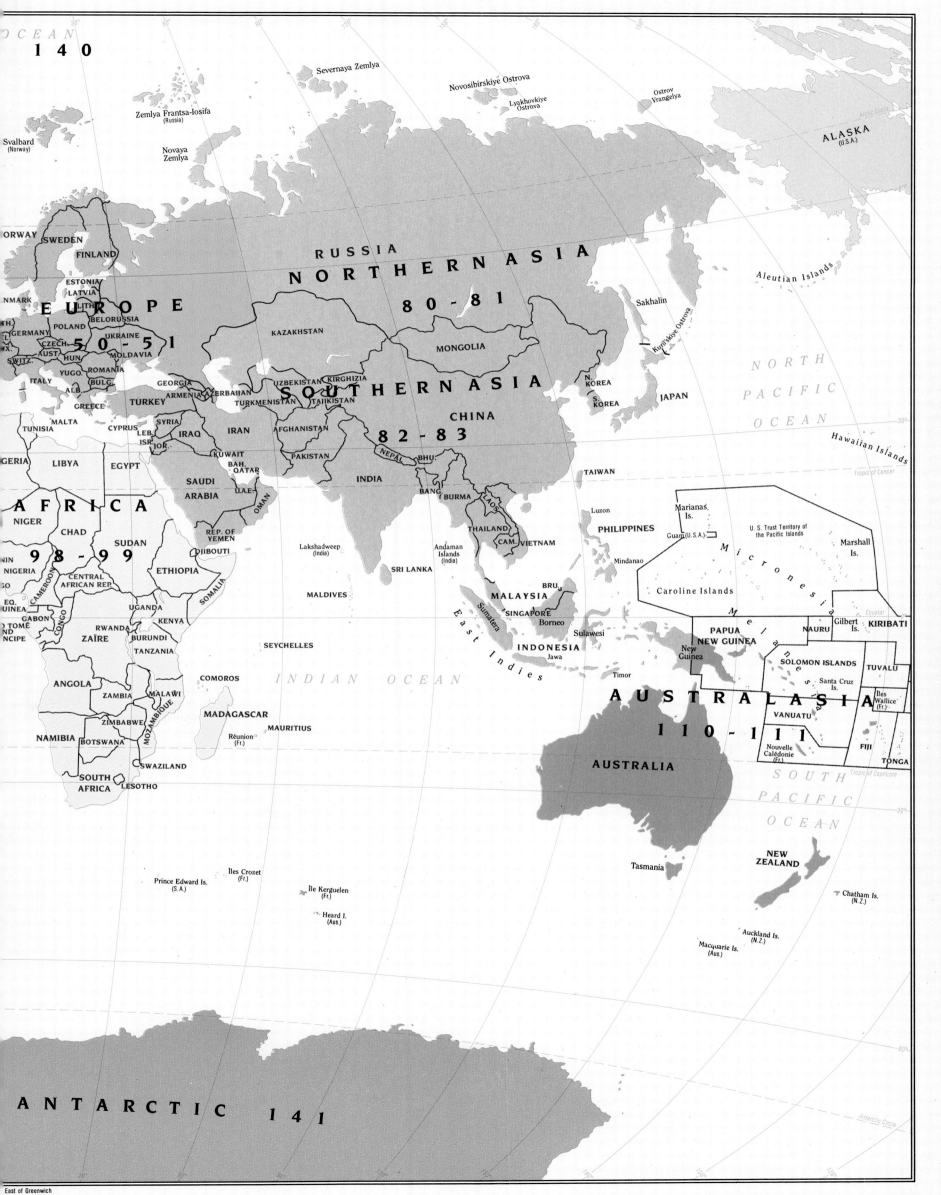

OCEAN

Svalbard
(Norway)

Zemlya Frantsa-Iosifa
(Russia)

Novaya
Zemlya

Severnaya Zemlya

Novosibirskiye Ostrova

Lyakhovskiye
Ostrova

Ostrov
Vrangelya

Arctic Circle

ALASKA
(U.S.A.)

ORWAY
SWEDEN
FINLAND

NMARK

ESTONIA
LATVIA
LITH.

BELORUSSIA

EUROPE
GERMANY   POLAND
50-51
CZECH   UKRAINE
AUST.   HUN.
SWITZ.   MOLDAVIA
ITALY   ROMANIA
ALB.   BULG.
GREECE
MALTA
CYPRUS
TUNISIA

RUSSIA

NORTHERN ASIA

80-81

KAZAKHSTAN

MONGOLIA

Aleutian Islands

Sakhalin

Kuril'skiye Ostrova

SOUTHERN ASIA

UZBEKISTAN   KIRGHIZIA
GEORGIA
ARMENIA AZERBAIJAN
TURKEY   TURKMENISTAN TAJIKISTAN
SYRIA
LEB.   IRAQ   IRAN   AFGHANISTAN
ISR. JOR.
KUWAIT
BAH.
QATAR   PAKISTAN
U.A.E.

CHINA

82-83

N.
KOREA
S.
KOREA

JAPAN

NORTH

PACIFIC

OCEAN

Hawaiian Islands

Tropic of Cancer

GERIA
LIBYA
EGYPT

SAUDI
ARABIA

OMAN

INDIA

NEPAL
BHU.
BANG.
BURMA
LAOS

TAIWAN

AFRICA
NIGER
CHAD   SUDAN
98-99
NIGERIA
CAMEROON CENTRAL
AFRICAN REP.
EQ.
GUINEA
GABON   CONGO   ZAIRE
TOMÉ
AND
NCIPE

REP. OF
YEMEN

DJIBOUTI

ETHIOPIA

SOMALIA

UGANDA
KENYA
RWANDA
BURUNDI
TANZANIA

Lakshadweep
(India)

Andaman
Islands
(India)

SRI LANKA

MALDIVES

THAILAND

CAM. VIETNAM

Luzon

PHILIPPINES

Mindanao

Marianas
Is.

Guam (U.S.A.)

Micronesia

U.S. Trust Territory of
the Pacific Islands

Marshall
Is.

MALAYSIA
SINGAPORE
Sumatera
Borneo
BRU.

Melanesia

Caroline Islands

Equator

SEYCHELLES

INDIAN   OCEAN

East Indies

INDONESIA
Jawa
Sulawesi
Timor

New
Guinea

PAPUA
NEW GUINEA

NAURU

Gilbert
Is.

KIRIBATI

COMOROS

MADAGASCAR

MAURITIUS

Réunion
(Fr.)

ANGOLA
ZAMBIA
MALAWI
ZIMBABWE
MOZAMBIQUE
NAMIBIA
BOTSWANA
SWAZILAND
SOUTH
AFRICA   LESOTHO

SOLOMON ISLANDS

Santa Cruz
Is.

TUVALU

AUSTRALASIA

110-111

VANUATU

Nouvelle
Calédonie
(Fr.)

Iles
Wallice
(Fr.)

FIJI

TONGA

SOUTH

PACIFIC

OCEAN

Tropic of Capricorn

AUSTRALIA

Tasmania

**NEW
ZEALAND**

Iles Crozet
(Fr.)

Prince Edward Is.
(S.A.)

Ile Kerguelen
(Fr.)

Heard I.
(Aus.)

Auckland Is.
(N.Z.)

Chatham Is.
(N.Z.)

Macquarie Is.
(Aus.)

ANTARCTIC   141

Antarctic Circle

Designed and produced by E.S.R.

THE SOLAR SYSTEM

Modern scientific and astronomical studies have increased our knowledge of the universe and the Earth's place within it immensely. Space exploration has solved many mysteries, but there is still much to be learnt.

The Earth is one of nine planets and numerous smaller bodies that orbit the Sun. The Sun is part of a much larger group of perhaps 100 billion stars that make up the Milky Way. This in turn is only one of the billions of galaxies in an incomprehensibly large universe.

Orbiting the Sun
Under the control of the Sun's gravitational force each planet maintains an elliptical orbit. Except for Mercury and Pluto, which are inclined 7° and 17° respectively, the orbits of the other planets lie within 3° of the plane of the Sun's equator.

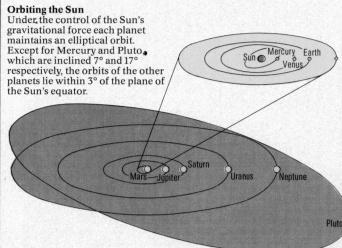

	Sun	Mercury	Venus	Earth	Mars	Jupiter	Saturn
Distance from the Sun (mean) millions of km	-	57·9	108·2	149·6	227·9	778·3	1427
Orbit (sidereal period) days		88	224·7	365·25	687	4332·5	10759·2
Rotation d=days hr=hours	24·6d	58·65d	243d	23·93hr	24·62hr	9·8hr	10·2hr
Orbital inclination	-	7°	3°23'	0°	1°52'	1°18'	2°29'
Equatorial diameter km	1392530	4878	12104	12756	6787	142800	120600
Mass (Earth=1)	333000	0·055	0·815	1 5·97x10²⁴kg	0·012	317·8	92·2
Density (water=1)	1·41	5·43	5·24	5·52	3·94	1·32	0·7
Number of satellites	-	0	0	1	2	16	17

The Sun is a huge, brilliant star at the centre of the Solar System. It is thought to be about five billion years old; halfway through its stable period of existence. The source of the Sun's immense energy is the continuous fusion of hydrogen into helium. Temperatures in the photosphere can reach 5500°C. Above the photosphere lies the chromosphere, the top layer of which contains numerous spicules that reach into the lower corona. The corona extends far beyond the Sun and produces a bright glow. Solar prominences often appear as great arches extending into the corona. The most conspicuous features on the surface of the Sun are dark blemishes called sunspots. These groups may be associated with violent solar flares.

Mercury is the smallest of the terrestrial planets and the closest to the Sun. The surface is distinctly lunar in appearance, extensively cratered, with smoother volcanic plains. Long lines of cliffs and scarps cut across the plains and craters alike. These probably resulted from crustal shortening as the planet cooled and shrank. Mercury has the greatest temperature extremes of any planet, rising to 480°C during daylight and falling to −180°C at night. This, as well as the virtual lack of atmosphere, indicates that no known form of life could survive there.

Venus is the planet most similar to Earth in both size and mass. However, it is altogether a more hostile world. A dense atmosphere (96 per cent carbon dioxide) obscures the surface under permanent cloud whilst maintaining a temperature of about 480°C. Radar mapping has revealed a landscape of highland 'continents', 'lowlands' and undulating plains. There are also shallow craters, large volcanoes and some rift valleys and trenches. Space probes have shown that the surface is strewn with smooth rocks.

Earth is the largest of the inner planets. The lower atmosphere consists mainly of nitrogen and oxygen. Ozone in the upper layers protects the Earth from the Sun's harmful radiation. The Earth is unique in having a surface largely covered with water (70 per cent), the remainder by continental land masses. Plate tectonics is the dominant process responsible for the structure of the surface, which is then subjected to erosional forces, creating a changing landscape.

Mars has a thin atmosphere which is mainly carbon dioxide (95 per cent). The mean surface temperature is about −40°C, ranging from −138°C at the winter pole to 27°C at the equator, causing strong atmospheric circulation. Dust storms can occur, enveloping the planet, and may take months to settle. Surface features include craters that are often filled with dust, lava plains and giant volcanoes such as Olympus Mons (25km high and 500km across its base), immense canyons, winding river-like valleys, the formation of which is subject to speculation, and polar ice caps which expand and contract with the seasons.

Asteroids are probably the remains of the debris from which the planets formed. They range in diameter from 1000km (the largest, Ceres), to less than 1km. The orbits of most asteroids lie between Mars and Jupiter.

Jupiter is the largest and most massive of the planets. It rotates faster than any other planet. This causes the equatorial region to bulge and the poles to flatten. The atmosphere is composed primarily of hydrogen and helium. The immense heat emanating from the planet's interior produces huge convection currents in the atmosphere. This drives strong wind systems that generate the alternate light- and dark-coloured bands of cloud that encircle the planet. A prominent feature is the Great Red Spot, which was first seen in the 17th century. It is thought to be a huge storm. Other storms have been observed, but none have survived for more than a few days. Jupiter's ring system appears to consist of particles temporarily entrapped by the planet's intense magnetic field. Its satellite system has at least 16 moons.

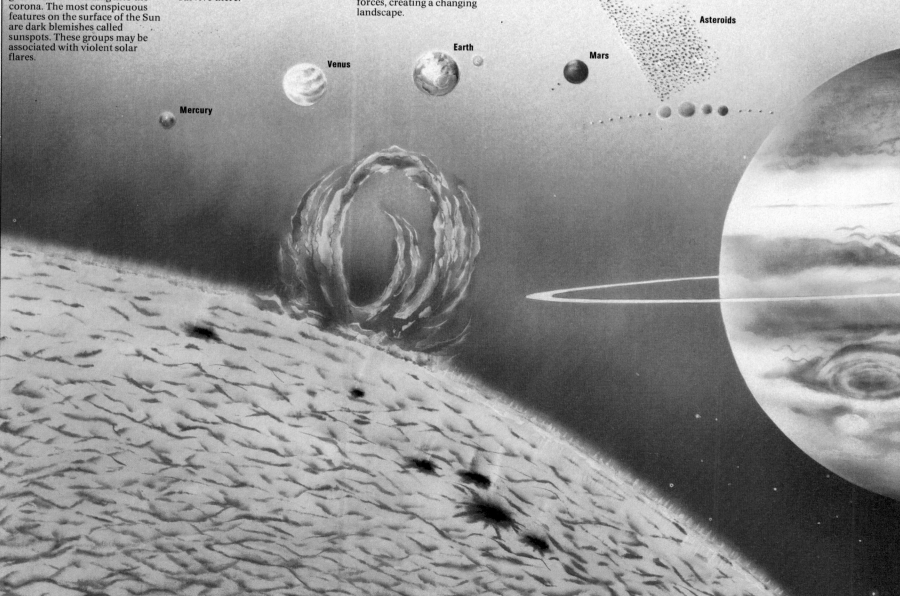

Uranus	Neptune	Pluto
1870	4497	5900
30684·8	60190·5	90465
16·3hr	18·2hr	6·38d
0°46′	1°46′	17°12′
51800	48600	3000
14·5	·17·2	0·002
1·27	1·76	1·1?
5	2	1

Saturn, broadly similar in structure and composition to Jupiter, has a significantly lower mean density, and a greater degree of polar flattening. The atmosphere consists mainly of hydrogen, with some helium. It is thought that droplets of helium formed in Saturn's upper atmosphere sink towards the core, heating the interior as they descend. This may explain why the planet emits over twice as much heat as it receives. Saturn's belt-zone pattern is less conspicuous, and large cloud features are scarce. Strong zonal winds are symmetrical about the equator. The equatorial jet can blow at a speed of 1800km per hour. The most prominent feature of Saturn is its ring system, which is composed of small particles coated with water ice orbiting the planet in nearly circular paths. Seventeen satellites have so far been detected.

Uranus is thought to have a rocky, metallic core surrounded by a deep envelope of water, methane and ammonia 'ices', with a deep atmosphere composed mainly of hydrogen, helium and methane. Its axis is inclined by 98°, causing strong seasonal effects. The poles receive more solar radiation during each orbit than the equator. This, coupled with the lack of an internal heat source, suggests that atmospheric circulation is weak. Uranus has nine slightly elliptical rings of debris orbiting its equatorial region. It is also known to have five satellites.

Neptune was discovered due to the irregularities in the motion of Uranus's orbit which indicated the existence of another planet. Its composition is thought to be very similar to that of Uranus. However, as it emits twice as much heat as it receives, an internal heat source is thought to be responsible. Neptune has a 'bluish' appearance that has been attributed to the methane in the atmosphere. It has two satellites: Triton and Nereid.

Pluto lies on the fringe of the Solar System. Although a planet was believed to exist beyond the orbit of Neptune, Pluto was not found until 1930. Its satellite, Charon, was not discovered until 1978. The planet is thought to be made up of a mixture of frozen gases and rock. It has an eccentric orbit, which is presently inside the orbit of Neptune, where it will remain until the end of the century.

Pluto

Neptune

Uranus

Saturn

Jupiter

Designed and produced by E.S.R.

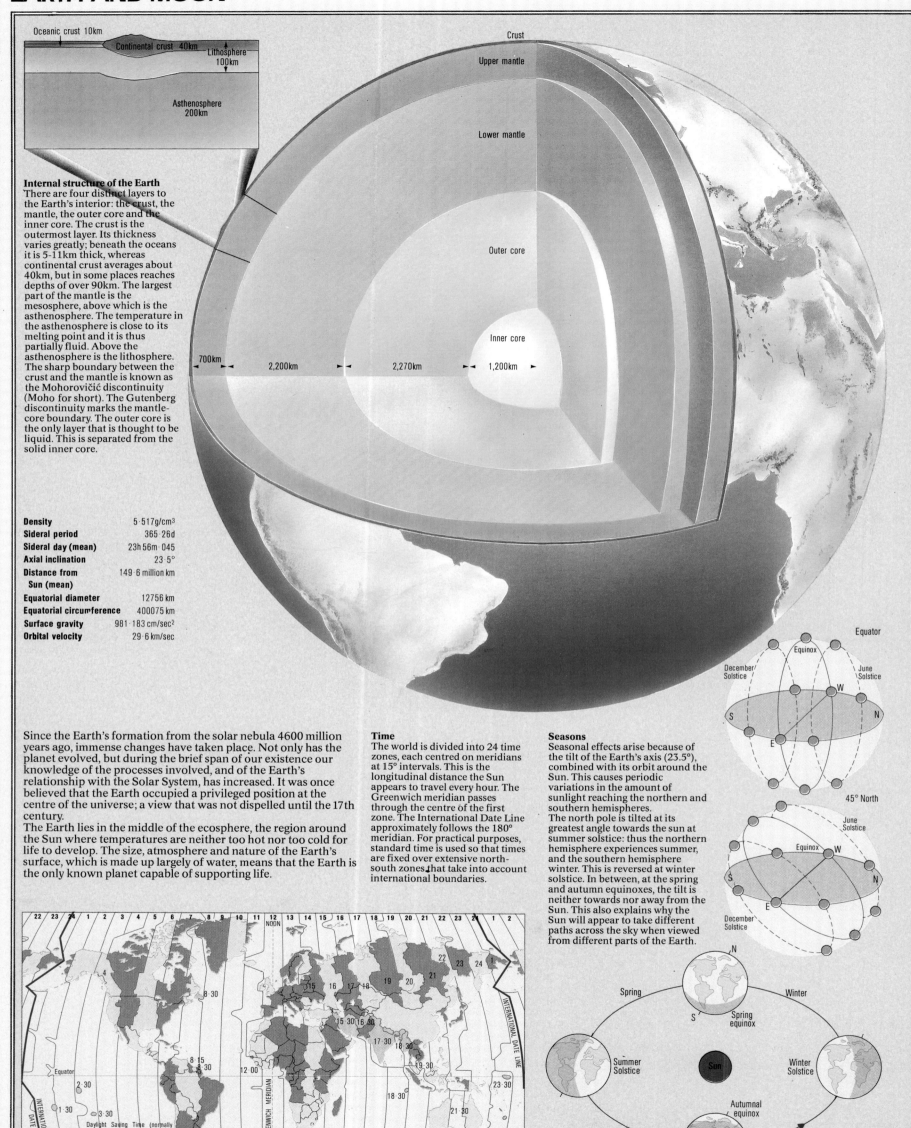

Oceanic crust 10km

Continental crust 40km

Lithosphere 100km

Asthenosphere 200km

Crust

Upper mantle

Lower mantle

Outer core

Inner core

700km | 2,200km | 2,270km | 1,200km

Internal structure of the Earth

There are four distinct layers to the Earth's interior: the crust, the mantle, the outer core and the inner core. The crust is the outermost layer. Its thickness varies greatly; beneath the oceans it is 5-11km thick, whereas continental crust averages about 40km, but in some places reaches depths of over 90km. The largest part of the mantle is the mesosphere, above which is the asthenosphere. The temperature in the asthenosphere is close to its melting point and it is thus partially fluid. Above the asthenosphere is the lithosphere. The sharp boundary between the crust and the mantle is known as the Mohorovičić discontinuity (Moho for short). The Gutenberg discontinuity marks the mantle-core boundary. The outer core is the only layer that is thought to be liquid. This is separated from the solid inner core.

Density	5·517g/cm³
Sideral period	365·26d
Sideral day (mean)	23h 56m·04s
Axial inclination	23·5°
Distance from Sun (mean)	149·6 million km
Equatorial diameter	12756 km
Equatorial circumference	400075 km
Surface gravity	981·183 cm/sec²
Orbital velocity	29·6 km/sec

Since the Earth's formation from the solar nebula 4600 million years ago, immense changes have taken place. Not only has the planet evolved, but during the brief span of our existence our knowledge of the processes involved, and of the Earth's relationship with the Solar System, has increased. It was once believed that the Earth occupied a privileged position at the centre of the universe; a view that was not dispelled until the 17th century.

The Earth lies in the middle of the ecosphere, the region around the Sun where temperatures are neither too hot nor too cold for life to develop. The size, atmosphere and nature of the Earth's surface, which is made up largely of water, means that the Earth is the only known planet capable of supporting life.

Time

The world is divided into 24 time zones, each centred on meridians at 15° intervals. This is the longitudinal distance the Sun appears to travel every hour. The Greenwich meridian passes through the centre of the first zone. The International Date Line approximately follows the 180° meridian. For practical purposes, standard time is used so that times are fixed over extensive north-south zones that take into account international boundaries.

Seasons

Seasonal effects arise because of the tilt of the Earth's axis (23.5°), combined with its orbit around the Sun. This causes periodic variations in the amount of sunlight reaching the northern and southern hemispheres. The north pole is tilted at its greatest angle towards the sun at summer solstice: thus the northern hemisphere experiences summer, and the southern hemisphere winter. This is reversed at winter solstice. In between, at the spring and autumn equinoxes, the tilt is neither towards nor away from the Sun. This also explains why the Sun will appear to take different paths across the sky when viewed from different parts of the Earth.

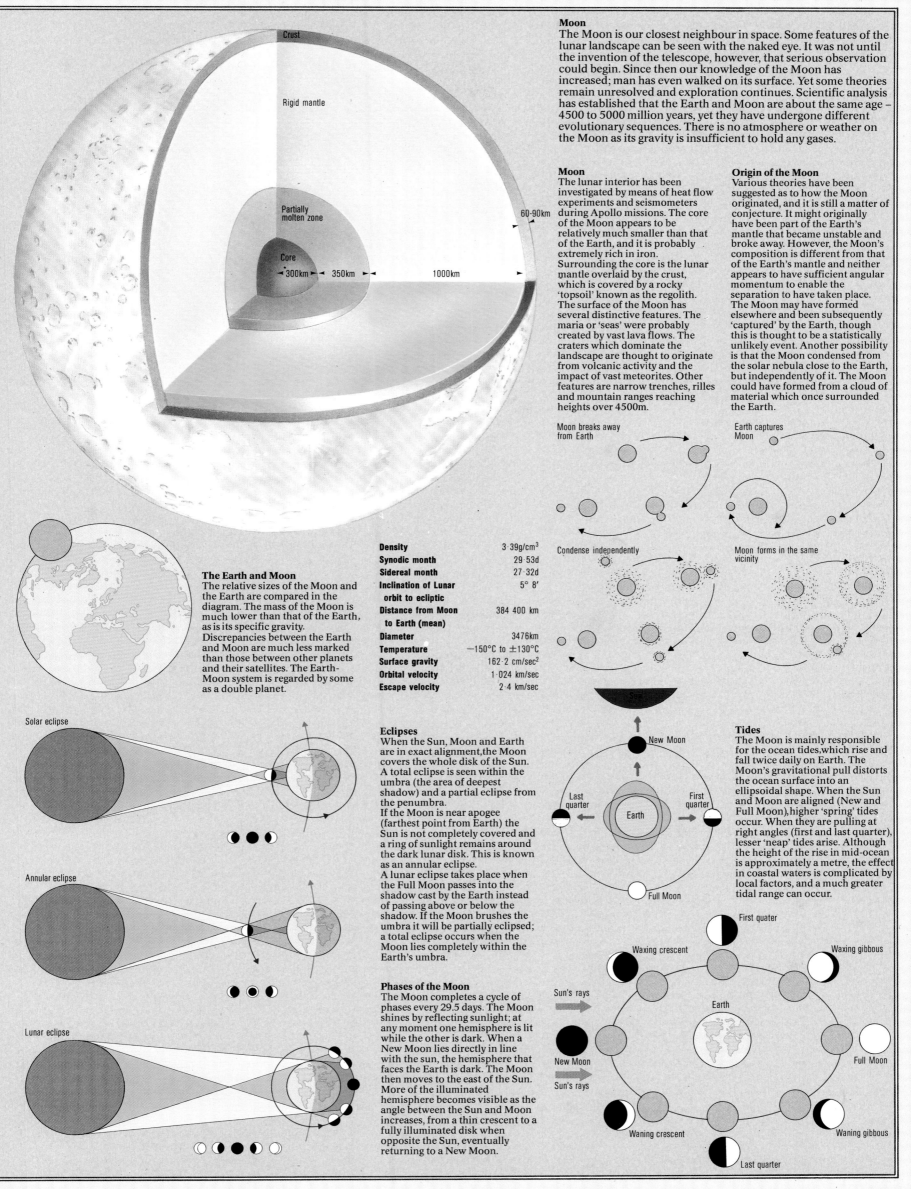

Crust

Rigid mantle

Partially molten zone

Core

←300km→ ←350km→ ←1000km→ 60-90km

Moon

The Moon is our closest neighbour in space. Some features of the lunar landscape can be seen with the naked eye. It was not until the invention of the telescope, however, that serious observation could begin. Since then our knowledge of the Moon has increased; man has even walked on its surface. Yet some theories remain unresolved and exploration continues. Scientific analysis has established that the Earth and Moon are about the same age – 4500 to 5000 million years, yet they have undergone different evolutionary sequences. There is no atmosphere or weather on the Moon as its gravity is insufficient to hold any gases.

Moon

The lunar interior has been investigated by means of heat flow experiments and seismometers during Apollo missions. The core of the Moon appears to be relatively much smaller than that of the Earth, and it is probably extremely rich in iron. Surrounding the core is the lunar mantle overlaid by the crust, which is covered by a rocky 'topsoil' known as the regolith. The surface of the Moon has several distinctive features. The maria or 'seas' were probably created by vast lava flows. The craters which dominate the landscape are thought to originate from volcanic activity and the impact of vast meteorites. Other features are narrow trenches, rilles and mountain ranges reaching heights over 4500m.

Origin of the Moon

Various theories have been suggested as to how the Moon originated, and it is still a matter of conjecture. It might originally have been part of the Earth's mantle that became unstable and broke away. However, the Moon's composition is different from that of the Earth's mantle and neither appears to have sufficient angular momentum to enable the separation to have taken place. The Moon may have formed elsewhere and been subsequently 'captured' by the Earth, though this is thought to be a statistically unlikely event. Another possibility is that the Moon condensed from the solar nebula close to the Earth, but independently of it. The Moon could have formed from a cloud of material which once surrounded the Earth.

Moon breaks away from Earth

Earth captures Moon

Condense independently

Moon forms in the same vicinity

The Earth and Moon

The relative sizes of the Moon and the Earth are compared in the diagram. The mass of the Moon is much lower than that of the Earth, as is its specific gravity. Discrepancies between the Earth and Moon are much less marked than those between other planets and their satellites. The Earth-Moon system is regarded by some as a double planet.

Density	3·39g/cm³
Synodic month	29·53d
Sidereal month	27·32d
Inclination of Lunar orbit to ecliptic	5° 8'
Distance from Moon to Earth (mean)	384 400 km
Diameter	3476km
Temperature	−150°C to ±130°C
Surface gravity	162·2 cm/sec²
Orbital velocity	1·024 km/sec
Escape velocity	2·4 km/sec

Eclipses

When the Sun, Moon and Earth are in exact alignment, the Moon covers the whole disk of the Sun. A total eclipse is seen within the umbra (the area of deepest shadow) and a partial eclipse from the penumbra.
If the Moon is near apogee (farthest point from Earth) the Sun is not completely covered and a ring of sunlight remains around the dark lunar disk. This is known as an annular eclipse.
A lunar eclipse takes place when the Full Moon passes into the shadow cast by the Earth instead of passing above or below the shadow. If the Moon brushes the umbra it will be partially eclipsed; a total eclipse occurs when the Moon lies completely within the Earth's umbra.

Solar eclipse

Annular eclipse

Lunar eclipse

Phases of the Moon

The Moon completes a cycle of phases every 29.5 days. The Moon shines by reflecting sunlight; at any moment one hemisphere is lit while the other is dark. When a New Moon lies directly in line with the sun, the hemisphere that faces the Earth is dark. The Moon then moves to the east of the Sun. More of the illuminated hemisphere becomes visible as the angle between the Sun and Moon increases, from a thin crescent to a fully illuminated disk when opposite the Sun, eventually returning to a New Moon.

New Moon

Last quarter

First quarter

Earth

Full Moon

Tides

The Moon is mainly responsible for the ocean tides, which rise and fall twice daily on Earth. The Moon's gravitational pull distorts the ocean surface into an ellipsoidal shape. When the Sun and Moon are aligned (New and Full Moon), higher 'spring' tides occur. When they are pulling at right angles (first and last quarter), lesser 'neap' tides arise. Although the height of the rise in mid-ocean is approximately a metre, the effect in coastal waters is complicated by local factors, and a much greater tidal range can occur.

Sun's rays

Waxing crescent

First quarter

Waxing gibbous

New Moon

Earth

Full Moon

Waning crescent

Last quarter

Waning gibbous

Designed and produced by E.S.R.

MOVING CONTINENTS

The Earth's development is still a matter of much conjecture and debate. Until comparatively recently the view that the structure of the Earth has remained essentially fixed throughout geological time was common. The matching of many pairs of coastlines (strictly, continental shelves) led to the first detailed geological and structural comparisons. Palaeomagnetism has probably proved to be the most influential proof of continental drift, in conjunction with palaeontology, palaeoclimatology and other geological evidence.

Plate tectonics, the field of Earth studies which encompasses the theory of continental drift, offers an explanation for many of the Earth's varied structural and geophysical phenomena. According to theory, the lithosphere consists of rigid segments called plates. These can contain both oceanic and continental crust, which 'float' across the more mobile asthenosphere. Major interactions occur along the plate margins.

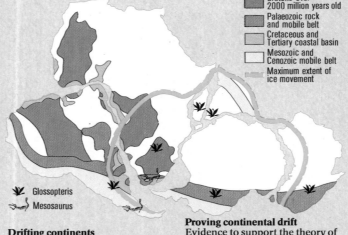

Cratons over 2000 million years old
Palaeozoic rock and mobile belt
Cretaceous and Tertiary coastal basin
Mesozoic or Cenozoic mobile belt
Maximum extent of ice movement

Glossopteris
Mesosaurus

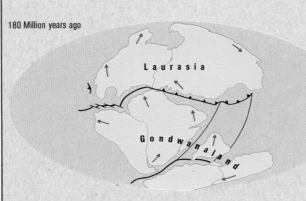

180 Million years ago

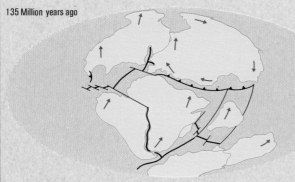

135 Million years ago

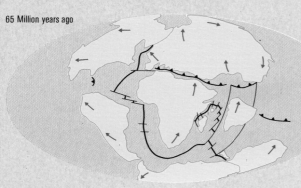

65 Million years ago

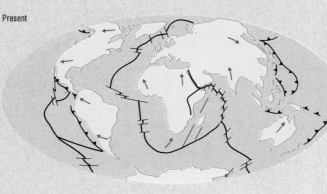

Present

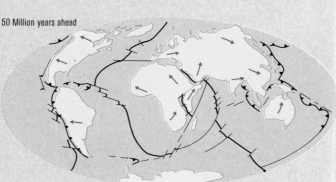

50 Million years ahead

Drifting continents
180 million years ago
The fragmentation of the supercontinent Pangaea began about 200 million years ago. Two major rifts initiated the breakup. The rift zone between North America and Africa generated a northern continental group, Laurasia. The rift that separated the southern landmass of Gondwanaland sent India in a northward direction and simultaneously split South America and Africa from Australia and Antarctica.

135 million years ago
Both Gondwanaland and Laurasia continued to drift northwards. Africa and South America began splitting apart to form the origins of the South Atlantic. India continued heading northwards to Asia. The southern part of the North Atlantic had widened considerably.

65 million years ago
South America had completely separated from Africa and the South Atlantic emerged as a full-fledged ocean. Madagascar had broken away from Africa. In the south, Australia was still connected to Antarctica.

Present
The northward movement of India has led to a collision with Asia, from which the Himalayas resulted. The separation of Greenland from Eurasia is also a recent event in geological time. South America has connected with North America, whilst Australia has drifted north away from Antarctica. Africa is moving away from the Arabian peninsula as the Red Sea rift widens.

50 million years ahead
By extrapolating plate movements into the future, important changes can be seen. A new sea emerges as East Africa parts company with the mainland. Australia and Papua New Guinea migrate north. The Baja peninsula slides past the North American plate along the San Andreas Fault. The continents will undoubtedly continue to change shape and position: exactly how must still be speculative.

Proving continental drift
Evidence to support the theory of continental drift and the idea that today's continents were once joined comes from various geological and geophysical investigations. Rocks from 'matching coastlines' such as South America and Africa, are often similar in age, type and structure. Fossil remains of the reptile *Mesosaurus* have been found on both sides of the South Atlantic. Similarly the remains of the fossil fern *Glossopteris* also indicates that the continents were once joined. Comparisons of palaeomagnetism in rocks of various ages and the Earth's changing magnetic field seems to confirm continental movement.

Plate tectonics
The mobile behaviour of the material within the asthenosphere allows the motion of lithospheric plates, which form a rigid outer shell to the Earth. Each plate moves as a distinct unit. Most earthquakes, volcanoes and mountain building occur along the plate margins.

There are three types of plate boundary: Divergent (constructive) where plates move apart and upwelling of material from the mantle creates oceanic ridges; Convergent (destructive) where plates collide, causing the lithosphere of one plate to be consumed along a subduction zone; Transform margin, along which plates slide, neither creating nor destroying the lithosphere.

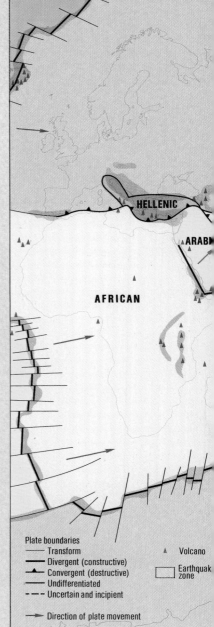

HELLENIC
ARAB
AFRICAN

Plate boundaries
— Transform
— Divergent (constructive)
— Convergent (destructive)
— Undifferentiated
--- Uncertain and incipient
→ Direction of plate movement
▲ Volcano
Earthquake zone

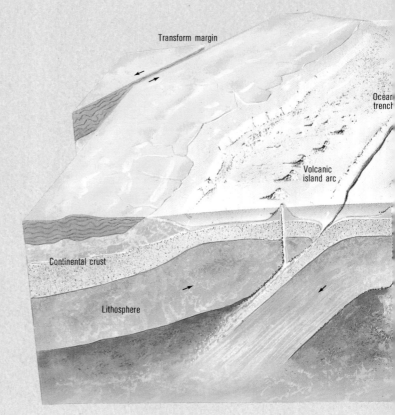

Transform margin
Ocean trench
Volcanic island arc
Continental crust
Lithosphere

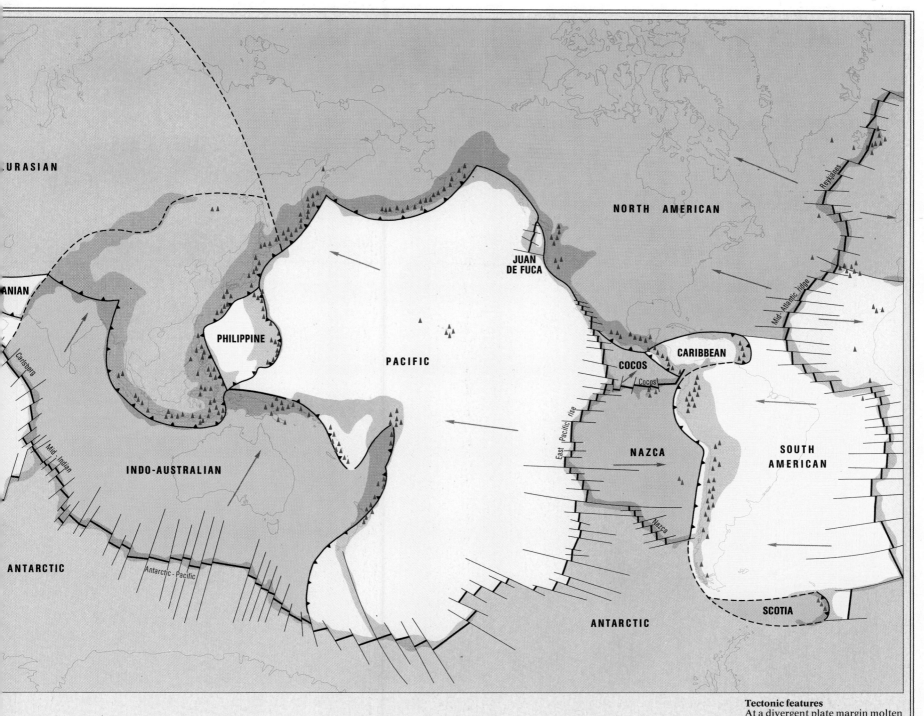

EURASIAN

URASIAN

ANIAN

Carlsberg

PHILIPPINE

JUAN
DE FUCA

NORTH AMERICAN

PACIFIC

COCOS

Cocos

CARIBBEAN

Mid-Atlantic ridge

Reykjanes

INDO-AUSTRALIAN

East Pacific rise

NAZCA

SOUTH
AMERICAN

Mid. Indian

Nazca

ANTARCTIC

Antarctic - Pacific

ANTARCTIC

SCOTIA

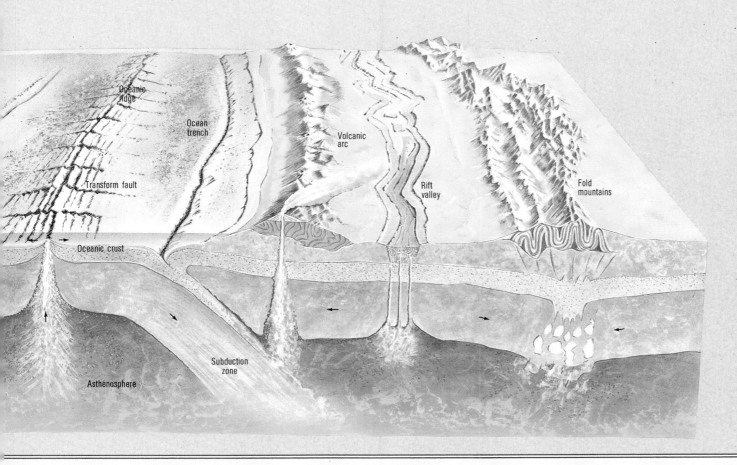

Oceanic
ridge

Ocean trench

Volcanic
arc

Transform fault

Rift
valley

Fold
mountains

Oceanic crust

Subduction
zone

Asthenosphere

Tectonic features

At a divergent plate margin molten material rises to form new lithosphere. When the magma reaches the surface it cools, solidifies and continues to diverge. The ocean floors are thus in a state of continuous creation and spreading. The Red Sea is believed to be the site of a recently formed divergent boundary. Lateral spreading within a continent can generate large down-faulted valleys, or rifts, like the Great Rift Valley of East Africa.

Plate destruction occurs along subduction zones, often indicated by seismic activity. Continents will remain at the surface while the denser oceanic lithosphere is consumed in an ocean trench. The subducting lithosphere re-enters the Earth's interior, slowly melts and becomes reassimilated. Some magma may eventually migrate to the surface producing volcanic arcs, of which the Andes are an example. Island arcs, such as the Aleutian Islands, are often associated with descending oceanic plates.

If continental plates converge new mountain ranges will result. These are composed of deformed sedimentary rocks and fragments of volcanic arc compressed together. The most recently formed are the Himalayas, but the Alps and the Urals are also thought to have originated in this manner. At transform margins tectonic effects are less dramatic as plates slide against one another. However, as in southern California increased seismic and volcanic activity occurs.

15

THE EARTH'S LANDSCAPE

The landscape around us is the result of a complex system of natural processes. Different rocks of igneous, sedimentary or metamorphic origin comprise the underlying structure. These can be brought to the surface of the Earth by various forces. When exposed to the elements of nature they are slowly weathered, leading to the disintegration and decomposition of the rock. The debris is then carried away and deposited elsewhere. In turn this may be acted upon by other agents. The Earth's surface reflects the processes at work at any given time. Although the forces which shape the landscape appear to act very slowly, in geological terms the alterations are very swift.

The number of people inhabiting the Earth has risen exponentially, and technology has expanded in conjunction with this growth. The human impact on the landscape has thus become increasingly significant. Construction, excavation, reclamation, hydrological work and farming create the most visible features of this changing environment.

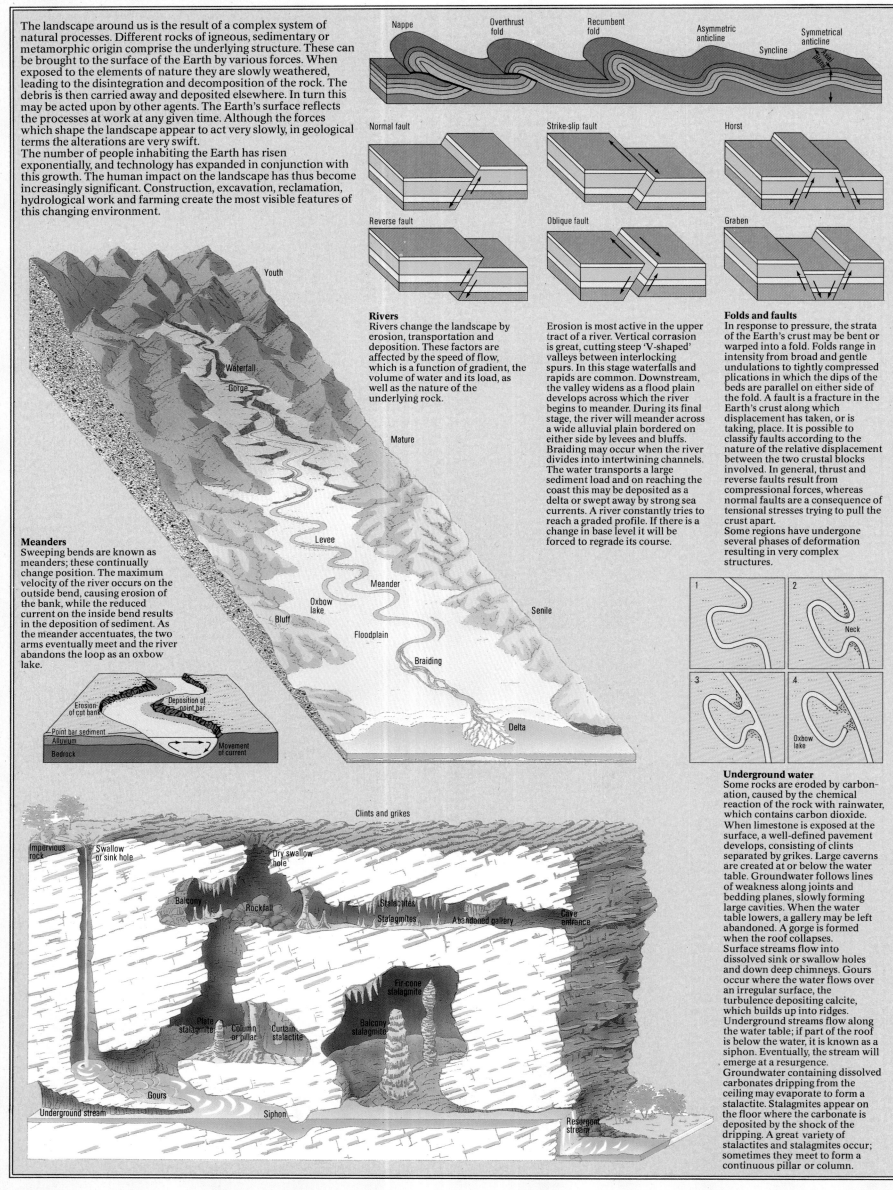

Meanders

Sweeping bends are known as meanders; these continually change position. The maximum velocity of the river occurs on the outside bend, causing erosion of the bank, while the reduced current on the inside bend results in the deposition of sediment. As the meander accentuates, the two arms eventually meet and the river abandons the loop as an oxbow lake.

Rivers

Rivers change the landscape by erosion, transportation and deposition. These factors are affected by the speed of flow, which is a function of gradient, the volume of water and its load, as well as the nature of the underlying rock.

Erosion is most active in the upper tract of a river. Vertical corrasion is great, cutting steep 'V-shaped' valleys between interlocking spurs. In this stage waterfalls and rapids are common. Downstream, the valley widens as a flood plain develops across which the river begins to meander. During its final stage, the river will meander across a wide alluvial plain bordered on either side by levees and bluffs. Braiding may occur when the river divides into intertwining channels. The water transports a large sediment load and on reaching the coast this may be deposited as a delta or swept away by strong sea currents. A river constantly tries to reach a graded profile. If there is a change in base level it will be forced to regrade its course.

Folds and faults

In response to pressure, the strata of the Earth's crust may be bent or warped into a fold. Folds range in intensity from broad and gentle undulations to tightly compressed plications in which the dips of the beds are parallel on either side of the fold. A fault is a fracture in the Earth's crust along which displacement has taken, or is taking, place. It is possible to classify faults according to the nature of the relative displacement between the two crustal blocks involved. In general, thrust and reverse faults result from compressional forces, whereas normal faults are a consequence of tensional stresses trying to pull the crust apart.

Some regions have undergone several phases of deformation resulting in very complex structures.

Underground water

Some rocks are eroded by carbonation, caused by the chemical reaction of the rock with rainwater, which contains carbon dioxide. When limestone is exposed at the surface, a well-defined pavement develops, consisting of clints separated by grikes. Large caverns are created at or below the water table. Groundwater follows lines of weakness along joints and bedding planes, slowly forming large cavities. When the water table lowers, a gallery may be left abandoned. A gorge is formed when the roof collapses.

Surface streams flow into dissolved sink or swallow holes and down deep chimneys. Gours occur where the water flows over an irregular surface, the turbulence depositing calcite, which builds up into ridges. Underground streams flow along the water table; if part of the roof is below the water, it is known as a siphon. Eventually, the stream will emerge at a resurgence.

Groundwater containing dissolved carbonates dripping from the ceiling may evaporate to form a stalactite. Stalagmites appear on the floor where the carbonate is deposited by the shock of the dripping. A great variety of stalactites and stalagmites occur; sometimes they meet to form a continuous pillar or column.

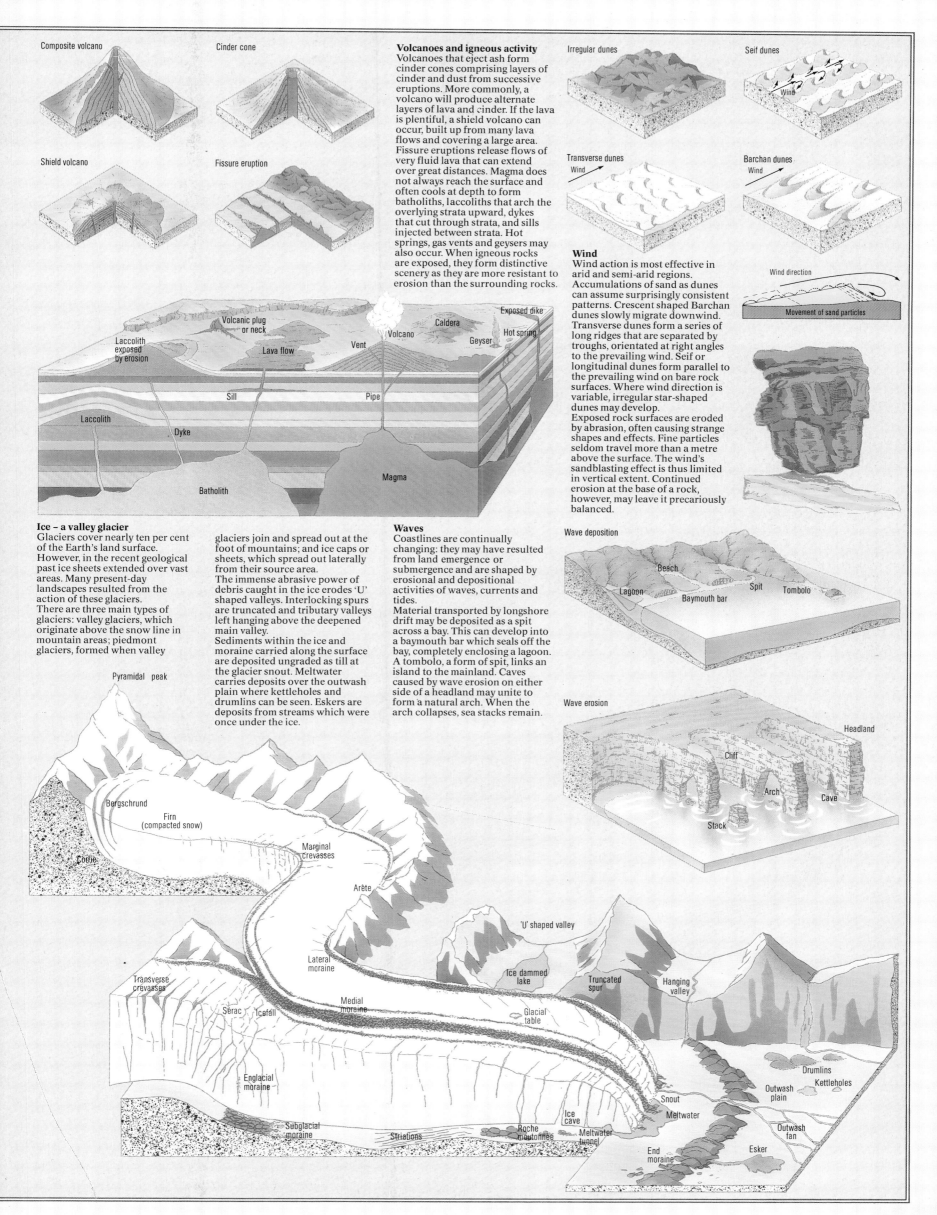

Composite volcano

Cinder cone

Shield volcano

Fissure eruption

Volcanoes and igneous activity

Volcanoes that eject ash form cinder cones comprising layers of cinder and dust from successive eruptions. More commonly, a volcano will produce alternate layers of lava and cinder. If the lava is plentiful, a shield volcano can occur, built up from many lava flows and covering a large area. Fissure eruptions release flows of very fluid lava that can extend over great distances. Magma does not always reach the surface and often cools at depth to form batholiths, laccoliths that arch the overlying strata upward, dykes that cut through strata, and sills injected between strata. Hot springs, gas vents and geysers may also occur. When igneous rocks are exposed, they form distinctive scenery as they are more resistant to erosion than the surrounding rocks.

Irregular dunes

Seif dunes

Wind

Transverse dunes
Wind

Barchan dunes
Wind

Wind

Wind action is most effective in arid and semi-arid regions. Accumulations of sand as dunes can assume surprisingly consistent patterns. Crescent shaped Barchan dunes slowly migrate downwind. Transverse dunes form a series of long ridges that are separated by troughs, orientated at right angles to the prevailing wind. Seif or longitudinal dunes form parallel to the prevailing wind on bare rock surfaces. Where wind direction is variable, irregular star-shaped dunes may develop.
Exposed rock surfaces are eroded by abrasion, often causing strange shapes and effects. Fine particles seldom travel more than a metre above the surface. The wind's sandblasting effect is thus limited in vertical extent. Continued erosion at the base of a rock, however, may leave it precariously balanced.

Wind direction

Movement of sand particles

Volcanic plug or neck
Caldera
Exposed dike
Laccolith exposed by erosion
Vent **Volcano** **Geyser** **Hot spring**
Lava flow
Sill
Pipe
Laccolith
Dyke
Magma
Batholith

Ice – a valley glacier

Glaciers cover nearly ten per cent of the Earth's land surface. However, in the recent geological past ice sheets extended over vast areas. Many present-day landscapes resulted from the action of these glaciers.
There are three main types of glaciers: valley glaciers, which originate above the snow line in mountain areas; piedmont glaciers, formed when valley glaciers join and spread out at the foot of mountains; and ice caps or sheets, which spread out laterally from their source area.
The immense abrasive power of debris caught in the ice erodes 'U' shaped valleys. Interlocking spurs are truncated and tributary valleys left hanging above the deepened main valley.
Sediments within the ice and moraine carried along the surface are deposited ungraded as till at the glacier snout. Meltwater carries deposits over the outwash plain where kettleholes and drumlins can be seen. Eskers are deposits from streams which were once under the ice.

Waves

Coastlines are continually changing: they may have resulted from land emergence or submergence and are shaped by erosional and depositional activities of waves, currents and tides.
Material transported by longshore drift may be deposited as a spit across a bay. This can develop into a baymouth bar which seals off the bay, completely enclosing a lagoon. A tombolo, a form of spit, links an island to the mainland. Caves caused by wave erosion on either side of a headland may unite to form a natural arch. When the arch collapses, sea stacks remain.

Wave deposition
Beach
Lagoon **Baymouth bar** **Spit** **Tombolo**

Wave erosion
Headland
Cliff
Arch **Cave**
Stack

Pyramidal peak
Bergschrund
Firn (compacted snow)
Corrie

Transverse crevasses
Marginal crevasses
Arête
Lateral moraine
Sérac **Icefall**
Medial moraine
'U' shaped valley
Ice dammed lake
Truncated spur
Hanging valley
Glacial table
Englacial moraine
Drumlins
Kettleholes
Snout
Outwash plain
Subglacial moraine
Striations
Roche moutonnée
Ice cave
Meltwater
Meltwater tunnel
End moraine
Outwash fan
Esker

Designed and produced by E.S.R.

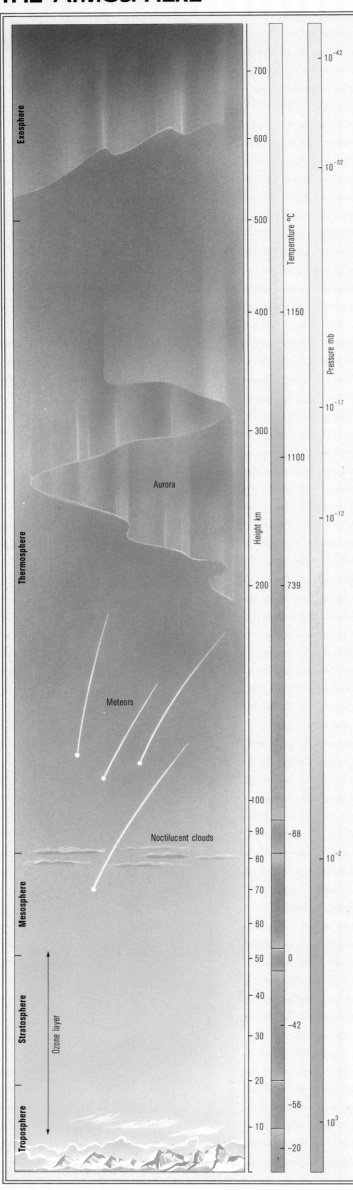

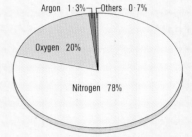

Exosphere, Thermosphere and Mesosphere
Stratosphere
Troposphere

Earth

The atmosphere, which is unlike that of any other planet, encircles and protects the Earth. Changes in the composition of the atmosphere are closely associated with the evolution of the Earth. One of the most important transitions was the increase in oxygen when photosynthetic plants evolved.

The atmosphere is a mixture of gases, the largest proportion of which is nitrogen. The most important is oxygen, without which life could not be sustained; other gases are present in quite small quantities.

Near the Earth's surface, gravitational pull increases the density of the atmosphere. We do not feel this air pressure because of the equal air pressure inside our bodies. Variation in air pressure has a major influence on weather, as does the amount of water vapour in the atmosphere. These elements are in turn affected by a number of factors such as the evaporation of water from the oceans, wind movements and the topography of the Earth.

Structure of the atmosphere
The atmosphere can be divided into various layers, depending on its physical properties. Variations in temperature and pressure result from the distribution of solar heating and help to distinguish the different zones.

Atmospheric composition
The composition of the Earth's atmosphere has changed as the planet has evolved. At present the largest proportion is formed of nitrogen followed by oxygen. Argon and carbon dioxide can also be found, as well as other inert gases such as neon and helium. The atmosphere also contains variable amounts of water vapour, up to three per cent, and small quantities of sulphur dioxide.

Argon 1·3% — Others 0·7%
Oxygen 20%
Nitrogen 78%

Exosphere merges into the vacuum of space. It is extremely rarefied and is composed mainly of hydrogen and helium.

Thermosphere absorbs ultraviolet radiation. Temperatures rise steeply with height to several thousand degrees. This region is the source of the ionosphere, disturbances in this region appear as glowing lights of varying colours – aurorae. They occur primarily over the poles because the charged particles from the Sun are channelled there by the Earth's magnetic field. Short-wave and long-wave radio transmissions are also reflected at various layers within the ionosphere.

It would appear that human activities are altering the natural atmospheric conditions of the planet. To what extent this is happening is still a matter of great debate.

The ozone (a form of oxygen), in the upper atmosphere, screens the Earth from the Sun's ultraviolet rays and is deteriorating. The use of man-made refrigerant gases such as chlorofluorocarbons (CFCs) are a contributing factor. Conversely, other pollutants, such as methane, are by a complex set of chemical reactions increasing ozone levels nearer the ground, which may be adding to the 'greenhouse effect', a phrase which has been used to describe a general warming of the atmosphere.

Since the industrial revolution, carbon dioxide levels have increased by 30 per cent. This is a direct result of burning fossil fuel and destroying vast tracts of forest. The carbon dioxide traps outgoing radiation, which leads to an increase in temperatures. It has been predicted that an average rise of 3°C is possible, and as much as 8-10°C at the poles. Sea levels would rise as a result of melting ice and thermal expansion of the oceans. Many areas of low-lying land would then be flooded and island nations swamped. Accompanying these temperature rises would be changes in rainfall patterns which could affect agricultural productivity. In general it is also thought that tropical conditions would gradually extend northwards.

Other forms of atmospheric pollution are also causing concern. Industrial emissions of sulphur oxide and nitrogen oxide dissolve in rain, which is often transported great distances before returning to Earth as sulphuric and nitric acids. Their deposition as 'acid rain' can have dire effects on ecosystems. Forests are affected, soils leached and water supplies contaminated. Exhaust-caused smogs and lead emitted from vehicles also have a detrimental effect on the atmosphere.

It is known that the atmosphere and climate of the planet have changed with time. Our knowledge, however, is far from complete in many areas. Whether changes in atmospheric conditions are natural or man-made is to some degree still a matter of speculation and controversy.

Mesosphere extends to a height of about 80km and in it there is a marked fall in temperature to −120°C. Meteorites from space tend to burn out in this region as they meet increased air resistance.

Stratosphere contains the ozone layer, which absorbs the Sun's harmful ultraviolet light. As a result, the temperature rises to about 10°C before decreasing again in the stratopause. Noctilucent clouds may form from compressed meteoric dust in this region.

Troposphere is the lowest layer of the atmosphere and contains all the climatic activities that affect us. It reaches about 8km above the poles and 15km above the equator. Pressure is at its greatest due to the weight of the layers above, and 80 per cent of the mass of the atmosphere is found here. Near ground level, visible and infrared radiation is absorbed. Temperature decreases with height until the tropopause is reached.

Greenhouse effect
The balance of the incoming and outgoing solar radiation is disturbed by the increased amount of carbon dioxide which traps infrared radiation. This causes a general warming of the atmosphere known as the greenhouse effect.

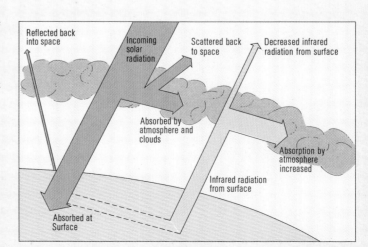

Reflected back into space
Incoming solar radiation
Scattered back to space
Decreased infrared radiation from surface
Absorbed by atmosphere and clouds
Absorption by atmosphere increased
Infrared radiation from surface
Absorbed at Surface

Clouds

Clouds can be classified on the basis of their appearance and height. The basic forms are cirrus, stratus and cumulus. Other clouds reflect one of these forms or are combinations or modifications of them.

Cirrus thin, delicate, fibrous ice-crystal clouds. Sometimes appear as hooked filaments called 'mares tails', often the first sign of an approaching depression.

Cirrocumulus thin, white ice-crystal clouds in the form of ripples, waves or globular masses all in a row. May produce a 'mackerel sky'.

Cirrostratus thin sheet of white ice-crystal clouds that may give the sky a milky look. Sometimes produce haloes around the Sun or Moon.

Altocumulus white to grey clouds often composed of separate globules. Frequently indicates unsettled weather.

Altostratus stratified veil of clouds that are generally thin and may produce very light precipitation.

Stratocumulus soft, grey clouds in globular patches or rolls. Rolls may join together to make a continuous cloud.

Stratus low uniform layer, forms dull, overcast skies. Associated with depressions, may often produce drizzle and rain.

Nimbostratus amorphous layer of dark grey clouds. One of the chief precipitation-producing clouds.

Cumulus dense, billowy clouds often characterised by flat bases. May occur as isolated clouds or closely packed.

Cumulonimbus towering cloud sometimes spreading out on top to form an 'anvil head'. Associated with heavy rainfall, thunder, lightning, hail and tornadoes.

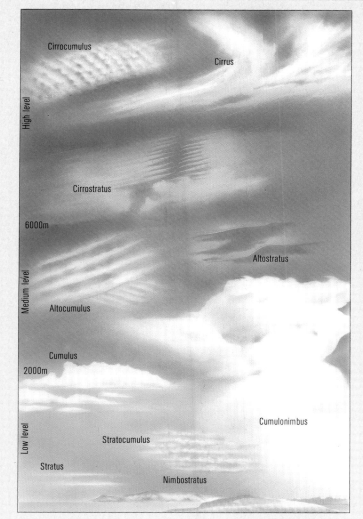

Clouds

Without clouds there would be no precipitation. Variations in the amount of precipitation from place to place as well as local differences from time to time have a significant impact not only on the nature of the physical landscape but also on people's lifestyles.

Clouds consist of microscopic drops of water or ice crystals suspended in the atmosphere. Formation occurs when air that contains water vapour becomes saturated and reaches its dew point. This is usually the result of the air rising and thus cooling. The water vapour then condenses around dust particles.

Wind

The unequal heating of the Earth by solar radiation generates pressure differences. These inequalities cause the movement of air from areas of higher pressure to areas of lower pressure. A system of general circulation is thus generated by semipermanent cells of high and low pressure over the oceans. Wind direction is then subject to deflection by the Coriolis effect, to the right in the northern hemisphere, to the left in the southern hemisphere. This is complicated by seasonal pressure changes over land, which can give rise to seasonal reversals of wind known as monsoons.

Circulation of the air

The temperature differences between the poles and the equator provide the thermal energy to drive atmospheric circulation. Warm air at the equator rises and flows towards the poles at high levels. Cold polar air moves towards the equator at low levels to replace it. Once the effect of rotation is added, the Coriolis effect, this simple convection system breaks down into smaller cells.

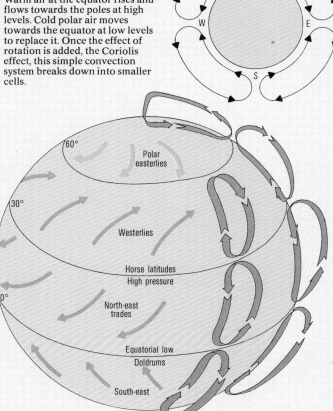

A Depression

Variable weather in the middle latitudes often results from the development of low pressure areas known as depressions, a common feature of which is the formation of warm and cold fronts. The warm, light air rises above the cool air along the warm front. Behind, the cold air forces its way under the warm air along the cold front. Gradually, the cold front catches up with the warm front and the warm air is pushed above the cold in an occlusion. In the northern hemisphere, the air circulates in an anticlockwise direction and in the southern, it circulates clockwise.

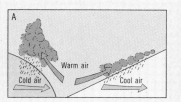
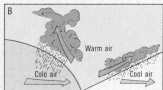

Climate

The climate of an area is its characteristic weather considered over a long period of time. Differences in latitude, prevailing air masses, either local or regional, the relative distribution of land and sea, as well as the topography, will all have an effect on the climatic conditions experienced. The most popular climatic classification is that devised by Wladimir Köppen. It is based on the seasonal variations of temperature and rainfall and their effect on vegetation growth. The range of climates can broadly be defined according to latitude. Hot, tropical climates are dominated by equatorial air masses throughout the year. Temperate climates of the mid-latitudes are very variable, subjected alternately to subpolar and subtropical air masses as well as seasonal shifts. Polar climates of high latitudes are strongly seasonal, influenced by subpolar and polar air masses.

Geological evidence suggests that during other periods the planet experienced a more uniform climate. The present variable pattern may be due, in part, to the fact that the earth is still recovering from the last Ice Age, although opinion varies as to whether fluctuations in climate should be regarded as abnormal.

Tropical climate
- Equatorial rain forest
- Monsoon
- Tropical rain savannah

Dry climate
- Desert
- Steppe

Warm temperate climate
- Dry summer
- Dry winter
- Rain in all seasons

Cool temperate climate
- Dry winter
- Rain in all seasons

→ Tropical cyclone track

Cold climate
- Highland
- Polar

Designed and produced by E.S.R.

EVOLUTION OF LIFE

All living things have a common ancestry – dating as far back as the origin of life itself. It is believed that the first flickerings of life began over 3500 million years ago. Since then species have become ever more numerous and diverse, to produce the present vast array of life. Through successive geological periods the variety of life forms preserved as fossils is both astonishing and informative. It is possible to tell not only what plants and animals looked like, but also, to some extent, how they lived.

The theory of evolution helps to explain how the different kinds of flora and fauna came into existence, how they are related to each other and how they have changed. Charles Darwin was the first person to propound the theory of evolution in a scientific manner. He suggested that a process of natural selection takes place. Those plants and animals best adapted to their environment are more likely to survive and reproduce than others. As time passes an increasing proportion of individuals will have inherited the particular advantageous characteristics.

Geological time scale
Geological time is divided into named intervals. These are separated from each other by major changes in rock type, obvious breaks in succession, and abrupt changes in fossil groups.

Various dating methods place rocks and geological events in the correct chronological order. The particular fossil content in successive strata is one such method. Today, radioactive dating is the most reliable way of determining the absolute age of rocks. The basis of this involves analysis of the atomic decay of elements within the rock minerals.

Chronology of human evolution
Little is known about the very earliest hominids. One possible early ancestor was *Ramapithecus*. The evolution to modern man was the subject of a long, complex process, much of which is still the subject of controversy. The notable stages of human evolution are an erect posture and bipedal gait, and an increase in body and brain size.

Tracing the origins of man
Evidence for tracing the evolution of man comes essentially from the fossil record. Remains of early man have been found in many places. However, the distribution of sites reflects the preservation of human remains and their discovery rather than any reliable population pattern. Little is known about the actual period of the populations from which the fossils are derived.

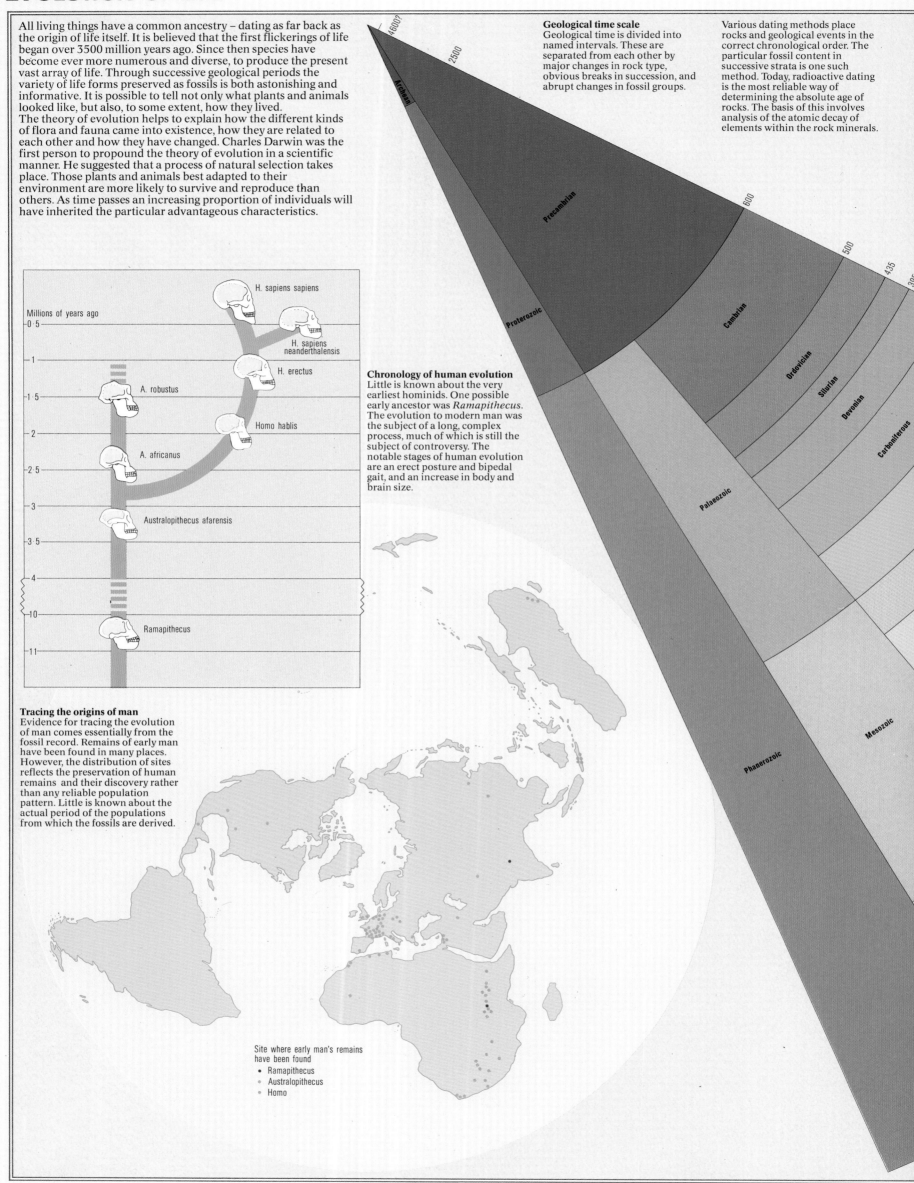

Millions of years ago

H. sapiens sapiens
H. sapiens neanderthalensis
H. erectus
A. robustus
Homo hablis
A. africanus
Australopithecus afarensis
Ramapithecus

Site where early man's remains have been found
- Ramapithecus
- Australopithecus
- Homo

4600
2500
Archean
Precambrian
Proterozoic
600
500
435
395
Cambrian
Ordovician
Silurian
Devonian
Carboniferous
Palaeozoic
Mesozoic
Phanerozoic

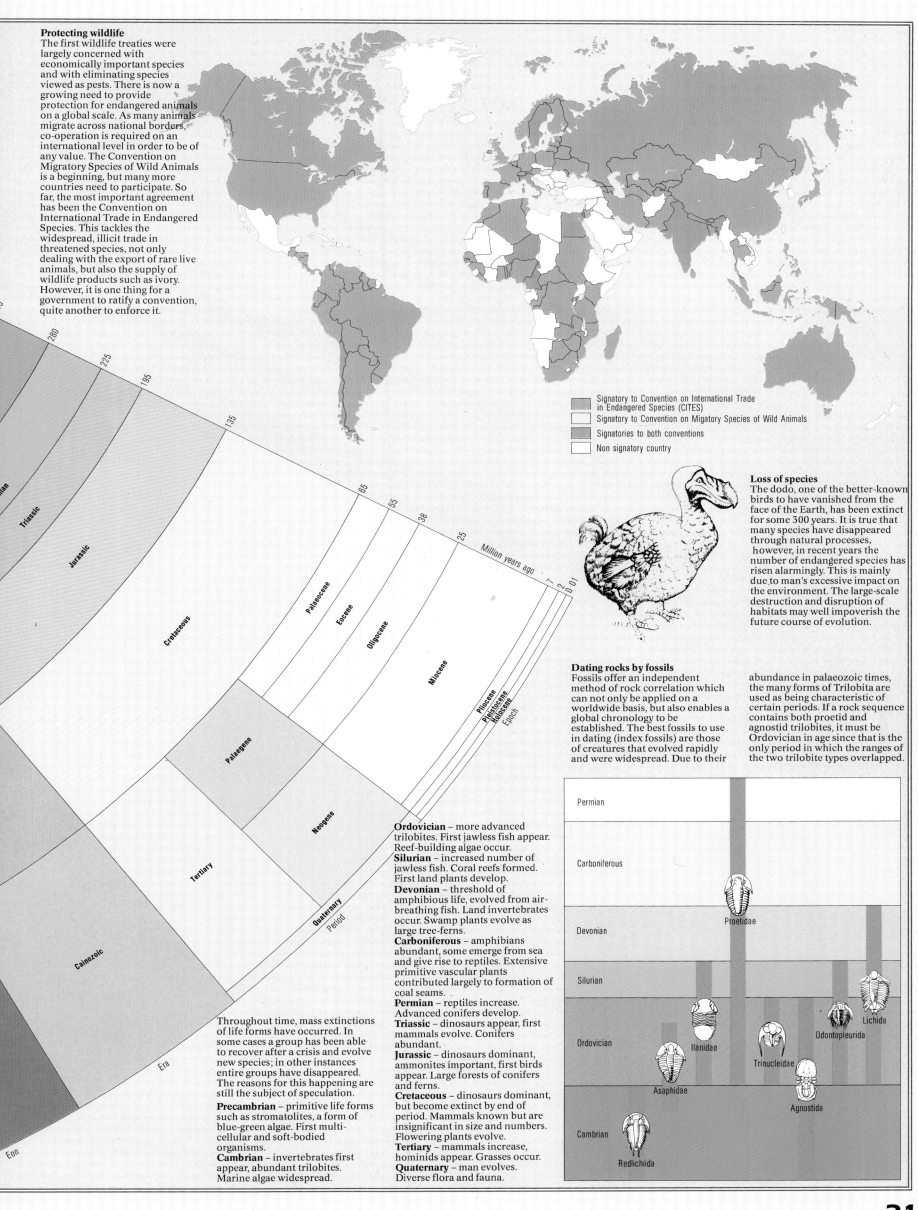

Protecting wildlife
The first wildlife treaties were largely concerned with economically important species and with eliminating species viewed as pests. There is now a growing need to provide protection for endangered animals on a global scale. As many animals migrate across national borders, co-operation is required on an international level in order to be of any value. The Convention on Migratory Species of Wild Animals is a beginning, but many more countries need to participate. So far, the most important agreement has been the Convention on International Trade in Endangered Species. This tackles the widespread, illicit trade in threatened species, not only dealing with the export of rare live animals, but also the supply of wildlife products such as ivory. However, it is one thing for a government to ratify a convention, quite another to enforce it.

Signatory to Convention on International Trade in Endangered Species (CITES)
Signatory to Convention on Migratory Species of Wild Animals
Signatories to both conventions
Non signatory country

Loss of species
The dodo, one of the better-known birds to have vanished from the face of the Earth, has been extinct for some 300 years. It is true that many species have disappeared through natural processes, however, in recent years the number of endangered species has risen alarmingly. This is mainly due to man's excessive impact on the environment. The large-scale destruction and disruption of habitats may well impoverish the future course of evolution.

Dating rocks by fossils
Fossils offer an independent method of rock correlation which can not only be applied on a worldwide basis, but also enables a global chronology to be established. The best fossils to use in dating (index fossils) are those of creatures that evolved rapidly and were widespread. Due to their abundance in palaeozoic times, the many forms of Trilobita are used as being characteristic of certain periods. If a rock sequence contains both proetid and agnostid trilobites, it must be Ordovician in age since that is the only period in which the ranges of the two trilobite types overlapped.

Ordovician – more advanced trilobites. First jawless fish appear. Reef-building algae occur.
Silurian – increased number of jawless fish. Coral reefs formed. First land plants develop.
Devonian – threshold of amphibious life, evolved from air-breathing fish. Land invertebrates occur. Swamp plants evolve as large tree-ferns.
Carboniferous – amphibians abundant, some emerge from sea and give rise to reptiles. Extensive primitive vascular plants contributed largely to formation of coal seams.
Permian – reptiles increase. Advanced conifers develop.
Triassic – dinosaurs appear, first mammals evolve. Conifers abundant.
Jurassic – dinosaurs dominant, ammonites important, first birds appear. Large forests of conifers and ferns.
Cretaceous – dinosaurs dominant, but become extinct by end of period. Mammals known but are insignificant in size and numbers. Flowering plants evolve.
Tertiary – mammals increase, hominids appear. Grasses occur.
Quaternary – man evolves. Diverse flora and fauna.

Throughout time, mass extinctions of life forms have occurred. In some cases a group has been able to recover after a crisis and evolve new species; in other instances entire groups have disappeared. The reasons for this happening are still the subject of speculation.

Precambrian – primitive life forms such as stromatolites, a form of blue-green algae. First multi-cellular and soft-bodied organisms.
Cambrian – invertebrates first appear, abundant trilobites. Marine algae widespread.

Permian
Carboniferous
Devonian — Proetidae
Silurian
Ordovician — Ilanidae, Trinucleidae, Odontopleurida, Lichida, Asaphidae, Agnostida
Cambrian — Redlichiida

Designed and produced by E.S.R.

EXPLORATION AND DISCOVERY

The early explorers who travelled beyond their own shores were accomplished shipbuilders and seamen. The Vikings, Chinese and Arabs were among those who first reached distant lands. Some merchants and missionaries reached remote inland areas. Within a relatively short space of time the great voyages of discovery had charted the vast expanses of sea and largely determined the extent and shape of the continental landmasses. These geographical explorations were later expanded and consolidated by expeditions of a more scientific nature.

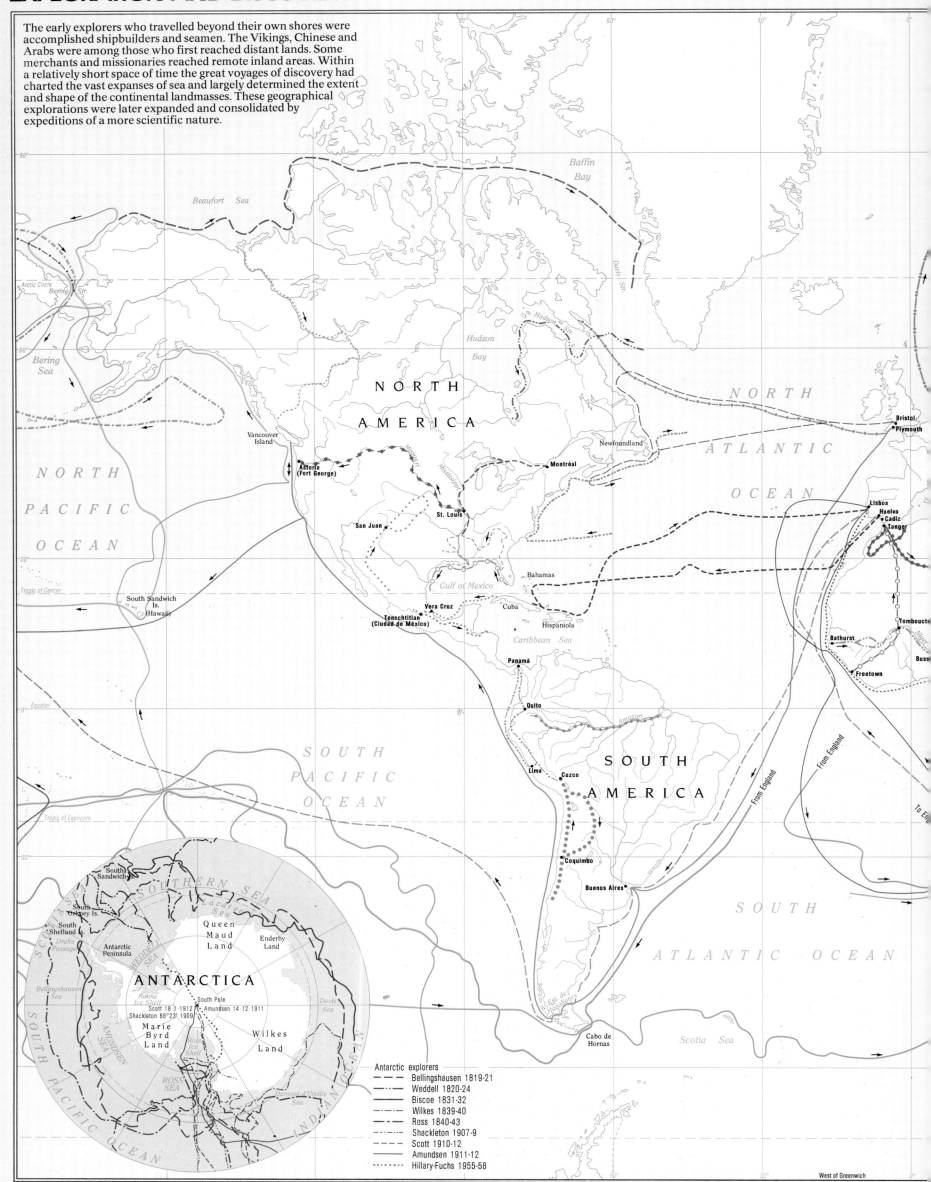

Antarctic explorers

- ─── Bellingshausen 1819-21
- ─ ·· ─ Weddell 1820-24
- ─── Biscoe 1831-32
- ─ · ─ Wilkes 1839-40
- ─ ·· ─ Ross 1840-43
- ─ · ─ Shackleton 1907-9
- ─ ─ ─ Scott 1910-12
- ─── Amundsen 1911-12
- ········ Hillary-Fuchs 1955-58

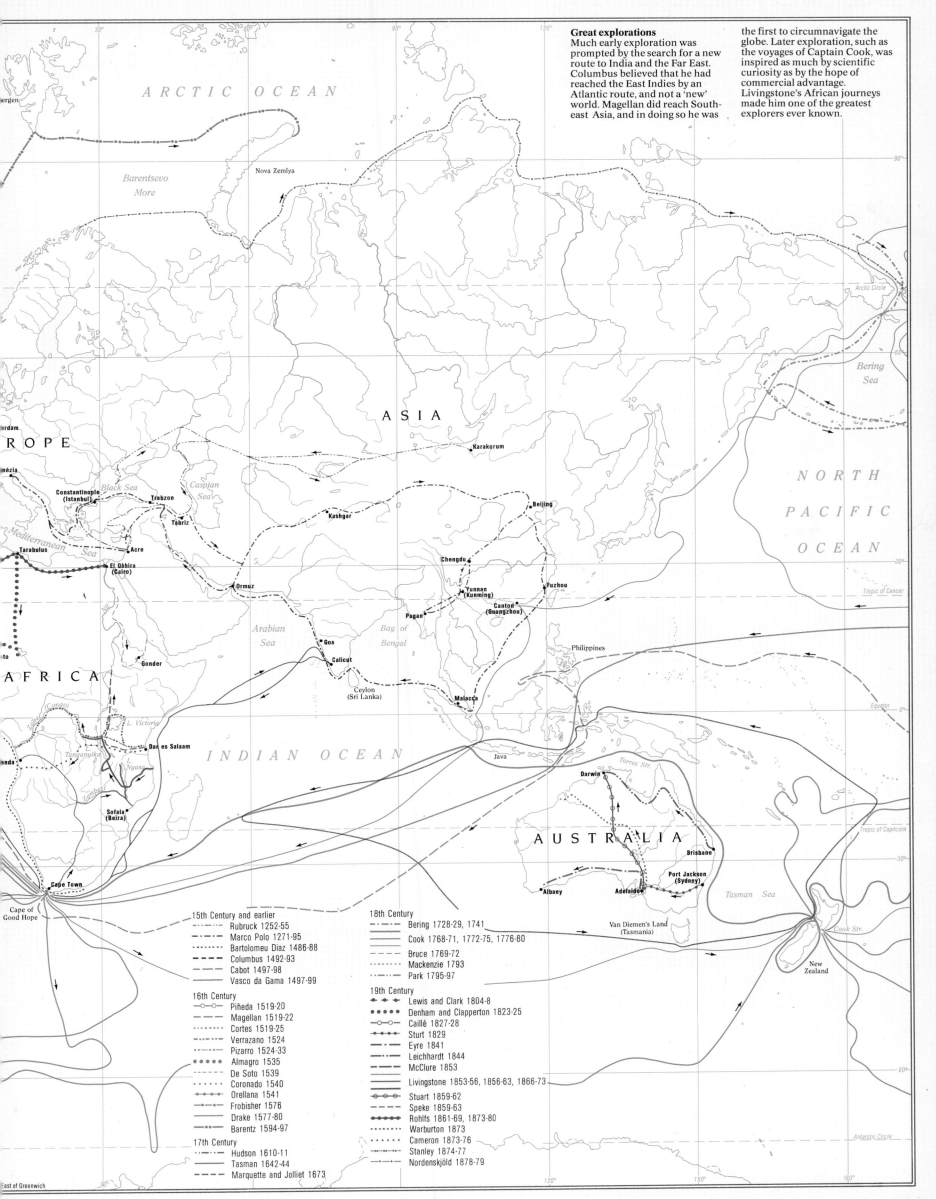

Great explorations
Much early exploration was prompted by the search for a new route to India and the Far East. Columbus believed that he had reached the East Indies by an Atlantic route, and not a 'new' world. Magellan did reach Southeast Asia, and in doing so he was the first to circumnavigate the globe. Later exploration, such as the voyages of Captain Cook, was inspired as much by scientific curiosity as by the hope of commercial advantage. Livingstone's African journeys made him one of the greatest explorers ever known.

15th Century and earlier
- Rubruck 1252-55
- Marco Polo 1271-95
- Bartolomeu Diaz 1486-88
- Columbus 1492-93
- Cabot 1497-98
- Vasco da Gama 1497-99

16th Century
- Piñeda 1519-20
- Magellan 1519-22
- Cortes 1519-25
- Verrazano 1524
- Pizarro 1524-33
- Almagro 1535
- De Soto 1539
- Coronado 1540
- Orellana 1541
- Frobisher 1576
- Drake 1577-80
- Barentz 1594-97

17th Century
- Hudson 1610-11
- Tasman 1642-44
- Marquette and Jolliet 1673

18th Century
- Bering 1728-29, 1741
- Cook 1768-71, 1772-75, 1776-80
- Bruce 1769-72
- Mackenzie 1793
- Park 1795-97

19th Century
- Lewis and Clark 1804-8
- Denham and Clapperton 1823-25
- Caillé 1827-28
- Sturt 1829
- Eyre 1841
- Leichhardt 1844
- McClure 1853
- Livingstone 1853-56, 1856-63, 1866-73
- Stuart 1859-62
- Speke 1859-63
- Rohlfs 1861-69, 1873-80
- Warburton 1873
- Cameron 1873-76
- Stanley 1874-77
- Nordenskjöld 1878-79

ARCTIC OCEAN

Barentsevo More

Nova Zemlya

ASIA

Karakorum

EUROPE

Constantinople (Istanbul)

Black Sea

Trabzon

Caspian Sea

Tabriz

Kashgar

Beijing

NORTH PACIFIC OCEAN

Bering Sea

Arctic Circle

Mediterranean Sea

Tarabulus

Acre

El Qâhira (Cairo)

Ormuz

Chengdu

Yunnan (Kunming)

Fuzhou

Tropic of Cancer

Pagan

Canton (Guangzhou)

AFRICA

Gonder

Arabian Sea

Goa

Bay of Bengal

Calicut

Philippines

Ceylon (Sri Lanka)

Malacca

Equator

(Congo)

L. Victoria

INDIAN OCEAN

Java

Dar es Salaam

Tanganyika

L. Nyasa

Zambezi

Torres Str.

Darwin

Sofala (Beira)

AUSTRALIA

Brisbane

Tropic of Capricorn

Cape Town

Port Jackson (Sydney)

Albany

Adelaide

Tasman Sea

Cape of Good Hope

Van Diemen's Land (Tasmania)

Cook Str.

New Zealand

East of Greenwich

Antarctic Circle

ORGANISATIONS AND AFFILIATIONS

Today's large number of nations is a relatively recent phenomenon. As colonialism declined, the number of independent nations grew. Some of the recently established national boundaries have created artificial divisions which often divide tribal lands and separate ethnic communities. Many newly emergent countries have been beset by instability, civil war and other turbulent events. The outcome of disputes within and between nations is now often dependent upon global opinion or intervention.

Nations are becoming more involved in each others affairs by virtue of trade, technology and aid. Also, problems such as terrorism, pollution, ecological issues and many more may be tackled more effectively through collaborative effort. An array of international and regional bodies, consultative agencies and other cohesive groupings reflect this growing interdependence of nations. There has been a rapid growth in recent years in the number of non-governmental organisations. They range from development groups like OXFAM to conservation groups such as Greenpeace and Friends of the Earth. These and other pressure groups seek to influence governments and international agencies. Some highly effective campaigns have increased world awareness of the disasters and problems faced in other parts of the globe as well as bringing to the fore many environmental issues.

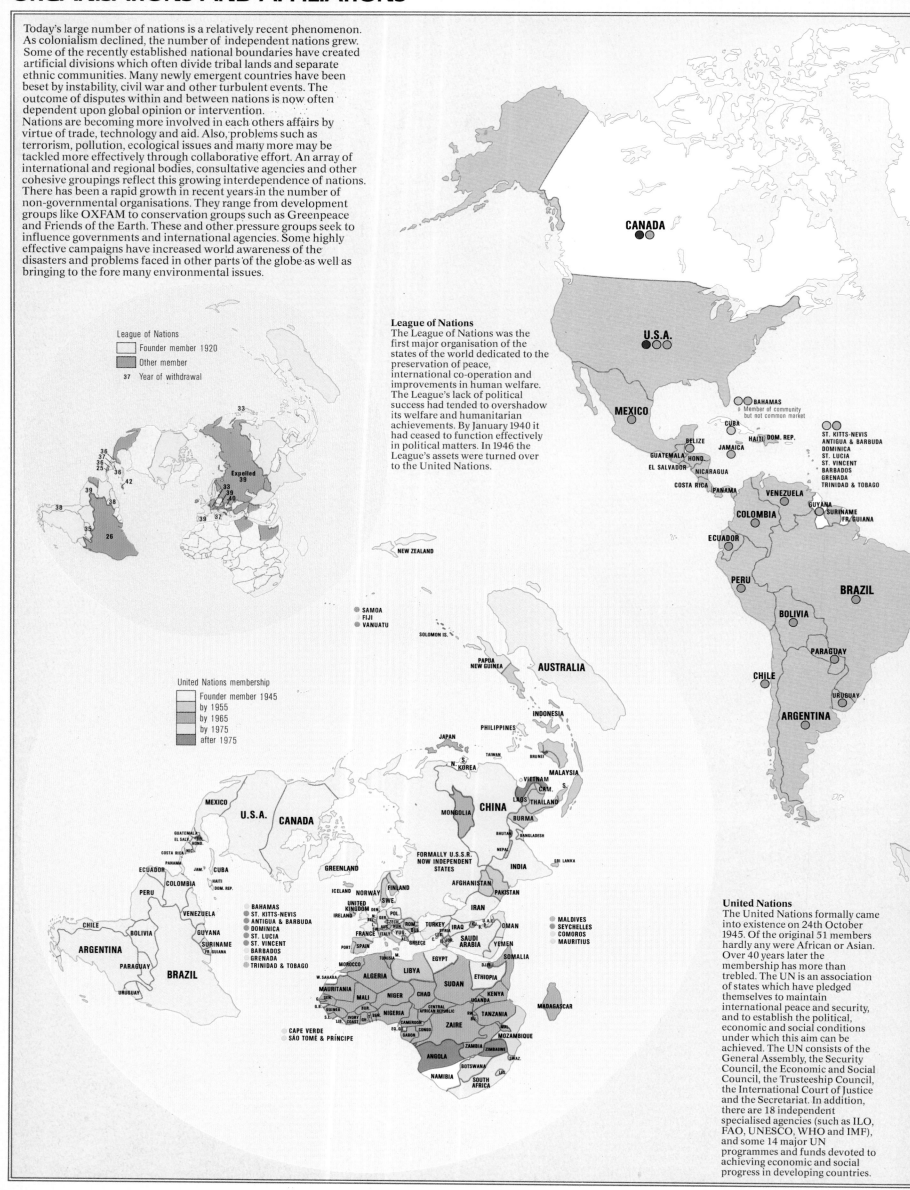

League of Notions

□ Founder member 1920
▨ Other member
37 Year of withdrawal

United Nations membership

□ Founder member 1945
▨ by 1955
▨ by 1965
□ by 1975
▨ after 1975

League of Nations

The League of Nations was the first major organisation of the states of the world dedicated to the preservation of peace, international co-operation and improvements in human welfare. The League's lack of political success had tended to overshadow its welfare and humanitarian achievements. By January 1940 it had ceased to function effectively in political matters. In 1946 the League's assets were turned over to the United Nations.

United Nations

The United Nations formally came into existence on 24th October 1945. Of the original 51 members hardly any were African or Asian. Over 40 years later the membership has more than trebled. The UN is an association of states which have pledged themselves to maintain international peace and security, and to establish the political, economic and social conditions under which this aim can be achieved. The UN consists of the General Assembly, the Security Council, the Economic and Social Council, the Trusteeship Council, the International Court of Justice and the Secretariat. In addition, there are 18 independent specialised agencies (such as ILO, FAO, UNESCO, WHO and IMF), and some 14 major UN programmes and funds devoted to achieving economic and social progress in developing countries.

24

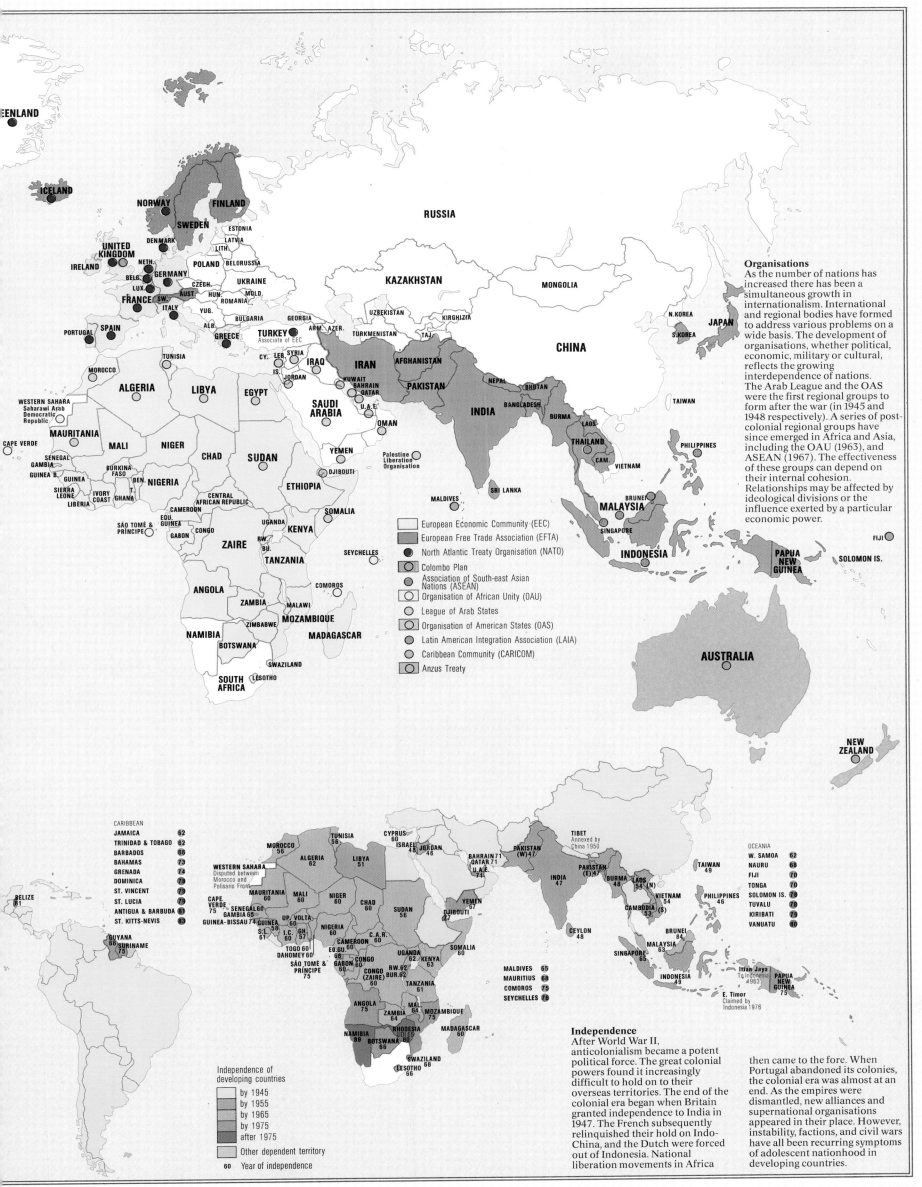

Organisations

As the number of nations has increased there has been a simultaneous growth in internationalism. International and regional bodies have formed to address various problems on a wide basis. The development of organisations, whether political, economic, military or cultural, reflects the growing interdependence of nations. The Arab League and the OAS were the first regional groups to form after the war (in 1945 and 1948 respectively). A series of post-colonial regional groups have since emerged in Africa and Asia, including the OAU (1963), and ASEAN (1967). The effectiveness of these groups can depend on their internal cohesion. Relationships may be affected by ideological divisions or the influence exerted by a particular economic power.

Legend (Organisations):
- European Economic Community (EEC)
- European Free Trade Association (EFTA)
- North Atlantic Treaty Organisation (NATO)
- Colombo Plan
- Association of South-east Asian Nations (ASEAN)
- Organisation of African Unity (OAU)
- League of Arab States
- Organisation of American States (OAS)
- Latin American Integration Association (LAIA)
- Caribbean Community (CARICOM)
- Anzus Treaty

Independence

After World War II, anticolonialism became a potent political force. The great colonial powers found it increasingly difficult to hold on to their overseas territories. The end of the colonial era began when Britain granted independence to India in 1947. The French subsequently relinquished their hold on Indo-China, and the Dutch were forced out of Indonesia. National liberation movements in Africa then came to the fore. When Portugal abandoned its colonies, the colonial era was almost at an end. As the empires were dismantled, new alliances and supernational organisations appeared in their place. However, instability, factions, and civil wars have all been recurring symptoms of adolescent nationhood in developing countries.

Legend (Independence of developing countries):
- by 1945
- by 1955
- by 1965
- by 1975
- after 1975
- Other dependent territory
- 60 Year of independence

CARIBBEAN
- JAMAICA 62
- TRINIDAD & TOBAGO 62
- BARBADOS 66
- BAHAMAS 73
- GRENADA 74
- DOMINICA 78
- ST. VINCENT 79
- ST. LUCIA 79
- ANTIGUA & BARBUDA 81
- ST. KITTS-NEVIS 83

OCEANIA
- W. SAMOA 62
- NAURU 68
- FIJI 70
- TONGA 70
- SOLOMON IS. 78
- TUVALU 78
- KIRIBATI 79
- VANUATU 80

POPULATION

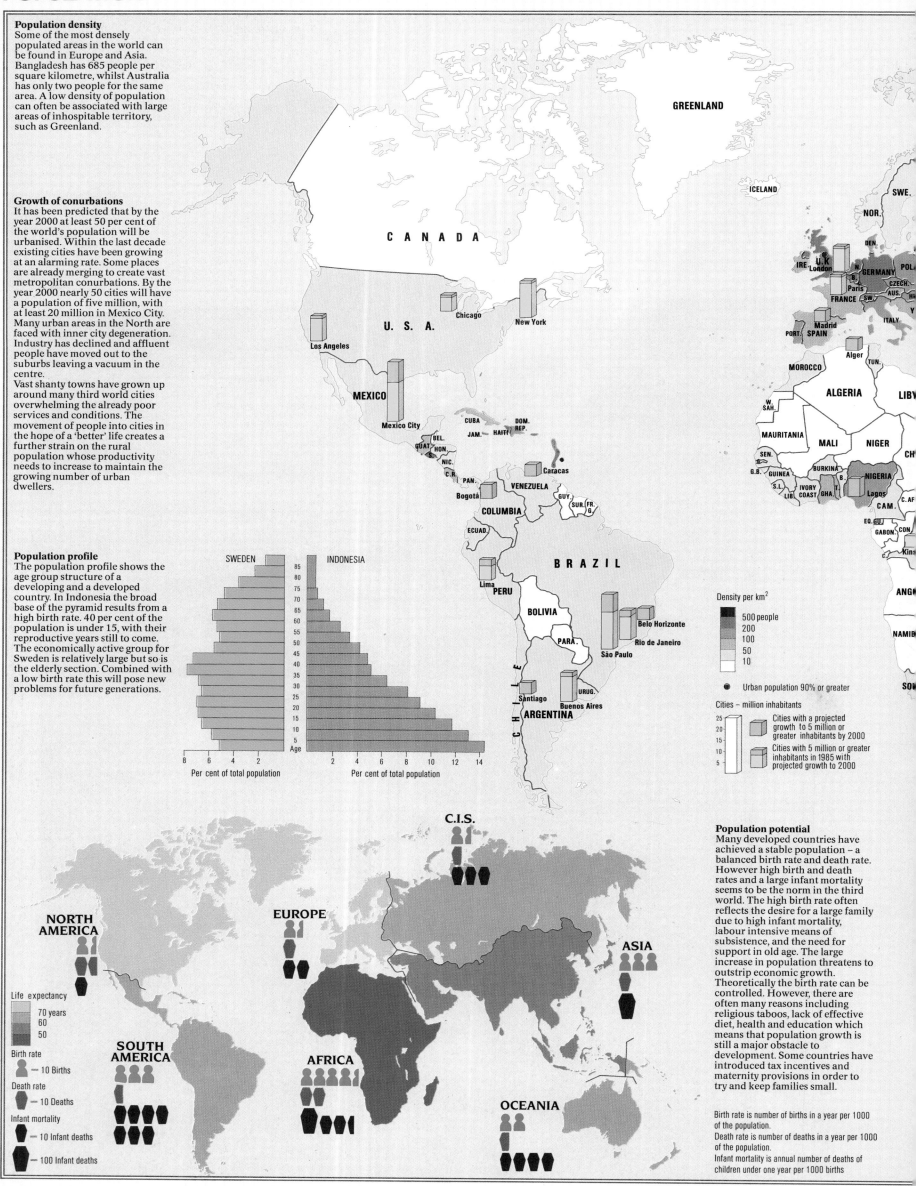

Population density
Some of the most densely populated areas in the world can be found in Europe and Asia. Bangladesh has 685 people per square kilometre, whilst Australia has only two people for the same area. A low density of population can often be associated with large areas of inhospitable territory, such as Greenland.

Growth of conurbations
It has been predicted that by the year 2000 at least 50 per cent of the world's population will be urbanised. Within the last decade existing cities have been growing at an alarming rate. Some places are already merging to create vast metropolitan conurbations. By the year 2000 nearly 50 cities will have a population of five million, with at least 20 million in Mexico City. Many urban areas in the North are faced with inner city degeneration. Industry has declined and affluent people have moved out to the suburbs leaving a vacuum in the centre.
Vast shanty towns have grown up around many third world cities overwhelming the already poor services and conditions. The movement of people into cities in the hope of a 'better' life creates a further strain on the rural population whose productivity needs to increase to maintain the growing number of urban dwellers.

Population profile
The population profile shows the age group structure of a developing and a developed country. In Indonesia the broad base of the pyramid results from a high birth rate. 40 per cent of the population is under 15, with their reproductive years still to come. The economically active group for Sweden is relatively large but so is the elderly section. Combined with a low birth rate this will pose new problems for future generations.

SWEDEN   INDONESIA

Per cent of total population   Per cent of total population

Density per km²
500 people
200
100
50
10

● Urban population 90% or greater

Cities – million inhabitants

Cities with a projected growth to 5 million or greater inhabitants by 2000

Cities with 5 million or greater inhabitants in 1985 with projected growth to 2000

Population potential
Many developed countries have achieved a stable population – a balanced birth rate and death rate. However high birth and death rates and a large infant mortality seems to be the norm in the third world. The high birth rate often reflects the desire for a large family due to high infant mortality, labour intensive means of subsistence, and the need for support in old age. The large increase in population threatens to outstrip economic growth. Theoretically the birth rate can be controlled. However, there are often many reasons including religious taboos, lack of effective diet, health and education which means that population growth is still a major obstacle to development. Some countries have introduced tax incentives and maternity provisions in order to try and keep families small.

Life expectancy
70 years
60
50

Birth rate
— 10 Births

Death rate
— 10 Deaths

Infant mortality
— 10 Infant deaths
— 100 Infant deaths

Birth rate is number of births in a year per 1000 of the population.

Death rate is number of deaths in a year per 1000 of the population.

Infant mortality is annual number of deaths of children under one year per 1000 births

26

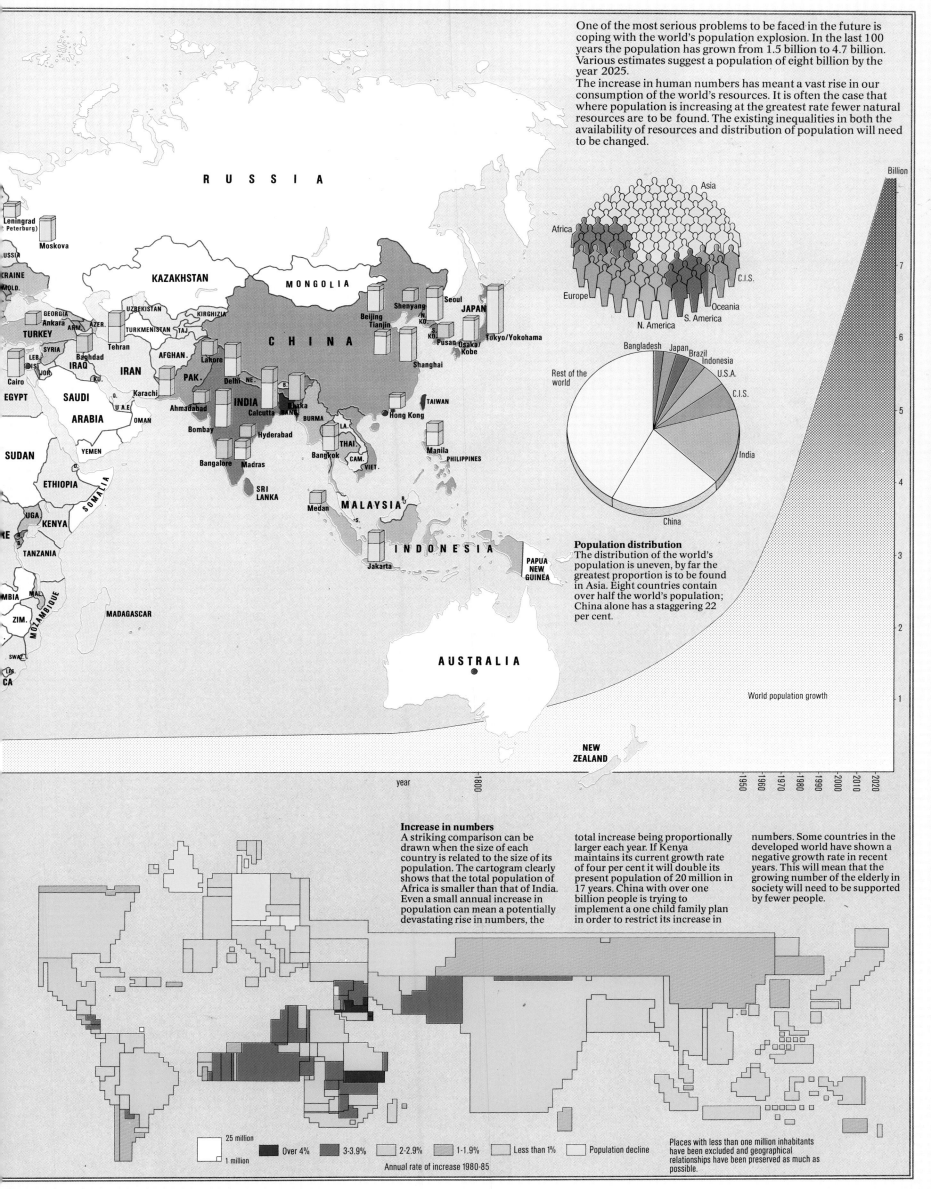

One of the most serious problems to be faced in the future is coping with the world's population explosion. In the last 100 years the population has grown from 1.5 billion to 4.7 billion. Various estimates suggest a population of eight billion by the year 2025.

The increase in human numbers has meant a vast rise in our consumption of the world's resources. It is often the case that where population is increasing at the greatest rate fewer natural resources are to be found. The existing inequalities in both the availability of resources and distribution of population will need to be changed.

Population distribution

The distribution of the world's population is uneven, by far the greatest proportion is to be found in Asia. Eight countries contain over half the world's population; China alone has a staggering 22 per cent.

World population growth

Increase in numbers

A striking comparison can be drawn when the size of each country is related to the size of its population. The cartogram clearly shows that the total population of Africa is smaller than that of India. Even a small annual increase in population can mean a potentially devastating rise in numbers, the total increase being proportionally larger each year. If Kenya maintains its current growth rate of four per cent it will double its present population of 20 million in 17 years. China with over one billion people is trying to implement a one child family plan in order to restrict its increase in numbers. Some countries in the developed world have shown a negative growth rate in recent years. This will mean that the growing number of the elderly in society will need to be supported by fewer people.

25 million — 1 million · Over 4% · 3-3.9% · 2-2.9% · 1-1.9% · Less than 1% · Population decline

Annual rate of increase 1980-85

Places with less than one million inhabitants have been excluded and geographical relationships have been preserved as much as possible.

27

Designed and produced by E.S.R.

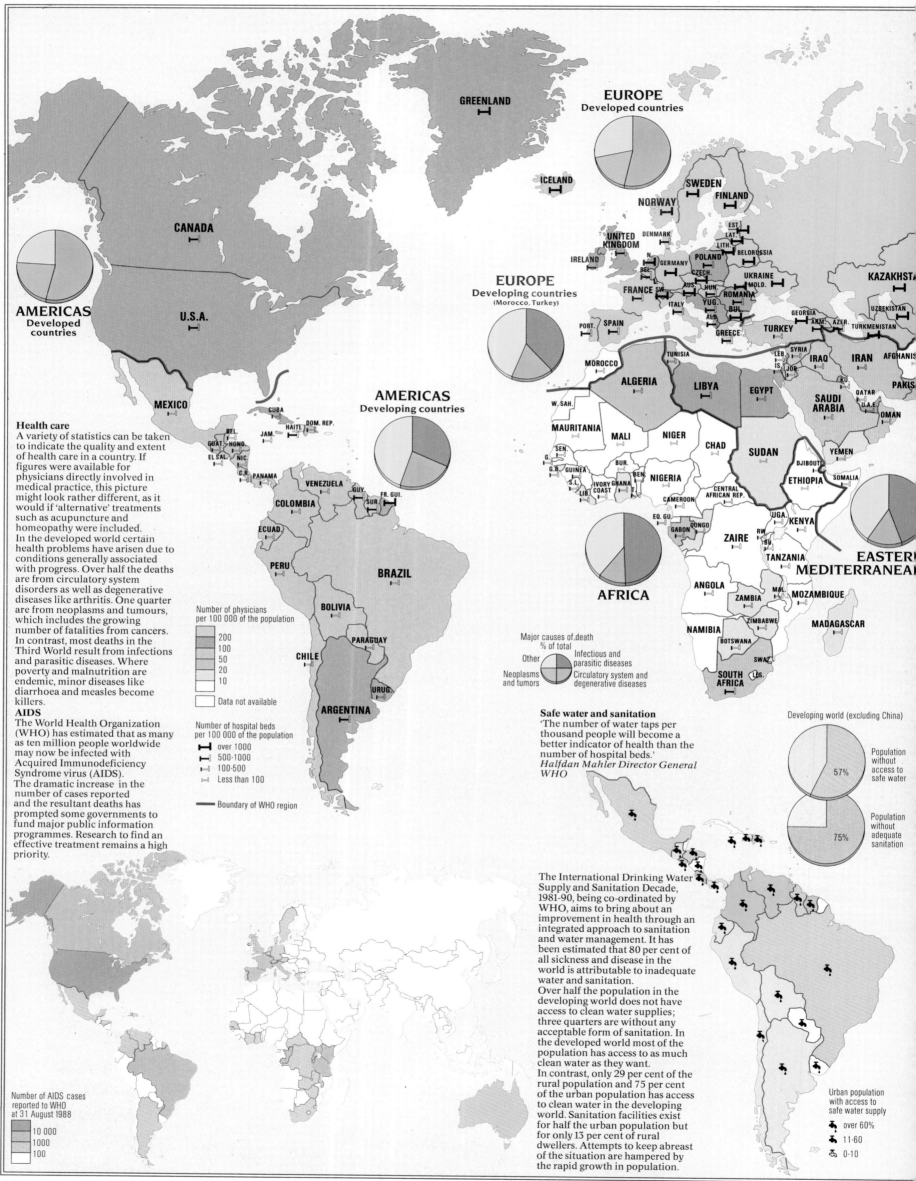

Health care

A variety of statistics can be taken to indicate the quality and extent of health care in a country. If figures were available for physicians directly involved in medical practice, this picture might look rather different, as it would if 'alternative' treatments such as acupuncture and homeopathy were included.
In the developed world certain health problems have arisen due to conditions generally associated with progress. Over half the deaths are from circulatory system disorders as well as degenerative diseases like arthritis. One quarter are from neoplasms and tumours, which includes the growing number of fatalities from cancers. In contrast, most deaths in the Third World result from infections and parasitic diseases. Where poverty and malnutrition are endemic, minor diseases like diarrhoea and measles become killers.

AIDS

The World Health Organization (WHO) has estimated that as many as ten million people worldwide may now be infected with Acquired Immunodeficiency Syndrome virus (AIDS).
The dramatic increase in the number of cases reported and the resultant deaths has prompted some governments to fund major public information programmes. Research to find an effective treatment remains a high priority.

Number of physicians
per 100 000 of the population

- 200
- 100
- 50
- 20
- 10
- Data not available

Number of hospital beds
per 100 000 of the population
- over 1000
- 500-1000
- 100-500
- Less than 100

— Boundary of WHO region

Major causes of death
% of total

Other | Infectious and parasitic diseases
Neoplasms and tumors | Circulatory system and degenerative diseases

Safe water and sanitation

'The number of water taps per thousand people will become a better indicator of health than the number of hospital beds.'
Halfdan Mahler Director General WHO

Developing world (excluding China)

57% — Population without access to safe water

75% — Population without adequate sanitation

The International Drinking Water Supply and Sanitation Decade, 1981-90, being co-ordinated by WHO, aims to bring about an improvement in health through an integrated approach to sanitation and water management. It has been estimated that 80 per cent of all sickness and disease in the world is attributable to inadequate water and sanitation.
Over half the population in the developing world does not have access to clean water supplies; three quarters are without any acceptable form of sanitation. In the developed world most of the population has access to as much clean water as they want.
In contrast, only 29 per cent of the rural population and 75 per cent of the urban population has access to clean water in the developing world. Sanitation facilities exist for half the urban population but for only 13 per cent of rural dwellers. Attempts to keep abreast of the situation are hampered by the rapid growth in population.

Number of AIDS cases
reported to WHO
at 31 August 1988
- 10 000
- 1000
- 100

Urban population
with access to
safe water supply
- over 60%
- 11-60
- 0-10

AMERICAS Developed countries

CANADA

U.S.A.

MEXICO

AMERICAS Developing countries

CUBA HAITI DOM. REP.
BEL. GUAT. HOND. JAM.
EL SAL. NIC.
C.R. PANAMA

VENEZUELA
GUY. SUR. FR. GUI.
COLOMBIA
ECUAD.
PERU
BRAZIL
BOLIVIA
PARAGUAY
CHILE
URUG.
ARGENTINA

GREENLAND

EUROPE Developed countries

ICELAND
NORWAY SWEDEN FINLAND
UNITED KINGDOM DENMARK EST. LAT. LITH.
IRELAND N. GERMANY POLAND BELORUSSIA
BEL. CZECH. UKRAINE
FRANCE SW. AUS. HUN. MOLD. ROMANIA
ITALY YUG. BUL.
PORT. SPAIN ALB. GREECE TURKEY GEORGIA AKM. AZER.

EUROPE Developing countries (Morocco, Turkey)

KAZAKHSTA
UZBEKISTAN
TURKMENISTAN
SYRIA IRAQ IRAN AFGHANIS
LEB. IS. JOR. KU. PAKIS
MOROCCO TUNISIA
ALGERIA LIBYA EGYPT SAUDI ARABIA QATAR U.A.E. OMAN
W. SAH.
MAURITANIA MALI NIGER CHAD SUDAN YEMEN
SEN. DJIBOUTI SOMALIA
G.B. GUINEA BUR. BEN. NIGERIA ETHIOPIA
S.L. IVORY GHANA CENTRAL AFRICAN REP.
LIB. COAST CAMEROON
EQ. GU. UGA. KENYA
GABON CONGO RW.
ZAIRE BU.
TANZANIA
ANGOLA ZAMBIA MAL. MOZAMBIQUE
NAMIBIA ZIMBABWE MADAGASCAR
BOTSWANA SWAZ.
SOUTH AFRICA LES.

AFRICA

EASTER MEDITERRANEA

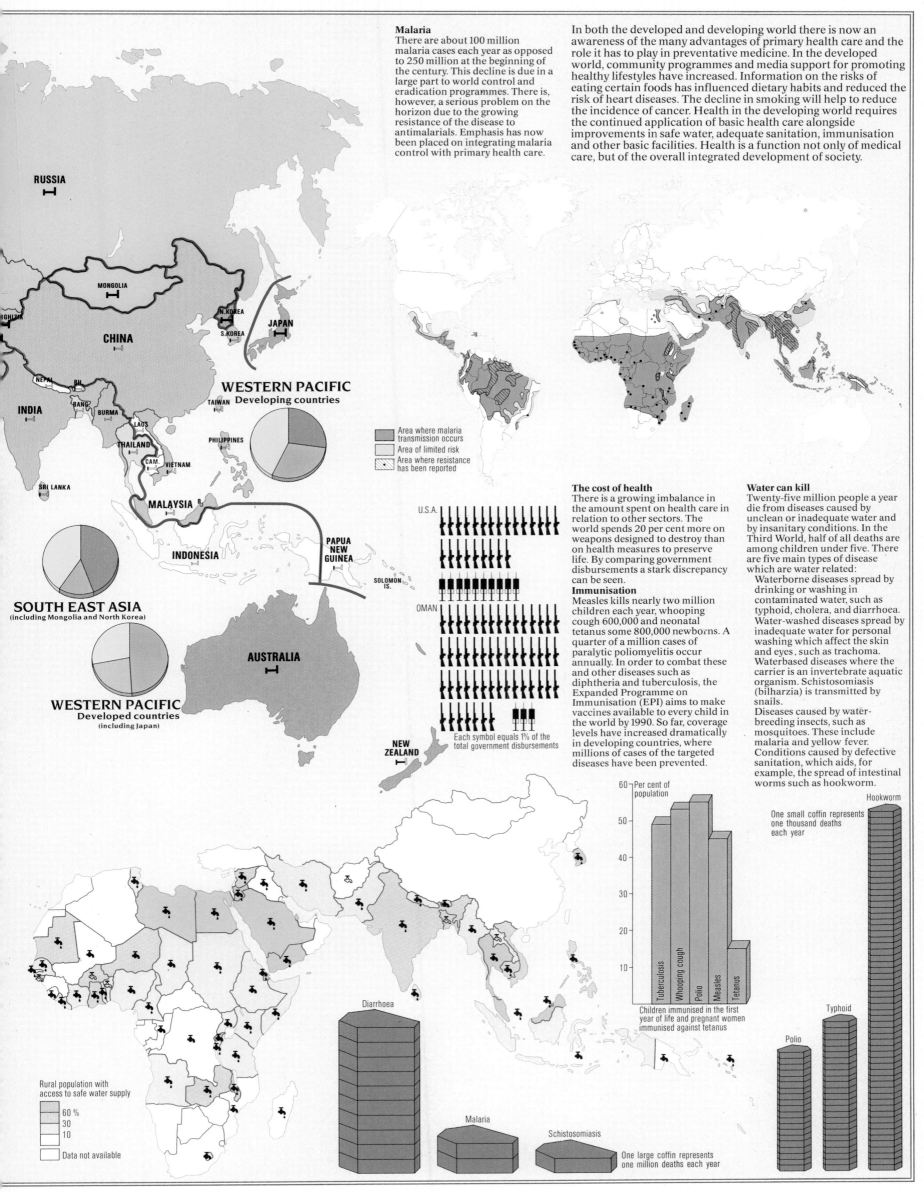

Malaria

There are about 100 million malaria cases each year as opposed to 250 million at the beginning of the century. This decline is due in a large part to world control and eradication programmes. There is, however, a serious problem on the horizon due to the growing resistance of the disease to antimalarials. Emphasis has now been placed on integrating malaria control with primary health care.

In both the developed and developing world there is now an awareness of the many advantages of primary health care and the role it has to play in preventative medicine. In the developed world, community programmes and media support for promoting healthy lifestyles have increased. Information on the risks of eating certain foods has influenced dietary habits and reduced the risk of heart diseases. The decline in smoking will help to reduce the incidence of cancer. Health in the developing world requires the continued application of basic health care alongside improvements in safe water, adequate sanitation, immunisation and other basic facilities. Health is a function not only of medical care, but of the overall integrated development of society.

RUSSIA

MONGOLIA

N. KOREA

S. KOREA

JAPAN

CHINA

NEPAL

BH

BANG

BURMA

INDIA

LAOS

THAILAND

TAIWAN

WESTERN PACIFIC
Developing countries

PHILIPPINES

CAM.

VIETNAM

SRI LANKA

MALAYSIA

INDONESIA

PAPUA NEW GUINEA

SOLOMON IS.

SOUTH EAST ASIA
(including Mongolia and North Korea)

AUSTRALIA

WESTERN PACIFIC
Developed countries
(including Japan)

NEW ZEALAND

Area where malaria transmission occurs

Area of limited risk

Area where resistance has been reported

The cost of health

There is a growing imbalance in the amount spent on health care in relation to other sectors. The world spends 20 per cent more on weapons designed to destroy than on health measures to preserve life. By comparing government disbursements a stark discrepancy can be seen.

U.S.A.

OMAN

Each symbol equals 1% of the total government disbursements

Immunisation

Measles kills nearly two million children each year, whooping cough 600,000 and neonatal tetanus some 800,000 newborns. A quarter of a million cases of paralytic poliomyelitis occur annually. In order to combat these and other diseases such as diphtheria and tuberculosis, the Expanded Programme on Immunisation (EPI) aims to make vaccines available to every child in the world by 1990. So far, coverage levels have increased dramatically in developing countries, where millions of cases of the targeted diseases have been prevented.

Water can kill

Twenty-five million people a year die from diseases caused by unclean or inadequate water and by insanitary conditions. In the Third World, half of all deaths are among children under five. There are five main types of disease which are water related:

Waterborne diseases spread by drinking or washing in contaminated water, such as typhoid, cholera, and diarrhoea.
Water-washed diseases spread by inadequate water for personal washing which affect the skin and eyes, such as trachoma.
Waterbased diseases where the carrier is an invertebrate aquatic organism. Schistosomiasis (bilharzia) is transmitted by snails.
Diseases caused by water-breeding insects, such as mosquitoes. These include malaria and yellow fever.
Conditions caused by defective sanitation, which aids, for example, the spread of intestinal worms such as hookworm.

60 Per cent of population

50

40

30

20

10

Tuberculosis

Whooping cough

Polio

Measles

Tetanus

Children immunised in the first year of life and pregnant women immunised against tetanus

One small coffin represents one thousand deaths each year

Hookworm

Typhoid

Polio

Diarrhoea

Malaria

Schistosomiasis

One large coffin represents one million deaths each year

Rural population with access to safe water supply

60 %
30
10

Data not available

EDUCATION AND WORK

It has been argued that the kind of education provided by schools may be less important than 'traditional' wisdom derived from experience, especially in cultures other than those in the industrialised world. Education in the Third World has often been modelled on imported curricula which reflect the needs and conditions of a different society. Though newly independent nations introduce more suitable subjects, they may often lack the resources for relevant teaching materials.

Illiteracy

An illiterate person, one who is unable to read or write, is at a basic disadvantage in a world where literacy is an increasingly critical skill. Despite many literacy programmes, the total number of illiterates – over 800 million people, most of them in developing countries – continues to grow. These nations have only 12 per cent of the world's education budget. Most African countries spend less than ten per cent of GNP on education. There is a noticeable gap between the levels of male and female illiteracy, the latter being higher. This is often due to cultural differences and religious attitudes.

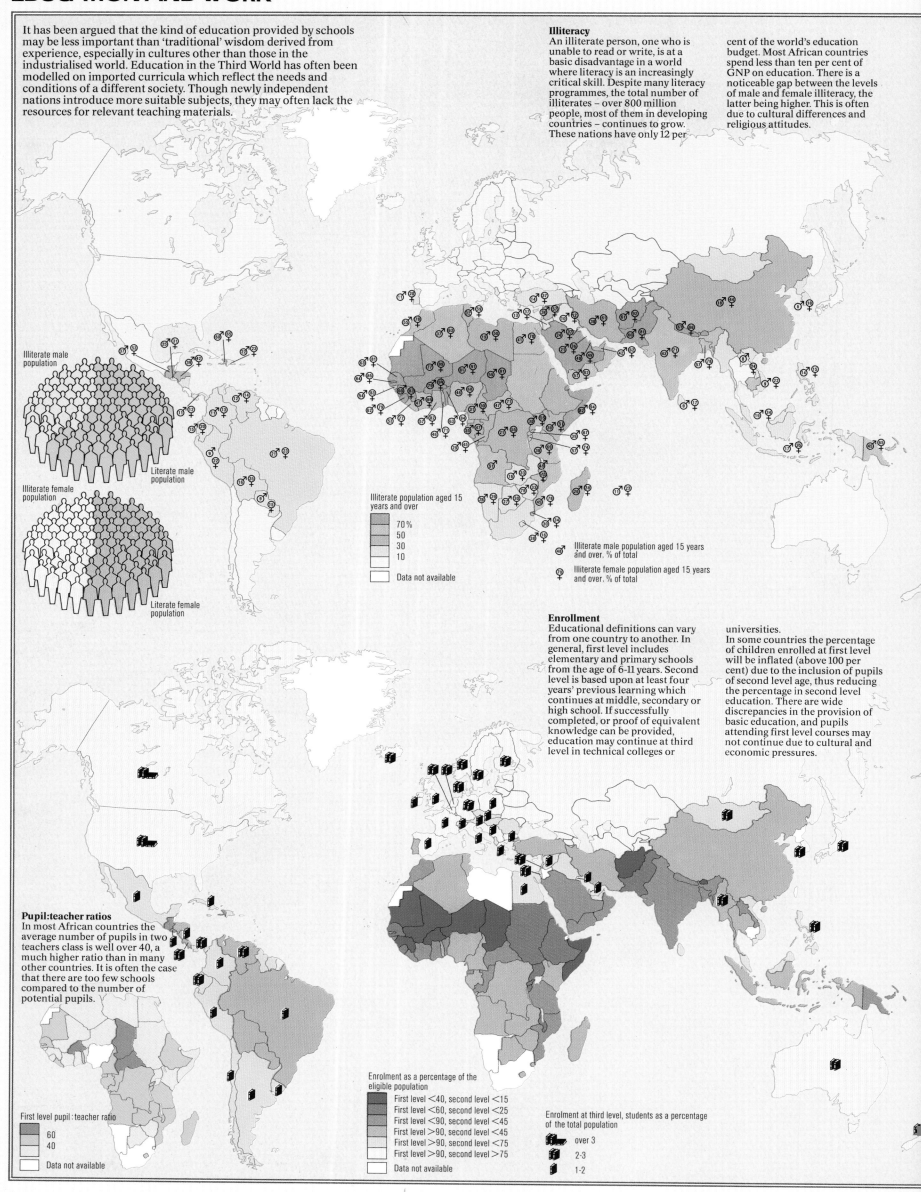

Illiterate male population

Literate male population

Illiterate female population

Literate female population

Illiterate population aged 15 years and over

70 %
50
30
10

Data not available

Illiterate male population aged 15 years and over, % of total

Illiterate female population aged 15 years and over, % of total

Enrollment

Educational definitions can vary from one country to another. In general, first level includes elementary and primary schools from the age of 6-11 years. Second level is based upon at least four years' previous learning which continues at middle, secondary or high school. If successfully completed, or proof of equivalent knowledge can be provided, education may continue at third level in technical colleges or universities.

In some countries the percentage of children enrolled at first level will be inflated (above 100 per cent) due to the inclusion of pupils of second level age, thus reducing the percentage in second level education. There are wide discrepancies in the provision of basic education, and pupils attending first level courses may not continue due to cultural and economic pressures.

Pupil:teacher ratios

In most African countries the average number of pupils in two teachers class is well over 40, a much higher ratio than in many other countries. It is often the case that there are too few schools compared to the number of potential pupils.

First level pupil : teacher ratio

60
40

Data not available

Enrolment as a percentage of the eligible population

First level <40, second level <15
First level <60, second level <25
First level <90, second level <45
First level >90, second level <45
First level >90, second level <75
First level >90, second level >75

Data not available

Enrolment at third level, students as a percentage of the total population

over 3
2-3
1-2

30

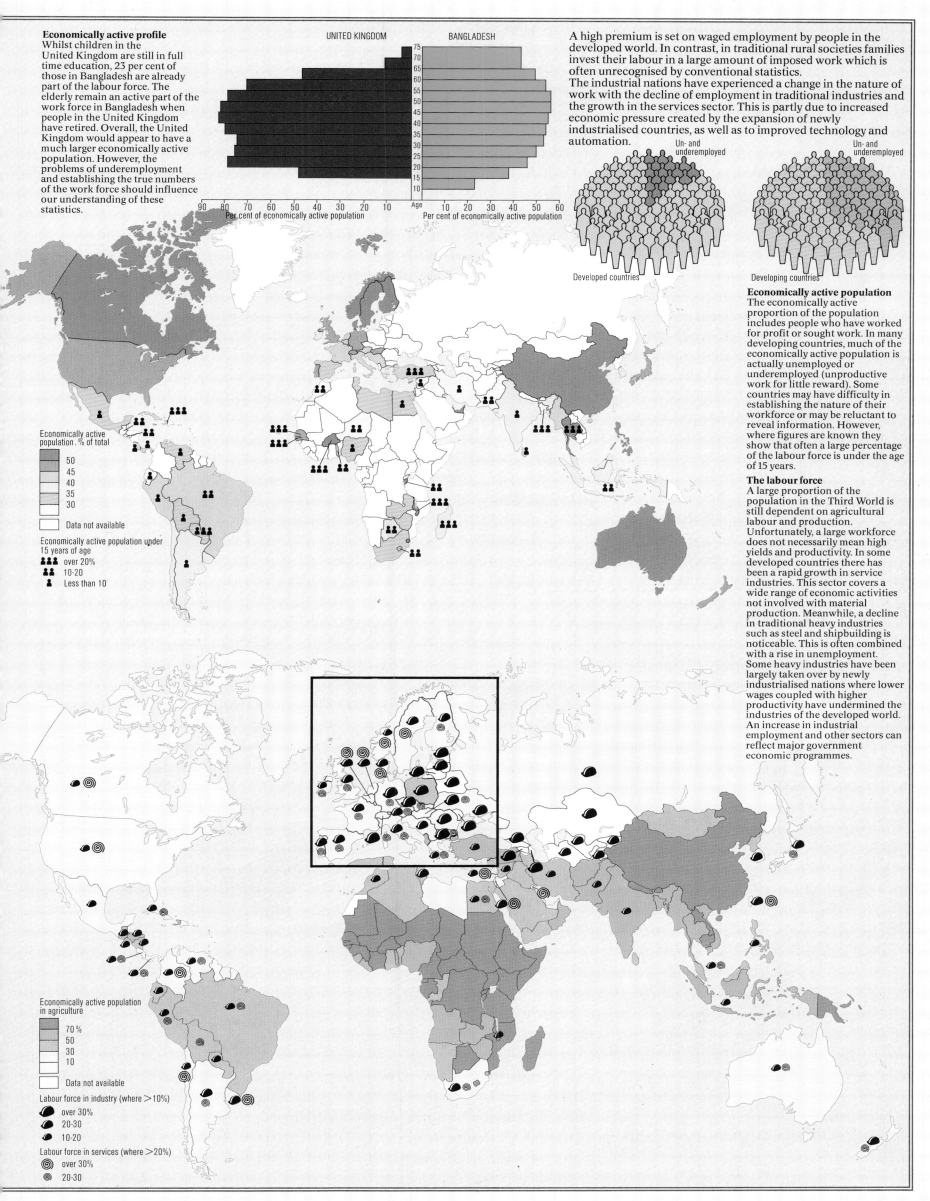

Economically active profile

Whilst children in the United Kingdom are still in full time education, 23 per cent of those in Bangladesh are already part of the labour force. The elderly remain an active part of the work force in Bangladesh when people in the United Kingdom have retired. Overall, the United Kingdom would appear to have a much larger economically active population. However, the problems of underemployment and establishing the true numbers of the work force should influence our understanding of these statistics.

UNITED KINGDOM BANGLADESH

Per cent of economically active population

A high premium is set on waged employment by people in the developed world. In contrast, in traditional rural societies families invest their labour in a large amount of imposed work which is often unrecognised by conventional statistics.

The industrial nations have experienced a change in the nature of work with the decline of employment in traditional industries and the growth in the services sector. This is partly due to increased economic pressure created by the expansion of newly industrialised countries, as well as to improved technology and automation.

Un- and underemployed

Developed countries

Un- and underemployed

Developing countries

Economically active population

The economically active proportion of the population includes people who have worked for profit or sought work. In many developing countries, much of the economically active population is actually unemployed or underemployed (unproductive work for little reward). Some countries may have difficulty in establishing the nature of their workforce or may be reluctant to reveal information. However, where figures are known they show that often a large percentage of the labour force is under the age of 15 years.

The labour force

A large proportion of the population in the Third World is still dependent on agricultural labour and production. Unfortunately, a large workforce does not necessarily mean high yields and productivity. In some developed countries there has been a rapid growth in service industries. This sector covers a wide range of economic activities not involved with material production. Meanwhile, a decline in traditional heavy industries such as steel and shipbuilding is noticeable. This is often combined with a rise in unemployment. Some heavy industries have been largely taken over by newly industrialised nations where lower wages coupled with higher productivity have undermined the industries of the developed world. An increase in industrial employment and other sectors can reflect major government economic programmes.

Economically active population . % of total

- 50
- 45
- 40
- 35
- 30
- Data not available

Economically active population under 15 years of age

- over 20%
- 10-20
- Less than 10

Economically active population in agriculture

- 70 %
- 50
- 30
- 10
- Data not available

Labour force in industry (where >10%)
- over 30%
- 20-30
- 10-20

Labour force in services (where >20%)
- over 30%
- 20-30

LAND USE

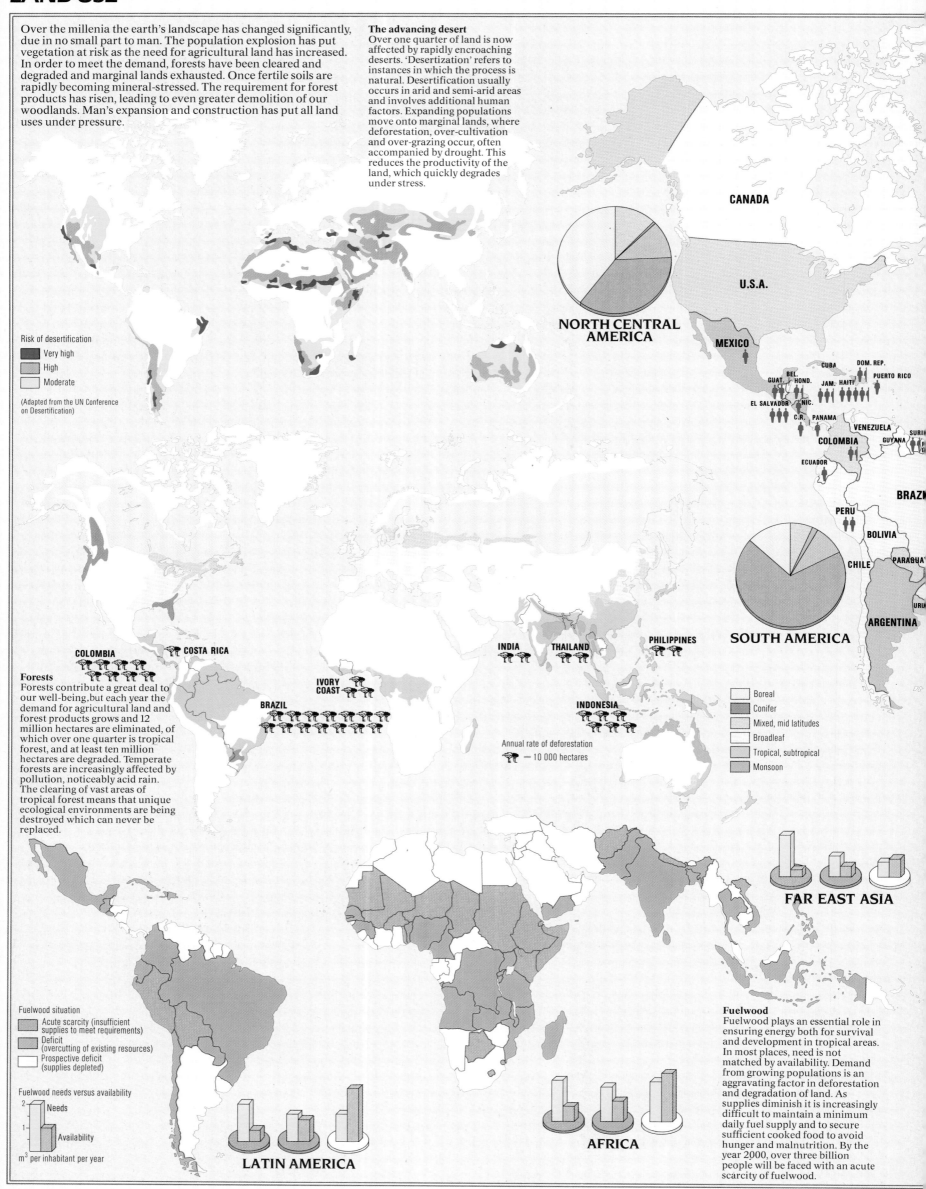

Over the millenia the earth's landscape has changed significantly, due in no small part to man. The population explosion has put vegetation at risk as the need for agricultural land has increased. In order to meet the demand, forests have been cleared and degraded and marginal lands exhausted. Once fertile soils are rapidly becoming mineral-stressed. The requirement for forest products has risen, leading to even greater demolition of our woodlands. Man's expansion and construction has put all land uses under pressure.

The advancing desert

Over one quarter of land is now affected by rapidly encroaching deserts. 'Desertization' refers to instances in which the process is natural. Desertification usually occurs in arid and semi-arid areas and involves additional human factors. Expanding populations move onto marginal lands, where deforestation, over-cultivation and over-grazing occur, often accompanied by drought. This reduces the productivity of the land, which quickly degrades under stress.

Risk of desertification

- ■ Very high
- ▨ High
- ☐ Moderate

(Adapted from the UN Conference on Desertification)

Forests

Forests contribute a great deal to our well-being, but each year the demand for agricultural land and forest products grows and 12 million hectares are eliminated, of which over one quarter is tropical forest, and at least ten million hectares are degraded. Temperate forests are increasingly affected by pollution, noticeably acid rain. The clearing of vast areas of tropical forest means that unique ecological environments are being destroyed which can never be replaced.

Annual rate of deforestation

🌳 = 10 000 hectares

Forest types

- ☐ Boreal
- ▨ Conifer
- ☐ Mixed, mid latitudes
- ☐ Broadleaf
- ▨ Tropical, subtropical
- ▨ Monsoon

NORTH CENTRAL AMERICA

SOUTH AMERICA

FAR EAST ASIA

CANADA · U.S.A. · MEXICO · CUBA · DOM. REP. · BEL · GUAT. · HOND. · JAM. · HAITI · PUERTO RICO · EL SALVADOR · NIC. · C.R. · PANAMA · VENEZUELA · SURI · COLOMBIA · GUYANA · ECUADOR · BRAZ · PERU · BOLIVIA · CHILE · PARAGUA · URU · ARGENTINA

COLOMBIA · COSTA RICA · IVORY COAST · BRAZIL · INDIA · THAILAND · PHILIPPINES · INDONESIA

Fuelwood

Fuelwood plays an essential role in ensuring energy both for survival and development in tropical areas. In most places, need is not matched by availability. Demand from growing populations is an aggravating factor in deforestation and degradation of land. As supplies diminish it is increasingly difficult to maintain a minimum daily fuel supply and to secure sufficient cooked food to avoid hunger and malnutrition. By the year 2000, over three billion people will be faced with an acute scarcity of fuelwood.

Fuelwood situation

- ▨ Acute scarcity (insufficient supplies to meet requirements)
- ▨ Deficit (overcutting of existing resources)
- ☐ Prospective deficit (supplies depleted)

Fuelwood needs versus availability

Needs · Availability

m³ per inhabitant per year

LATIN AMERICA

AFRICA

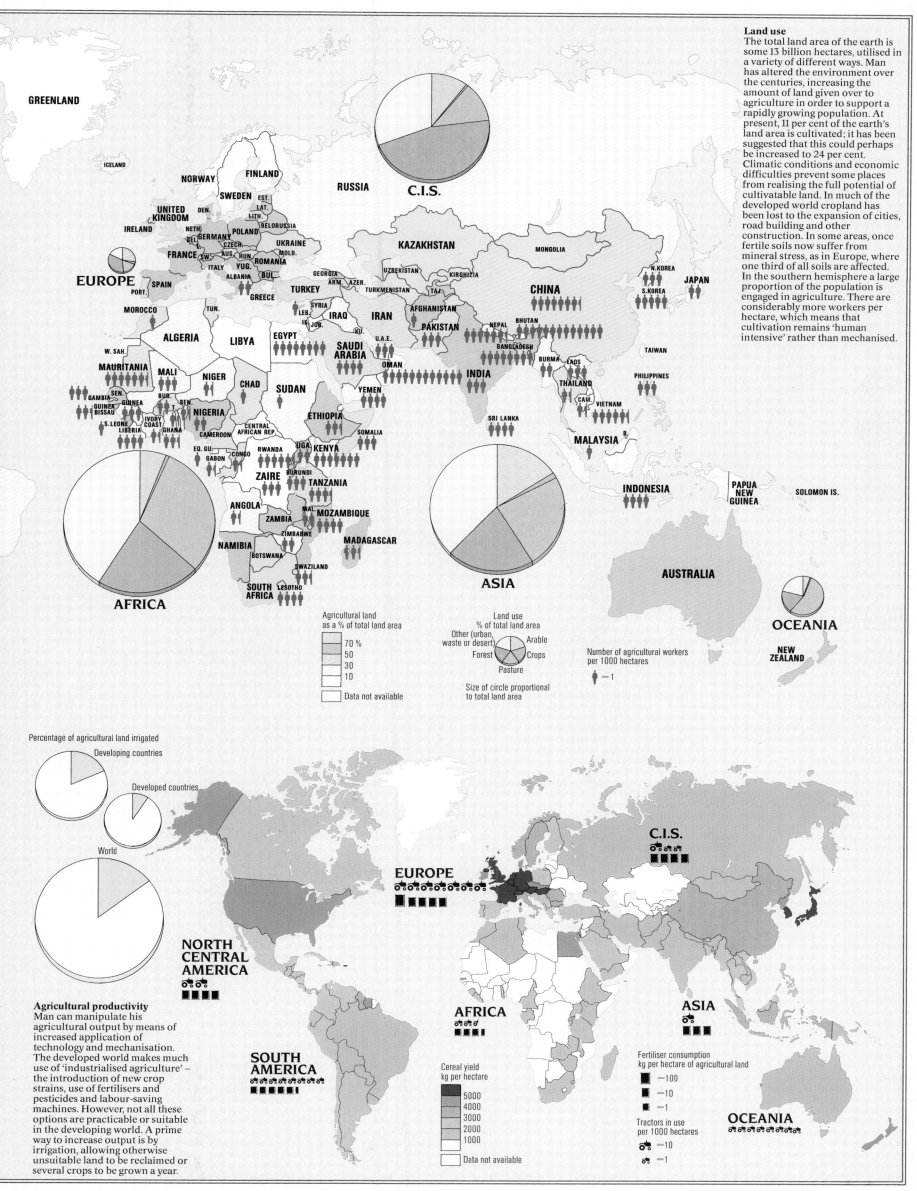

Land use

The total land area of the earth is some 13 billion hectares, utilised in a variety of different ways. Man has altered the environment over the centuries, increasing the amount of land given over to agriculture in order to support a rapidly growing population. At present, 11 per cent of the earth's land area is cultivated; it has been suggested that this could perhaps be increased to 24 per cent. Climatic conditions and economic difficulties prevent some places from realising the full potential of cultivatable land. In much of the developed world cropland has been lost to the expansion of cities, road building and other construction. In some areas, once fertile soils now suffer from mineral stress, as in Europe, where one third of all soils are affected. In the southern hemisphere a large proportion of the population is engaged in agriculture. There are considerably more workers per hectare, which means that cultivation remains 'human intensive' rather than mechanised.

Agricultural productivity

Man can manipulate his agricultural output by means of increased application of technology and mechanisation. The developed world makes much use of 'industrialised agriculture' – the introduction of new crop strains, use of fertilisers and pesticides and labour-saving machines. However, not all these options are practicable or suitable in the developing world. A prime way to increase output is by irrigation, allowing otherwise unsuitable land to be reclaimed or several crops to be grown a year.

Agricultural land as a % of total land area
70 %
50
30
10
Data not available

Land use % of total land area
Other (urban, waste or desert)
Forest
Arable
Crops
Pasture
Size of circle proportional to total land area

Number of agricultural workers per 1000 hectares = 1

Percentage of agricultural land irrigated
Developing countries
Developed countries
World

Cereal yield kg per hectare
5000
4000
3000
2000
1000
Data not available

Fertiliser consumption kg per hectare of agricultural land
= 100
= 10
= 1

Tractors in use per 1000 hectares
= 10
= 1

Designed and produced by E.S.R.

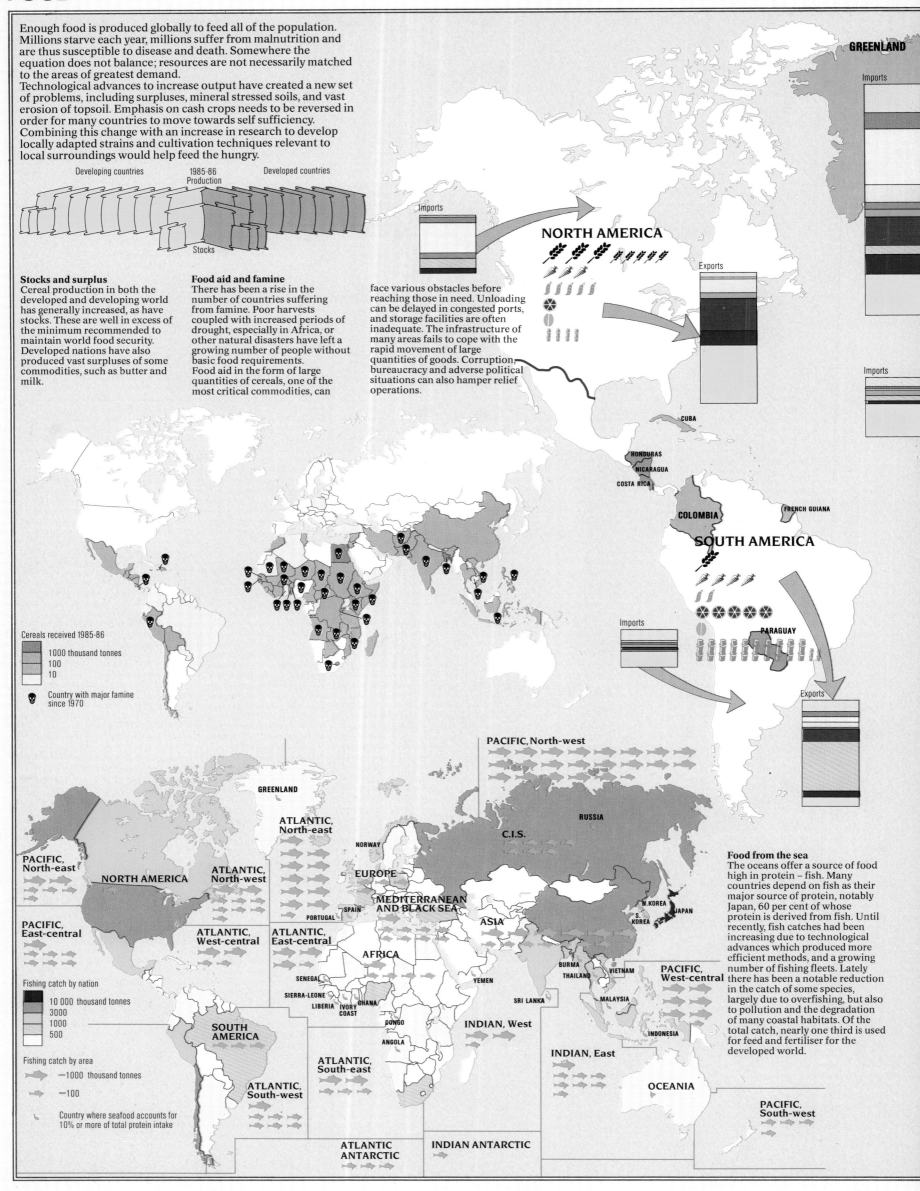

Enough food is produced globally to feed all of the population. Millions starve each year, millions suffer from malnutrition and are thus susceptible to disease and death. Somewhere the equation does not balance; resources are not necessarily matched to the areas of greatest demand.
Technological advances to increase output have created a new set of problems, including surpluses, mineral stressed soils, and vast erosion of topsoil. Emphasis on cash crops needs to be reversed in order for many countries to move towards self sufficiency. Combining this change with an increase in research to develop locally adapted strains and cultivation techniques relevant to local surroundings would help feed the hungry.

Developing countries   1985-86 Production   Developed countries

Stocks

Stocks and surplus
Cereal production in both the developed and developing world has generally increased, as have stocks. These are well in excess of the minimum recommended to maintain world food security. Developed nations have also produced vast surpluses of some commodities, such as butter and milk.

Food aid and famine
There has been a rise in the number of countries suffering from famine. Poor harvests coupled with increased periods of drought, especially in Africa, or other natural disasters have left a growing number of people without basic food requirements.
Food aid in the form of large quantities of cereals, one of the most critical commodities, can face various obstacles before reaching those in need. Unloading can be delayed in congested ports, and storage facilities are often inadequate. The infrastructure of many areas fails to cope with the rapid movement of large quantities of goods. Corruption, bureaucracy and adverse political situations can also hamper relief operations.

GREENLAND

Imports

NORTH AMERICA

Imports

Exports

CUBA

HONDURAS
NICARAGUA
COSTA RICA

COLOMBIA   FRENCH GUIANA

SOUTH AMERICA

Imports

PARAGUAY

Exports

Cereals received 1985-86
1000 thousand tonnes
100
10

● Country with major famine since 1970

Food from the sea
The oceans offer a source of food high in protein – fish. Many countries depend on fish as their major source of protein, notably Japan, 60 per cent of whose protein is derived from fish. Until recently, fish catches had been increasing due to technological advances which produced more efficient methods, and a growing number of fishing fleets. Lately there has been a notable reduction in the catch of some species, largely due to overfishing, but also to pollution and the degradation of many coastal habitats. Of the total catch, nearly one third is used for feed and fertiliser for the developed world.

PACIFIC, North-west

PACIFIC, North-east

NORTH AMERICA

ATLANTIC, North-west

ATLANTIC, North-east

GREENLAND

NORWAY

EUROPE

RUSSIA

C.I.S.

ASIA

N. KOREA
S. KOREA   JAPAN

PACIFIC, North-east

PACIFIC, East-central

ATLANTIC, West-central

ATLANTIC, East-central

MEDITERRANEAN AND BLACK SEA

SPAIN

PORTUGAL

AFRICA

SENEGAL

SIERRA-LEONE
LIBERIA IVORY GHANA
          COAST

CONGO

ANGOLA

SOUTH AMERICA

BURMA
THAILAND

VIETNAM

YEMEN

SRI LANKA

MALAYSIA

INDONESIA

PACIFIC, West-central

INDIAN, West

INDIAN, East

OCEANIA

Fishing catch by nation
10 000 thousand tonnes
3000
1000
500

Fishing catch by area
—1000 thousand tonnes
—100

Country where seafood accounts for 10% or more of total protein intake

ATLANTIC, South-west

ATLANTIC, South-east

PACIFIC, South-west

ATLANTIC ANTARCTIC

INDIAN ANTARCTIC

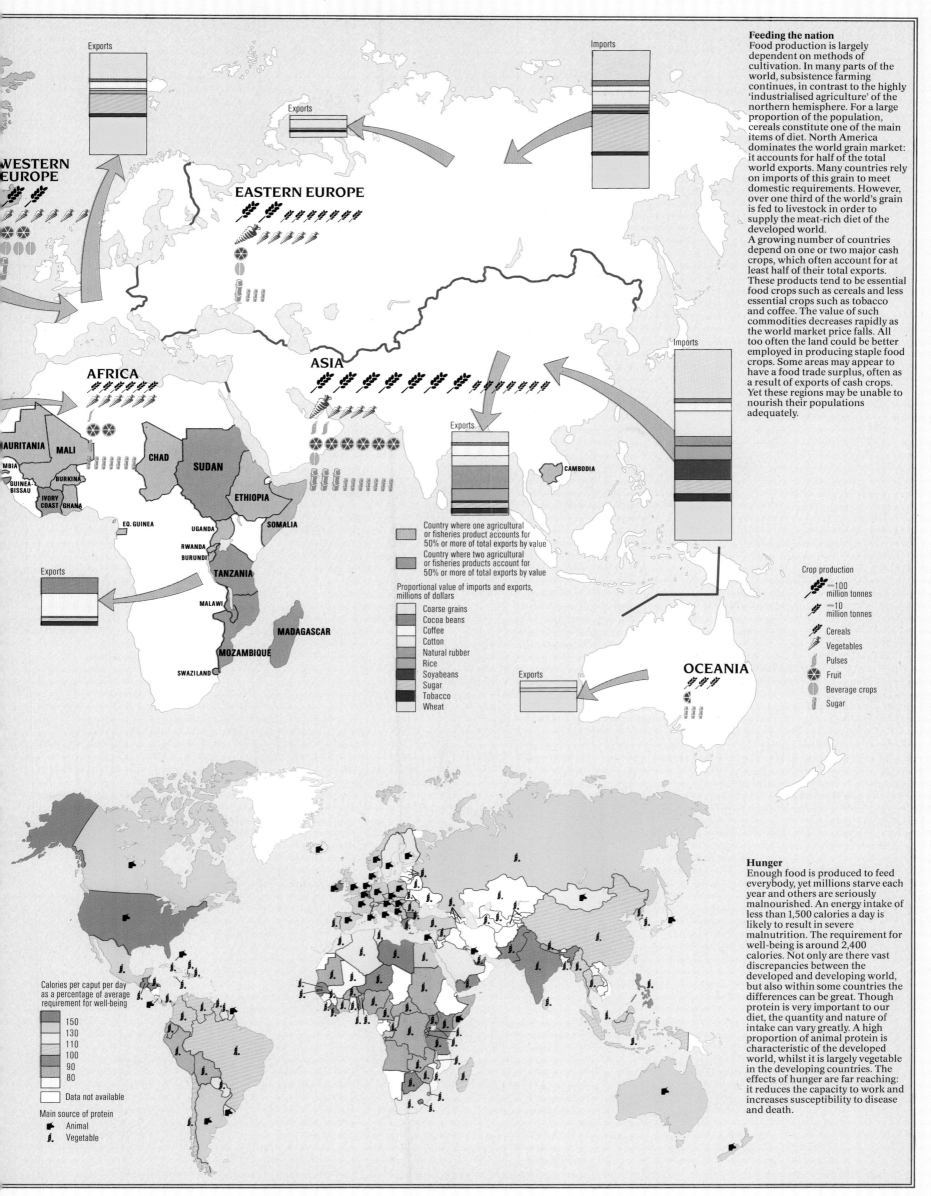

Feeding the nation
Food production is largely dependent on methods of cultivation. In many parts of the world, subsistence farming continues, in contrast to the highly 'industrialised agriculture' of the northern hemisphere. For a large proportion of the population, cereals constitute one of the main items of diet. North America dominates the world grain market: it accounts for half of the total world exports. Many countries rely on imports of this grain to meet domestic requirements. However, over one third of the world's grain is fed to livestock in order to supply the meat-rich diet of the developed world.
A growing number of countries depend on one or two major cash crops, which often account for at least half of their total exports. These products tend to be essential food crops such as cereals and less essential crops such as tobacco and coffee. The value of such commodities decreases rapidly as the world market price falls. All too often the land could be better employed in producing staple food crops. Some areas may appear to have a food trade surplus, often as a result of exports of cash crops. Yet these regions may be unable to nourish their populations adequately.

WESTERN EUROPE

EASTERN EUROPE

AFRICA

ASIA

OCEANIA

Exports
Imports
Exports
Imports
Exports
Exports
Imports
Exports

MAURITANIA
MALI
MBIA
GUINEA-BISSAU
BURKINA
IVORY COAST
GHANA
EQ. GUINEA
CHAD
SUDAN
ETHIOPIA
UGANDA
SOMALIA
RWANDA
BURUNDI
TANZANIA
MALAWI
MADAGASCAR
MOZAMBIQUE
SWAZILAND

CAMBODIA

Country where one agricultural or fisheries product accounts for 50% or more of total exports by value
Country where two agricultural or fisheries products account for 50% or more of total exports by value

Proportional value of imports and exports, millions of dollars
Coarse grains
Cocoa beans
Coffee
Cotton
Natural rubber
Rice
Soyabeans
Sugar
Tobacco
Wheat

Crop production
—100 million tonnes
—10 million tonnes
Cereals
Vegetables
Pulses
Fruit
Beverage crops
Sugar

Hunger
Enough food is produced to feed everybody, yet millions starve each year and others are seriously malnourished. An energy intake of less than 1,500 calories a day is likely to result in severe malnutrition. The requirement for well-being is around 2,400 calories. Not only are there vast discrepancies between the developed and developing world, but also within some countries the differences can be great. Though protein is very important to our diet, the quantity and nature of intake can vary greatly. A high proportion of animal protein is characteristic of the developed world, whilst it is largely vegetable in the developing countries. The effects of hunger are far reaching: it reduces the capacity to work and increases susceptibility to disease and death.

Calories per caput per day as a percentage of average requirement for well-being
150
130
110
100
90
80
Data not available

Main source of protein
Animal
Vegetable

35

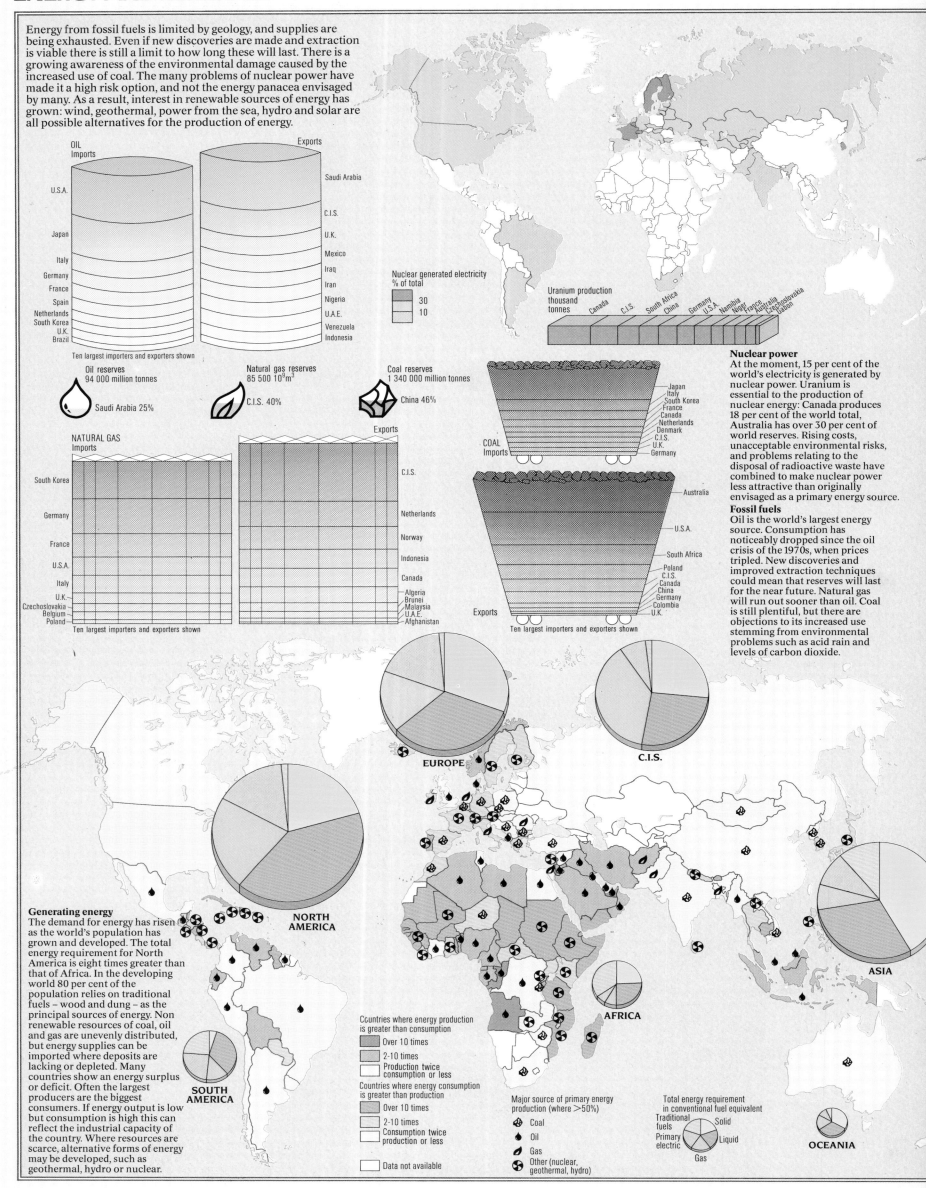

Energy from fossil fuels is limited by geology, and supplies are being exhausted. Even if new discoveries are made and extraction is viable there is still a limit to how long these will last. There is a growing awareness of the environmental damage caused by the increased use of coal. The many problems of nuclear power have made it a high risk option, and not the energy panacea envisaged by many. As a result, interest in renewable sources of energy has grown: wind, geothermal, power from the sea, hydro and solar are all possible alternatives for the production of energy.

OIL
Imports

Exports

U.S.A.
Japan
Italy
Germany
France
Spain
Netherlands
South Korea
U.K.
Brazil

Saudi Arabia
C.I.S.
U.K.
Mexico
Iraq
Iran
Nigeria
U.A.E.
Venezuela
Indonesia

Ten largest importers and exporters shown

Nuclear generated electricity
% of total
30
10

Uranium production
thousand
tonnes

Canada · C.I.S. · South Africa · China · Germany · U.S.A. · Namibia · Niger · France · Australia · Czechoslovakia · Gabon

Oil reserves
94 000 million tonnes
Saudi Arabia 25%

Natural gas reserves
85 500 10⁹m³
C.I.S. 40%

Coal reserves
1 340 000 million tonnes
China 46%

NATURAL GAS
Imports

Exports

South Korea
Germany
France
U.S.A.
Italy
U.K.
Czechoslovakia
Belgium
Poland

C.I.S.
Netherlands
Norway
Indonesia
Canada
Algeria
Brunei
Malaysia
U.A.E.
Afghanistan

Ten largest importers and exporters shown

COAL
Imports

Japan
Italy
South Korea
France
Canada
Netherlands
Denmark
C.I.S.
U.K.
Germany

Australia
U.S.A.
South Africa
Poland
C.I.S.
Canada
China
Germany
Colombia
U.K.

Exports

Ten largest importers and exporters shown

Nuclear power
At the moment, 15 per cent of the world's electricity is generated by nuclear power. Uranium is essential to the production of nuclear energy: Canada produces 18 per cent of the world total, Australia has over 30 per cent of world reserves. Rising costs, unacceptable environmental risks, and problems relating to the disposal of radioactive waste have combined to make nuclear power less attractive than originally envisaged as a primary energy source.

Fossil fuels
Oil is the world's largest energy source. Consumption has noticeably dropped since the oil crisis of the 1970s, when prices tripled. New discoveries and improved extraction techniques could mean that reserves will last for the near future. Natural gas will run out sooner than oil. Coal is still plentiful, but there are objections to its increased use stemming from environmental problems such as acid rain and levels of carbon dioxide.

EUROPE

C.I.S.

NORTH AMERICA

ASIA

Generating energy
The demand for energy has risen as the world's population has grown and developed. The total energy requirement for North America is eight times greater than that of Africa. In the developing world 80 per cent of the population relies on traditional fuels – wood and dung – as the principal sources of energy. Non renewable resources of coal, oil and gas are unevenly distributed, but energy supplies can be imported where deposits are lacking or depleted. Many countries show an energy surplus or deficit. Often the largest producers are the biggest consumers. If energy output is low but consumption is high this can reflect the industrial capacity of the country. Where resources are scarce, alternative forms of energy may be developed, such as geothermal, hydro or nuclear.

AFRICA

SOUTH AMERICA

Countries where energy production is greater than consumption
Over 10 times
2-10 times
Production twice consumption or less

Countries where energy consumption is greater than production
Over 10 times
2-10 times
Consumption twice production or less

Data not available

Major source of primary energy production (where >50%)
Coal
Oil
Gas
Other (nuclear, geothermal, hydro)

Total energy requirement in conventional fuel equivalent
Traditional fuels
Primary electric
Solid
Liquid
Gas

OCEANIA

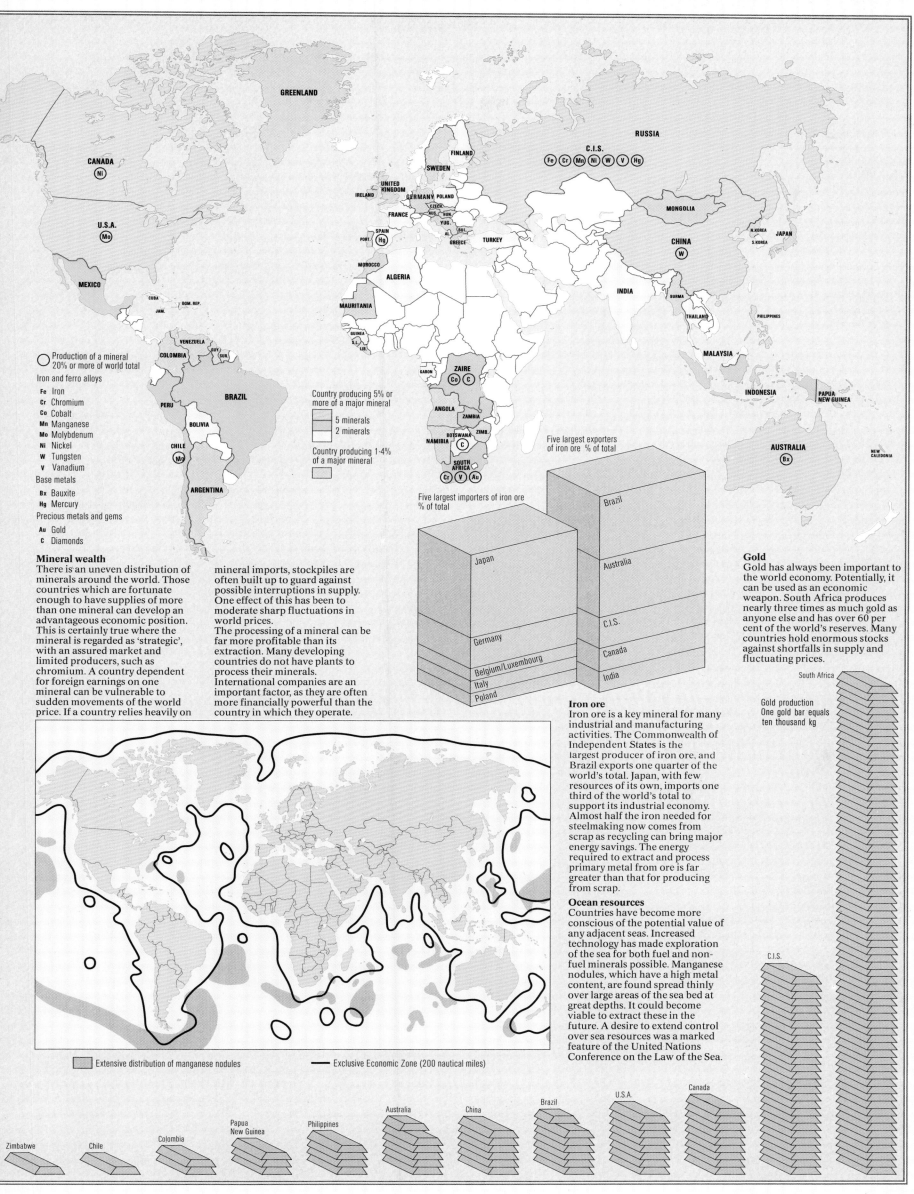

Mineral wealth

There is an uneven distribution of minerals around the world. Those countries which are fortunate enough to have supplies of more than one mineral can develop an advantageous economic position. This is certainly true where the mineral is regarded as 'strategic', with an assured market and limited producers, such as chromium. A country dependent for foreign earnings on one mineral can be vulnerable to sudden movements of the world price. If a country relies heavily on mineral imports, stockpiles are often built up to guard against possible interruptions in supply. One effect of this has been to moderate sharp fluctuations in world prices.

The processing of a mineral can be far more profitable than its extraction. Many developing countries do not have plants to process their minerals. International companies are an important factor, as they are often more financially powerful than the country in which they operate.

Production of a mineral 20% or more of world total

Iron and ferro alloys
- Fe Iron
- Cr Chromium
- Co Cobalt
- Mn Manganese
- Mo Molybdenum
- Ni Nickel
- W Tungsten
- V Vanadium

Base metals
- Bx Bauxite
- Hg Mercury

Precious metals and gems
- Au Gold
- C Diamonds

Country producing 5% or more of a major mineral
- 5 minerals
- 2 minerals

Country producing 1-4% of a major mineral

Five largest importers of iron ore % of total

Five largest exporters of iron ore % of total

Iron ore

Iron ore is a key mineral for many industrial and manufacturing activities. The Commonwealth of Independent States is the largest producer of iron ore, and Brazil exports one quarter of the world's total. Japan, with few resources of its own, imports one third of the world's total to support its industrial economy. Almost half the iron needed for steelmaking now comes from scrap as recycling can bring major energy savings. The energy required to extract and process primary metal from ore is far greater than that for producing from scrap.

Ocean resources

Countries have become more conscious of the potential value of any adjacent seas. Increased technology has made exploration of the sea for both fuel and non-fuel minerals possible. Manganese nodules, which have a high metal content, are found spread thinly over large areas of the sea bed at great depths. It could become viable to extract these in the future. A desire to extend control over sea resources was a marked feature of the United Nations Conference on the Law of the Sea.

Gold

Gold has always been important to the world economy. Potentially, it can be used as an economic weapon. South Africa produces nearly three times as much gold as anyone else and has over 60 per cent of the world's reserves. Many countries hold enormous stocks against shortfalls in supply and fluctuating prices.

Gold production
One gold bar equals ten thousand kg

Extensive distribution of manganese nodules

Exclusive Economic Zone (200 nautical miles)

TRADE

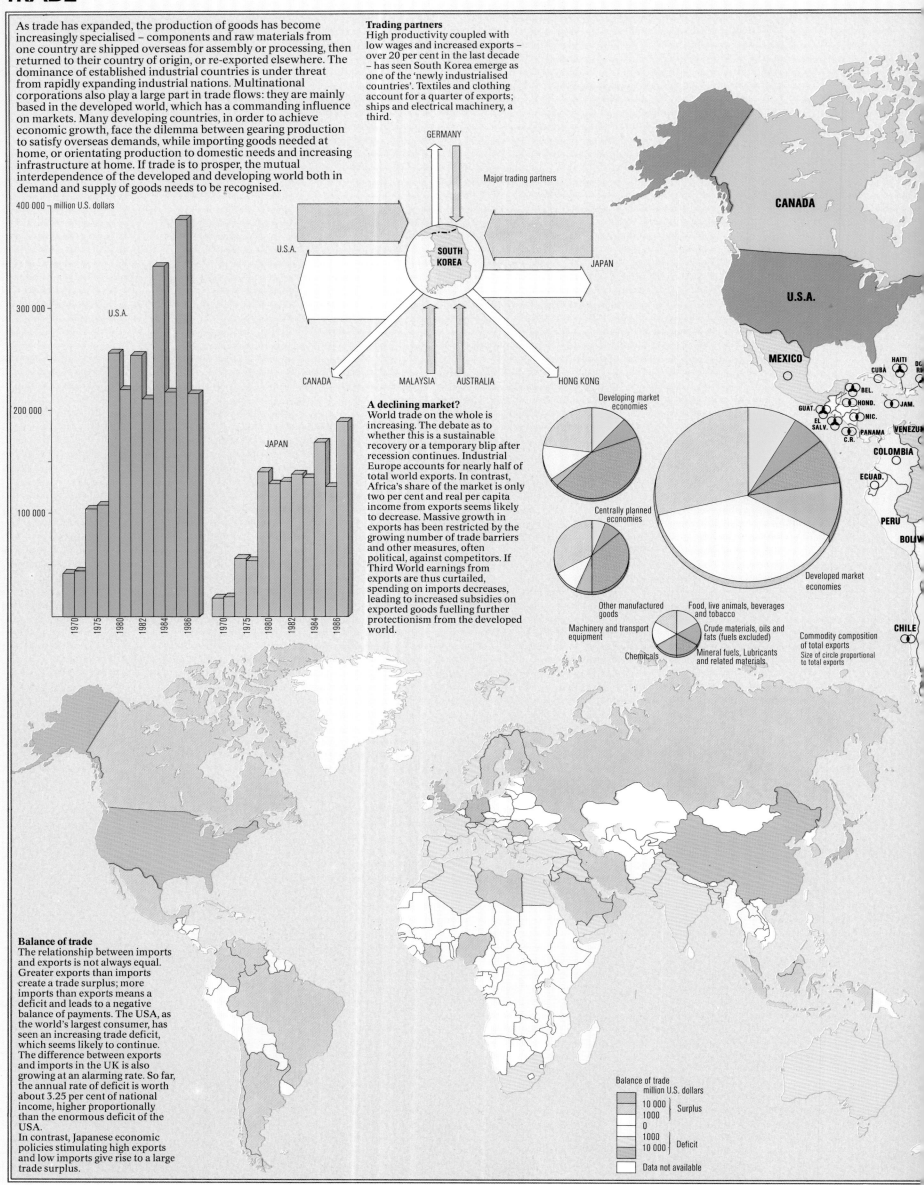

As trade has expanded, the production of goods has become increasingly specialised – components and raw materials from one country are shipped overseas for assembly or processing, then returned to their country of origin, or re-exported elsewhere. The dominance of established industrial countries is under threat from rapidly expanding industrial nations. Multinational corporations also play a large part in trade flows: they are mainly based in the developed world, which has a commanding influence on markets. Many developing countries, in order to achieve economic growth, face the dilemma between gearing production to satisfy overseas demands, while importing goods needed at home, or orientating production to domestic needs and increasing infrastructure at home. If trade is to prosper, the mutual interdependence of the developed and developing world both in demand and supply of goods needs to be recognised.

Trading partners

High productivity coupled with low wages and increased exports – over 20 per cent in the last decade – has seen South Korea emerge as one of the 'newly industrialised countries'. Textiles and clothing account for a quarter of exports; ships and electrical machinery, a third.

GERMANY

Major trading partners

U.S.A.

SOUTH KOREA

JAPAN

CANADA   MALAYSIA   AUSTRALIA   HONG KONG

A declining market?

World trade on the whole is increasing. The debate as to whether this is a sustainable recovery or a temporary blip after recession continues. Industrial Europe accounts for nearly half of total world exports. In contrast, Africa's share of the market is only two per cent and real per capita income from exports seems likely to decrease. Massive growth in exports has been restricted by the growing number of trade barriers and other measures, often political, against competitors. If Third World earnings from exports are thus curtailed, spending on imports decreases, leading to increased subsidies on exported goods fuelling further protectionism from the developed world.

400 000 — million U.S. dollars

300 000

U.S.A.

200 000

JAPAN

100 000

1970 1975 1980 1982 1984 1986   1970 1975 1980 1982 1984 1986

Developing market economies

Centrally planned economies

Developed market economies

Other manufactured goods

Machinery and transport equipment

Chemicals

Food, live animals, beverages and tobacco

Crude materials, oils and fats (fuels excluded)

Mineral fuels, Lubricants and related materials

Commodity composition of total exports
Size of circle proportional to total exports

CANADA

U.S.A.

MEXICO

HAITI   DO.
CUBA   R.
BEL.   JAM.
HOND.
GUAT.   NIC.
EL   PANAMA
SALV.   C.R.   VENEZU.

COLOMBIA

ECUAD.

PERU   BOLIV

CHILE

Balance of trade

The relationship between imports and exports is not always equal. Greater exports than imports create a trade surplus; more imports than exports means a deficit and leads to a negative balance of payments. The USA, as the world's largest consumer, has seen an increasing trade deficit, which seems likely to continue. The difference between exports and imports in the UK is also growing at an alarming rate. So far, the annual rate of deficit is worth about 3.25 per cent of national income, higher proportionally than the enormous deficit of the USA.
In contrast, Japanese economic policies stimulating high exports and low imports give rise to a large trade surplus.

Balance of trade
million U.S. dollars

10 000   Surplus
1000
0
1000
10 000   Deficit

Data not available

38

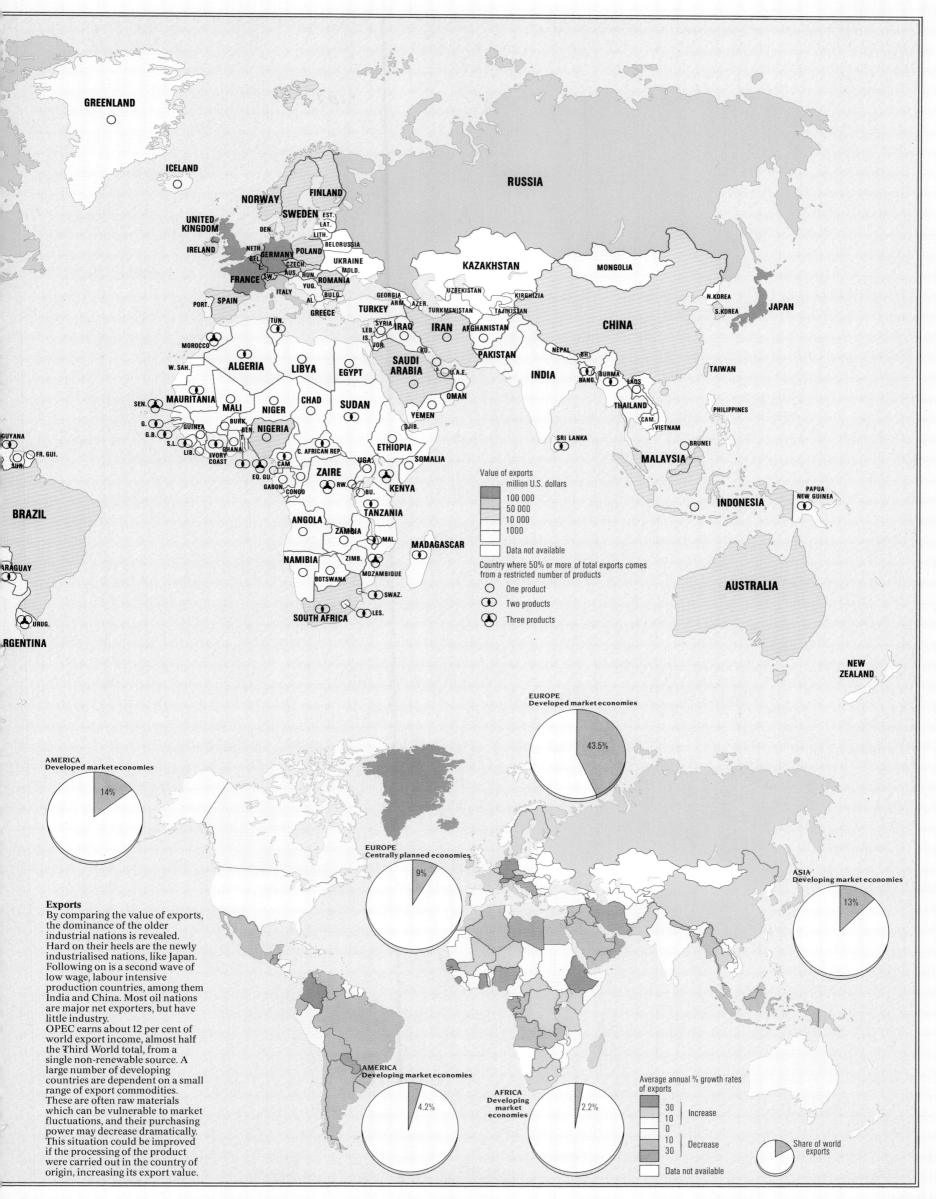

GREENLAND

ICELAND

NORWAY **FINLAND**
SWEDEN
UNITED
KINGDOM DEN. EST.
LAT.
IRELAND LITH.
NETH. GERMANY POLAND BELORUSSIA
BEL. CZECH. UKRAINE
FRANCE AUS. HUN. MOLD.
SW. ITALY ROMANIA
YUG.
PORT. SPAIN AL. BULG.
GREECE **TURKEY**
TUN. GEORGIA
MOROCCO ARM. AZER. UZBEKISTAN
SYRIA
LEB. IRAQ TURKMENISTAN
W. SAH. **ALGERIA** **LIBYA** **EGYPT** IS. JOR. **IRAN** **AFGHANISTAN**
KU.
SAUDI
SEN. **MAURITANIA** **ARABIA** U.A.E. **PAKISTAN**
G. **MALI** **NIGER** **CHAD** **SUDAN** OMAN
G.B. GUINEA BURK. YEMEN
S.L. BEN. **NIGERIA** DJIB.
LIB. GHANA C. AFRICAN REP. **ETHIOPIA**
IVORY CAM.
COAST UGA. SOMALIA
EQ. GU. **ZAIRE** KENYA
GABON RW.
CONGO BU.
ANGOLA TANZANIA
ZAMBIA MAL.
ZIMB. **MADAGASCAR**
NAMIBIA MOZAMBIQUE
BOTSWANA
SWAZ.
LES.
SOUTH AFRICA

RUSSIA

KAZAKHSTAN **MONGOLIA**

KIRGHIZIA N.KOREA **JAPAN**
TAJIKISTAN S.KOREA
CHINA
NEPAL TAIWAN
BH.
INDIA BANG. BURMA
LAOS
THAILAND PHILIPPINES
CAM.
VIETNAM
BRUNEI
SRI LANKA **MALAYSIA**

BRAZIL

GUYANA
FR. GUI.
SUR.

PARAGUAY

URUG.
ARGENTINA

INDONESIA **PAPUA**
NEW GUINEA

AUSTRALIA

NEW
ZEALAND

Value of exports
million U.S. dollars
100 000
50 000
10 000
1000

Data not available

Country where 50% or more of total exports comes
from a restricted number of products

◯ One product
◑ Two products
◕ Three products

Exports
By comparing the value of exports,
the dominance of the older
industrial nations is revealed.
Hard on their heels are the newly
industrialised nations, like Japan.
Following on is a second wave of
low wage, labour intensive
production countries, among them
India and China. Most oil nations
are major net exporters, but have
little industry.
OPEC earns about 12 per cent of
world export income, almost half
the Third World total, from a
single non-renewable source. A
large number of developing
countries are dependent on a small
range of export commodities.
These are often raw materials
which can be vulnerable to market
fluctuations, and their purchasing
power may decrease dramatically.
This situation could be improved
if the processing of the product
were carried out in the country of
origin, increasing its export value.

AMERICA
Developed market economies
14%

EUROPE
Developed market economies
43.5%

EUROPE
Centrally planned economies
9%

ASIA
Developing market economies
13%

AMERICA
Developing market economies
4.2%

AFRICA
Developing
market
economies
2.2%

Average annual % growth rates
of exports
30
10
0 Increase
10
30 Decrease

Data not available

Share of world
exports

Designed and produced by E.S.R.

WEALTH AND DEBT

The chasm between the rich and poor nations of the world is widening. Existing methods of reducing the difference involve loans and aid from governments, UN organisations and aid agencies. In the future the international economic system needs to be redesigned to finance and invest in sustainable development of national resources and programmes to combat poverty.

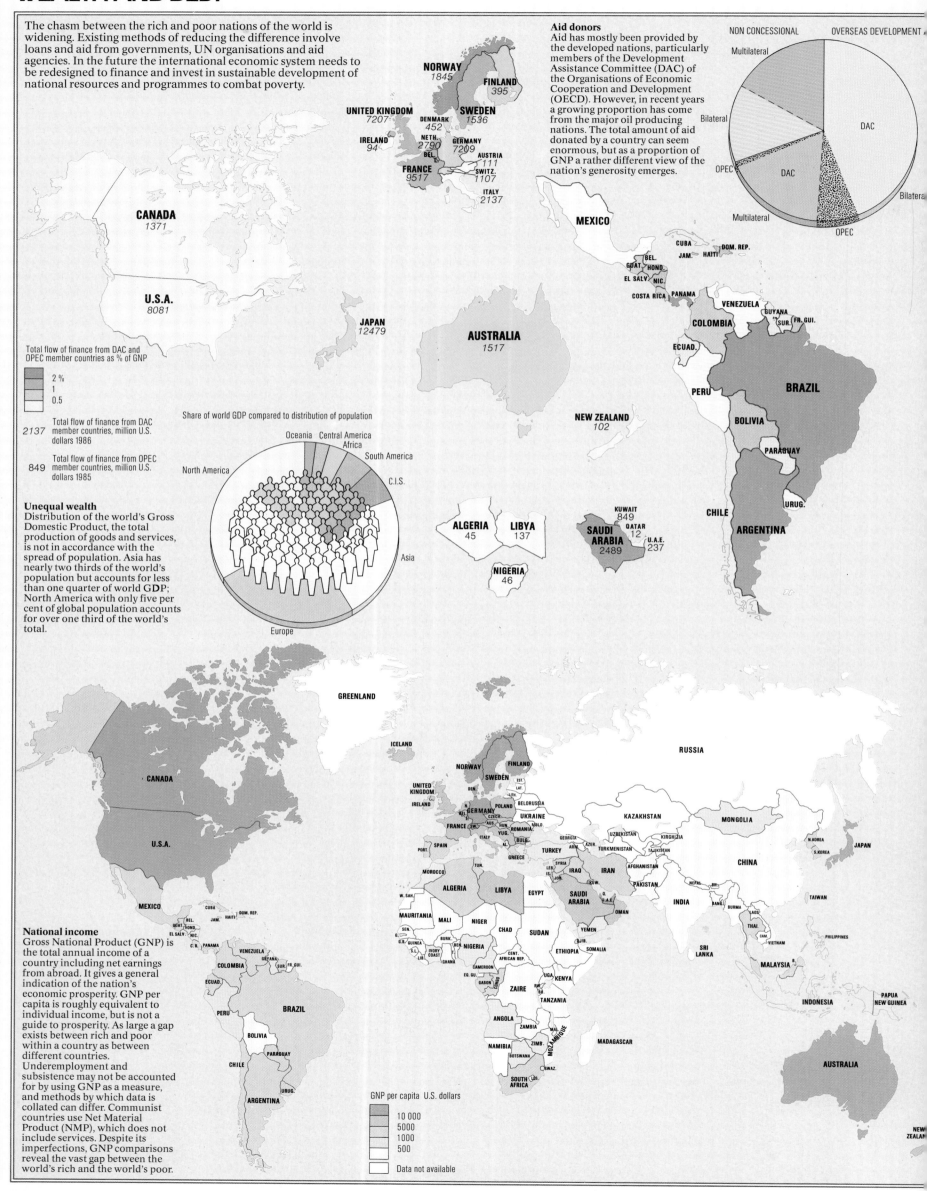

Aid donors
Aid has mostly been provided by the developed nations, particularly members of the Development Assistance Committee (DAC) of the Organisations of Economic Cooperation and Development (OECD). However, in recent years a growing proportion has come from the major oil producing nations. The total amount of aid donated by a country can seem enormous, but as a proportion of GNP a rather different view of the nation's generosity emerges.

NON CONCESSIONAL   OVERSEAS DEVELOPMENT
Multilateral
Bilateral   DAC
OPEC   DAC
Multilateral   Bilateral
OPEC

NORWAY *1845*
FINLAND *395*
UNITED KINGDOM *7207*
SWEDEN *1536*
DENMARK *452*
IRELAND *94*
NETH. *2790*
GERMANY *7209*
AUSTRIA *111*
BEL.
FRANCE *9517*
SWITZ. *1107*
ITALY *2137*

Total flow of finance from DAC and OPEC member countries as % of GNP
- 2 %
- 1
- 0.5

2137 Total flow of finance from DAC member countries, million U.S. dollars 1986

849 Total flow of finance from OPEC member countries, million U.S. dollars 1985

CANADA *1371*

U.S.A. *8081*

JAPAN *12479*

MEXICO

CUBA
BEL. DOM. REP.
GUAT. HOND. JAM. HAITI
EL SALV. NIC.
COSTA RICA PANAMA

VENEZUELA
GUYANA
COLOMBIA SUR. FR. GUI.
ECUAD.
PERU
BRAZIL
BOLIVIA
PARAGUAY
CHILE
URUG.
ARGENTINA

AUSTRALIA *1517*

NEW ZEALAND *102*

Unequal wealth
Distribution of the world's Gross Domestic Product, the total production of goods and services, is not in accordance with the spread of population. Asia has nearly two thirds of the world's population but accounts for less than one quarter of world GDP; North America with only five per cent of global population accounts for over one third of the world's total.

Share of world GDP compared to distribution of population

Oceania Central America
Africa
North America   South America
C.I.S.
Asia
Europe

ALGERIA *45*
LIBYA *137*
KUWAIT *849*
SAUDI ARABIA *2489*
QATAR *12*
U.A.E. *237*
NIGERIA *46*

GREENLAND

ICELAND
NORWAY FINLAND
UNITED KINGDOM SWEDEN EST.
DEN. LITH.
IRELAND BELORUSSIA
N. POLAND
GERMANY CZECH. UKRAINE
FRANCE SW. AUS. HUN. ROMANIA MOLD.
ITALY YUG. BULG.
SPAIN AL. GREECE TURKEY
PORT. GEORGIA ARM. AZER.
MOROCCO SYRIA IRAQ IRAN
TUN. LEB. JOR. KUW.
ALGERIA LIBYA EGYPT SAUDI ARABIA
W. SAH. Q.
MAURITANIA OMAN
MALI NIGER CHAD SUDAN YEMEN
SEN. BURK. CENT. DJIB.
G.B. GUINEA BEN. NIGERIA AFRICAN REP. ETHIOPIA SOMALIA
S.L. IVORY GHANA
LIB. COAST
CAMEROON
EQ. GU. UGA. KENYA
GABON ZAIRE RW.
TANZANIA
ANGOLA ZAMBIA
NAMIBIA ZIMB. MADAGASCAR
BOTSWANA MOZAMBIQUE
SOUTH SWAZ.
AFRICA

RUSSIA
KAZAKHSTAN MONGOLIA
UZBEKISTAN KIRGHIZIA N.KOREA
TURKMENISTAN TAJIKISTAN S.KOREA JAPAN
AFGHANISTAN CHINA
PAKISTAN NEPAL BH. TAIWAN
INDIA BANG. BURMA LAOS
THAI. PHILIPPINES
SRI VIETNAM CAM.
LANKA
MALAYSIA
INDONESIA PAPUA NEW GUINEA

AUSTRALIA

NEW ZEALAND

National income
Gross National Product (GNP) is the total annual income of a country including net earnings from abroad. It gives a general indication of the nation's economic prosperity. GNP per capita is roughly equivalent to individual income, but is not a guide to prosperity. As large a gap exists between rich and poor within a country as between different countries. Underemployment and subsistence may not be accounted for by using GNP as a measure, and methods by which data is collated can differ. Communist countries use Net Material Product (NMP), which does not include services. Despite its imperfections, GNP comparisons reveal the vast gap between the world's rich and the world's poor.

CANADA

U.S.A.

MEXICO
CUBA
GUAT. HOND. BEL. DOM. REP.
EL SALV. JAM. HAITI
NIC.
C.R. PANAMA
VENEZUELA
COLOMBIA GUYANA
SUR. FR. GUI.
ECUAD.
PERU BRAZIL
BOLIVIA
PARAGUAY
CHILE
URUG.
ARGENTINA

GNP per capita U.S. dollars
- 10 000
- 5000
- 1000
- 500
- Data not available

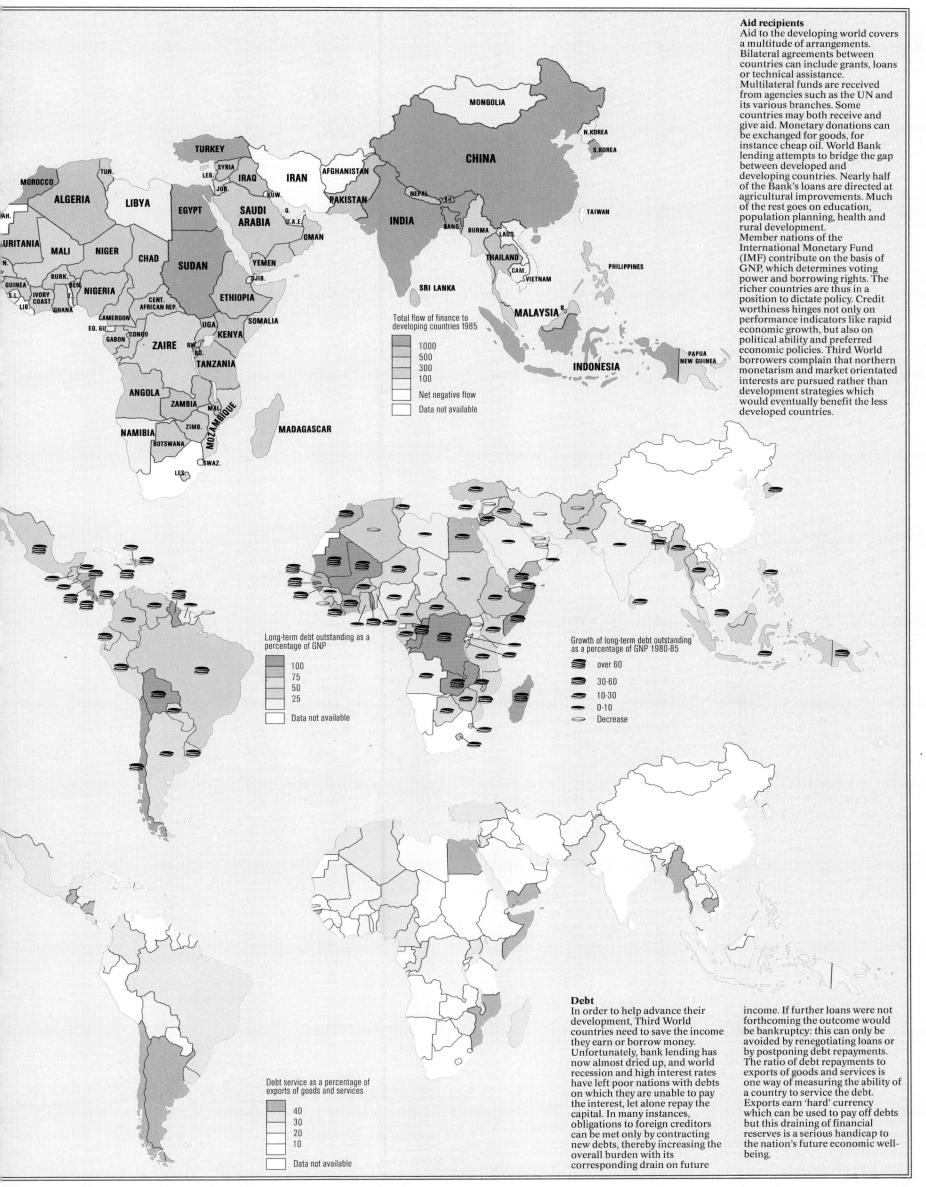

Aid recipients
Aid to the developing world covers a multitude of arrangements. Bilateral agreements between countries can include grants, loans or technical assistance. Multilateral funds are received from agencies such as the UN and its various branches. Some countries may both receive and give aid. Monetary donations can be exchanged for goods, for instance cheap oil. World Bank lending attempts to bridge the gap between developed and developing countries. Nearly half of the Bank's loans are directed at agricultural improvements. Much of the rest goes on education, population planning, health and rural development.
Member nations of the International Monetary Fund (IMF) contribute on the basis of GNP, which determines voting power and borrowing rights. The richer countries are thus in a position to dictate policy. Credit worthiness hinges not only on performance indicators like rapid economic growth, but also on political ability and preferred economic policies. Third World borrowers complain that northern monetarism and market orientated interests are pursued rather than development strategies which would eventually benefit the less developed countries.

Total flow of finance to developing countries 1985

- 1000
- 500
- 300
- 100
- Net negative flow
- Data not available

Long-term debt outstanding as a percentage of GNP

- 100
- 75
- 50
- 25
- Data not available

Growth of long-term debt outstanding as a percentage of GNP 1980-85

- over 60
- 30-60
- 10-30
- 0-10
- Decrease

Debt service as a percentage of exports of goods and services

- 40
- 30
- 20
- 10
- Data not available

Debt
In order to help advance their development, Third World countries need to save the income they earn or borrow money. Unfortunately, bank lending has now almost dried up, and world recession and high interest rates have left poor nations with debts on which they are unable to pay the interest, let alone repay the capital. In many instances, obligations to foreign creditors can be met only by contracting new debts, thereby increasing the overall burden with its corresponding drain on future income. If further loans were not forthcoming the outcome would be bankruptcy: this can only be avoided by renegotiating loans or by postponing debt repayments. The ratio of debt repayments to exports of goods and services is one way of measuring the ability of a country to service the debt. Exports earn 'hard' currency which can be used to pay off debts but this draining of financial reserves is a serious handicap to the nation's future economic well-being.

41

SETTLEMENT

For scales larger than 1:2,000,000   Population

 BIRMINGHAM   >1,000,000

GLASGOW   500,000–1,000,000

CARDIFF   250,000–500,000

LIMERICK   50,000–250,000

•   **Dover**   10,000–50,000

•   Lossiemouth   5,000–10,000

○   Church Stretton   <5,000

CROYDON   London Borough

For scales between 1:2,000,000 and 1:12,000,000

NEW YORK   >5,000,000

RANGOON   2,500,000–5,000,000

■   **KUYBYSHEV**   1,000,000–2,500,000

•   **Hyderabad**   500,000–1,000,000

•   Adelaide   100,000–500,000

○   Baden-Baden   <100,000

For scales smaller than 1:12,000,000

■   **DAR ES SALAAM**   >1,000,000

•   **Maracaibo**   500,000–1,000,000

•   Tiranë   <500,000

Lisboa   National capital   **Winnipeg**   State, provincial capital

COMMUNICATIONS

Motorway

Motorway under construction

Principal road

Principal road under construction

Other main road

Track, seasonal road

Road tunnel

Principal railway

Principal railway under construction

Railway tunnel

✈   International, main airport

BOUNDARIES

International

Undefined, disputed

Internal, state, provincial

Armistice, cease-fire line

The representation of a boundary in this atlas does not denote its international recognition and therefore the *defacto* situation has been depicted.

HYDROGRAPHIC FEATURES

River, stream

Intermittent watercourse

Waterfall, rapids

Dam, barrage

Irrigation, drainage channel

Canal

Lake, reservoir

Intermittent, seasonal lake

Salt pan, mud flat

Oasis

Marsh, swamp

Reef

Depth of sea in metres

Scales larger than 1:12,000,000

0
200
3000

Scales smaller than 1:12,000,000

0
1000
5000

OTHER FEATURES

▲ 3798   Elevation above sea level (metres)

▼ −133   Depression, below sea level (metres)

≍   Pass

Oil, gas pipeline with field

ENVIRONMENTAL TYPES

 Permanent ice and snow

 Mountain and moorland

 Tundra

 Coniferous forest

 Deciduous forest

 Tropical forest

 Prairie

 Temperate agriculture

 Mediterranean scrub

Savannah

Desert

This representation of the environment and its associated vegetation gives an overview of the landscape. It is not intended to be definitive.

CONVERSION SCALES

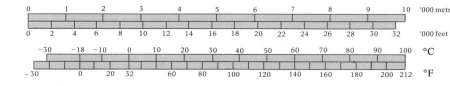

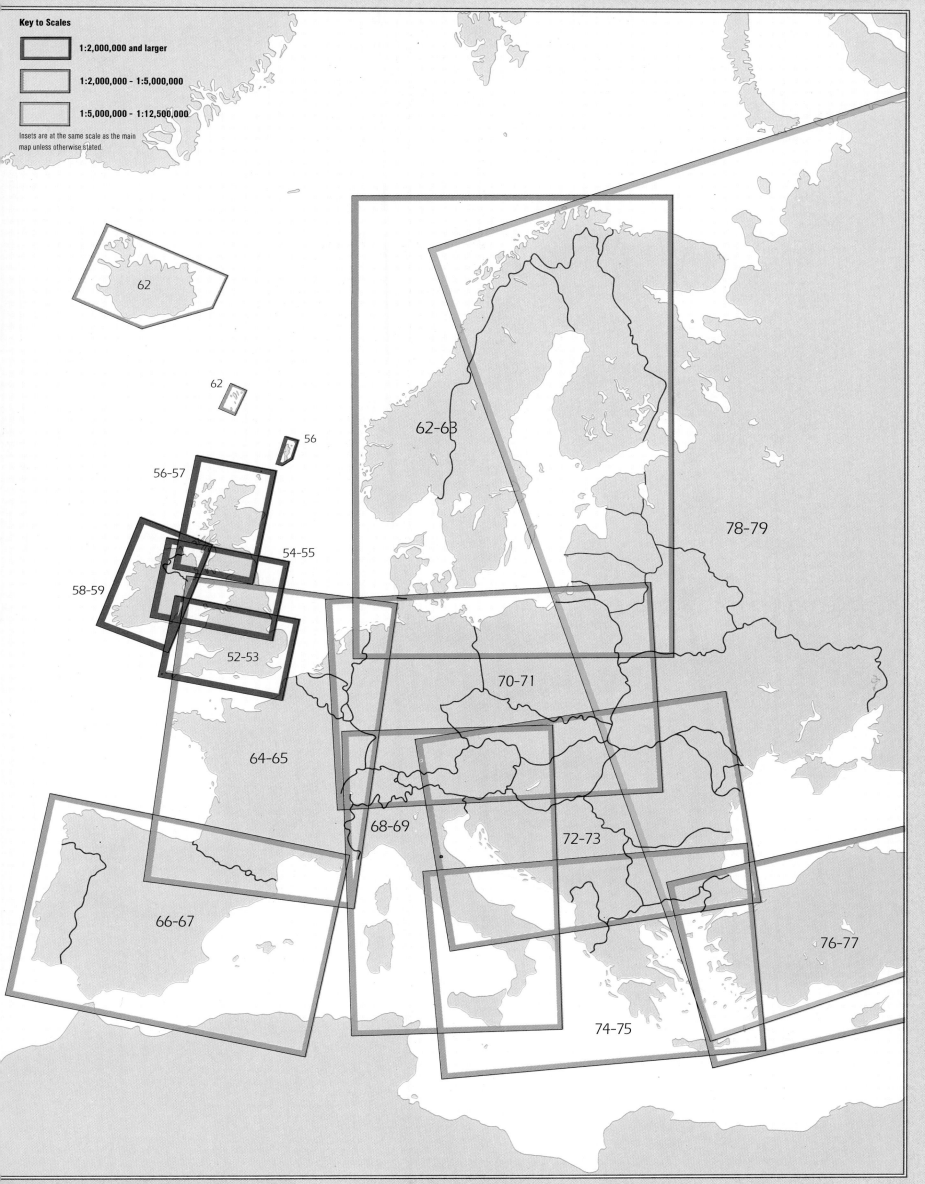

Key to Scales

	1:2,000,000 and larger
	1:2,000,000 - 1:5,000,000
	1:5,000,000 - 1:12,500,000

Insets are at the same scale as the main map unless otherwise stated.

62

62

56

56-57

54-55

58-59

52-53

62-63

78-79

70-71

64-65

68-69

72-73

66-67

74-75

76-77

Designed and produced by E.S.R.

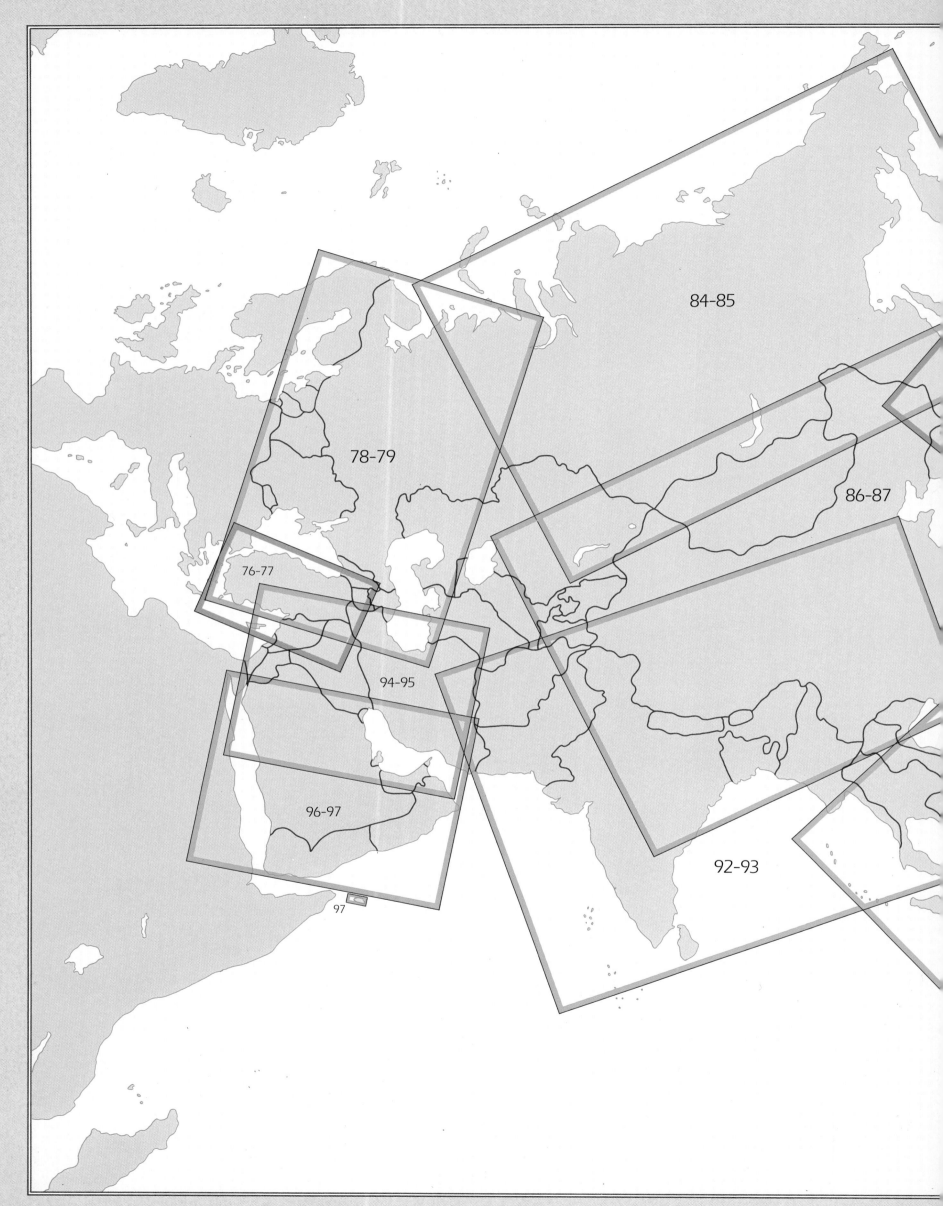

84-85

78-79

86-87

76-77

94-95

96-97

92-93

97

88-89

89

114

90-91

114

112-113

115

115

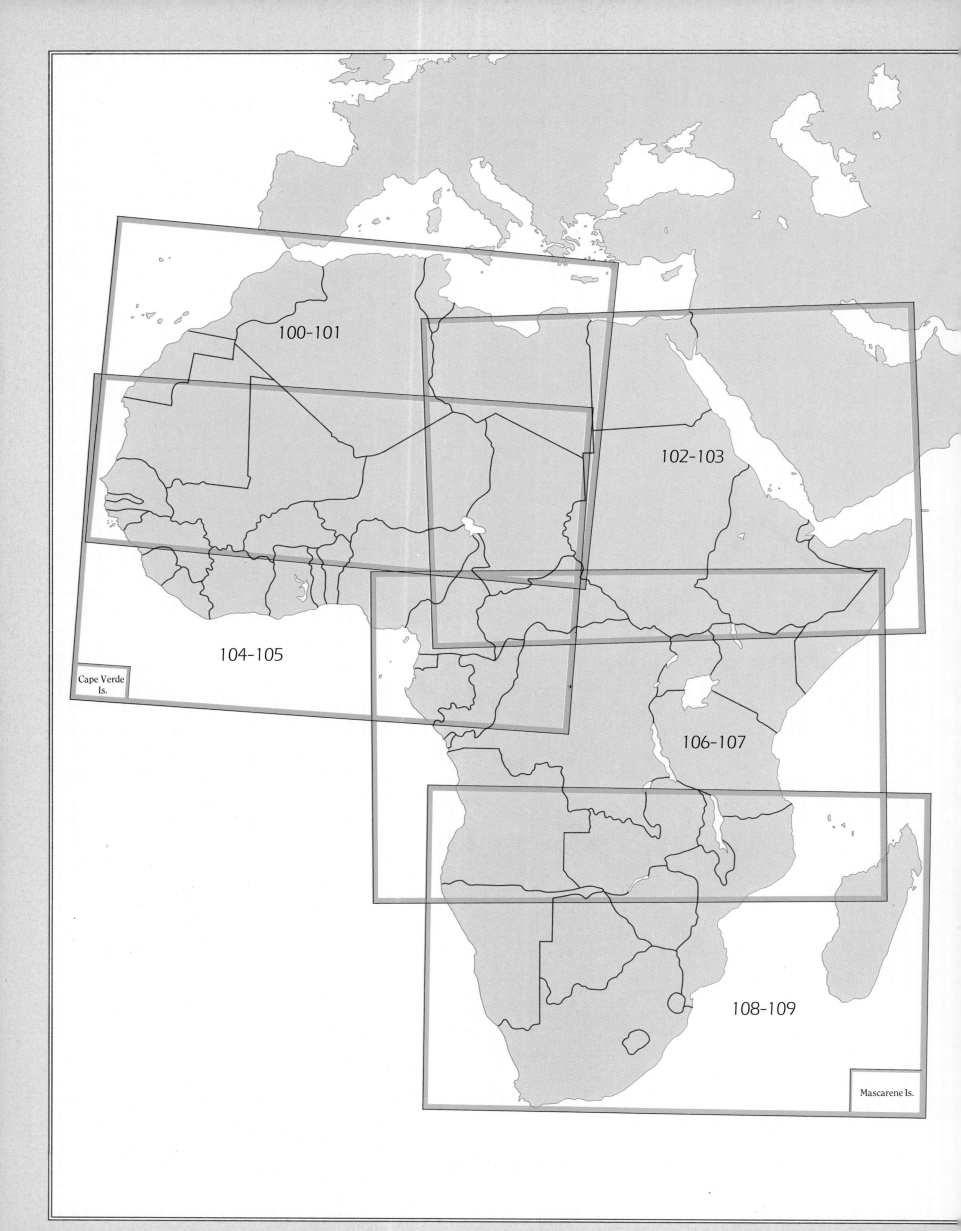

100-101

102-103

104-105

Cape Verde
Is.

106-107

108-109

Mascarene Is.

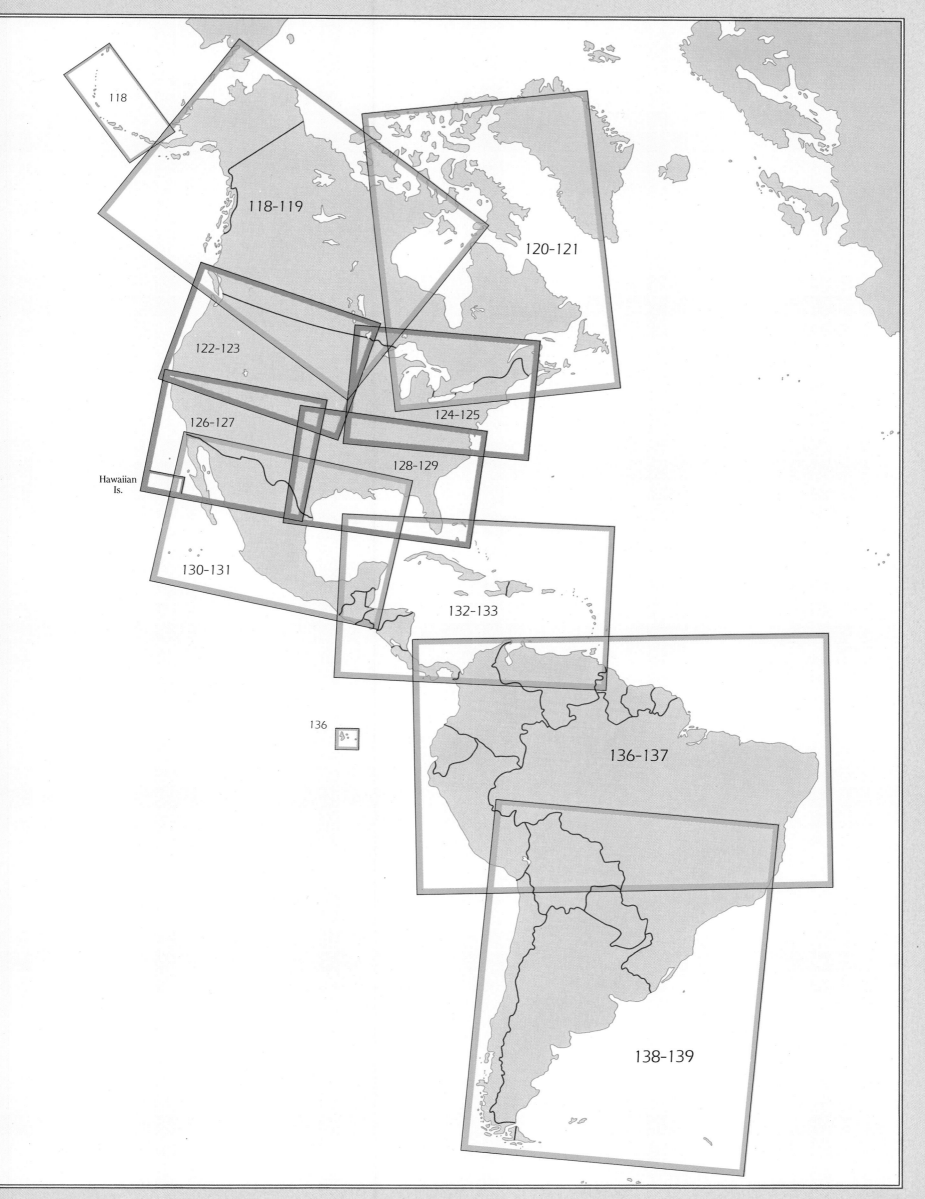

118

118-119

120-121

122-123

124-125

126-127

Hawaiian
Is.

128-129

130-131

132-133

136

136-137

138-139

West of Greenwich

A 150° **B** 120° **C** 90° **D** 60° **E** 30° **F**

1

ARCTIC OCEAN

Ellesmere
Island

Lincoln
Sea

Queen

Elizabeth

Islands

Kane
Basin

Viscount Melville
Sound

Baffin Bay

GREENLAND
(Denmark)

Jan Mayen
(Norway)

Banks
Island

Beaufort Sea

Amundsen
Gulf

Victoria Island

Ostrov Vrangelya

Pt. Barrow

Chucki
Sea

2

Brooks Range

ALASKA
(U.S.A.)

Mackenzie Mts.

Great Bear Lake

Oikiqtaluk

Davis Str.

Denmark Strait

Norwegian
Sea

ICELAND

Reykjavík

McKINLEY
6194 ▲

Alaska Range

Gulf of Alaska

Kodiak I.

Great Slave Lake

Reindeer Lake

Foxe
Basin

Hudson Str.

Labrador Sea

Kap Farvel

Fóroyar
(Denmark)

Shetland Is.
(U.K.)

Bering
Sea

Rocky Mountains

CANADA

Hudson Bay

Labrador

UNITED
KINGDOM

Nor

Aleutian   Islands

L. Winnipeg

Dublin
IRELAND

Amster
s'Gravenha

Aleutian   Trench

Vancouver I.

Missouri

Great
Lakes

Ottawa

Newfoundland

LONDON
Bru×e

BE

PARIS

3

NORTH

PACIFIC

OCEAN

Gt. Salt Lake

Great
Plains

UNITED STATES
OF
AMERICA

CHICAGO

Appalachian Mts.

NEW YORK
PHILADELPHIA
Washington

NORTH

ATLANTIC

OCEAN

FRAN

AND.

PORTUGAL

Açores
(Port.)

Madrid

SPAIN

FRAN

SAN FRANCISCO

Mississippi

Lisboa

El Dja

LOS ANGELES

Bermuda
(U.K.)

Rabat

MOROCCO

Isla de Guadalupe
(Mex.)

Madeira
(Port.)

30°

Hawaiian

Islands

Tropic of Cancer

Gulf of Mexico

BAHAMAS
Nassau

Ilas Canarias
(Sp.)

WESTERN
SAHARA

Al Aaiún

ALGE

Atlas Mountains

HAWAII
(U.S.A.)

MEXICO
CIUDAD DE
MÉXICO

La Habana

CUBA
West Indies

DOMINICAN REP.

MAURITANIA

Nouakchott

CAPE
VERDE
IS.

Dakar

Islas de Revillagigedo
(Mex.)

Belmopan
BELIZE
GUATEMALA
Guatemala
EL SALVADOR
San Salvador

Port au Prince
HAITI
Kingston
JAMAICA
HONDURAS
Tegucigalpa
NICARAGUA

Puerto Rico(U.S.A.)
Santo Domingo

Caribbean Sea

Leeward Is.

BARBADOS

Praia

SEN
THE
GAMBIA
GUINEA-
BISSAU

Banjul
Bissau

MALI

BUR
FASO
N
Bamako
GUINEA
Ouagadougou

4

Polynesia

Line Islands

Christmas I.

Managua
San José
COSTA RICA
PANAMA

Panamá

Caracas
VENEZUELA

Windward Is.

TRINIDAD
AND TOBAGO

Georgetown
Paramaribo
Cayenne
FRENCH GUIANA

SIERRA LEONE
Conakry Freetown
Monrovia
LIBERIA

IVORY
COAST

Lome
Accra

Phoenix Is.

KIRIBATI

Equator

COLOMBIA
Bogotá

GU
SUR

SÃO TO
AND PRINC

W.
SOMOA
Apia Samoa
(U.S.A.)

Cook Islands
(N.Z.)

Iles Marquises
(Fr.)

French Polynesia
(Fr.)

SOUTH

PACIFIC

Quito
ECUADOR

Islas Galápagos
(Ecuador)

Isla Fernando
de Noronha
(Brazil)

Ascension
(U.K.)

5

TONGA
Nuku'alofa

Tahiti

Iles de la
Société

Iles Tuamotu

OCEAN

PERU

Cordillera

LIMA

BRAZIL
Planalto do
Mato Grosso

Brasília

St. Helena
(U.K.)

Iles Gambier

Pitcairn I.
(U.K.) Ducie I.
(U.K.)

La Paz
BOLIVIA

Ilha da Trindade
(Brazil)

SOUTH

Tropic of Capricorn

Isla de Pascua
(Easter I.)
(Chile)

PARAGUAY
Asunción

SÃO PAULO

RIO DE JANEIRO

ATLANTIC

30°

ACONCAGUA
6960 ▲

Los Andes

URUGUAY
Montevideo

OCEAN

Islas Juan
Fernández
(Chile)

Santiago

BUENOS AIRES
ARGENTINA

Tristan da Cunha
(U.K.)

Gough I.
(U.K.)

Chatham Is.
(N.Z.)

Cordillera de los Andes

Patagonia

6

Falkland Is.
(U.K.)

South Georgia
(U.K.)

South
Sandwich
Is. (U.K.)

Cabo de Hornos

Scotia Sea

A 150° **B** 120° **C** 90° **D** 60° **E** 30° **F**

1:85,000,000 (Scale at the Equator)

Designed and produced by E.S.R.

West of Greenwich | East of Greenwich

1:12,500,000

© COLOUR LIBRARY BOOKS

Miller Oblated Stereographic Projection

Designed and produced by E.S.R.

SOUTHERN ENGLAND AND WALES

Transverse Mercator Projection

1:1,175,000

© COLOUR LIBRARY BOOKS

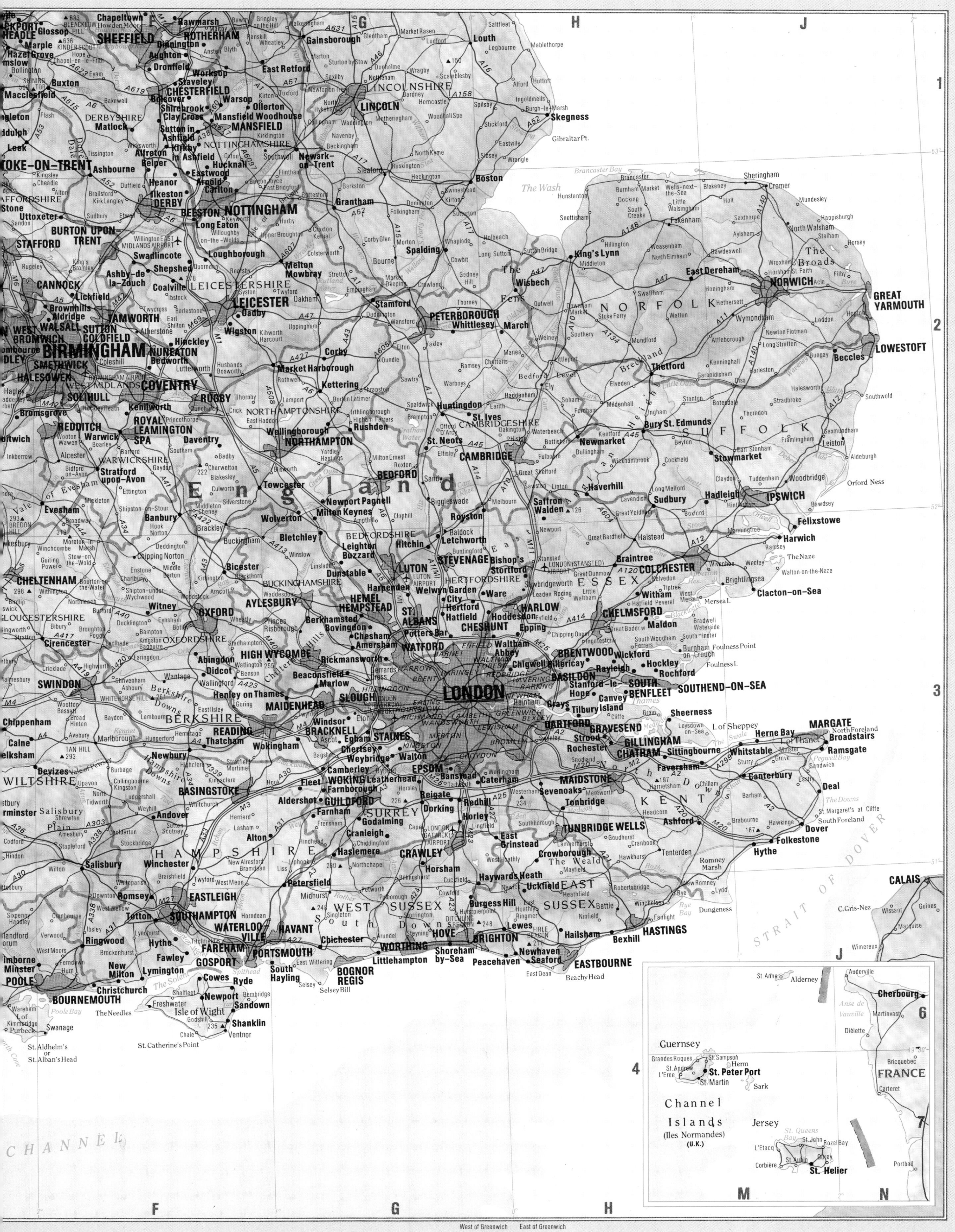

Designed and produced by E.S.R.

Transverse Mercator Projection

1:1,175,000

© COLOUR LIBRARY BOOKS

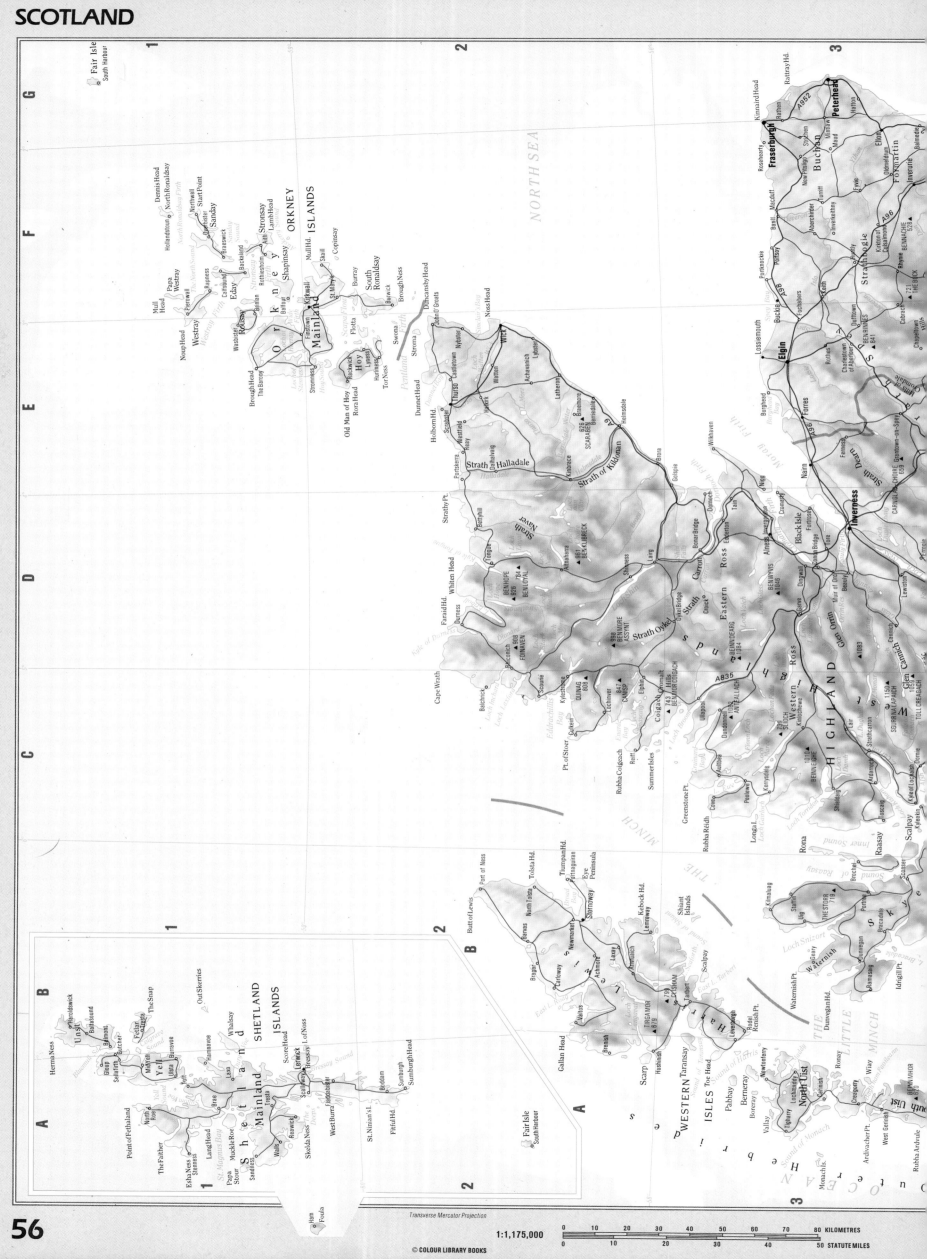

West of Greenwich

57

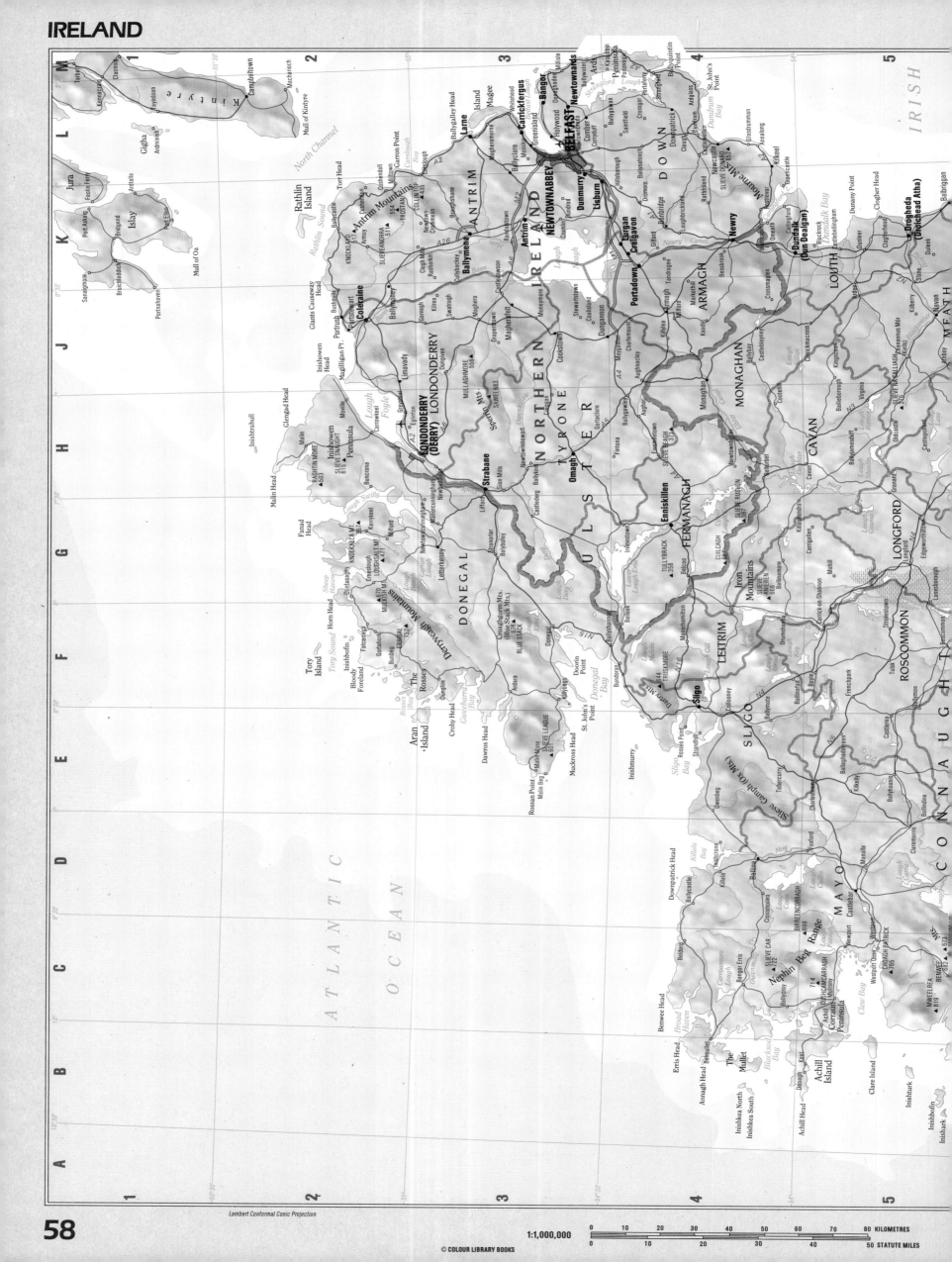

Lambert Conformal Conic Projection

1:1,000,000

© COLOUR LIBRARY BOOKS

80 KILOMETRES

50 STATUTE MILES

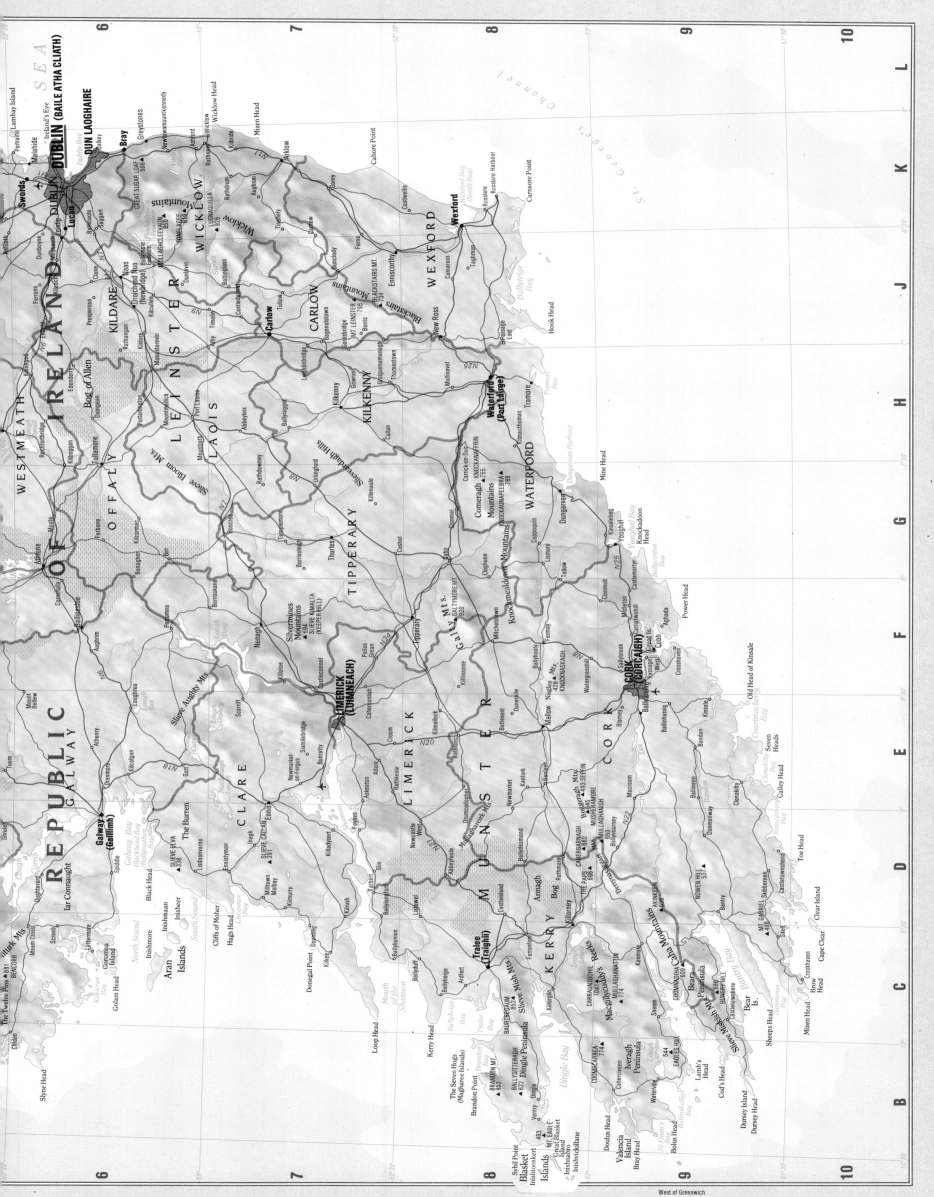

IRELAND

REPUBLIC OF IRELAND

1:5,000,000

© COLOUR LIBRARY BOOKS

West of Greenwich   East of Greenwich

| 0 | 50 | 100 | 150 | 200 | 250 | 300 | 350 | 400 KILOMETRES |

| 0 | 50 | 100 | 150 | 200 | 250 STATUTE MILES |

61

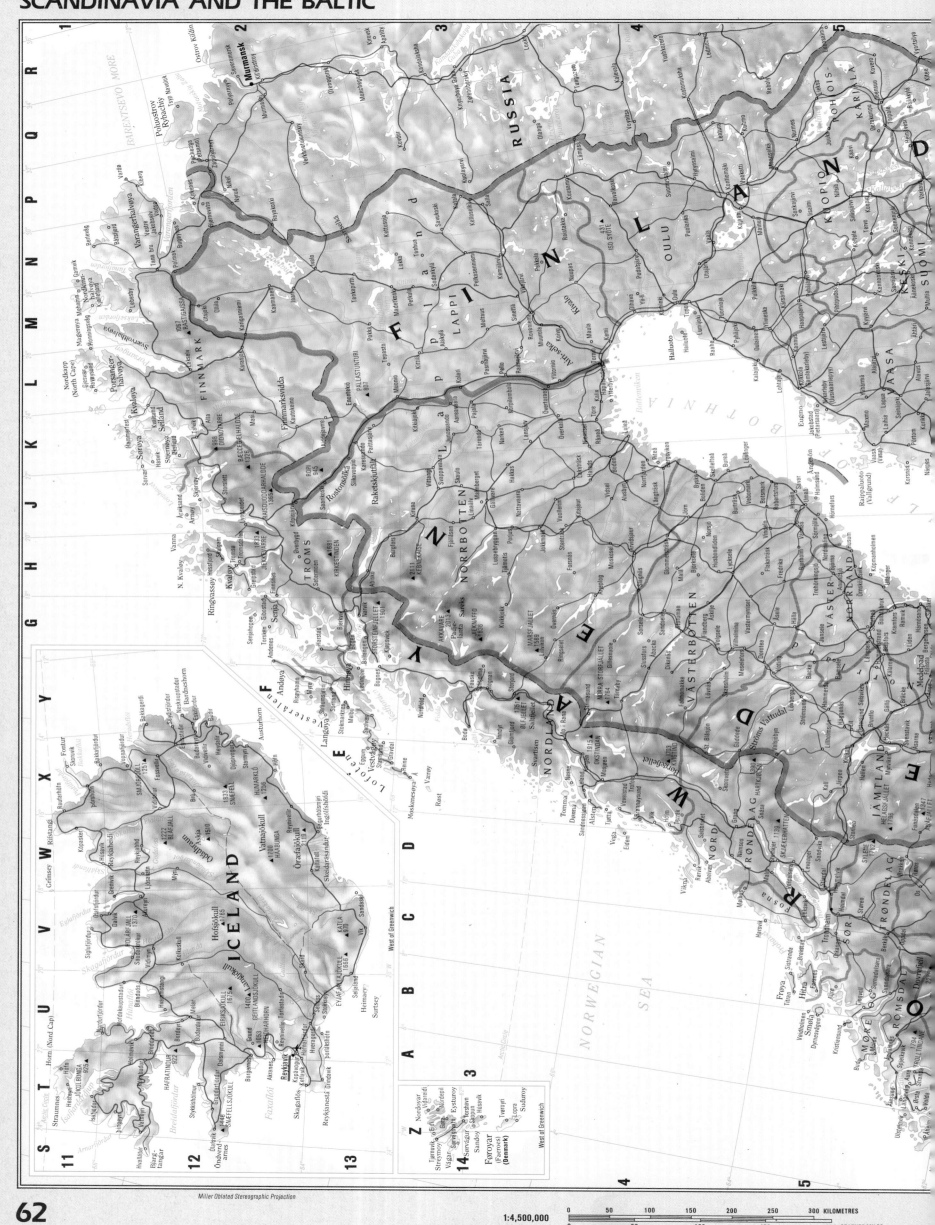

Miller Oblated Stereographic Projection

1:4,500,000

© COLOUR LIBRARY BOOKS

63

BENELUX AND FRANCE

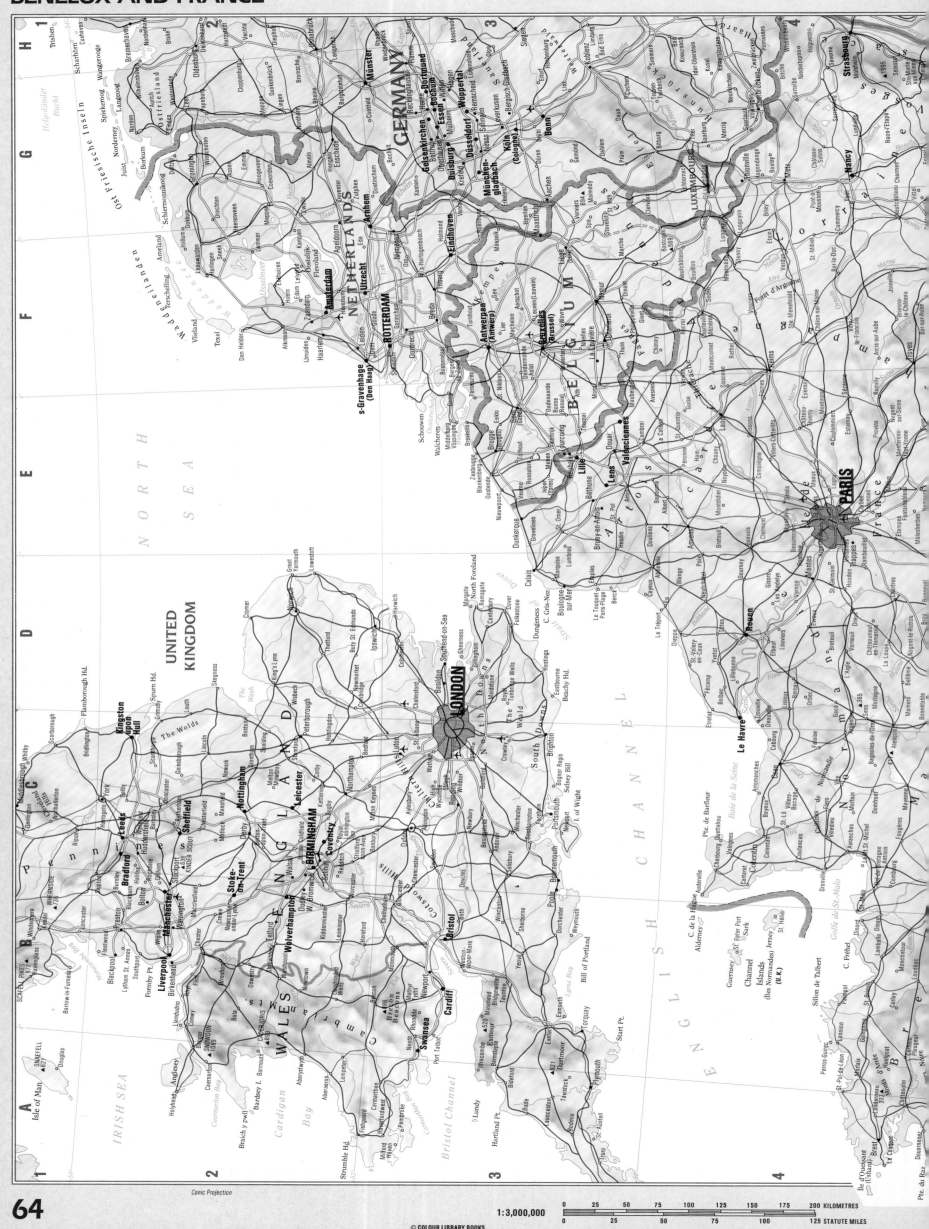

Conic Projection

1:3,000,000

| 0 | 25 | 50 | 75 | 100 | 125 | 150 | 175 | 200 KILOMETRES |

| 0 | 25 | 50 | 75 | 100 | 125 STATUTE MILES |

© COLOUR LIBRARY BOOKS

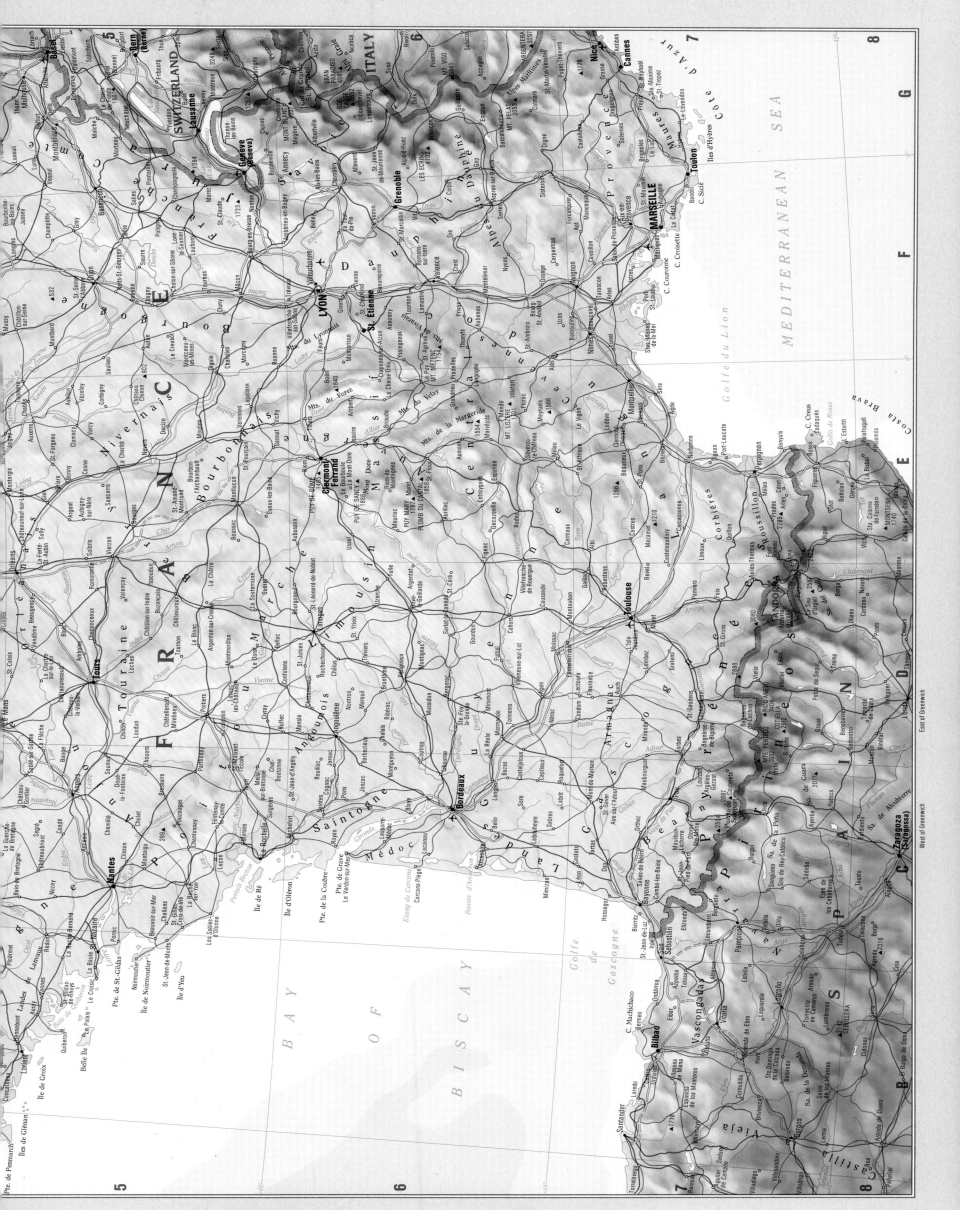

THE IBERIAN PENINSULA

Conic Projection

1:3,000,000

© COLOUR LIBRARY BOOKS

Golfe de Gascuña

F Labrit Roquefort Castelsarrasin Montauban Carmaux Le Vigan Avignon Apt Manosque K
Léon Castets Tartas Mont-de-Marsan Condom Lectoure Fleurance Gaillac Albi Nîmes Beaucaire Tarascon Cavaillon Salernes Draguignan

Hossegor Dax Aire-sur-l'Adour Armagnac Auch L'Isle-Jourdain Montauban St-Affrique Le Vigan Lodève Montpellier Arles Salon-de-Provence Aix-en-Provence Provence Brignoles Le Luc Fréjus

Biarritz Bayonne Orthez Salies-de-Béarn Mirande Lombez Toulouse Muret Revel Mazamet 1210 St-Pons Béziers Agde Sète Stes-Maries-de-la-Mer Port-St-Louis Istres Martigues MARSEILLE St-Maximin Aubagne La Ciotat St-Tropez Maures Le Lavandou

Cambo-les-Bains Pau Tarbes St-Gaudens Gratens Carcassonne Narbonne C. Couronne C. Croisette Toulon Bandol Hyères Iles d'Hyères

San Sebastián Mauléon-Licharre Lourdes Bagnères-de-Bigorre St-Girons Pamiers Limoux Corbières Port-Leucate C. Sicié 1

Elizondo St-Jean-Pied-de-Port Oloron-Ste-Marie Argelès-Gazost Cauterets 2887 Foix Ax-les-Thermes Quillan Golfe du Lion

Navarra Pirineos Puertode Somport 2887 Bagnères-de-Luchon 2880 3080 Roussillon Font-Romeu Prades Perpignan Banyuls

Pamplona Burgui Jaca MTE. PERDIDO 3352 PIC D'ANETO 3404 Viella Espot ANDORRA Andorra la Vella 2765 Céret C. Creus Cadaqués

Estella Sangüesa Sos del Rey Católico COTIELLA ▲2912 Vielha Puigcerdá 2923 Ripoll Figueras Roses Golfo de Roses

Olite Sa. de la Peña Ayerbe Sa. de Guara 2077 Graus Pobla de Segur La Seu d'Urgell 2557 Sa. del Cadí Berga Olot L'Estartit

Tafalla Calahorra Sádaba Huesca Tremp Oliana Navars Vich Sta. Coloma de Farnés Gérona La Bisbal Palafrugell

Tudela Ejea de los Caballeros Tardienta Barbastro Benabarre Ponts Cardona MONTSENY 1740 Bañolas Palamós

Agreda ▲2316 Borja Tarazona Tauste Monzón Tamarite de Litera Balaguer Manresa Granollers Blanes Calella de la Costa Costa Brava

Ciria Ricla La Almunia de Doña Godina Zuera Binéfar Lérida Tárrega Cervera Igualada 1236▲ Sabadell Tarrasa Sta. Coloma de Gramanet Mataró

Ateca Calatayud Belchite Fraga Llanos de Urgel Bellpuig Martorell Badalona BARCELONA Hospitalet

Cariñena Pina Bujaraloz Mequinenza Villafranca del Penedés Sitges 2

Daroca Muniesa Caspe Flix Falset Valls Reus Vilanueva y Geltrú

Calamocha Montalbán 1522 Castellote Valderrobres Gandesa Tarragona Cambrils Costa Dorada

4518 Molina de Aragón ▲1393 Perelló Tortosa Golfo de San Jorge

Monreal del Campo Aliaga Morella Amposta La Cava C. de Tortosa

SIERRA ALTA 1855 Alfambra Sa. de Gúdar PEÑARROYA 2019 Vinaroz Benicarló San Carlos de la Rápita

Albarracín 1839 Teruel Mora de Rubielos Peñíscola

Mts. Universales Albocácer Torreblanca C. Caballeria Ciudadela Alayor Menorca (Minorca)

N Torre ▲2020 Albentosa Castellón de la Plana Islas Columbretes Puerto de Pollensa C. de Formentor C. d'Artrutx Mahón

Cañete Santa Cruz de Moya Viver Burriana P. MAYOR ▲1445 Alcudia

Carboneras de Guadazaón Talayuelas Segorbe Alcublas Sagunto Sóller La Puebla Inca Artá

Motilla del Palancar Minglanilla Chelva Liria I. Dragonera Palma Manacor

Requena Chiva Torrente VALENCIA Andraitx Lluchmayor Felanitx Mallorca (Majorca) 3

Tarazona de la Mancha Casas Ibáñez San Martés Golfo de Valencia Baia de Palma Campos del Puerto

Albacete Ayora Enguera Alberique Cullera C. de Salinas

Chinchilla Sa. de Enguera 1245 Alcira Ibiza (Iviza) San Juan Bautista Cabrera

Almansa Gandia San Antonio Abad Sta. Eulalia del Río

Pozohondo Yecla Villena Denia Ibiza Islas Baleares

Alcoy 1588 C. de la Nao San Francisco Javier (Balearic Islands)

Elche de la Sierra Monóvar Calpe Formentera Pta. Rotja (Spain)

Hellín Jumilla 1371 Benidorm Villajoyosa

Murcia Crevillente Alicante Costa Blanca

Caravaca de la Cruz Elche

Mula Molina de Segura Orihuela

Librilla MURCIA Torrevieja

Totana Lorca La Unión Cartagena C. de Palos

Vélez Rubio Mazarrón

Huércal Overa Aguilas 4

C. de Gata

MEDITERRANEAN SEA

Dellys Golfe de Bejaia Jijel

EL DJAZAÏR (ALGIERS) Borg El Bahri Tigzirt Azazga Bejaia (Bougie) Ziama-Mansouria

Cherchell Tizi Ouzou Thénia Lakhdaria Kherrata Petite Kabylie

Tipaza Bou Ismaïl Larba Djurdjura 2308 Akbou

Ténès Sidi Akacha 1415 El Affroun Blida LALLA KHEDIDJA Sétif

Tarzout Khemis Miliana Medéa Bir Ghbalou Ain Bessem Bouira Mansoura

Dahra Miliana Aïn Defla Sour al Ghozlane Mts. du Hodna Borj Bou Arreridj Ain Oulmene

Bouhalloufa Ech Cheliff Bou Kadir Boghar Ksar El Boukhari 1863 M'Sila Chott El Hodna

Mostaganem ▲1985 Theniet El Had ▲1464

El Had ALGERIA Boghar Bordj Bou Arréridj 5

C. Ferrat Golfe d'Arzew Idiouia Massif de l'Ouarsenis Bougzoul Barika

Arzew Relizane Zemmora Chahbounia M'Sila Aïn El Hadjel

Kristel Oran Yellel Bou Kadir

F West of Greenwich East of Greenwich G H J

67

Designed and produced by E.S.R.

Conic Projection

1:3,000,000

0 25 50 75 100 125 150 175 200 KILOMETRES

0 25 50 75 100 125 STATUTE MILES

© COLOUR LIBRARY BOOKS

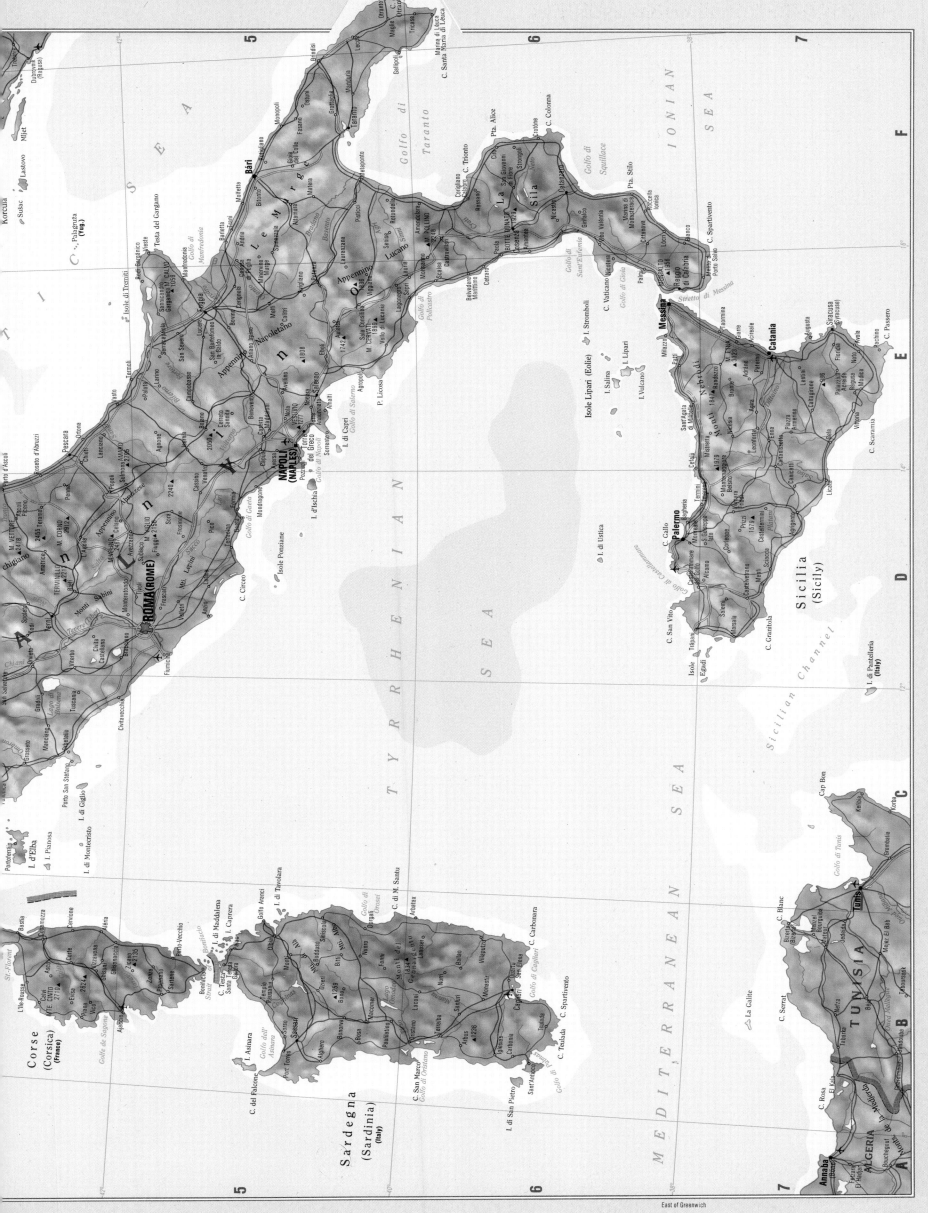

69

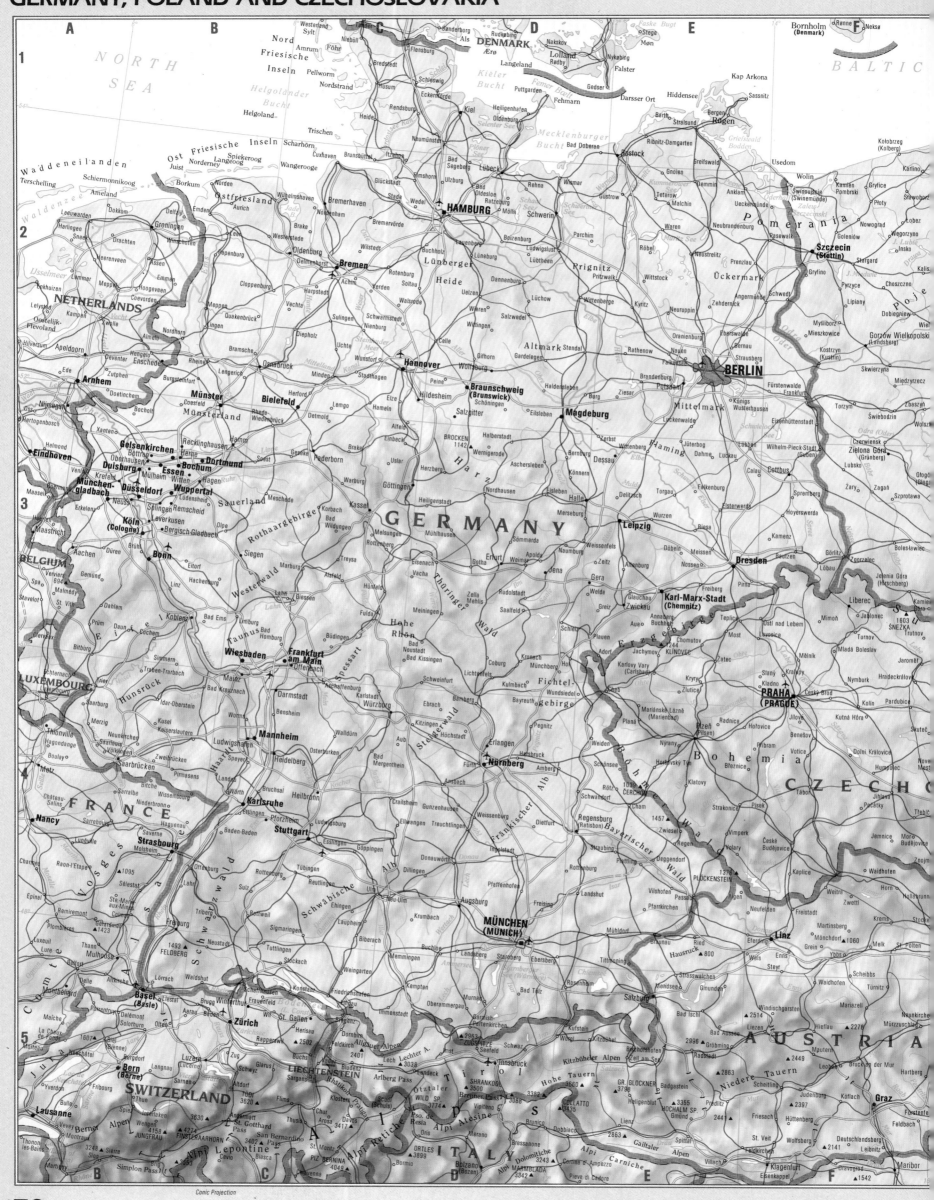

Conic Projection

1:3,000,000

0   25   50   75   100   125   150   175   200 KILOMETRES

0   25   50   75   100   125 STATUTE MILES

© COLOUR LIBRARY BOOKS

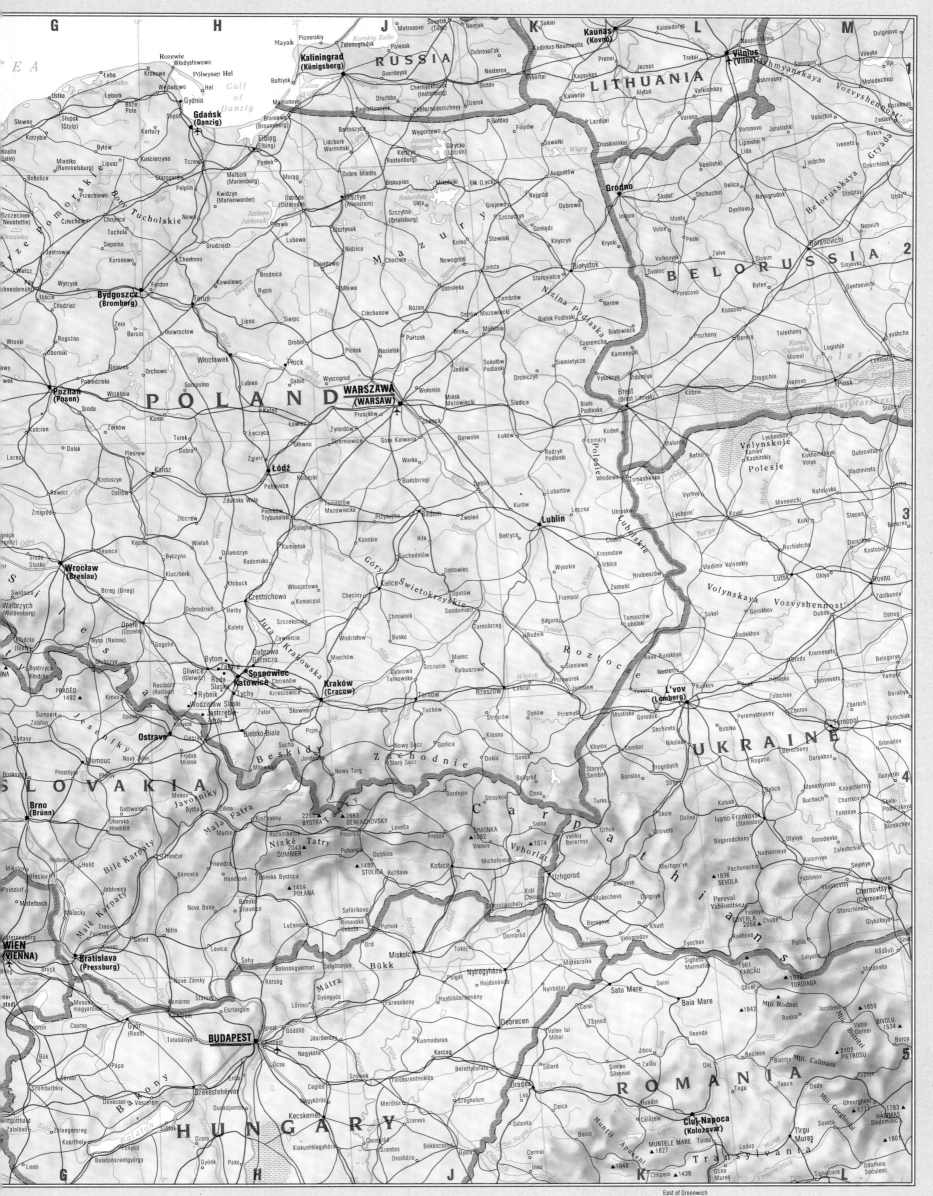

Designed and produced by E.S.R.

East of Greenwich

YUGOSLAVIA, HUNGARY, ROMANIA AND BULGARIA

Conic Projection

1:3,000,000

© COLOUR LIBRARY BOOKS

| 0 | 25 | 50 | 75 | 100 | 125 | 150 | 175 | 200 KILOMETRES |
| 0 | 25 | 50 | 75 | 100 | 125 STATUTE MILES |

Conic Projection

1:3,000,000

| 0 | 25 | 50 | 75 | 100 | 125 | 150 | 175 | 200 KILOMETRES |
| 0 | 25 | 50 | 75 | 100 | 125 STATUTE MILES |

© COLOUR LIBRARY BOOKS

GREECE

BULGARIA

TURKEY

LAVIA

AEGEAN SEA

BLACK SEA

Marmara Denizi (Sea of Marmara)

Thrakikón Pélagos

Thermaïkós Kólpos

Peloponnisos

Kikladhes (Cyclades)

Dhodhekánisos (Dodecanese)

Kritikón Pélagos (Sea of Crete)

Kríti (Crete)

SOFIYA (SOFIA)

Plovdiv

Skopje

Thessaloniki (Saloníki)

ATHÍNAI (ATHENS)

Varna

İZMİR (SMYRNA)

Balıkesir

Lésvos (Lesbos)

Khíos (Chios)

Límnos (Lemnos)

Thásos

Samothráki

Évvoia (Euboea)

Sámos

Ródhos (Rhodes)

Kárpathos (Scarpanto)

Kos (Cos)

Kálimnos (Calino)

Thíra (Santorini)

Náxos

Páros

Mílos

Kíthira (Cerigo)

Zákinthos (Zante)

Pátrai (Patras)

Kórinthos (Corinth)

Spárti (Sparta)

Kalámata

Ákr. Taínaron (C.Matapán)

Iráklion (Candia)

Khaniá (Canea)

MUSALA ▲2926

ÓLIMBOS (OLYMPUS) ▲2917

Voríai Sporádhes (Northern Sporades)

Skópelos

Skíros

Andros

Tínos

Míkonos

Síros

Sérifos

Sífnos

Amorgós

İstanbul

Varna

East of Greenwich

75

Lambert Conformal Conic Projection

1:3,500,000

© COLOUR LIBRARY BOOKS

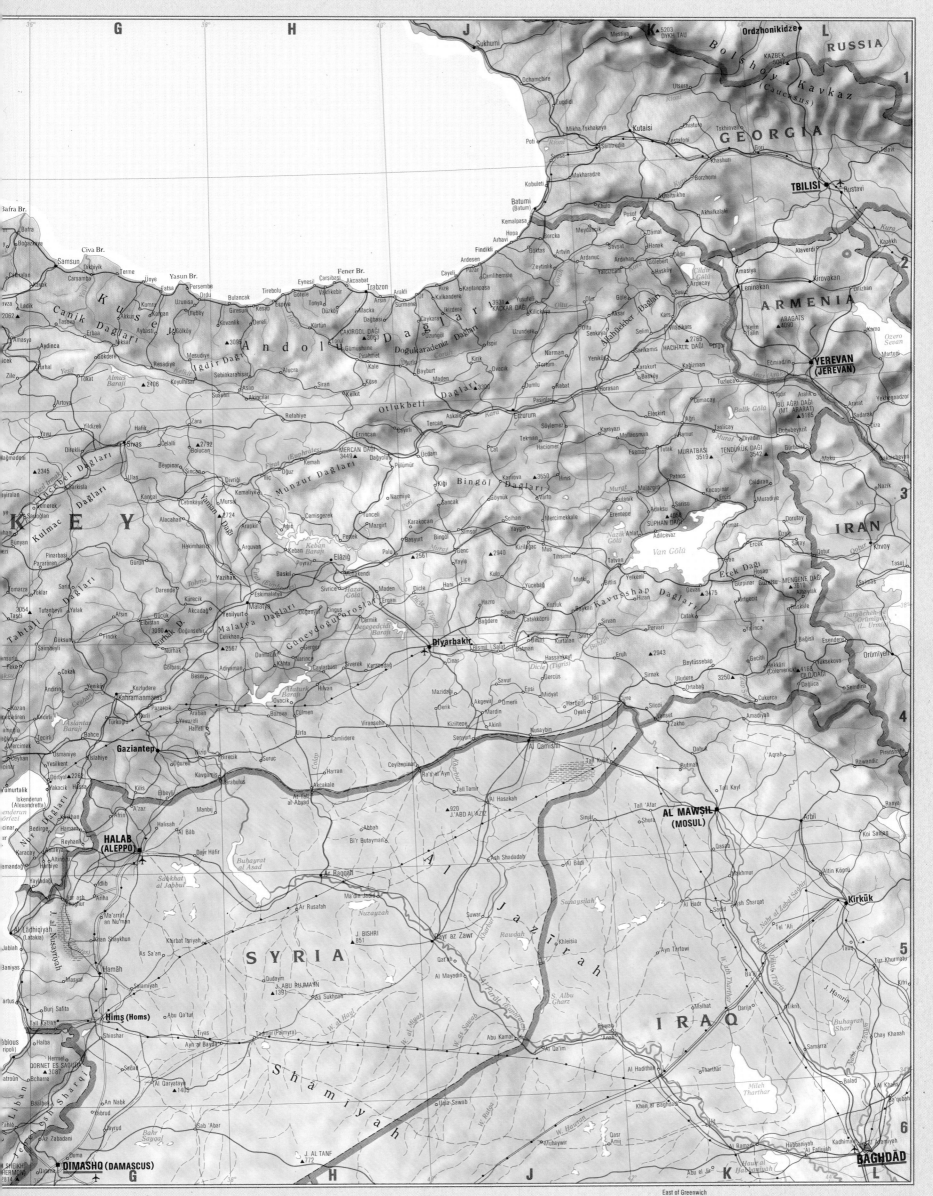

Miller Obiated Stereographic Projection

1:8,000,000

© COLOUR LIBRARY BOOKS

East of Greenwich

79

Conic Projection

1:17,000,000

| 0 | 100 | 200 | 300 | 400 | 500 | 600 | 700 | 800 KILOMETRES |

| 0 | 100 | 200 | 300 | 400 | 500 STATUTE MILES |

© COLOUR LIBRARY BOOKS

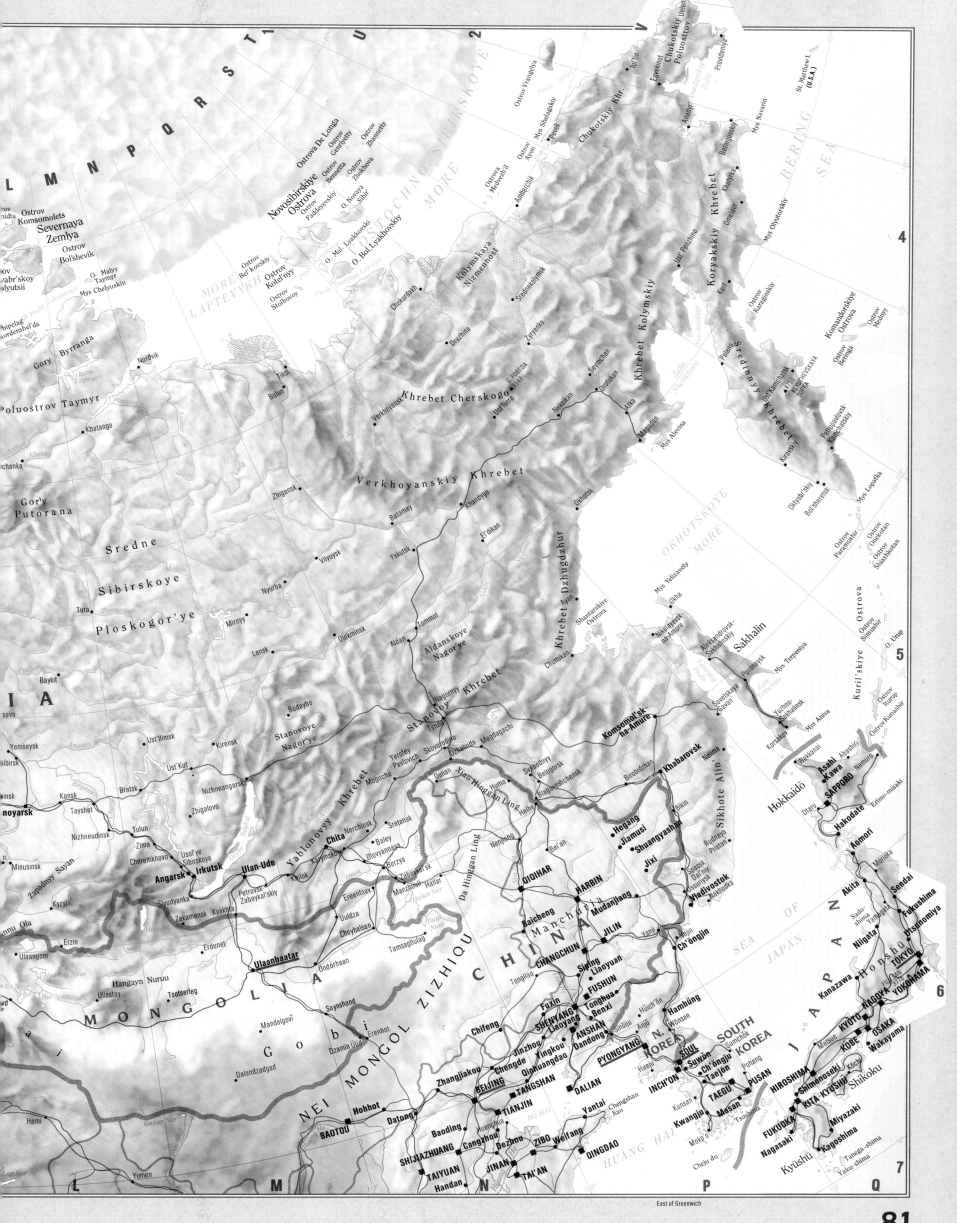

Lambert Azimuthal Equal Area Projection

1:25,000,000

| 0 | 200 | 400 | 600 | 800 | 1000 KILOMETRES |

| 0 | 100 | 200 | 300 | 400 | 500 | 600 STATUTE MILES |

© COLOUR LIBRARY BOOKS

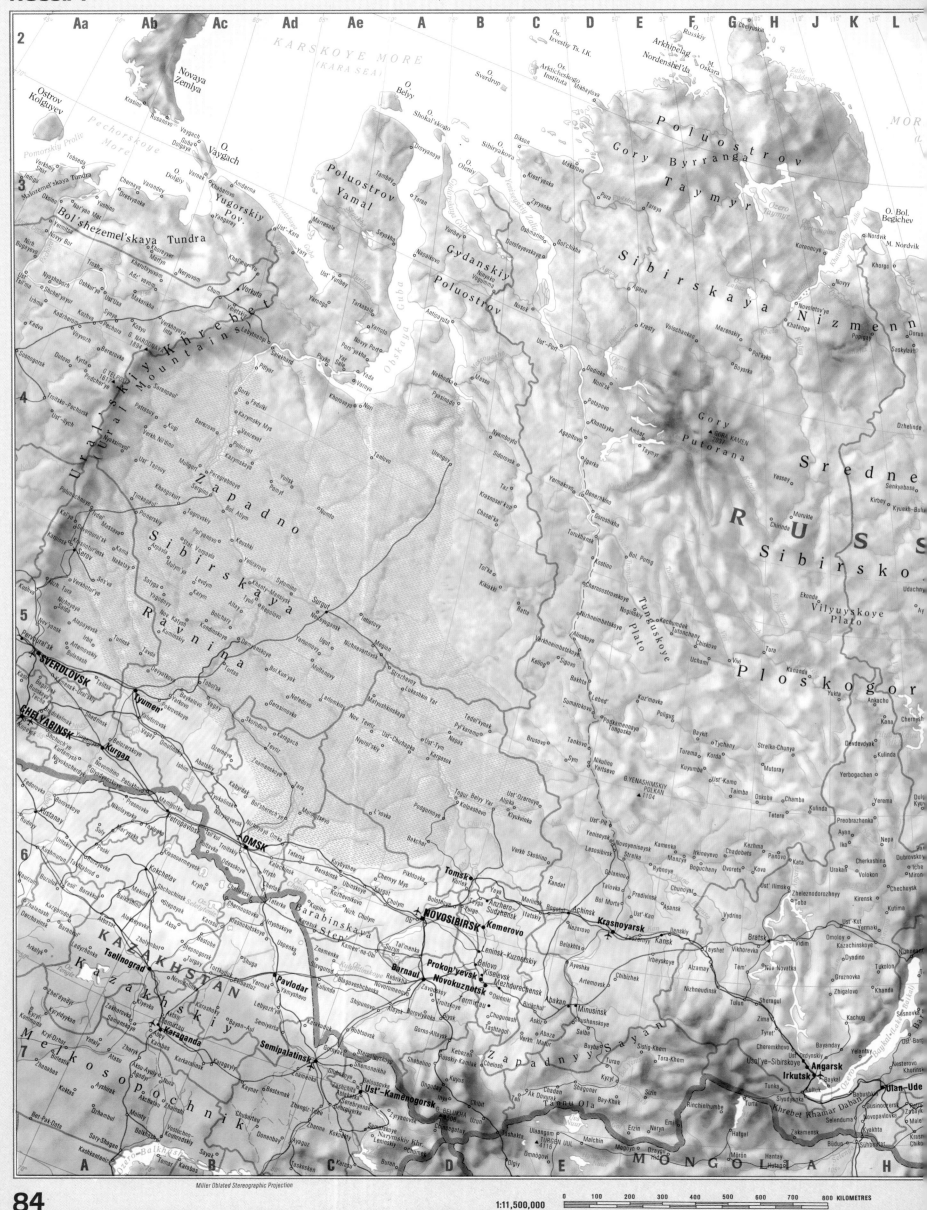

KARSKOYE MORE
(KARA SEA)

MONGOLIA

Miller Oblated Stereographic Projection

1:11,500,000

© COLOUR LIBRARY BOOKS

| 0 | 100 | 200 | 300 | 400 | 500 | 600 | 700 | 800 KILOMETRES |
| 0 | 50 | 100 | 150 | 200 | 250 | 300 | 350 | 400 | 450 | 500 STATUTE MILES |

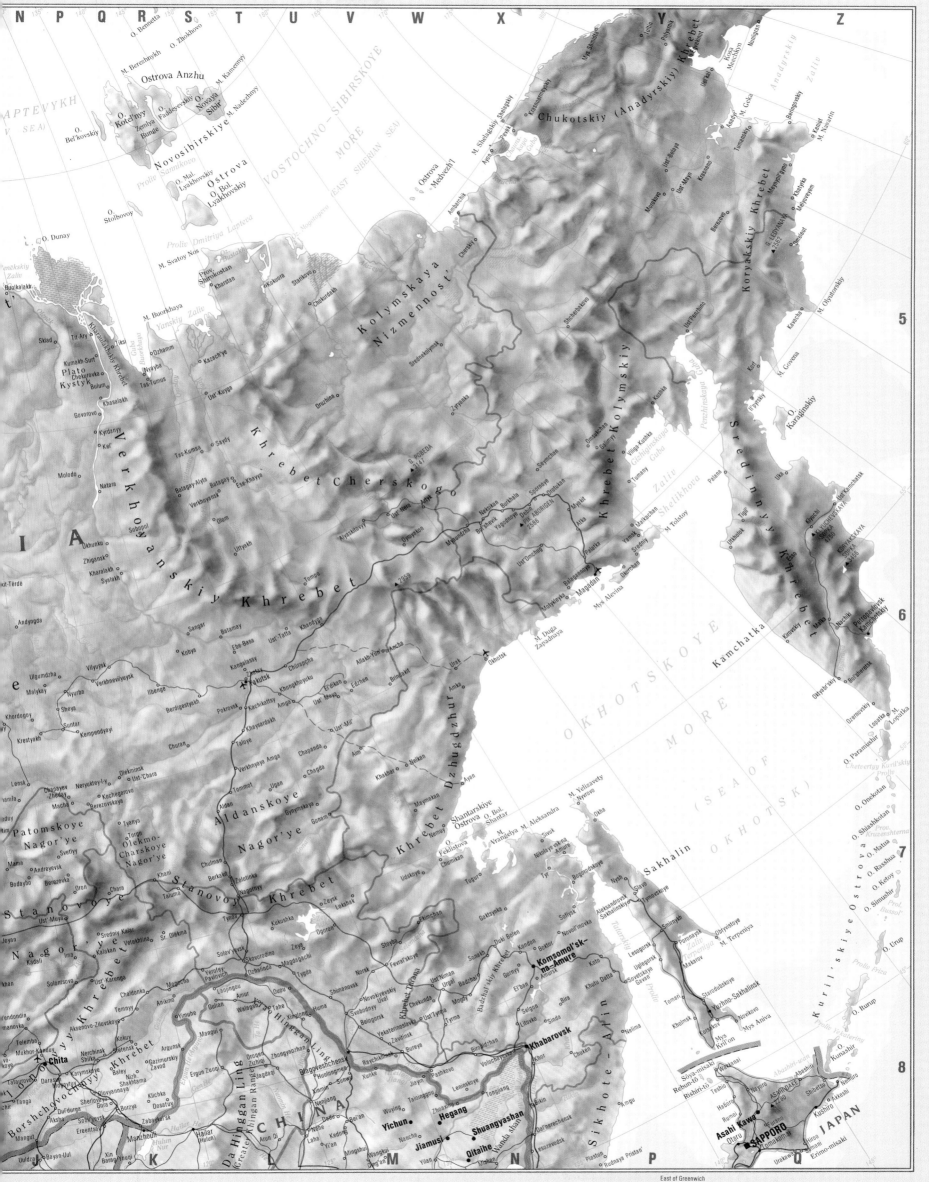

East of Greenwich

85

Miller Oblated Stereographic Projection

1:11,500,000

© COLOUR LIBRARY BOOKS

| 0 | 100 | 200 | 300 | 400 | 500 | 600 | 700 | 800 KILOMETRES |

| 0 | 50 | 100 | 150 | 200 | 250 | 300 | 350 | 400 | 450 | 500 STATUTE MILES |

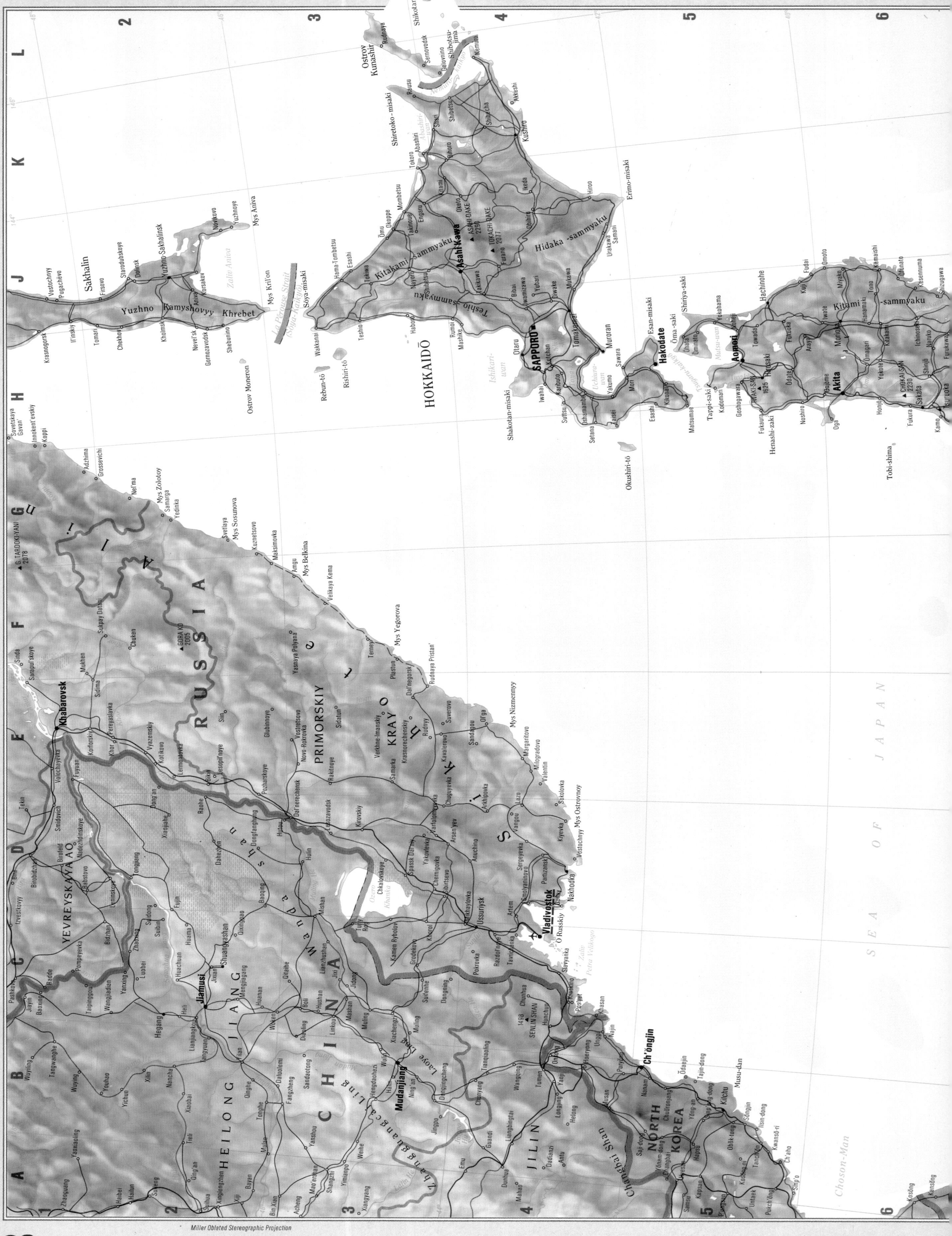

Sakhalin

Yuzhno-Sakhalinsk

Yuzhno Kamyshovyy Khrebet

Mys Krilon

La Pérouse Strait

HOKKAIDŌ

Asahi-kawa

ASAHI-DAKE 2290

TOKACHI-DAKE 2077

Hidaka - sammyaku

Teshio - sammyaku

Kitakami - sammyaku

SAPPORO

Hakodate

Aomori

Akita

Ishikari-wan

Uchiura-wan

Erimo-misaki

Shiretoko - misaki

Ostrov Kunashir

Kushiro

RUSSIA

Khabarovsk

PRIMORSKIY KRAY

Vladivostok

Nakhodka

Ussuriysk

YEVREYSKAYA AO

HEILONG JIANG

CHINA

Jiamusi

Mudanjiang

JILIN

NORTH KOREA

Ch'ŏngjin

SEA OF JAPAN

Zaliv Petra Velikogo

Changbai Shan

G. TARDOKI-YANI 2078

GORA KO 2005

SENJUN SHAN

Choson-Man

Miller Oblated Stereographic Projection

1:4,500,000

| 0 | 50 | 100 | 150 | 200 | 250 | 300 KILOMETRES |

| 0 | 50 | 100 | 150 | 200 STATUTE MILES |

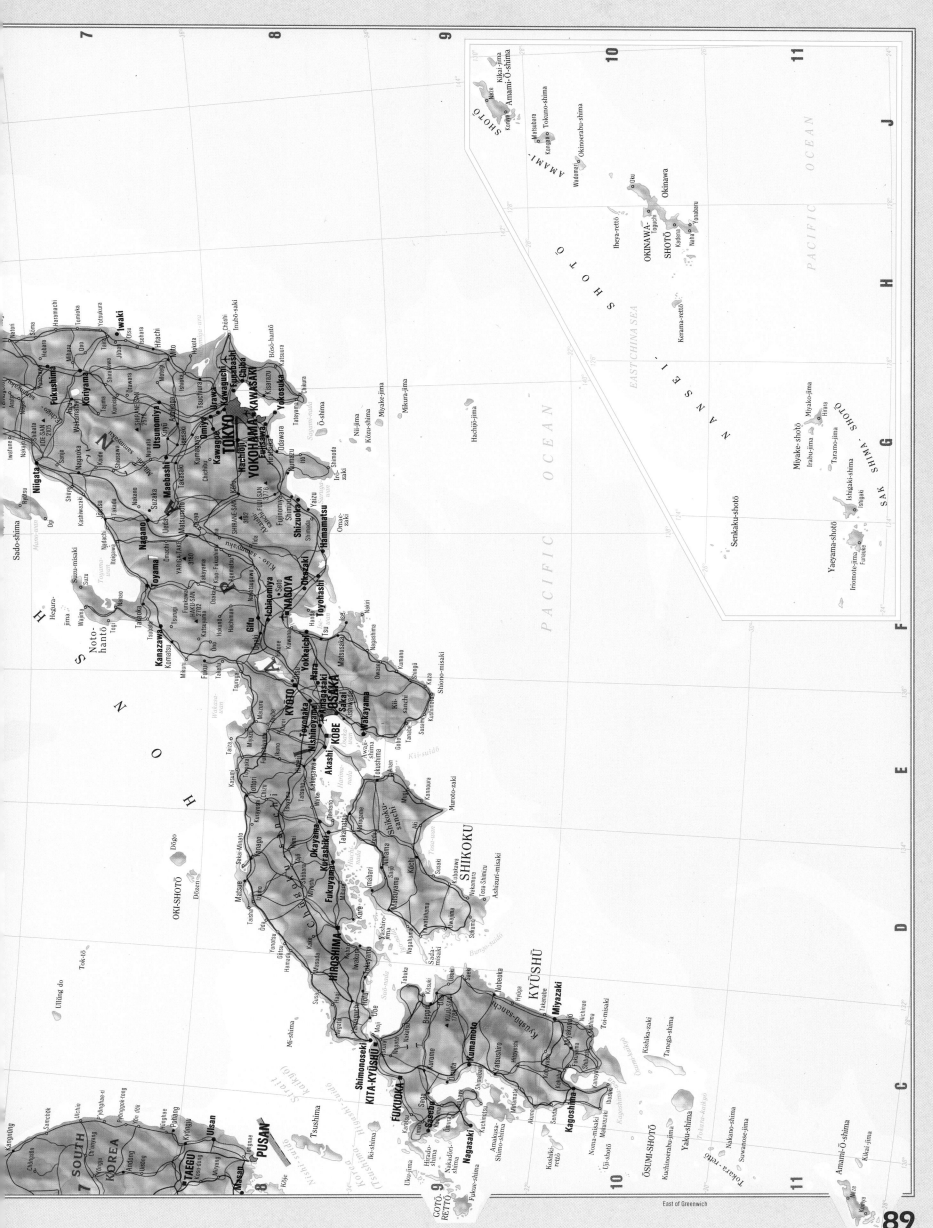

East of Greenwich

Designed and produced by E.S.R.

BANGLADESH
CHITTAGONG

BURMA

BAY
OF
BENGAL

Andaman
Islands
(India)

Nicobar
Islands
(India)

RANGOON

ANDAMAN
SEA

Mandalay

THAILAND

KRUNG THEP (BANGKOK)

Gulf
of
Thailand

LAOS

Viangchan
(Vientiane)

HANOI
HAIPHONG

Beibu Wan
(Gulf
of
Tongking)

CHINA

MACAO
(AOMEN)
(Port.)

Victoria
HONG KONG
(U.K.)

Maoming

Zhanjiang

Haikou

Hainan Dao

Da Nang

Parcel Islands
Xisha Qundao
(Claimed by China
and Vietnam)

NAN HAI

(SOUTH CHINA
SEA)

CAMBODIA

Phnom
Penh

VIETNAM

HO CHI MINH (SAIGON)

Nanshan Islands
Nansha Qundao
(Claimed by China, Vietnam and Philippines)

MALAYSIA

BRUNEI

George Town
(Pinang)

Kuala Terengganu

Malay
Peninsula

KUALA LUMPUR

MEDAN

SINGAPORE
Johor Baharu

Kuching

SARAWAK

KALIMANTAN
Borneo

Pontianak

Balikpapan

Banjarmasin

S U M A T E R A

Padang

Palembang

INDIAN

OCEAN

Tanjungkarang
Telukbetung

JAKARTA

Bogor
BANDUNG

SEMARANG
Surakarta

SURABAYA

Malang

LAUT JAWA

Jawa (Java)

Bali

Lombok

Mercator Projection

90

1:12,000,000

0 100 200 300 400 500 600 700 800 KILOMETRES
0   100   200   300   400   500 STATUTE MILES

© COLOUR LIBRARY BOOKS

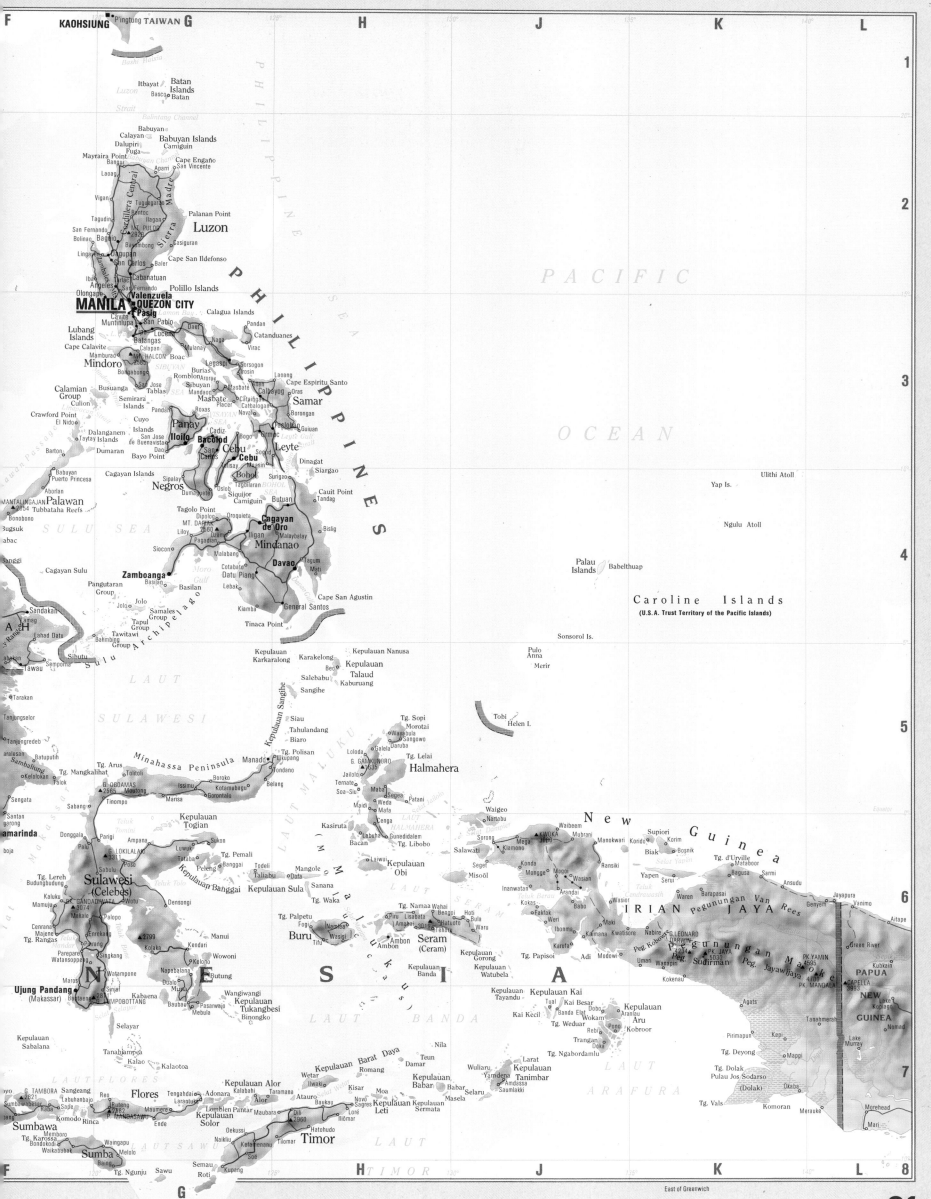

KAOHSIUNG P'ingtung TAIWAN **G**

F **G** **H** **J** **K** **L**

Itbayat
Batan Islands
Basco Batan

Babuyan
Calayan Babuyan Islands
Dalupiri Fuga Camiguin
Mayraira Point Bangui Cape Engaño
Bangui San Vincente
Laoag Aparri

Vigan Tuguegarao
Taguding Bontoc Ilagan Palanan Point
San Fernando Bangued Casiguran
Bolinao Baguio MT. PULOG 2920
Linga-yen Cape San Ildefonso
San Carlos Dagupan Baler
Ibaan Tarlac Cabanatuan
Angeles San Fernando
Olongapo **VALENZUELA** Polillo Islands
MANILA QUEZON CITY
Cavite **Pasig** Calagua Islands
Muntinlupa San Pablo Daet Pandan
Lubang Batangas Lucena Catanduanes
Islands Calapan Naga Virac
Cape Calavite Mamburao Boac Legaspi
Mindoro MT. HALCON 2585 Laoang Cape Espiritu Santo
Bongabong Burias Sorsogon Oras
Calamian Romblon Masbate Catbalogan Samar
Group Busuanga Sibuyan Mandaon Borongan
Culion Semirara San Jose Tablas Catbalogan
Islands Pandan Placer Tacloban Guiuan
Crawford Point Cuyo Roxas Cadiz Cebu
El Nido Islands San Jose Bacolod
Dalanganem Tay tay de Buenavista Cebu Leyte
Barton Islands Bayo Point Dao Maasin Dinagat
Dumaran Panay Iloilo Dumaguete Siargao
Babuyan Negros Siquijor Surigao
Puerto Princesa Cagayan Islands Sipalay Tagbilaran Bohol Cauit Point
Aborlan Palawan Camiguin Butuan Tandag
MANTALINGAJAN Tagolo Point Dipolog Oroquieta Bislig
2054 Tubbataha Reefs MT. DAPIAK Dumanquilas Malaybalay
Bononao 2560 Iligan Cagayan de Oro
Bugsuk SULU SEA Liloy Pagadian Mindanao
abac Cagayan Sulu Siocon Malabang Tagum
Banggi Datu Piang Davao
Sandakan Zamboanga Cotabato Lebak Mati
Pangutaran Basilan Cape San Agustin
Group Basilan Kiamba
Lahad Datu Jolo General Santos
Samales Tinaca Point
Tapul Group
Tawitawi Group
Sibutu Kepulauan Kepulauan Nanusa
Tawau Sempurna Karkaralong Karakelong

Kepulauan Talaud
Salebabu Kaburuang
Sangihe

LAUT
SULAWESI
Kepulauan Sangihe Siau
Tahulandang Biaro
Tg. Mangkalihat Tg. Arus Manado Tg. Polisan
Minahassa Peninsula

PHILIPPINES

PACIFIC

OCEAN

Ulithi Atoll

Yap Is.

Ngulu Atoll

Palau Islands Babelthuap

Caroline Islands
(U.S.A. Trust Territory of the Pacific Islands)

Sonsorol Is.

Pulo Anna
Merir

Tobi
Helen I.

Tg. Sopi
Morotai
Wayabula Sangowo
Galela Daruba

New Guinea

Waigeo Supiori
Nartabu Korido Korim Biak Bosnik
Waibem Yapen Serui
Mega KWOKA 3090 Mubrani Manokwari
Klamono Ransiki Tg. d'Urville Mataboor
Salawati Sorong Konda Wasian Bagusa Sarmi Ansudu
Seget Misoöl Mongge Magoi Wandu Nabire Waren Barapasai
Inanwatan Arandai Teluk Cendrawasih Warmbo G. LEONARD Jayapura Vanimo
Kasiruta Labuha Gunedidalem Kokas Fakfak Weri Ibonma Maki Peg. Kobowre DARWIN Peg. Van Rees Genyem Aitape
Bacan Kepulauan Obi Laiwui Bula Waru Karufa Umari PK. YAMIN Green River
Tg. Palpetu Tg. Namaa Wahai Hoti Modowi Peg. Sudirman 5030 Kubkain
Fogi Namea 908 Platuoto Tehoru Adi Tg. Papisoi Kokenau Peg. Jayawijaya 4760 PAPUA
Buru Tifu Wasisi Ambon Seram (Ceram) Kepulauan Gorong Agats PK. MANDALA NEW
Ambon Kepulauan Banda Kepulauan Watubela Pirimapun CAPELLA 3993 GUINEA
Kepulauan Kai Kepi
Kepulauan Tayandu Tual Kai Besar Tanahmerah Lake Murray
Kai Kecil Kepulauan Aru Mappi Nomad
Tg. Weduar Wokam Tg. Deyong
Rebi Kobroor
Trangan Tg. Ngabordamlu Okaba
Nila Larat Tg. Dolak Komoran
Teun Damar Wuliaru Kepulauan Tanimbar Pulau Jos Sodarso Merauke Mari
Romang Kisar Moa Yamdena Amdassa (Dolak) Morehead
Wetar Iliwaki Saumlakki Tg. Vals

PACIFIC Elevator

LAUT
MALUKU
(MOLUCCA SEA)

LAUT
HALMAHERA

Halmahera
Loloda
Tondano G. GAMKUNORO 1635
Tobelo
Jailolo
Ternate Kao
Soa-Siu Maba
Weda Lelai
Patani
Segea Mafa
Maidi

Kau
Tg. Lelai

LAUT SERAM

LAUT BANDA

Kepulauan Barat Daya

LAUT ARAFURA

I R I A N J A Y A

Pegunungan Maoke

Timor

LAUT TIMOR

91

East of Greenwich

Designed and produced by E.S.R.

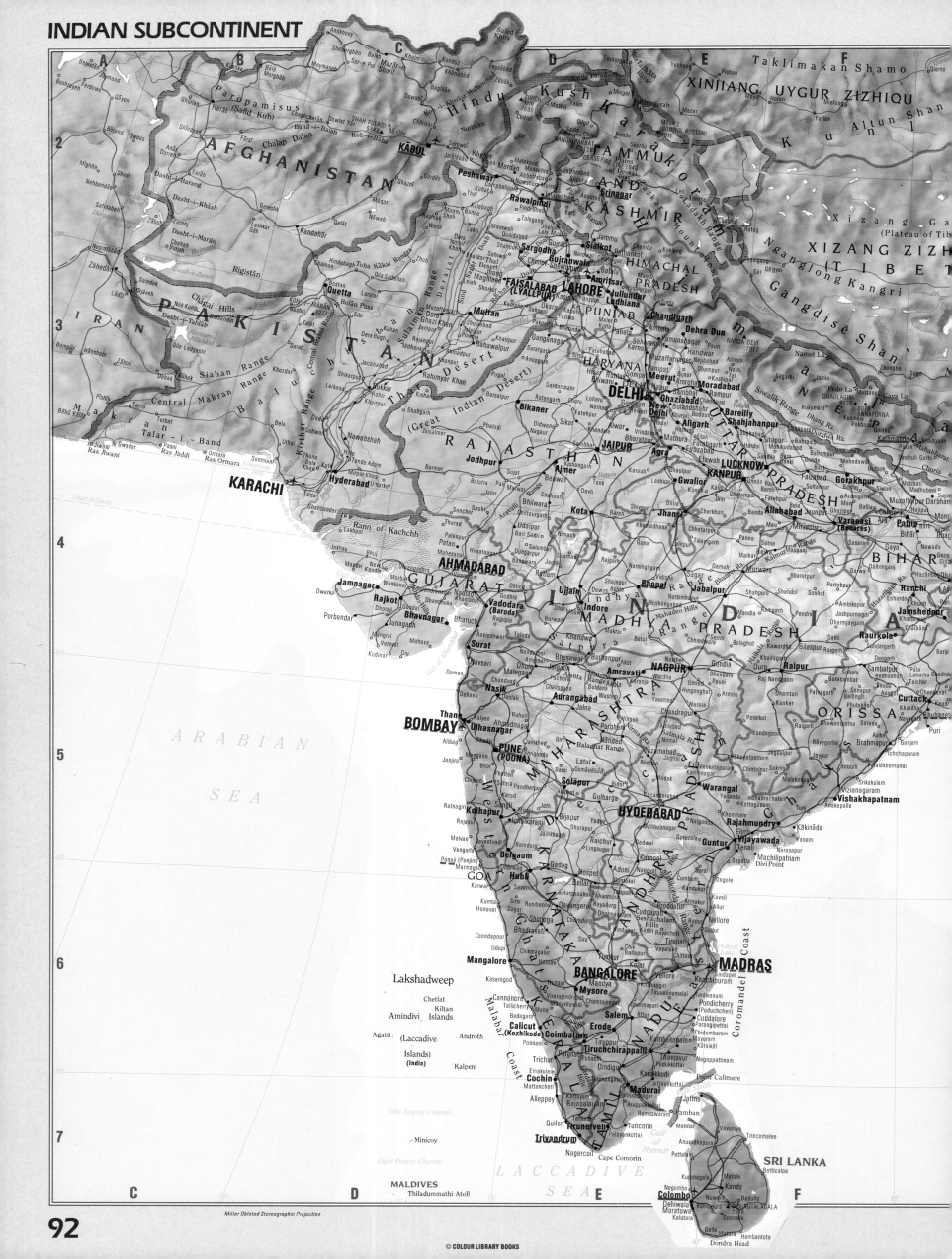

Miller Oblated Stereographic Projection

© COLOUR LIBRARY BOOKS

93

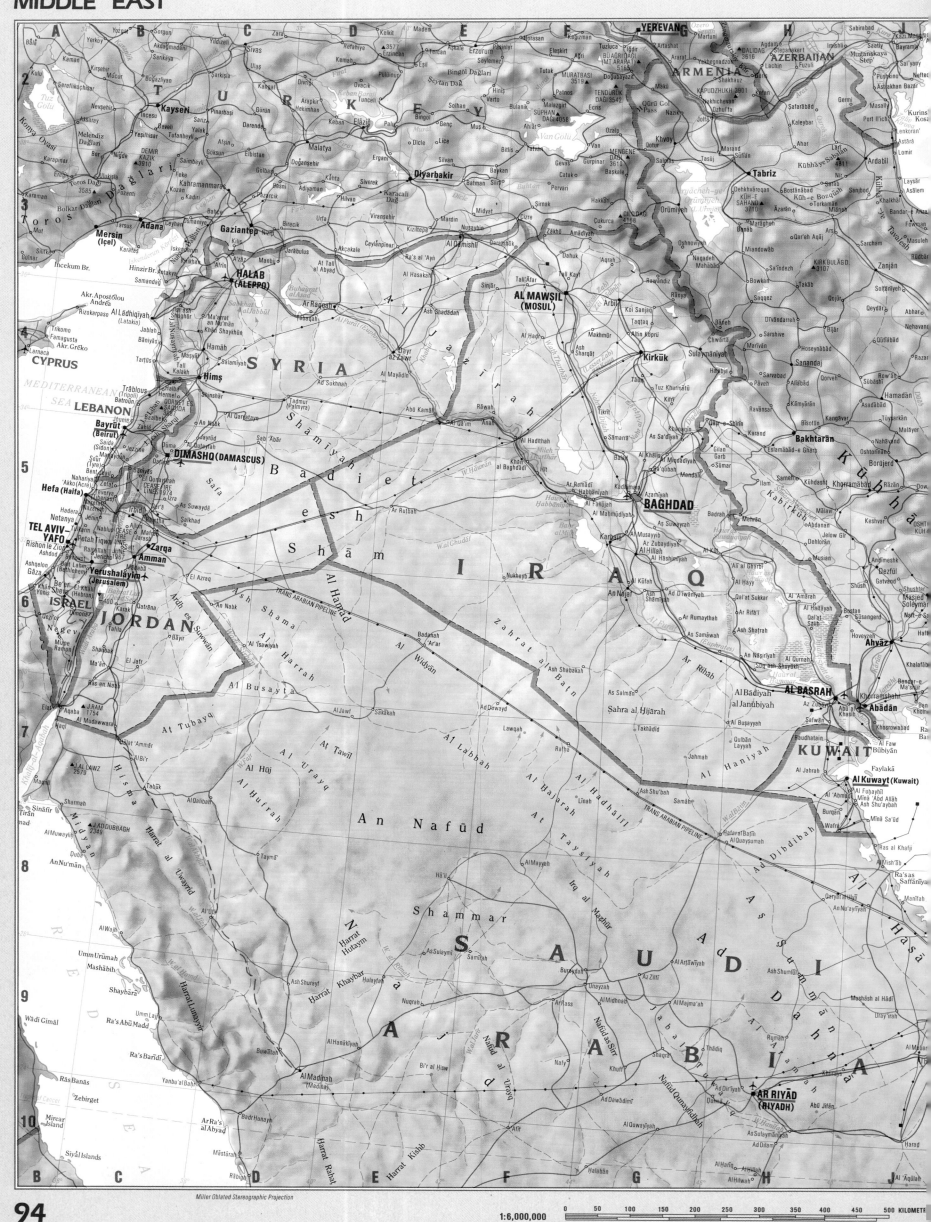

Miller Oblated Stereographic Projection

1:6,000,000

© COLOUR LIBRARY BOOKS

| 0 | 50 | 100 | 150 | 200 | 250 | 300 | 350 | 400 | 450 | 500 KILOMETRE |

| 0 | 50 | 100 | 150 | 200 | 250 | 300 STATUTE MILES |

Designed and produced by E.S.R.

East of Greenwich

ARABIAN PENINSULA

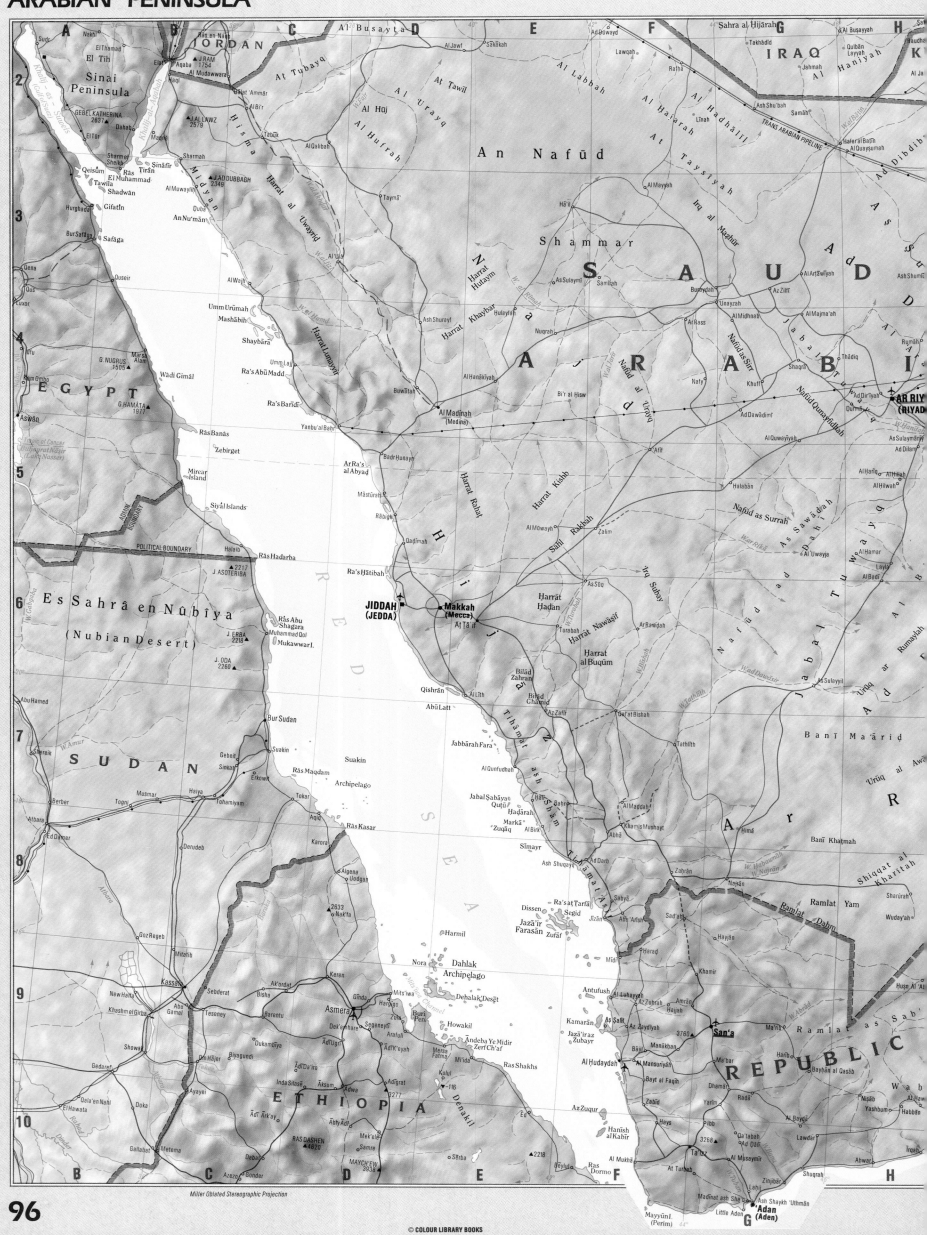

Miller Oblated Stereographic Projection

© COLOUR LIBRARY BOOKS

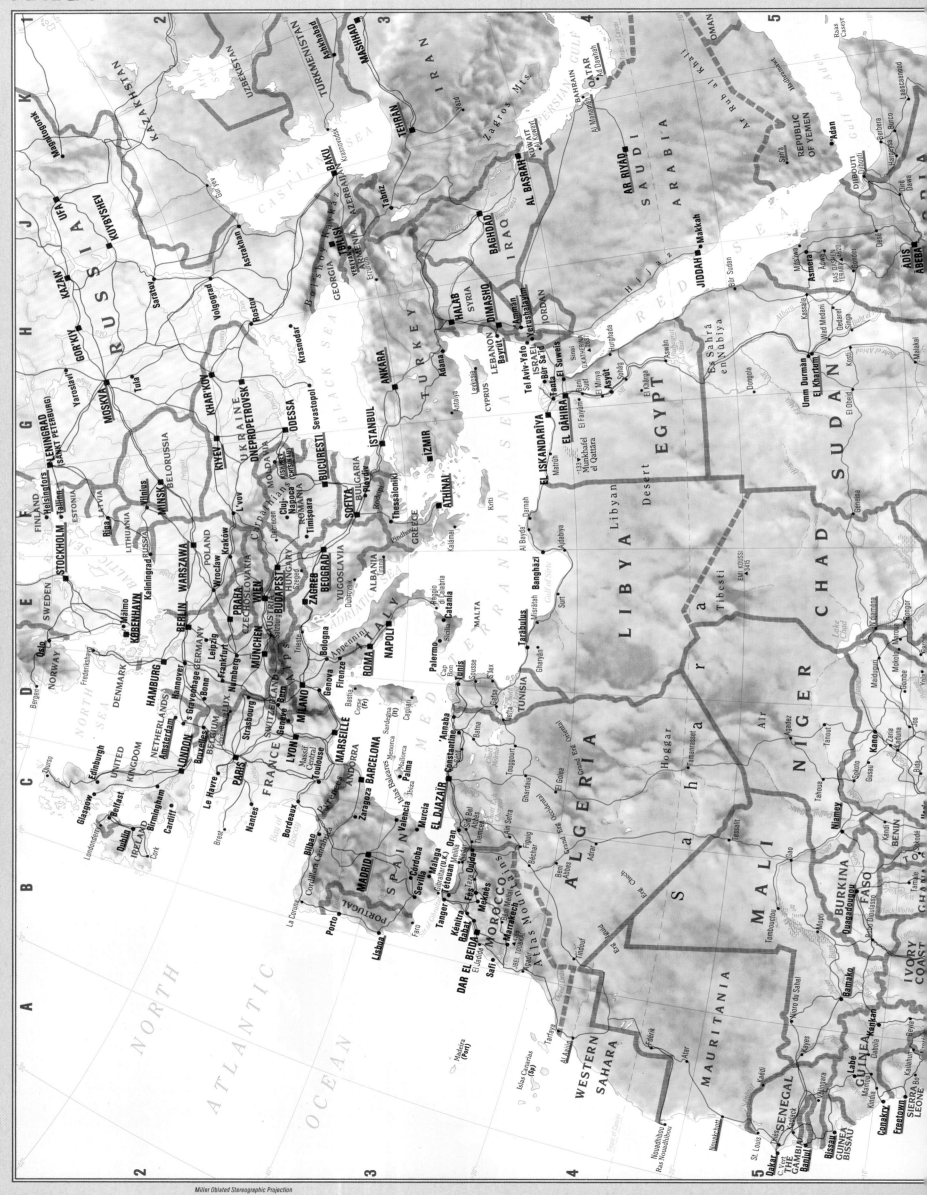

Miller Oblated Stereographic Projection

1:23,000,000

© COLOUR LIBRARY BOOKS

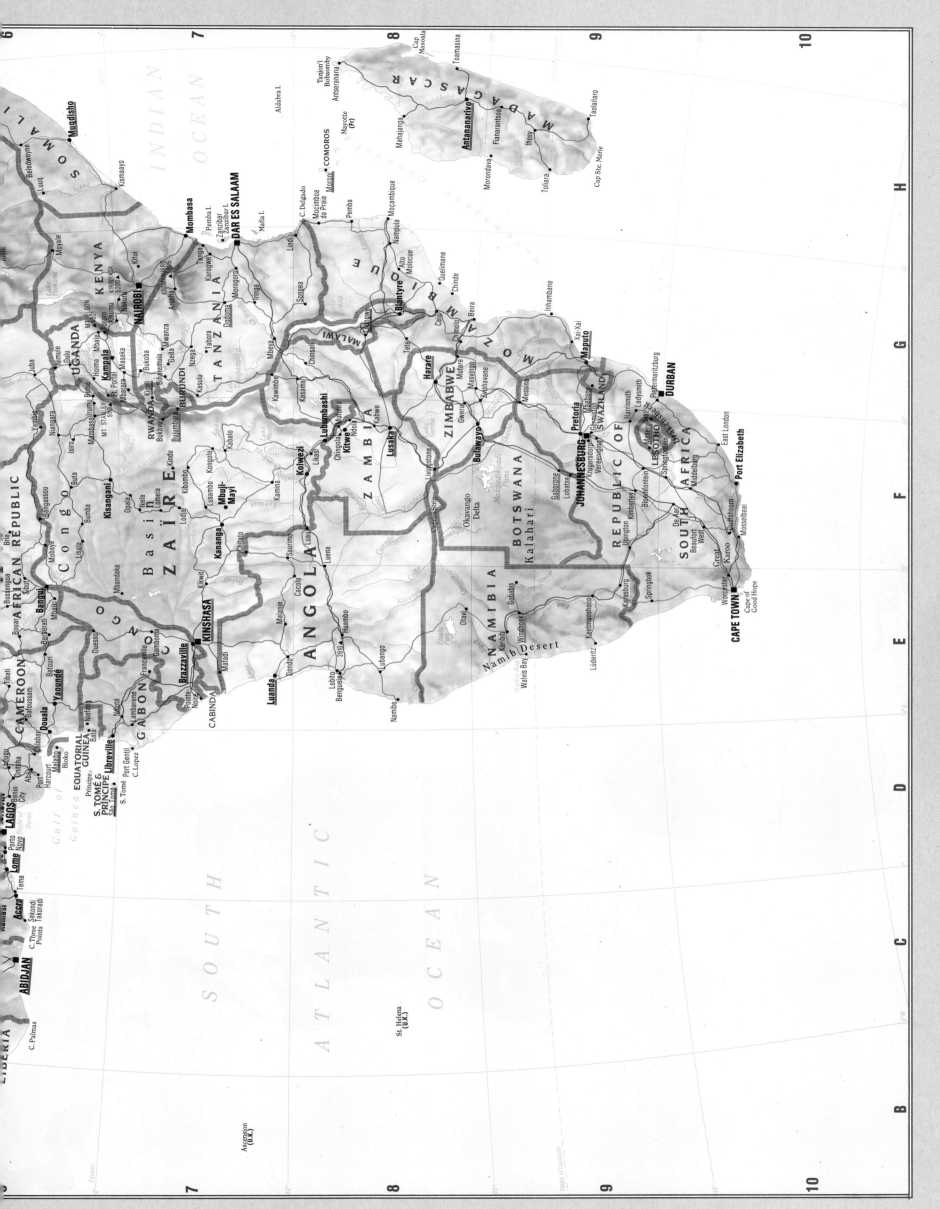

A B C D E

SPAIN

NORTH
ATLANTIC

OCEAN

Madeira
(Portugal)
Funchal

Cádiz
Málaga
Almería
Gibraltar (U.K.)
Ceuta (Sp.)
Tanger
Tétouan
Cap Spartel
Cap des Trois
Fourches
Melilla
(Spain)
Oran
Larache
(El Araiche)
Ksar el kebir
Ouezzane
Nador
Sidi Bel
Abbès
Tlemcen
Oujda

DAR EL BEIDA
(CASABLANCA)
Kénitra
Rabat
Salé
Meknès
Fès
Taza
El Jadida
Khemisset
Safi
Settat
Khouribga
Oued Zem
Youssoufia
Kasba Tadla
Beni Mellal
MOROCCO
Moyen Atlas
Essaouira
Demnate
Marrakech
(Marrakesh)
JEBEL
TOUBKAL
Cap Rhir
Agadir
Taroudannt
Ouarzazate
Anti-Atlas
Tiznit
Sidi Ifni

Ilhas Selvagens
(Portugal)

Islas Canarias (Canary Is.)
(Spain)
La Palma
Sta. Cruz
de la Palma
Gomera
Lanzarote
Arrecife
Fuerteventura
Valverde
Tenerife
Sta. Cruz
de Tenerife
Las Palmas
Hierro
Gran Canaria
Puerto del
Rosario
Tarfaya
(Villa Bens)
Cap Juby
Al Aaiún
(Laâyoune)

Béchar

Grand Erg Occid

Hamada du Dra
Oued Drâa
Oued Tigzerte
Tan-Tan

ALGE

Tindouf

Es Semara
El Saquia al Hamra
Boujdour

WESTERN
SAHARA

Bir Moghrein
(Fort Trinquet)

Erg Iguidi

Adrar

Tropic of Cancer

Ad Dakhla
(Villa Cisneros)
Baie de
Rio de Oro

Reggane

Timimoun

Ksabi

C. Barbas

Fderik
Zouerate

Maktéir

Erg Chech

Taoudenni

Tanezrouft

S a h

Nouadhibou
(Pt. Etienne)
Ras Nouadhibou
(C. Blanc)

Atar
Chinguetti

Ouarâne

Irharen

C. Timiris

Akjoujt

MAURITANIA

El Djouf

Aguelhok

Ad
Ifo

Tessalit

Nouakchott
Beila

Tidjikdja
Tichitt

Araouane

M A L I

Boutilimit
Moudjéria
Aouker
Tamchaket
Oualata

L. Faguibine
Tombouctou
(Timbuktu)
Ras el Ma
Niger
Bourem
Gourma-
Rharous
Bamba

Mederdra
Aleg
Kiffa
Aïoun el Atrouss
Néma
Timbédra

St. Louis
Louga
Dagana
Podor
Bogué
Kaédi
Diorbivol
Mbout
Sélibabi
Guidimaka
Niafunké
Goundam
Gao
Ansongo

Kébémer
Linguère
Matam
Bakel
Balé
Nara
Douentza

Tivaouane
Thiès
Diourbel
Bassé Santa Su
Kayes
Nioro du Sahel
Sokolo
Niono
Bandiagara
Dori

Cape Vert
Dakar
Mbour
Fatick
Kaolack
(Kaffrine)
SENEGAL
Tambacounda
Kaffrine
Kaffa
Ségou
Mopti
Ouahigouya
Yako

Banjul
(Bathurst)
Brikama
THE GAMBIA
Georgetown
Maka
Vélingara
Kolda
Satadougou
Kéniéba
Kita
Djenné
Tougan

Ziguinchor
C. Roxo
GUINEA
BISSAU
Bissau
Bolama
Arquipelago
dos Bijagos

Bafoulabé
Kati
Bamako
Koutiala
San
Dédougou

BURKINA FASO

Ouagadougou

Labé
GUINEA
Kankan

GHANA

Miller Oblated Stereographic Projection   West of Greenwich

1:9,000,000

0 100 200 300 400 500 600 KILOMETRES
0   50 100 150 200 250 300 350 400 STATUTE MILES

© COLOUR LIBRARY BOOKS

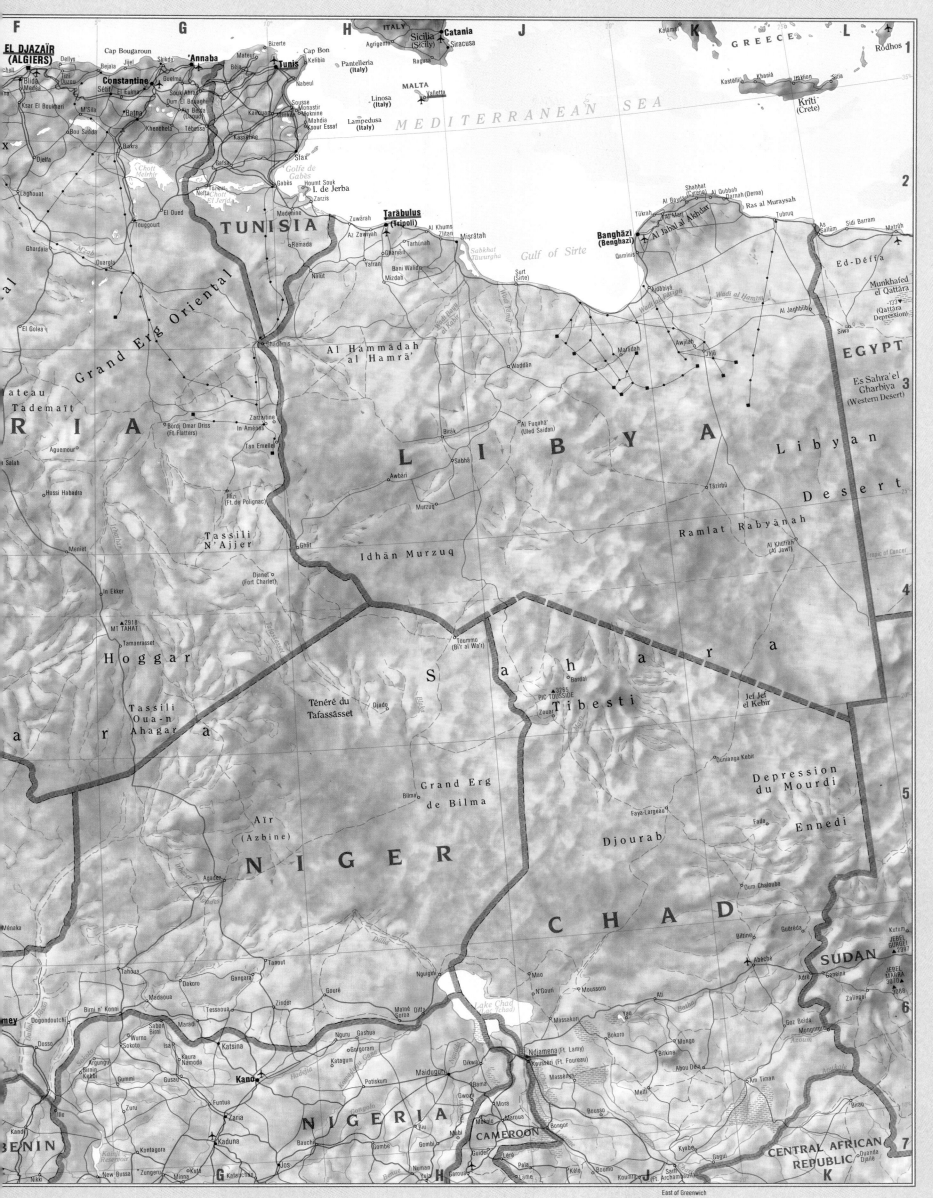

F **G** **H** **J** **K** **L**

1

EL DJAZAÏR
(ALGIERS)
Dellys Cap Bougaroun
Bejaia Jijel Skikda 'Annaba Bizerte Cap Bon GREECE Ródhos
Tizi Ouzou Guelma Mateur Kelibia Kastélli Khaniá Iráklion Sitía
Constantine El Eulma Tunis Pantelleria (Italy) Kríti (Crete)
Sétif Batna Souk Ahras Nabeul ITALY Catania
M'Sila Aïn Beïda Oum El Bouaghi Sousse Agrigento Sicilia (Sicily) Siracusa
Bou Saâda Khenchela Tébessa Kasserine Monastir Ragusa
Barika Moknine Mahdia MALTA
Kairouan Makthar Ksour Essaf Valletta
Djelfa Biskra Linosa (Italy) MEDITERRANEAN SEA
Laghouat Gafsa Sfax Lampedusa (Italy)
Chott Golfe de Gabès **2**
Meirhir Sousse Houmt Souk I. de Jerba
Ghardaïa Tozeur Netta Gabès Zarzis Tarābulus Shahhat (Cyrene) Al Qubbah
El Oued Chott El Jerid Zuwārah (Tripoli) Al Bayda Darnah (Derna)
Touggourt Medenine Az Zawiyah Al Khums Ras al Muraysah
Ouargla Remada Gharyān Zliten Misrātah Banghāzī Al Jabal al Akhdar Tubruq As Sallūm Sidi Barrani
El Golea Nālūt Yafran Tarhūnah (Benghazi) Matrūh
Mizdah Bani Walid Qaminis Ed-Déffa
Ghadāmis Surt (Sirte) Sabkhat Tāwurgha Gulf of Sirte Munkhafed el Qattāra
Al Hammādah Wadi Tamit Ajdābiyā -133 (Qattāra Depression)
al Hamrā' Waddān Al Jaghbūb Siwa EGYPT **3**
Zarzaïtine Birāk Al Fuqahā' (Uled Saidan) Marādah Awjilah Jālū
Bordj Omar Driss (Ft. Flatters) In Amenas Tan Emellel **L I B Y A** Es Sahra'el Gharbiya (Western Desert)
Aguemour Sabhā Libyan
Hassi Habadra Awbāri Desert
Salah Illizi (Ft. de Polignac) Murzuq Tāzirbū Ramlat Rabyānah Al Khufrah (Al Jawf)
Tassili N'Ajjer Ghāt Tropic of Cancer **4**
Meniet Idhān Murzuq
In Ekker Djanet (Fort Charlet)
MT TAHAT ▲2918 Toummo (Bi'r al Wa'r) Bardai Jef Jef el Kebir
Tamanrasset S a h a r a PIC TOUSSIDE ▲3265
Hoggar Zouar Tibesti
Tassili Ténéré du Tafassâsset Djado Dunianga Kebir
Oua-n Bilma Depression du Mourdi
Ahagar Grand Erg Faya-Largeau Fada Ennedi **5**
Aïr (Azbine) de Bilma Djourab Oum Chalouba
Agadez **N I G E R** Kutum JEBEL GÜRGEI ▲2397
Tahoua **C H A D** Biltine Guéréda SUDAN
Ménaka Tanout Abéché JEBEL MARRA ▲3070
Dakoro Gangara Nguigmi Mao Adré Geneina Zalingei **6**
Madaoua Zinder N'Gouri Ati Goz Beida
Birni n' Konni Goure Massakori Yao Mongo Mongororo
Tessaoua Maïné Soroa Moussoro Bokoro Bitkine Am Timan
Tanout Diffa Lake Chad (Lac Tchad) Bousso Abou Déïa Birao
7

101

Designed and produced by E.S.R.

East of Greenwich

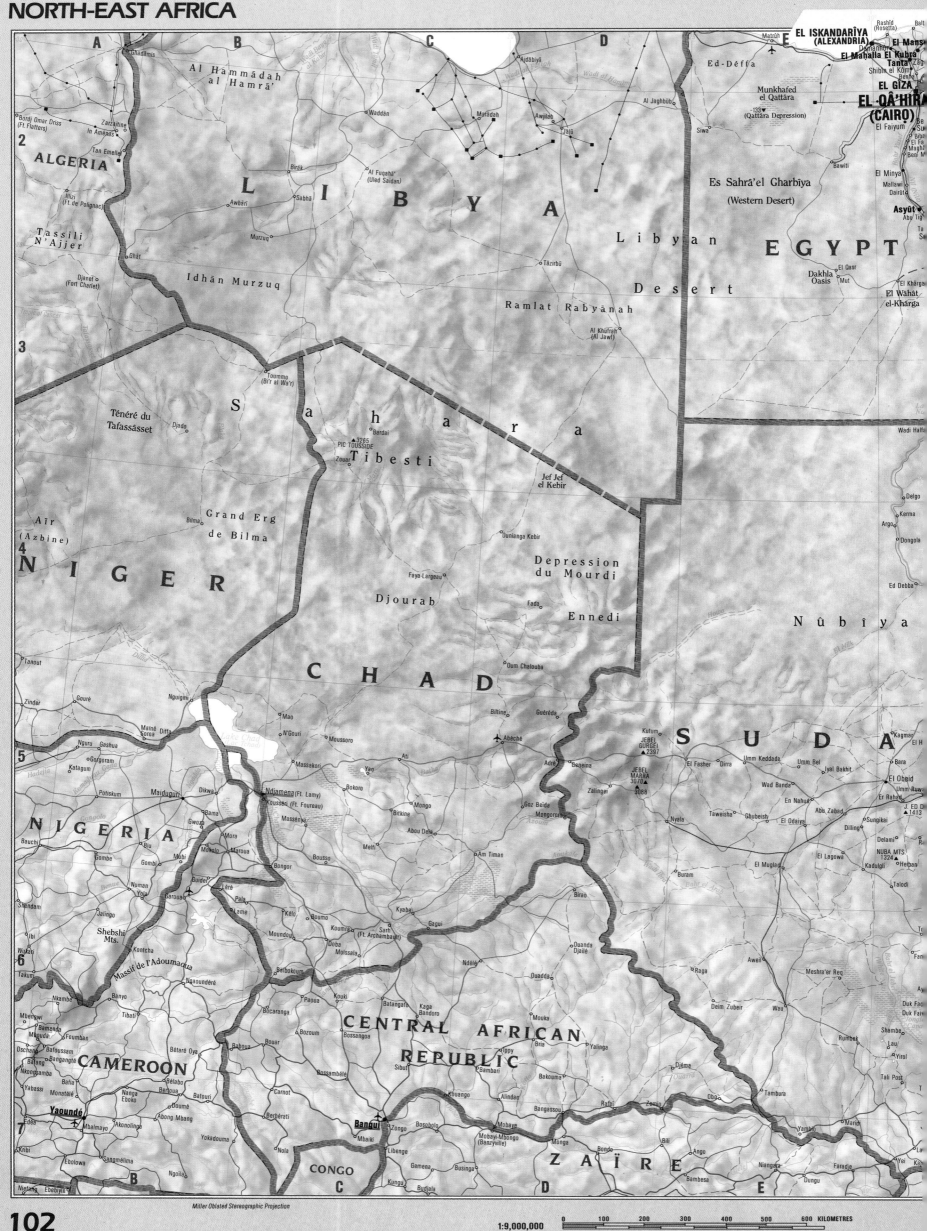

Miller Oblated Stereographic Projection

1:9,000,000

| 0 | 100 | 200 | 300 | 400 | 500 | 600 KILOMETRES |

| 0 | 50 | 100 | 150 | 200 | 250 | 300 | 350 | 400 STATUTE MILES |

© COLOUR LIBRARY BOOKS

F | G | H | J | K

ISRAEL
JORDAN
IRAQ
KUWAIT
Al Kuwayt (Kuwait)
IRAN

(Damietta)
ūr Sa'īd
(Port Said)
El 'Arīsh
Ismā'īliya
El Suweis (Suez)
Sinai Peninsula
GEBEL KATHERINA ▲2637
El Tûr
Maqnā
J AL LAWZ ▲2579
Tabūk
Ma'ān
Ra's en Naqb
Elat
'Aqaba
Al Mudawwara

Al Busayyah
Ad Duwayd
Al Jahrah
Ash Shu'bah
TRANS ARABIAN PIPELINE
Hafar al Bāṭin
Ra's al Khafji
Borāzjān
Farrāshband
Fīrūzābād
Fasā
Dārāb
Jahrom

An Nafūd
As Sahrā Esh Sharqīya (Arabian Desert)
Ras Muhammad
Hurghada
Duba
Al 'Ulā
Taymā'
Sakākah
Al Jawf
Al Mayyah
Hā'il
Ad Dahnā
Ad Dammām
Az Zahrān
Al Manāmah
BAHRAIN
Kharg Is.
Būshehr
Khvormūj
Kangān
Nāy Band
Lāvān
Bandar-e Lengeh
Bastak
Lār
Khonj

Mashābih
Shaybārā
Umm Lajj
Al Wajh
Ra's Abū Madd
Ra's Barīdī
Yanbu'al Baḥr
Al Madīnah (Medina)
BadrHunayn
Rābigh
Ra's Ḥātibah
Ra's al Abyaḍ
ArRa's al Abyaḍ

Buraydah
'Unayzah
'ArRass
Ash Shuray'
Nuqrah
Hulaylah
Al Hanākīyah
Shaqrā
Ad Dir'īyah
Ar Riyāḍ (Riyadh)
Ad Dilam
Ad Dawādimī
Afīf
Al Ḥāriq
'Aflaj
Al Jubayl
Al Muharraq
Al Hufūf
Buqayq
Al Mubarraz
Ra's Tannūrah
Dukhān
Al Khobar
QATAR
Ad Dawhah (Doha)
Az Zarqā
Musay'id
Ra's al Udayd
Harad
Abū Zabī (Abu Dhabi)
Mutlah
UNITED ARAB EMIRATES

SAUDI ARABIA

RED SEA

Aswān
Sadd-al-Aswān (Aswan High Dam)
1977 GEBEL HAMATA ▲
Lake Nasser (Buhayrat Nasr)
Es Sahrâ en Nûbīya (Nubian Desert)

An Nafūd
Ḥā'il
Ad Dahnā
Ad Dawādimī
Tropic of Cancer
Sabkhat Matti
Al 'Ubaylah

Halāban
Zalim
As Sūq
Laylā
ARABIA
Ar Rub al Khālī
OMAN

Makkah (Mecca)
JIDDAH (JEDDA)
Aṭ Ṭā'if
Al Līth
Hijaz
Turabah
Da'at Bishah
As Sulayyil
Darb

Muhammad Qol
JEBEL ODA ▲2260
Al Qunfudhah
Hali
Abhā
Khamis Mushayt
Sharūrah
Thamūd
Damqawt

Port Sudan
Suakin
Sinkat
Tohamiyam
Tokar
Abū Hamed
Berber
Musmar
Derudeb
Karora
Najrān
W. Najran
Sabyā
Abū 'Arīsh
Jīzān
Sa'dah
Al Qaṭn
Tarīm
Ra's Fartak
Sayhūt
Ūishn
Ash Shiḥr
Riyan
Al Mukallā
Hadhramawt
REPUBLIC OF YEMEN

Es Sahrâ en Nûbīya
Jazā'ir Farasān
Nak'fa
Nora
Dehalak Deset

Ed Damer
Athara
Merowe
Shendi
Kassala
Keren
Mits'iwa
Sebderat
Barentu
Asmera
Ak'ordat
Ādī Ugrī
Ādī K'eyah
Teseney
Az Zuhrah
Az Zaydīyah
Amrān
San'a ▲3760
Hariḍ
Bayhān al Qasāb
Al Bayḍā
Lawdar
Al Mukallā
Habbān

Khartoum North
El Khartum (Khartoum)
El Kamlin
Wad Rawa
El Geteina
Rufa'a
Wad Medani
El Hawata
Gedaref
Al Hudaydah
Bayt al Faqīh
Zabīd
Dhamār
Ibb
Ad Dāli'
'Irqah
Shuqrah
Habbān

Āksum ▲3277
Adigrat
Adwa
Ābiy Adi
Mek'elē
Denakil
Ēd
Ta'izz
Aṭ Ṭurbah
Al Mukhā
Madīnat ash Sha'b
Little Aden
Ash Shaykh 'Uthmān
Adan (Aden)
Lahij
Ash Shaykh 'Uthmān

El Hawata
Sennar
El Host
Hag 'Abdulla
Singa
Gallabat
Metema
▲4620
Dabat
Gonder
Sek'ot'a
▲4247
Debre Tabor
Lalibela ▲4284
Weldiya
Desē
GULF OF ADEN
Caluula
Raas Caluula
Bereeda
Qandala ▲1510

Kosti
Renk
Ed Damazin
El Jebelein
Dynkur
Guba
▲3533
BIRHAN ▲4154
Debre Mark'os
Mot'a
Debre Birhan
Ankober
Ras el Bir
Dbock
Tadjoura
Djibouti
DJIBOUTI
Saylac
Boosaaso (Bender Qaasim)
CAL 1810 ▲
Hurdiyo
Xaafuun
Raas Xaafuun

Melut
Nasir
Nyerol
Waat
Dembī Dolo
Metu
Gorē
Jima
Nek'emtē
ĀDĪS ĀBEBA
▲3298 DENDI
A Nazrēt
Mi'eso
Dirē Dawa
Jeldēsa
▲3138
Ahmar Mountains
Hārer
Jijiga
Hargeysa
▲995 Sheekh
Cadaadley
Burco
SOMALIA
Berbera
Laas Dhuure
Karin
▲2410 Ceerigaabo
Maydh
Qardho
Bandarbeyla

Pibor Post
Nagīshot
▲3187
Didinga Hills
Kapoeta
KENYA
Lake Turkana Lake Rudolf
Moyale
Hosa'ina
Shewa Gimira
K'ECH'A TERARA ▲4190
Shashemenē
Yirga Alem
▲4307 BATU
Goba
Gīnīr
Negēlē
ETHIOPIA
Ogadēn
K'ebrī Dehar
K'orahē
Denan
Geladī
Goalkacyo
Jirriiban
Eyl
Raas Gabbac
Kails
Hobyo

 galla
3568 ▲
Gīdolē
Bako
Maji
Dolo Odo
Luug
Xuddur
Tayeeglow
Buulobarde
Mareeg
Ceelbuur
Xarardheere
Ceeldheer

East of Greenwich

Designed and produced by E.S.R.

A   B   C   D   E

WESTERN
SAHARA

C. Barbas

Nouadhibou
(Pt. Etienne)
Ras Nouadhibou
(C. Blanc)

Makteir

Tropic of Cancer

Erg   Chech

Tanezrouft

Ouarâne

Taoudenni

Atar   Chinguetti

MAURITANIA

El   Djouf

S   a

C. Timiris

Akjoujt

Araouane

Agueh

Nouakchott   Beila

Tidjikdja

Tichitt

Aouker

Moudjéria

Tamchaket

MALI

Boutilimit

Mederdra   Aleg

Bogué

Oualata

Tes

St.Louis   Dagana   Podor

Kaédi

Kiffa   Aïoun el Atrouss   Néma

Timbédra

L. Faguibine   Tombouctou
(Timbuktu)   Gourma-
Rharous   Bamba

Bourem

Louga
Kébémer   Diorbivol   Matam

Ras el Ma   Niger

Gao

Linguère

Sélibaby

Goundam

Tivaouane   Thiès
Cape Vert
Dakar   Diourbel

Bakel   Balé

Ayoro du Sahel

Niafounké

Mbour   Fatick
Foundiougne   Kaolack

SENEGAL

Nioro   Nara

Sokolo

Douentza

Mbout

Kayes

Bandiagara   Dori

Banjul
(Bathurst)   Georgetown   Maka
THE GAMBIA   Brikama   Basse-santa Su
Gambia   Tambacounda

Kaffrine

Bafoulabé

Niono

Djenné   Ségou   San

Mopti

Ouahigouya

Yako

Tougan

Déboug ou

BURKINA FASO

Diouloulou
Ziguinchor
C. Roxo   Kolda   Vélingara

Bissau   GUINEA
BISSAU   Bafatá
Fulacunda
Bolama   Koundara
Foulá Moise

Koukounkoun   Kédougou

Satadougou
Bafing
Makana

Kita

Kati
Bamako

Koutiala   Sikasso

Boromo   Koudougou   Ouagadougou

Léo   Po   Faga
N'Gourm

Arquipelago
dos Bijagos

Gaoual

Yambering

Siguiri

Bougouni

Hounde
Diébougou   Tumu

Tenkodogo

Bawku
Navrongo   Dapaong

Boké   Télimélé
Labé
Dalaba   Dinguiraye

Massigui

Bobo
Dioulasso

Bolgatanga

Dabola   Kouroussa

Banfora

Lawra

Pita   Dionso

GUINEA

Bougouni   Wa

Cap Verga   Boffa

Mamou   Timbo   Dabola

Kankan

Gaoua

Batié

Daboya

Tamale

Kindia

Faranah

Odienné   Boundiali   Kong

Bole

Damongo   Yendi

Conakry   Dubréka
Forécariah   Kabala

Kissidougou   Boundiali   Korhogo

Bouna

Kintampo   Kete

Kambia   SIERRA
Port Loko   LEONE   Makeni
Freetown   Magburaka

Sefadu   Guékédou   Macenta   1236▲   Beyla

Ferkessédougou   Katiola   Bondoukou

Dabakala

Salaga

Moyamba   Shenge
Kailahun   Pendembu
Segbwema   Kenema

Touba   Ségbéla

Bouaké

IVORY   COAST   GHANA

Yauri Bay   Shgrbro   Bo
Sherbro Island   Kongma   Pujehun

Wologisi
Mts.   Nzérékoré   Lola
R52   Bankouma
MTS. NIMBA   Man

Séguéla

Katiola

Bouaké   Sunyani   Mampong
Kumasi

Bouaflé   Daloa   Bouaflé

Yamoussoukro   Dimbokro
Sinfra   Toumodi

Aya-Yemahino
Bekwai   Akosombo
Dam

Robertsport   Gbarnga   Zuénoula   Bagnoa   Agboville

Ho

LIBERIA   Guiglo   Sassandra

Tototo

Monrovia   Zwedru   Soubré

Anyama
Bingerville
ABIDJAN

Nsuta   Koforidua   Akuse
Tarkwa   Cape Coast

Buchanan   Timbo

Grand
Lahou

Enchi
Oda   Dunkwa   Saltpond
Winneba   Tema
Accra

Greenville (Sinoe)   Sassandra   San Pédro

Cape Three Points   Axim   Dixcove   Sekondi Takoradi

Greenville
(Sinoe)   Sasstown   Harper   Tabou
C. Palmas

A   T   L   A   N   T   I   C

O   C   E   A   N

B

Santo
Antão
Porto Novo
São Vincente   Mindelo

Sal

São Nicolau

CAPE
VERDE

Boa Vista

Equator

São
Tiago
Fogo   Maio

Brava   Praia

L

Miller Oblated Stereographic Projection

West of Greenwich

104

1:9,000,000

0   100   200   300   400   500   600 KILOMETRES

0   50   100   150   200   250   300   350   400 STATUTE MILES

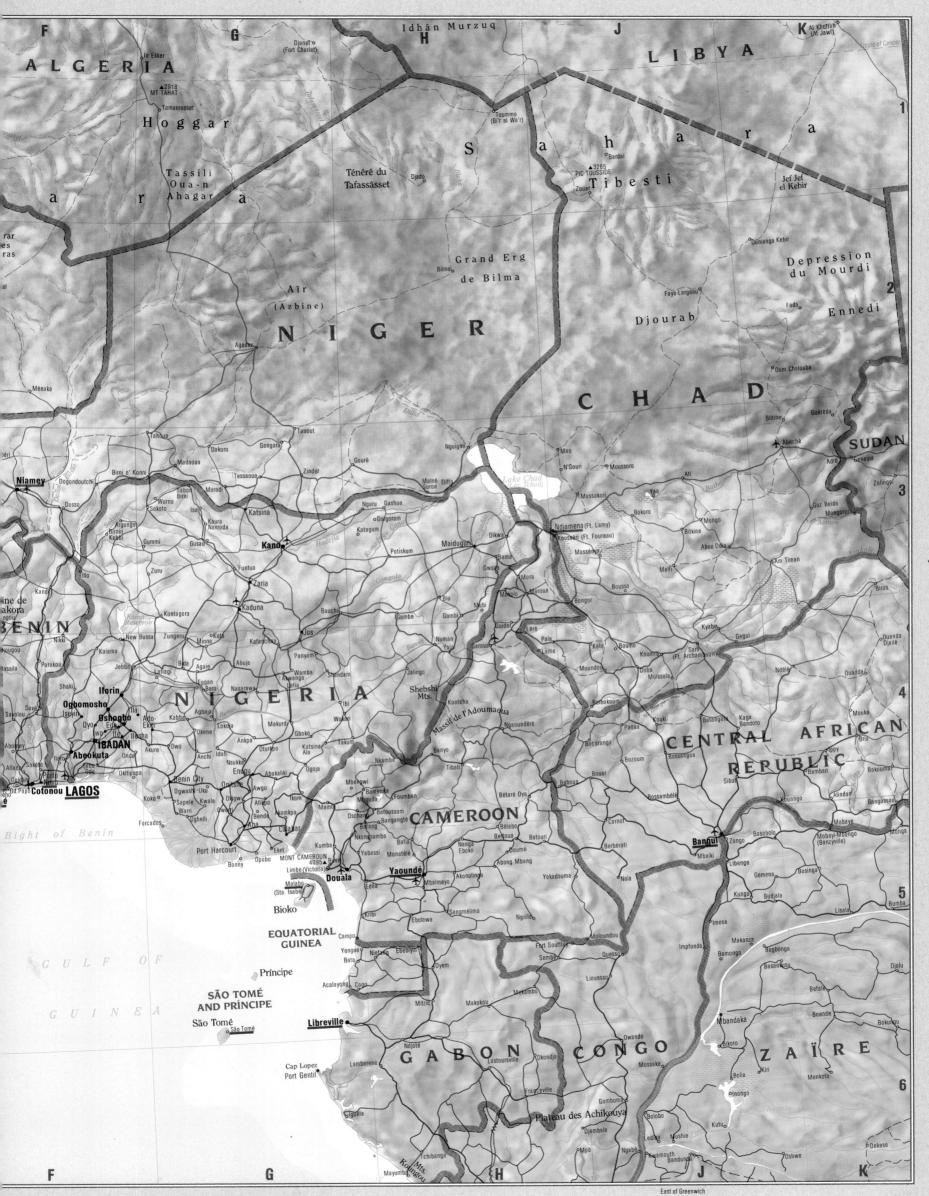

ALGERIA

In Ekker

▲2918
MT TAHAT
Tamanrasset

Hoggar

Tassili
Oua-n
Ahagar

Idhān Murzuq

Djanet
(Fort Charlet)

LIBYA

S a h a r a

Toummo
(Bi'r al Wa'r)

Bardai

▲3265
PIC TOUSSIDE
Zouar

Tibesti

Al Khufrah
(Al Jawf)

Tropic of Cancer

Ténéré du
Tafassâsset

Djado

Bilma

Grand Erg
de Bilma

Jef Jef
el Kebir

Depression
du Mourdi

Aïr
(Azbine)

N I G E R

Agadez

Ménaka

C H A D

Faya-Largeau

Djourab

Fada

Ennedi

Oum Chalouba

Ounianga Kebir

Biltine

Guéréda

SUDAN

Tahoua

Tanout

Nguigmi

Mao

N'Gouri

Moussoro

Abéché

Adré

Geneina

Niamey

Dogondoutchi

Birni n' Konni

Dakoro

Gangara

Madaoua

Tessaoua

Zinder

Gouré

Maïné
Soroa

Diffa

Lake Chad
(Lac Tchad)

Massakori

Yao

Bokoro

Mongo

Ati

Bathor

Goz Beida

Mongororo

Zalingei

Dosso

Sokoto

Wurno

Maradi

Sabon
Birni

Isa

Katsina

Kaura
Namoda

Nguru

Gashua

Gorgoram

Massénya

Ndjamena (Ft. Lamy)
Koussiri (Ft. Foureau)

N'Djamena

Bokoro

Abou Deïa

Am Timan

Birao

BENIN

Argungu
Birnin
Kebbi

Illo

Kandi

Gummi

Gusau

Zuru

Kano

Funtua

Katagum

Potiskum

Maiduguri

Dikwa

Bama

Gwoza

Mora

Maroua

Bousso

Melfi

Mfollowi

Ndélé

Ouanda
Djalé

Ouadda

Kaïne de
Makora

Kainji
Reservoir

Nikki

Ilugou

Kontagora

New Bussa

Zungeru

Minna

Kaduna

Zaria

Kafanchan

Bauchi

Gombe

Gombi

Biu

Mubi

Maroua

Bongor

Guider

Léré

Kélo

Boumo

Kyabé

Sarh
(Ft. Archambault)

Gagui

Parakou

Kaiama

Jebba

Bida

Agaie

Baro

Abuja

Panyam

Jos

Wamba
Kaja

Shendam

Jalingo

Shebshi
Mts.

Numan

Yola

Garoua

Pala

Lame

Moundou

Doba

Moïssala

Gagui

Koumra

Baïbokoum

Koukou

Batangafo

Kaga
Bandoro

Mouka

Bria

Shaki
Iseyin
Oyo

Iwo

Iforin

Ogbomosho

Oshogbo

Ila

Ife

Ilesha

Ado-
Ekiti

IBADAN

Abeokuta

N I G E R I A

Kabba

Okene

Lokoja

Idah

Ankpa

Oturkpo

Katsina
Ala

Takum

Wukari

Ibi

Kontcha

Massif de l'Adoumaoua

Ngaoundéré

Tibati

Banyo

Nkambé

CENTRAL AFRICAN

REPUBLIC

Bambari

Bakouma

Alindao

Bangassou

Sibut

Bozoum

Bocaranga

Paoua

Bossangoa

Kouango

 Bambari

Allada
Sakété
Ouidah
Porto-
Novo

Cotonou LAGOS

Benin City

Ogwashi-Uku

Onitsha

Asaba

Sapele

Kwale

Agbor

Okigwi

Enugu

Awgu

Afikpo

Abakaliki

Ikom

Mamfé

Mbengwi

Bamenda

Mbouda

Foumban

Bafoussam

Bangangté

Dschang

Bafia

CAMEROON

Bélabo

Bertoua

Bouar

Baboua

Baoro

Carnot

Berbérati

Bossembélé

Bangui

Zongo

Bosobolo

Mbaïki

Libenge

Gemena

Businga

Mobaye

Mobayi-Mbongo
(Banzyville)

Monga

Forcados

Bight of Benin

Port Harcourt

Bonny

Opobo

Eket

MONT CAMEROUN
4095▲

Kumba

Limbe (Victoria)

Buéa

Nkongsamba

Yabassi

Nanga
Eboko

Doumé

Abong Mbang

Batouri

Yokadouma

Nola

Gamena

Kungu

Budjala

Lisala

Bumba

GULF OF

Malabo
(Sta. Isabel)

Bioko

Douala

Edéa

Monatélé

Yaoundé

Mbalmayo

Akonolinga

Ngoïla

Moloundou

Impfondo

Imese

Makanza

Bomongo

Bogbonga

Basankusu

Djolu

EQUATORIAL
GUINEA

Campo

Yengue

Bata

Nietang

Ebolowa

Ebebiyin

Oyem

Sangmélima

Fort Soufflay

Sembé

Quesso

Liouesso

Befale

Boende

Bokungu

GUINEA

Príncipe

SÃO TOMÉ
AND PRÍNCIPE

São Tomé

São Tomé

Acalayong

Cogo

Mitzic

Makokou

Mekambo

Owando

Mbandaka

Bikoro

Inongo

Libreville

Cap Lopez
Port Gentil

Lambaréné

Ndjolé

Lastoursville

Okondja

GABON

Franceville

CONGO

Mossaka

Gamboma

Bolobo

Kutu

Mushie

ZAÏRE

Bolia

Kiri

Monkoto

Oshwe

Dekese

Iguela

Tchibanga

Mayumba

Mts.
Koumgou

Plateau des Achikouya

Mpe

Ngabé

Djambala

Léding

Kwamouth
Bandundu

East of Greenwich

Miller Oblated Stereographic Projection

1:9,000,000

© COLOUR LIBRARY BOOKS

SUDAN

Meshra'er Req · Fangak · Abwong · Nyerol · Nasir · F · 3298 DENOI · G · A. Nazrēt · H · Degeh Bur · J · Domo
Ayod · Waat · Metu · Gorē · Jima · Hosa'ina · K'ECH'A TERARA 4190 · Ginit · Geladi · Gaalkacyo

ETHIOPIA

Rumbek · Shambe · Lau · Yirol · Duk Fadiat · Duk Fawiil · Pibor Post · Shewa Gimira · 4170 · Shashemenē · Goba · 4307 BATU · Denan · K'orahē · Ogadēn
Tali Post · Tombe · Bor · Hongli Canal · Maji · Bako · Gidolē · 3568 · Yirga 'Alem · Negelē · Genalē Wenz · K'ebri Dehar · Hobyo

Mongalla · Kapoeta · Didinga Hills · Nagishat · Lokichokio · Moyale · Dolo Odo · Luuq · El K'oran · Beledweyne · Ceelbuur · Xarardheere

SOMALIA

Yambio · Maridi · Juba · Lalyo · Kajo Kaji · Nimule · 3187 · Lake Turkana (Lake Rudolf) · Moyale · Xuddur · Tayeeglow · Buulobarde · Cadale · Mareeq
Faradje · Yei · Kajo Kaji · Kitgum · Kakamari · Lodwar · Marsabit · Diinsoor · Baardheere · Bayhabo · Mahaddayweyne · Jawhar · Warshiikh

UGANDA

Dungu · Watsa · Arua · Rhino Camp · 2448 · Bunaba · Lira · MT. KULAL 2285 · Wanlaweyn · Afgooye · Muqdisho (Mogadishu)
Mungbere · Mambasa · Monts Bleus · Atura · Soroti · 3325 · MONT NYIRU 2742 · Wajir · Buurhakaba · Marka
Beni 5110 STANLEY · Ft. Portal · Masindi · Hoima · MONT ELGON 4321 · 3581 · 2637 BOKOL · Matthews Peak 2375 · Bilesha Plain · Baraawe

KENYA

Lubero · Kasese · Mubende · Bukloto · Namasagali · Mbale · Cherangany Hills · Eldoret · Mado Gashi
Masisi · Rutshuru · Kabale · Kampala · Entebbe · Jinja · Tororo · Kitale · Kakamega · Nyahururu · Nanyuki · Isiolo · Afmadow
Gome 4510 · Ruhengeri · Masaka · Kisumu · Kericho · Nakuru 3999 · Nyeri · 5200 KIRINYAGA · Embu · Garissa · Goob Weyn · Kismaayo

RWANDA

Bukavu · Nyanza · Kigali · Sese Is. · Kisii · Sotik · Murang'a (Ft. Hall) · Meru · Kitui · Witu · Lamu
Mwenga · Butare · Ngozi · Biharamulo · Lake Victoria · NAIROBI · Ngong · Machakos · Yatta Plateau · Kipini
Uvira · Bujumbura · Gitega · Bukoba · Musoma · Mwanza · Magadi · Kibwezi · Chyulu Range · Malindi

BURUNDI

Fizi · Bubanza · Hutana · Kibondo · Geita · Serengeti Plain · 3648 · KILIMANJARO 5895 · Voi · Kilifi
Kanambare · Bururi · Kahama · Shinyanga · Ngorongoro Crater · 4565 Moshi · Takaungu
2575 · Kigoma · Ujiji · Nzega · 3417 · Arusha · Pare Mts. · Mombasa · Vanga · Pemba I.

TANZANIA

Kalemie (Albertville) · Uvinza · Tabora · Singida · Kondoa · Masai Steppe · Lushoto · Usambara Mts. · Tanga
Nyunzu · Kaliua · Manyoni · Dodoma · Handeni · Pangani · Zanzibar I.
Moba (Baudouinville) · Mpanda · Kitunda · Morogoro · Sadani · Zanzibar

Lake Tanganyika · Sumbawanga · Kasanga · Chunya · Kilosa · Uluguru Mountains · Bagamoyo · DAR ES SALAAM
Kipili · Mbala · Kawimbe · 2828 · Makambako · 2454 · Mahenge · Mohoro · Mafia I.
Pweto · Ikomba · Mbeya · Tukuyu · Kipengere Range · Njombe · Lombe

INDIAN OCEAN

Kasanga · Kawambwa · Luwingu · Kasama · Chinsali · Chilumba · Songea · Tunduru · Kilwa Masoko
Mansa (Fort Rosebery) · Mpika · Mzuzu · Cobue · Mecula · Lindi · Mikindani · Mtwara
Lake Bangweulu · Bangweulu Swamps · Lundazi · Nkhotakota · Lichinga · Mataca · Masasi · 945 · Makondi Kitangari Plateau · C. Delgado

ZAMBIA · **MALAWI**

Chipata (Ft. Jameson) · Mchinji (Ft. Manning) · Lilongwe · Dowa · Marrupa · Montepuez · Ancuabe · Pemba
Petauke · Kasungu · Salima · Chipoka · Mataca · Balama · Mecufi · Moroni · Grande Comore
Furancungo · Ulongue · Nsanje · Mangochi · Cuamba · Namapa · Lurio · Moheli · Anjouan

COMOROS

Zumbo · Fingoe · Zomba · Maua · Memba · Dzaoudzi · Mayotte (France)

MOZAMBIQUE

Cabora Bassa Dam · Tete · Moatize · Blantyre · Limbe · NAMULI 2419 · Gurué · Napata · Nametil · Nacala-a-Velha
Kariba · Mhangura · Bindura · CHIPERONE 2054 · Chiromo · Alto Molócue · Lugela · Gile · Angoche · Moçambique

ZIMBABWE

Nsanje (Port Herald) · Chemba · Mutarara · Namacurra · Quelimane · Mocuba · Moma

HARARE (Salisbury) · Chitungwiza · Marondera · Morrumbala · Caia · Morua Velha · Pebane · Besalampy · Mahabe

MADAGASCAR

Juan de Nova (France) · Toraka Vestale · C. St. André · Mahajanga · Marovoay · Soalala
Analalava · Antsohihy · Mahabe · Tsaratanana

East of Greenwich

107

Designed and produced by E.S.R.

Miller Oblated Stereographic Projection

1:9,000,000

| 0 | 100 | 200 | 300 | 400 | 500 | 600 KILOMETRES |

| 0 | 50 | 100 | 150 | 200 | 250 | 300 | 350 | 400 STATUTE MILES |

© COLOUR LIBRARY BOOKS

TANZANIA

Songea · Tunduru · Masasi · Kitangari · 945 · Makondi Plateau · Lindi · Mikindani · Mtwara · C. Delgado · Palma

Mueda · Mocimboa da Praia

Mataca · Mecula · Marrupa · Montepuez · Ibo · Quissanga · Pemba · Mecufi

Lichinga · Belama · Namapa · L'urio · Memba · Maaia · Nacala-a-Velha

Mangochi · Cuamba · Malema · Iapala · Moçambique

Namarroi · Alto Moloue · Namapanda · Mogincual · Angoche

Gurué · Errego Lugela · Gilé · Moma · Pebane

Chinde

Quelimane · Mocuba

M O Z A M B I Q U E

COMOROS
Moroni · Grande Comore
Moheli · Anjouan
Dzaoudzi · Mayotte (France)

Juan de Nova (France)

Bassas da India (France)

I. de l'Europa (France)

MADAGASCAR

Tanjon'i Bobaomby

Antseranana (Diégo-Suarez)
Nosy Mitsio
Nosy Bé · Hell-Ville · Ambilobe · Vohimarina (Vohémar)
Massif du Tsaratanana · 2876 · Sambava
Analalava · Antsohihy · Bealanana · Andapa · Antalaha
Mahajanga · Port-Bergé · Maroantsetra · C. Masoala
C. St. André · Soalala · Marovoay · Mananara
Toraka Vestale · Besalampy · Ambato-Boeny · Miarinarivo · Nosy Boraha (Sainte-Marie)
Stampiky · Maevatanana · Tsaratanana · Ambodifototra
Mahabe · Vavatenina · Fenoarivo Atsinanana
Maintirano · Morafenobe · A'tomainty · Toamasina (Tamatave)
Antsalova · Tsiroanomandidy · Ankazobe · Anjozorobe · A'tondrazaka · Andevoranto
Bekopaka · Miarinarivo · Muramanga
Belo-Tsiribihina · Arivonimamo · **Antananarivo (Tananarive)** · Anosibe an'Ala
Soavinandriana · Ambatolampy · Vatomandry
Morondava · Mahabo · Betafo · Antsirabe · Fandriana · Marolambo
A'tofinandrahana · Ambositra · Nosy-Varika
Manja · Tsitondroina · Fianarantsoa · Vohilava
Morombe · Béroroha · Ifanadiana · Mananjary
Ankiliabo · Ambalavao · Ikongo · Manakara
Ankazoabo · Ihosy · Andringitra · Vohipeno
Fitsitika · Farafangana
Toliara (Tuléar) · Betroka · Vangaindrano
Soalara · Mt. de l'Ivakoany · Midongy Atsimo
Betioky · Bekily · 1956 · Beampingaratra
Itampolo · Ampanihy · Taolañaro (Fort Dauphin)
Ambovombe
C. Sainte Marie · Faux Cap

Plateau du Bemaraha
Massif du Makay

MALAŴI
Chilumba · Mzuzu · Lundazi · Kasungu · Lilongwe · Dowa · Salima · Chipoka · Balaka · Zomba · **Blantyre** · Limbe · NAMULI · 2419 · Chiromo · 2054 · CHIPERONE
Ntcheu · Chipata (Ft. Jameson) · Mchinji (Ft. Manning)

Livingstone Mts.
Chilwa

Cobue · Furancungo · Ulongué · Tete · Moatize · Cabora Bassa Dam · Chimuara
Mutoko · Macossa · Gorongoza · Chemba · Caia · Mopeia Velha
Nova Vanduzi · Muanza · Dombe · Buzi · **Beira** · Nova Sofala
Chipinge · Chimanimani · Machanga · Nova Mambone
Espungabera · Algueirão · Jofane · Inhassôro · I. do Bazaruto
Chibuto · Chicualacuala · Madade · Vilanculos · I. Benguérua · P. S. Sebastião
Massangena · Homoine · Massinga
Mabalane · Panda · Inhambane
Massingir · Chókwè · Inharrime
Magude · Xai-Xai
Manhiça
Maputo · Baía de Maputo · C. de Santa Maria · Bela Vista
Makatini Flats · Ubombo
Lake St. Lucia · Cape Saint Lucia · Empangeni

Lebombo Mountains

I N D I A N   O C E A N

MAURITIUS
Port Louis · Beau Basin · Curepipe · Mahébourg
Réunion (France) · St. Denis · St. Benoit · St. Pierre
Mascarene Islands

Bonne Projection

1:19,000,000

East of Greenwich

| 0 | 200 | 400 | 600 | 800 KILOMETRES |

| 0 | 100 | 200 | 300 | 400 | 500 STATUTE MILES |

© COLOUR LIBRARY BOOKS

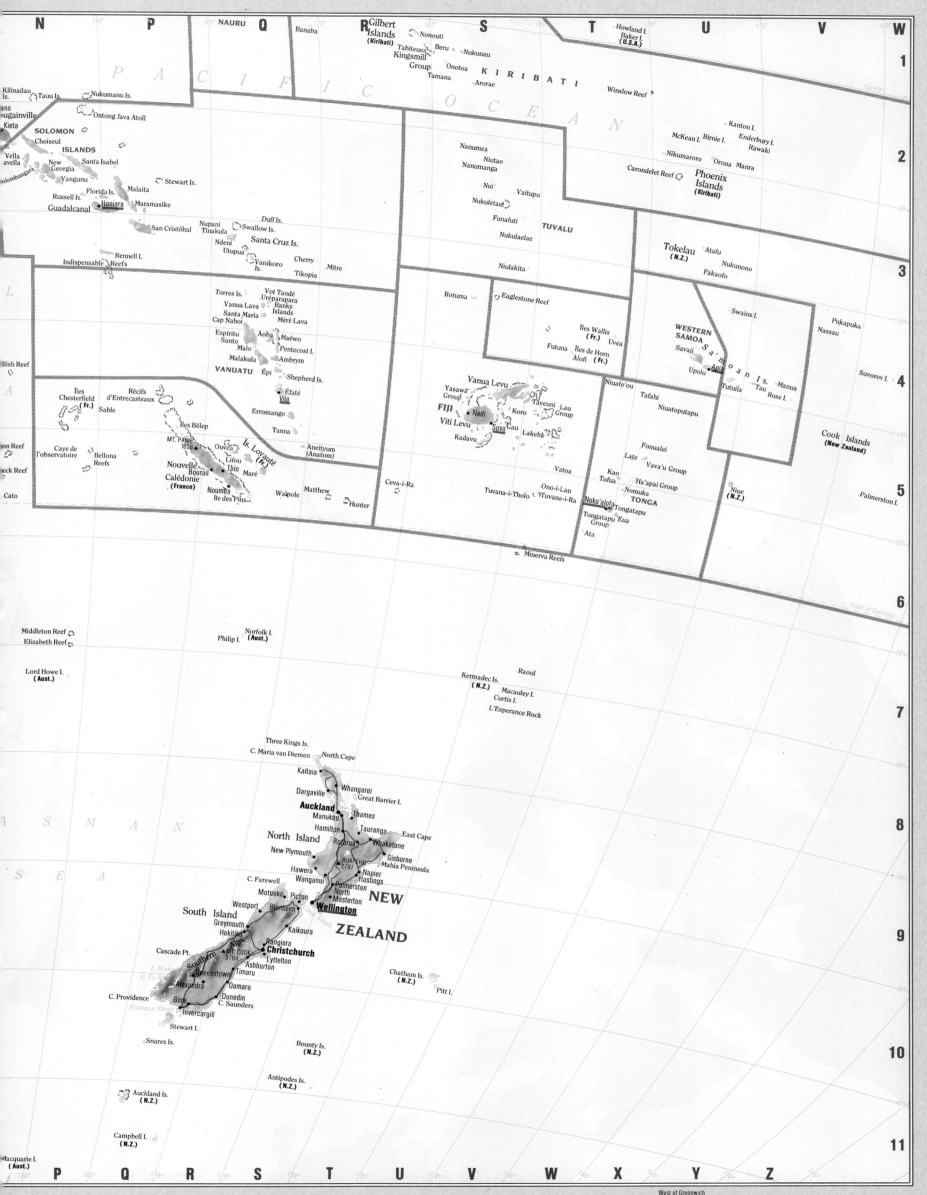

AUSTRALIA

INDIAN

OCEAN

TIMOR SEA

Ashmore Reef

Seringapatum Reef

Scott Reef

Beegle Reef

C. Bougainville

C. Londonderry

Joseph Bonaparte Gulf

Melville I.

C. Van Diemen

Bathurst I.

Darwin

Batchelor

Burrundie

Pine Creek

Edith F.

Willeroo

Birrindu

MT. HANN
854

Wyndham

Kununurra

Auvergne

Coolibah

Wave Hill

King Leopold Ranges

MT. ORD
936

Kimberley Plateau

MT. LUSH
786

Turkey Creek

Dampier Land

C. Lévêque

Derby

Broome

Yeeda River

Ellendale

Fitzroy Crossing

Halls Creek

Antrim Plateau

Rowley Shoals

Mermaid Reef

Clerke Reef

Imperieuse Reef

Christmas Creek

Margaret River

McClintock Range

NOR

Eighty Mile Beach

Anna Plains

Wallal Downs

Canning Basin

Tanami

Larrey Pt.

Port Hedland

Goldsworthy

Great Sandy Desert

Lake White

MT. SINGLETON
844

MT. ZIEL
1511

TER

Dampier Archipelago

Dampier

Karratha

Marble Bar

Lake Waukarlycarly

Percival Lakes

Lake Tobin

Lake Wills

MT. DOREEN

Yuendumu

Barrow I.

Yarraloola

Mulga Downs

Chichester Range

Lake Dora

MT. LEISIER
1005

Macdonnell Ran

North West Cape

Onslow

Hammersley Range

MT. BROCKMAN
1114

MT. BRUCE
1228

Roy Hill

Lake Disappointment

Lake Neale

Lake Amadeus

Pt. Cloates

MT. NEWMAN
1228

Newman

WESTERN

Lake Hopkins

Petermann Ranges

AYERS ROCK
860

Winning Pool

Lyndon

Gibson Desert

MT. DEERING
1220

MT. MORRIS
1255

Lake McLeod

Gifford Creek

MT. AUGUSTUS
1106

MT. EGERTON
994

Milgun

MT METHWIN
908

Barrow Range

MT. BURT
663

MT. WOODR
1514

MT. ILLBILLE
917

Carnarvon

Jimba Jimba

Landor

MT. STEERE

MT. FRASER
802

Peak Hill

Robinson Ranges

Lake Carnegie

Tomkinson Ranges

Musgrave Ranges

Birksgate Ra.

Wooramel

Berringarra

AUSTRALIA

Dirk Hartog I.

Meeberrie

Meekatharra

Wiluna

Lake Way

MT. SHENTON
595

Great Victoria Desert

Edel Land

Billabalong

Cue

Lake Austin

Sandstone

Lake Rason

Lake Dey-Dey

Lake Maurice

Bluff Pt.

Ajana

Edah Wagga

Mt. Magnet

Laverton

Lake Carey

Houtman Rocks

Mullewa

Wurarga

Lake Barlee

Lake Rebecca

Nullarbor

Oldea

Geraldton

Dongara

Morawa

Paynes Find

Lake Moore

Lake Minigwal

Rawlinna

Loongana

Forrest

Cook

Arrino

Perenjori

Lake Yindarlgooda

Zanthus

Deakin

Nullarbor

Wubin

Bonnie Rock

Kalgoorlie

Karonie

Plain

Moopna

Head of Bight

Pt. Fow

Watheroo

Moora

Southern Cross

Kambalda

Lake Lefroy

Eyre

Madura

Fowl

Bay

Gingin

Northam

Merredin

Lake Cowan

Great Australian Bight

Perth

Cunderdin

Quairading

Norseman

Fremantle

Rockingham

MT. COOKE
582

Beverley

Kondinin

The Johnston Lakes

Balladonia

Mandurah

Pingelly

Bremer Ra.

Lake Dundas

Narrogin

Lake King

Harvey

Williams

Wagin

Newdegate

Lake Grace

Ravensthorpe

Esperance

C. Pasley

Bunbury

Collie

Lake Magenta

Ongerup

Archipelago of the Recherche

C. Naturaliste

Busselton

Bridgetown

Kojonup

Katanning

Stirling Ra.

BLUFF KNOLL
1110

Pt. Henry

Esperance Bay

Augusta

Jardee

Northcliffe

Nornalup

Albany

C. Leeuwin

Pt. D'Entrecasteaux

Pt. Nuyts

King George Sound

Miller Oblated Stereographic Projection

1:10,500,000

© COLOUR LIBRARY BOOKS

0 100 200 300 400 500 600 700 800 KILOMETRES

0 100 200 300 400 500 STATUTE MILES

Map of eastern Australia and surrounding regions.

PAPUA NEW GUINEA

Louisiade Archipelago

Misima I.

Tagula

CORAL SEA

Osprey Reef

Bougainville Reef

Holmes Reefs

Mellish Reef

Lihou Reefs

Îles Chesterfield

Marion Reefs

Kenn Reef

Saumarez Reef

Wreck Reef

Tropic of Capricorn

Middleton Reef

Elizabeth Reef

Lord Howe I.

TASMAN SEA

East of Greenwich

QUEENSLAND

NEW SOUTH WALES

SOUTH AUSTRALIA

VICTORIA

TASMANIA

AUSTRALIAN CAPITAL TERRITORY

Gulf of Carpentaria

Simpson Desert

Great Artesian Basin

Great Dividing Range

BRISBANE

SYDNEY

Canberra

MELBOURNE

Adelaide

Newcastle

Wollongong

Gold Coast

Fraser Island

Moreton I.

Bribie I.

North Stradbroke I.

Kangaroo I.

King I.

Flinders I.

Furneaux Group

Bass Strait

Hobart

C. York

Cape York

Peninsula

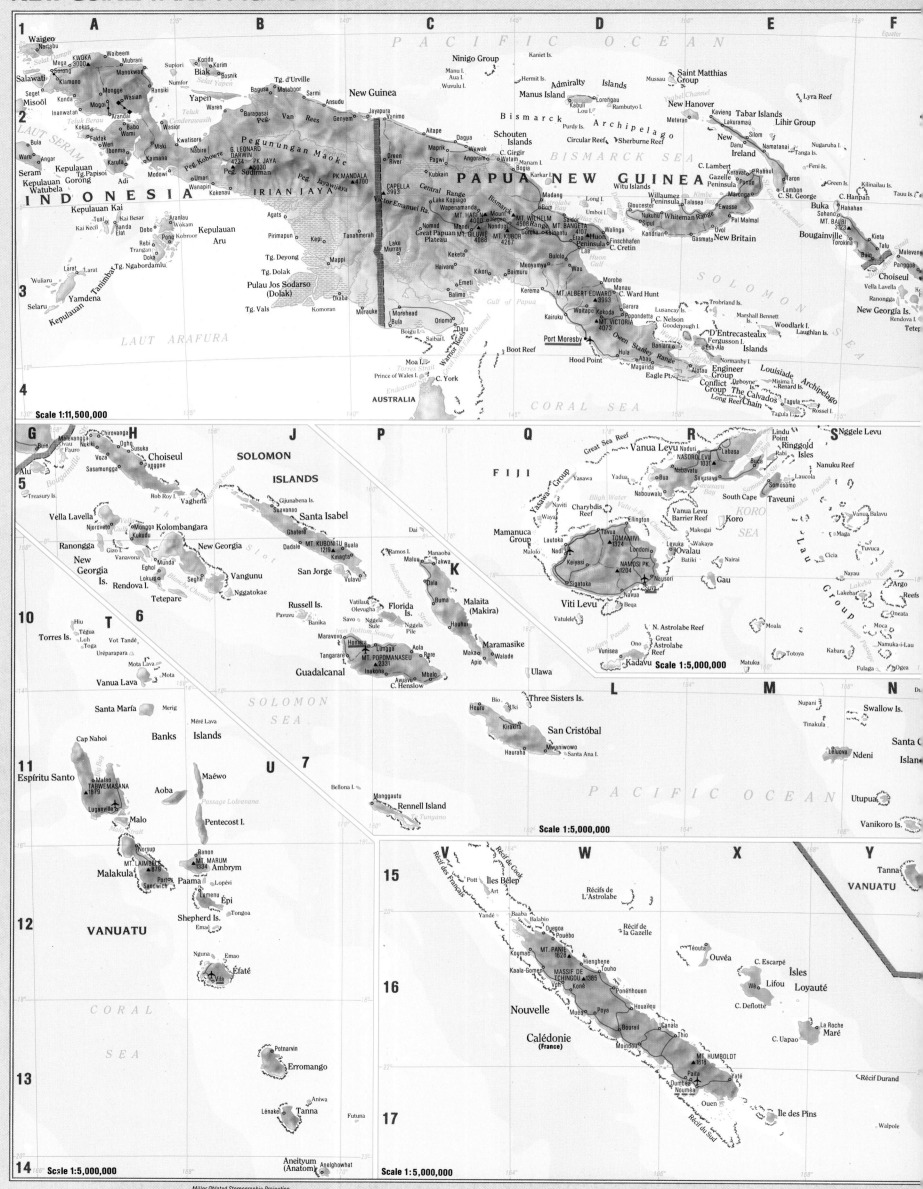

NEW

ZEALAND

North Island

South Island

Southern Alps

TASMAN SEA

PACIFIC OCEAN

Stewart Island

Chatham Islands

1:4,500,000

Designed and produced by E.S.R.

East of Greenwich

Lambert Azimuthal Equal Area Projection

1:20,000,000

| 0 | 100 | 200 | 300 | 400 | 500 | 600 | 700 | 800 | 900 | 1000 KILOMETRES |

| 0 | 100 | 200 | 300 | 400 | 500 | 600 STATUTE MILES |

© COLOUR LIBRARY BOOKS

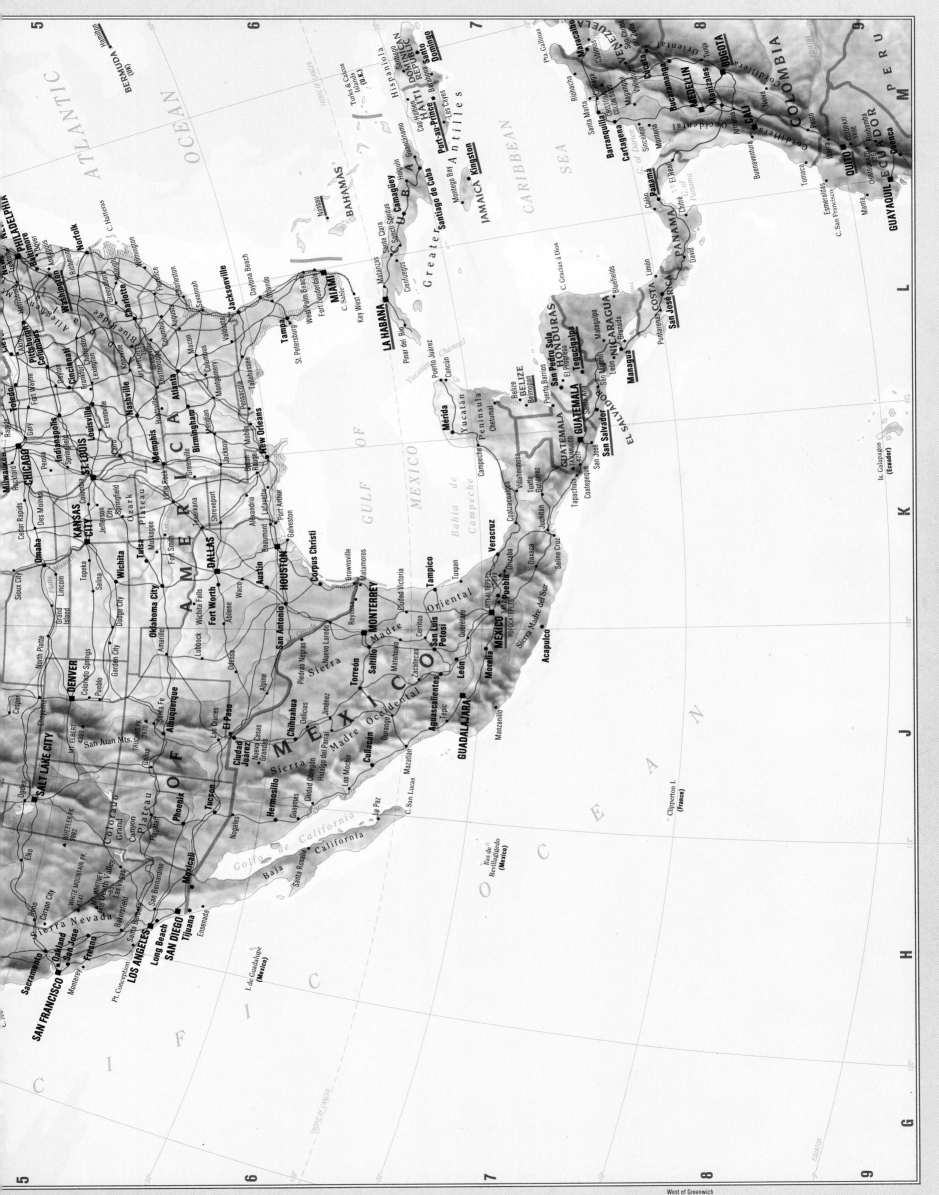

ALASKA

A B C D E F G H J K L

RUSSIA
Chukotskiy
Poluostrov
O. Arakamchechen

BEAUFORT
SEA

Chukchi
Sea

Bering
Strait

Seward
Peninsula

Norton
Sound

BERING
SEA

De Long Mts.
Baird Mountains

Brooks

Endicott Range Mts.

ALASKA
(U.S.A.)

Kuskokwim Mountains

Alaska Range

Kilbuck Mts.

Prudhoe Bay

INUVIK

Davidson Mts.
Richardson Mts.

Ogilvie Mts.

Mackenzie

YUKON

Dawson Range

Aleutian Range

Kenai Peninsula
Kenai Mts.

Chugach Mts.

St. Elias Mountains

Pelly Mountains

Cassiar Mts.

Mackenzie Mountains

Kodiak I.

GULF OF ALASKA

PACIFIC OCEAN

Alexander
Archipelago

Queen
Charlotte
Islands

ROCK

BRITI
COLUM

Vancouver
Island

Aa Ab Ac Ad Ae Af Ag
E F G H

St. Paul I.
Pribilof Is.
St. George I.

BERING SEA

Aleutian Islands

Near Islands
Rat Islands
Andreanof Islands
Islands of the Four Mts.
Fox Islands

Alaska Peninsula

Shumagin
Is.

8

9

1:12,500,000

Bipolar Oblique Conic Conformal Projection

118

1:9,000,000

0 100 200 300 400 500 600 KILOMETRES
0 50 100 150 200 250 300 350 400 STATUTE MILES

© COLOUR LIBRARY BOOKS

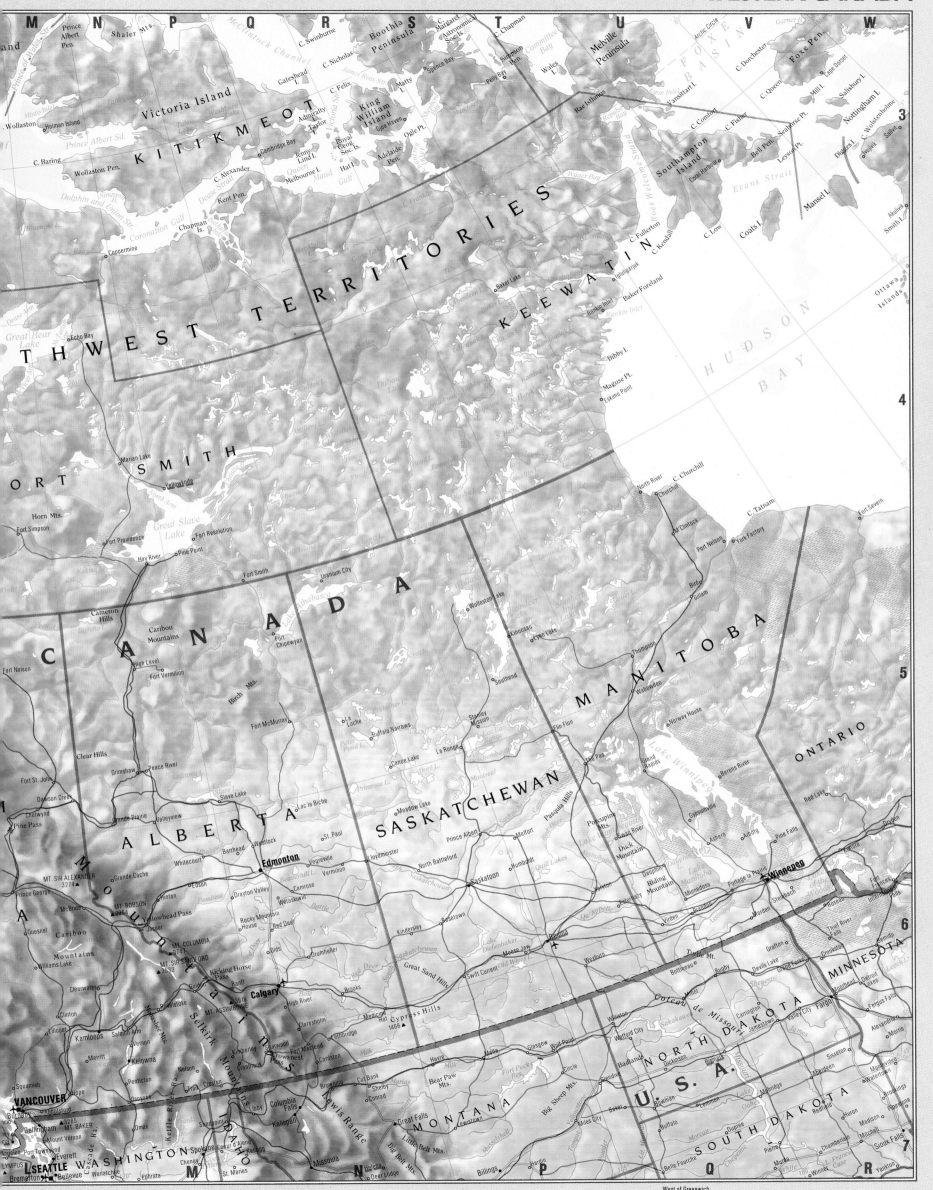

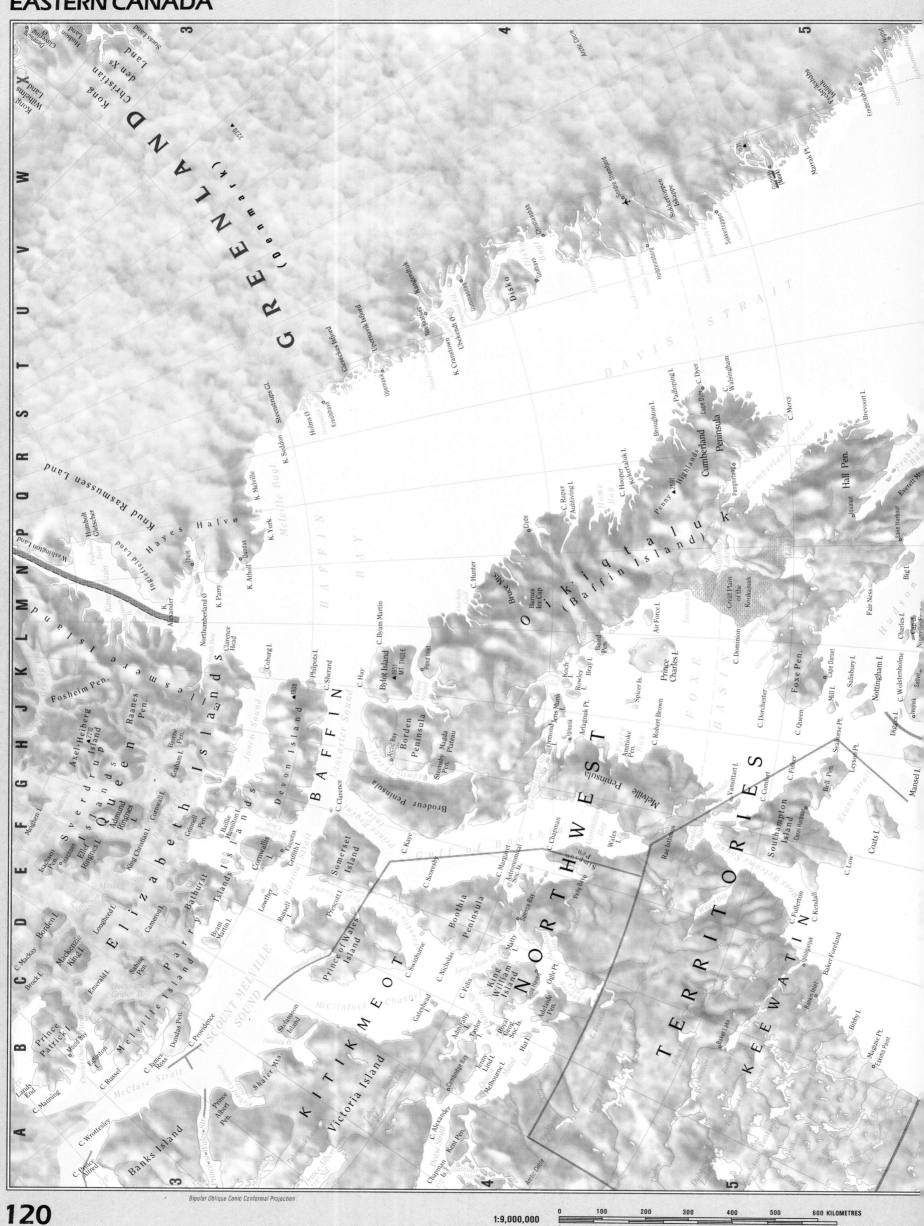

Bipolar Oblique Conic Conformal Projection

© COLOUR LIBRARY BOOKS

1:9,000,000

| 0 | 100 | 200 | 300 | 400 | 500 | 600 KILOMETRES |
| 0 | 50 | 100 | 150 | 200 | 250 | 300 | 350 | 400 STATUTE MILES |

West of Greenwich

Designed and produced by E.S.R.

Bipolar Oblique Conic Conformal Projection

1:5,000,000

© COLOUR LIBRARY BOOKS

0   50   100   150   200   250   300   350   400 KILOMETRES
0   50   100   150   200   250 STATUTE MILES

West of Greenwich

Designed and produced by E.S.R.

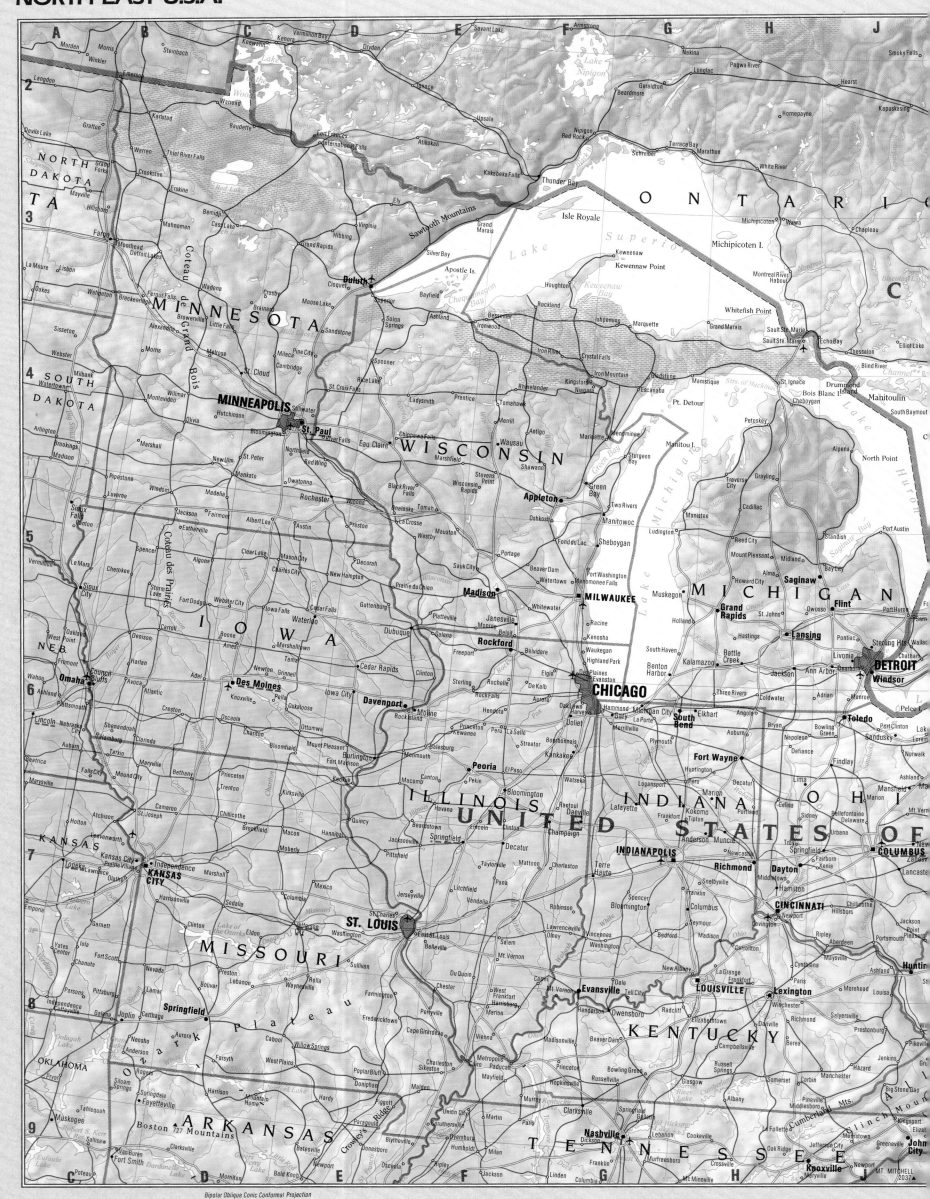

Bipolar Oblique Conic Conformal Projection

1:5,000,000

© COLOUR LIBRARY BOOKS

125

1:5,000,000

© COLOUR LIBRARY BOOKS

| 0 | 50 | 100 | 150 | 200 | 250 | 300 | 350 | 400 KILOMETRES |

| 0 | 50 | 100 | 150 | 200 | 250 STATUTE MILES |

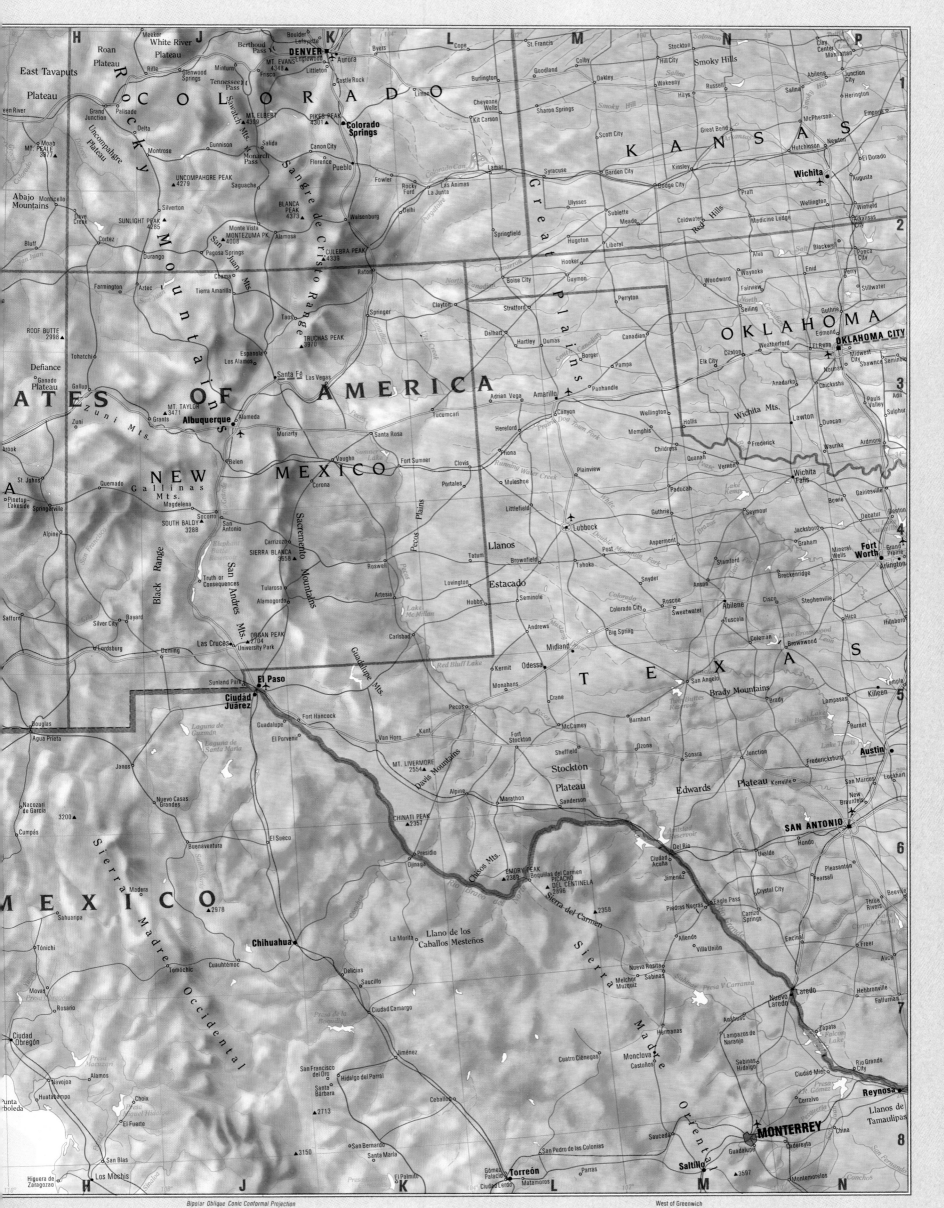

Bipolar Oblique Conic Conformal Projection

West of Greenwich

Designed and produced by E.S.R.

SOUTH-EAST U.S.A.

Bipolar Oblique Conic Conformal Projection

1:5,000,000

© COLOUR LIBRARY BOOKS

129

MEXICO

Bipolar Oblique Conic Conformal Projection

1:6,500,000

0 50 100 150 200 250 300 350 400 KILOMETRES
0   50   100   150   200 250 STATUTE MILES

© COLOUR LIBRARY BOOKS

This is a map of the Gulf of Mexico region, showing parts of the southern United States (Texas, Louisiana, Mississippi, Alabama, Georgia, Florida), Mexico, Guatemala, Belize, and Honduras.

United States cities and features:
Jacksboro, Denton, Garland, Irving, Fort Worth, Arlington, DALLAS, Terrell, Greenville, Mount Pleasant, Atlanta, L. O'the Pines, Longview, Marshall, Minden, Monroe, Canton, Forest, Meridian, Demopolis, Selma, Cuthbert, Albany, Anson, Breckenridge, Stephenville, Hillsboro, Corsicana, Longview, Jackson, MISSISSIPPI, Vicksburg, ALABAMA, GEORGIA, Chattahoochee, Abilene, Cisco, Hico, Waco, Jacksonville, Henderson, Nacogdoches, Natchez, St. Joseph, Brookhaven, Laurel, Opp, Dothan, Bainbridge, Sweetwater, S.A., Coleman, Brownwood, Killeen, Temple, Buffalo, Lufkin, Alexandria, Ville Platte, Bude, Hattiesburg, Southern Pine Hills, Poplarville, Lucedale, FLORIDA, De Funiak Springs, Valparaiso, Crawfordville, Tallahassee, Brady Mts., Brady, Lampasas, Cameron, Bryan, Livingston, Sam Rayburn Res., Jasper, De Ridder, Hammond, Picayune, Biloxi, Pascagoula, Mobile, Pensacola, Fort Walton Beach, Panama City, Port St. Joe, C. San Blas, St. George I., Apalachicola, Junction, Kerrville, AUSTIN, San Marcos, Columbus, Brenham, Hempstead, Huntsville, Cleveland, Silsbee, Lake Charles, New Iberia, Lafayette, Baton Rouge, La Place, NEW ORLEANS, Chandeleur Is., Edwards Plateau, Sonora, San Angelo, X, Uvalde, Hondo, SAN ANTONIO, Seguin, Port Arthur, Beaumont, HOUSTON, Pasadena, White L., Marsh I., Houma, West Bay, Mississippi Delta, Rio, Eagle Pass, Carrizo Springs, Pearsall, Three Rivers, Beeville, Victoria, Galveston, Freeport, Encinal, Freer, Alice, Sinton, Matagorda I., Corpus Christi, Baffin Bay, Falfurrias, Kingsville, Raymondville, San Benito

Mexico cities and features:
Nuevo Laredo, Laredo, Zapata, Falcon L., Rio Grande City, McAllen, Reynosa, Rio Bravo, Matamoros, MONTERREY, Guadalupe, China, Llanos de Tamaulipas, La Madre, Saltillo, Lampazos de Naranjo, Sabinas Hidalgo, Mier, Cerralvo, Gómez, Presa M.R., Montemorelos, San Fernando, Linares, Jiménez, Padilla, Matehuala, Ciudad Victoria, Presa de las Adjuntas, Aldama, Manuel, Arrecife Alacrán, Tula, Ciudad Mante, Ciudad Madero, Tampico, San Luis Potosí, Ciudad del Maíz, Ciudad Valles, Pánuco, Laguna de Tamiahua, Cabo Rojo, San Felipe, Jalpan, Tamazunchale, Tantoyuca, Tuxpan, San Miguel de Allende, Zimapán, Querétaro, San Juan del Río, Huichapan, Actopan, Pachuca, Tulancingo, Poza Rica, Papantla, Nautla, Celaya, Valle de Santiago, Acámbaro, Salvatierra, Salamanca, Teziutlán, Zempoala, Pta. Delgada, Morelia, Zinapécuaro, Atlacomulco, Acambay, Tejeda, Zumpango, Jalapa, COFRE DE PEROTE 4282, Apizaco 3506, Perote, Veracruz, CIUDAD DE MÉXICO, Texcoco, Calpulalpan, Xochimilco, Puebla, VOL. CITLALTÉPETL 5699, Toluca, NEVADO DE TOLUCA 4577, VOL. POPOCATÉPETL 5452, Amecameca, Cuautla, Atlixco, Córdoba, Orizaba, Pta. Roca Partida, Tuzantla, Cuernavaca, Azúcar de Matamoros, Tehuacán, Tierra Blanca, Alvarado, San Andrés Tuxtla, Huetamo, Temascaltepec, Taxco, Iguala, Chiautla, Acatlán, Cosamaloapan, Pta. Roca Partida, Álvaro Obregón, Frontera, Ciudad del Carmen, Tlapehuala, Huajuapan de León, 2896, Cuicatlán, Uxpepec, Yogope, Yaveo, Coatzacoalcos, Minatitlán, Cárdenas, Villahermosa, Jalapa, Macuspana, Tenosique, Tuxtepec, Llanos de Tabasco y Campeche, Tichapa, Chilpancingo, Tlapa, Tlaxiaco, ZEMPOALTÉPEC 3395, El Tule, Oaxaca, Paso Real, Raudales, Tuxtla Gutiérrez, San Cristóbal de las Casas, Comitán, Acapulco, Cruz Grande, Pinotepa Nacional, Miahuatlán, Ejutla, Pochutla, Tehuantepec, Juchitán, Ciudad Ixtepec, Sierra Madre del Sur, Pta. Maldonado, Sierra Cimaltepec, Golfo de Tehuantepec, Puerto Escondido, Istmo de Tehuantepec, Pijijiapan, 3703, Atoyac, San Marcos, 2949, Arriaga, Chahuites, Tonalá, Venustiano Carranza, Tonalá, Tapachula, Progreso, Mérida, Umán, Celestún, Ticul, Peto, Valladolid, Cozumel, I. de Cozumel, Campeche, Hopelchén, Polyuc, Felipe Carrillo Puerto, Pta. Herrero, Champotón, Yucatán, Pta. Morros, Francisco Escárcega, Xpujil, Chetumal, Banco Chinchorro, Dzilam de Bravo, Tizimin, Pta. Yalkubul, Río Lagartos, Cabo Catoche, Pto. Juárez, Bá. de la Ascensión

Guatemala / Belize / Honduras:
GUATEMALA, Tikal, Flores, La Libertad, Cobán, San Luis, Pta. Gorda, Punta Sal, BELIZE, Belize, Belmopan, Orange Walk, La Unión, San Antonio Nuevo, Hicks Cays, Turneffe Is., Lighthouse Reef, Glover Reef, Ambergris Cay, Stann Creek, Golfo de Honduras, Puerto Barrios, ALTO CUCHUMATANES 3993, Huehuetenango, Salamá, Sa. de las Minas, 3140, Sta. Rosa de Copán, Sta. Bárbara, Quezaltenango, Antigua Guatemala, VOLCÁN DE TAJUMULCO 4210, VOLCÁN DE AGUA 3752, Mazatenango, Retalhuleu, Escuintla, Metapán, Chalchuapa, Sta. Ana, Guazacapán, Cuilapa, HONDURAS, Comayagua, Colomoncagua, San Pedro Sula, El Progreso, Yoro, Morales, Zacapa, Puerto Cortés, Teta, San Cristóbal de las Casas, Montañas Mayas, GULF OF MEXICO, BAHÍA DE CAMPECHE

Madre Oriental (Sierra Madre Oriental), Sierra Madre, Sierra Madre del Sur, MÉXICO

West of Greenwich

Designed and produced by E.S.R.

131

CENTRAL AMERICA AND THE CARIBBEAN

Bipolar Oblique Conic Conformal Projection

1:7,000,000

© COLOUR LIBRARY BOOKS

Map grid references (top and bottom): K L M N P Q R S T
Row numbers (right side): 1 2 3 4 5 6 7 8 9 10 11

ATLANTIC

OCEAN

Tropic of Cancer

BAHAMAS

Arthur's Town
Cat I.
Hawknest Pt.
Conception I.
San Salvador (Watling I.)
Rum Cay
Long I.
Clarence Town
Samana Cray
South Pt.
Crooked I.
Snug Corner
Abraham's Bay
Mayaguana I.
Acklins I.
Ragged Cays
Kew
Caicos Is. (U.K.)
Hogsty Reef
Little Inagua I.
Turks I. (U.K.)
Great Inagua
Salt Cay
Matthew Town
Cabo Lucrecia
Moa
Baracoa
Cabo Maisí
Guantánamo
Santiago de Cuba
Île de la Tortue
Monte Cristi
C. Isabela
Port-de-Paix
Cap-Haïtien
Puerto Plata
Ba. de Escocesa
Gonaïves
Hinche
Santiago
San Francisco de Macoris
C. Samaná
La Vega
Ba. de Samaná
Sabana de la Mar
St Marc
PICO DUARTE 3175
Cordillera
Central
SANTO DOMINGO
C. Engaño
Golfe de la Gonâve
Île de la Gonâve
HAITI
San Juan
Higüey
La Romana
I. Saona
C. Dame Marie
Jérémie
PORT-AU-PRINCE
Barahona
San Pedros de Macoris
Dame Marie
Massif de la Hotte 2347
LA SELLE 2680
Baní
DOMINICAN REPUBLIC
Navassa I. (U.S.A.)
Les Cayes
Jacmel
Pedernales
Isla Beata
Cabo Beata
Pte.-à-Gravois
Île-à-Vache

Puerto Rico Trench

Aguadilla
Arecibo
Bayamon
SAN JUAN
Mona Passage
Mayagüez
CERRO DE PUNTA 1336
Caguas
I. Mona
C. Rojo
Ponce
Vieques
Puerto Rico (U.S.A.)
Frederiksted
St. Croix (U.S.A.)

Virgin Islands
St. Thomas (U.S.A.)
Charlotte Amalie
Road Town
Tortola (U.K.)
St. John (U.S.A.)
Anegada (U.K.)
Virgin Gorda (U.K.)
Anguilla (U.K.)
Saint Martin (Fr.)
Sint Maarten (Neth.)
Saba (Neth.)
St Eustatius (Neth.)
Basseterre
ST. KITTS-NEVIS
Montserrat (U.K.)
Plymouth

Leeward Islands

Barbuda
Antigua
St. John's
ANTIGUA AND BARBUDA

Guadeloupe (France)
La Désirade
Pointe-à-Pitre
Basse Terre
Marie Galante (France)
Iles des Saintes
I. de Aves (Bird I.) (Ven.)
DOMINICA
Marigot
Roseau

Lesser
Antilles

Martinique (France)
Fort-de-France

Windward Islands

ST. LUCIA
Castries

Kingstown
ST. VINCENT
The Grenadines
GRENADA
St. George's
Carriacou
BARBADOS
Bridgetown

CARIBBEAN SEA

Antilles

Lesser Antilles

Punta Gallinas
Pto. Estrella
Oranjestad
Aruba (Neth.)
Curaçao (Neth.)
Bonaire (Neth.)
Is. Las Aves (Ven.)
Kralendijk
Willemstad
I. Blanquilla (Ven.)
Tobago
Scarborough
Carrizal
Península de Guajira
Castilletes
Amuay
Penin. de Paraguaná
Punto Fijo
Pto. Cumarebo
Is. Los Roques (Ven.)
I. Orchila (Ven.)
Los Testigos (Ven.)
Isla de Margarita (Ven.)
Los Testigos (Ven.)
TRINIDAD AND TOBAGO
Barranquilla
Santa Marta
Cabo de la Aguja
Ríohacha
Maicao
San Rafael
Coro
Mirimire
I. La Tortuga (Ven.)
La Asunción
Porlamar
Port of Spain
Toco
Arima
Trinidad
Soledad
Sabanalarga
Valledupar
Maracaibo
Capatárida
Churuguara
Maiquetía
CARACAS
Guarenas
Cabo Codera
Cumaná
Carúpano
Río Caribe
Penín. de Paria
Güiria
Pto. Fortín
Galeota Pt.
Cartagena
Robles La Paz
Sta. Rita
San Felipe
Valencia
Maracay
Los Teques
Guanoco
Pedernales
Turbaco
Machiques
Cabimas
Carora
Barquisimeto
Yaritagua
San Juan de los Morros
Villa de Cura
Pto. Cabello
Pto. La Cruz
Barcelona 2660
Maturín
Arjona
Calamar
Lagunillas
Ciudad Ojeda
Tinaco
San Carlos
Mata Negra
San Mateo
Anaco
Carmen
Sincelejo
Since
Ciénaga
La Ceiba
El Tocuyo
Acarigua
Las Mercedes
Aragua de Barcelona
El Tigre
Tucupita
Mompós
Barranca
Trujillo
Valera
Guanare
Valle de la Pascua
Zaraza
Pariaguán
Barrancas
Planeta Rica
Magangué
San Carlos del Zulia
El Vigía
Nueva Florida
Calabozo
San José de Amacuro
PICO CRISTÓBAL COLON 5775
El Banco
Bobures
Mérida
Barinas
Boca del Pao
Pto. Ordaz
Ciudad Guayana
El Callao
Ocaña
PICO BOLÍVAR 5007
San Silvestre
Cabruta
Ciudad Bolívar
Guasipati
Caucasia
San Cristóbal
Mantecal
San Fernando de Apure
Mapire
Ciudad Piar
Zaragoza
ALTO DE TAMAR 2350
Cúcuta
EL VIEJO 4100
San Antonio de Caparo
Cerro Mato 1863
Maripa
CERRO BOLÍVAR 802
Las Trincheras
Yarumal
Barrancabermeja
Bucaramanga
Piedecuesta
Cúcuta
Pamplona
Guasdualito
La Urbana
La Paragua
San Pedro de las Bocas
El Dorado
COLOMBIA
Rubio
Banadía
Arauca
Santa María
Elorza
VENEZUELA
GUYANA
Port Kaituma
Kartuni

West of Greenwich

Designed and produced by E.S.R.

133

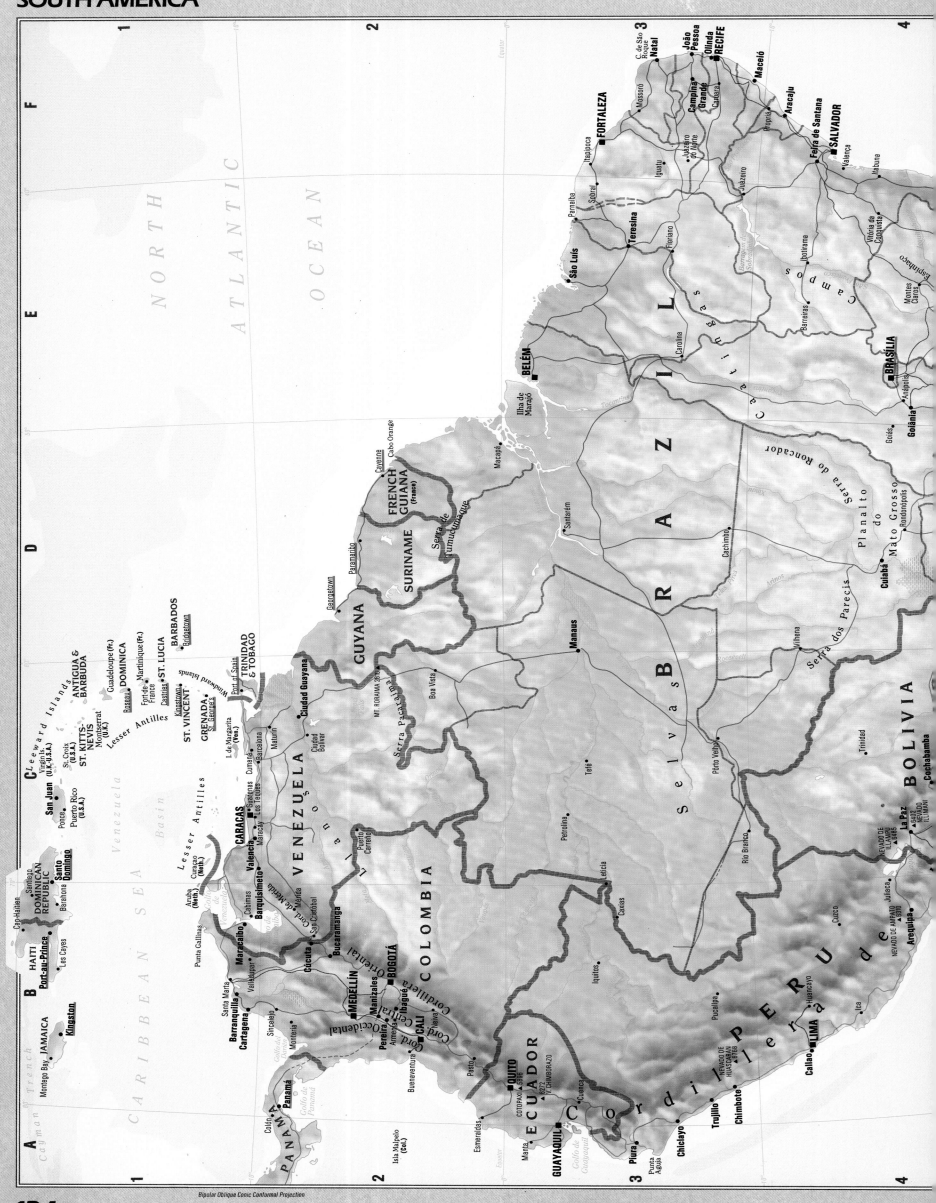

Bipolar Oblique Conic Conformal Projection

1:16,000,000

© COLOUR LIBRARY BOOKS

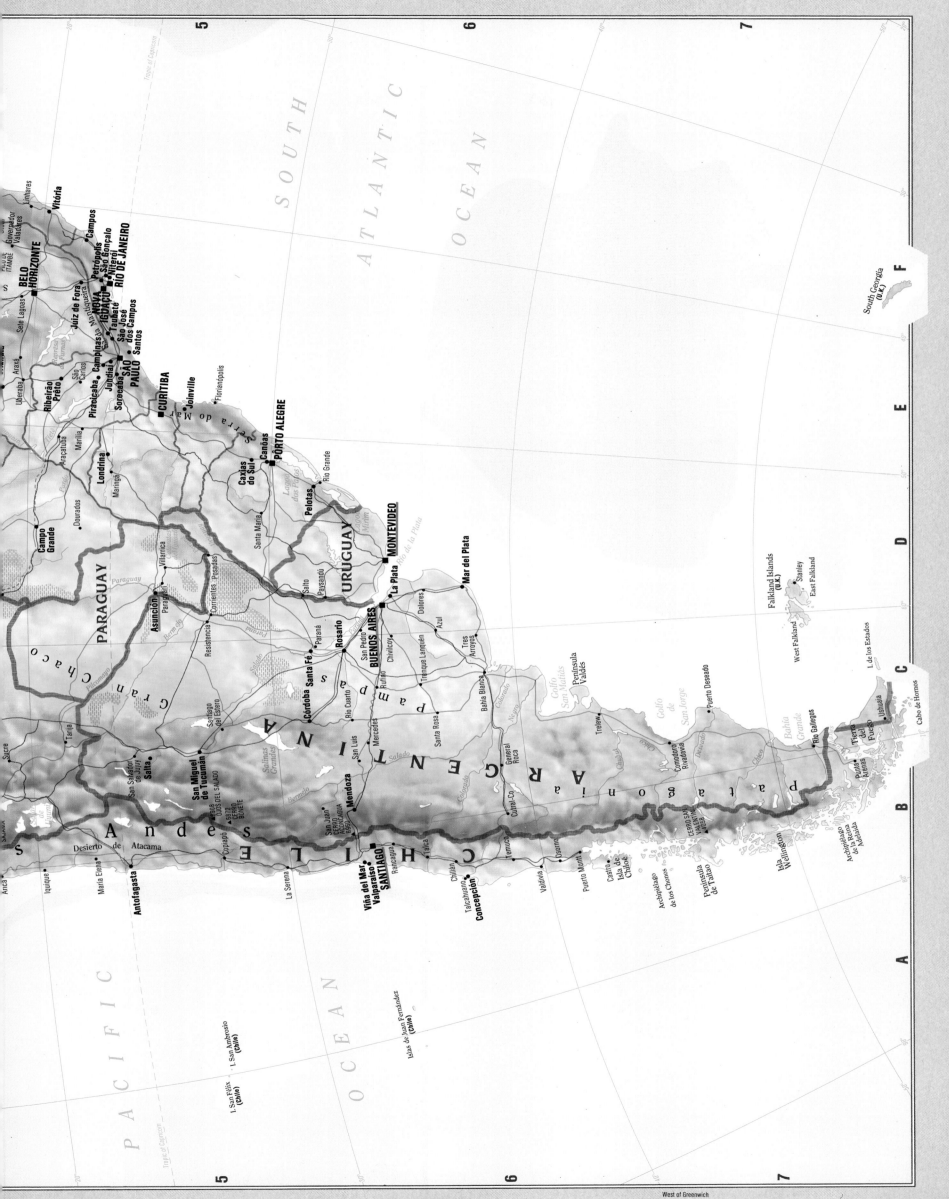

SOUTH

ATLANTIC

OCEAN

PACIFIC

OCEAN

South Georgia
(U.K.)

Falkland Islands
(U.K.)
Stanley
West Falkland   East Falkland

I. de los Estados

Cabo de Hornos

Ushuaia
Tierra del Fuego
Punta Arenas
Río Gallegos
Bahía Grande
Archipiélago
de la Reina
Adelaida
CERRO SAN
VALENTÍN
3,058
Puerto Deseado
Golfo
de
San Jorge
Comodoro
Rivadavia
Península
de Taitao
Archipiélago
de los Chonos
Isla
Wellington
Península Valdés
Golfo San Matías
Trelew
P a t a g o n i a
Castro
Isla de Chiloé
Puerto Montt
Osorno
Valdivia
Temuco
Bahía Blanca
Concepción
Talcahuano
Chillán
Talca
Rancagua
SANTIAGO
Valparaíso
Viña del Mar
San Juan
CERRO
ACONCAGUA
6,960
Mendoza
General
Roca
Cutral-Có
Santa Rosa
Tres
Arroyos
Azul
Dolores
Mar del Plata
La Plata
BUENOS AIRES
Tranque Lauquén
Rufino
Mercedes
San Luis
Río Cuarto
Córdoba   Santa Fé
Rosario
Paraná
San Pedro
Chivilcoy
MONTEVIDEO
URUGUAY
Paysandú
Salto
Santa María
Río Grande
Pelotas
Canoas
PÔRTO ALEGRE
Caxias do Sul
Florianópolis
Joinville
CURITIBA
Londrina
Maringá
Posadas
Corrientes
Resistencia
Paraguarí
Asunción
PARAGUAY
Villarrica
Concepción
Dourados
Campo Grande
Araçatuba
Marília
Santiago
del Estero
San Miguel
de Tucumán
Salta
San Salvador
de Jujuy
Tarija
Sucre
Antofagasta
María Elena
La Serena
Copiapó
Iquique
Arica
Desierto de Atacama
A n d e s
S A L A D O
CERRO
OJOS DEL
6,872
Salinas
Grandes
Gran Chaco
Pampa
ARGENTINA
C H I L E

Islas de Juan Fernández
(Chile)

I. San Ambrosio
(Chile)

I. San Félix
(Chile)

BELO
HORIZONTE
Vitória
Linhares
Governador
Valadares
Araxá
Uberaba
Ribeirão
Prêto
São
Carlos
Piracicaba
Campinas
Jundiaí
Sorocaba
SÃO
PAULO
Taubaté
NOVA
IGUAÇÚ
Petrópolis
Campos
São Gonçalo
Niterói
RIO DE JANEIRO
São José
dos Campos
Santos
Sete Lagoas
Juiz de Fora
Tropic of Capricorn

SOUTH
ATLANTIC
OCEAN

West of Greenwich

Designed and produced by E.S.R.

135

Bipolar Oblique Conic Conformal Projection

1:11,000,000

© COLOUR LIBRARY BOOKS

North Atlantic Ocean

SURINAME

FRENCH
GUIANA
(France)

Paramaribo · Nieuw Amsterdam
Totness · Moengo · Albina · Iracoubo
Groningen · Saint · Sinnamary
Saint Laurent · Kourou
Matapica · Kaw · Cayenne · Roura
Affobakka · Grand Santi · Guisanbourg

Serra de Haan Geh · Oranje · Gebergte · Malavate · Bienveneu
Pontoetoe · Kapiting · Regina
Serra Tumucumaque · Serra Lombarda

Cabo Orange
Oiapoque · Cabo Caciporé
Punta Grande

AMAPÁ

Merirumã
Serra do Navio
Amapá
Ilha de Maracá
Ponta Grossa
Azuari
Macapá

Mouths of the Amazon

Ilha Grande do Gurupá
Ilha de Marajó
Chaves · Soure · Salinópolis
Almeirim · Gurupá · Ponta de Pedras · Curuça · Marapanim
Melgaço · Curralinho · Vigia · Capanema · Tijoca · Viseu
BELÉM · Abaetetuba · São José do Gurupi
Igarapé Miri · Mojú · Turiaçu · Ilhas de São João
Cametá · Mocajuba · Marassumé
Baião · Alcântara · Ilha de São Marcos

PARÁ

Oriximiná · Alenquer · Prainha
Faro · Óbidos · Monte Alegre
Juruti · Santarém · Belterra
Parintins · Tauari

Vila Nova · Itaituba · Carajari
Tucuruí · São Luís · Rosário · Tutóia · Araioses
Camocim · Acaraú
Cajapió · Viana · Itapecuru Mirim · Paranaíba
Chapadinha · Brejo · Luzilândia · Tianguá · Sobral · Itapipoca · Caucaia · FORTALEZA
Pimentel · Bacabal · Coroatá · Piracuruca · Ipu · Massapê · Maranguape · Cascavel
Coari · Miguel Alves · Pinpiri · Baturité · Punta da Maceió
Altamira · Areão · Jacundá · Pedreiras · Perçoré · Codó · Cáxias · Campo Maior · Tamboril · Quixadá
Serra do Caracas · Sobrado · Maraba · Presidente Dutra · Teresina · Crateús · Senador Pompeu · Russas · Areia Branca
Tucuperê · São João do Araguaia · Imperatriz · Barra do Corda · São Miguel do Tapuio · Arneiroz · Jaguaribe · Mossoró · Macau · Touros · Pta. do Calcanhar
MARANHÃO · Xambioa · Colinas · Pastos Bons · PIAUÍ · Várzea Grande · Campos Sales · Iguatu · Icó · RIO GRANDE · Natal · Cabo de São Roque
Paranaidji · Serra das Alpercatas · Floriano · Picos · Jaicós · Juázeiro do Norte · Cajazeiras · Patos · DO NORTE · Angicos · Ceará Mirim
São Félix · Serra das Araras · Loreto · Uruçuí · Flores · Simplício Mendes · Oricuri · CEARÁ · Chapada do Araripe · Pombal · Sta. Luzia · Nova Cruz
Conceição do Araguaia · TRANS AMAZONIAN HIGHWAY · Balsas · Eliseu Martins · São João do Piauí · Paulistana · PARAÍBA · Serra Talhada · João Pessoa
Araguaçema · Couto Magalhães · Pedro Afonso · Serra do Uruçuí · Bom Jesús · Serra do Piauí · Rajada · Parnamirim · AMAZONIAN · Campina Grande · Cabo Branco
Araguaína · Miracema do Norte · Lizardo · Gilbués · Bom Jesús da Lapa · Nova Remanso · São Raimundo Nonato · HIGHWAY · Cabrobó · Floresta · Limoeiro · Olinda
BRAZIL · Serra do Cachimbo · Cristalândia · Pôrto Nacional · Redenção · Juázeiro · Santa Maria da Boa Vista · Carpina · RECIFE · Jaboatão
Serra · Cachimbo · Ilha do Bananal · Formosa do Rio Prêto · Barra · Petrolina · Tabuleiro · PERNAMBUCO · Vitória de · Sta. Antão · Cabo
dos Apiacás · Planalto do · Serra da Tabatinga · Xique-Xique · Uauá · Canudos · Pão de Açúcar · Palmares · Garanhuns · União dos Palmares
Campo de Diauarum · Natividade · Peixe · Capixaba · Irecê · Morro do Chapéu · Senhor do Bonfim · Euclides da Cunha · Itabaiana · ALAGOAS · Maceió
Mato Grosso · Alvorada · Barreiras · Santana · Ipupiara · Mundo Novo · Queimadas · Tucano · Propriá · Penedo · São Miguel dos Campos
Pôrto dos Gauchos · Arraias · BAHIA · Angical · Ibotirama · Andaraí · Jacobina · Ribeiro do Pombal · Estância · SERGIPE · Pontal do Manguinha
DO GROSSO · San Miguel do Araguaia · Cavalcante · Bom Jesús da Lapa · Macaúbas · Palmeiras · Serrinha · Inhambupe · Itaporanga · Aracaju
de Pedra · Chavantina · Aruanã · São Domingos · Riacho de Santana · Caetité · Novo Acre · Alagoinhas · Santo Amaro
Nobres · Guia · GOIÁS · Ceres · Formosa · Niquelândia · Cocos · Manga · Brumado · Jequié · Valença · Feira de Santana · Cachoeira
Barra do Bugres · Alto Coité · 1678 · Sítio da Abadia · Carinhanha · Vitória da · Taperoá · Nazaré · SALVADOR · I. de Tinharé
Cuiabá · Garças · Iporá · Serra Bonita · Urandi · Condeúba · Conquista · Ubaitaba · I. Boipeba · Baía de Todos os Santos
Rondonópolis · Jaraguá · Itaberaí · DISTRITO · Januária · Monte Azul · Itabuna · Ponta do Mutá
Poconé · Guiratinga · Goiás · FEDERAL · BRASÍLIA · Pedra Azul · Itapetinga · Ilhéus · Cabo Tromba Grande
Anhumas · Iporã · Luziânia · Brasília · Rio Pardo de Minas · Salto da Divisa · Una · Ponta Santo Antônio
MATO GROSSO · Caiaponia · Anápolis · Barrocão · Pirapora · Jequitinhonha · Pôrto Seguro
Alto Araguaia · Goiânia · Leopoldo de Bulhões · Cristalina · Paracatu · Bocaiúva · Escondido
Pantanal do · Hidrolândia · Leopoldina · Montes Claros · Salto · Serra · Ponta da Baleia
Rio Negro · Rio Verde · Bela Vista · Serra do · Capelinha · Caravelas
DO SUL · Morrinhos · Piro do Rio · Paracatu · Diamantina · Teófilo Otôni · Caravelas
Pantanal do Taquari · Itumbiara · Coromandel · PICO DE ITAMBÉ · Campanário · ESPÍRITO SANTO
Taquari · Araguari · Patos de Minas · 2040 · Governador · São Mateus
da Esperança · Baús · MINAS · Guanhães · Valadares
Serra das Araras · Prata · Patrocínio · Carlos Chagas
Uberlândia · GERAIS · Corinto · Helvécia
Itumirim · Abaeté · Três Marias · Sabará

137

West of Greenwich

Designed and produced by E.S.R.

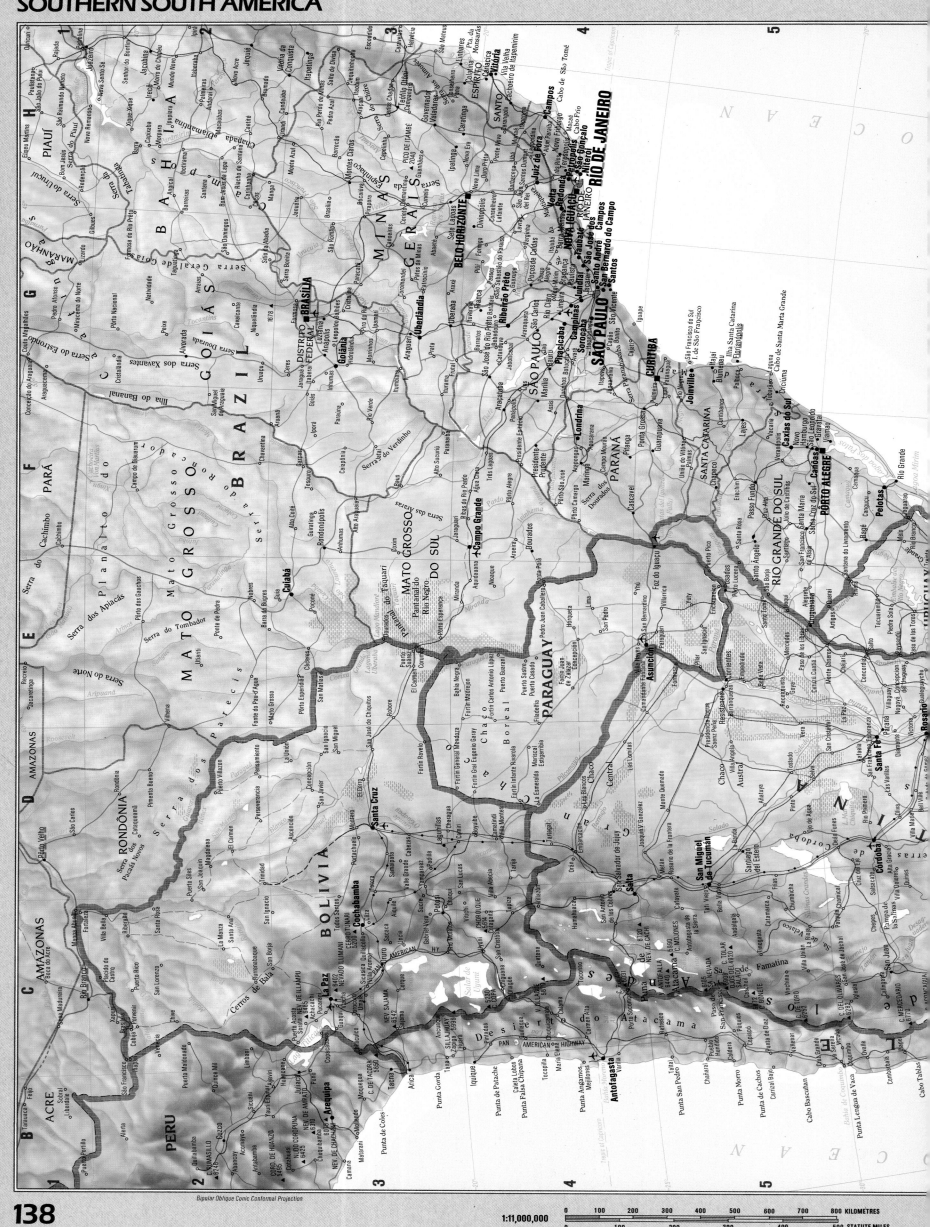

Bipolar Oblique Conic Conformal Projection

1:11,000,000

© COLOUR LIBRARY BOOKS

| 0 | 100 | 200 | 300 | 400 | 500 | 600 | 700 | 800 KILOMETRES |
| 0 | 100 | 200 | 300 | 400 | 500 STATUTE MILES |

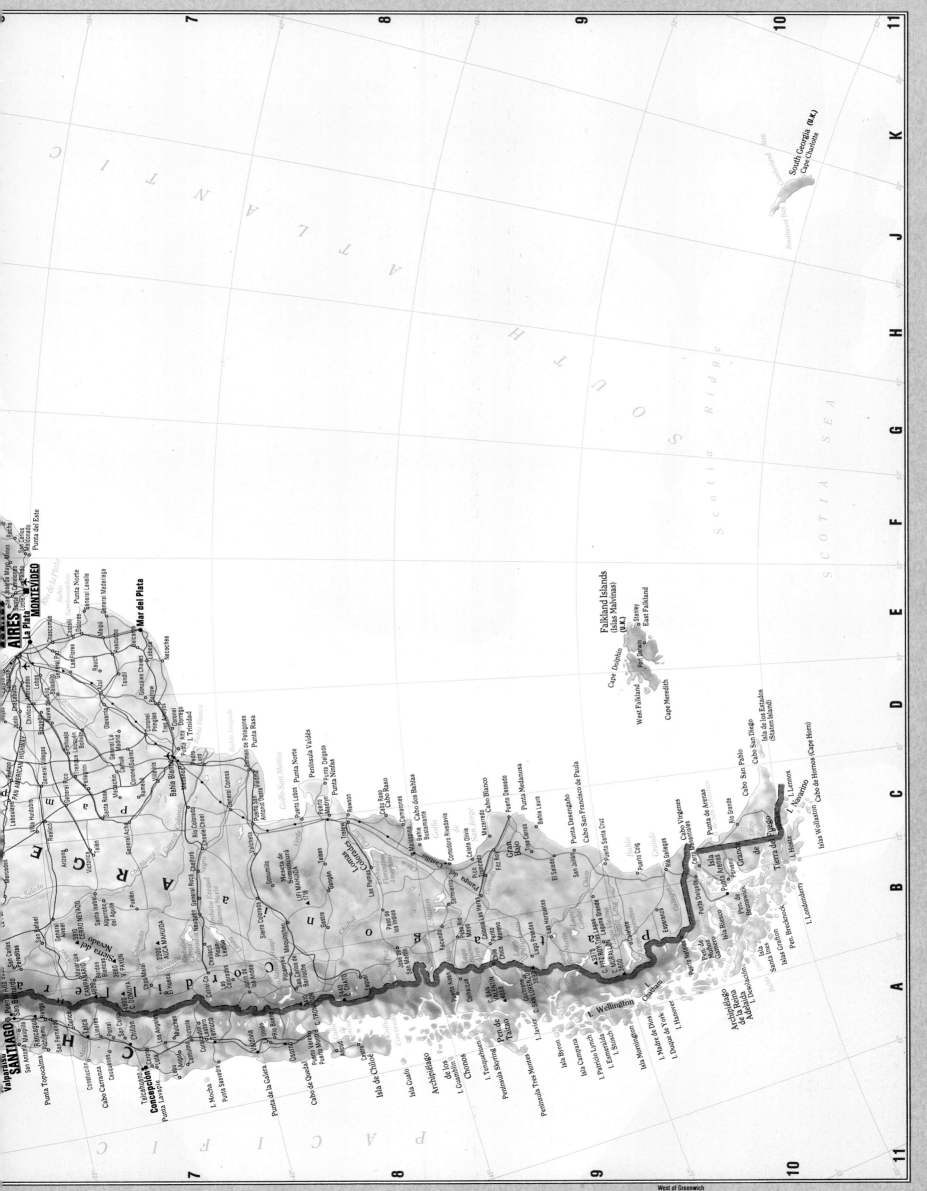

Designed and produced by E.S.R.

THE ARCTIC

Polar Stereographic Projection

Scale 1:30,000,000 (Approx.)

| 0 | 250 | 500 | 750 | 1000 | 1250 | 1500 KILOMETRES |

| 0 | 250 | 500 | 750 | 1000 STATUTE MILES |

© COLOUR LIBRARY BOOKS

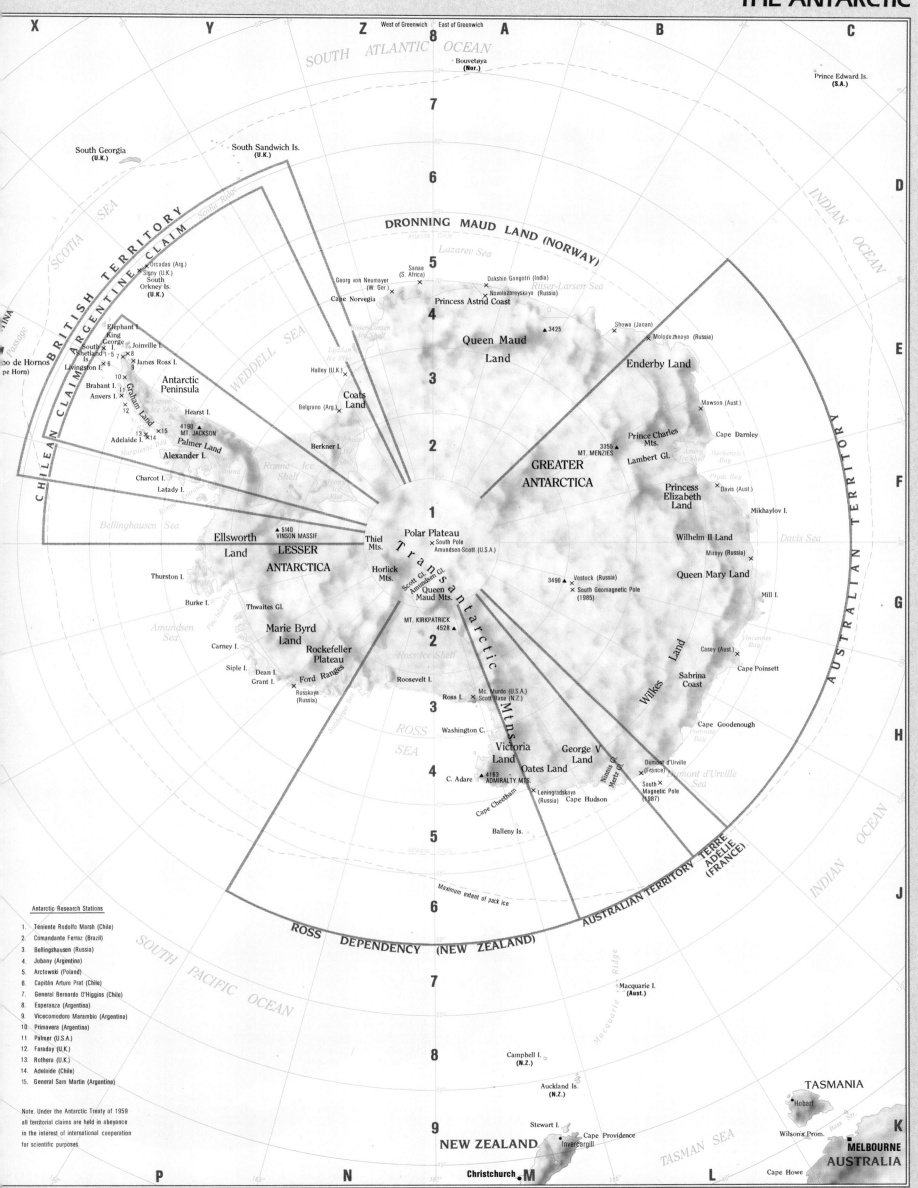

SOUTH ATLANTIC OCEAN

Bouvetøya (Nor.)

Prince Edward Is. (S.A.)

South Georgia (U.K.)

South Sandwich Is. (U.K.)

DRONNING MAUD LAND (NORWAY)

Lazarev Sea

Antarctic Circle

Georg von Neumayer (W. Ger.)
Sanae (S. Africa)
Dakshin Gangotri (India)
Novolazareyskaya (Russia)
Showa (Japan)
Molodezhnaya (Russia)

Cape Norvegia
Princess Astrid Coast

Orcadas (Arg.)
Signy (U.K.)
South Orkney Is. (U.K.)

Riiser-Larsen Sea

Queen Maud Land

▲ 3425

Enderby Land

Mawson (Aust.)

Elephant I.
King George I.
South Shetland Is. 1–5
Joinville I.
James Ross I.
Livingston I.
Brabant I.
Anvers I.

Weddell Sea

Halley (U.K.)

Coats Land

Belgrano (Arg.)

Cape Darnley

Prince Charles Mts.
3355 ▲ MT. MENZIES
Lambert Gl.

Antarctic Peninsula

Graham Land

Hearst I.

Berkner I.

Princess Elizabeth Land

Mikhaylov I.

Amery Ice Shelf

Prydz Bay

Davis (Aust.)

GREATER ANTARCTICA

4190 ▲ MT. JACKSON
Palmer Land

Adelaide I.

Larsen Ice Shelf

Ronne Ice Shelf

Wilhelm II Land

Davis Sea

Alexander I.

Charcot I.

Latady I.

Filchner Ice Shelf

Mirnyy (Russia)

Ellsworth Land

5140 ▲ VINSON MASSIF

Thiel Mts.

Polar Plateau
× South Pole
Amundsen-Scott (U.S.A.)

Queen Mary Land

LESSER ANTARCTICA

Horlick Mts.

3490 ▲ × Vostock (Russia)
× South Geomagnetic Pole (1985)

Thurston I.

Bellingshausen Sea

Burke I.

Transantarctic

Scott Gl.
Amundsen Gl.
Queen Maud Mts.

Thwaites Gl.

MT. KIRKPATRICK 4528 ▲

Marie Byrd Land

Carney I.

Rockefeller Plateau

Ross Ice Shelf

Amundsen Sea

Siple I.
Dean I.
Grant I.
Ford Ranges
Russkaya (Russia)

Roosevelt I.

Mtns.

Wilkes Land

Casey (Aust.)
Cape Poinsett

Sabrina Coast

Cape Goodenough

ROSS SEA

Mc. Murdo (U.S.A.)
Scott Base (N.Z.)
Ross I.

Washington C.

Victoria Land

George V Land

Nimis Gl.
Mertz Gl.

Dumont d'Urville (France)
Dumont d'Urville Sea

Oates Land

4163 ▲ ADMIRALTY MTS.
C. Adare

Leningradskaya (Russia)
Cape Hudson

South Magnetic Pole (1987)

Cape Cheetham

Balleny Is.

Maximum extent of pack ice

Antarctic Circle

TERRE ADÉLIE (FRANCE)

AUSTRALIAN TERRITORY

ROSS DEPENDENCY (NEW ZEALAND)

Macquarie I. (Aust.)

SOUTH PACIFIC OCEAN

Macquarie Ridge

Campbell I. (N.Z.)

Auckland Is. (N.Z.)

TASMANIA

Hobart

Stewart I.
Cape Providence

Wilson's Prom.
Bass Str.

NEW ZEALAND
Invercargill

MELBOURNE
AUSTRALIA

Christchurch M

TASMAN SEA

Cape Howe

INDIAN OCEAN

SCOTIA SEA

BRITISH TERRITORY
ARGENTINE CLAIM
CHILEAN CLAIMS

Cabo de Hornos (Cape Horn)
Drake Passage

ARGENTINA

Polar Stereographic Projection

Designed and produced by E.S.R.

Antarctic Research Stations

1. Teniente Rodolfo Marsh (Chile)
2. Comandante Ferraz (Brazil)
3. Bellingshausen (Russia)
4. Jubany (Argentina)
5. Arctowski (Poland)
6. Capitán Arturo Prat (Chile)
7. General Bernardo O'Higgins (Chile)
8. Esperanza (Argentina)
9. Vicecomodoro Marambio (Argentina)
10. Primavera (Argentina)
11. Palmer (U.S.A.)
12. Faraday (U.K.)
13. Rothera (U.K.)
14. Adelaide (Chile)
15. General Sam Martin (Argentina)

Note. Under the Antarctic Treaty of 1959 all territorial claims are held in abeyance in the interest of international cooperation for scientific purposes.

A   West of Greenwich   East of Greenwich   B   C   D   E   F

1

Svalbard
(Norway)

Zemlya Frantsa-Iosifa
(U.S.S.R.)

Severnaya Zemlya

Novosibirskiye Ostrov

GREENLAND
(Denmark)

Karskoye
More

Byrranga

More
Laptevykh

Kolmsk
Nizmen

Lyakhovkiye
Ostrova

2

Jan Mayen
(Norway)

Nordkapp

Lappland

Poluostrov
Yamal

Gydanskiy
Poluostrov

Plato
Putorana

Sredne

Verkhoyanskiy

Khrebet Cherskogo

More
Laptevykh

ICELAND

Reykjavik

Føroyar
(Denmark)

Norwegian
Sea

Barentsevo
More

Beloye
More

Sibirskoye

Denmark Strait
Arctic Circle

Shetland Is.
(U.K.)

SWEDEN

FINLAND

Oslo Stockholm
Helsingfors
Tallinn

Ozero Taymyr

Sibirskaya

Ploskogor'ye

Ravnina

Okhotskoye
More

Sakhalin

NORWAY

UNITED
KINGDOM

Dublin
IRELAND

København

DENMARK

LENINGRAD
(Sankt Peterburg)

MOSKVA

Zapadno

RUSSIA

Baykal

Sikhote Alin'

Kuril'skiye Ostrova

3

North
Sea

LONDON
Amsterdam
NETH.
BEL.
Bruxelles
LUX.
FRANCE PARIS

Berlin
GERMANY
Praha
CZECH.

ESTONIA
LATVIA
Riga
LITH.
Vilnius
Minsk
BELORUSSIA

Warszawa
POLAND

Kiyev
(Kiev)
UKRAINE

Prikaspiyskaya
Nizmennost'

Aral'skoye
More

Kirgiz
Step'

KAZAKHSTAN

Ozero Balkhash

Tashkent
UZBEKISTAN
Kyzylkum
Karakumy

Alma-Ata
Bishkek
KIRGHIZIA

Tyan Shan

MONGOLIA
Ulaanbaatar

Gobi

BEIJING

TIANJIN

N. KOREA
Pyŏngyang
SŎUL
S. KOREA

Sea of
Japan

JAPAN

TŌKYŌ

NORTH
ATLANTIC
OCEAN

PORTUGAL
Lisboa

Madrid
SPAIN

Açores
(Port.)

Bern
SWITZ.
AND.

Wien
AUST.
HUNG.
Budapest
YUGO.
Beograd
ROM.

MOLDAVIA
Kishinev
(Chişinău)
Bucuresti
BULG.

GEORGIA
Tbilisi
El'BRUS
5642
ARMENIA
Yerevan
AZER.
Baku

Ashkhabad
TURKMENISTAN

Dushanbe
TAJIKI.

Hindu
Kush

Tarim
Pendi
Takli makan
Shamo

Xizang
Gaoyuan

Kunlun Shan

-154

CHINA

Huang He

SHANGHAI

4

MOROCCO
Rabat

Madeira
(Port.)

El Djazair
Tunis
TUNISIA
Tarābulus
MALTA
Valletta

Atlas Mountains

Roma
Mediterranean Sea

GREECE
Athínai

Tirana
ALB.

CYPRUS
LEB.
Bayrūt
ISRAEL
Yerushalayim
JOR.
Amman

Levkosia
SYRIA
Dimashq
IRAQ
Baghdād

TEHRĀN

Kūhhā-ye Zagros

IRAN

Kābul
AFGHANISTAN

Islamabad

PAKISTAN

Himalaya

New DELHI
Kathmandu
NEPAL
8848
EVEREST

Thar
Desert

BHU.
Thimpu
BANG.

BURMA

Hanoi

HONG KONG
(U.K.)

Tā-pei
TAIWAN

Marianas
Is.

Guam (U.S.A.)

Ilas Canarias
(Sp.)

Al Aaiún

WESTERN
SAHARA

ALGERIA

Hoggar

LIBYA

Sahara

Tibesti

EGYPT

El Khartum

Red Sea

SAUDI
ARABIA

Ar Riyād

Al Kuwayt
KUW.
Al Manamah
QAT.
BAH.
Ad Dawhah
U.A.E.
Abū Zabi

Masqat

OMAN

Arabian
Sea

Suqutrā
(S. Yem.)

Lakshadweep
(India)

KARACHI

INDIA

BOMBAY

Deccan

CALCUTTA
Dhaka

MADRAS

Bay of
Bengal

Rangoon

Andaman
Islands
(India)

LAOS
Viangchan
THAI-
LAND
KRUNG THEP
CAM.
Phnom Penh

VIETNAM

MANILA

Luzon

PHILIPPINES

Mindanao

Caroline Islands

Micro

4 (cont.)

CAPE
VERDE
Praia

Dakar
SEN.
Banjul
THE
GAMBIA
GUINEA-
BISSAU
Conakry

MAURITANIA
Nouakchott

MALI
Bamako

NIGER
Niamey

BUR.
FASO
Ouagadougou

CHAD
N'djaména

SUDAN

Lac
Chad

San'ā
YEMEN

ETHIOPIA
Ādis Abeba

DJIB.

SOMALIA

Muqdisho

Colombo
SRI LANKA

Malé
MALDIVES

East Indies

MALAYSIA
Kuala Lumpur
SINGAPORE

Bandar Seri
Begawan
BRU.

Sumatera

Borneo

Sulawesi

Maluku

New
Guinea

PAPUA
NEW
GUINEA

Port Mor

GUINEA
SIERRA LEONE
Freetown
Monrovia
LIBERIA

IVORY
COAST
Abidjan

GH.
Accra

TOGO
BEN.
Lomé
Porto Novo
NIGERIA
Lagos

CENTRAL
AFRICAN REP.
Bangui

CAMEROON
Yaoundé
Malabo
EQ. GUINEA

UGANDA
Kampala
KENYA
Nairobi

5

Ascension
(U.K.)

St. Helena
(U.K.)

Ilha da Trindade
(Brazil)

SOUTH
ATLANTIC
OCEAN

Libreville
GABON

Congo
Basin
ZAIRE
Brazzaville
Kinshasa

CONGO
São Tomé
AND PRÍNCIPE

Luanda

ANGOLA

NAMIBIA
Windhoek

ZAMBIA
Lusaka

ZIMBABWE
Harare

RW.
Kigali
BU.
Bujumbura
Dodoma
TANZANIA

6895
KILIMANJARO

Victoria

SEYCHELLES

COMOROS
Moroni

MALAWI
Lilongwe

MOZAMBIQUE

MADAGASCAR
Antananarivo

Réunion
(Fr.)

MAURITIUS
Port Louis

INDIAN OCEAN

Laut
Timor

JAKARTA
Jawa

INDONESIA

Timor

Laut Arafura

AUSTRALIA

Gt. Barrier Reef

Gt. Dividing Range

BOTSWANA
Gaborone
Kalahari
Pretoria
Mbabne
SWAZILAND
Maputo
Maseru
LESOTHO
SOUTH
AFRICA

Cape of Good Hope

Tropic of Capricorn

Gt. Victoria Desert

L. Eyre

C. Leeuwin

Canberra

Tasmania

6

Tristan da Cunha
(U.K.)

Gough I.
(U.K.)

Prince Edward Is.
(S.A.)

Îles Crozet
(Fr.)

Île Kerguelen
(Fr.)

Heard I.
(Aus.)

South
Sandwich Is.
(U.K.)

A   B   C   D   E   F

Mercator Projection

1:85,000,000 (Scale at the Equator)

A R C T I C   O C E A N

Vostochno Sibirskoye More

Ostrov Vrangelya

Khrebet Kolymskiy

Anadyrskiy Zaliv

amchatka

Bering Sea

Chucki Sea

Pt. Barrow

Brooks Range

ALASKA (U.S.A.)

McKINLEY 6194 ▲

Alaska Range

Kodiak I.

Gulf of Alaska

Beaufort Sea

Banks Island

Amundsen Gulf

Victoria Island

Great Bear Lake

Mackenzie Mts

Gt. Slave Lake

Reindeer Lake

Viscount Melville Sound

Queen

Elizabeth

Islands

Ellesmere Island

Kane Basin

Lincoln Sea

Oikiqtaluk

Foxe Basin

Baffin Bay

Hudson Str.

Davis Str.

GREENLAND (Denmark)

Denmark Strait

Arctic Circle

Reykjavík
ICELAND

Kap Farvel

Labrador Sea

Labrador

Newfoundland

Aleutian Islands

Aleutian Trench

N O R T H
P A C I F I C
O C E A N

Hawaiian

Islands

HAWAII (U.S.A.)

Gulf of Alaska

Vancouver I.

Rocky Mountains

CANADA

Gt. Salt Lake

SAN FRANCISCO

LOS ANGELES

Isla de Guadalupe (Mex.)

Columbia

Missouri

L. Winnipeg

Great Plains

UNITED STATES
OF
AMERICA

Mississippi

Great Lakes

Ottawa

CHICAGO

NEW YORK

PHILADELPHIA

Washington

Appalachian Mts.

Bermuda (U.K.)

N O R T H
A T L A N T I C
O C E A N

Açores (Port.)

ust Territory of Pacific Islands

Marshall Is.

NAURU

Tarawa

Gilbert Is.

Phoenix Is.

Christmas I.

Line Islands

Ducie I. (U.K.)

P o l y n e s i a

KIRIBATI

Iles Marquises (Fr.)

BAHAMAS
Nassau

Gulf of Mexico

MEXICO
CIUDAD DE MÉXICO

Islas de Revillagigedo (Mex.)

La Habana

CUBA

West Indies

Belmopan
BELIZE
GUATEMALA
Guatemala
San Salvador
EL SALVADOR

Kingston
JAMAICA
HONDURAS
Tegucigalpa
Managua
NICARAGUA
San José
COSTA RICA

Port au Prince
HAITI

Santo Domingo

DOMINICAN REP.
Puerto Rico (U.S.A.)

Leeward Is.

Caribbean Sea

Windward Is.

BARBADOS

TRINIDAD
AND TOBAGO

CAPE
VERDE

Praia

Panamá
PANAMA

Caracas

VENEZUELA

Georgetown
GUY.
SUR
Paramaribo
Cayenne
FRENCH GUIANA

SOLOMON ISLANDS

Honiara

Santa Cruz Is.

TUVALU
Fanafuti

Iles Wallice (Fr.)

W.
SAMOA
Apla

Samoa (U.S.A.)

Cook Islands (N.Z.)

Tahiti

French Polynesia (Fr.)

Iles Tuamotu

Iles de la Société

Iles Gambier

Pitcairn I. (U.K.)

S O U T H
P A C I F I C
O C E A N

Bogotá

COLOMBIA

Islas Galápagos (Ecuador)

Quito
EQUADOR

Orinoco

Equator

Isla Fernando de Noronha (Brazil)

VANUATU

velle donie Fr.)

Vila

FIJI

Suva

TONGA

Nuku'alofa

Tonga Trench

Isla de Pascua (Easter I.) (Chile)

PERU

LIMA

Peru

BRAZIL

Planalto do

Mato Grosso

Cordillera

La Paz
BOLIVIA

Brasília

Ilha da Trindade (Brazil)

NEW ZEALAND

Wellington

Chatham Is. (N.Z.)

Islas Juan Fernández (Chile)

Santiago

Chile

ACONCAGUA 6960

Paraguay
PARAGUAY

Asunción

Cordillera de los Andes

SÃO PAULO

RÍO DE JANEIRO

Tropic of Capricorn

Auckland Is. (N.Z.)

Macquarie Is. (Aus.)

sman Sea

URUGUAY
Montevideo

BUENOS AIRES

ARGENTINA

Patagonia

S O U T H
A T L A N T I C
O C E A N

Falkland Is. (U.K.)

Cabo de Hornos

South Georgia (U.K.)

Scotia Sea

South Sandwich Is. (U.K.)

GLOSSARY AND ABBREVIATIONS

Language abbreviations in glossary

Afr	Afrikaans	*Dut*	Dutch	*I-C*	Indo-Chinese	*Mal*	Malay
Alb	Albanian	*Fin*	Finnish	*Ice*	Icelandic	*Mlg*	Malagasy
Ar	Arabic	*Fr*	French	*Ind*	Indonesian	*Mon*	Mongolian
Ber	Berber	*Gae*	Gaelic	*It*	Italian	*Nor*	Norwegian
Bul	Bulgarian	*Ger*	German	*Jap*	Japanese	*Per*	Persian
Bur	Burmese	*Gr*	Greek	*Khm*	Khmer	*Pol*	Polish
Ch	Chinese	*Heb*	Hebrew	*Kor*	Korean	*Por*	Portuguese
Cz	Czechoslovakian	*Hin*	Hindi	*Lao*	Laotian	*Rom*	Romanian
Dan	Danish	*Hun*	Hungarian	*Lat*	Latvian	*Rus*	Russian

S-C	Serbo-Croat	*Th*	Thai
Som	Somali	*Tib*	Tibetan
Sp	Spanish	*Tu*	Turkish
Swe	Swedish	*Vt*	Vietnamese
		Wel	Welsh

Glossary

A

Abar (*Ar*) – wells
Abyar (*Ar*) – wells
Adasi (*Tu*) – island
Adrar (*Ber*) – mountains
Ain (*Ar*) – spring, well
Akra (*Gr*) – cape, point
Alb (*Ger*) – mountains
Alpen (*Ger*) – mountains
Alpes (*Fr*) – mountains
Alpi (*It*) – mountains
Alto (*Por*) – high
-alv (*Swe*) – river
-alven (*Swe*) – river
Appenino (*It*) – mountain range
Aqabat (*Ar*) – pass
Archipielago (*Sp*) – archipelago
Arquipielago (*Por*) – archipelago
Arrecife (*Sp*) – reef
Ayia (*Gr*) – saint
Ayios (*Gr*) – saint
Ayn (*Ar*) – spring, well

B

Bab (*Ar*) – strait
Bad (*Ger*) – spa
Badiyah (*Ar*) – desert
Bælt (*Dan*) – strait
Baharu (*Mal*) – new
Bahia (*Sp*) – bay
Bahr (*Ar*) – bay, canal, lake, stream
Bahrat (*Ar*) – lake
Baia (*Por*) – bay
Baie (*Fr*) – bay
Baja (*Sp*) – lower
Ban (*Khm, Lao, Th*) – village
-bana (*Jap*) – cape, point
Banco (*Sp*) – bank
-bandao (*Ch*) – peninsula
Bandar (*Per*) – bay
Baraji (*Tu*) – reservoir
Barqa (*Ar*) – hill
Barragem (*Por*) – reservoir
Bassin (*Fr*) – basin, bay
Batin (*Ar*) – depression
Beinn (*Gae*) – mountain
Beloyy (*Rus*) – white
Ben (*Gae*) – mountain
Bereg (*Rus*) – bank, shore
Berg (*Ger*) – mountain
Berge (*Afr*) – mountains
Bheinn (*Gae*) – mountain
Biar (*Ar*) – wells
Bir (*Ar*) – well
Bi'r (*Ar*) – well
Birkat (*Ar*) – well
Birket (*Ar*) – well
Boca (*Sp*) – river mouth
Bocche (*It*) – mouths, estuary
Bodden (*Ger*) – bay
Bogazi (*Tu*) – strait
Boka (*S-C*) – gulf, inlet
Bol'shoy (*Rus*) – big
Bol'shoye (*Rus*) – big
Bory (*Pol*) – forest
Bratul (*Rom*) – river channel
Bucht (*Ger*) – bay
Bugt (*Dan*) – bay
Buhayrat (*Ar*) – lagoon, lake
Bukit (*Mal*) – hill, mountain
Bukt (*Nor*) – bay
Bulak (*Rus*) – spring
Burnu (*Tu*) – cape, point
Burun (*Tu*) – cape, point
Busen (*Ger*) – bay
Buyuk (*Tu*) – big

C

Cabo (*Por, Sp*) – cape, point
Cachoeira (*Sp*) – waterfall
Cap (*Fr*) – cape, point
Campos (*Sp*) – plain
Cao Nguyen (*Th*) – plateau, tableland
Cataratas (*Sp*) waterfall
Cayi (*Tu*) – stream
Cayo (*Sp*) – islet, rock
Cerro (*Sp*) – hill
Chaco (*Sp*) – jungle
Chaine (*Fr*) – mountain chain
Chapada (*Por*) – hills
Ch'eng (*Ch*) – town
Chiang (*Ch*) – river
Chiang (*Th*) – town
Chott (*Ar*) – marsh, salt lake
Chute (*Fr*) – waterfall
Cienaga (*Sp*) – marshy lake
Ciudad (*Sp*) – city, town
Co (*Tib*) – lake
Col (*Fr*) – pass
Colinas (*Sp*) – hills
Cordillera (*Sp*) – mountain range
Costa (*Sp*) – coast, shore
Cote (*Fr*) – coast, slope
Coteau (*Fr*) – hill, slope
Coxilha (*Por*) – mountain pasture
Cuchillas (*Sp*) – hills

D

Dag (*Tu*) – mountain
Dagi (*Tu*) – mountain
Daglari (*Tu*) – mountains
-dake (*Jap*) – peak
-dal (*Nor*) – valley
Dao (*Ch*) – island
Darreh (*Per*) – valley
Daryacheh (*Per*) – lake
Dasht (*Per*) – desert
Denizi (*Tu*) – sea
Desierto (*Sp*) – desert
Djebel (*Ar*) – mountain
-djik (*Dut*) – dyke
Do (*Kor, Jap, Vt*) – island
Dolina (*Rus*) – valley
Dolok (*Ind*) – mountain
Dolna (*Bul*) – lower
Dolni (*Cz*) – lower
-dong (*Kor*) – village
-dorp (*Afr*) – village
Dur (*Ar*) – mountains

E

Eiland (*Dut*) – island
Eilanden (*Dut*) – islands
-elva (*Nor*) – river
Embalse (*Sp*) – reservoir
Erg (*Ar*) – sandy desert
Estero (*Sp*) – bay, estuary, inlet
Estrecho (*Sp*) – strait
Etang (*Fr*) – lagoon, pond
Ezers (*Lat*) – lake

F

Feng (*Ch*) – mountain, peak
Fels (*Ger*) – rock
Firth (*Gae*) – estuary
-fjall (*Swe*) – mountains
Fjeld (*Dan*) – mountain
-fjell (*Nor*) – mountain
-floi (*Ice*) – bay
-fjoraur (*Ice*) – fjord
Forde (*Ger*) – inlet
Foret (*Fr*) – forest
-foss (*Ice*) – waterfall

G

-gan (*Jap*) – rock
Gang (*Ch*) – harbour
Ganga (*Hin*) – river
Gata (*Jap*) – inlet, lagoon
Gave (*Fr*) – torrent
Gebel (*Ar*) – mountain
Gebirge (*Ger*) – mountains
Ghat (*Hin*) – range of hills
Ghubbat (*Ar*) – bay
Glen (*Gae*) – valley
Gletscher (*Ger*) – glacier
Gobi (*Mon*) – desert
Golfe (*Fr*) – bay, gulf
Golfo (*It, Sp*) – bay, gulf
Golu (*Tu*) – lake
Gora (*Bul*) – forest
Gora (*Pol, Rus*) – mountain
-gorod (*Rus*) – small town
Gory (*Pol, Rus*) – mountains
Grada (*Rus*) – mountain range
Grad (*Bul, Rus, S-C*) – city, town
Gross (*Ger*) – big
Gryada (*Rus*) – ridge
Guba (*Rus*) – bay
-gunto (*Jap*) – island group
Gunung (*Ind, Mal*) – mountain

H

Hadh (*Ar*) – sand dunes
Hafen (*Ger*) – harbour, port
Haff (*Ger*) – bay, lagoon
Hai (*Ch*) – sea
Haixia (*Ch*) – strait
-holm (*Dan*) – island
Halvo (*Dan*) – peninsula
-hama (*Jap*) – beach
Hamada (*Ar*) – plateau
-hamar (*Ice*) – mountain
Hammadah (*Ar*) – plain, stony desert
Hamun (*Per*) – marsh
-hanto (*Jap*) – peninsula
Harrat (*Ar*) – lava field
Hav (*Swe*) – gulf
Havet (*Nor*) – sea
-havn (*Dan, Nor*) – harbour
Hawr (*Ar*) – lake
He (*Ch*) – river
Heide (*Ger*) – heath, moor
-hisar (*Tu*) – castle
Ho (*Ch*) – river
Hohe (*Ger*) – hills
Horn (*Ger*) – peak, summit
Hu (*Ch*) – lake
-huk (*Swe*) – cape, point

I

Idd (*Ar*) – well
Idhan (*Ar*) – sand dunes
Ile (*Fr*) – island
Iles (*Fr*) – islands
Ilha (*Por*) – island
Ilhas (*Por*) – islands
Insel (*Ger*) – island
Inseln (*Ger*) – islands
Irq (*Ar*) – sand dunes
Irmak (*Tu*) – large river
Isfjord (*Dan*) – glacier
Iskappe (*Dan*) – icecap
Isla (*Sp*) – island
Islas (*Sp*) – islands
Isola (*It*) – island
Isole (*It*) – islands
Istmo (*Sp*) – isthmus

J

Jabal (*Ar*) – mountain
-jarvi (*Fin*) – lake
Jaza 'ir (*Ar*) – islands
Jazirat (*Ar*) – island
Jazovir (*Bul*) – reservoir
Jbel (*Ar*) – mountain
Jebel (*Ar*) – mountain
Jezero (*Alb, S-C*) – lake
Jezioro (*Pol*) – lagoon, lake
Jezirat (*Ar*) – island
-jiang (*Ch*) – river
Jibal (*Ar*) – mountain
Jiddat (*Ar*) gravel plain
-jima (*Jap*) – island
-joki (*Fin*) – river
-jokull (*Ice*) – glacier

K

Kaap (*Afr*) – cape, point
-kai (*Jap*) – bay, sea
-kaikyo (*Jap*) – strait
Kanaal (*Dut*) – canal
Kap (*Ger*) – cape, point
-kapp (*Nor*) – cape, point
Kas (*Khm*) – island
Kavir (*Per*) – desert
-kawa (*Jap*) – river
Kenet (*Alb*) – inlet
Kep (*Alb*) – cape, point
Kepulauan (*Ind*) – archipelago, islands
Kereb (*Ar*) – hill, ridge
Khalij (*Ar*) – bay, gulf
Khawr (*Ar*) – wadi
Khrebet (*Ru*) – mountain range
Kiang (*Ch*) – river
Klein (*Afr, Ger*) – small
Ko (*Th*) – island
-ko (*Jap*) – inlet, lake
Koh (*Khm*) – island
Kolpos (*Gr*) – gulf
Kolymskoye (*Rus*) – mountain range
Korfezi (*Tu*) – bay, gulf
Kosa (*Rus*) – spit
Kotlina (*Cz, Pol*) – basin, depression
Kraj (*Cz, Pol, S-C*) – region
Krasnyy (*Rus*) – red
Kray (*Rus*) – region
Kreis (*Ger*) – district
Kryazh (*Rus*) – mountains
Kucuk (*Tu*) – small
Kuh (*Per*) – mountain
Kuhha (*Per*) – mountains
Kum (*Rus*) – sandy desert
Kyst (*Dan*) – coast
Kyun (*Bur*) – island
Kyunzu (*Bur*) – islands

L

La (*Tib*) – pass
Lac (*Fr*) – lake
Lacul (*Rom*) – lake
Laem (*Th*) – point
Lago (*It, Por, Sp*) – lake
Lagoa (*Por*) – lagoon
Laguna (*Sp*) – lagoon, lake
Lam (*Th*) – stream
Lande (*Fr*) – heath, sandy moor
Laut (*Ind*) – sea
Ling (*Ch*) – mountain range
Liman (*Rus*) – bay, gulf
Limni (*Gr*) – lagoon, lake
Llano (*Sp*) – plain, prairie
Llanos (*Sp*) – plains, prairies

M

Mae Nam (*Th*) – river
Mala (*S-C*) – small
Malaya (*Rus*) – small
Male (*Cz*) – small
Maloye (*Rus*) – small
Malyy (*Rus*) – small
Mar (*Por, Sp*) – sea
Mare (*It*) – sea
Masirah (*Ar*) – channel
Massif (*Fr*) – mountains
Mato (*Por*) – forest
Meer (*Afr, Dut, Ger*) – lake, sea
Menor (*Por, Sp*) – lesser, smaller
Mer (*Fr*) – sea
Mesa (*Sp*) – tableland
Minami (*Jap*) – south
-misaki (*Jap*) – cape, point
Mont (*Fr*) – mountain
Montagna (*It*) – mountain
Montagne (*Fr*) – mountain
Montagnes (*Fr*) – mountains
Montana (*Sp*) – mountain
Montanas (*Sp*) – mountains
Monte (*It, Por, Sp*) – mountain
Monti (*It*) – mountains
More (*Rus*) – sea
Mull (*Gae*) – cape, point, promontory
Munkhafad (*Ar*) – depression
Muntii (*Rom*) – mountains
Mynydd (*Wel*) – mountain
Mys (*Rus*) – cape, point

N

-nada (*Jap*) – gulf, sea
Nadrz (*Cz*) – reservoir
Nafud (*Ar*) – desert, dune
Nagor'ye (*Rus*) – highland, uplands
Nagy- (*Hun*) – great
Nahr (*Ar*) – river
Namakzar (*Per*) – desert, salt flat
Nei (*Ch*) – inner
Ness (*Gae*) – cape, promontory
Neu (*Ger*) – new
Nevada (*Sp*) – snow capped mountains
Nevado (*Sp*) – mountain
Ngoc (*Vt*) – mountain peak
-nisi (*Gr*) – island
Nisoi (*Gr*) – islands
Nisos (*Gr*) island
Nizhnyaya (*Rus*) – lower
Nizina (*Pol*) – depression, lowland
Nizmennost' (*Rus*) – lowland
Noord (*Dut*) – north
Nord (*Dan, Fr, Ger*) – north
Norte (*Por, Sp*) – north
Nos (*Bul, Rus*) – point, spit
Nosy (*Mlg*) – island
Nova (*Bul*) – new
Nova (*Cz*) – new
Novaya (*Rus*) – new
Nove (*Cz*) – new
Novi (*Bul*) – new
Nudo (*Sp*) – mountain
Nuruu (*Mon*) – mountain range
Nuur (*Mon*) – lake

O

Ø (*Dan*) – island
Oblast' (*Rus*) – province

L

Llyn (*Wel*) – lake
Loch (*Gae*) – lake
Lough (*Gae*) – lake

Occidental (*Fr, Rom, Sp*) – western
Oki (*Jap*) – bay
-oog (*Ger*) – island
Ojo (*Sp*) spring
Orasul (*Rom*) – city
Ori (*Gr*) – mountains
Oriental (*Fr, Rom, Sp*) – eastern
Ormos (*Gr*) – bay
Oros (*Gr*) – island
Ort (*Ger*) – cape, point
Ostrov (*Rus*) – island
Ostrova (*Rus*) – islands
Otok (*S-C*) – island
Otoki (*S-C*) – islands
Ouadi (*Ar*) – wadi, dry watercourse
Oued (*Ar*) – dry river bed, wadi
Ovasi (*Tu*) – plain
Ozero (*Rus*) – lake

P
Pampa (*Sp*) – plain
Paniai (*Ind*) – lake
Paso (*Sp*) – pass
Passage (*Fr*) – pass
Passo (*It*) – pass
Pasul (*Rom*) – pass
Pelagos (*Gr*) – sea
Pendi (*Ch*) – basin
Pengunungnan (*Ind*) – mountain range
Peninsola (*It*) – peninsula
Peninsule (*Fr*) – peninsula
Pereval (*Rus*) – pass
Peski (*Rus*) – desert, sands
Phnom (*Khm*) – hill, mountain
Phu (*Vt*) – mountain
Pic (*Fr*) – peak
Picacho (*Sp*) – peak
Pico (*Sp*) – peak
Pik (*Rus*) – peak
Pingyuan (*Ch*) – plain
Pizzo (*It*) – peak
Planalto (*Por*) – plateau
Plana (*S-C, Sp*) – plain
Planina (*Bul, S-C*) – mountains
Plato (*Afr, Bul, Rus*) – plateau
Ploskogor'ye (*Rus*) – plateau
Ploskogorje (*Rus*) – plateau
Poco (*Ind*) – peak

Pohorie (*Cz*) – mountain range
Pointe (*Fr*) – cape, point
Pojezierze (*Pol*) – plateau
Poluostrov (*Rus*) – peninsula
Polwysep (*Pol*) – peninsula
Ponta (*Por*) – cape, point
Presa (*Sp*) – reservoir
Proliv (*Sp*) – strait
Pueblo (*Sp*) – village
Puerto (*Sp*) – harbour, pass
Pulau (*Ind, Mal*) – island
Puna (*Sp*) – desert plateau
Puncak (*Ind*) – peak
Punta (*It, Sp*) – cape, point
Puy (*Fr*) – peak

Q
Qalamat (*Ar*) – well
Qalib (*Ar*) – well
Qararat (*Ar*) – depression
Qolleh (*Per*) – mountain
Qornet (*Ar*) – peak
Qundao (*Ch*) – archipelago

R
Ramlat (*Ar*) – dunes
Ra's (*Ar, Per*) – cape, point
Ras (*Ar*) – cape, point
Rass (*Som*) – cape, point
Ravnina (*Rus*) – plain
Recife (*Por*) – reef
Represa (*Por*) – dam
Reshteh (*Per*) – mountain range
-retto (*Jap*) – island chain
Rijeka (*S-C*) – river
Rio (*Por, Sp*) – river
Riviere (*Fr*) – river
Rt (*S-C*) – cape, point
Rubha (*Gae*) – cape, point
Ruck (*Ger*) – mountain
Rucken (*Ger*) – ridge
Rud (*Per*) – river
Rudohorie (*Cz*) – mountains
Rzeka (*Pol*) – river

S
Sabkhat (*Ar*) – salt flat
Sagar (*Hin*) – lake
Sahara (*Ar*) – desert

Sahl (*Ar*) – plain
Sahra (*Ar*) – desert
Sa'id (*Ar*) highland
-saki (*Jap*) – cape, point
Salar (*Sp*) – salt pan
Salina (*Sp*) – salt pan
San (*Sp*) – saint
-san (*Jap*) – mountain
-sanchi (*Jap*) – mountainous area
Sankt (*Ger, Swe*) – saint
-sanmyaku (*Jap*) – mountain range
Santa (*Sp*) – saint
Sao (*Por*) – saint
Sar (*Kur*) – mountain
Satu (*Rom*) – village
Sawqirah (*Ar*) – bay
Se (*I-C*) – river
See (*Ger*) – lake
-sehir (*Tu*) – town
Selat (*Ind*) – channel, strait
-selka (*Fin*) – bay
Selva (*Sp*) – forest
Serra (*Por*) – mountain range
Serrania (*Sp*) – mountains
-seto (*Jap*) – channel, strait
Severnaya (*Rus*) – southern
Sfintu (*Rus*) – saint
Shamo (*Ch*) – desert
Shan (*Ch*) – mountains
Shandi (*Ch*) – mountainous area
Shatt (*Ar*) – river mouth, river
-shima (*Jap*) – islands
Shiqqat (*Ar*) – interdune trough
Sierra (*Sp*) – mountain range
Sint (*Afr, Dut*) – saint
Slieve (*Gae*) – range of hills
So (*Dan, Nor*) – lake
Soder- (*Swe*) – southern
Sondre (*Dan, Nor*) – southern
Song (*Vt*) – river
Spitze (*Ger*) – peak
Sredne (*Rus*) – middle
Stadt (*Ger*) – town
Stara (*Cz*) – old
Staraya (*Rus*) – old
Stenon (*Gr*) – strait, pass
Step' (*Rus*) – plain, steppe
Strelka (*Rus*) – spit
Stretto (*It*) – strait

-suido (*Jap*) – channel, strait
Sund (*Swe*) – sound, strait
Szent- (*Hun*) – saint

T
-take (*Jap*) – peak
Tall (*Ar*) – hill
Tallat (*Ar*) – hills
Tanggula (*Tib*) – pass
Tanjong (*Ind, Mal*) – cape, point
Tanjon'i (*Mlg*) – cape, point
Tanjung (*Ind, Mal*) – cape, point
Tao (*Ch*) – island
Taraq (*Ar*) – hills
Tassili (*Ber*) – rocky plateau
Tau (*Rus*) – mountains
Taung (*Bur*) – mountain, south
Tekojarvi (*Fin*) – reservoir
Tell (*Ar*) – hill
Teluk (*Ind*) – bay
Tenere (*Fr*) – desert
Terre (*Fr*) – land
Thale (*Th*) – lake
Thamad (*Ar*) – well
Tirat (*Ar*) – canal
Tjarn (*Swe*) – lake
Tso (*Tib*) – lake
Tonle (*Khm*) – lake
Tutul (*Ar*) – hills

U
Ujung (*Ind*) – cape, point
-ura (*Jap*) – inlet
Urayq (*Ar*) – sand ridge
Uruq (*Ar*) – dunes
Ust (*Rus*) – river mouth
Uul (*Mon*) – mountain

V
Valea (*Rom*) – valley
-varos (*Hun*) – town
-varre (*Nor*) – mountain
-vatten (*Swe*) – lake
Vaux (*Fr*) – valleys
Velika (*S-C*) – big
Velikaya (*Rus*) – big
Verkhne (*Rus*) – upper
-vesi (*Fin*) – lake, water
Ville (*Fr*) – town
Vinh (*Vt*) – bay

Virful (*Rom*) – peak
Vodokhranilishche (*Rus*) – reservoir
Volcan (*Sp*) – volcano
Vorota (*Rus*) – strait
Vostochnyy (*Rus*) – eastern
Vozvyshennost' (*Rus*) hills, upland
Vpadina (*Rus*) – depression

W
Wadi (*Ar*) – river, stream
Wahat (*Ar*) – oasis
Wai (*Ch*) – outer
Wald (*Ger*) – forest
Wan (*Ch*) – bay
Wasser (*Ger*) – lake, water
Wenz (*Ar*) – river
Wielka (*Pol*) – big

X
Xan (*Ch*) – strait
Xi (*Ch*) – stream, west
Xia (*Ch*) – gorge, lower
Xian (*Ch*) – county
Xiao (*Ch*) – small
Xu (*Ch*) – island

Y
Yam (*Heb*) – lake
-yama (*Jap*) – mountain
Yarimadasi (*Tu*) – peninsula
Yazovir (*Bul*) – reservoir
Ye (*Bur*) – island
Yoma (*Bur*) – mountain range
Yugo- (*Rus*) – southern
Yuzhnyy (*Rus*) – southern

Z
Zaki (*Jap*) – cape, point
Zalew (*Pol*) – bay, inlet
Zaliv (*Rus*) – bay
-zan (*Jap*) – mountain
Zapadno (*Rus*) – western
Zatoka (*Pol*) – bay
Zee (*Dut*) – sea
Zemiya (*Rus*) – island, land
-zhen (*Ch*) – town

Abbreviations

A
A. – Alp, Alpen, Alpi
Akr. – Akra
And. – Andorra
Arch. – Archipelago
Arr. – Arrecife
Aust. – Australia
Ay. – Ayios

B
B. – Bahia, Baia, Baie, Bay, Bucht, Bukt
Ba. – Bahia
Bang. – Bangladesh
Bah. – Bahrain
Bel. – Belgium
Ben. – Benin
Bg. – Berg
Bhu. – Bhutan
Bk. – Bukit
Bol. – Bol'shoy, Bol'shoye
Br. – Burnu, Burun
Bru. – Brunei
Bt. – Bukit
Bu. – Burundi
Bü. – Büyük
Bulg. – Bulgaria
Bur. Faso – Burkina Faso

C
C. – Cabo, Cap, Cape, Cerro
Can. – Canal, Canale
Cga. – Cienaga
Chan. – Channel
Co. – Cerro
Col. – Columbia
Cord. – Cordillera
Cr. – Creek
Czech. – Czechoslovakia

D
D. – Dag, Dagi, Daglari, Daryacheh
D.C. – District of Columbia
Den. – Denmark
Djib. – Djibouti

E
E. – East
Eq. – Equatorial
Est. – Estrecho

F
Fd. – Fjord
Fk. – Fork
Fr. – France
Ft. – Fort

G
G. – Golfe, Golfo, Guba, Gulf, Gora, Gunung
Gd. – Grand
Gde. – Grande
Geb. – Gebirge
Gen. – General
Geog. – Geographical
Ger. – Germany
Gh. – Ghana
Gl. – Glacier
Gr. – Grande, Gross
Gt. – Great
Guy. – Guyana

H
Har. – Harbour
Hd. – Head
Hung. – Hungary

I
I. – Ile, Ilha, Insel, Isla, Island, Isle, Isola, Isole

Is. – Ilhas, Iles, Islands, Islas, Isles
Isth. – Isthmus

J
J. – Jabal, Jbel, Jebel, Jezioro, Jezero, Jazair
Jor. – Jordan

K
K. – Kap, Kuh, Kuhha, Koh, Kolpos
Kam. – Kampuchea
Kan. – Kanal, Kanaal
Kep. – Kepulauan
Khr. – Khrebet
Kör. – Körfezi
Kuw. – Kuwait

L
L. – Lac, Lacul, Lago, Lake, Limni, Llyn, Loch, Lough
Lag. – Lagoon, Laguna
Leb. – Lebanon
Liech. – Liechtenstein
Lit. – Little
Lux. – Luxembourg

M
M. – Mys
Mal. – Malawi
Mex. – Mexico
Mgne. – Montagne
Mt. – Mont, Mount, Mountain
Mti. – Monti
Mtii. – Muntii
Mts. – Monts, Mounts, Mountains

N
N. – Nord, North, Nos
Neb.– Nebraska

Neth. – Netherlands
Nev. – Nevado
N.H. – New Hampshire
Nizh. – Nizhnyaya
Nizm. – Nizmennost
Nor. – Norway
N.Z. – New Zealand

O
O. – Ost, Ostrov
Os. – Ostova
Oz. – Ozero

P
P. – Point
Pass. – Passage
Penn. – Pennsylvania
Peg. – Peganungan
Pen. – Peninsola, Peninsula, Peninsule
Pk. – Peak, Puncak
Pl. – Planina
Pol. – Poluostrov
Port. – Portugal
Prom. – Promontory
Pt. – Point
Pta. – Ponta, Punta
Pte. – Pointe
Pto. – Puerto, Punto

Q
Qat. – Qatar

R
R. – Reshteh
Ra. – Range
Rep. – Republic
Res. – Reservoir
Rés. – Réservoir
Rom. – Romania
Rw. – Rwanda

S
S. – Shatt, South
Sa. – Serra, Sierra
S.A. – South Africa
Sd. – Sound, Sund
Sp. – Spain
Sprs. – Springs
St. – Saint, Sint
Sta. – Santa
Ste. – Sainte
Str. – Strait
Sur. – Suriname
Switz. – Switzerland

T
Tg. – Tanjong, Tanjung
Tk. – Teluk

U
U.A.E. – United Arab Emirates
U.K. – United Kingdom
U.S.A. – United States of America

V
V. – Volcano
Vdkhr. – Vodokhranilishche
Ven. – Venezuela
Verkh. – Verkhne
Vn. – Volcan
Vol. – Volcan, Volcano

W
W. – Wadi, Wald, West

Y
Y. – Yarimadasi
Yug. – Yugoslavia

Z
Zal. – Zaliv

INDEX

The index includes an alphabetical list of all names appearing in the map section of the atlas. Names on the maps and in the index are generally in the local language. For names in languages not written in the Roman alphabet, the officially accepted transliteration system has been used.

Most features are indexed to the largest scale map on which they appear. Extensive features are usually indexed to maps that show the features completely or show them in their relationship to surrounding areas. For extensive regional features, locations are given for the approximate centre of the feature, those for linear features are given at the position of the name.

Each entry in the index is located by a page number and an alphanumeric grid reference on that particular page. The grid is defined by letters, positioned at the top and at the bottom of the map spread, and numbers, shown at the sides of the spread. For example, Bandung in Indonesia has the reference 90 D7. It can thus be found on page 90 in the grid square D7.

Where two identical names are referenced to the same page and grid square, it should be noted that they relate to different adjacent features. For example, the name Avon appears twice in the index and in both cases it is referenced to 52 E3. These two entries locate firstly the county of Avon and secondly the River Avon.

A

A	62	E3
Aachen	70	B3
Aalst	64	F3
Aanekoski	62	L5
Aarau	68	B2
Aare	68	A2
Aareavaara	62	K3
Aarschot	64	F3
Aba *China*	93	K2
Aba *Nigeria*	105	G4
Abacaxis	136	F4
Abacka	62	G4
Abadan	94	J6
Abadeh	95	L6
Abaete	138	G3
Abaetetuba	137	H4
Abag Qi	87	M3
Abaid, Bahr el	103	F5
Abajo Mountains	127	H2
Abakaliki	105	G4
Abakan	84	E6
Abana	76	E2
Abancay	136	C6
Abarqu	95	L6
Abarqu, Kavir-e	95	L6
Abashiri	88	K3
Abashiri-wan	88	K4
Abatskiy	84	A5
Abau	114	D4
Abay	86	C2
Abay Wenz	103	G5
Abaza	84	E6
Abbadia San Salvatore	69	C4
Abbah	77	H4
Abberton Reservoir	53	H3
Abbeville *France*	64	D3
Abbeville *U.S.A.*	128	F6
Abbeyfeale	59	D8
Abbey Head	54	F2
Abbeyleix	59	H7
Abbot Ice Shelf	141	T4
Abbot, Mount	113	K3
Abbotsbury	52	E4
Abbotsford	122	C3
Abbottabad	92	D2
Abd Al Aziz, Jbel	77	H4
Abd al Kuri	97	N10
Abdanan	94	H5
Abdulino	78	J5
Abeche	102	D5
Abelvaer	62	H4
Abengourou	104	E4
Abenra	63	C9
Abeokuta	105	F4
Aberaeron	52	C2
Abercarn	52	D3
Aberchirder	56	F3
Abercraf	52	D3
Aberdare	52	D3
Aberdaron	52	C2
Aberdeen *South Africa*	108	D6
Aberdeen *U.K.*	57	F3
Aberdeen *Maryland, U.S.A.*	125	M7
Aberdeen *Mississippi, U.S.A.*	128	H4
Aberdeen *Ohio, U.S.A.*	124	J7
Aberdeen *S.Dakota, U.S.A.*	123	Q5
Aberdeen *Washington, U.S.A.*	122	C4
Aberdeen Lake	119	R3
Aberfoyle	57	D4
Abergavenny	52	D3
Abergele	55	F3
Abergwaun	52	C3
Abergwynft	52	D3
Aberhonddu	52	D3
Abermo	52	D2
Abersoch	52	C2
Abersychan	52	D3
Abertawe	52	D3
Aberteifi	52	C2
Abertillery	52	D3
Aberystwyth	52	C2
Abez	78	L2
Abha	96	F7
Abhar	94	J3
Abhar Rud	95	K4
Abide	76	B2
Abidjan	104	E4
Abilene *Kansas, U.S.A.*	123	R8
Abilene *Texas, U.S.A.*	127	N4
Abingdon	53	F3
Abingdon Island	136	A7
Abington	57	E5
Abisko	62	H2
Abitibi	125	K2
Abitibi, Lake	125	L2
Abiy Adi	96	D10
Ablaketka	86	E2
Abo	63	M6
Aboisso	104	E4
Abomey	105	F4
Abongabong, Gunung	90	B5
Abong Mbang	105	H5
Aborigen, Pik	85	R4
Aborlan	91	F4
Abou Deia	102	C5
Aboyne	57	F3
Abrad, Wadi	96	G9
Abraham's Bay	133	L3
Abrantes	66	B3
Abruzzese, Appennino	69	D4
Abu Ali	97	J3
Abu al Khasib	94	H6
Abu Arish	96	F8
Abu Dhabi	97	M4
Abu el Jir	77	K6
Abu Gamel	96	C9
Abu Hamed	96	A7
Abuja	105	G4
Abu Jifan	97	H4
Abu Kamal	94	E4
Abu Latt	96	E7
Abu Madd, Ra's	96	C4
Abu Musa	95	M9
Abu Qatur	77	G5
Abu Shagara, Ras	96	C6
Abut Head	115	C5
Abu Tig	102	F2
Abu Zabad	102	E5
Abu Zabi	97	M4
Abwong	103	F6
Aby	63	G7
Abyad, Ar Ra's al	96	D5
Abyalven	62	J4
Abybro	63	C8
Abyek	95	K3
Acalayong	105	G5
Acambaro	131	J7
Acambay	131	K8
Acandi	132	J10
Acaponeta	130	G6
Acapulco	131	K9
Acarai, Serra	136	F3
Acarau *Brazil*	137	J4
Acarau *Brazil*	137	J4
Acarigua	136	D2
Acatlan *Mexico*	130	H7
Acatlan *Mexico*	131	K8
Acatzingo	131	L8
Acayucan	131	M9
Acceglio	68	A3
Accra	104	E4
Accrington	55	G3
Achacachi	138	C3
Achavanich	56	E2
Acheng	88	A3
Achikouya, Plateau des	106	B3
Achill	58	C5
Achill Head	58	B5
Achill Island	58	B5
Achim	70	C2
Achinsk	84	E5
Achmore	56	B2
Achnacroish	57	C4
Achosnich	57	B4
Acigol	76	F3
Acipayam	76	C4
Acireale	69	E7
Acklins Island	133	K3
Acle	53	J2
Acomayo	136	C6
Aconcagua, Cerro	139	C6
Aconchi	127	G6
Acores	48	F3
Acoyapa	132	E9
Acqui Terme	68	B3
Acre *Brazil*	136	C5
Acre *Brazil*	136	D5
Acre *Israel*	94	B5
Actopan	131	K7
Acu	137	K5
Ada *Ghana*	104	F4
Ada *Oklahoma, U.S.A.*	128	D3
Adair, Bahia de	126	F5
Adaja	66	D2
Adak	118	Ac9
Adak Island	118	Ac9
Adaksu	77	K3
Adalia	76	D4
Adam	97	N5
Adaminaby	113	K6
Adan	96	G10
Adana	76	F4
Adapazari	76	D2
Adare	59	E7
Adda	68	B2
Adda	68	B3
Ad Dakhla	100	B4
Ad Dali	96	G10

Name	Page	Ref
Ad Dammam	97	K3
Ad Darb	96	F8
Ad Dawadimi	96	G4
Ad Dawhah	97	K4
Ad Dila	97	K7
Ad Dilam	96	H5
Ad Diriyah	96	H4
Ad Duwaniyah	94	G6
Ad Duwayd	96	F1
Adel	124	C6
Adelaide *Antarctic*	141	V5
Adelaide *Australia*	113	H5
Adelaide *Bahamas*	129	P8
Adelaide Island	141	V5
Adelaide Peninsula	120	G4
Aden	96	G10
Aden, Gulf of	103	J5
Adh Dhayd	97	M4
Adi	114	A2
Adi Ark'ay	96	C10
Adi Dairo	96	D9
Adige	68	C3
Adigrat	96	D9
Adiguzel Baraji	76	C3
Adi Keyah	96	D9
Adilabad	92	E5
Adilcevaz	77	K3
Adin	122	D7
Adirondack Mountains	125	N4
Adis Abeba	103	G6
Adi Ugri	96	D9
Adiyaman	77	H4
Adjud	73	J2
Adjuntas, Presa de las	131	K6
Adka	118	Ac9
Adlington	55	G3
Admello	68	C2
Admiralty Gulf	112	F1
Admiralty Inlet	120	J3
Admiralty Island *Canada*	119	Q2
Admiralty Island *U.S.A.*	118	J4
Admiralty Islands	114	D2
Admund Ringnes Island	120	G2
Ado-Ekiti	105	G4
Adonara	91	G7
Adoni	92	E5
Adorf	70	E3
Adoumaoua, Massif de l'	105	H4
Adour	65	C7
Adra	66	E4
Adrano	69	E7
Adrar	100	E3
Adre	102	D5
Adria	68	D3
Adrian *Michigan, U.S.A.*	124	J6
Adrian *Texas, U.S.A.*	127	L3
Adriatic Sea	68	E4
Adwa	96	D9
Adwick le Street	55	H3
Adycha	85	P3
Adzhima	88	G1
Adzvavom	78	K2
Aegean Sea	75	H3
Afafura, Laut	91	K7
Afanasevo	78	J4
Affobakka	137	F3
Affric	56	C3
Afghanistan	92	B2
Afgooye	107	J2
Afif	96	F5
Afikpo	105	G4
Afmadow	107	H2
Afognak Island	118	E4
Afon Efyrnwy	52	D2
Afrin	77	G4
Afsin	77	G3
Afyon	76	D3
Agadez	101	G5
Agadir	100	D2
Agadyr	86	C2
Agaie	105	G4
Agalta, Sierra de	132	E7
Agano	89	G7
Agapa *Russia*	84	D2
Agapa *Russia*	84	D2
Agapitovo	84	D3
Agartala	93	H4
Agaruut	87	K3
Agats	114	B3
Agatti	92	D6
Agattu Island	118	Aa9
Agbaja	105	G4
Agboville	104	E4
Agdam	94	H2
Agde	65	E7
Agematsu	89	F8
Agen	65	D6
Aghada	59	F9
Agha Jari	95	J6
Agiabampo, Estero de	130	E4
Agin	77	H3
Agira	69	E7
Aglasun	76	D4
Agnanda	75	F4
Agno	68	C3
Agnone	69	E5
Agout	65	D7
Agra	92	E3
Agram	72	C3
Agreda	67	F2
Agri	69	F5
Agri	77	K3
Agrigento	69	D7
Agrinion	75	F3
Agropoli	69	E5
Agua Clara	138	F4
Aguadas	136	B2
Aguadilla	133	P5
Aguanaval	130	H5
Agua Prieta	127	H5
Aguascalientes	130	H4
Agua, Volcan de	132	B7
Aguelhok	100	F5
Aguemour	101	F3
Aguilar de Campoo	66	D1
Aguilas	67	F4
Aguja, Cabo de la	133	K9
Aguja, Punta	136	A5
Agulhas, Kaap	108	D6
Agusan	91	H4
Ahar	94	H2
Aheim	62	A5
Ahipara Bay	115	D1
Ahititi	115	E3
Ahlat	77	K3
Ahmadabad	92	D4
Ahmadi	95	N8
Ahmadnagar	92	D5
Ahmadpur	92	D3
Ahmar Mountains	103	H6
Ahoskie	129	P2
Ahram	95	K7
Ahtari	62	L5
Ahtarinjarvi	62	L5
Ahuachapan	132	C8
Ahvaz	94	J6
Ahvenanmaa	63	H6
Ahwar	96	H10
Aiddejavrre	62	K2
Aidhipsos	75	G3
Aigen	68	D1
Aigues	65	F6
Aiken	129	M4
Ailao Shan	93	K4
Ailsa Craig	57	C5
Aim	85	N5
Aimores, Serra dos	138	H3
Ain	65	F5
Ain Beida	101	G1
Ain Bessem	67	H4
Ain Defla	67	G4
Ain El Hadjel	67	H5
Ain Oulmene	67	J5
Ain Sefra	100	E2
Ainsworth	123	Q6
Aioun el Atrouss	100	D5
Aiquile	138	C3
Air	101	G5
Airbangis	90	B5
Airdrie	57	E5
Aire *France*	64	F4
Aire *U.K.*	55	J3
Airedale	55	H3
Aire-sur-l'Adour	65	C7
Air Force Island	120	M4
Airgin Sum	87	L3
Airi-selka	62	L3
Aisne	64	E4
Aitape	114	C2
Aith	56	F1
Aix-en-Provence	65	F7
Aix-les-Bains	65	F6
Aiyina	75	G4
Aiyinion	75	G2
Aiyion	75	G3
Aizawl	93	H4
Aizpute	63	J8
Aizu-Wakamatsu	89	G7
Ajaccio	69	B5
Ajana	112	C4
Ajanta Range	92	E4
Ajdabiya	101	K2
Ajlun	94	B5
Ajman	97	M4
Ajmer	92	D3
Akaishi-sanchi	89	G8
Akalkot	92	E5
Akamkpa	105	G4
Akaroa Head	115	D5
Akbou	67	J4
Akbulak	79	K5
Akcaabat	77	H2
Akcaakale	77	H4
Akcadag	77	G3
Akcakoca	76	D2
Akcaova	76	C4
Akcay	76	C4
Akchatau	86	C2
Ak Daglari	76	C4
Akdagmadeni	77	F3
Ak Dovurak	84	E6
Akershus	63	D6
Akeshir Golu	76	D3
Aketi	101	J4
Akgevir	77	J4
Akhalkalaki	77	K2
Akhaltsikhe	77	K2
Akhdar, Al Jabal al	101	K2
Akhdar, Jabal	97	N5
Akhdar, Wadi	96	C3
Akheloos	75	F3
Akhiok	118	E4
Akhisar	76	B3
Akhmim	103	F2
Akhtubinsk	79	H6
Akhtyrka	79	E5
Aki	89	D9
Akimiski Island	121	K7
Akincilar	77	H2
Akinkeen	59	D9
Akinli	77	J4
Akita	88	H6
Akjoujt	100	C5
Akkavare	62	J3
Akkeshi	88	K4
Akko	94	B5
Akkoy	76	B4
Akkus	77	G2
Aklavik	118	H2
Akniste	63	L8
Akola	92	E4
Akonolinga	105	H5
Akordat	96	C9
Akosombo Dam	104	F4
Akot	92	E4
Akpatok Island	121	N5
Akpinar	76	E3
Akqi	86	D3
Akranes	62	T12
Akron	125	K6
Aksar	77	K2
Aksaray	76	E3
Aksay *China*	86	G4
Aksay *Kazakhstan*	79	J5
Aksehir	76	D3
Akseki	76	D4
Aksenovo-Zilovskoye	85	K6
Aks-e Rostam	95	M7
Aksha	85	J6
Akshimrau	79	J7
Aksu *China*	86	E3
Aksu *Turkey*	76	D4
Aksu *Kazakhstan*	79	J5
Aksu-Ayuly	86	C2
Aksu Cayi	76	D4
Aksum	96	D9
Aksumbe	86	B3
Aktau	84	A6
Akti	75	H2
Aktogay	86	D2
Akulivik	120	L5
Akune	89	C9
Akun Island	118	Ae9
Akure	105	G4
Akureyri	62	V12
Akuse	104	F4
Akutan Island	118	Ae9
Akwanga	105	G4
Akyab	93	H4
Akyatan Golu	76	F4
Akyazi	76	D2
Akyurt	76	E2
Akzhar	86	C3
Al Aaiun	100	C3
Alabama *U.S.A.*	129	J4
Alabama *U.S.A.*	129	J4
Alaca	76	F2
Alacahan	77	G3
Alacam	77	F2
Alacran, Arrecife	131	Q6
Alagoas	137	K5
Alagoinhas	137	K6
Alagon *Spain*	66	C2
Alagon *Spain*	67	F2
Al Ahmadi	97	J2
Al Ajaiz	97	N7
Alajarvi	62	K5
Alajuela	132	E9
Alakanuk	118	C3
Alakol, Ozero	86	E2
Alakyla	62	L3
Al Amarah	94	H6
Alameda *California, U.S.A.*	126	A2
Alameda *New Mexico, U.S.A.*	127	J3
Alamicamba	132	E8
Alamo	126	E2
Alamogordo	127	K4
Ala, Monti di	69	B5
Alamos	127	H7
Alamosa	127	K2
Aland	63	H6
Alands hav	63	M6
Alanya	76	E4
Alaotra, Lake	109	J3
Alapayevsk	84	Ad5
Al Aqulah	97	J5
Alarcon, Embalse de	66	E3
Al Artawiyah	96	G3
Alasehir	76	C3
Al Ashkhirah	97	P6
Alaska	118	E3
Alaska, Gulf of	118	F4
Alaska Peninsula	118	Af8
Alaska Range	118	E3
Alassio	68	B4
Alatna	118	E2
Alatyr	78	H5
Alausi	136	B4
Alaverdi	77	L2
Alavus	62	K5
Al Ayn	97	M4
Alayor	67	J3
Alayskiy Khrebet	86	C4
Al Azamiyah	77	L6
Alazeya	85	S2
Alba	68	B3
Al Bab	77	G4
Albacete	67	F3
Alba de Tormes	66	D2
Al Badi	96	H5
Al Badi	77	J5
Alba Iulia	73	G2
Albak	63	D8
Alba, Mount	115	B6
Albanel, Lake	121	M7
Albania	74	E2
Albano	137	F4
Albany *Australia*	112	D5
Albany *Canada*	121	K7
Albany *Georgia, U.S.A.*	129	K5
Albany *Kentucky, U.S.A.*	124	H8
Albany *New York, U.S.A.*	125	P5
Albany *Oregon, U.S.A.*	122	C5
Albarracin	67	F2
Al Basrah	94	H6
Albatross Bay	113	J1
Albatross Point	115	E3
Al Bayda	96	G10
Albayrak	77	L3
Albemarle	129	M3
Albemarle Island	136	A7
Albemarle Sound	129	P2
Albenga	68	B3
Albentosa	67	F2
Alberche	66	D2
Alberga	113	G4
Albergaria-a-Velha	66	B2
Alberique	67	F3
Albert	64	E3
Alberta	119	M5
Albert Edward, Mount	114	D3
Albert Kanaal	64	F3
Albert, Lake	107	F2
Albert Lea	124	D5
Albert Nile	107	F2
Albertville *France*	65	G6
Albertville *Zaire*	107	E4
Albi	65	E7
Albina	137	G2
Al Bir	96	C2
Al Birk	96	E7
Albocacer	67	G2
Albo, Monti	69	B5
Alboran, Isla de	66	E5
Alborg	63	D8
Alborg Bugt	63	D8
Alborz, Reshteh-ye Kuhta ye	95	K3
Albro	113	K3
Albufeira	66	B4
Albu Gharz, Sabkhat	77	J5
Albuquerque	127	J3
Al Buraymi	97	M4
Albury	113	K6
Al Busayyah	94	H6
Al Buzun	97	K9
Alcacer do Sal	66	B3
Alcala de Henares	66	E2
Alcamo	69	D7
Alcanices	66	C2
Alcaniz	67	F2
Alcantara	66	C3
Alcantara	137	J4
Alcantara, Embalse de	66	C3
Alcaraz	66	E3
Alcaraz, Sierra de	66	E3
Alcaudete	66	D4
Alcazar de San Juan	66	E3
Alcester	53	F2
Alcolea del Pinar	66	E2
Alcoutim	66	C4
Alcoy	67	F3
Alcubierre, Sierra de	67	F2
Alcublas	67	F3
Alcudia	67	H3
Aldabra Islands	82	C7
Aldama	131	K6
Aldan *Russia*	85	M5
Aldan *Russia*	85	N4
Aldanskoye Nagorye	85	M5
Alde	53	J2
Aldeburgh	53	J2
Aldeia Nova	66	C4
Alderley Edge	55	G3
Alderney	53	M6
Aldershot	53	G2
Aldridge	53	F2
Aleg	100	C5
Alegrete	138	E5
Aleksandra, Mys	85	P6
Aleksandriya	79	E6
Aleksandrov	78	F4
Aleksandrovac	73	F4
Aleksandrov Gay	79	H5
Aleksandrovsk	78	K4
Aleksandrovskoye	79	G7
Aleksandrovsk-Sakhalinskiy	85	Q6
Aleksandry, Ostrov	80	F1
Alekseyevka *Kazakhstan*	84	A6
Alekseyevka *Russia*	79	F5
Aleksin	78	F5
Alem Paraiba	138	H4
Alencon	64	D4
Alenquer	137	G4
Alentejo	66	C3
Alenuihaha Channel	126	S10
Aleppo	77	G4
Aleria	69	B4
Alerta	136	C6
Ales	65	F6
Aleshki	78	H2
Alessandria	68	B3
Alessio	74	E2
Alesund	62	B5

Name	Page	Grid
Aleutian Islands	118	Ab9
Aleutian Range	118	D4
Aleutian Trench	143	H3
Alevina, Mys	85	S5
Alexander Archipelago	118	J4
Alexander Bay	108	C5
Alexander, Cape	119	P2
Alexander City	129	K4
Alexander Island	141	V4
Alexander, Kap	120	M2
Alexandra *Australia*	113	K6
Alexandra *New Zealand*	115	B6
Alexandretta	77	G4
Alexandria *Egypt*	102	E1
Alexandria *Romania*	73	H4
Alexandria *South Africa*	108	E6
Alexandria *U.K.*	57	D5
Alexandria *Louisiana, U.S.A.*	128	F5
Alexandria *Minnesota, U.S.A.*	124	C4
Alexandria *Virginia, U.S.A.*	125	M7
Alexandroupolis	75	H2
Aleysk	84	C6
Al Fallujah	77	K6
Alfambra *Spain*	67	F2
Alfambra *Spain*	67	F2
Alfaro	136	B4
Alfatar	73	J4
Al Faw	94	J7
Alfeld	70	C3
Alfios	75	F4
Alford *Grampian, U.K.*	56	F3
Alford *Lincolnshire, U.K.*	55	K3
Alfreton	55	H3
Al Fuhayhil	97	J2
Al Fujayrah	97	N4
Al Fuqaha	101	J3
Al Furat	77	J5
Algard	63	A7
Algarrobo del Aguila	139	C7
Algarve	66	B4
Algatart	86	C3
Algeciras	66	D4
Algena	96	D8
Alger, Baie d	67	H4
Algeria	101	F3
Al Ghaydah	97	P5
Alghero	69	B5
Algiers	101	F1
Algoa Bay	108	E6
Algodoes	137	K5
Algodonales	66	D4
Algona	124	C5
Algonquin Park	125	L4
Algueirao	109	F4
Al Hadd	97	P5
Al Hadithah	94	F4
Al Hadr	77	K5
Al Halfayah	94	H6
Al Hallaniyah	97	N8
Al Hamar	96	H5
Alhambra	66	E3
Al Hanakiyah	96	E4
Al Hariq	96	H5
Al Hasa	97	J3
Al Hasakah	77	J4
Al Hashimiyah	94	G5
Al Hawtah	96	H9
Al Hayy	94	H5
Al Hillah *Iraq*	94	G5
Al Hillah *Saudi Arabia*	96	H5
Al Hilwah	96	H5
Al Hudaydah	96	F9
Al Hufuf	96	J4
Al Huraydah	97	J9
Aliabad	94	H4
Aliabad	95	M7
Aliaga	76	B3
Aliaga	67	F2
Aliakmon	75	G2
Ali al Gharbi	94	H5
Alibag	92	D5
Alibey, Ozero	73	L3
Alibunar	73	F3
Alicante	67	F3
Alice	128	C7
Alice, Punta	69	F6
Alice Springs	113	G3
Aligarh	92	E3
Aligudarz	95	J5
Alijuq, Kuh-e	95	K6
Al Ikhwan	97	N10
Alima	106	C3
Alindao	102	D6
Alingsas	63	E8
Alinskoye	84	D4
Alipka	84	D5
Al Isawiyah	94	C6
Alisos	126	G5
Alistati	75	G2
Aliwal North	108	E6
Al Jaghbub	101	K2
Al Jahrah	97	H2
Al Jawarah	97	N7
Al Jawf *Libya*	101	K4
Al Jawf *Saudi Arabia*	96	D2
Al Jazirah	77	J4
Al Jubayl	97	J3
Aljustrel	66	B4
Al Kalban	97	P6
Al Kamil	97	P5
Al Khaburah	97	N5
Al Khalis	94	G5
Al Khaluf	97	P6
Al Khasab	97	N3
Al Khatt	97	N4
Al Khawr	97	K4
Al Khubar	97	K3
Al Khufrah	101	K4
Al Khums	101	H2
Al Khuraybah	97	J9
Al Khuwayr	97	K3
Alkmaar	64	F2
Al Kufah	94	G5
Al Kut	94	G5
Al Kuwayt	97	H2
Allada	105	F4
Al Ladhiqiyah	77	F5
Allahabad	92	F3
Allahuekber Daglari	77	K2
Allakh-Yun	85	P4
Allanmyo	93	J5
Allanridge	108	E5
Allaqi, Wadi	103	F2
Allariz	66	C1
Alldays	108	E4
Allegheny	125	L6
Allegheny Mountains	124	J8
Allegheny Plateau	125	K7
Allen *Philippines*	91	G3
Allen *U.K.*	52	C4
Allen, Bog of	59	H6
Allendale	129	M4
Allende	127	M6
Allen, Lough	58	F4
Allenstein	71	J2
Allentown	125	N6
Alleppey	92	E7
Aller	70	D2
Allerston	55	J2
Allevard	65	G6
Allgauer Alpen	68	C2
Alliance *Nebraska, U.S.A.*	123	N6
Alliance *Ohio, U.S.A.*	125	K6
Allier	65	E5
Allik	121	Q6
Al Lith	96	E6
Alloa	57	E4
Al Luhayyah	96	F9
Allur	92	F6
Alma *Canada*	125	Q2
Alma *Michigan, U.S.A.*	124	H5
Alma *Nebraska, U.S.A.*	123	Q7
Alma-Ata	86	D3
Almaciles	66	E4
Almada	66	B3
Al Maddah	96	F7
Almaden	66	D3
Al Madinah	96	D4
Almagro	66	E3
Al Mahmudiyah	94	G5
Al Majmaah	96	G4
Almalyk	86	B3
Al Manamah	97	K3
Almanor, Lake	122	D7
Almansa	67	F3
Al Mansuriyah	96	F9
Almanzor, Pic de	66	D2
Al Mariyah	97	L5
Al Marj	101	K2
Al Masnaah	97	N5
Al Mawsil	77	K4
Al Mayadin	77	J5
Al Mayyah	96	F3
Almazan	66	E2
Almeirim	137	G4
Almelo	64	G2
Almendra, Embalse de	66	C2
Almeria	66	E4
Almeria, Golfo de	66	E4
Almetyevsk	78	J5
Almhult	63	F8
Al Midhnab	96	G4
Almina, Punta	66	D5
Al Miqdadiyah	94	G5
Almiropotamos	75	H3
Almiros	75	G3
Almirou, Kolpos	75	H5
Al Mishab	96	J3
Almodovar	66	B4
Almond	57	E4
Almonte	66	D3
Almora	92	E3
Al Mubarraz	97	J4
Al Mudawwara	94	B7
Al Mudaybi	97	P5
Al Mudayrib	97	P5
Al Muharraq	97	K3
Al Mukalla	97	J9
Al Mukha	96	F10
Almuradiel	66	E3
Al Musaymir	96	G10
Al Musayyib	94	G5
Almus Baraji	77	G2
Al Muwayh	96	E5
Al Muwaylih	96	B3
Alness	57	G5
Alnwick	55	H1
Alofi	111	T4
Alor	91	G7
Alora	66	D4
Alor, Kepulauan	91	G7
Alotau	114	E4
Alpe-d'Huez	65	G6
Alpena	124	J4
Alpercatas, Serra das	137	J5
Alpine *Arizona, U.S.A.*	127	H4
Alpine *Texas, U.S.A.*	127	L5
Alps	50	J6
Alpu	76	D3
Al Qaffay	97	K4
Al Qaim	77	J5
Al Qalibah	96	C2
Al Qamishli	94	E3
Al Qaryatayn	77	G5
Al Qatif	97	J3
Al Qatn	97	J9
Al Qaysumah	96	H2
Al Qubbah	101	K2
Alqueva, Barragem de	66	C3
Alquippa	125	K6
Al Qunfudhah	96	E7
Al Qurayni	97	L6
Al Qurayyat	97	P5
Al Qurnah	94	H6
Al Qutayfah	94	C5
Al Quwayiyah	96	G4
Al Quzah	97	J9
Al Ramadi	77	K6
Als	70	C1
Alsace	64	G4
Alsask	123	K2
Alsasua	67	E1
Alsek	118	H4
Alsfeld	70	C3
Alsten	62	E4
Alstermo	63	F8
Alston	55	G2
Alta	62	P2
Altaelv	62	K2
Altafjord	62	K1
Alta Gracia	138	D6
Altagracia	133	M9
Altai	86	G2
Altamaha	129	M5
Altamira	137	G4
Altamura	69	F5
Altamura, Isla de	130	E5
Alta, Sierra	67	C2
Altay *Russia*	84	Ae4
Altay *China*	86	F2
Altay *Mongolia*	86	H2
Altdorf	68	B2
Altenburg	70	E3
Altinekin	76	E3
Altinhisar	76	F3
Altinkaya	76	D4
Altin Kopru	77	L5
Altinova	76	B3
Altinozu	77	G4
Altintas	76	D3
Altkirche	65	G5
Altmark	70	D2
Altmuhl	70	D4
Altnaharra	56	D2
Alto Araguaia	138	F3
Alto Coite	138	F3
Alto Molocue	109	G3
Alton *Hampshire, U.K.*	53	G3
Alton *Staffordshire, U.K.*	53	F2
Altoona	125	L6
Alto Sucuriu	138	F3
Altrincham	55	G3
Altun Shan	92	F1
Alturas	122	D7
Al Ubaylah	97	K6
Alucra	77	H2
Aluksne	63	M8
Al Ula	96	C3
Alumine	139	B7
Al Uqayr	97	K4
Alur Setar	90	C4
Al Uwayja	96	G5
Alva	128	C2
Alvarado	131	M8
Alvaro Obregon	131	N8
Alvdal	63	H5
Alvdalen	63	F6
Alvito	66	C3
Alvorada	137	H6
Alvsborg	63	E8
Alvsbyn	62	J4
Al Wajh	96	C3
Alwar	92	E3
Alwen Reservoir	55	F3
Alwinton	57	F5
Al Wusayl	97	K4
Alyaskitovyy	85	Q4
Alyat	94	J2
Alyth, Forest of	57	E4
Alytus	71	L1
Alzamay	84	F5
Amadeus, Lake	112	G3
Amadiyah	77	K4
Amadjuak Lake	120	M5
Amagasaki	89	E8
Amager	63	E9
Amahai	91	H6
Amakusa-Shimo-shima	89	C9
Amal	63	E7
Amalfi	69	E5
Amalias	75	F4
Amalner	92	E4
Amami-O-shima	89	B11
Amami-shoto	89	J10
Amandola	69	D4
Amantea	69	F6
Amanzimtoti	108	F6
Amapa	137	G3
Amapa	137	G3
Amarante	66	B2
Amarapura	93	J4
Amargosa	126	D3
Amarillo	127	M3
Amaro	69	E4
Amasiya	77	K2
Amasra	76	E2
Amasya	77	F2
Amatignak Island	118	Ac9
Amatrice	69	D4
Amazon	137	G4
Amazonas	137	G4
Amazon, Mouths of the	137	G4
Ambala	92	E2
Ambalavao	109	J4
Ambanja	109	J2
Ambar	84	E3
Ambarchik	85	U3
Ambarnyy	78	E2
Ambato	136	B4
Ambato-Boeny	109	J3
Ambatolampy	109	J3
Amberg	70	D4
Ambergris Cay	132	D5
Amberieu-en-Bugey	65	F6
Ambert	65	E6
Ambikapur	92	F4
Ambilobe	109	J2
Amble-by-the-Sea	55	H1
Ambleside	55	G2
Ambodifototra	109	J3
Amboise	65	D5
Ambon *Indonesia*	91	H6
Ambon *Indonesia*	91	H6
Ambositra	109	J4
Ambovombe	109	J5
Ambriz	106	B4
Ambrym	114	U12
Amchitka Island	118	Ab9
Amchitka Pass	118	Ab9
Amdassa	91	J7
Amderma	84	Ad3
Amdo	93	H2
Ameca	130	G7
Amecameca	131	K8
Amendolara	69	F6
Ameralik	120	R5
American	122	D8
American Falls Reservoir	122	H6
American Samoa	111	U4
Americus	129	K4
Amersham	53	G3
Amery Ice Shelf	141	E5
Ames	124	D5
Amesbury	53	F3
Amfiklia	75	G3
Amfilokhia	75	F3
Amfipolis	75	G2
Amfissa	75	G3
Amga *Russia*	85	N4
Amga *Russia*	85	N4
Amgu	88	F3
Amguema	85	Y3
Amgun	85	P6
Amherst *Canada*	121	P8
Amherst *U.S.A.*	125	L8
Amiata, Monte	69	C4
Amiens	64	E4
Amikino	85	L6
Amilhayt, Wadi al	97	L7
Amindivi Islands	92	D6
Amirante Islands	82	D7
Amistad Reservoir	127	M6
Amitioke Peninsula	120	K4
Amka	85	Q5
Amland	64	F2
Amlia Island	118	Ad9
Amlwch	55	E3
Amman	94	B6
Ammanford	52	C4
Ammer	70	D4
Ammersee	70	D5
Amol	95	L3
Amorgos *Greece*	75	H4
Amorgos *Greece*	75	J4
Amos	125	L2
Amot *Buskerud, Norway*	63	C7
Amot *Telemark, Norway*	63	C7
Amotfors	63	E7
Ampana	91	G6
Ampanihy	109	H4
Ampato, Nevado de	138	B3
Amposta	67	G2
Ampthill	53	G2
Amqui	125	S2
Amran	96	F9
Amravati	92	E4
Amritsar	92	D2
Amroha	92	E3
Amrum	70	C1
Amsterdam *Netherlands*	64	F2
Amsterdam *U.S.A.*	125	N5
Am Timan	102	D5
Amuay	133	M9
Amundsen Glacier	141	P1
Amundsen-Scott	141	A1
Amundsen Sea	141	S5
Amuntai	90	F6
Amur *China*	87	N1
Amur *Russia*	85	Q6
Amuri Pass	115	D5
Amursk	85	P6
Amurskaya Oblast	85	M6
Amur, Wadi	103	F4

Name	Page	Ref
Amvrakikos Kolpos	75	F3
Amvrosiyevka	79	F6
Anabar	84	J2
Anaco	133	Q10
Anaconda	122	H4
Anadarko	128	C3
Anadyr *Russia*	85	W4
Anadyr *Russia*	85	X4
Anadyrskiy Khrebet	85	W3
Anafi *Greece*	75	H4
Anafi *Greece*	75	H4
Anafjallet	62	E5
Anah	77	J5
Anaheim	126	D4
Anahuac	128	B7
Anakapalle	92	F5
Anaktuvuk	118	E2
Analalava	109	J2
Anambas, Kepulauan	90	D5
Anamur	76	E4
Anamur Burun	76	E4
Anan	89	E9
Ananes	75	H4
Anantapur	92	E6
Anantnag	92	E2
Ananyev	73	K2
Ananyevo	86	D3
Anapolis	138	J3
Anapu	137	G4
Anar	95	M6
Anarak	95	L5
Anar Darreh	95	Q5
Anatuya	138	D5
Anaua	136	E3
Anavilhanas, Arquipielago das	136	E4
A Nazret	103	G6
Anbei	86	H3
Ancenis	65	C5
Ancha	85	P4
Anchi	105	G4
Anchorage	118	F3
Anchor Island	115	A6
Ancohuma, Nevado	138	C3
Ancona	68	D4
Ancrum	57	F4
Ancuabe	109	G2
Ancuaque	138	C3
Ancud	139	B8
Ancud, Golfo de	139	B8
Anda	87	P2
Andalgala	138	C5
Andalsnes	62	B5
Andalucia	66	D4
Andalusia	129	J5
Andaman Islands	93	H6
Andaman Sea	93	J6
Andamarca	136	C6
Andam, Wadi	97	P6
Andanga	78	H4
Andapa	109	J2
Andarai	137	J6
Andeba Ye Midir Zerf Chaf	96	E9
Andeg	78	J2
Andenes	62	G2
Andermatt	68	B2
Anderson *Canada*	118	K2
Anderson *Indiana, U.S.A.*	124	H6
Anderson *Missouri, U.S.A.*	124	C8
Anderson *S.Carolina, U.S.A.*	129	L3
Anderson Bay	113	K7
Andes	136	B2
Andevoranto	109	J3
Andfjorden	62	G2
Andhra Pradesh	92	E5
Andikithira	75	G5
Andimeshk	94	J5
Andimilos	75	H4
Andiparos	75	H4
Andipaxoi	75	F3
Andirin	77	G4
Andizhan	86	C3
Andkhvoy	95	S3
Andoas	136	B4
Andong	89	B7
Andongwei	87	M4
Andorra	66	G1
Andorra la Vella	67	G1
Andover	53	F3
Andoya	62	F2
Andraitx	67	H3
Andrascoggin	125	Q4
Andravidha	75	F4
Andreafsky	118	C3
Andreanof Islands	118	Ac9
Andrews	127	L4
Andreyevka	79	J5
Andreyevo Ivanovka	73	L2
Andreyevsk	85	J5
Andria	69	F5
Andrijevica	72	E4
Andringitra	109	J4
Andropov	78	F4
Andros	132	H2
Andros *Greece*	75	H4
Andros *Greece*	75	H4
Androth	92	D6
Andujar	66	D3
Andulo	106	C5
Andyngda	85	K3
Anegada	133	Q5
Anegada, Bahia	139	D8
Aneho	105	F4
Aneityum	114	U13
Anelghowhat	114	U14
Aneto, Pic D'	67	G1
Angamos, Punta	138	B4
Angar	114	A2
Angara	84	E5
Angara Basin	140	A1
Angarsk	84	G6
Ange	62	F5
Angel de la Guarda, Isla	126	F6
Angeles	91	G2
Angel Falls	136	E2
Angelholm	63	E8
Angelino	128	E5
Angellala	113	K4
Angermanalven	62	G5
Angermunde	70	F2
Angers	65	C5
Angeson	62	J5
Angical	138	J6
Angicos	137	K5
Angikuni Lake	119	R3
Anglesey	54	E4
Ango	106	E2
Angoche	109	G3
Angohran	95	N8
Angol	139	B7
Angola	106	C5
Angola *U.S.A.*	124	H6
Angoram	114	C2
Angostura, Presa de la	131	N9
Angouleme	65	D6
Angoumois	65	D6
Angren	86	B3
Anguila Islands	132	H3
Anguilla	133	R5
Angus, Braes of	57	E4
Anholt	63	D8
Anhua	93	M3
Anhui	93	N2
Anhumas	138	F3
Aniak	118	D3
Anidhros	75	H4
Animas, Punta de las	126	F6
Anina	73	F3
Aniva	88	J2
Aniva, Mys	88	J2
Aniva, Zaliv	88	J2
Aniwa	114	U13
Anjalankoski	63	M6
Anjou	65	C5
Anjouan	109	H2
Anjozorobe	109	J3
Anju	87	P4
Ankacho	84	H4
Ankang	93	L2
Ankara	76	E3
Ankazoabo	109	H4
Ankazobe	109	J3
Ankiliabo	109	H4
Anklam	70	E2
Ankleshwar	92	D4
Ankober	103	G6
Ankpa	105	G4
Anlong	93	L3
Anlu	93	M2
Anna	79	G5
Annaba	101	G1
Annaberg-Buchholz	70	E3
An Nabk *Saudi Arabia*	94	C6
An Nabk *Syria*	94	C4
Anna Creek	113	H4
Annagh Bog	59	D8
Annagh Head	58	B4
Annagh Island	59	C5
An Najaf	94	G6
Annalong	58	L4
Annan *U.K.*	57	E5
Annan *U.K.*	55	F2
Annandale	57	E5
Anna Plains	112	E2
Annapolis	125	M7
Annapurna	92	F3
Ann Arbor	124	J5
An Nasiriyah	94	H6
Ann, Cape	125	Q5
Annecy	65	G6
Annenskiy-Most	78	F3
Annfield Plain	55	H2
An Nhon	93	L6
Anniston	129	K4
Annonay	65	F6
An Nuayriyah	97	J3
An Numan	96	B3
Ano Arkhanai	75	H5
Anosibe an Ala	109	J3
Ano Viannos	75	H5
Anoyia	75	H5
Anqing	87	M5
Ansbach	70	D4
Anshan	87	N3
Anshun	93	L3
Ansley	123	Q7
Anson	127	N4
Anson Bay	112	G1
Ansongo	100	F5
Anston	55	H3
Anstruther	57	F4
Ansudu	114	B2
Antabamba	136	C6
Antakya	77	G4
Antalaha	109	K2
Antalya	76	D4
Antalya Korfezi	76	D4
Antananarivo	109	J3
Antarctic Peninsula	141	W5
An Teallach	56	C3
Antequera	66	D4
Anti-Atlas	100	D3
Antibes	65	G7
Anticosti Island	121	P8
Antigo	124	F4
Antigua	133	S6
Antigua and Barbuda	133	S6
Antigua Guatemala	132	B7
Antioch	126	B2
Antipayuta	84	B3
Antipodes Islands	111	S11
Antlers	128	E3
Antofagasta	138	B4
Antofagasta de la Sierra	138	C5
Antofalla, Salar de	138	C5
Antofalla, Volcan	138	C5
Antonio, Ponta Santo	137	K7
Antonovo	73	J4
Antrain	64	C4
Antrim *U.K.*	58	K3
Antrim *U.K.*	58	K3
Antrim Mountains	58	K2
Antrim Plateau	112	F2
Antsalova	109	H3
Antseranana	109	J2
Antsirabe	109	J3
Antsohihy	109	J2
Antu	88	B4
Antufush	96	F9
An-tung	87	N7
Antwerp	64	F3
Antwerpen	64	F3
Anuchino	88	D4
Anugul	92	F4
Anundsjo	62	H5
Anupgarh	92	D3
Anuradhapura	92	F7
Anvers Island	141	V6
Anxi	86	H3
Anxious Bay	113	G5
Anyama	104	E4
Anyang	87	L4
Anyemaqen Shan	93	J2
Anyudin	78	K3
Anzhero-Sudzhensk	84	D5
Anzhu, Ostrova	85	Q1
Anzio	69	D5
Aoba	114	T11
Aola	114	K6
Aomori	88	H5
Aosta	68	A3
Aoukale	102	D5
Aouker	100	D5
Apalachee Bay	129	K6
Apalachicola	129	K6
Apaporis	136	D4
Aparri	91	G2
Apatity	62	Q3
Apatzingan	130	H8
Apeldoorn	64	F2
Apia	111	U4
Apiacas, Serra dos	137	F5
Apin-Apin	90	F4
Apio	114	K6
Apizaco	131	K8
Apolda	70	D3
Apollonia	75	H4
Apopka, Lake	129	M6
Apostle Islands	124	E3
Apostolou Andrea, Akra	76	F5
Apostolovo	79	E6
Appennino	68	C4
Appleby-in-Westmorland	55	G2
Appleton	124	F4
Apsheronsk	79	F7
Apt	65	F7
Apucarana	138	F4
Apure	136	D2
Apurimac	136	C6
Apuseni, Muntii	73	G2
Aq	77	L3
Aqaba	94	B7
Aqaba, Gulf of	103	F2
Aqaba, Khalij-al-	96	B2
Aqal	86	D3
Aqda	95	L5
Aqiq	96	D7
Aqrah	77	K4
Aqueda	66	C2
Aquidauana	138	E4
Ara	92	F3
Arabad	95	N5
Araban	77	G4
Arabatskaya Strelkha, Kosa	79	F6
Araba, Wadi	94	B6
Arab, Bahr el	102	E5
Arabelo	136	E3
Arabian Desert	103	F2
Arabian Sea	97	N8
Arab, Shatt al	94	H6
Arac	76	E2
Aracaju	137	K6
Aracati	137	K4
Aracatuba	138	F4
Aracena	66	C4
Aracena, Sierra de	66	C4
Aracuai *Brazil*	138	H3
Aracuai *Brazil*	137	H3
Arad	73	F2
Aradah	97	L5
Arafuli	96	D9
Aragats	77	L2
Aragon	67	F1
Araguacema	137	H5
Aragua de Barcelona	136	E2
Araguaia	137	H5
Araguaine	137	H5
Araguari	137	G3
Araioses	137	J4
Arak	95	J4
Arakamchechen, Ostrov	118	A3
Arakan Yoma	93	H5
Arakhthos	75	F3
Arakli	77	J2
Araks	77	K2
Aral	86	E3
Aralik	77	L3
Aralqi	86	F4
Aral Sea	98	J2
Aralsk	86	A2
Aralskoye More	80	G5
Aramah, Al	96	H4
Aranda de Duero	66	E2
Arandai	114	A2
Aran Island	58	E3
Aran Islands	59	C6
Aranjuez	66	E2
Aranlau	114	A3
Araouane	100	E5
Arapahoe	123	Q7
Arapawa Island	115	E4
Arapiraca	137	K5
Arapkir	77	H3
Arapongas	138	F4
Ar'ar	94	E6
Araracuara	136	C4
Araraquara	138	G4
Araras, Serra das *Maranhao, Brazil*	137	H5
Araras, Serra das *Mato Grosso do Sul, Brazil*	138	F3
Ararat	77	L3
Araripe, Chapada do	137	K5
Arar, Wadi	94	E6
Aras	77	K2
Arato	89	H6
Arauca *Colombia*	136	C2
Arauca *Venezuela*	136	D2
Aravalli Range	92	D3
Araxa	138	G3
Araya	88	H5
Araya, Peninsula de	136	E1
Arba	67	F1
Arbatax	69	B6
Arbil	77	L4
Arboga	63	F7
Arboleda, Punta	127	H7
Arborg	119	R5
Arbra	63	G6
Arbroath	57	F4
Arbus	69	B6
Arcachon	65	C6
Arcachon, Bassin d	65	C6
Arcadia	129	M7
Arcata	122	B7
Arc Dome	122	F8
Archidona	66	D4
Arcis-sur-Aube	64	F4
Arco	122	H6
Arcos de la Frontera	66	D4
Arctic Bay	120	J3
Arctic Ocean	140	A1
Arctic Red	118	J2
Arctic Red River	118	J2
Arctowski	141	W6
Arda	73	H5
Ardabil	94	J2
Ardahan	77	K2
Ardalstangen	63	B6
Ardanuc	77	K2
Ardara	58	F3
Ardarroch	56	C3
Ardee	58	J5
Ardennes	64	F3
Ardentinny	57	D4
Ardesen	77	J2
Ardestan	95	L5
Ardfert	59	C8
Ardglass	58	L4
Ardgour	57	C4
Ardh es Suwwan	94	C6
Ardila	66	C3
Ardino	73	H5
Ardivacher Point	56	A3
Ardlussa	57	C4
Ardminish	57	C5
Ardmore	128	D3
Ardnacross Bay	57	C5
Ardnamurchan	57	B4
Ardnamurchan Point	57	B4
Ardnave Point	57	B5
Ardrossan	57	D5
Ards Peninsula	58	L3
Ardtalla	57	B5
Ardvasar	57	C3
Ardvule, Rubha	56	A3
Areao	137	H4
Arecibo	133	P5
Areia Branca	137	K4
Arena de las Ventas, Punta	130	E5
Arena, Point	122	B8
Arena, Punta	130	E6
Arenas de San Pedro	66	D2
Arenas, Punta de	139	C10

Name	Page	Ref
Arendal	63	C7
Areopolis	75	G4
Arequipa	138	A3
Arevalo	66	D2
Arezzo	68	C4
Arfersiorfik	120	R4
Arga	67	F1
Argan	86	F3
Arganil	66	B2
Argeles-Gazost	65	C7
Argens	65	G7
Argent	65	E5
Argenta	68	C3
Argentan	64	C4
Argentat	65	D6
Argentera	68	A3
Argenteuil	64	E4
Argentina	139	C7
Argentino, Lago	139	B10
Argenton-sur-Creuse	65	D5
Arges	73	H3
Argo	102	F4
Argolikos Kolpos	75	G4
Argonne, Foret d'	64	F4
Argopuro, Gunung	90	E7
Argo Reefs	114	S9
Argos	75	G4
Argostolion	75	F3
Arguello, Point	126	B3
Argun	85	K6
Argungu	105	F3
Argunsk	85	L6
Arguvan	77	H3
Argyle, Lake	112	F2
Argyll	57	C4
Arhavi	77	J2
Ar Horqin Qi	87	M3
Arhus	63	D8
Ariano Irpino	69	E5
Arica	138	B3
Ariege	65	D7
Ariha	77	G5
Arilje	72	F4
Arima	136	E1
Arinagour	57	B4
Arinos	137	F6
Aripuana	136	E5
Arisaig, Sound of	57	C4
Aristazabal Island	118	K5
Arivonimamo	109	J3
Arivruaich	56	B2
Ariza	67	E2
Arizaro, Salar de	138	C4
Arizona *Argentina*	139	C7
Arizona *U.S.A.*	126	F3
Arjang	63	E7
Arjeplog	62	H3
Arjona	136	B1
Arkadak	79	G5
Arkadelphia	128	F3
Arkaig, Loch	57	B4
Arkalyk	84	Ae6
Arkansas *U.S.A.*	128	E3
Arkansas *U.S.A.*	128	F3
Arkansas City	128	D2
Arkhangelos	75	K4
Arkhangelsk	78	G3
Arkhipovka	88	D4
Arklow	59	K7
Arkoi	75	J4
Arkona, Kap	70	E1
Arkticheskogo Instituta, Ostrova	84	C1
Arlagnuk Point	120	K4
Arlanza	66	E1
Arlberg Pass	68	C2
Arles *France*	65	E7
Arles *France*	65	F7
Arlington *Oregon, U.S.A.*	122	D5
Arlington *S.Dakota, U.S.A.*	123	R5
Arlington *Virginia, U.S.A.*	125	M7
Arlon	64	F4
Armadale	57	E5
Armagh *U.K.*	58	J4
Armagh *U.K.*	58	J4
Armagnac	65	D7
Armah, Wadi	97	K8
Arman	85	S4
Armancon	65	E5
Armathia	75	J5
Armavir	79	G6
Armenia	79	G7
Armenia *Colombia*	136	B3
Armenis	73	G3
Armidale	113	L5
Armori	92	E4
Armoy	58	K2
Armstrong	124	F1
Armthorpe	55	H3
Armu	88	F2
Armutlu	76	C2
Armutova	76	B3
Armyansk	79	E6
Arnaia	75	G2
Arnarfjordur	62	S12
Arnaud	121	M5
Arnauti, Akra	76	K3
Arnedo	67	E1
Arneiroz	137	J5
Arnhem	64	F2
Arnhem, Cape	113	H1
Arnhem Land	113	G1
Arno	68	C4
Arnold	53	F2
Arnon	65	E5
Arnoy	62	J1
Arnprior	125	M4
Aro	70	D1
Aroab	108	C5
Aroeira	138	F4
Arona	68	B3
Aroostook	125	R3
Arorae	111	S2
Aroroy	91	G3
Arosa	68	B2
Arpa	77	K2
Arpacay	77	K2
Arpavla	84	Ad4
Arraias	137	H6
Ar Ramadi	94	F5
Arran	57	C5
Ar Raqqah	77	H5
Arras	64	E3
Ar Rass	96	F4
Ar Rawdah	96	F6
Ar Rawuk	97	J9
Arrecife	100	C3
Arree, Monts d'	64	B4
Arriaga	131	N9
Ar Rifai	94	H6
Arrino	112	D4
Ar Riyad	96	H4
Arromanches	64	C4
Arroux	65	F5
Arrow	52	E2
Arrow, Lough	58	F4
Arrowtown	115	B6
Arroyo Verde	139	C8
Ar Ruays	97	L4
Ar Rub al Khali	97	L6
Ar Rumaytha	97	K4
Ar Rumaythah	94	G6
Ar Rusafah	77	H5
Ar Rustaq	97	N5
Ar Rutbah	94	E5
Ars	63	C8
Ars	94	H3
Arsaynshand	87	L3
Arsenajan	95	L7
Arsenyev	88	D3
Arsin	77	H2
Arsk	78	H4
Arslankoy	76	F4
Art	114	V15
Arta	75	F3
Arta	67	H3
Artashat	130	H8
Arteaga	88	D4
Artem	132	F3
Artemisa	79	J7
Artem-Ostrov	79	F6
Artemovsk	84	Ad5
Artemovskiy	65	D4
Artenay	127	K4
Artesia	115	C5
Arthur's Pass	133	K2
Arthur's Town	78	K4
Arti	138	E6
Artigas	119	P3
Artillery Lake	64	E3
Artois	77	G2
Artova	67	H3
Artrutx, Cabo 'd	79	D6
Artsiz	86	D4
Artux	77	J2
Artvin	85	R4
Artyk	107	F2
Arua	137	G6
Aruana	133	N8
Aruba	114	A3
Aru, Kepulauan	136	E4
Aruma	53	G4
Arun	93	H3
Arunachal Pradesh	53	G4
Arundel	87	N2
Arun Qi	92	E7
Aruppukkottai	107	G3
Arusha	91	G5
Arus, Tanjung	90	F6
Aru, Tanjung	106	E2
Aruwimi	87	J2
Arvayheer	62	M4
Arvidsjaur	63	E7
Arvika	62	J1
Arviksand	64	G2
Arxang	86	F3
Arys	86	B3
Arzamas	78	G4
Arzanah	97	L4
Arzew	100	E1
Arzew, Golfe 'd	67	F5
Arzua	66	B1
As	63	D7
Asadabad	94	J4
Asad, Buhayrat al	77	H5
Asagipinar	76	E3
Asahi-Dake	88	J4
Asahi Kawa	88	J4
Asalem	94	J3
Asamankese	104	E4
Asansk	84	F5
Asansol	92	G4
Asap	77	H2
Asarna	62	F3
Asbestos Mountains	108	D5
Asbury Park	125	P6
Ascencion	138	D3
Ascension	99	B7
Ascension, Bahia de la	131	R8
Aschaffenburg	70	C4
Aschersleben	70	D3
Asco	69	B4
Ascoli Piceno	69	D4
Ascot	53	G3
Aseb	103	H5
Aseda	63	F8
Asele	62	G4
Asenovgrad	73	H5
Asha	78	K4
Ashbourne *Ireland*	59	K5
Ashbourne *U.K.*	55	H3
Ashburton *Australia*	112	D3
Ashburton *New Zealand*	115	C5
Ashburton *U.K.*	52	D4
Ashbury	53	F3
Ashby-de-la-Zouch	53	F2
Ashcroft	122	D2
Ashdod	94	B6
Ashdown	128	E4
Asheboro	129	N3
Ashern	119	R5
Asheville	129	L3
Ashford *Ireland*	59	K6
Ashford *U.K.*	53	H3
Ashikaga	89	G7
Ashington	55	H1
Ashizuri-misaki	89	D9
Ashkazar	95	M6
Ashkhabad	95	P3
Ashkinak	95	R6
Ashland *California, U.S.A.*	122	C6
Ashland *Kentucky, U.S.A.*	124	J7
Ashland *Montana, U.S.A.*	123	L5
Ashland *Nebraska, U.S.A.*	123	R7
Ashland *Ohio, U.S.A.*	124	J6
Ashland *Wisconsin, U.S.A.*	124	E3
Ashqelon	94	B6
Ash Shabakah	94	F6
Ash Shadadah	77	J4
Ash Shamiyah	94	G6
Ash Shariqah	97	M4
Ash Sharqat	77	K5
Ash Shatrah	94	H6
Ash Shaykh Uthman	96	G10
Ash Shihr	97	J9
Ash Shisar	97	L7
Ash Shuaybah	97	J2
Ash Shubah	96	G2
Ash Shumlul	96	H3
Ash Shuqayq	96	F8
Ash Shurayf	96	D4
Ashta	92	E4
Ashtabula	125	K6
Ashton-under-Lyne	55	G3
Ashuanipi Lake	121	N7
Asi	94	C4
Asika	92	F5
Asilah	100	D1
Asinara, Golfo dell	69	B5
Asinara, Isola	69	B5
Askale	77	J3
Askeaton	59	E7
Asker	63	H7
Askersund	63	F7
Askilje	62	G4
Askim	63	D7
Askiz	84	E6
Askja	62	W12
Askola	63	L6
Aslantas Baraji	77	G4
Asmera	96	D9
Asmera	103	G4
Asnen	63	F8
Asoteriba, Jebel	96	C6
Aspatria	55	F2
Aspermont	127	M4
Aspres-sur-Buech	65	F6
As Saan	77	G5
As Sadiyah	94	G4
As Salif	96	F9
As Sallum	101	L2
As Salman	94	G6
Assam	93	H3
As Samawah	94	G6
As Saquia al Hamra	100	C3
Assateague Island	125	N7
As Sawda	97	M8
Assen	64	G2
Assens	63	C9
Assers	63	D8
Assiniboia	123	A3
Assiniboine	123	Q3
Assiniboine, Mount	122	G2
Assis	138	F4
Assisi	69	D4
As Sukhnah	77	H5
As Sulaymaniyah	96	H4
As Sulaymi	96	E3
As Sulayyil	96	G6
As Suq	96	F6
As Suwayda	94	C5
As Suwayh	97	P5
As Suwayrah	94	G5
Astakidha	75	J5
Astara	94	J2
Asti	68	B3
Astin Tagh	92	G1
Astipalaia *Greece*	75	J4
Astipalaia *Greece*	75	J4
Astorga	66	C1
Astoria	122	C4
Astrakhan	79	H6
Astrakhan Bazar	94	J2
Astrolabe Bay	114	D3
Astronomical Society Islands	120	H4
Astros	75	G4
Astudillo	66	D1
Asturias	66	D1
Asuncion	138	E5
Asuncion, Bahia de	126	E7
Aswan	103	F3
Aswan High Dam	103	F3
Asyut	102	F2
Ata	111	T6
Atabey	76	D4
Atacama, Desierto do	138	C4
Atacama, Puna de	138	C4
Atacama, Salar de	138	C4
Atafu	111	U3
Atakora, Chaine de l	105	F3
Atakpame	104	F4
Atalandi	75	G3
Atar	100	C4
Atasu	86	C2
Ataturk Baraji	77	H4
Atauro	91	H7
Atbara *Sudan*	103	F4
Atbara *Sudan*	103	G4
Atbasar	84	Ae6
At-Bashi	86	D3
Atchafalaya	128	G5
Atchafalaya Bay	128	G6
Atchison	124	C7
Ateca	67	F2
Aterno	69	D4
Atesine, Alpi	68	C2
Ath	64	E3
Athabasca	119	N4
Athabasca, Lake	119	P4
Athboy	58	J5
Athenry	59	E6
Athens *Greece*	75	G3
Athens *Georgia, U.S.A.*	129	L4
Athens *Ohio, U.S.A.*	124	J7
Athens *Tennessee, U.S.A.*	129	K3
Athens *Texas, U.S.A.*	128	E4
Atherstone	53	F2
Atherton	113	K2
Athinai	75	G4
Athlone	59	G6
Athol	115	B6
Atholl, Forest of	57	E4
Atholl, Kap	120	N2
Athos	75	H2
Athy	59	J7
Ati	102	C5
Atiabad	95	P4
Atiamuri	115	F3
Atico	136	C7
Atienza	66	E2
Atikokan	124	E2
Atikonak Lake	121	P7
Atka *U.S.A.*	118	Ad9
Atka *Russia*	85	S4
Atka Island	118	Ad9
Atkarsk	79	H5
Atlacomulco	131	K8
Atlanta *Georgia, U.S.A.*	129	K4
Atlanta *Texas, U.S.A.*	128	E4
Atlantic	124	C6
Atlantic City	125	N7
Atlantic Ocean, North	48	E3
Atlantic Ocean, South	48	F5
Atlin, Lake	118	J4
Atlixco	131	K8
Atmakur	92	E6
Atofinandrahana	109	J4
Atoka	128	D3
Atomainty	109	J3
Atondrazaka	109	J3
Atotonilco	130	H7
Atoyac	131	J9
Atrak	95	N3
Atran	63	E8
Atrato	136	B2
Atrek	95	M3
Atsumi	88	G6
At Taif	96	E6
At Tall al Abyad	77	H4
Attawapiskat *Canada*	121	K7
Attawapiskat *Canada*	121	K7
Attemovsk	84	E6
Attila Line	76	E5
Attleboro	125	Q6
Attleborough	53	J2
Attopeu	93	L6
Attu	118	Ae9
Attu Island	118	Aa9
Attur	92	E6
At Turbah	96	G10
At Tuwayrifah	97	J6
Atuel	139	C7
Atura	107	F2
Atvidaberg	63	G7
Aua Island	114	C2
Auas Mountains	108	C4
Aub	70	D4
Aubagne	65	F7
Aube	64	F4
Aubenas	65	F6
Aubigny-sur-Nere	65	E5
Aubry Lake	118	K2
Auburn *Australia*	113	L4
Auburn *Alabama, U.S.A.*	129	K4
Auburn *California, U.S.A.*	126	B1

Name	Page	Grid
Auburn *Indiana, U.S.A.*	124	H6
Auburn *Maine, U.S.A.*	125	Q4
Auburn *Nebraska, U.S.A.*	124	C6
Auburn *New York, U.S.A.*	125	M5
Aubusson	65	E6
Auca Mahuida	139	C7
Auce	63	K8
Auch	65	D7
Auchavan	57	E4
Auchengray	57	E5
Auchterarder	57	E4
Auckland	115	E2
Auckland Islands	141	M8
Aude	65	E7
Auderville	64	C4
Audierne, Baie 'd	65	A5
Aue	70	E3
Augher	58	H4
Aughnacloy	58	J4
Aughrim *Galway, Ireland*	59	F6
Aughrim *Wicklow, Ireland*	59	K7
Aughton	55	H3
Augsburg	70	D4
Augusta *Australia*	112	D5
Augusta *Georgia, U.S.A.*	129	M4
Augusta *Italy*	69	E7
Augusta *Kansas, U.S.A.*	128	D2
Augusta *Maine, U.S.A.*	125	R4
Augusta *Montana, U.S.A.*	122	H4
Augustine Island	118	E4
Augustow	71	K2
Augustus, Mount	112	D3
Auletta	69	E5
Aulia	103	F4
Aulitiving Island	120	N4
Aulne	64	B4
Aultbea	56	C3
Aultgrish	65	E6
Aupalak	121	N6
Aurangabad	92	E5
Auray	65	B5
Aurdal	63	C6
Aure *Norway*	62	B5
Aure *Norway*	62	C5
Aurich	70	B2
Aurillac	65	E6
Aurkuning	90	E6
Aurora *Colorado, U.S.A.*	123	M8
Aurora *Illinois, U.S.A.*	124	F6
Aurora *Missouri, U.S.A.*	124	D8
Aurora *Nebraska, U.S.A.*	123	R7
Au Sable	124	J4
Auskerry Sound	56	F1
Aust-Agder	63	D7
Austin *Minnesota, U.S.A.*	124	D5
Austin *Nevada, U.S.A.*	126	D1
Austin *Texas, U.S.A.*	128	D5
Austin, Lake	112	D4
Australia	110	F6
Australian Capital Territory	113	K6
Austria	68	D2
Austurhorn	62	X12
Autazes	136	F4
Authie	64	D3
Autlan	130	G8
Autun	65	F5
Auvergne *Australia*	112	G2
Auvergne *France*	65	E6
Auxerre	65	E5
Avallon	65	E5
Avanos	76	F3
Avare	138	G4
Avas	75	H2
Avcilar	76	C2
Avebury	53	F3
Aveiro *Portugal*	66	B2
Aveiro *Portugal*	66	B2
Avellino	69	E5
Avelon Peninsula	121	R8
Aversa	69	E5
Aves, Isla de	133	R7
Avesnes	64	E3
Avesta	63	G6
Aveyron	65	E6
Avezzano	69	D4
Avgo	75	H5
Aviemore	57	E3
Aviemore, Lake	115	C6
Avigliano	69	E5
Avignon	65	F7
Avila	66	D2
Avila, Sierra de	66	D2
Aviles	66	D1
Avisio	68	C2
Aviz	66	C3
Avlum	63	C8
Avoca *Australia*	113	J6
Avoca *Iowa, U.S.A.*	124	C6
Avola	69	E7
Avon *Devon, U.K.*	52	D4
Avon *Hampshire, U.K.*	53	F4
Avon *U.K.*	52	E3
Avon *U.K.*	52	E3
Avonmouth	52	E3
Avon Park	129	M7
Avon Water	57	D5
Avranches	64	C4
Avrig	73	H3
Avuavu	114	K6
Awaji-shima	89	E8
Awali	97	K3
Awanui	115	D1
Awarik, Uruq al	96	H7
Awarua Point	115	A6
Awa-shima	89	G6
Awash Wenz	103	H5
Awaso	104	E4
Awatere	115	D4
Awbari	101	H3
Aweil	102	E6
Awe, Loch	57	C4
Awful, Mount	115	B6
Awgu	105	G4
Awjilah	101	K2
Axbridge	52	E3
Axe *Dorset, U.K.*	52	E4
Axe *Somerset, U.K.*	52	E3
Axel-Heiberg Island	120	H2
Axim	104	E5
Axios	75	G2
Ax-les-Thermes	65	D7
Axminster	52	D4
Ayabe	89	E8
Ayacucho *Argentina*	139	E7
Ayacucho *Peru*	136	C6
Ayaguz	86	F2
Ayamonte	66	C4
Ayan *Russia*	84	H5
Ayan *Russia*	85	P5
Ayancik	76	F2
Ayas	76	E3
Ayaviri	136	C6
Ayayei	96	C10
Aya-Yenahin	104	E4
Aybasti	77	G2
Aydarkul , Ozero	86	B3
Aydere	95	N2
Aydin	76	B4
Aydinca	77	G2
Aydincik	76	E4
Aydin Daglari	76	C3
Ayerbe	67	F1
Ayers Rock	112	G4
Ayeshka	84	E6
Ayia Anna	75	G3
Ayia Marina	75	J5
Ayios	75	G4
Ayios Andreas	75	G4
Ayios Evstratios	75	H3
Ayios Kirikos	75	J4
Ayios Nikolaos *Greece*	75	F3
Ayios Nikolaos *Greece*	75	H5
Ayios Petros	75	F3
Aykathonisi	75	J4
Aykhal	84	J3
Aylesbury	53	G3
Ayllon	66	E2
Aylmer, Lake	119	P3
Aylsham	53	J2
Ayn al Bayda	77	G5
Ayni	86	B4
Ayn Tarfawi	77	K5
Ayn, Wadi al	97	M5
Ayod	102	F6
Ayon	85	V3
Ayon, Ostrov	85	V3
Ayora	67	F3
Ayr *U.K.*	57	D5
Ayr *U.K.*	57	D5
Ayranci	76	E4
Ayre, Point of	54	E2
Aysgarth	55	H2
Ayshirak	86	C2
Aytos	73	J4
Ayun	97	L8
Ayutthaya	93	K6
Ayvacik	76	B3
Ayvali	76	D4
Azambuja	66	B3
Azamgarh	92	F3
Azaran	94	H3
Azaz	77	G4
Azazga	67	J4
Azbine	101	G5
Azerbaijan	79	H7
Azezo	96	C10
Azogues	136	B4
Azoum	102	D5
Azov, Sea of	79	F6
Azovskoye More	79	F6
Azpeitia	66	E1
Azraq, Bahr el	103	F5
Azrou	100	D2
Aztec	127	H2
Azuaga	66	D3
Azuari	137	G3
Azuero, Peninsula de	132	G11
Azul *Argentina*	139	E7
Azul *Mexico*	131	Q9
Azul, Cordillera	136	B5
Azur, Cote d'	65	G7
Azvaday	76	E2
Az Zabadani	77	G6
Az Zafir	96	E7
Az Zahran	97	K3
Az Zarqa	97	L4
Az Zawiyah	101	H2
Az Zaydiyah	96	F9
Az Zilfi	96	G3
Az Zubaydiyah	94	G5
Az Zubayr	94	H6
Az Zuhrah	96	F9
Az Zuqur	96	F9

B

Name	Page	Grid
Baaba	114	W16
Baalbek	77	G5
Baamonde	66	C1
Baardheere	107	H2
Babadag	73	K3
Babaeski	76	B2
Babahoyo	136	B4
Babai Gaxun	87	J3
Baba, Koh-i-	92	C2
Babar	91	H7
Babar, Kepulauan	91	H7
Babayevo	78	F4
Babbacombe Bay	52	D4
Babelthuap	91	J4
Babine Lake	118	K5
Babo	114	A2
Babol	95	L3
Babol Sar	95	L3
Baboua	102	B6
Babstovo	88	D1
Babushkin	84	H6
Babuyan *Philippines*	91	F4
Babuyan *Philippines*	91	G2
Babuyan Channel	91	G2
Babuyan Islands	91	G2
Bacabal	137	J4
Bacan	91	H6
Bacau	73	J2
Baccegalhaldde	62	J2
Back	119	R2
Backa	63	E6
Backaland	56	F1
Backa Topola	72	E3
Backe	62	G5
Bac Ninh	93	L4
Bacolod	91	G3
Bacup	55	G3
Badagara	92	E6
Badajoz	66	C3
Badalona	67	H2
Badanah	94	E6
Bad Aussee	68	C3
Badby	53	F2
Bad Doberan	70	D1
Bad Ems	70	B3
Baden	68	B2
Baden-Baden	70	C4
Badenoch	57	D4
Badgastein	68	D2
Bad Homburg	70	C3
Badiet esh Sham	94	D5
Bad Ischl	68	D2
Bad Kissingen	70	D3
Bad Kreuznach	70	B4
Bad Lands	123	N4
Bad Mergentheim	70	C4
Badminton	52	E3
Bad Neustadt	70	D3
Bad Oldesloe	70	D2
Ba Don	93	L5
Badong	93	M2
Badrah	94	G5
Badr Hunayn	96	D5
Bad Segeberg	70	D2
Bad Tolz	70	D5
Badulla	92	F7
Bad Wildungen	70	C3
Badzhal	85	N6
Badzhalskiy Khrebet	85	N6
Bae Can	93	L4
Baena	66	D4
Baeza	136	B4
Bafa Golu	76	B4
Bafang	105	H4
Bafata	104	C3
Baffin	120	H3
Baffin Bay *Canada*	120	N3
Baffin Bay *U.S.A.*	128	D7
Baffin Island	120	L3
Bafia	105	H5
Bafing Makana	100	C6
Bafoulabe	100	C6
Bafoussam	105	H4
Bafq	95	M6
Bafra	77	F2
Bafra Burun	77	F2
Baft	95	N7
Bafwasende	106	E2
Bagamoya	107	G4
Bagan Datuk	90	C5
Bagansiapiapi	90	C5
Baganyuvam	78	K2
Bagaryak	84	Ad5
Bagdad	126	F3
Bagdere	77	J3
Bage	138	F6
Bagenalstown	59	J7
Baggs	123	L7
Baghdad	77	L6
Bagherhat	93	G4
Bagheria	69	D6
Baghlan	95	C1
Bagh nam Faoilean	56	A3
Bagisli	77	L4
Bagneres-de-Bigorre	65	D7
Bagneres-de-Luchon	65	D7
Bagnoles-de-l'Orne	64	C4
Bagnolo Mella	68	C3
Bagoe	104	D3
Bagrationovsk	71	J1
Bagshot	53	G3
Baguio	91	G2
Bagusa	114	B2
Bahamas	132	J2
Baharampur	93	G4
Bahau	90	C5
Bahaur	90	E6
Bahawalpur	92	D3
Bahce	77	G4
Bahia	137	J6
Bahia Blanca	139	D7
Bahia Bustamante	139	C9
Bahia, Islas de la	132	D6
Bahia Kino	126	G6
Bahia Laura	139	C9
Bahia Negra	138	E4
Bahias, Cabo dos	139	C8
Bahr	96	E7
Bahr, Abu	97	J6
Bahraich	92	F3
Bahrain	97	K3
Bahrain, Gulf of	97	K4
Bahr Sayqal	77	G6
Bahu Kalat	95	Q9
Baia de Maputo	109	F5
Baia Mare	73	G2
Baian, Band-i-	92	C2
Baiao	137	H4
Baiazeh	95	M5
Baibokoum	102	C6
Baicheng *Jilin, China*	87	N2
Baicheng *Xinjiang Uygur Zizhiqu, China*	86	E3
Baie Comeau	125	R2
Baie-du-Poste	121	M7
Baiji	77	K5
Baiju	87	N5
Baikal, Lake	84	H6
Baile Atha Cliath	59	K6
Baile Herculane	73	G3
Bailieborough	58	J5
Baillie Hamilton Island	120	H2
Baillie Island	118	C1
Bailundo	106	C5
Baimuru	114	C3
Bainbridge	129	K5
Bain-de-Bretagne	65	C5
Baing	91	G8
Bains-les-Bains	65	G4
Baird Inlet	118	C3
Baird Mountains	118	C2
Baird Peninsula	120	L4
Bairin Youqi	87	M3
Bairin Zuoqi	87	M3
Bairnsdale	113	K6
Baise	65	D7
Baixingt	87	N3
Baiyanghe	86	F3
Baja	72	E2
Baja, Punta	126	E6
Bajgiran	95	P3
Bajil	96	F9
Bajmok	72	E3
Bakchar	84	C5
Bakel	104	C3
Baker *Chile*	139	B9
Baker *California, U.S.A.*	126	E3
Baker *Montana, U.S.A.*	123	M4
Baker *Oregon, U.S.A.*	122	F5
Baker Foreland	119	S3
Baker Island	111	T1
Baker Lake	119	R3
Baker, Mount	122	D3
Bakersfield	126	C3
Bakewell	55	H3
Bakharden	95	N2
Bakhardok	95	P2
Bakharz	95	P4
Bakhchisaray	79	E7
Bakhmach	79	E5
Bakhta	84	D4
Bakhtaran	94	H4
Bakhtegan, Daryacheh-ye	95	L7
Bakhty	86	F2
Bakinskikh Komissarov	95	M2
Bakir	76	B3
Bakkafjordur	62	X11
Bakkafloi	62	X11
Bakkagerdi	62	Y12
Baklan	76	C4
Bako	103	G6
Bakongan	90	B5
Bakony	72	D2
Bakouma	102	D6
Baku	79	H7
Bakwanga	106	D4
Bala	52	D2
Bala	76	E3
Balabac	91	F4
Balabac Strait	90	F4
Balabio	114	W16
Bala, Cerros de	136	D6
Balacita	73	G3
Balad	77	L6
Baladch	95	K3
Balagannoye	85	R5
Balaghat	92	F4
Balaghat Range	92	E5
Balaguer	67	G2
Balaikarangan	90	E5
Balaka	107	F5
Balakhta	84	E5
Balakleya	79	F6
Balakovo	79	H5
Bala Lake	52	D2
Balama	109	G2
Balambangan	91	F4
Bala Morghab	95	R4
Balangir	92	F4

Name	Page	Grid
Balashov	79	G5
Balassagyarmat	72	E1
Balaton	72	D2
Balatonszentgyorgy	72	D2
Balazote	66	E3
Balbi, Mount	114	E3
Balboa	132	H10
Balbriggan	58	K5
Balcarce	139	E7
Balchik	73	K4
Balchrick	56	C2
Balclutha	115	B7
Bald Knob	128	G3
Baldock	53	G3
Baleares, Islas	67	H3
Balearic Islands	67	H3
Baleia, Ponta da	137	K7
Baleine, Grande Riviere de la	121	L6
Baleine, Riviere a la	121	N6
Baler	91	G2
Balerno	57	E5
Balestrand	63	B6
Baley	85	K6
Balfes Creek	113	K3
Balfour	56	F1
Balguntay	86	F3
Balhaf	97	J10
Bali	90	F7
Baligrod	71	K4
Balikesir	76	B3
Balik Golu	77	K3
Balikpapan	90	F6
Bali, Laut	90	F7
Balimbing	91	F4
Balimo	114	C3
Balinqiao	87	M3
Balintang Channel	91	G2
Balkashino	84	Ae6
Balkh	92	C1
Balkhash	86	C2
Balkhash, Ozero	86	C2
Balladonia	112	E5
Ballaghaderreen	58	E5
Ballandean	113	L4
Ballangen	62	G2
Ballantrae	57	C5
Ballao	69	B6
Ballarat	113	J6
Ballard, Lake	112	E4
Ballasalla	54	E2
Ballash	92	F4
Ballater	57	E3
Balle	100	D5
Ballenas, Bahia de	126	F7
Ballenas, Canal de las	126	F6
Balleny Islands	141	L5
Ballia	92	F3
Ballina	58	D4
Ballinafad	58	F4
Ballinamore	58	G4
Ballinasloe	59	F6
Ballincollig	59	E9
Ballindine	58	E5
Ballineen	59	E9
Ballinhassig	59	E9
Ballinluig	57	E4
Ballinskelligs Bay	59	B9
Ball Peninsula	120	K5
Ballsh	74	E2
Ballybay	58	J4
Ballybofey	58	G3
Ballybunion	59	C7
Ballycastle Ireland	58	D4
Ballycastle U.K.	58	K2
Ballyclare	58	L3
Ballycotton Bay	59	G9
Ballycroy	58	C4
Ballydesmond	59	D8
Ballyduff	59	C8
Ballygalley Head	58	L3
Ballygawley	58	H4
Ballygowan	58	L4
Ballyhaunis	58	E5
Ballyheige	59	C8
Ballyheige Bay	59	C8
Ballyhooly	59	F8
Ballyjamesduff	58	H5
Ballykeel	58	H3
Ballylongford	59	D7
Ballymahon	59	G5
Ballymena	58	K3
Ballymoe	58	F5
Ballymoney	58	J2
Ballymore Eustace	59	J6
Ballymote	58	E4
Ballynahinch	58	L4
Ballyquintin Point	58	M4
Ballyragget	59	H7
Ballyshannon	58	F3
Ballysitteragh	59	B8
Ballyteige Bay	59	J8
Ballyvaghan Bay	59	D6
Ballyvourney	59	D9
Ballywater	58	M3
Balmedie	56	F3
Balonne	113	K4
Balotra	92	D3
Balrampur	92	F3
Balranald	113	J5
Bals	73	H3
Balsas Brazil	137	H5
Balsas Mexico	131	J8
Balsas Peru	136	B5
Balsta	63	G7

Name	Page	Grid
Balta	79	D6
Baltanas	66	D2
Baltasound	56	A1
Baltic Sea	63	G9
Baltim	102	F1
Baltimore	125	M7
Baltinglass	59	J7
Baluchistan	92	C3
Balurghat	93	G3
Balvicar	57	C4
Balya	76	B3
Balykshi	79	J6
Bam	95	N3
Bam	95	P7
Bama	105	H3
Bamako	100	D6
Bamba	102	D6
Bambari	102	D6
Bamberg U.S.A.	129	M4
Bamberg W.Germany	70	D4
Bambesa	106	E2
Bamenda	105	H4
Bami	95	N2
Bamian	92	C2
Bam Posht	95	R8
Bampton	53	F3
Bampur	95	Q8
Banaba	111	Q2
Banadia	133	M11
Banagher	59	G6
Banalia	106	E2
Banam	93	L6
Ban Aranyaprathet	93	K6
Banas	92	E3
Banas, Ras	96	C5
Bana, Wadi	96	G10
Banaz	76	C3
Banbridge	58	K4
Banbury	53	F2
Banchory	57	F3
Bancroft	125	M4
Banda	92	F3
Banda Aceh	90	B4
Banda Elat	91	J7
Banda, Kepulauan	91	H6
Banda, Laut	91	H7
Bandama Blanc	104	D4
Bandan Kuh	95	Q6
Banda, Punta la	126	D5
Bandar Abbas	95	N8
Bandarbeyla	103	K6
Bandar-e Anzali	94	J3
Bandar-e Deylam	95	K6
Bandar-e Lengeh	95	M8
Bandar e Mashur	94	J6
Bandar-e Moghuyeh	95	M8
Bandar-e Rig	95	K7
Bandar-e Torkeman	95	M3
Bandar Khomeyni	94	J6
Bandar Seri Begawan	90	E5
Bande	66	C1
Band-e-pay	95	L3
Bandiagara	100	E6
Bandirma	76	B2
Bandol	65	F7
Bandon Ireland	59	E9
Bandon Ireland	59	E9
Bandundu	106	C3
Bandung	90	D7
Baneh	94	G4
Banes	133	K4
Banff Canada	122	G2
Banff U.K.	56	F3
Banfora	104	E3
Bangalore	92	E6
Bangangte	105	H4
Bangassou	102	D7
Bangeta, Mount	114	D3
Banggai	91	G6
Banggai, Kepulauan	91	G6
Banggi	91	F4
Banghazi	101	K2
Bangka	90	D6
Bangkalan	90	E7
Bangkaru	90	B5
Bangka, Selat	90	D6
Bangko	90	D6
Bangkok	93	K6
Bangkok, Bight of	93	K6
Bangladesh	93	G4
Bangor Down, U.K.	58	L3
Bangor Gwynedd, U.K.	54	E3
Bangor U.S.A.	125	R4
Bangor Erris	58	C4
Bang Saphan Yai	93	J6
Bangui Central African Rep.	102	C7
Bangui Philippines	91	G2
Bangweulu, Lake	107	E5
Bangweulu Swamps	107	E5
Ban Hat Yai	93	K7
Ban Houei Sai	93	K4
Bani	100	D6
Bani	133	M5
Baniara	114	D3
Banika	114	J6
Bani Khatmah	96	G7
Bani Maarid	96	H7
Bani Walid	101	H2
Baniyas	94	B5
Baniyas	94	B4
Bani´Zaynan, Hadh	97	J6
Banja Luka	72	D3
Banjarmasin	90	E6

Name	Page	Grid
Banjul	104	B3
Banka Banka	113	G2
Ban Kantang	93	J7
Ban Keng Phao	93	L6
Bankfoot	57	E4
Ban Khemmarat	93	L5
Ban Khok Kloi	93	J7
Banks Island Australia	114	C4
Banks Island British Columbia, Canada	118	J5
Banks Island NW.Territories, Canada	119	L1
Banks Islands	111	Q4
Banks Peninsula	115	D5
Banks, Point	118	E4
Banks Strait	113	K7
Ban Kui Nua	93	J6
Bankura	93	G4
Bankya	73	G4
Ban Mae Sariang	93	J5
Banmauk	93	J4
Ban Me Thuot	93	L6
Bann	58	K3
Ban Nabo	93	L5
Ban Na San	93	J7
Bannockburn	108	E4
Bannu	92	D2
Banolas	67	H1
Banovce	71	H4
Ban Pak Chan	93	J6
Ban Sao	93	K5
Banska Bystrica	71	H4
Banska Stiavnica	71	H4
Bansko	73	G5
Banstead	53	G3
Banswara	92	D4
Bantaeng	91	F7
Ban Takua Pa	93	J7
Ban Tan	93	K6
Banteer	59	E8
Ban Tha Sala	93	J7
Bantry	59	D9
Bantry Bay	59	C9
Banya	73	H4
Banyak, Kepulauan	90	B5
Banyo	105	H4
Banyuls	65	E7
Banyuwangi	90	E7
Banzyville	106	D2
Baoding	87	M4
Baofeng	93	M2
Baoji	93	L2
Baoqing	88	D2
Baoshan	93	J4
Baoting	93	L5
Baotou	87	L3
Baoxing	88	C1
Bapatla	92	F5
Bapaume	64	E3
Baqubah	77	L6
Bar Ukraine	73	J1
Bar Yugoslavia	77	E1
Bara	102	F5
Baraawe	107	H2
Barabai	90	F6
Bara Banki	92	F3
Barabinsk	84	B5
Barabinskaya Step	84	B6
Baracoa	133	K4
Baraganul	73	J3
Barahona	133	M5
Barail Range	93	H3
Baraka	96	C8
Barakkul	84	Ae6
Baram	90	E5
Baran	92	E3
Barang, Dasht-i-	95	Q5
Barankul	84	Ae6
Baranof Island	118	H4
Baranovichi	71	L2
Baraoltului, Muntii	73	H2
Barapasai	114	B2
Barat Daya, Kepulauan	91	H7
Barbacena	138	H4
Barbados	133	T6
Barbas, Cap	100	B4
Barbastro	67	G1
Barberton South Africa	108	F5
Barberton U.S.A.	125	K6
Barbezieux	65	C6
Barbuda	133	S6
Barcaldine	113	K3
Barcelona Spain	67	H2
Barcelona Venezuela	136	E2
Barcelonnette	65	G6
Barcelos Brazil	136	E4
Barcelos Portugal	66	B2
Barcin	71	G2
Barcoo	113	J3
Barcs	72	D3
Barda	79	H7
Bardai	102	C3
Bardas Blancas	139	C7
Barddhaman	93	G4
Bardejov	71	J4
Bardneshorn	62	Y12
Bardney	55	J3
Bardsey Island	52	C2
Bareilly	92	E3
Barentsevo More	78	F2
Barentsoya	80	D2
Barents Sea	78	F2
Barentu	103	G4
Bareo	90	F5

Name	Page	Grid
Barfleur, Point de	64	C4
Barford	53	F2
Bargrennan	57	D5
Barguzinskiy Khrebet	84	H6
Barh	92	G3
Barhaj	92	F3
Bari	53	J3
Bar Harbor	125	R4
Bari	69	F5
Baridi, Ra's	96	C4
Barika	67	J5
Barinas	136	C2
Baring, Cape	119	M1
Baripada	92	G4
Bari Sadri	92	D4
Barisal	93	H4
Barisan, Pegunungan	90	C6
Barito	90	E6
Barka	97	N5
Barkan, Ra's-e	95	J7
Barking	53	H3
Barkley Sound	122	B3
Barkly East	108	E6
Barkly Tableland	113	H2
Barkol	86	F3
Barkston	53	G2
Barle	52	D3
Bar-le-Duc	64	F4
Barlee, Lake	112	D4
Barlestone	53	F2
Barletta	69	F5
Barmby Moor	55	J3
Barmer	92	D3
Barmouth	52	D2
Barnard Castle	55	H2
Barnaul	84	C6
Barnes Ice Cap	120	M3
Barnet	53	G3
Barnhart	127	M5
Barnoldswick	55	G3
Barnsley	55	H3
Barnstaple	52	C3
Barnstaple Bay	52	C3
Baro	105	G4
Baroda	92	D4
Barony, The	56	E1
Barquilla	66	D3
Barquinha	66	B3
Barquisimeto	136	D1
Barra Brazil	137	J6
Barra U.K.	57	A4
Barra do Bugres	138	E3
Barra do Corda	137	H5
Barra Head	57	A4
Barra Mansa	138	H4
Barranca Peru	136	B4
Barranca Venezuela	133	L10
Barrancabermeja	136	C2
Barrancas	133	R10
Barrancos	66	C3
Barranqueras	138	E5
Barranquilla	136	C1
Barra, Sound of	57	A3
Barre	125	P4
Barreiras	137	H6
Barreiro	66	B3
Barren Island, Cape	110	L10
Barren Islands	118	E4
Barren River Lake	124	H8
Barretos	138	G4
Barrhead Canada	119	N5
Barrhead U.K.	57	F4
Barrhill	57	D5
Barrie	125	L4
Barrier, Cape	115	E2
Barriere	122	D2
Barrington Tops	113	L5
Barrocao	138	H3
Barrow Argentina	139	D7
Barrow Ireland	59	H8
Barrow U.S.A.	118	D1
Barrowford	55	G3
Barrow-in-Furness	55	F2
Barrow Islands	112	D3
Barrow, Point	118	D1
Barrow Range	112	F4
Barrow Strait	120	G3
Barry	52	D3
Barry's Bay	125	M4
Barsalpur	92	D3
Barsi	92	E5
Barstow	126	D3
Bar-sur-Aube	64	F4
Bar-sur-Seine	64	F4
Barth	70	E1
Bartica	136	F2
Bartin	76	E2
Bartle Frere, Mount	113	K2
Bartlesville	128	D2
Barton Philippines	91	F3
Barton U.S.A.	125	P4
Barton-upon-Humber	55	J3
Bartoszyce	71	J1
Barumun	90	C5
Barus	90	B5
Baruun Urt	87	L2
Barvas	56	B2
Barwani	92	D4
Barwon	113	K4
Barysh	79	H5
Basaidu	95	M8
Basankusu	106	C2
Basco	91	G1
Bascunan, Cabo	138	B5

Name	Page	Ref
Basel	68	A2
Basento	69	F5
Bashakerd, Kuhha-ye	95	P8
Bashi Haixia	87	N7
Basht	95	K6
Basilan *Philippines*	91	G4
Basilan *Philippines*	91	G4
Basildon	53	H3
Basingstoke	53	F3
Baskale	77	L3
Baskatong, Reservoir	125	N3
Baskil	77	H3
Baskoy	77	K2
Basle	68	A2
Basoko	106	D2
Bassano del Grappa	68	C3
Bassar	104	F4
Bassas da India	109	G4
Bassein	93	H5
Bassenthwaite	55	F2
Bassenthwaite Lake	55	F2
Basse Santa Su	104	C3
Basseterre	133	R6
Basse Terre	133	S6
Bassett	123	Q6
Bassila	105	F4
Bass Strait	113	K6
Bastad	63	E8
Bastak	95	M8
Bastam	95	M3
Basti	92	F3
Bastia	69	B4
Bastogne	64	F4
Bastrop *Louisiana, U.S.A.*	128	G4
Bastrop *Texas, U.S.A.*	128	D5
Basyurt	77	J3
Bata	105	G5
Batabano, Golfo de	132	F3
Batagay	85	N3
Batagay-Alyta	85	N3
Batakan	90	E6
Bataklik Golu	76	E4
Batala	92	E2
Batalha	66	B3
Batamay	85	M4
Batan	91	G1
Batang	93	J2
Batangafo	102	C6
Batangas	91	G3
Batanghari	90	C6
Batan Islands	91	G1
Batatais	138	G4
Batavia	125	L5
Bataysk	79	F6
Batchelor	112	G1
Batesville	128	G3
Bath *U.K.*	52	E3
Bath *U.S.A.*	125	M5
Batha	102	C5
Bathgate	57	E5
Bathurst *Australia*	113	K5
Bathurst *Canada*	125	T3
Bathurst *The Gambia*	104	B3
Bathurst Inlet	119	P2
Bathurst Island	112	G1
Bathurst Islands	120	F2
Batie	104	E4
Batiki	114	R8
Batinah, Al	97	N4
Batin, Wadi al	96	H2
Batiscan	125	P3
Batitoroslar	76	D4
Batlaq-e Gavkhuni	95	L5
Batley	55	H3
Batman *Turkey*	77	J4
Batman *Turkey*	77	J4
Batna	101	G1
Baton Rouge	128	G5
Batouri	105	H5
Batroun	77	F5
Batsfjord	62	N1
Battambang	93	K6
Batticaloa	92	F7
Battle *Canada*	119	N5
Battle *U.K.*	53	H4
Battle Creek	124	H5
Battle Harbour	121	Q7
Battle Mountain	122	F7
Batu	103	G6
Batubetumbang	90	D6
Batum	77	J2
Batumi	77	J2
Batu Pahat	90	C5
Batuputih	91	F5
Baturaja	90	D6
Baturite	137	K4
Baubau	91	G7
Bauchi	105	G3
Bauda	92	F4
Baudette	124	C2
Baudo	136	B2
Baudouinville	107	E4
Bauge	65	C5
Bauhinia Downs	113	K3
Baukau	91	H7
Bauld, Cape	121	Q7
Baumann Fjord	120	J2
Baunie	113	L4
Baurtregaum	59	C8
Bauru	138	G4
Baus	138	F3
Bautzen	70	F3
Bawdeswell	53	J2
Bawdsey	53	J2
Bawean	90	E7
Bawiti	102	E2
Bawku	104	E3
Bawtry	55	H3
Baxley	129	L5
Bayamo	132	J4
Bayamon	133	P5
Bayan	88	A2
Bayan-Aul	84	B6
Bayandalay	87	J3
Bayanday	84	H6
Bayan Harshan	93	J2
Bayanhongor	86	J2
Bayan Mod	87	J3
Bayan Obo	87	K3
Bayano, Laguna	132	H10
Bayan-Ondor	86	H3
Bayantsagaan	86	H3
Bayantsogt	87	K2
Bayan-Uul	87	L2
Bayard *Nebraska, U.S.A.*	123	N7
Bayard *New Mexico, U.S.A.*	127	H4
Bayat *Turkey*	76	D3
Bayat *Turkey*	76	F2
Bayburt	77	J2
Bay City *Michigan, U.S.A.*	124	J5
Bay City *Texas, U.S.A.*	128	E6
Baydaratskaya Guba	84	Ae3
Baydhabo	107	H2
Baydon	53	F3
Bayerischer Wald	70	E4
Bayeux	64	C4
Bayfield	124	E3
Bayhan al Qasab	96	G9
Bayindir	76	B3
Bayir	94	C6
Baykadam	86	B3
Baykal	84	G6
Baykalovo	84	Ae5
Baykal, Ozero	84	H6
Baykan	77	J3
Bay-Khak	84	E6
Baykit	84	F4
Baynunah	97	L5
Bayombong	91	G2
Bayona	66	B1
Bayonne	65	C7
Bayo Point	91	G3
Bayram-Ali	95	R3
Bayramic	76	B3
Bayramiy	94	J2
Bayramtepe	76	C2
Bayreuth	70	D4
Bayrut	76	F6
Bay Saint Louis	128	H5
Bayt al Faqih	96	F9
Baytown	128	E6
Bayy al Kabir, Wadi	101	H2
Baza	66	E4
Bazaliya	71	M4
Bazar-Dyuzi	79	H7
Bazaruto, Ilha do	109	G4
Bazas	65	C6
Bazman	95	Q8
Bazman, Kuh-e-	95	Q7
Bcharre	77	F5
Beach	123	N4
Beachy Head	53	H4
Beaconsfield	53	G3
Beadnell Bay	55	H1
Beagh, Lough	58	G2
Beagle Gulf	112	G1
Beagle Reef	112	E2
Beal	57	G5
Bealanana	109	J2
Beaminster	52	E4
Beampingaratra	109	J4
Bear	122	J6
Beara Peninsula	59	C9
Beardmore	124	G2
Beardstown	124	E6
Bear Island *Canada*	121	K7
Bear Island *Ireland*	59	C9
Bear Lake	122	J7
Bearley	53	F2
Bearn	65	C7
Bear Paw Mount	122	K3
Bearsden	57	D5
Beartooth Range	123	K5
Beata, Cabo	133	M6
Beata, Isla	133	M6
Beatrice	123	R7
Beatty	126	D2
Beattyville	125	M2
Beau Basin	109	L7
Beaucaire	65	F7
Beaufort *Malaysia*	90	F4
Beaufort *U.S.A.*	129	M4
Beaufort Sea	118	H1
Beaufort West	108	D6
Beaugency	65	D5
Beauly *U.K.*	56	D3
Beauly *U.K.*	56	D3
Beauly Firth	56	D3
Beaumaris	54	E3
Beaumont *France*	64	E4
Beaumont *California, U.S.A.*	126	D4
Beaumont *Texas, U.S.A.*	128	E5
Beaune	65	F5
Beaurepaire	65	F6
Beauvais	64	E4
Beauvoir-sur-Mer	65	B5
Beaver *Saskatchewan, Canada*	119	P5
Beaver *Yukon, Canada*	118	K3
Beaver Dam *Kentucky, U.S.A.*	124	G8
Beaver Dam *Wisconsin, U.S.A.*	124	F5
Beaverhill Lake	119	N5
Beawar	92	D3
Beazley	139	C6
Bebedouro	138	G4
Bebington	55	F3
Beccles	53	J2
Becej	72	F3
Becerrea	66	C1
Bechar	100	E2
Becharof Lake	118	D4
Bechet	73	G4
Beckingham	55	J3
Beckley	125	K8
Beclean	73	H2
Bedale	55	H2
Bedarieux	65	E7
Bede, Point	118	E4
Bedford *U.K.*	124	G7
Bedford *U.S.A.*	53	G2
Bedford Level	53	H2
Bedfordshire	53	G2
Bedlington	55	H1
Bedwas	52	D3
Bedworth	53	F2
Beer Sheva	94	B6
Beeston	53	F2
Beeswing	57	E5
Beeville	128	D6
Befale	106	D2
Befandriana	109	J3
Begejska Kanal	72	F3
Begoml	63	N10
Behbehan	95	K6
Behraamkale	76	B3
Behshahr	95	L3
Beian	87	P2
Beibu Wan	93	L4
Beihai	93	L4
Beijing	87	M4
Beila	100	B5
Beinn a' Ghlo	57	E4
Beinn Bheigier	57	B5
Beinn Dearg *Highland, U.K.*	56	D3
Beinn Dearg *Tayside, U.K.*	57	E4
Beinn Dorain	57	D4
Beinn Eighe	56	C3
Beinn Fhada	56	C3
Beinn Ime	57	D4
Beinn Mhor	56	A3
Beinn na Caillich	57	C3
Beinn Resipol	57	C4
Beinn Sgritheall	57	C3
Beipiao	87	N3
Beira	109	F3
Beirut	76	F6
Bei Shan	86	H3
Beit Lahm	94	B6
Beius	73	G2
Beja	66	C3
Beja	101	G1
Bejaia	101	G1
Bejaia, Golfe de	67	J4
Bejar	66	D2
Bejestan	95	P4
Beji	92	C3
Bekdast	79	J7
Bekescsaba	73	F2
Bekily	109	J4
Bekopaka	109	H3
Bekwai	104	E4
Bela India	92	F3
Bela Pakistan	92	C3
Belabo	105	H5
Belaga	90	E5
Belang	91	G5
Bela Palanka	73	G4
Bela Vista	109	F5
Belawan	90	B5
Belaya *Russia*	78	K4
Belaya *Russia*	85	W3
Belaya-Kalitva	79	G6
Belaya Kholunitsa	78	J4
Belayan	90	F5
Belaya Tserkov	79	E6
Belcher Channel	120	G2
Belcher Islands	121	L6
Belchiragh	94	S4
Belchite	67	F2
Belcoo	58	G4
Belderg	58	C4
Belebey	78	J5
Beledweyne	103	J7
Belem	137	H4
Belen *Turkey*	76	E4
Belen *U.S.A.*	127	J3
Belep, Iles	114	V15
Belesar, Embalse de	66	C1
Belev	79	F5
Belfast *New Zealand*	115	D5
Belfast *U.K.*	58	L3
Belfast Lough	58	L3
Belfield	123	N4
Belford	57	G5
Belfort	65	G5
Belgaum	92	D5
Belgium	64	E3
Belgorod	79	F5
Belgorod-Dnestrovskiy	79	E6
Belgrade	72	F3
Belgrano	141	X3
Belica	71	L2
Beli Lom	73	J4
Beli Manastir	72	E3
Belimbing	90	C7
Belin	65	C6
Belinskiy	79	G5
Belinyu	90	D6
Belitsa	73	G5
Belitung	90	D6
Belize	132	C6
Belkina, Mys	88	F3
Belknap, Mount	122	H8
Belkovskiy, Ostrov	85	P1
Bella Bella	118	K5
Bellac	65	D5
Bella Coola	118	K5
Bellaire	128	E6
Bellary	92	E5
Bella Vista *Argentina*	138	C5
Bella Vista *Argentina*	138	E5
Belleek	58	F4
Bellefontaine	124	J6
Belle Fourche *South Dakota, U.S.A.*	123	N5
Belle Fourche *Wyoming, U.S.A.*	123	M5
Belle Glade	129	M7
Belle Ile	65	B5
Belle Isle	121	Q7
Belleme	64	D4
Belleville *Canada*	125	M4
Belleville *Illinois, U.S.A.*	124	F7
Belleville *Kansas, U.S.A.*	123	R8
Bellevue *Idaho, U.S.A.*	122	G6
Bellevue *Washington, U.S.A.*	122	C4
Belley	65	F6
Bellingham *U.K.*	57	F5
Bellingham *U.S.A.*	122	C3
Bellinghaussen Sea	141	U5
Bellingshausen	141	W6
Bellinzona	68	B2
Bello	136	B2
Bellona Island	114	J7
Bellona Reefs	111	N6
Bellpuig	67	G2
Bellshill	57	D5
Belluno	68	D2
Bell Ville	138	D6
Belly	122	H3
Belmont	56	A1
Belmonte *Portugal*	66	C2
Belmonte *Spain*	66	E3
Belmopan	132	C6
Belmullet	58	B4
Belogorsk	79	E6
Belogorsk	71	M4
Belogradchik	73	G4
Belo Horizonte	138	K4
Beloit	124	F5
Belokorovichi	79	D5
Belorado	66	E1
Belorechensk	79	F7
Beloren	76	E4
Belorussia	71	L2
Belorusskaya Gryada	71	L2
Belot, Lac	118	K2
Belo-Tsiribihina	109	H3
Belousovka	84	C6
Belovo	84	D6
Beloye More	78	F2
Beloye Ozero	78	F3
Belozersk	78	F4
Belozerskoye	84	Ae5
Belper	55	H3
Belsay	57	G5
Belterra	137	F4
Belton	55	J3
Beltsy	73	J2
Belturbet	58	H4
Belukha, Gora	86	F2
Belvedere Marittimo	69	E6
Belvidere	124	F5
Belvoir, Vale of	53	G2
Belyando, River	113	K3
Belyayevka	73	L2
Belyy, Ostrov	85	A2
Belyy Yar	84	D5
Belzyce	71	K3
Bemaraha, Plateau du	109	J3
Bembridge	53	F4
Bemidji	124	C3
Benabarre	67	G1
Ben Alder	57	D4
Benalla	113	K6
Benares	92	F3
Benavente	66	D2
Ben Avon	57	E3
Benbaun	59	C5
Ben Chonzie	57	E4
Bencorr	59	C5
Ben Cruachan	57	C4
Bend	122	D5
Bende	105	G4
Bender Qaasim	103	J5
Bendery	79	D6
Bendigo	113	J6
Benesov	70	F4
Benevento	69	E5
Bengbu	87	M5
Benghazi	101	K2
Bengkalis	90	C5
Bengkulu	90	C6
Bengo, Baia do	106	B4
Bengoi	91	J6
Bengtsfors	63	E7

Name	Page	Ref
Benguela	106	B5
Benguerua, Ilha	109	G4
Benha	102	F1
Ben Hope	56	D2
Beni *Bolivia*	136	D6
Beni *Zaire*	107	E2
Beni Abbes	100	E2
Benicarlo	67	G2
Benidorm	67	F3
Beni Mazar	102	F2
Beni Mellal	100	D2
Benin	105	F4
Benin, Bight of	105	F4
Benin City	105	G4
Beni Saf	100	E1
Beni Suef	102	F2
Ben Klibreck	56	D2
Ben Lawers	57	D4
Ben Ledi	57	D4
Ben Lomond	57	D4
Ben Loyal	56	D2
Ben Lui	57	D4
Ben Macdui	57	E3
Ben MorCoigach	56	C3
Ben More *Central, U.K.*	57	D4
Ben More *Strathclyde, U.K.*	56	B4
Ben More Assynt	56	D2
Benmore, Lake	115	C6
Bennachie	56	F3
Benn Cleuch	57	E4
Bennetta, Ostrov	85	R1
Ben Nevis	57	C4
Bennington	125	P5
Benoni	108	E5
Be, Nosy	109	J2
Ben Rinnes	56	E3
Bensheim	70	C4
Benson *U.K.*	53	F3
Benson *U.K.*	126	G5
Ben Starav	57	C4
Bent	95	P8
Bentinck Island	93	J6
Bent Jbail	94	B5
Bentley	55	H3
Benton	128	F3
Benton Harbor	124	G5
Bentung	90	C5
Benue	105	G4
Ben Venue	57	D4
Ben Vorlich	57	D4
Benwee	58	C5
Benwee Head	58	C4
Ben Wyvis	56	D3
Benxi	87	N3
Beo	91	H5
Beograd	72	F3
Beppu	89	C9
Beqa	114	R9
Berat	74	E2
Berau, Teluk	114	A2
Berber	103	F4
Berbera	103	J5
Berberati	102	C7
Berck	64	D3
Berdichev	79	D6
Berdigestyakh	85	M4
Berdyansk	79	F6
Berea	124	H8
Bereeda	103	K5
Beregovo	79	C6
Berens	119	R5
Berens River	119	R5
Bere Regis	52	E4
Berettyo	73	F2
Berettyoujfalu	73	F2
Bereza	71	L2
Berezhany	71	L4
Berezhnykh, Mys	85	Q1
Berezina	78	D5
Berezino	78	D5
Berezna	79	E5
Berezniki	78	K4
Berezno	71	M3
Berezovka *Russia*	78	K3
Berezovka *Russia*	85	K5
Berezovka *Russia*	85	T3
Berezovka *Ukraine*	79	E6
Berezovo *Russia*	84	Ae4
Berezovo *Russia*	85	W4
Berezovskaya	85	K5
Berg	108	C6
Berga	67	G1
Bergama	76	B3
Bergamo	68	B3
Bergeforsen	62	G5
Bergen *E. Germany*	70	E1
Bergen *Norway*	63	J6
Bergen op Zoom	64	F3
Bergerac	65	D6
Bergfors	62	H2
Bergisch-Gladbach	70	B3
Bergsviken	62	J4
Berhala, Selat	90	C6
Beringa, Ostrov	81	T4
Bering Glacier	118	G3
Beringovskiy	85	X4
Bering Sea	143	H3
Bering Strait	118	B2
Berislav	79	E6
Beris, Ra's	95	Q9
Berja	66	E4
Berkak	62	C5
Berkakit	85	L5
Berkeley *U.K.*	52	E3
Berkeley *U.S.A.*	126	A2
Berkhamsted	53	G3
Berkner Island	141	W3
Berkovitsa	73	G4
Berkshire	53	F3
Berkshire Downs	53	F3
Berkshire Mountains	125	P5
Berlevag	62	N2
Berlin *E. Germany*	70	E2
Berlin *U.S.A.*	125	Q4
Bermeja, Sierra	66	D4
Bermejo *Argentina*	138	C6
Bermejo *Argentina*	138	D4
Bermeo	66	E1
Bermillo de Sayago	66	C2
Bermuda	117	N5
Bern	68	A2
Bernau	70	E2
Bernay	64	D4
Bernburg	70	D3
Berne	68	A2
Berner Alpen	68	A2
Berneray *U.K.*	57	A4
Berneray *U.K.*	56	A3
Bernina, Piz	68	B2
Beroroha	109	J4
Berounka	70	E4
Berre, Etang de	65	F7
Berriedale	56	E2
Berriedale Water	56	E2
Berrigan	113	K6
Berringarra	112	D4
Berrouaghia	67	H4
Berry *Australia*	113	L5
Berry *France*	65	E5
Berryessa, Lake	122	C8
Berry Head	52	D4
Berry Islands	132	J1
Bershad	73	K1
Berthoud Pass	123	L8
Bertoua	105	H5
Beru	111	S2
Beruri	136	E4
Berwick	125	M6
Berwick-upon-Tweed	57	F5
Berwyn Mountains	52	D2
Berzence	72	D2
Besalampy	109	H3
Besancon	65	G5
Besar, Kai	91	J7
Besbre	65	E5
Beshneh	95	M7
Besiri	77	J4
Beskidy Zachodnie	71	H4
Beslan	79	G7
Besni	77	G4
Bessarabia	73	K2
Bessarabka	73	K2
Bessbrook	58	K4
Bessemer *Alabama, U.S.A.*	129	J4
Bessemer *Winconsin, U.S.A.*	124	F3
Bestamak *Kazakhstan*	86	D2
Bestamak *Kazakhstan*	79	K6
Bestobe	84	A6
Bestuzhevo	78	G3
Betafo	109	J3
Betanzos	66	B1
Betare Oya	105	H4
Bethal	108	E5
Bethanie	108	C5
Bethany	124	C6
Bethel	118	C3
Bethel Park	125	L6
Bethesda *U.K.*	54	E3
Bethesda *U.S.A.*	125	M7
Bethlehem *Israel*	94	B6
Bethlehem *South Africa*	108	E5
Bethulie	108	E6
Bethune *France*	64	D4
Bethune *France*	64	E3
Betioky	109	H4
Betpak-Dala	86	B2
Bet-Pak-Data	86	B2
Betroka	109	J4
Betsiamites	125	R2
Betsiboka	109	J3
Bettiah	92	F3
Bettyhill	56	D2
Betul	92	E4
Betwa	92	E4
Betws-y-coed	54	F3
Beuvron	65	D5
Beverley *Australia*	112	D5
Beverley *U.K.*	55	J3
Beverly Hills	126	C3
Bexhill	53	H4
Beykoz	76	C2
Beyla	104	D4
Beylul	96	F10
Beyneu	79	K6
Beypazari	76	D2
Beypinar	77	G3
Beysehir	76	D4
Beysehir Golu	76	D4
Beyton	53	H2
Beytussebap	77	K4
Bezhetsk	78	F4
Beziers	65	E7
Bezmein	95	P2
Bhadgaon	92	G3
Bhadrachalam	92	F5
Bhadrakh	92	G4
Bhadravati	92	E6
Bhagalpur	92	G3
Bhakkar	92	D2
Bhamo	93	J4
Bhandara	92	E4
Bhanrer Range	92	F4
Bharatpur *Pradesh, India*	92	F4
Bharatpur *Rajasthan, India*	92	E3
Bharuch	92	D4
Bhatinda	92	D2
Bhatpara	93	G4
Bhavnagar	92	D4
Bhawanipatna	92	F5
Bhilwara	92	D3
Bhima	92	E5
Bhiwani	92	E3
Bhopal	92	E4
Bhopalpatnam	92	F5
Bhor	92	D5
Bhubaneshwar	92	G4
Bhuj	92	C4
Bhumiphol Dam	93	J5
Bhusawal	92	E4
Bhutan	93	G3
Bia	136	D4
Biaban	95	N8
Biabanak	95	S5
Biak	91	H5
Biala Podlaska	71	K2
Bialobrzegi	71	J3
Bialowieza	71	K2
Bialystok	71	K2
Bianco	69	F6
Biankouma	104	D4
Biaro	91	H5
Biarritz	65	C7
Biasca	68	B2
Biba	102	F2
Bibai	88	H4
Bibala	106	B5
Bibby Island	119	S3
Biberach	70	C4
Bibury	53	F3
Bicester	53	F3
Bicheno	113	K7
Bickle Knob	125	L7
Bida	105	G4
Bidar	92	E5
Biddeford	125	Q5
Biddulph	55	G3
Bidean Nam Bian	57	C4
Bideford	52	C3
Bideford Bay	52	C3
Bidford-on-Avon	53	F2
Bidokht	95	P4
Bidzhan *Russia*	88	C1
Bidzhan *Russia*	88	C2
Biebrza	71	K2
Biel	68	A2
Bielefeld	70	C2
Biella	68	B3
Bielsko-Biala	71	H4
Bielsk Podlaski	71	K2
Bien Hoa	93	L6
Bienne	68	A2
Bienveneu	137	G3
Bienville, Lac	121	M6
Biferno	69	E5
Biga	76	B2
Bigadic	76	C3
Big Bay	114	T11
Big Belt Mountains	122	J4
Big Blue	123	R7
Bigbury Bay	52	D4
Biggar *Canada*	123	K1
Biggar *U.K.*	57	E5
Biggleswade	53	G2
Big Horn	123	K5
Big Horn Mountains	123	L5
Big Island	120	M5
Big Pine	126	C2
Big Piney	123	J6
Big Sheep Mountains	123	L4
Big Sioux	123	R5
Big Snowy Mount	122	K4
Big Spring	127	M4
Big Stone Gap	124	J8
Big Timber	123	J5
Big Trout Lake	119	T4
Bihac	72	C3
Bihar	92	G4
Bihar	92	G3
Biharamulo	107	F3
Bihoro	88	K4
Bihu	87	M6
Bijagos, Arquipelago dos	104	B3
Bijapur	92	E5
Bijar	94	H4
Bijeljina	72	E3
Bijelo Polje	72	E4
Bijie	93	L3
Bijnor	92	E3
Bikaner	92	D3
Bikin *Russia*	88	E2
Bikin *Russia*	88	F2
Bikoro	106	C3
Bilad Bani Bu Ali	97	P5
Bilad Ghamid	96	E6
Bilad Zahran	96	E6
Bilaspur	92	F4
Bilauktaung Range	93	J6
Bilbao	66	E1
Bilchir	85	J6
Bilecik	76	C2
Biled	73	F3
Bile Karpaty	71	G4
Bilesha Plain	107	H2
Bilgoraj	71	K3
Bili	106	E2
Bilin	93	J5
Billabalong	112	D4
Billericay	53	H3
Billingham	55	H2
Billings	123	K5
Billingshurst	53	G3
Bilma	101	H5
Bilma, Grand Erg de	101	H5
Biloela	113	L3
Bilo Gora	72	D3
Biloxi	128	H5
Biltine	102	D5
Bilugyun	93	J5
Binalud, Kuh-e	95	P3
Binatang	90	E5
Binder	87	L2
Bindloe Island	136	A7
Bindura	108	F3
Binefar	67	G2
Binga	108	E3
Bingara	113	L4
Bingerville	104	E4
Bingham	125	R4
Binghamton	125	N5
Bingley	55	H3
Bingol	77	J3
Bingol Daglari	77	J3
Binjai *Indonesia*	90	B5
Binjai *Indonesia*	90	D5
Binongko	91	G7
Bintan	90	C5
Bintuhan	90	C6
Bintulu	90	E5
Bin Xian *Heilongjiang, China*	88	A3
Bin Xian *Shaanxi, China*	93	L2
Binyang	93	L4
Bio	114	K7
Biobio	139	B7
Biograd	72	C4
Bioko	105	G5
Bir	92	E5
Bira *Russia*	88	D1
Bira *Russia*	88	D1
Bira *Russia*	85	P7
Birag, Kuh-e	95	Q8
Birak	101	H3
Bir al Hisw	96	E4
Bir al War	101	H4
Birao	102	D5
Biratnagar	93	G3
Bir Butayman	77	H4
Birca	73	G4
Birch Island	122	D2
Birch Mountains	119	N4
Bird	119	S4
Bird Island	133	R7
Birdlip	53	E3
Birdum	113	G2
Birecik	77	G4
Bireun	90	B4
Bir Fardan	97	J5
Bir Ghabalou	67	H4
Bir Hadi	97	K7
Birhan	103	G5
Birikchul	84	D6
Birjand	95	P5
Birkenhead *New Zealand*	115	E2
Birkenhead *U.K.*	55	F3
Birksgate Range	112	F4
Birlad *Romania*	73	J2
Birlad *Romania*	73	J2
Birlestik	86	B2
Birmingham *U.K.*	53	F2
Birmingham *U.S.A.*	129	J4
Bir Moghrein	100	C3
Birnie Island	111	U2
Birni Kebbi	105	F3
Birni nKonni	101	G6
Birobidzhan	88	D1
Birofeld	88	D1
Birr	59	G6
Bir, Ras el	103	H5
Birreencorragh	58	C5
Birrimbah	112	G2
Birsk	78	K4
Birtle	123	P2
Birtley	55	H2
Biryusa	84	F5
Birzai	63	L8
Biscay, Bay of	65	B6
Bischofshofen	68	D2
Biscotasi Lake	124	J3
Bisert	78	K4
Bisevo	72	D4
Bisha	96	C9
Bishah, Wadi	96	F6
Bishkek	86	C3
Bishnupur	93	G4
Bishop	126	C2
Bishop Auckland	55	H2
Bishop Burton	55	J3
Bishop's Castle	52	D2
Bishops Falls	121	Q8
Bishop's Stortford	53	H3
Bishri, Jbel	77	H5
Biskra	101	G2
Biskupiec	71	J2
Bislig	91	H4
Bismarck Archipelago	114	D2
Bismarck Range	114	D3
Bismark	123	P4

Bismil 77 J4
Bismo 63 C6
Bisotun 94 H4
Bispfors 62 G5
Bissau 104 B3
Bissett 123 S2
Bistcho Lake 119 M4
Bistretu 73 G4
Bistrita *Romania* 73 H2
Bistrita *Romania* 73 J2
Bistritei, Muntii 73 H2
Bitburg 70 B3
Bitche 64 G4
Bitik 79 J5
Bitkine 102 C5
Bitlis 77 K3
Bitola 73 F5
Bitonto 69 F5
Bitterfontein 108 C6
Bitterroot 122 G4
Bitterroot Range 122 G4
Bitti 69 B5
Biu 105 H3
Bivolu 73 H2
Biwa-ko 89 E8
Biyad, Al 96 H5
Biyagundi 96 C9
Biysk 84 D6
Bizerta 69 B7
Bizerte 101 G1
Bjargtangar 62 S12
Bjelovar 72 D3
Bjerkvik 62 L2
Bjorklinge 63 G6
Bjorksele 62 H4
Bjorna 62 H5
Bjorneborg *Finland* 63 J6
Bjorneborg *Sweden* 63 F7
Bjornevatn 62 N2
Bjornoya 80 C2
Bjurholm 62 H5
Bjursas 63 F6
Bla Bheinn 56 B3
Black *Alaska, U.S.A.* 118 G2
Black *Arizona, U.S.A.* 127 H4
Black *Arkansas, U.S.A.* 128 G3
Black *New York, U.S.A.* 125 N5
Blackadder Water 57 F5
Blackall 113 K3
Black Bay 124 F2
Black Belt 129 J4
Blackburn 55 G3
Black Canyon City 126 F3
Blackdown Hills 52 D4
Blackfoot 122 H6
Blackford 57 E4
Black Head 59 D6
Blackhead Bay 59 D6
Blackhill 55 H3
Black Hills 123 N5
Black Isle 56 D3
Black Mesa 126 G2
Blackmill 52 D3
Black Mountain 52 D3
Black Mountains 52 D3
Blackpool 55 F3
Black Range 127 J4
Black River Falls 124 E4
Blackrock 58 K5
Black Rock Desert 122 E7
Black Sea 51 P7
Blacksod Bay 58 B4
Blackstairs Mount 59 J7
Blackstairs Mountains 59 J7
Blackthorn 53 F3
Black Volta 104 E4
Black Water 57 E4
Blackwater *Australia* 113 K3
Blackwater *Meath, Ireland* 58 J5
Blackwater *Waterford, Ireland* 59 F8
Blackwater *Essex, U.K.* 53 H3
Blackwater *Hampshire, U.K.* 53 G3
Blackwaterfoot 57 C5
Blackwater Lake 119 L3
Blackwater Reservoir *Highland, U.K.* 57 D4
Blackwater Reservoir *Tayside, U.K.* 57 E4
Blackwell 128 D2
Blackwood 112 D5
Blaenavon 52 D3
Blafjall 62 W12
Blagodarnyy 79 G6
Blagoevgrad 73 G4
Blagoveshchensk *Russia* 78 K4
Blagoveshchensk *Russia* 85 M6
Blagoyevo 78 H3
Blair Atholt 57 E4
Blairgowrie 57 E4
Blaka 101 H4
Blakely 129 K5
Blakeney 53 J2
Blakesley 53 F2
Blanca, Bahia 139 D7
Blanca, Costa 67 F3
Blanca Peak 127 K2
Blanca, Punta 126 E6
Blanca, Sierra 127 K4
Blanc, Cap 69 B7
Blanche Channel 114 H6
Blanche, Lake 113 H4
Blanchland 55 G2
Blanc, Mont 65 G6
Blanco 136 E7
Blanco, Cabo 139 C9
Blanco, Cape 122 B6
Blanda 62 V12
Blandford Forum 53 E4
Blanes 67 H2
Blangy 64 D4
Blankenberge 64 E3
Blanquilla, Isla 136 E1
Blantyre 107 G6
Blarney 59 E9
Blasket Islands 59 A8
Blavet 65 B5
Blaydon 55 H2
Blaye 65 C6
Bleadon 52 E3
Bleaklow Hill 55 H3
Bled 72 C2
Blekinge 63 F8
Bletchley 53 G3
Bleus, Monts 107 F2
Blida 101 F1
Bligh Water 114 R8
Blind River 124 J3
Blisworth 53 G2
Block Island 125 Q6
Bloemfontein 108 E5
Blois 65 D5
Blonduos 62 U12
Bloodvein 123 R2
Bloody Foreland 58 F2
Bloomfield 124 D6
Bloomington *Illinois, U.S.A.* 124 F6
Bloomington *Indiana, U.S.A.* 124 G7
Bloomington *Minnesota, U.S.A.* 124 D4
Bloomsbury 113 K3
Blouberg 108 E4
Blubberhouses 55 H3
Bludenz 68 B2
Bluefield 125 K8
Bluefields 132 F9
Blue Mountain Lake 125 N5
Blue Mountain Peak 132 J5
Blue Mountains 122 E5
Bluemull Sound 56 A1
Bluenose Lake 119 M2
Blue Ridge 129 K3
Blue Ridge Mountains 129 L3
Blue Stack 58 F3
Blue Stack Mountains 58 F3
Bluff *New Zealand* 115 B7
Bluff *U.S.A.* 127 H2
Bluff Knoll 112 D5
Bluff Point 112 C4
Bluff, Punta 126 F6
Blumenau 138 G5
Blunt 123 Q5
Blyth *Northumberland, U.K.* 55 H1
Blyth *Nottinghamshire, U.K.* 55 H3
Blyth *Suffolk, U.K.* 53 J2
Blythe 126 E4
Blythe Bridge 53 E2
Blytheville 128 H3
Bo 104 C4
Boac 91 G3
Boa Fe 136 C5
Boa Vista *Cape Verde* 104 L7
Boa Vista *Amazonas, Brazil* 136 D4
Boa Vista *Roraima, Brazil* 136 E3
Bobai 93 M4
Bobaomby, Tanjoni 109 J2
Bobbili 92 F5
Bobbio 68 B3
Bobo Dioulasso 104 E3
Bobolice 71 G2
Bobr 70 F3
Bobrinents 79 E6
Bobrka 71 L4
Bobrov 79 G5
Bobruysk 79 D5
Bobures 133 M10
Boca del Pao 136 E2
Boca do Acre 136 D5
Boca Grande 136 E2
Bocaiuva 138 H3
Boca Mavaca 136 D3
Bocaranga 102 C6
Boca Raton 129 M7
Bochnia 71 J4
Bocholt 70 B3
Bochum 70 B3
Bodalla 113 L6
Bodaybo 85 J5
Boddam 56 A2
Boden 62 J4
Bodensee 70 C5
Bodhan 92 E5
Bodmin 52 C4
Bodmin Moor 52 C4
Bodo 62 F3
Bodrum 76 B4
Bodva 71 J4
Bodza, Pasul 73 J3
Boen 65 F6
Boende 106 D3
Boffa 104 C3
Bogalusa 128 H5
Bogan 113 K5
Bogaz 76 E2
Bogazkale 76 F2
Bogazkaya 77 F2
Bogazkopru 76 F3
Bogazliyan 76 F3
Bogbonga 106 C2
Bogen 62 L2
Boggeragh Mountains 59 E8
Boghar 67 H5
Bogia 114 D2
Bognes 62 G2
Bognor Regis 53 G4
Bogo 91 G3
Bogodukhov 79 F5
Bogong, Mount 113 K6
Bogor 90 D7
Bogorodchany 71 L4
Bogorodskoye *Russia* 78 J4
Bogorodskoye *Russia* 85 Q6
Bogota 136 C3
Bogotol 84 D5
Bogra 93 G4
Boguchany 84 F5
Boguchar 79 G6
Bogue 100 C5
Bogue Chitto 128 G5
Boguslav 79 E6
Bo Hai 87 K4
Bohemia 70 E4
Bohmer Wald 70 E4
Bohol 91 G4
Bohol Sea 91 G4
Boiano 69 E5
Boigul 114 C3
Boipeba, Ilha 137 K6
Bois Blanc Island 124 H4
Boisdale, Loch 57 A3
Boise *U.S.A.* 122 F6
Boise *U.S.A.* 122 F6
Boise City 127 L2
Bois, Lac des 118 K2
Boissevain 123 P3
Boizenburg 70 D2
Bojana 74 E2
Bojnurd 95 N3
Boka 73 F3
Boka Kotorska 72 E4
Boke 104 C3
Bokhara 113 K4
Boknafjord 63 A7
Bokol 107 G2
Bokoro 102 C5
Boksitogorsk 78 E4
Boktor 85 P6
Bokungu 106 D3
Bolama 104 B3
Bolanos 130 H7
Bolan Pass 92 C3
Bolbec 64 D4
Bolchary 84 Ae5
Bole 104 E4
Boleslawiec 70 F3
Bolgatanga 104 E3
Bolgrad 79 D6
Boli 88 C3
Bolia 106 C3
Boliden 62 J4
Bolinao 91 F2
Bol Irgiz 79 H5
Bolivar 139 D7
Bolivar *Missouri, U.S.A.* 124 D8
Bolivar *Tennessee, U.S.A.* 128 H3
Bolivar, Cerro 133 R11
Bolivar, Pico 133 M10
Bolivia 138 C3
Boljevac 73 F4
Bolkhov 79 F5
Bollington 55 G3
Bollnas 63 G6
Bollon 113 K4
Bollstabruk 62 G5
Bolmen 63 E8
Bolobo 106 C3
Bologna 68 C3
Bologoye 78 E4
Bolotnoye 84 C5
Boloven, Cao Nguyen 93 L5
Bolsena, Lago di 69 C4
Bolsherechye 84 A5
Bolsheretsk 85 T6
Bolshevik 85 R4
Bolshevik, Ostrov 81 M2
Bolshezemelskaya Tundra 78 K2
Bolshoy Anyuy 85 U3
Bolshoy Atlym 84 Ae4
Bolshoy Balkhan, Khrebet 95 M2
Bolshoy Begichev, Ostrov 84 J2
Bolshoy Chernigovka 79 J5
Bolshoy Kavkaz 77 L1
Bolshoy Kunyak 84 A5
Bolshoy Lyakhovskiy, Ostrov 85 Q2
Bolshoy Murta 84 E5
Bolshoy Pit 84 E5
Bolshoy Porog 84 E3
Bolshoy Shantar, Ostrov 85 P5
Bolshoy Usa 78 K4
Bolshoy Yenisey 84 E6
Bolshoy Yugan 84 A5
Bolsover 55 H3
Boltana 67 G1
Bolt Head 52 D4
Bolton *Greater Manchester, U.K.* 55 G3
Bolton *Northumberland, U.K.* 57 G5
Bolu 76 D2
Bolucan 77 G3
Bolus Head 59 B9
Bolvadin 76 D3
Bolyarovo 73 J4
Bolzano 68 C2
Bom 114 D3
Boma 106 B4
Bombala 113 K6
Bombay 92 D5
Bomili 106 E2
Bom Jesus 137 J5
Bom Jesus da Lapa 137 J6
Bomlafjord 63 A7
Bomlo 63 A7
Bomongo 106 C2
Bonab 94 H3
Bonaire 133 N8
Bonaire Trench 133 N9
Bona, Mount 118 G3
Bonar Bridge 56 D3
Bonavista 121 R8
Bonavista Bay 121 R8
Bon, Cap 101 H1
Bondo 106 D2
Bondokodi 91 F7
Bondoukou 104 E4
Bone 69 A7
Bo'ness 57 E4
Bonete, Cerro 138 C5
Bone, Teluk 91 G6
Bongabong 91 G3
Bongor 102 C5
Bonham 128 D4
Bonifacio 69 B5
Bonifacio, Strait of 69 B5
Bonn 70 B3
Bonners Ferry 122 F3
Bonnetable 64 D4
Bonneval 64 D4
Bonneville 65 G5
Bonneville Salt Flats 122 H7
Bonnie Rock 112 D5
Bonny *France* 65 E5
Bonny *Nigeria* 105 G5
Bonnyrigg 57 E5
Bono 69 B5
Bonobono 91 F4
Bonorva 69 B5
Bonthe 104 C4
Bontoc 91 G2
Booligal 113 J5
Boologooro 112 C3
Boone *Iowa, U.S.A.* 124 D5
Boone *N. Carolina, U.S.A.* 129 M2
Booneville *Mississippi, U.S.A.* 128 H3
Booneville *New York, U.S.A.* 125 N5
Booroorban 113 J5
Boosaaso 103 J5
Boothia, Gulf of 120 J4
Boothia Peninsula 120 H3
Bootle 55 F3
Boot Reefs 114 C3
Bopeechee 113 H4
Boquilla, Presa de la 127 K7
Boquillas del Carmen 127 L6
Bor *Sudan* 102 F6
Bor *Turkey* 76 F4
Bor *Yugoslavia* 73 G3
Boraha, Nosy 109 J3
Borah Peak 122 H5
Boras 63 E8
Borasambar 92 F4
Borazjan 95 K7
Borba 136 F4
Borborema, Planalto da 137 K5
Borca 73 H2
Borcka 77 J2
Bordeaux 65 C6
Borden Island 120 D2
Borden Peninsula 120 K3
Borders 57 F5
Bordertown 113 J6
Bordeyri 62 U12
Bordj-Bou-Arreridj 67 J4
Bordj Bounaama 67 G5
Bordj Omar Driss 101 G3
Borensberg 63 F7
Boreray 56 A3
Borga 63 L6
Borgarnes 62 U12
Borgefjellet 62 E4
Borger 127 M3
Borgholm 63 G8
Borgo San Lorenzo 68 C4
Borgosesia 68 B3
Borgo Val di Taro 68 B3
Borgo Valsugana 68 C2
Borislav 71 K4
Borisoglebsk 79 G5
Borisov 63 Q9
Borispol 79 E5
Borja 67 F2
Borkovskaya 78 H2
Borkum 70 B2
Borlange 63 F6
Borlu 76 C3
Bormida 68 B3
Bormio 68 C2
Borneo 90 E5
Bornholm 70 F1
Bornholmsgattet 63 F9
Bornova 76 B3
Borohoro Shan 86 E3
Boroko 91 G5
Boromo 104 E3
Boronga Islands 93 H5
Borongan 91 H3
Borovichi 78 E4
Borovlyanka 84 C6
Borovsk 78 K4
Borovskoye 84 Ad6

Name	Page	Grid
Borrika	113	J6
Borris	59	J7
Borrisokane	59	F7
Borrisoleigh	59	G7
Borroloola	113	H2
Borrowdale	55	F2
Borshchev	73	J1
Borshchovochnyy Khrebet	85	J6
Borth	52	C2
Borujen	95	K6
Borujerd	94	J5
Borve	57	A4
Borzhomi	77	K2
Borzya	85	K7
Bosa	69	B5
Bosanski Brod	72	E3
Bosanski Novi	72	D3
Bosanski Petrovac	72	D3
Boscastle	52	C4
Bose	93	L4
Bos Gradiska	72	D3
Boshruyeh	95	N5
Bosilegrad	73	G4
Boskovice	71	G4
Bosna	72	E3
Bosnik	114	B2
Bosobolo	106	C2
Boso-hanto	89	H8
Bosphorus	76	C2
Bossambele	102	C6
Bossangoa	102	C6
Bossier City	128	F4
Bostan Iran	94	H6
Bostan Pakistan	92	C2
Bostanabad	94	H3
Bosten Bagrax Hu	86	F3
Boston U.S.A.	53	G2
Boston U.S.A.	125	Q5
Boston Mountains	128	E3
Botesdale	53	J2
Botev	73	H4
Botevgrad	73	G4
Bothel	55	F2
Bothnia, Gulf of	62	J5
Botna	73	K2
Botosani	73	J2
Botsmark	62	J4
Botswana	108	D4
Botte Donato	69	F6
Bottenhavet	63	H6
Bottenviken	62	K4
Bottesford	53	G2
Bottineau	123	P3
Bottisham	53	H2
Bottrop	70	B3
Botucatu	138	G4
Bouafle	104	D4
Bouake	104	D4
Bouar	102	C6
Bouarfa	100	E2
Boucant Bay	113	G1
Bouchegouf	69	A7
Bougainville	114	E3
Bougainville, Cape	112	F1
Bougainville Reef	113	K2
Bougainville Strait	114	J5
Bougaroun, Cap	101	G1
Bougie	67	J4
Bougouni	100	D6
Bougzdul	67	H5
Bouhalloufa	67	G4
Bouillon	64	F4
Bouira	67	H4
Bou Ismail	67	H4
Boujdour	100	C3
Bou Kadir	67	G4
Boulay	64	G4
Boulder	123	M8
Boulder City	126	E3
Boulogne-sur-Mer	64	D3
Boumbe I	102	C7
Boumbe II	102	C7
Boumo	102	C6
Bouna	104	E4
Boundiali	104	D4
Boung Long	93	L6
Boun Tai	93	K4
Bountiful	122	J7
Bounty Islands	111	S11
Bourail	114	W16
Bourbon-l'Archambault	65	E5
Bourbonnais France	65	E5
Bourbonnais U.S.A.	124	G6
Bourbonne-les-Bains	65	F5
Bourem	100	E5
Bourganeuf	65	D6
Bourg-en-Bresse	65	F5
Bourges	65	E5
Bourgogne	65	F5
Bourgogne, Canal de	65	E5
Bourg-Saint-Andeol	65	F6
Bourke	113	K5
Bourne	53	G2
Bournemouth	53	F4
Bou Saada	101	F1
Boussac	65	E5
Bousso	102	C5
Boutilimit	100	C5
Boves	68	A3
Bovey	52	D4
Bovey Tracy	52	D4
Bovingdon	53	G3
Bovino	69	E5
Bow	122	H2

Name	Page	Grid
Bowbells	123	N3
Bowen	113	K3
Bowers Bank	118	Ab9
Bowes	55	G2
Bowfell	55	F2
Bowie	128	D4
Bow Island	122	J3
Bowkan	94	H3
Bowland, Forest of	55	G2
Bowling Green Kentucky, U.S.A.	124	G8
Bowling Green Ohio, U.S.A.	124	J6
Bowman	123	N4
Bowman Bay	120	M4
Bowness	55	G2
Bowness-on-Solway	55	F2
Bowraville	113	L5
Boxford	53	H2
Bo Xian	93	N2
Boxing	87	M4
Box Tank	113	J5
Boyabat	76	F2
Boyang	87	M6
Boyarka	84	F2
Boyd Lake	119	Q3
Boyer	124	C6
Boyle	58	F5
Boyne	58	K5
Boynton Beach	129	M7
Boyuibe	138	D4
Bozburun	76	C4
Bozcaada	75	H3
Bozdogan	76	C4
Boz Daglari	76	B3
Bozeman	122	J5
Bozen	68	C2
Boze Pole	71	G1
Bozkir	76	E4
Bozkurt	76	E2
Bozoum	102	C6
Bozova	77	H4
Bozqush, Kuh-e	94	H3
Bozuyuk	76	D3
Bra	68	A3
Brabant Island	141	V6
Brabourne	53	H3
Brac	72	D4
Bracadale	56	B3
Bracadale, Loch	56	B3
Bracciano	69	D4
Bracke	62	F5
Brackley	53	F2
Bracknell	53	G3
Brad	73	G2
Bradano	69	F5
Bradda Head	54	E2
Bradenton	129	L7
Bradford U.K.	55	H3
Bradford U.S.A.	125	L6
Bradford-on-Avon	52	E3
Bradwell Waterside	53	H3
Brady	127	N5
Brady Mountains	127	N5
Brae	56	A1
Braemar	57	E3
Braemore	56	E2
Braeswick	56	F1
Braga	66	B2
Bragado	139	D7
Braganca	66	C2
Braganca Paulista	138	G4
Bragar	56	B2
Brahman Baria	93	H4
Brahmani	92	G4
Brahmapur	92	F5
Brahmaputra	93	H3
Braidwood	113	K6
Braila	73	J3
Brailsford	53	F2
Brainerd	124	C3
Braintree	53	H3
Braishfield	53	F3
Brake	70	C2
Brakel	70	C3
Brallos	75	G3
Bramdean	53	F3
Bramham	55	H3
Bramming	63	C9
Brampton Canada	125	L5
Brampton U.K.	55	G2
Bramsche	70	B2
Brancaster	53	H2
Brancaster Bay	53	H2
Branco	136	E3
Branco, Cabo	137	L5
Brandberg	108	B4
Brandbu	63	D6
Brande	63	C9
Brandenburg	70	E2
Brandesburton	55	J3
Brandon Canada	123	Q3
Brandon U.S.A.	125	P5
Brandon Bay	59	B8
Brandon Mount	59	B8
Brandon Point	59	B8
Brandval	63	E6
Branesti	73	J3
Braniewo	71	H1
Bran, Pasul	73	H3
Brantford	125	L5
Brantley	129	J5
Brantome	65	D6
Brasileia	136	D6
Brasilia Distrito Federal, Brazil	138	F3

Name	Page	Grid
Brasilia Minas Gerais, Brazil	138	H3
Braslav	63	M9
Brasov	73	H3
Brassey Range	91	F5
Brates, Lacul	73	K3
Bratislava	71	G4
Bratsk	84	G5
Bratslav	73	K1
Braunau	68	D1
Braunsberg	71	H1
Braunschweig	70	D2
Braunton	52	C3
Brava	104	L7
Brava, Costa	67	H2
Bravo del Norte, Rio	127	L6
Brawley	126	E4
Bray	59	K6
Bray Head	59	B9
Bray Island	120	L4
Brazil	137	G5
Brazos	128	D5
Brazzaville	106	C3
Brcko	72	E3
Brda	71	G2
Breadalbane	57	D4
Breaksea Sound	115	A6
Brean	52	D3
Brebes	90	D7
Brechfa	52	C3
Brechin	57	F4
Breckenridge Texas, U.S.A.	128	C4
Breckenridge Minnesota, U.S.A.	124	B3
Breckland	53	H2
Brecknock, Peninsula	139	B10
Breclav	71	G4
Brecon	52	D3
Brecon Beacons	52	D3
Breda	64	F3
Bredon Hill	53	F3
Bredstedt	70	C1
Breezewood	125	L7
Bregenz	68	B2
Bregovo	73	G3
Breidafjordur	62	T12
Brejo	137	J4
Brekken	62	D5
Brekstad	62	C5
Bremen U.S.A.	129	K4
Bremen W. Germany	70	C2
Bremerhaven	70	C2
Bremer Range	112	E5
Bremerton	122	C4
Bremervorde	70	C2
Brendon Hills	52	D3
Brenham	128	D5
Brenig, Llyn	55	F3
Brenish	56	A2
Brenner Pass	68	C2
Breno	68	C3
Brenta	68	C3
Brentford	53	G2
Brentwood U.K.	53	H3
Brentwood U.S.A.	125	P6
Brescia	68	C3
Breskens	64	E3
Breslau	71	G3
Bressanone	68	C2
Bressay	56	A2
Bressay Sound	56	A2
Bressuire	65	C5
Brest France	64	A4
Brest Belorussia	71	K2
Brestlitovsk	79	E5
Brest Litovsk	71	K2
Bretagne	64	B4
Bretcu	73	J2
Breteuil France	64	D4
Breteuil France	64	E4
Breton, Cape	121	Q8
Breton Sound	128	H6
Brett, Cape	115	E1
Breueh	90	B4
Brevoort Island	120	P5
Brewer	125	R4
Brewster	122	E3
Brewton	129	J5
Brezhnev	78	J4
Breznice	70	E4
Brezo, Sierra del	66	D1
Bria	102	D6
Briancon	65	G6
Brianne, Llyn	52	D2
Briare	65	E5
Bribie Island	113	L4
Brichany	73	J1
Bricquebec	53	N7
Bride	54	E2
Bridestowe	52	C4
Bridgend Mid Glamorgan, U.K.	52	D3
Bridgend Strathclyde, U.K.	57	B5
Bridge of Allan	57	E4
Bridge of Gaur	57	D4
Bridge of Orchy	57	D4
Bridge of Weir	57	D5
Bridgeport Alabama, U.S.A.	129	K3
Bridgeport California, U.S.A.	126	C1
Bridgeport Connecticut, U.S.A.	125	P6
Bridgeport Nebraska, U.S.A.	123	N7
Bridgeton	125	N7
Bridgetown Australia	112	D5
Bridgetown Barbados	133	T8
Bridgetown Canada	121	N9

Name	Page	Grid
Bridgewater	121	P9
Bridgnorth	52	E2
Bridgwater	52	D3
Bridgwater Bay	52	D3
Bridlington	55	J2
Bridlington Bay	55	J2
Bridport	52	E4
Brieg	71	G3
Brienne-le-Chateau	64	F4
Brier Island	125	S4
Briey	64	F4
Brig	68	A2
Brigg	55	J3
Brighouse	55	H3
Brightlingsea	53	J3
Brighton	53	G4
Brignoles	65	G7
Brihuega	66	E2
Brikama	104	B3
Brindakit	85	P4
Brindisi	69	F5
Brinian	56	F1
Brinkley	128	G3
Brioude	65	E6
Brisbane	113	L4
Bristol U.K.	52	E3
Bristol U.S.A	125	P6
Bristol Bay	118	D4
Bristol Channel	52	D2
Bristol Lake	126	E3
Bristow	128	D3
British Columbia	118	L4
Brits	108	E5
Britstown	108	D6
Brittle, Lake	57	B3
Brive-la-Gaillarde	65	D6
Briviesca	66	E1
Brixham	52	D4
Brlik	86	C3
Brno	71	G4
Broad	129	M3
Broadback	121	L7
Broad Bay	56	B2
Broad Cairn	57	E4
Broad Haven	58	C4
Broad Hinton	53	F3
Broadhurst Range	112	E3
Broad Sound Australia	113	K3
Broad Sound U.K.	52	B3
Broadstairs	53	J3
Broads, The	53	J2
Broadus	123	M5
Broadway	53	F2
Brochel	56	B3
Brocken	70	D3
Brockenhurst	53	F4
Brock Island	120	D2
Brockman, Mount	112	D3
Brockton	125	Q5
Brod	73	F5
Broddanes	62	U12
Brodeur Peninsula	120	J3
Brodick	57	C5
Brodick Bay	57	C5
Brodnica	71	H2
Brodokalmak	84	Ad5
Brody	79	D5
Brok	71	J2
Broken Bay	113	L5
Broken Bow Nebraska, U.S.A.	123	Q7
Broken Bow Oklahoma, U.S.A.	128	E3
Broken Bow Lake	128	E3
Broken Hill Australia	113	J5
Broken Hill Zambia	107	E5
Bromberg	71	G2
Bromley	53	H3
Bromsgrove	53	E2
Bromyard	52	E2
Bronderslev	63	C8
Bronnoysund	62	E4
Bronte	69	E7
Brookfield	124	D7
Brookhaven	128	G5
Brookings Oregon, U.S.A.	122	B6
Brookings S. Dakota, U.S.A.	123	R5
Brookneal	125	L8
Brooks	122	H2
Brooks Range	118	D2
Brooksville	129	L6
Broome	112	E2
Broom, Loch	56	C3
Brora U.K.	56	D2
Brora U.K.	56	E2
Brosteni	73	G3
Broto	67	F1
Brotton	55	J2
Brou	64	D4
Brough	55	G2
Brough Head	56	E1
Brough Ness	56	F2
Broughshane	58	K3
Broughton	55	E5
Broughton in Furness	55	F2
Broughton Island	120	P4
Broughton Poggs	53	F3
Browerville	124	C3
Brow Head	59	C10
Brownfield	127	L4
Brownhills	53	F2
Browning	122	H3
Brownsville	128	D8
Brownwood	128	C5
Brownwood, Lake	127	N5
Bru	62	Y12

156

Bruar, The Falls of 57 E4
Bruay-en-Artois 64 E3
Bruce Bay 115 B5
Bruce, Mount 112 D3
Bruce Mountains 120 M3
Bruchsal 70 C4
Bruck 68 F1
Bruck an der Mur 68 E2
Brue 52 E3
Bruernish Point 57 A4
Bruges 64 E3
Brugg 68 B2
Brugge 64 E3
Bruhl 70 B3
Bruichladdich 57 B5
Brumado 137 J6
Brumunddal 63 D6
Brunei 90 E4
Brunette Downs 113 H2
Brunflo 62 F5
Brunico 68 C2
Brunkeberg 63 C7
Brunn 71 G4
Brunsbuttel 70 C2
Brunswick *Georgia, U.S.A.* 129 M5
Brunswick *Maine, U.S.A.* 121 N9
Brunswick *Maryland, U.S.A.* 125 M7
Brunswick *W. Germany* 70 D2
Brunswick Bay 112 E2
Brunswick, Peninsula 139 B10
Bruny Island 111 L10
Brusa 76 C2
Brush 123 N7
Brusilovka 79 J5
Brusovo 84 D4
Brussel 64 F3
Bruthen 113 K6
Bruton 52 E3
Bruxelles 64 F3
Bryan *Ohio, U.S.A.* 124 H6
Bryan *Texas, U.S.A.* 128 D5
Bryan, Mount 113 H5
Bryansk 79 E5
Bryanskoye 79 H7
Bryher 52 K5
Bryne 63 D6
Brynmawr 52 D3
Brynzeny 73 J1
Brza Palanka 73 G3
Brzava 73 F3
Brzeg 71 G3
Bua *Fiji* 114 R8
Bua *Sweden* 63 E8
Buala 114 J6
Bubanza 107 E3
Bubiyan 97 J2
Buca *Fiji* 114 R8
Buca *Turkey* 76 B3
Bucak 76 D4
Bucaramanga 136 C2
Buchach 79 D6
Buchan 56 F3
Buchanan 104 C4
Buchanan, Lake 127 N5
Buchan Gulf 120 M3
Buchannan Bay 120 L2
Bucharest 73 J3
Buchholz 70 C2
Buchlgvie 57 D4
Buchloe 70 D4
Buchon, Point 126 B3
Buchs 68 B2
Buckeye 126 F4
Buckfastleigh 52 D4
Buckhannon 125 K7
Buckhaven 57 E4
Buckie 56 F3
Buckingham 53 G3
Buckingham Bay 113 H1
Buckinghamshire 53 G3
Buckkisla 76 E4
Buckley 55 F3
Bucksburn 57 F3
Buck, The 56 F3
Bucuresti 73 J3
Bud 62 B5
Budapest 72 E2
Budardalur 62 U12
Budareyri 62 X12
Budaun 92 E3
Budduso 69 B5
Bude *U.K.* 52 C4
Bude *U.S.A.* 128 G5
Bude Bay 52 B4
Budennovsk 79 G7
Budingen 70 C3
Budir 62 Y12
Budjala 106 C2
Budleigh Salterton 52 D4
Budogoshch 78 E4
Budun 87 K1
Budungbudung 91 F6
Budu, Sabkhat al 97 J5
Buea 105 G5
Buenaventura *Colombia* 136 B3
Buenaventura *Mexico* 127 J6
Buenaventura, Bahia 136 B3
Buena Vista 125 L8
Buena Vista Lake Bed 126 C3
Buenos Aires 139 D6
Buenos Aires, Lago 139 B9
Buffalo *New York, U.S.A.* 125 L5
Buffalo *S. Dakota, U.S.A.* 123 N5
Buffalo *Texas, U.S.A.* 128 D5

Buffalo *Wyoming, U.S.A.* 123 L5
Buffalo Lake 119 M3
Buffalo Narrows 119 P4
Buftea 73 H3
Bug 71 K2
Buga 136 B3
Bugdayli 95 M2
Bugel, Tanjung 90 E7
Bugoynes 62 N2
Bugrino 78 H2
Bugsuk 91 F4
Bugulma 78 J5
Buguruslan 78 J5
Buhl 122 G6
Buhusi 73 J2
Buie, Loch 57 B4
Builth Wells 52 D2
Buin 114 G5
Buinsk 78 H5
Buin Zahra 95 K4
Buitrago del Lozoye 66 E2
Bujaraloz 67 F2
Buje 72 B3
Bujumbura 107 E3
Buk 72 D2
Buka 114 E3
Bukama 106 E4
Bukavu 107 E3
Bukhara 80 H6
Bukittinggi 90 D6
Bukk 72 F1
Bukoba 107 F3
Bukoloto 107 F2
Bula 114 A2
Bulanash 84 Ad5
Bulancak 77 H2
Bulandshahr 92 E3
Bulanik 77 K3
Bulanovo 79 K5
Bulawayo 108 E4
Buldan 76 C3
Buldana 92 E4
Buldir Island 118 Ab9
Buldurty 79 J6
Bulgan *Mongolia* 86 G2
Bulgan *Mongolia* 87 J2
Bulgaria 73 G4
Buliluyan, Cape 91 F4
Bulkeley 55 G3
Bulle 68 A2
Buller 115 C4
Bullhead City 126 E3
Bull Shoals Lake 128 F2
Bulolo 114 D3
Bulum 85 M2
Buma 114 K6
Bumba 106 D2
Buna 74 E2
Bunbeg 58 F2
Bunbury 112 D5
Bunclody 59 J7
Buncrana 58 H2
Bundaberg 113 L3
Bundoran 58 F4
Bungalaut, Selat 90 B6
Bungay 53 J2
Bungo-suido 89 D9
Bunguran Utara, Kepulauan 90 D5
Bunia 107 F2
Bunkie 128 F5
Bunratty 59 E7
Buntingford 53 G3
Buntok 90 E6
Bunyan 77 F3
Buolkalakh 85 K2
Buol Kheyr 95 K7
Buorkhaya, Guba 85 N2
Buorkhaya, Mys 85 N2
Buqayq 97 J2
Buqum, Harrat al 96 F6
Buram 102 E5
Buran 86 F2
Buraydah 96 F3
Burbage 53 F3
Burbank 126 C3
Burco 103 J6
Burdalyk 95 S2
Burdekin 113 K3
Burdur 76 D4
Burdur Golu 76 D4
Bure 53 J2
Burea 62 J4
Burentsogt 87 L2
Bureya *Russia* 85 M7
Bureya *Russia* 85 N6
Burg 70 D2
Burgas 73 J4
Burgdorf 68 A2
Burgeo 121 Q8
Burgersdorp 108 E6
Burgess Hill 53 G4
Burghead 56 E3
Burghead Bay 56 E3
Burgh-le-Marsh 55 K3
Burgos 66 E1
Burgsteinfurt 70 B2
Burgsvik 63 H8
Burguete 67 F1
Burhan Budai Shan 93 J1
Burhaniye 76 B3
Burhanpur 92 E4
Burias 91 G3
Burica, Punta 132 F10
Burin Peninsula 121 Q8

Buri Peninsula 96 D9
Buriram 93 K5
Burj Safita 77 G5
Burke Island 141 S4
Burketown 113 H2
Burkhala 85 R4
Burkina Faso 104 E3
Burley 122 H6
Burli 79 J5
Burlington *Canada* 124 C6
Burlington *Colorado, U.S.A.* 123 N8
Burlington *Iowa, U.S.A.* 124 E6
Burlington *N. Carolina, U.S.A.* 129 N2
Burlington *Vermont, U.S.A.* 125 P4
Burlington *Washington, U.S.A.* 122 C3
Burlton 52 E2
Burlyu-Tobe 86 D2
Burma 93 J4
Burmantovo 78 L3
Burnaby 122 C3
Burneston 55 H2
Burnet 128 C5
Burnham-on-Crouch 53 H3
Burnham-on-Sea 52 E3
Burnie 113 K7
Burnley 55 G3
Burns 122 E6
Burntwood 119 R4
Burqan 97 H2
Burqin 86 F2
Burra 113 H5
Burravoe 56 A1
Burray 56 F2
Burren, The 59 D6
Burriana 67 F3
Burrow Head 54 E2
Burrs Junction 122 F6
Burrundie 112 G1
Burry Port 52 C3
Bursa 76 C2
Bur Safaga 103 F2
Bur Said 103 F1
Bur Sudan 96 C7
Burt, Mount 112 F4
Burton Joyce 53 F2
Burton Lake 121 L7
Burton Latimer 53 G2
Burton upon Stather 55 J3
Burton-upon-Trent 53 F2
Burtrask 62 J4
Buru 91 H6
Burum 97 J9
Burundi 107 E3
Burunnoye 79 J5
Bururi 107 E3
Burwick 56 F2
Bury 55 G3
Burylbaytal 86 C2
Burynshik 79 J6
Bury Saint Edmunds 53 H2
Busayta, Al 96 D1
Bushat 74 E2
Bushehr 95 K7
Bushimaie 106 D4
Bushmills 58 J2
Businga 106 D2
Busira 106 C3
Busk 71 L4
Buskerud 63 C6
Busko 71 J3
Busselton 112 D5
Bussol , Proliv 85 S7
Bustakh, Ozero 85 Q2
Busto Arsizio 68 B3
Busuanga 91 G3
Buta 106 D2
Butare 107 E3
Bute 57 C5
Bute, Sound of 57 C5
Butiaba 107 F2
Butler 125 L6
Butmah 77 K4
Butte 122 H5
Buttermere 55 F2
Butterworth *Malaysia* 90 C4
Butterworth *South Africa* 108 E6
Buttevant 59 E8
Button Islands 121 P5
Butuan 91 H4
Butung 91 G7
Buturlinovka 79 G5
Buulobarde 103 J7
Buurhakaba 107 H2
Buwatah 96 D4
Buxton 55 H3
Buy 78 G4
Buyba 84 E6
Buynaksk 79 H7
Buyr Nuur 87 M2
Buyuk Agri Dagi 77 L3
Buyuklacin 76 F2
Buyuk Menderes 76 C4
Buzancais 65 D5
Buzau *Romania* 73 J3
Buzau *Romania* 73 J3
Buzi 109 F3
Buzovyazy 78 K5
Buzuluk 84 Ae6
Buzuluk 79 J5
Byam Martin, Cape 120 L3
Byam Martin Island 120 F2
Byczyna 71 H3
Bydgoszcz 71 G2

Byers 123 M8
Byfleet 53 G3
Byglandsfjord 63 B7
Bykhov 79 E5
Bykovo *Russia* 79 H6
Bykovo *Russia* 78 H3
Byla Slatina 73 G4
Bylot Island 120 L3
Byrock 113 K5
Byron, Cape 113 L4
Byron, Isla 139 A9
Byrranga, Gory 84 E2
Byrum 63 D8
Byserovo 78 J4
Byske 62 J4
Byskealven 62 J4
Bystra 71 H4
Bystraya 85 T6
Bystrzyca Klodzka 71 G3
Bytantay 85 N3
Bytca 71 H4
Byten 71 L2
Bytom 71 H3
Bytow 71 G1
Byxelkrok 63 G8

C

Caala 106 C5
Caatingas 137 H5
Caballos Mestenos, Llano de los 127 K6
Caballeria, Cabo 67 J2
Cabanatuan 91 G2
Cabano 125 R3
Cabeza de Buey 66 D3
Cabeza Lagarto, Punta 136 B6
Cabezas 138 D3
Cabimas 136 C1
Cabinda *Angola* 106 B4
Cabinda *Angola* 106 B4
Cabo 137 L5
Cabo Colnet 126 D5
Cabo Gracias a Dios, Punta 132 F7
Cabonga, Reservoir 125 M3
Cabool 124 D8
Caboolture 113 L4
Cabora Bassa Dam 109 F3
Cabo Raso 139 C8
Caborca 126 F5
Cabot Strait 121 P8
Cabourg 64 C4
Cabourne 55 J3
Cabrach 56 E3
Cabra del Santo Cristo 66 E4
Cabrera 67 H3
Cabrera, Sierra 66 C1
Cabriel 67 F3
Cabrobo 137 K5
Cabruta 136 D2
Cacak 72 F4
Caceres *Spain* 66 C3
Caceres *Brazil* 138 E3
Caceres *Colombia* 136 B2
Cache Creek 122 C8
Cache Peak 122 H6
Cachimbo 137 G5
Cachimbo, Serra do 137 G5
Cachi, Nevado de 138 C4
Cachoeira 138 K6
Cachoeiro de Itapemirim 138 H4
Cachos, Punta de 138 B5
Cacinci 72 D3
Cacipore, Cabo 137 G3
Cacolo 106 C5
Caconda 106 C5
Cacula 106 B5
Cadadley 103 H6
Cadale 107 J2
Cadaques 67 H1
Cadereyta 128 C8
Cader Idris 52 D2
Cadibarrawirracana, Lake 113 H4
Cadillac *Canada* 123 L3
Cadillac *U.S.A.* 124 H4
Cadi, Sierra del 67 G1
Cadiz 66 C4
Cadiz 91 G3
Cadiz, Baia de 66 C4
Cadiz, Golfo de 66 C4
Caen 64 C4
Caerdydd 52 D3
Caerfyrddin 52 C3
Caergybi 54 E3
Caernarfon 54 E3
Caernarfon Bay 54 E3
Caerphilly 52 D3
Caersws 52 D2
Caetite 137 J6
Cafayate 138 C5
Cagayan 91 G2
Cagayan de Oro 91 G4
Cagayan Islands 91 G4
Cagayan Sulu 91 F4
Cagliari 69 B6
Cagliari, Golfo di 69 B6
Caguan 136 C3
Caguas 133 P5
Cahama 106 B6
Caha Mountains 59 C9
Caherbarnagh 59 D8
Caherciveen 59 B9
Caherconlish 59 F7

Cahir 59 G8
Cahore Point 59 K7
Cahors 65 D6
Caia 109 G3
Caiaponia 138 F3
Caibarien 132 H3
Cai Be 93 L6
Caicos Islands 133 M4
Caicos Passage 133 L3
Cairndow 57 D4
Cairn Gorm 57 E3
Cairngorm Mountains 57 E3
Cairnryan 54 D2
Cairns 113 K2
Cairn Water 57 E5
Cairo *Egypt* 102 F1
Cairo *U.S.A.* 124 F8
Caiundo 106 C6
Caiwarro 113 J4
Cajamarca 136 B5
Cajapio 137 J4
Cajatambo 136 B6
Cajati 138 G4
Cajazeiras 137 K5
Cakiralan 77 F2
Cakirgol Dagi 77 H2
Cal 76 C3
Cal 103 J5
Cala 73 G2
Calabar 105 G5
Calabozo 136 D2
Calafat 73 G4
Calafate 139 B10
Calafell 67 G2
Calagua Islands 91 G3
Calahorra 67 F1
Calais *France* 64 D3
Calais *U.S.A.* 125 S4
Calama 138 C4
Calamar *Colombia* 136 C1
Calamar *Colombia* 136 C3
Calamian Group 91 G3
Calamocha 67 F2
Calandula 106 C4
Calang 90 B5
Calapan 91 G3
Calarasi 73 J3
Calatayud 67 F2
Calatele 73 G2
Calatrava, Campo de 66 E3
Calau 70 F3
Calavite, Cape 91 G3
Calayan 91 G2
Calbayog 91 G3
Calcanhar, Ponta do 137 K5
Calcasieu 128 F5
Calcasieu Lake 128 F6
Calcutta 93 G4
Caldararu 73 H3
Caldas da Rainha 66 B3
Caldbeck 55 F2
Caldeirao, Sierra do 66 B4
Calder 55 H3
Caldera 138 B5
Caldew 55 G2
Caldicot 52 E3
Caldiran 77 K3
Caldwell 122 F6
Caledon 108 E6
Calella de la Costa 67 H2
Caleta Lobos 138 C4
Caleta Olivia 139 C9
Calexico 126 E4
Calf of Man 54 E2
Calfsound 56 F1
Calgary 122 G2
Cali 136 B3
Caliach Point 57 B4
Calicut 92 E6
Calienta 126 E2
California 126 B1
California, Golfo de 126 G7
Calimani, Muntii 73 H2
Calimere, Point 92 E6
Calingasta 139 C6
Calino 75 J4
Calitri 69 E5
Callabonna, Lake 113 J4
Callan 59 H7
Callander 57 D4
Callao 136 B6
Callington 52 C4
Calne 53 E3
Caloosahatchee 129 M7
Calpe 67 G3
Calpulalpan 131 K8
Caltagirone 69 E7
Caltanissetta 69 E7
Caltilbuk 76 C3
Calulo 106 B5
Caluula 103 K5
Caluula, Raas 103 K5
Calvados Chain, The 114 T10
Calvert 113 H2
Calvert Hills 113 H2
Calvert Island 118 K5
Calvi 69 B4
Calvinia 108 C6
Calvo, Monte 69 E6
Cam 53 G2
Camabatela 106 C4
Camacupa 106 C5
Camaguey 132 J4
Camaguey, Archipielago de 132 H3
Camalan 76 F4
Camana 138 B3
Camaqua 138 F6
Camardi 76 F4
Camaron, Cabo 132 E7
Camarones 139 C8
Camaross 59 J8
Camas 122 C5
Camatindi 138 D4
Cambados 66 B1
Camberley 53 G3
Cambodia 93 K6
Cambo-les-Bains 65 C7
Camborne 52 B4
Cambrai 64 E3
Cambrian Mountains 52 D2
Cambridge *New Zealand* 115 E2
Cambridge *U.K.* 52 H2
Cambridge *Maryland, U.S.A.* 125 M7
Cambridge *Massachusetts, U.S.A.* 125 Q5
Cambridge *Minnesota, U.S.A.* 124 D4
Cambridge *Ohio, U.S.A.* 125 K6
Cambridge Bay 119 Q2
Cambridge Gulf 112 F1
Cambridgeshire 53 G2
Cambrils 67 G2
Cambundi-Catembo 106 C5
Camden *Arkansas, U.S.A.* 128 F4
Camden *New Jersey, U.S.A.* 125 N7
Camden *S. Carolina, U.S.A.* 129 M3
Cameia 106 D5
Camelford 52 C4
Cameli 76 C4
Camerino 68 D4
Cameron *Arizona, U.S.A.* 126 G3
Cameron *Missouri, U.S.A.* 124 C7
Cameron *Texas, U.S.A.* 128 D5
Cameron Hills 119 M4
Cameron Island 120 F2
Cameron Mountains 115 A7
Cameroon 105 H4
Cameroun, Mont 105 G5
Cameta 137 H4
Camiguin *Philippines* 91 G2
Camiguin *Philippines* 91 G4
Camilla 129 K5
Caminha 66 B2
Camiri 138 D4
Camissombo 106 D4
Camlidere 76 E2
Camlidere 77 H4
Camlihemsin 77 J2
Camliyayla 76 F4
Camocim 137 J4
Camooweal 113 H2
Camorta 93 H7
Campana 139 E6
Campana, Isla 139 A9
Campanario 138 H3
Campanario *Argentina* 139 B7
Campanario *Spain* 66 D3
Campbell 108 D5
Campbell, Cape 115 E4
Campbell Island 141 M8
Campbellpore 92 D2
Campbell River 122 B2
Campbellsville 124 H8
Campbellton 125 S3
Campbelltown 113 L5
Campbeltown 57 C5
Campeche 131 P8
Campeche, Bahia de 131 N8
Camperdown 113 J6
Campillo de Arenas 66 E4
Campillos 66 D4
Campina Grande 137 K5
Campinas 138 G4
Campo 105 G5
Campoalegre 136 B3
Campobasso 69 E5
Campo de Diauarum 137 G6
Campo Grande 138 F4
Campo Maior *Brazil* 137 J4
Campo Maior *Portugal* 66 C3
Campo Mourao 138 F4
Campos *Bahia, Brazil* 137 J6
Campos *Rio de Janeiro, Brazil* 138 H4
Campos del Puerto 67 H3
Campos Sales 137 J5
Campos, Tierra de 66 D1
Campsie Fells 57 D4
Camrose 119 N5
Can 76 B2
Canada 116 F5
Canada de Gomez 138 D6
Canadian 127 M3
Canadian Shield 116 K3
Canakkale 76 B2
Canakkale Bogazi 76 B2
Canala 114 W16
Canal Casiquiare 136 D3
Canal Cockburn 139 B10
Cananea 126 G5
Canarias, Islas 100 B3
Canarreos, Archipielago de los 132 G4
Canary Islands 100 B3
Canastota 125 N5
Canaveral, Cape 129 M6
Canaveras 66 E2
Canberra 113 K6
Cancarli 76 B3
Candarli Korfezi 75 J3
Cande 65 C5
Candelaria 131 P8
Candia 75 H5
Candir 76 E2
Cando 123 Q3
Canea 75 H5
Canelones 139 E6
Canete 67 F2
Caney 128 E2
Cangallo 136 C6
Cangamba 106 C5
Cangas de Narcea 66 C1
Cangas de Onis 66 D1
Canguaretama 137 K5
Cangucu 138 F6
Cangzhou 87 M4
Caniapiscau *Canada* 121 N7
Caniapiscau *Canada* 121 N6
Caniapiscau, Lac 121 N7
Canicatti 69 D7
Canik Daglari 77 G2
Canisp 56 C2
Canjayar 66 E4
Cankaya 76 E3
Cankiri 76 E2
Canna 57 B3
Cannanore 92 E6
Canna, Sound of 57 B3
Cannes 65 G7
Cannich *U.K.* 56 D3
Cannich *U.K.* 56 D3
Canning 118 F2
Canning Basin 112 E2
Cannington 52 D3
Cannock 53 E2
Cann River 113 K6
Canoas 138 F5
Canoas 138 F5
Canoeiros 138 G3
Canoe Lake 119 P4
Canon City 127 K1
Canosa di Puglia 69 F5
Canta 136 B6
Cantabrica, Cordillera 66 D1
Cantabrico, Mar 66 D1
Cantanhede 66 B2
Canterbury 53 J3
Canterbury Bight 115 D6
Canterbury Plains 115 C6
Can Tho 93 L6
Canton *China* 93 M4
Canton *Illinois, U.S.A.* 124 E6
Canton *Mississippi, U.S.A.* 128 H4
Canton *New York, U.S.A.* 125 N4
Canton *Ohio, U.S.A.* 125 K6
Canton *S. Dakota, U.S.A.* 123 R6
Canudos *Amazonas, Brazil* 136 F5
Canudos *Bahia, Brazil* 137 K5
Canuma 136 F4
Canutama 136 E5
Canvey Island 53 H3
Canyon 127 M3
Cao Bang 93 L4
Caombo 106 C4
Capanaparo 136 D2
Capanema 137 H4
Capao Bonito 138 G4
Capatarida 136 C1
Cap de la Madeleine 125 P3
Cape Breton Island 121 P8
Cape Coast 104 E4
Cape Coral 129 M7
Cape Dorset 120 L5
Cape Dyer 120 P4
Cape Egmont 115 D3
Cape Girardeau 124 F8
Capel 53 G3
Capelinha 138 H3
Capella 114 C2
Cape Town 108 C6
Cape Verde 104 L7
Cape York Peninsula 113 J1
Cap-Haitien 133 L5
Capim 137 H4
Capitan Arturo Prat 141 V6
Capixaba 138 J6
Cappoquin 59 G8
Capraia, Isola di 68 B4
Caprera, Isola 69 B5
Capricorn Channel 113 L3
Capri, Isola di 69 E5
Caprivi Strip 108 D3
Captieux 65 C6
Capua 69 E5
Caqueta 136 C4
Carabinani 136 E4
Caracal 73 H3
Caracarai 136 E3
Caracas 136 D1
Carajari 137 G4
Carajas, Serra dos 137 G5
Carangola 138 H4
Caratasca 132 F7
Caratasca, Laguna 132 F7
Caratinga 138 H3
Carauari 136 D4
Caravaca de la Cruz 67 F3
Caravelas 137 K7
Carballo 66 B1
Carbonara, Capo 69 B6
Carbondale 125 N6
Carbonear 121 R8
Carboneras de Guadazaori 67 F3
Carbonia 69 B6
Carcans, Etang de 65 C6
Carcans-Plage 65 C6
Carcarana 138 D6
Carcassonne 65 E7
Carcross 118 J3
Cardak 76 C4
Cardamon Hills 92 E7
Cardenas 131 N9
Cardiel, Lago 139 B9
Cardiff 52 D3
Cardigan 52 C2
Cardigan Bay 52 C2
Cardona 67 G2
Cardston 122 H3
Carei 73 G2
Carentan 64 C4
Carey, Lake 112 E4
Carhaix-Plouguer 64 B4
Carhue 139 D7
Cariacica 138 H4
Caribbean Sea 132 H7
Cariboa Lake 124 F1
Cariboo Mountains 119 L5
Caribou *Canada* 119 R4
Caribou *U.S.A.* 125 S3
Caribou Mountains 119 M4
Carinena 67 F2
Carinhanha 137 J6
Carinish 56 A3
Caripito 133 R9
Carleton, Mount 125 S3
Carlingford 58 K4
Carlingford Lough 58 K4
Carlisle *U.K.* 55 G2
Carlisle *U.S.A.* 125 M6
Carlos Chagas 138 H3
Carlow *Ireland* 59 J7
Carlow *Ireland* 59 J7
Carloway 56 C2
Carlsbad *Czechoslovakia* 70 E3
Carlsbad *California, U.S.A.* 126 D4
Carlsbad *New Mexico, U.S.A.* 127 K4
Carlton *Nottinghamshire, U.K.* 53 F2
Carlton *N. Yorkshire, U.K.* 55 H2
Carlyle 123 N3
Carmacks 118 H3
Carmagnola 68 A3
Carmarthen 52 C3
Carmarthen Bay 52 C3
Carmaux 65 E6
Carmel Head 54 E3
Carmelo 139 E6
Carmen 136 B2
Carmen Alto 138 C4
Carmen de Patagones 139 D8
Carmen, Isla 126 G8
Carmen, Sierra del 127 L6
Carmi 124 F7
Carmona 66 D4
Carnarvon *Australia* 112 C3
Carnarvon *South Africa* 108 D6
Carn Ban 57 D3
Carnedd Llewelyn 54 F3
Carnegie, Lake 112 E4
Carnew 59 K7
Carney Island 141 R4
Carnforth 55 G2
Carn Glas-choire 56 E3
Carniche, Alpi 68 D2
Car Nicobar 93 H7
Carnlough 58 L3
Carnlough Bay 58 L3
Carnot 102 C7
Carnsore Point 59 K8
Carnwath 118 K2
Carolina 137 H5
Caroline Islands 91 K4
Carondelet Reef 111 U3
Caroni 136 E2
Carora 133 M9
Carpathians 73 F1
Carpatii Meridionali 73 G3
Carpentaria, Gulf of 113 H1
Carpentras 65 F6
Carpi 68 C3
Carpina 137 K5
Carra, Lough 58 D5
Carranza, Cabo 139 B7
Carranza, Presa V. 127 M7
Carrara 68 C3
Carrauntoohil 59 C9
Carriacou 133 S8
Carrick 57 D5
Carrickfergus 58 L3
Carrickmacross 58 J5
Carrick-on-Shannon 58 F5
Carrick-on-Suir 59 H8
Carrigallen 58 G5
Carrigtwohill 59 F9
Carrington 123 Q4
Carrion 66 D1
Carrizal 136 C1
Carrizal Bajo 138 B5
Carrizo Springs 127 N6
Carrizozo 127 K4
Carroll 124 C5
Carrollton *Georgia, U.S.A.* 129 K4
Carrollton *Kentucky, U.S.A.* 124 H7
Carron 56 D3
Carron, Loch 56 C3
Carrot 119 Q5
Carrowkeel 58 H2
Carrowmore Lough 58 C4
Carryduff 58 L3

Name	Page	Grid
Carsamba	76	E4
Carsamba	77	G2
Carsibasi	77	H2
Carson City	126	C1
Carson Sink	122	E8
Carsphairn	57	D5
Cartagena *Colombia*	136	B1
Cartagena *Spain*	67	F4
Cartago *Colombia*	136	B3
Cartago *Costa Rica*	132	F10
Cartaret	53	N7
Cartaxo	66	B3
Cartaya	66	C4
Carteret	64	C4
Carterton	115	E4
Carthage *Missouri, U.S.A.*	124	C8
Carthage *Texas, U.S.A.*	128	E4
Cartier Island	110	F4
Cartwright	121	Q7
Caruara	137	K5
Carumbo	106	C4
Carupano	136	E1
Caruthersville	128	H2
Carvoeiro, Cabo	66	B3
Cary	52	E3
Casablanca	100	D2
Casa Grande	126	G4
Casale Monferrato	68	B3
Casalmaggiore	68	C3
Casamance	104	B3
Casanare	136	C2
Casas Ibanez	67	F3
Cascade	122	F5
Cascade Mountains	122	D3
Cascade Point	115	B5
Cascade Range	122	C6
Cascais	66	B3
Cascapedia	125	S2
Cascavel *Ceara, Brazil*	137	K4
Cascavel *Parana, Brazil*	138	F4
Caschuil	138	C5
Caserta	69	E5
Casey	141	H5
Cashel	59	G7
Casiguran	91	G2
Casilda	138	D6
Casma	136	B5
Casnewydd	52	E3
Caspe	67	F2
Casper	123	L6
Caspian Sea	51	S7
Cass	124	J5
Cassamba	106	D5
Casse, Grande	65	G6
Cassiar Mountains	118	J3
Cassinga	106	C6
Cassino	69	D5
Cass Lake *U.S.A.*	124	C3
Cass Lake *U.S.A.*	124	C3
Cassongue	106	B5
Casteljaloux	65	D6
Castellammare del Golfo	66	D6
Castellammare, Golfo di	69	D6
Castellane	65	G7
Castellar de Santiago	66	E3
Castellar de Santisteban	66	E3
Castelli	139	E7
Castellnedd	52	D3
Castellon de la Plana	67	F3
Castellote	67	F2
Castelnaudary	65	D7
Castelo Branco	66	C3
Castelsarrasin	65	D6
Casteltermini	69	D7
Castelvetrano	69	D7
Castets	65	C7
Castilla la Nueva	66	E3
Castilla la Vieja	66	D2
Castilletes	136	C1
Castillo, Pampa del	139	C9
Castillos	139	F6
Castlebar	58	D5
Castlebay	57	A4
Castlebellingham	58	K5
Castleblayney	58	J4
Castle Bolton	55	H2
Castle Carrock	55	G2
Castleconnel	59	F7
Castledawson	58	J3
Castlederg	58	G3
Castledermot	59	J7
Castle Douglas	54	F2
Castleellis	59	K8
Castleford	55	H3
Castleisland	59	D8
Castlemaine	113	J6
Castlemaine	59	F9
Castlepollard	58	H5
Castlerea	58	E5
Castle Rock	123	M8
Castleside	55	H2
Castleton	55	H3
Castletown *Highland, U.K.*	56	E2
Castletown *Isle of Man, U.K.*	54	E2
Castletownbere	59	C9
Castletownshend	59	D9
Castlewellan	58	L4
Castonos	127	M7
Castor	122	J1
Castres	65	E7
Castries	133	S7
Castro	139	B8
Castro Alves	137	K6
Castro del Rio	66	D4
Castropol	66	C1
Castro Urdiales	66	E1
Castro Verde	66	B4
Castrovillari	69	F6
Castuera	66	D3
Caswell Sound	115	A6
Cat	77	J3
Catacamas	132	E7
Catacaos	136	A5
Cataingan	91	G3
Catak	77	K3
Catakkopru	77	J3
Catalca	76	C2
Cataluna	67	G2
Catalzeytin	76	F2
Catamarca	138	C5
Catanduanes	91	G3
Catanduva	138	G4
Catania	69	E7
Catanzaro	69	F6
Cataqueama	136	E6
Catastrophie, Cape	113	H5
Catatumbo	133	L10
Catbalogan	91	G3
Caterham	53	G3
Catete	106	B4
Cathcart	108	E6
Cat Island	133	K2
Cato	111	N6
Catoche, Cabo	131	R7
Catria, Monte	68	D4
Catrimani *Brazil*	136	E3
Catrimani *Brazil*	136	E3
Catskill	125	P5
Catskill Mountains	125	N5
Catwick Islands	93	L6
Cauca	133	K11
Caucaia	137	K4
Caucasia	133	K11
Caucasus	77	L1
Cauit Point	91	H4
Caulkerbush	55	F1
Caungula	106	C4
Cauquenes	139	B7
Caura	133	Q11
Causapscal	125	S2
Caussade	65	D6
Cauterets	65	C7
Cauto	132	J4
Cauvery	92	E6
Cavado	66	B2
Cavaillon	65	F7
Cavalcante	138	H6
Cavally	104	D4
Cavan *Ireland*	58	H5
Cavan *Ireland*	58	H5
Cavdir	76	C4
Cavendish	53	H2
Cavite	91	G3
Caxias	136	C4
Caxias	137	J4
Caxias do Sul	138	E5
Caxito	106	B4
Cay	76	D3
Cayagzi	76	F2
Caycuma	76	E2
Cayeli	77	J2
Cayenne	137	G3
Cayeux	64	D3
Caygoren Baraji	76	C3
Cayiralan	77	F3
Cayirli	77	H3
Caykara	77	J2
Caylarbasi	77	H4
Cayman Brac	132	H5
Cayman Trench	132	F5
Caynabo	103	J6
Cayuga Lake	125	M5
Cazalla de la Sierra	66	D4
Cazma *Yugoslavia*	72	D3
Cazma *Yugoslavia*	72	D3
Cazombo	106	D5
Cazorla	66	E4
Cea	66	D1
Ceahlau	73	H2
Ceanannus Mor	58	J5
Ceara	137	K5
Ceara-Mirim	137	K5
Ceballos	127	K7
Cebollera	66	E1
Cebu *Philippines*	91	G3
Cebu *Philippines*	91	G3
Cecina	68	C4
Cedar	124	D5
Cedar City	126	F2
Cedar Creek Lake	128	D4
Cedar Falls	124	D5
Cedar Lake	119	Q5
Cedar Rapids	124	E6
Cedartown	129	K3
Cedros, Isla de	126	E6
Ceduna	113	G5
Ceelbuur	103	J7
Ceeldheer	103	J7
Ceerigaabo	103	J5
Cefalu	69	E6
Cega	66	D2
Cegled	72	E2
Ceica	73	G2
Cekerek *Turkey*	77	F2
Cekerek *Turkey*	76	F2
Celalli	77	G3
Celano	69	D4
Celaya	131	J7
Celebes	91	G6
Celebi	76	E3
Celestun	131	P7
Celikhan	77	H3
Celina	124	H6
Celje	72	C2
Celle	70	D2
Celtik	76	D3
Celyn, Llyn	52	D2
Cemaes Head	52	C2
Cemilbey	76	F2
Cemisgezek	77	H3
Cendrawasih, Teluk	91	K6
Cenga	91	H6
Cenrana	91	F6
Center	128	E5
Centinela, Picacho Del	127	L6
Cento	68	C3
Central	57	D4
Central African Republic	102	D6
Central Brahui Range	92	C3
Central, Cordillera *Colombia*	136	B3
Central, Cordillera *Dominican Republic*	133	M5
Central, Cordillera *Peru*	136	B5
Central, Cordillera *Philippines*	91	G2
Central Heights	126	G4
Centralia	122	C4
Central Makran Range	92	B3
Central, Massif	65	E6
Central Range	114	C2
Central Siberian Plateau	84	H3
Cephalonia	75	F3
Cepu	90	E7
Ceram	91	H6
Cercal	66	B4
Cerchov	70	E4
Ceres	138	G3
Ceret	65	E7
Cerignola	69	E5
Cerigo	75	G4
Cerkes	76	E2
Cerkeskoy	76	B2
Cermei	73	F2
Cermik	77	H3
Cerna *Romania*	73	G3
Cerna *Romania*	73	K3
Cerne Abbas	52	E4
Cerralvo	128	C7
Cerralvo, Isla	130	E5
Cerreto Sannita	69	E5
Cerro Azul	136	B6
Cerro de Pasco	136	B6
Cerro Machin	131	L9
Cerro Manantiales	139	C10
Cerros Colorados, Embalse	139	C7
Cervaro	69	E5
Cervera	67	G2
Cervera de Pisuerga	66	D1
Cervia	68	D3
Cervione	69	B4
Cesar	133	L9
Cesena	68	D3
Cesenatico	68	D3
Cesis	63	L8
Ceske Budejovice	70	F4
Cesky Brod	70	F3
Cesme	76	B3
Cessnock	113	L5
Cetate	73	G3
Cetinje	72	E4
Cetinkaya	77	G3
Cetraro	69	E6
Ceuta	66	D4
Ceva-i-Ra	111	R6
Cevennes	65	F6
Cevherli	76	F4
Cevio	68	B2
Cevizli	76	D4
Ceyhan *Turkey*	76	F4
Ceyhan *Turkey*	77	F4
Ceylanpinar	77	J4
Chaadayevka	79	H5
Chablis	65	E5
Chacabuco	139	D6
Chachani, Nevado de	138	B3
Chachapoyas	136	B5
Chachoengsao	93	K6
Chaco Austral	138	D5
Chaco Boreal	138	E4
Chaco Central	138	D4
Chad	102	C5
Chad *Russia*	78	K4
Chadan	84	E6
Chadderton	55	G3
Chaddesley Corbett	53	E2
Chadileovu	139	C7
Chad, Lake	102	B5
Chadobets	84	F5
Chadron	123	N6
Chagai Hills	92	B3
Chagda	85	N5
Chaghcharan	95	S4
Chagny	65	F5
Chagoda	78	F4
Chagos Archipelago	82	F7
Chahah Burjak	95	R6
Chah Bahar	95	Q9
Chahbounia	67	H5
Chaho	88	B5
Chahuites	131	M9
Chaibasa	92	G4
Chai Buri	93	K5
Chaiya	93	J7
Chaiyaphum	93	K5
Chala	136	C7
Chalais	65	D6
Chalap Dalan	92	B2
Chala, Punta	136	B7
Chalatenango	132	C7
Chaldonka	85	K6
Chale	53	F4
Chaleur, Baie de	121	N8
Chaleur Bay	125	T3
Chalhuanca	136	C6
Chalisgaon	92	E4
Challaco	139	C7
Challacombe	52	D3
Challans	65	C5
Challis	122	G5
Chalmny Varre	78	F2
Chalna	93	G4
Chalon-sur-Marne	64	F4
Chalon-sur-Saone	65	F5
Chalus	65	D6
Chalus	95	K3
Cham	70	E4
Chama	127	J2
Chaman	92	C2
Chamba *India*	92	E2
Chamba *Russia*	84	G4
Chambal	92	E3
Chamberlain *Australia*	112	F2
Chamberlain *U.S.A.*	123	Q6
Chambersburg	125	M7
Chambery	65	F6
Chamela	130	G8
Chamical	138	C6
Chamonix	65	G6
Chamouchouane	125	P2
Champagne	64	F4
Champagnole	65	F5
Champaign	124	F6
Champflower	52	D3
Champlain, Lake	125	P4
Champlitte	65	F5
Champoton	131	P8
Chamrajnagar	92	E6
Chamusca	66	B3
Chanaral	138	B5
Chanaran	95	P3
Chanca	66	C4
Chandalar	118	F2
Chandausi	92	E3
Chandeleur Islands	128	H6
Chandigarh	92	E2
Chandler	121	P8
Chandmani *Mongolia*	86	G2
Chandmani *Mongolia*	86	H2
Chandpur	93	H4
Chandrapur	92	E5
Chandvad	92	D4
Chanf	95	Q8
Changan	93	L2
Changane	109	F4
Changbai	88	B5
Changbai Shan	88	B4
Changchun	87	P3
Changde	93	M3
Chang-hua	87	N7
Chang Jiang	87	M5
Chang, Ko	93	K6
Changle	87	M4
Changling	87	N3
Changma	86	H4
Changnyon	87	P4
Changsan-got	87	N4
Changsha	93	M3
Changshan	87	M6
Changtai	87	M7
Changting	87	M6
Changwu	93	L1
Changxing	87	M5
Changyi	87	M4
Changzhi	87	L4
Changzhou	87	M5
Channel Islands	53	M7
Channel-Port-aux-Basques	121	Q8
Chantada	66	C1
Chanthaburi	93	K6
Chantilly	64	E4
Chantonnay	65	C5
Chantrey Inlet	120	G4
Chanute	128	E2
Chany, Ozero	84	B6
Chao	136	B5
Chao Hu	87	M5
Chao Phraya	93	K5
Chaor He	87	N2
Chaouen	100	D1
Chaoyang *China*	87	N3
Chaoyang *China*	87	N3
Chaozhou	87	M7
Chapadinha	137	J4
Chapala, Laguna de	130	H7
Chapanda	85	N5
Chapayevo	79	J5
Chapayevsk	79	H5
Chapayev-Zheday	85	K4
Chapchachi	79	H6
Chapeco	138	F5
Chapel-en-le-Frith	55	H3
Chapel Hill	129	N3
Chapeltown *Grampian, U.K.*	56	E3
Chapeltown *S. Yorkshire, U.K.*	55	H3
Chapleau	124	J3

Chaplygin 79 F5
Chapman 112 F2
Chapman, Cape 120 J4
Chapman Islands 119 P2
Chaqui 138 C3
Chara *Russia* 85 K5
Chara *Russia* 85 K5
Charagua 138 D3
Charak 95 M8
Charambira, Punta 136 B3
Charcot Island 141 U5
Chard 52 E4
Chardzhou 80 H6
Charente 65 C6
Chari 102 C5
Charikar 92 C1
Chariton *U.S.A.* 124 D6
Chariton *U.S.A.* 124 D6
Charkhari 92 E3
Charlemount 58 J4
Charleroi 64 F3
Charlesbourg 125 Q3
Charles, Cape 125 N8
Charles City 124 D5
Charles Island *Canada* 120 M5
Charles Island *Ecuador* 136 A7
Charleston *Illinois, U.S.A.* 124 F7
Charleston *Missouri, U.S.A.* 124 F8
Charleston *S. Carolina, U.S.A.* 129 N4
Charleston *W. Virginia, U.S.A.* 125 K7
Charlestown 58 E5
Charlestown of Aberlour 56 E3
Charleville 113 K4
Charleville-Mezieres 64 F4
Charlotte 129 M3
Charlotte Amalie 133 Q5
Charlotte, Cape 139 J10
Charlotte Harbour 129 L7
Charlottesville 125 L7
Charlottetown 121 P8
Charlton 113 J6
Charlton Island 121 L7
Charmes 64 G4
Charnley 112 F2
Charolles 65 F5
Charters Towers 113 K3
Chartres 64 D4
Charwelton 53 F2
Charybdis Reef 114 Q8
Charyn 86 D3
Chascomus 139 E7
Chaselka 84 C3
Chaslands Mistake 115 B7
Chasong 87 P3
Chasovo 78 J3
Chasseeneuil 65 D6
Chat 95 M3
Chateaubriant 65 C5
Chateau Chinon 65 E5
Chateaudun 65 D4
Chateau-Gontier 65 C5
Chateau-la-Valliere 65 D5
Chateaulin 64 A4
Chateauneuf-en-Thimerais 64 D4
Chateauneuf-sur-Loire 65 E5
Chateaurenault 65 D5
Chateauroux 65 D5
Chateau-Salins 64 G4
Chateau-Thierry 64 E4
Chatellerault 65 D5
Chatham *New Brunswick, Canada* 125 T3
Chatham *Ontario, Canada* 124 J5
Chatham *U.K.* 53 H3
Chatham, Isla 139 B10
Chatham Island *Ecuador* 136 A7
Chatham Island *New Zealand* 115 F7
Chatham Islands 115 G7
Chatillon 68 A3
Chatillon-sur-Indre 65 D5
Chatillon-sur-Seine 65 F5
Chato, Cerro 139 B8
Chattahoochee 129 K5
Chattanooga 129 K3
Chatteris 53 H2
Chatyrtash 86 D3
Chaudiere 125 Q3
Chaumont 64 F4
Chaunskaya Guba 85 V3
Chauny 64 E4
Chautauqua Lake 125 L5
Chavantina 138 G6
Chaves *Brazil* 137 H4
Chaves *Portugal* 66 C2
Chaviva 136 C3
Chay Khanah 77 L5
Chaykovskiy 78 J4
Chazhegovo 78 J3
Cheadle 55 G3
Cheb 70 E3
Cheboksary 78 H4
Cheboygan 124 H4
Chechen , Ostrov 79 H7
Chech, Erg 100 E3
Chechuysk 84 H5
Checiny 71 J3
Chedabucto Bay 121 P8
Cheddar 52 E3
Cheduba 93 H5
Cheetham, Cape 141 L4
Chef-Boutonne 65 C5
Chehalis 122 C4
Chehel Dokhtaran 95 R4
Cheju 87 P5
Cheju do 87 P5
Chekhov 88 H2
Chekunda 85 N6
Chekurovka 85 M2
Chekuyevo 78 F3
Chelan 122 D4
Chelan, Lake 122 D3
Chela, Serra da 106 B6
Cheleken 95 L2
Chelforo 139 C7
Cheliff, Oued 100 F1
Chelkar 51 U6
Chelm 71 K3
Chelmsford 53 H3
Chelmuzhi 78 F3
Chelosh 84 D6
Cheltenham 53 E3
Chelva 67 F3
Chelyabinsk 84 Ad5
Chelyuskin 84 G1
Chelyuskin, Mys 81 M2
Chemba 109 F3
Chemille 65 C5
Chemnitz 70 E3
Chenab 92 D2
Cheney 122 F4
Chengde 87 M3
Chengdu 93 K2
Chenghai 87 M7
Chengjiang 93 K4
Chengshan Jiao 87 N4
Chenonceaux 65 D5
Chen Xian 93 M3
Chepen 136 B5
Chepes 139 C6
Chepstow 52 E3
Chequamegon Bay 124 E3
Cher 65 E5
Cherangany Hills 107 G2
Cheraw 129 N3
Cherbourg 64 C4
Cherchell 101 F1
Cherdyn 78 K3
Cheremkhovo 84 G6
Cheremosh 71 L4
Cherepovets 78 F4
Cherevkovo 78 H3
Cherkashina 84 H5
Cherkassy 79 E6
Cherkessk 79 G7
Cherlak 84 A6
Cherlakskiy 84 A6
Cherlmno 71 H2
Chermoz 78 K4
Chernaya *Russia* 78 K2
Chernaya *Russia* 78 K2
Cherni 73 G4
Chernigov 79 E5
Chernigovka *Russia* 88 D3
Chernigovka *Ukraine* 79 F6
Chernikovsk 78 K5
Cherni Lom 73 J4
Chernobyl 79 E5
Chernoostrovskoye 84 D4
Chernousovka 84 A6
Chernovtsy 73 H1
Chernushka 78 K4
Chernutyevo 78 H3
Chernyakhovsk 71 J1
Chernyshevskiy 85 J4
Chernyye Zemli 79 H6
Chernyy Mys 84 C5
Chernyy Otrog 79 K5
Cherokee 124 C5
Cherokee Sound 129 P7
Cherry 111 Q4
Cherskiy 85 U3
Cherskogo, Khrebet 85 Q3
Chertkovo 79 G6
Chertsey *New Zealand* 115 C5
Chertsey *U.K.* 53 G3
Chervonograd 79 C5
Chervonoznamenka 73 L2
Cherwell 53 F3
Chesapeake 125 M8
Chesapeake Bay 125 M8
Chesham 53 G3
Cheshire 55 G3
Cheshkaya Guba 78 H2
Cheshunt 53 G3
Chesil Beach 52 E4
Chester *U.K.* 55 G3
Chester *Illinois, U.S.A.* 124 F8
Chester *Montana, U.S.A.* 122 J3
Chester *S. Carolina, U.S.A.* 129 M3
Chesterfield 55 H3
Chesterfield, Iles 113 M2
Chesterfield Inlet 119 S3
Chester-le-Street 55 H2
Chesters 57 F5
Chesterton Range 113 K4
Chesuncook Lake 125 R3
Chetlat 92 D6
Chetumal 131 Q8
Chetvertyy Kurilskiy Proliv 85 S7
Chetwynd 119 L4
Cheviot Hills 57 F5
Cheviot, The 57 F5
Chew 52 E3
Chew Valley Lake 52 E3
Cheyenne *S. Dakota, U.S.A.* 123 P5
Cheyenne *Wyoming, U.S.A.* 123 M7
Cheyenne Wells 127 L1
Chhapra 92 F3
Chhatarpur 92 E4
Chhindwara 92 E4
Chia-i 87 N7
Chiange 106 B6
Chiani 69 D4
Chiari 68 B3
Chiatura 77 K1
Chiautla 131 K8
Chiavari 68 B3
Chiavenna 68 B2
Chiba 89 H8
Chibia 106 B6
Chibit 84 D6
Chibizhek 84 E6
Chibougamau 125 N2
Chibougamau Lake 125 N2
Chibuto 109 F4
Chicago 124 G6
Chicama 136 B5
Chicapa 106 D4
Chichagof Island 118 H4
Chichester 53 G4
Chichester Range 112 D3
Chichibu 89 G8
Chichigalpa 132 D8
Chickasha 128 D3
Chicko 119 L5
Chiclayo 136 B5
Chico *Argentina* 139 C10
Chico *Argentina* 139 C8
Chico *U.S.A.* 122 D8
Chicoutimi 125 Q2
Chicualacuala 109 F4
Chidambaram 92 E6
Chiddingfold 53 G3
Chidley, Cape 121 P5
Chiefland 129 L6
Chiemsee 70 E5
Chieng-Mai 93 J5
Chienti 68 D4
Chieti 69 E4
Chifeng 87 M3
Chifre, Serra do 138 H3
Chiguana 138 C4
Chigubo 109 F4
Chigwell 53 H3
Chihli, Gulf of 87 K4
Chihuahua 127 J6
Chihuatlan 130 G8
Chiili 86 B3
Chijinpu 86 H3
Chik Ballapur 92 E6
Chikishlyer 95 L3
Chikmagalur 92 E6
Chikura 89 G8
Chi, Lam 93 K5
Chilamate 132 E8
Chilapa 131 K9
Chilas 92 D1
Chilca 136 B6
Chilca, Punta 136 B6
Childers 113 L4
Childress 127 M3
Chile 139 B7
Chile Chico 139 B9
Chilete 136 B5
Chilham 53 H3
Chilia, Bratul 73 K3
Chilik *Kazakhstan* 86 D3
Chilik *Kazakhstan* 79 J5
Chililabombwe 107 E5
Chillagoe 113 J2
Chillan 139 B7
Chillicothe *Missouri, U.S.A.* 124 D7
Chillicothe *Ohio, U.S.A.* 124 J7
Chilliculco 138 C3
Chiloe, Isla de 139 B8
Chilpancingo 131 K9
Chiltern Hills 53 G3
Chilumba 107 F5
Chi-lung 87 N6
Chilwa, Lake 107 G6
Chimanimani 109 F3
Chimay 64 F3
Chimborazo, Volcan 136 B4
Chimbote 136 B5
Chimishliya 73 K2
Chimkent 86 B3
Chimoio 109 F3
China 128 C8
Chinandega 132 D8
Chinati Peak 127 K6
Chinchilla 113 L4
Chinchilla de Monte Aragon 67 F3
Chinchon 66 E2
Chinchorro, Banco 131 R8
Chindagatuy 86 F2
Chinde 109 G3
Chindwin 93 H4
Chingola 107 E5
Chinguetti 100 C4
Chin Hills 93 H4
Chiniot 92 D2
Chinju 87 P4
Chinon 65 D5
Chinsali 107 F5
Chintalnar 92 F5
Chioggia 68 D3
Chios 75 H3
Chipata 107 F5
Chiperone 109 G3
Chipinge 109 F4
Chiplun 92 D5
Chipoka 107 F5
Chi Pou 93 L6
Chippenham 53 E3
Chippewa 124 E4
Chippewa Falls 124 E4
Chipping 55 G3
Chipping Norton 53 F3
Chipping Ongar 53 H3
Chipping Sodbury 52 E3
Chiputneticook Lakes 125 S4
Chiquinquira 136 C2
Chirchik 86 B3
Chiredzi 109 F4
Chirikof Island 118 D4
Chirimba 84 E5
Chirinda 84 G3
Chirique, Golfo de 132 F11
Chirk 52 D2
Chiromo 107 G6
Chirovanga 114 H5
Chirpan 73 H4
Chirripo 132 F10
Chishmy 78 K5
Chisinau 79 D6
Chisinau 73 K2
Chiskovo 84 F4
Chisone 68 A3
Chisos Mountains 127 L6
Chistopol 78 J4
Chita 85 J6
Chitato 106 D4
Chitembo 106 C5
Chitina 118 G3
Chitinskaya Oblast 85 K6
Chitradurga 92 E6
Chitral 92 D1
Chittagong 93 H4
Chittaurgarh 92 D4
Chittoor 92 E6
Chitungwiza 108 F3
Chiume 106 D6
Chiusi 69 C4
Chiva 67 F3
Chivasso 68 A3
Chivato, Punta 126 G7
Chive 136 D6
Chivhu 108 F3
Chivilcoy 139 D6
Chizha 78 G2
Chizha Vtoraya 79 H5
Chizu 89 E8
Chkalovskoye 88 D3
Chmielnik 71 J3
Choctawhatchee 129 K5
Chodziez 71 G2
Choele-Choel 139 C7
Choire, Loch 56 D2
Choiseul 114 H5
Choix 127 H7
Chojnice 71 G2
Chokai-san 88 H6
Chokurdakh 85 R2
Chokwe 109 F4
Cholderton 53 F3
Cholet 65 C5
Chollerton 57 F5
Choluteca 132 D8
Choma 106 E6
Chomutov 70 E3
Chona 84 H4
Chon Buri 93 K6
Chongan 87 M6
Chongjin 88 B5
Chongju 87 P4
Chongli 87 M3
Chongming Dao 87 M5
Chongqing 93 L3
Chongren 87 M6
Chongson 89 B7
Chongyang 93 M3
Chonos, Archipielago de los 139 B8
Chon Thanh 93 L6
Chop 79 C6
Chorley 55 G3
Chorolque 138 C4
Chortkov 79 D6
Chorzele 71 J2
Choshi 89 H8
Chosica 136 B6
Chos-Malal 139 B7
Choson-Man 87 P4
Choszczno 70 F2
Chota 136 B5
Choteau 122 H4
Choybalsan 87 L2
Christchurch *New Zealand* 115 D5
Christchurch *U.K.* 53 F4
Christiansfeld 63 C9
Christianshab 120 R4
Christie Bay 119 N3
Christmas Creekq 112 F2
Christmas Island *Australia* 83 J8
Christmas Island *Kiribati* 143 H4
Chrzanow 71 H3
Chu 86 C3
Chubartau 86 D2
Chubut 139 C8
Chudleigh 52 D4
Chudovo 78 E4
Chudskoye Ozero 63 M7
Chugach Mountains 118 G3
Chugoku-sanchi 89 D8
Chugunash 84 D6
Chuguyevka 88 D3
Chukchi Sea 118 B2

Chuken 88 F2
Chukhloma 78 G4
Chukotat 121 L5
Chukotskiy Khrebet 85 W3
Chukotskiy Poluostrov 81 V3
Chulak-Kurgan 86 B3
Chula Vista 126 D4
Chulman 85 L5
Chulmleigh 52 D4
Chulym *Russia* 84 C5
Chulym *Russia* 84 C5
Chum 78 L2
Chumbicha 138 C5
Chumek 86 F2
Chumikan 85 P6
Chumphon 93 J6
Chuna 84 F5
Chunchon 87 P4
Chungju 87 P4
Chunhua 88 C4
Chunoyar 84 F5
Chunya 107 F4
Chunyang 88 B4
Chunyang 89 B7
Chuquibamba 138 B3
Chuquicamata 138 B4
Chur 68 B2
Churan 85 L4
Churapcha 85 N4
Churchill *Canada* 119 S4
Churchill *Canada* 119 S4
Churchill *Newfoundland, Canada* 121 P7
Churchill, Cape 119 S4
Churchill Falls 121 P7
Churchill Peak 118 L4
Church Stretton 52 E2
Churia Ghati Hills 92 G3
Churin 136 B6
Churu 92 D3
Churuguara 136 D1
Chushevitsy 78 G3
Chushul 92 E2
Chusovaya 78 K4
Chusovov 78 K4
Chust 86 C3
Chute des Passes 125 Q2
Chuuronjang 88 B5
Chuxiong 93 K4
Chu Yang Sin 93 L6
Chwarta 94 G4
Chyulu Range 107 G3
Cianjur 90 D7
Cicekdagi 76 F3
Cicia 114 S8
Cide 76 E2
Cidones 66 E2
Ciechanow 71 J2
Ciego de Avila 132 H4
Cienaga 136 C1
Cienfuegos 132 G3
Cieszyn 71 H4
Cieza 67 F3
Ciftehan 76 F4
Cifteler 76 D3
Cifuentes 66 E2
Cihanbeyli 76 E3
Cijara, Embalse de 66 D3
Cilacap 90 D7
Cildir 77 K2
Cildir Golu 77 K2
Cilo Dagi 77 L4
Cimarron 128 A2
Cimone, Monte 68 C3
Cimpeni 73 G2
Cimpina 73 H3
Cimpulung 73 H3
Cimpuri 73 J2
Cinar 77 J4
Cinaruco 136 D2
Cina, Tanjung 90 C7
Cinca 67 G2
Cincer 72 D4
Cincinnati 124 H7
Cinderford 52 E3
Cine 76 C4
Cingus 77 H3
Cinto, Monte 69 B4
Circeo, Capo 69 D5
Circle *Alaska, U.S.A.* 118 G2
Circle *Montana, U.S.A.* 123 M4
Circular Reef 114 D2
Cirebon 90 D7
Cirencester 53 F3
Ciri 136 E5
Ciria 67 E2
Ciro 69 F6
Cisco 128 C4
Cislau 73 J3
Cisna 71 K4
Cisneros 136 B2
Cistierna 66 D1
Citac, Nevado 136 C6
Citlaltepetl, Volcan 131 L8
Citt a di Castello 68 D4
Cittanova 69 F6
Ciucului, Muntii 73 H2
Ciudad Acuna 127 M6
Ciudad Bolivar 136 E2
Ciudad Camargo 127 K7
Ciudad Cuauhtemoc 131 P10
Ciudad del Carmen 131 P8
Ciudad del Maiz 131 K6
Ciudad de Mexico 131 K8
Ciudadela 67 H3
Ciudad Guayana 136 E2
Ciudad Guzman 130 H8
Ciudad Ixtepec 131 M9
Ciudad Juarez 127 J5
Ciudad Lerdo 127 L8
Ciudad Madero 131 L6
Ciudad Mante 131 K6
Ciudad Mier 128 C7
Ciudad Obregon 127 H7
Ciudad Ojeda 133 M9
Ciudad Piar 133 R11
Ciudad Real 66 E3
Ciudad Rodrigo 66 C2
Ciudad Valles 131 K7
Ciudad Victoria 131 K6
Civa Burun 77 G2
Cividale del Friuli 68 D2
Civita Castellana 69 D4
Civitanova Marche 68 D4
Civitavecchia 69 C4
Civray 65 D5
Civril 76 C3
Cizre 77 K4
Clach Leathad 57 D4
Clacton-on-Sea 53 J3
Cladich 57 C4
Claerwen Reservoir 52 D2
Clain 65 D5
Claire, Lac a lEau 121 M6
Claire, Lake 119 N4
Clamecy 65 E5
Clane 59 J6
Clanton 129 J4
Clanwilliam 108 C6
Claonaig 57 C5
Clare *Australia* 113 H5
Clare *Ireland* 59 D7
Clare Island 58 B5
Claremont 125 P5
Claremorris 58 D5
Clarence *New Zealand* 115 D5
Clarence *New Zealand* 115 D5
Clarence, Cape 120 H3
Clarence Head 120 L2
Clarence Strait *Australia* 112 G1
Clarence Strait *U.S.A.* 118 J4
Clarence Town 133 K3
Clarinda 124 C6
Clarion 125 L6
Clark 123 K5
Clarke River 113 K2
Clark Fork *Montana, U.S.A* 122 H4
Clark Fork *Washington, U.S.A.* 122 F3
Clark, Lake 118 E3
Clarksburg 125 K7
Clarksdale 128 G3
Clarks Hill Lake 129 L4
Clarkston 122 F4
Clarksville *Arkansas, U.S.A.* 128 F3
Clarksville *Tennessee, U.S.A.* 129 J2
Clar, Loch nan 56 D2
Clatteringshaws Loch 57 D5
Claughton 55 G2
Clavering O 120 X3
Claxton 129 M4
Clay Center 123 R8
Clay Cross 55 H3
Claydon 53 J2
Clayton *Georgia, U.S.A.* 129 L3
Clayton *New Mexico, U.S.A.* 127 L2
Clear, Cape 59 C10
Clearfield *Pennsylvania, U.S.A.* 125 L6
Clearfield *Utah, U.S.A.* 122 J7
Clear Fork 127 N4
Clear Hills 119 M4
Clear Island 59 D10
Clear Lake *California, U.S.A.* 122 C8
Clear Lake *Iowa, U.S.A.* 124 D5
Clear Lake Reservoir 122 D7
Clearwater *Canada* 122 G1
Clearwater *Canada* 119 P4
Clearwater *Florida, U.S.A.* 129 L7
Clearwater *Idaho, U.S.A.* 122 F4
Clearwater Mountains 122 G4
Cleethorpes 55 J3
Clerke Reef 112 D2
Clermont *Australia* 113 K3
Clermont *France* 64 E4
Clermont-Ferrand 65 E6
Clermont-l'Herault 65 E7
Clervaux 64 G3
Cleve 113 H5
Clevedon 52 E3
Cleveland *U.K.* 55 H2
Cleveland *Mississippi, U.S.A.* 128 G4
Cleveland *Ohio, U.S.A.* 125 K6
Cleveland *Tennessee, U.S.A.* 129 K3
Cleveland *Texas, U.S.A.* 128 E5
Cleveland, Cape 113 K2
Cleveland Hills 55 H2
Cleveland, Mount 122 H3
Cleveleys 55 F3
Clew Bay 58 C5
Clifden *Ireland* 59 B6
Clifden *New Zealand* 115 A7
Cliffe 53 H3
Cliffs of Moher 59 D7
Clifton 55 G2
Clincha Alta 136 B6
Clinch Mountains 129 L2
Clingmans Dome 129 L3
Clinton *Canada* 122 D2
Clinton *Illinois, U.S.A.* 124 F6
Clinton *Iowa, U.S.A.* 124 E6
Clinton *Mississippi, U.S.A.* 128 G4
Clinton *Missouri, U.S.A.* 124 D7
Clinton *N. Carolina, U.S.A.* 129 N3
Clinton *Oklahoma, U.S.A.* 128 C3
Clinton-Colden Lake 119 P3
Clipperton Island 117 J7
Clisham 56 B3
Clisson 65 C5
Clitheroe 55 G3
Cliza 138 C3
Cloates, Point 112 C3
Clogheen 59 G8
Clogherhead 58 K5
Clogher Head 58 K5
Clogh Mills 58 K3
Clonakilty 59 E9
Clonakilty Bay 59 E9
Cloncurry *Australia* 113 J3
Cloncurry *Australia* 113 J3
Clonmel 59 G8
Clonmult 59 F9
Clophill 53 G2
Cloppenburg 70 C2
Cloquet 124 D3
Cloud Peak 123 L5
Cloudy Bay 115 E4
Clough 58 L4
Cloughton 55 J2
Clovelly 52 C3
Clovis 127 L3
Cloyes 65 D4
Cluanie, Loch 57 C3
Cluj-Napoca 73 G2
Clun 52 E2
Cluny 65 F5
Cluses 65 G5
Clusone 68 B3
Clutha 115 B7
Clwyd *U.K.* 55 F3
Clwyd *U.K.* 55 F3
Clwydian Range 55 F3
Clyde *Canada* 120 N3
Clyde *U.K.* 57 E5
Clydebank 57 D5
Clyde, Firth of 57 D5
Clydesdale 57 E5
Clynnog-fawr 54 E3
Clywedog, Llyn 52 D2
Coa 66 C2
Coachella 126 D4
Coachella Canal 126 E4
Coaldale 126 D2
Coalinga 126 B2
Coalisland 58 J3
Coal River 118 K4
Coalville 53 F2
Coan, Cerro 136 B5
Coari *Brazil* 136 E4
Coari *Brazil* 136 E4
Coast Mountains 122 B2
Coast Range 122 C5
Coatbridge 57 D5
Coaticook 125 Q4
Coats Island 120 K5
Coats Land 141 Y3
Coatzacoalcos *Mexico* 131 M8
Coatzacoalcos *Mexico* 131 M9
Coban 132 B7
Cobar 113 K5
Cobh 59 F9
Cobija 136 D6
Cobourg 125 L5
Cobram 113 K6
Cobue 109 F2
Coburg 70 D3
Coburg Island 120 L2
Cochabamba 138 C3
Cochem 70 B3
Cochin 92 E7
Cochrane *Canada* 122 G2
Cochrane *Chile* 139 B9
Cock Bridge 57 E3
Cockburn 113 J5
Cockburnspath 57 F5
Cockenzie 57 F4
Cockerham 55 G3
Cockermouth 55 F2
Cockfield *Durham, U.K.* 55 H2
Cockfield *Suffolk, U.K.* 53 H2
Coco 132 E7
Cocoa 129 M6
Coco Channel 93 H6
Coco Islands 93 H6
Cocoparra Range 113 K5
Cocos 137 J6
Cocula 130 H7
Codajas 136 E4
Cod, Cape 125 R6
Codera, Cabo 136 D1
Codfish Island 115 A7
Codford 53 E3
Codigoro 68 D3
Cod Island 121 P6
Codo 137 J4
Codogno 68 B3
Cod's Head 59 B9
Coen 113 J1
Coeroeni 137 F3
Coesfeld 70 B3
Coeur d'Alene 122 F4
Coeur d'Alene Lake 122 F4
Coevorden 64 G2
Coffeyville 128 E2
Coffin Bay 113 H5
Coff's Harbour 113 L5
Cogealac 73 K3
Coghinas 69 B5
Cognac 65 C6
Cogo 105 G5
Cogolludo 66 E2
Cohuna 113 J6
Coiba, Isla 132 G11
Coigach 56 C2
Coigeach, Rubha 56 C2
Coihaique 139 B9
Coimbatore 92 E6
Coimbra 66 B2
Coipasa, Salar de 138 C3
Cokak 77 G4
Colac 113 J6
Colap 77 H4
Colatina 138 E3
Colby 123 P8
Colchester 53 H3
Cold Ashton 52 E3
Coldstream 57 F5
Coldwater *Kansas, U.S.A.* 127 N2
Coldwater *Michigan, U.S.A.* 124 H6
Colebrook 125 Q4
Coleman *Australia* 113 J1
Coleman *U.S.A.* 127 N5
Colemerick 77 K4
Coleraine *Australia* 113 J6
Coleraine *U.K.* 58 J2
Colesberg 108 E6
Coleshill 53 F2
Coles, Punta de 139 B3
Colfax 122 F4
Colgrave Sound 56 B1
Colhue Huapi, Lago 139 C9
Colima 130 H8
Colima, Nevado de 130 H8
Colinas 137 J5
Colintraive 57 C5
Coll 57 C4
Collatto 68 D2
College Park 129 K4
Collie 112 D5
Collier Bay 112 E2
Colliford Lake Reservoir 52 C4
Collingbourne Kingston 53 F3
Collingham 55 J3
Collingwood *Canada* 125 K4
Collingwood *New Zealand* 115 D4
Collins 128 H5
Collin Top 58 K3
Collooney 58 F4
Colmar 64 G4
Colmars 65 G6
Colmenar 66 D4
Colmenar Viejo 66 E2
Colne *Essex, U.K.* 53 H3
Colne *Lancashire, U.K.* 55 G3
Cologne 70 B3
Colombia 136 C3
Colombo 92 E7
Colomoncagua 132 C7
Colon *Cuba* 132 G3
Colon *Panama* 132 H10
Colonia Las Heras 139 C9
Colonna, Capo 69 F6
Colonsay 57 B4
Colorado *Argentina* 139 D7
Colorado *Arizona, U.S.A.* 126 E4
Colorado *Texas, U.S.A.* 127 M4
Colorado *U.S.A.* 123 L8
Colorado Canal 123 N8
Colorado, Cerro 126 E5
Colorado City 127 M4
Colorado River Aqueduct 126 D4
Colorado Springs 127 K1
Colsterworth 53 G2
Coluene 137 G6
Columbia *Missouri, U.S.A.* 124 D7
Columbia *Pennsylvania, U.S.A.* 125 M7
Columbia *S. Carolina, U.S.A.* 129 M4
Columbia *Tennessee, U.S.A.* 129 J3
Columbia *Washington, U.S.A.* 122 D5
Columbia, District of 125 M7
Columbia Falls 122 G3
Columbia, Mount 119 M5
Columbine, Cape 108 C6
Columbus *Georgia, U.S.A.* 129 K4
Columbus *Indiana, U.S.A.* 124 H7
Columbus *Mississippi, U.S.A.* 128 H4
Columbus *Montana, U.S.A.* 123 K5
Columbus *Nebraska, U.S.A.* 123 R7
Columbus *Ohio, U.S.A.* 124 J7
Columbus *Texas, U.S.A.* 128 D6
Colville *Alaska, U.S.A.* 118 D2
Colville *Washington, U.S.A.* 122 F3
Colville, Cape 115 E2
Colville Channel 115 E2
Colville Lake 118 K2
Colwyn Bay 54 F3
Comacchio 68 D3
Comana 73 J3
Comandante Ferraz 141 W6
Comandante Fontana 138 E5
Comayagua 132 D7
Combarbala 138 B6
Combe Martin 52 C3
Comber 58 L3
Combermere Bay 93 H5
Combourg 64 C4
Comeragh Mountains 59 G8
Comfort, Cape 120 K4

Comilla 93 H4
Comitan 131 N9
Committee Bay 120 J4
Como 68 B3
Comodoro Rivadavia 139 C9
Como, Lago di 68 B3
Comorin, Cape 92 E7
Comoros 109 H2
Compiegne 64 E4
Comporta 66 B3
Compostela 130 G7
Conakry 104 C4
Conara Junction 113 K7
Concarneau 65 B5
Conceicao do Araguaia 137 H5
Concepcion *Bolivia* 138 D3
Concepcion *Chile* 138 B7
Concepcion *Panama* 132 F10
Concepcion *Paraguay* 138 E4
Concepcion del Oro 130 J5
Concepcion del Uruguay 138 E6
Concepcion, Punta 126 G7
Conception Bay 121 R8
Conception Island 133 K3
Conception, Point 126 B3
Concho 127 M5
Conchos *Mexico* 128 C8
Conchos *Mexico* 127 K6
Concord *California, U.S.A.* 126 A2
Concord *N. Carolina, U.S.A.* 129 M3
Concord *New Hampshire, U.S.A.* 125 Q5
Concordia *Argentina* 138 E6
Concordia *U.S.A.* 123 R8
Condamine 113 L4
Condeuba 138 J6
Condolobin 113 K5
Condom 65 D7
Conecuh 129 J5
Conegliano 68 D3
Conflict Group 114 E4
Confolens 65 D5
Congjiang 93 L3
Congleton 55 G3
Congo 106 B3
Congo 106 D2
Congo Basin 99 E6
Conisbrough 55 H3
Coniston 55 F2
Coniston Water 54 E2
Connah's Quay 55 F3
Connaught 58 D5
Conneaut 125 K6
Connecticut *U.S.A.* 125 P6
Connecticut *U.S.A.* 125 P6
Connellsville 125 L6
Conn, Lough 58 D4
Connors Range 113 K3
Conon 56 D3
Conon Bridge 56 D3
Conrad 122 J3
Conselheiro Lafaiete 138 H4
Conselheiro Pena 138 H3
Consett 55 H2
Con Son 93 L7
Constance, Lake 70 C5
Constancia dos Baetas 136 E5
Constanta 73 K3
Constantina 66 D4
Constantine 101 G1
Constantine Bay 52 B4
Constantine, Cape 118 D4
Constantinople 76 C2
Constitucion 139 B7
Contamana 136 C5
Contas 137 J6
Contratacion 136 C2
Contrexeville 64 F4
Contulmo 139 B7
Contwoyto Lake 119 N2
Conway *Arkansas, U.S.A.* 128 F3
Conway *New Hampshire, U.S.A.* 125 Q5
Conway *S. Carolina, U.S.A.* 129 N4
Conway Bay 54 F3
Conwy 54 F3
Coober Pedy 113 G4
Cook 112 G5
Cook, Cape 122 A2
Cookeville 129 K2
Cook Inlet 118 E3
Cook Islands 143 H5
Cook, Mount 115 C5
Cook, Recif de 114 W15
Cookstown 58 J3
Cook Strait 115 C4
Cooktown 113 K2
Coolibah 112 G2
Coolidge 126 G4
Cooma 113 K6
Coomnadiha 59 C9
Coomscarrea 59 B9
Coonamble 113 K5
Coondapoor 92 D6
Coongan 112 D3
Coopers Creek 113 H4
Cooroy 113 L4
Coosa 129 J4
Coos Bay *U.S.A.* 122 B6
Coos Bay *U.S.A.* 122 B6
Cootamundra 113 K5
Cootehill 58 H4
Copacabana 138 C3
Copa, Cerro 138 C4

Cope 123 N8
Copenhagen 63 E9
Copiapo 138 B5
Copinsay 56 F2
Copkoy 76 B2
Copper 118 G3
Copper Center 118 F3
Coppermine *Canada* 119 M2
Coppermine *Canada* 119 N2
Copper Mount 122 F2
Copplestone 52 D4
Copsa Mica 73 H2
Coquet 57 G5
Coquimbo 138 B5
Coquimbo, Bahia de 138 B5
Corabia 73 H4
Coracora 136 C7
Coral Harbour 120 K5
Coral Sea Plateau 113 K2
Corantijn 136 F3
Corbeil-Essonnes 64 E4
Corbiere 53 M7
Corbieres 65 E7
Corbigny 65 E5
Corbin 124 H8
Corby 53 G2
Corby Glen 53 G2
Corcaigh 59 E9
Corcubion 66 B1
Cordele 129 L5
Cordoba 131 L8
Cordoba *Argentina* 138 D6
Cordoba *Spain* 66 D4
Cordoba, Sierras de 138 D6
Cordova 136 B6
Cordova 118 F3
Corfe 52 D4
Corfu *Greece* 74 E3
Corfu *Greece* 74 E3
Coria 66 C2
Corigliano Calabro 69 F6
Corinda 113 H2
Corinth *Greece* 75 G4
Corinth *U.S.A.* 128 H3
Corinth, Gulf of 75 G3
Corinto *Brazil* 138 H3
Corinto *Nicaragua* 132 D8
Corixa Grande 138 E3
Cork *Ireland* 59 E9
Cork *Ireland* 59 E9
Corlay 64 B4
Corleone 69 D7
Corlu 76 B2
Cornafulla 59 F6
Corner Brook 121 Q8
Cornhill-on-Tweed 57 F4
Corning 125 M5
Corn Islands 132 F8
Cornudilla 66 E1
Cornwall *U.K.* 52 C4
Cornwall *U.K.* 125 N4
Cornwallis Island 120 H2
Cornwall Island 120 H2
Coro 136 D1
Coroata 137 J4
Corocoro 138 C3
Coromandel *Brazil* 138 G3
Coromandel *New Zealand* 115 E2
Coromandel Coast 92 F6
Coromandel Peninsula 115 E2
Corona 127 K3
Coronado, Bahia de 132 E10
Coronation Gulf 119 N2
Coronel 139 B7
Coronel Dorrego 139 D7
Coronel Pringles 139 D7
Coronel Suarez 139 D7
Corovode 75 F2
Corps 65 F6
Corpus Christi 128 D7
Corpus Christi Bay 128 D7
Corpus Christi, Lake 128 D6
Corque 138 C3
Corran 57 C4
Corraun Peninsula 58 C5
Corrib, Lough 59 D6
Corrientes *Argentina* 138 E5
Corrientes *Peru* 136 B4
Corrientes, Cabo *Colombia* 136 B2
Corrientes, Cabo *Cuba* 132 E4
Corrientes, Cabo *Mexico* 130 G7
Corrigan 128 E5
Corrigin 112 D5
Corry 125 L6
Corryvreckan, Gulf of 57 C4
Corse 69 B4
Corse, Cap 68 B4
Corsewall Point 57 C5
Corsica 69 B4
Corsicana 128 D4
Corte 69 B4
Cortegana 66 C4
Cortez 127 H2
Cortina d'Ampezzo 68 D2
Cortland 125 M5
Cortona 68 C4
Corubal 104 C3
Coruche 66 B3
Coruh 77 J2
Corum 76 F2
Corumba 138 E3

Corumba 138 G3
Corunna 66 B1
Corvallis 122 C5
Corve 52 E2
Corwen 52 D2
Cos 75 J4
Cosamaloapan 131 M8
Cosamozza 69 B4
Cosenza 69 F6
Cosiguina, Volcan 132 D8
Cosmoledo Islands 82 C7
Cosne 65 E5
Costa, Cordillera de la 133 N9
Costa Rica 132 E9
Costesti 73 H3
Cotabato 91 G4
Cotacachi 136 B3
Cotagaita 138 C4
Cotahuasi 138 B3
Cotentin 64 C4
Cotiella 67 G1
Cotonou 105 F4
Cotopaxi 136 B4
Cottage Grove 122 C6
Cottbus 70 F3
Cottingham 55 J3
Cottonwood 126 F3
Coubre, Pointe de la 65 C6
Coulommiers 64 E4
Coulonge 125 M3
Council Bluffs 124 C6
Coupar Angus 57 E4
Courantyne 136 F3
Courchevel 65 G6
Couronne, Cap 65 F7
Courtenay 122 B3
Courtmacsherry Bay 59 E9
Coutances 64 C4
Couto Magalhaes 137 H5
Coutras 65 C6
Cove 56 C3
Coventry 53 F2
Covilha 66 C2
Covington *Kentucky, U.S.A.* 124 H7
Covington *Virginia, U.S.A.* 125 L8
Cowal 57 C4
Cowan, Lake 112 E5
Cowbit 53 G2
Cowbridge 52 D3
Cowdenbeath 57 E4
Cowes 53 F4
Cowfold 53 G4
Cowlitz 122 C4
Cowra 113 K5
Coxim 138 F3
Cox's Bazar 93 H4
Coxwold 55 H2
Cozumel 131 R7
Cozumel, Isla de 131 R7
Cracow 71 H3
Cradock 108 E6
Craig 123 L7
Craigavon 58 K4
Craignure 57 C4
Crail 57 F4
Crailsheim 70 D4
Craiova 73 G3
Cramlington 55 H1
Cranborne 53 F4
Cranbrook 122 G3
Crane 127 L5
Cranleigh 53 G3
Cranstown, Kap 120 Q3
Craponne-sur-Arzon 65 E6
Crasna *Romania* 73 G2
Crasna *Romania* 73 J2
Crater Lake 122 C6
Crateus 137 J5
Crati 69 F6
Crato 137 K5
Cravo Norte 136 C2
Crawford 123 N6
Crawford Point 91 F3
Crawfordville 129 K5
Crawley 53 G3
Crazy Mountains 123 J4
Creach Bheinn 57 C4
Creag Meaghaidh 57 D3
Creagorry 56 A3
Crediton 52 D4
Cree *Canada* 119 P4
Cree *U.K.* 57 D5
Cree Lake 119 P4
Creeslough 58 G2
Creetown 54 E2
Creggan 58 H3
Creggs 58 F5
Crema 68 B3
Cremona 68 B3
Crepaja 72 F3
Cres *Yugoslavia* 72 C3
Cres *Yugoslavia* 72 C3
Crescent 122 D6
Crescent City 122 B7
Crest 65 F6
Creston 124 C6
Crestview 129 J5
Crete 75 H5
Cretin, Cape 114 D3
Creus, Cap 67 H1
Creuse 65 D5
Crevillente 67 F3
Crewe 55 G3

Crewkerne 52 E4
Crianlarich 57 D4
Criccieth 52 C2
Criciuma 138 G5
Crick 53 F2
Crickhowell 52 D3
Cricklade 53 F3
Crieff 57 E4
Criffel 55 F2
Crikvenica 72 C3
Crimea 79 E6
Cristalandia 137 H6
Cristalina 138 G3
Cristobal Colon, Pico 136 C1
Crisu Alb 73 F2
Crisu Negru 73 F2
Crisu Repede 73 G2
Crna Reka 73 F5
Crni Drim 72 F5
Croaghgorm Mountains 58 F3
Croagh Patrick 58 C5
Croatia 72 C3
Crocketford 57 E5
Crockett 128 E5
Croggan 57 C4
Crohy Head 58 F3
Croick 56 D3
Croisette, Cap 65 F7
Croke, Mount 112 D5
Croker Island 112 G1
Cromalt Hills 56 C2
Cromar 57 F3
Cromarty 56 D3
Cromarty Firth 56 D3
Cromdale, Hills of 56 E3
Cromer 53 J2
Cromwell 115 B6
Crook 55 H2
Crooked *Canada* 122 D5
Crooked *U.S.A.* 119 L4
Crooked Island 133 K3
Crooked Island Passage 133 K3
Crookham 57 F4
Crookhaven 59 C10
Crookston 124 B3
Croom 59 E7
Crosby *Isle of Man, U.K.* 54 E2
Crosby *Merseyside, U.K.* 55 F3
Crosby *U.S.A.* 124 D3
Cross 105 G4
Crossett 128 G4
Cross Fell 55 G2
Crossgar 58 L4
Cross Hands 52 C3
Crosshaven 59 F9
Cross Lake 119 R5
Crossmaglen 58 J4
Crossmolina 58 D4
Cross Sound 118 H4
Crossville 129 K3
Crotone 69 F6
Crouch 53 H3
Crowborough 53 H3
Crowle 55 J3
Crowley's Ridge 128 G3
Crowsnest Pass 119 N6
Croxton Kerrial 53 G2
Croydon *Australia* 113 J2
Croydon *U.K.* 53 G2
Crozet, Iles 142 C6
Crozier Channel 120 C2
Cruces, Punta 136 B2
Crudgington 52 E2
Crumlin 58 K3
Cruz Alta 138 F5
Cruz, Cabo 132 J5
Cruz del Eje 138 C6
Cruzeiro do Sul 136 C5
Cruz Grande *Chile* 138 B5
Cruz Grande *Mexico* 131 K9
Crymych 52 C3
Crystal City 127 N6
Crystal Falls 124 F3
Csongrad 72 F2
Csorna 72 D2
Cuamba 109 G2
Cuando 106 D6
Cuangar 106 C6
Cuango 106 C4
Cuanza 106 C4
Cuatro Cienegas 127 L7
Cuauhtemoc 127 J6
Cuautla 131 K8
Cuba 132 G4
Cubango 106 C6
Cubara 133 L11
Cubuk 76 E2
Cuchi 106 C5
Cuchilla Grande 138 E6
Cuchivero 136 D2
Cuchumatanes, Alto 132 B7
Cuckfield 53 G3
Cucui 136 C2
Cucuta 136 C2
Cuddalore 92 E6
Cuddapah 92 E6
Cudgwa 113 K6
Cue 112 D4
Cuellar 66 D2
Cuenca 136 B4
Cuencame 130 D4
Cuenca, Serrania de 66 E2
Cuernavaca 131 K8
Cuero 128 D6
Cuiaba *Brazil* 138 E3

Cuiaba *Brazil*	138	E3
Cuicatlan	131	L9
Cuilcagh	58	G4
Cuillin Hills	56	B3
Cuillin Sound	57	B3
Cuito	106	C6
Cuito Cuanavale	106	C6
Cuitzeo, Laguna de	131	J8
Cuiuni	136	E4
Cukai	90	C5
Cukurca	77	K4
Cu Lao Hon	93	L6
Culbertson	123	M3
Culebra Peak	127	K2
Culebra, Sierra de la	66	C2
Culiacan	130	F5
Culion	91	F3
Culiseui	137	G6
Culkein	56	C2
Cullera	67	F3
Cullin, Lough	58	D5
Cullman	129	J3
Culm	52	D4
Culmen	77	H4
Culpeper	125	L7
Cults	57	F3
Culverden	115	D5
Culworth	53	F2
Culzean Bay	57	D5
Cumacay	77	K3
Cumali	76	B2
Cumana	136	E1
Cumbal, Nevado de	136	B3
Cumberland *Kentucky, U.S.A.*	124	H8
Cumberland *W. Virginia, U.S.A.*	125	L7
Cumberland Bay	139	J10
Cumberland Mountains	129	K2
Cumberland Peninsula	120	P4
Cumberland Plateau	129	J3
Cumberland Sound	120	N4
Cumbernauld	57	E5
Cumbria	55	G2
Cumbrian Mountains	55	F2
Cumbum	92	E5
Cumina	137	F4
Cummings	122	C8
Cumnock	57	D5
Cumpas	127	H5
Cumra	76	E4
Cunderdin	112	D5
Cunene	106	B6
Cuneo	68	A3
Cunnamulla	113	K4
Cunningham	57	D5
Cuorgne	68	A3
Cupar	57	E4
Cupica	136	B2
Cuprija	73	F4
Cupula, Pico	130	D5
Curacao	133	N8
Curacautin	139	B7
Curaco	139	C7
Curaray	136	B4
Curepipe	109	L7
Curico	139	B7
Curitiba	138	F5
Curitibanos	138	F5
Currais Novos	137	K5
Curralinho	137	H4
Curra, Lough	59	E6
Currane, Lough	59	B9
Currelo	138	H3
Curtici	73	F2
Curtis *Canada*	120	J4
Curtis *U.S.A.*	123	P7
Curtis Channel	113	L3
Curtis Island *Australia*	113	L3
Curtis Island *New Zealand*	111	T8
Curua *Brazil*	137	G4
Curua *Brazil*	137	G5
Curuca	137	G4
Curupira	136	E4
Curupira, Sierra de	136	E3
Curuzu Cuatia	138	E5
Cushcamcarragh	58	C5
Cushendall	58	K2
Cushendun	58	K2
Cusiana	136	C3
Cut Bank	122	H3
Cuthbert	129	K5
Cutral-Co	139	B7
Cuttack	92	G4
Cuvelai	106	C6
Cuxhaven	70	C2
Cuyo Islands	91	G3
Cuyuni	136	F2
Cuzco	136	C6
Cvrsnica	72	D4
Cwmbran	52	D3
Cwmffrwd	52	C3
Cyclades	75	H4
Cynthiana	124	H7
Cypress Hills	123	K3
Cyprus	76	E5
Cyrene	101	K2
Czarna	71	J3
Czechoslovakia	70	F4
Czeremcha	71	K2
Czernowitz	73	H1
Czerwiensk	70	F2
Czestochowa	71	H3
Czluchow	71	G2

D

Dabakala	104	E4
Daban Shan	93	K1
Daba Shan	93	L2
Dabat	103	G5
Dabeiba	136	B2
Dabie Shan	93	N2
Dabola	104	C3
Daboya	104	E4
Dabrowa	71	K2
Dabrowa Gornicza	71	H3
Dabrowa Tarnowska	71	J3
Dabsan	86	G2
Da Cabreira, Sierra	66	B2
Dacca	93	G4
Dadale	114	J6
Daday	76	E2
Dadianzi	88	B4
Dadu	92	C3
Daeni	73	K3
Daer Reservoir	57	E5
Daet	91	G3
Dafla Hills	93	H3
Dafrah, Ad	97	L5
Dagana	104	B2
Dagardi	76	C3
Dagbasi	77	H2
Dagbeli	76	D4
Dagenham	53	H3
Daggs Sound	115	A6
Daglica	77	L4
Daglingworth	53	E3
Dagongcha	86	H4
Dagua	114	C2
Dagupan	91	G2
Dagyolu	77	H3
Dahab	96	B2
Dahanu	92	D5
Dahezhen	88	D2
Dahi, Nafud ad	96	G5
Da Hinggan Ling	87	N2
Dahlak Archipelago	96	E9
Dahlem	70	B3
Dahme	70	E3
Dahm, Ramlat	96	G8
Dahna, Ad *Saudi Arabia*	96	H6
Dahna, Ad *Saudi Arabia*	96	H4
Dahod	92	D4
Dahra	67	G4
Dahuk	77	K4
Dai	114	K5
Daia	73	J4
Daik	90	D6
Daimiel	66	E3
Daingean	59	H6
Dair, Jebel ed	102	F5
Dairut	102	F2
Daito-jima	83	M4
Dajarra	113	H3
Dakar	104	B3
Dakhla Oasis	102	E2
Dak Kon	93	L6
Dakoro	101	G6
Dakovica	72	F4
Dakovo	72	E3
Dakshin Gangotri	141	A5
Dala	114	K6
Dalaba	104	C3
Dalab, Chalp	95	S5
Dalad Qi	87	K3
Dala-Jarna	63	F6
Dalalven	63	G6
Dalaman	76	C4
Dalandzadgad	87	J3
Dalanganem Islands	91	G3
Dalaoba	86	E3
Da Lat	93	L6
Dalbandin	92	B3
Dalbeattie	54	F2
Dalby	113	L4
Dalch	52	D4
Dale *Norway*	63	A6
Dale *U.S.A.*	124	G7
Dalhalvaig	56	E2
Dalhart	127	L2
Dalhousie	125	S2
Dalhousie, Cape	118	K1
Dali	93	K3
Dalian	87	N4
Dalidag	94	H2
Dalkeith	57	E5
Dalkey	59	K6
Dallas	128	D4
Dalles, The	122	D5
Dall Island	118	J4
Dallol Bosso	101	F6
Dalma	97	L4
Dalmally	57	D4
Dalmatia	72	C3
Dalnaspidal	57	D4
Dalnegorsk	88	E3
Dalnerechensk	88	D3
Daloa	104	D4
Dalou Shan	93	L3
Dalrymple	57	D5
Dalrymple, Mount	113	K3
Dalsmynni	62	U12
Daltenganj	92	F4
Dalton	129	K3
Daluolemi	88	B3
Dalupiri	91	G2
Dalvik	62	V12

Daly	112	G1
Daly Waters	113	G2
Damal	77	K2
Daman	92	D4
Damanhur	102	F1
Damar	91	H7
Damascus	77	G6
Damavand	95	L4
Damba	106	C4
Dame Marie	133	K5
Dame Marie, Cabo	133	K5
Damghan	95	M3
Damh, Loch	56	C3
Damietta	103	F1
Daming	87	M4
Damlacik	77	H4
Damodar	92	G4
Damoh	92	E4
Damongo	104	E4
Dampier	112	D3
Dampier Archipelago	112	D3
Dampier Land	112	E2
Dampier, Selat	91	J6
Dampier Strait	114	D3
Damqawt	97	L8
Da Nang	93	L5
Danau Toba	90	B5
Danba	93	K2
Danbury	125	P6
Danby Lake	126	E3
Dandong	87	N3
Daneborg	120	X3
Dangchang	93	K2
Dangori	93	J3
Dangrek, Phnom	93	K6
Dangshan	93	N2
Daniel	123	J6
Danilov	78	G4
Danilovgrad	72	E4
Dank	97	N5
Danli	132	D7
Dannenburg	70	D2
Dannevirke	115	F4
Dansville	125	M5
Danu	114	E2
Danube	71	H5
Danumparai	90	F5
Danville *Illinois, U.S.A.*	124	G6
Danville *Kentucky, U.S.A.*	124	H8
Danville *Virginia, U.S.A.*	125	L8
Dan Xian	93	L5
Dany	113	J6
Danzig, Gulf of	71	H1
Dao	91	G3
Daoud	101	G1
Dao Xian	93	M3
Dapaong	104	F3
Dapiak, Mount	91	G4
Daqing	87	N2
Daqm	97	N7
Daqq-e-Patargan	95	Q5
Dara	94	C5
Darab	95	M7
Darabani	73	J1
Daran	95	K5
Dar Anjir, Kavir-e	95	M5
Darasun	85	J6
Daravica	74	F1
Darband	95	N6
Darbhanga	92	G3
Darby, Cape	118	C3
Dardanelle Lake	128	F3
Dardanelles	75	J2
Dar El Beida	100	D2
Darende	77	G3
Dar Es Salaam	107	G4
Dargaville	115	D1
Darica	76	C2
Darien, Golfo del	136	B2
Darija	77	K5
Darjeeling	93	G3
Darjiling	93	G3
Dar Lac, Cao Nguen	93	L6
Darlag	93	J2
Darling	113	J5
Darling Downs	113	K4
Darling Range	112	D5
Darlington *U.K.*	55	H2
Darlington *U.S.A.*	129	N3
Darmanesti	73	J2
Darmstadt	70	C4
Darnah	101	K2
Darnick	113	J5
Darnley Bay	118	L2
Darnley, Cape	141	E5
Daroca	67	F2
Darokhov	71	L4
Darovskoye	78	H4
Darreh Gaz	95	P3
Darsa	97	N10
Darsi	92	E5
Darsser Ort	70	E1
Dart	52	D4
Dartford	53	H3
Dartmoor	52	D4
Dartmouth *Canada*	121	P9
Dartmouth *U.K.*	52	D4
Darton	55	H3
Darty Mountains	58	F4
Daru	114	C3
Daruba	91	H5
Daruvar	72	D3
Darvel	57	D5

Darvi	86	G2
Darwen	55	G3
Darwin	112	G1
Darwin, Mount	126	C2
Daryacheh-ye Orumiyeh	77	L4
Darzin	95	P7
Das	97	L4
Dashitou	86	F3
Dashizhai	87	N2
Dasht *Iran*	95	N3
Dasht *Pakistan*	92	B3
Dashti-oburdon	86	B4
Da, Song	93	K4
Datca	76	B4
Datia	92	E3
Datong	87	L3
Datong Shan	93	J1
Datuk, Tanjung	90	D5
Datu Piang	91	G4
Daugava	63	M8
Daugavpils	63	P9
Daule *Ecuador*	136	B4
Daule *Ecuador*	136	B3
Daun	70	B3
Dauphin	119	Q5
Dauphine	65	F6
Dauphine, Alpes du	65	F6
Dauphin Lake	119	R5
Davangere	92	E6
Davao	91	H4
Davao Gulf	91	H4
Davarzan	95	N3
Dave Creek	127	H2
Davenport	124	E6
Daventry	53	F2
David	132	F10
David-Gorodok	79	D5
Davidson	123	L2
Davidson Mountains	118	G2
Davington	57	E5
Davis *Antarctic*	141	F5
Davis *Australia*	112	E3
Davis *U.S.A.*	126	B1
Davis Mountains	127	K5
Davis Sea	141	F6
Davis Strait	120	P4
Davlekanovo	78	K5
Davos	68	B2
Davulga	76	D3
Dawa	87	N3
Dawasir, Wadi al	96	G6
Dawa Wenz	103	H7
Dawhat Salwah	97	K4
Dawley	52	E2
Dawlish	52	D4
Dawna Range	93	J5
Dawqah	97	M7
Dawros Head	58	E3
Dawson *Australia*	113	K3
Dawson *Canada*	118	H3
Dawson *Georgia, U.S.A.*	129	K5
Dawson *N. Dakota, U.S.A.*	123	Q4
Dawson Creek	119	L4
Dawson, Mount	122	F2
Dawson Range	118	H3
Dawu	93	M2
Dawusi	93	H1
Dawwah	97	P6
Dax	65	C7
Da Xian	93	L2
Daxue Shan	93	K2
Dayr az Zawr	77	J5
Dayr Hafir	77	G4
Dayton *Ohio, U.S.A.*	124	H7
Dayton *Tennessee, U.S.A.*	129	K3
Dayton *Washington, U.S.A.*	122	F4
Daytona Beach	129	M6
Dayu	93	M3
Da Yunhe	87	M4
Dayville	122	E5
Dazkiri	76	C4
De Aar	108	D6
Dead Sea	94	B6
Deakin	112	F5
Deal	53	J3
Dean	93	N3
Dean *Canada*	118	K5
Dean *U.K.*	55	G3
Dean, Forest of	52	E3
Dean Funes	138	D6
Dean Island	141	R4
Dearborn	124	J5
Dease Arm	119	L2
Dease Inlet	118	D1
Dease Lake	118	J4
Dease Strait	119	P2
Death Valley	126	D2
Deauville	64	D4
Deben	53	J2
Debin	85	S4
Deblin	71	J3
Deboyne Islands	114	E4
Debre Birhan	103	G6
Debrecen	73	F2
Debre Markos	103	G5
Debre Tabor	103	G5
Decatur *Alabama, U.S.A.*	129	J3
Decatur *Georgia, U.S.A.*	129	K4
Decatur *Illinois, U.S.A.*	124	F7
Decatur *Indiana, U.S.A.*	124	H6
Decatur *Texas, U.S.A.*	128	D4
Decazeville	65	E6
Deccan	92	E5
Deception	108	D4

Deception	120	M5	Dengqen	93	J2	Dewas	92	E4	Dinard	64	B4
Dechang	93	K3	Den Haag	64	F2	De Witt	128	G3	Dinas Head	52	C2
Decize	65	E5	Den Helder	64	F2	Dewsbury	55	H3	Dinbych	55	F3
Decorah	124	E5	Denia	67	G3	Dey-Dey, Lake	112	G4	Dinbych-y-pysgod	52	C3
Deda	73	H2	Deniliquin	113	K6	Deyhuk	95	N5	Dinder	96	B10
Deddington	53	F3	Denio	122	E7	Deylaman	95	J3	Dindigul	92	E6
Dedeagach	75	H4	Denison *Iowa, U.S.A.*	124	C6	Deyong, Tanjung	114	B3	Dinek	76	E4
Dedegol Daglari	76	D4	Denison *Texas, U.S.A.*	128	D4	Deyyer	95	K8	Dinggye	93	G3
Dedekoy	76	E2	Denison, Mount	118	E4	Dez	94	J5	Dingle	59	B8
Dedougou	104	E3	Denizli	76	C4	Dezful	94	J5	Dingle Bay	59	B8
Dedu	87	P2	Denmark	63	B9	Dezhneva, Mys	118	B2	Dingle Peninsula	59	B8
Dee *Cheshire, U.K.*	55	G3	Denmark Strait	116	S2	Dezhou	87	M4	Dinguiraye	104	C3
Dee *Dumfries and Galloway*, U.K.	54	F2	Dennis Head	56	F1	Dhaka	93	G4	Dingwall	56	D3
Dee *Grampian*, U.K.	57	F3	Denny	57	E4	Dhamar	96	G9	Dingxi	93	K1
Dee, Linn of	57	E4	Denpasar	90	F7	Dhampur	92	E3	Dingxin	86	H3
Deep River	125	M3	Densongi	91	G6	Dhamtari	92	F4	Dingxing	87	M4
Deeps, The	56	A2	Denta	73	F3	Dhanbad	92	G4	Dinh Lap	93	L4
Deering, Mount	112	F4	Denton	128	D4	Dhandhuka	92	D4	Dinnington	55	H3
Deer Lake	121	Q8	D'Entrecasteaux Islands	114	E3	Dhang Range	92	F3	Dinosaur	123	K7
Deer Lodge	122	H4	D'Entrecasteaux, Point	112	D5	Dhankuta	93	G3	Dionard	56	D2
Defiance	124	H6	Denver	123	M8	Dhar	92	E4	Diorbivol	104	C2
Defiance Plateau	127	H3	Deogarh	92	F4	Dharmapuri	92	E6	Diouloulou	104	B3
Deflotte, Cape	114	X16	Deoghar	92	G4	Dharmavaram	92	E6	Diourbel	104	B3
De Funiak Springs	129	J5	Deolali	92	D5	Dharmjaygarh	92	F4	Dipolog	91	G4
Degeberga	63	F9	Deosai, Plains of	92	E2	Dharwad	92	D5	Dir	92	D1
Degeh Bur	103	H6	Dep	85	M6	Dhaulagiri	92	F3	Direction, Cape	113	J1
Degelis	125	R3	Deqen	93	J3	Dhaulpur	92	E3	Dire Dawa	103	H6
Degerhamn	63	G8	Deqing	93	M4	Dhenkanal	92	G4	Direkli	77	G3
Deggendorf	70	E4	De Queen	128	E3	Dhenousa	75	H4	Dirk Hartogs Island	112	C4
De Grey	112	E3	Dera Bugti	92	C3	Dhermatas, Akra	75	G5	Dirra	102	E5
Dehaj	95	M6	Dera Ghazikhan	92	D2	Dhermi	74	E2	Dirranbandi	113	K4
Dehak	95	R8	Dera Ismail Khan	92	D2	Dheskati	75	F3	Disappointment, Cape	122	B4
Dehalak Deset	103	H4	Derajat	92	D2	Dhespotiko	75	H4	Disappointment, Lake	112	E5
Deh Bid	95	L6	Derazhno	71	M3	Dhialvos Zakinthou	75	F4	Discovery Bay	113	J6
Deh-Dasht	95	K6	Derazhnya	73	J1	Dhidhimotikhon	75	J2	Dishna *Egypt*	103	F2
Deheq	95	K5	Derbent	79	H7	Dhikti Ori	75	H5	Dishna *U.S.A.*	118	D3
Dehiwala	92	E7	Derby *Australia*	112	E2	Dhirfis	75	G3	Disko	120	R4
Dehkhvareqan	94	G3	Derby *U.K.*	53	F2	Dhodhekanisos	75	J4	Disko Bay	120	R4
Dehloran	94	H5	Derbyshire	55	H3	Dhomokos	75	G3	Disna *Belorussia*	63	M9
Dehra Dun	92	E2	Derekoy	76	B2	Dhoraji	92	D4	Disna *Belorussia*	63	N9
Deh Salm	95	P6	Dereli	77	H2	Dhrangadhra	92	D4	Dispur	93	H3
Dehui	87	P3	Derg	58	G3	Dhrepanon, Akra	75	G3	Diss	53	J2
Deim Zubeir	102	E6	Dergachi	79	F5	Dhuburi	93	G3	Dissen	96	E8
Dej	73	G2	Derg, Lough *Donegal, Ireland*	58	G3	Dhule	92	D4	Distrito Federal	138	G3
De Kalb *Illinois, U.S.A.*	124	F6	Derg, Lough *Tipperary, Ireland*	59	F7	Dia	75	H5	Ditchling Beacon	53	G4
De Kalb *Texas, U.S.A.*	128	E4	De Ridder	128	F5	Diamante	138	D6	Ditinn	104	C3
Dekemhare	96	D9	Derik	77	J4	Diamantina *Australia*	113	H4	Dittaino	69	E7
Dekese	106	D3	Derinkuyu	76	F3	Diamantina *Brazil*	138	H3	Ditton Priors	52	E2
Delami	102	F5	Derna	101	K2	Diamantina, Chapada	137	J6	Diu	92	D4
Delano	126	C3	Derong	93	J3	Diamond Lake Junction	122	D6	Divandarreh	94	H4
Delaram	95	R5	Derravaragh, Lough	58	H5	Diavata	75	G2	Divinopolis	138	G4
Delaware *Ohio, U.S.A.*	124	J6	Derry	58	H2	Diba al Hisn	97	N4	Divi Point	92	F5
Delaware *Pennsylvania, U.S.A.*	125	N6	Derrynasaggart Mountains	59	D9	Dibaya	106	D4	Divisor, Serra do	136	C5
Delaware *U.S.A.*	125	N7	Derryveagh Mountains	58	F2	Dibdibah, Ad	96	H2	Divnoye	79	G6
Delaware Bay	125	N7	Derudeb	103	G4	Dibrugarh	93	H3	Divrigi	77	H3
Delcevo	73	G5	Derveni	75	G3	Dickinson	123	N4	Dixcove	104	E5
Delemont	68	A2	Derventa	72	D3	Dickson	129	J2	Dixon Entrance	118	J5
Delft	64	F2	Derwent *Australia*	113	K7	Dicle	77	J4	Diyadin	77	K3
Delfzijl	64	G2	Derwent *Derbyshire, U.K.*	55	H3	Didcot	53	F3	Diyala	94	G4
Delgada, Punta	131	L8	Derwent *N. Yorkshire, U.K.*	55	J2	Didinga Hills	103	F7	Diyarbakir	77	J4
Delgado, Cabo	109	H2	Derwent Reservoir	55	H2	Didnovarre	62	K1	Diza	77	L3
Delgerhaan	87	J2	Derwent Water	54	E2	Didwana	92	D3	Dja	105	H5
Delgo	102	F3	Derzhavinsk	84	Ae6	Die	65	F6	Djado	101	H4
Delhi *India*	92	E3	Desaguadero *Argentina*	138	C6	Diebougou	104	E3	Djambala	106	B3
Delhi *India*	92	E3	Desaguadero *Bolivia*	138	C3	Diefenbaker, Lake	123	L2	Djanet	101	G4
Delhi *Colorado, U.S.A.*	127	L2	Descanso	126	D4	Diego-Suarez	109	J2	Djelfa	101	F2
Delhi *New York, U.S.A.*	125	N5	Deschambault Lake	119	Q5	Dielette	53	N6	Djema	102	E6
Delice *Turkey*	76	E3	Deschutes	122	D5	Dien Bien Phu	93	K4	Djenne	100	E6
Delice *Turkey*	76	F2	Dese	103	G5	Diepholz	70	C2	Djibouti	103	H5
Delicias	127	K6	Deseado	139	C9	Dieppe	64	D4	Djibouti	103	H5
Delijan	95	K4	Desemboque	126	F5	Dietfurt	70	D4	Djolu	106	D2
Delingha	93	J1	Desengano, Punta	139	C9	Diffa	101	H6	Djougou	105	F4
Delitzsch	70	E3	Desert Center	126	E4	Digby	121	N9	Djourab	102	C4
Delle	65	G5	Desert Peak	122	H7	Digges Island	120	L5	Djupivogur	62	X12
Dellys	101	F1	Des Moines *U.S.A.*	124	D6	Digne	65	G6	Djurdjura	67	J4
Delmenhorst	70	C2	Des Moines *U.S.A.*	124	D6	Digoin	65	F5	Djursland	63	D8
Delnice	72	C3	Desna	79	E5	Digor	77	K2	Dmitriya Lapteva, Proliv	85	Q2
De Long Mountains	118	C2	Desolacion, Isla	139	B10	Digul	114	C3	Dmitrov	78	F4
Deloraine	113	K7	Des Plaines	124	G5	Diinsoor	107	H2	Dnepr	79	E6
Delray Beach	129	M7	Dessau	70	E3	Dijlah, Nahr	77	K5	Dneprodzerzhinsk	79	E6
Del Rio	127	M6	Destna	71	G3	Dijon	65	F5	Dnepropetrovsk	79	F6
Delsbo	63	G6	Dete	108	E3	Dikakah, Ad	97	K7	Dneprovskaya Nizmennost	79	D5
Delta *Colorado, U.S.A.*	127	H1	Detmold	70	C3	Dikanas	62	G4	Dneprovsko-Bugskiy Kanal	71	L2
Delta *Utah, U.S.A.*	126	F1	Detour, Point	124	G4	Dikbiyik	77	G2	Dnestr	73	K2
Delta Junction	118	F3	Detroit	124	J5	Dikili	76	B3	Dnestrovskiy Liman	73	L2
Delvin	58	H5	Detroit Lakes	124	C3	Dikson	84	C2	Dno	78	E4
Dema	78	J5	Deutschlandsberg	68	E2	Dikwa	105	H3	Doaktown	125	T3
Demanda, Sierra de la	66	E1	Deva	73	G3	Dili	91	H7	Doba	102	C6
Demba	106	D4	Devakottai	92	E7	Di Linh	93	L6	Dobbiaco	68	D2
Dembi Dolo	103	F6	Devdevdyak	84	H4	Dilizhan	77	L2	Dobeln	70	E3
Demer	64	F3	Devecikonagi	76	C3	Dillia	101	H5	Dobiegniew	70	F2
Demerara	136	F2	Devecser	72	D2	Dilling	102	E5	Dobo	114	A3
Deming	127	J4	Devegecidi Baraji	77	H3	Dillingen	70	D4	Doboj	72	E3
Demini	136	E3	Develi	76	F3	Dillingham	118	D4	Dobra	71	H3
Demirci	76	C3	Deventer	64	G2	Dillon	122	H5	Dobre Miasto	71	J2
Demir Kazik	76	F4	Deveron	56	F3	Dilolo	106	D5	Dobric	73	J4
Demirkoy	76	B2	Devils	127	M5	Dimapur	93	H3	Dobrodzien	71	H3
Demmin	70	E2	Devil's Bridge	52	D2	Dimashq	77	G6	Dobrogea	73	K3
Demnate	100	D2	Devils Lake	123	Q3	Dimbelenge	106	D4	Dobrovolsk	71	K1
Demopolis	129	J4	Devils Paw	118	J4	Dimbokro	104	E4	Dobrush	79	E5
Dempo, Gunung	90	C6	Devils Tower	123	M5	Dimbo vita	73	H3	Dobryanka	78	K4
Demyanskoye	84	Ae5	Devin	73	H5	Dimitrovgrad *Bulgaria*	73	H4	Dobsina	71	J4
Denakil	103	H5	Devizes	53	F3	Dimitrovgrad *Russia*	78	H5	Dobson	115	C5
Denan	103	H6	Devli	92	E3	Dimona	94	B6	Dochart	57	D4
Denau	86	B4	Devnya	73	J4	Dimovo	73	G4	Docking	53	H2
Denbigh	55	F3	Devoll	75	F2	Dinagat	91	H3	Dodecanese	75	J4
Denbigh, Cape	118	C3	Devon	52	D4	Dinajpur	93	G3	Dodge City	127	M2
Denby Dale	55	H3	Devon Island	120	J2	Dinan	64	B4	Dodman Point	52	C4
Dendang	90	D6	Devonport	115	E2	Dinanagar	92	E2	Dodoma	107	G4
Dendermonde	64	F3	Devrek	76	D2	Dinant	64	F3	Doetinchem	64	G3
Dendi	103	G6	Devrekani	76	E2	Dinar	76	D3	Dofa	91	H6
Denezhkino	84	D3	Devrez	76	E2	Dinara Planina	72	D3	Dogai Coring	93	G2
Dengkou	87	K3	Devyatkova	84	Ae5				Doganbey	76	D4
			Dewangiri	93	H3				Doganhisar	76	D3

Name	Page	Grid
Dogankent	76	F4
Dogansehir	77	G3
Doganyol	77	H3
Doganyurt	76	E2
Dog Creek	122	C2
Dogen Co	93	H2
Dog Lake	124	F2
Dogo	89	D7
Dogondoutchi	101	F6
Dogubeyazit	77	L3
Dogukardeniz Daglari	77	J2
Doha	97	K4
Doi Luang	93	K5
Dojran	73	G5
Dojransko Jezero	73	G5
Doka *Indonesia*	114	A3
Doka *Sudan*	96	B10
Dokkum	64	G2
Dokshitsy	63	M9
Dokurcun	76	D2
Dolak	114	B3
Dolak, Tanjung	91	K7
Dolanog	52	D2
Dolbeau	125	P2
Dol-de-Bretagne	64	C4
Dole	65	F5
Dolgellau	52	D2
Dolginovo	71	M1
Dolgiy, Ostrov	84	Ac3
Dolgoye	71	K4
Dolina	79	C6
Dolinsk	88	J2
Dolinskaya	79	E6
Dollar	57	E4
Dollar Law	57	E5
Dolni Kralovice	70	F4
Dolok, Tanjung	114	A3
Dolomitiche, Alpi	68	C2
Dolo Odo	103	H7
Dolores *Argentina*	139	E7
Dolores *Uruguay*	139	E6
Dolores *U.S.A.*	122	K8
Dolphin and Union Strait	119	N1
Dolphin, Cape	139	E10
Dolsk	71	G3
Domanic	76	C3
Dombas	63	C5
Dombe	109	F3
Dombe Grande	106	B5
Dombovar	72	E2
Dombrad	73	F1
Dome, Puy de	65	E6
Domett	115	D5
Domfront	64	C4
Dominica	133	S7
Dominical	132	F10
Dominican Republic	133	M5
Dominion, Cape	120	M4
Domo	103	J6
Domodossola	68	B2
Domuya, Cerro	139	B7
Don *Grampian, U.K.*	56	F3
Don *S. Yorkshire, U.K.*	55	H3
Don *Russia*	79	G6
Donaghadee	58	L3
Donaldsville	128	G5
Donau	68	E1
Donauworth	70	D4
Don Benito	66	D3
Doncaster	55	H3
Dondo	106	B4
Dondra Head	92	F7
Donegal *Ireland*	58	F3
Donegal *Ireland*	58	G3
Donegal Bay	58	F3
Donegal Point	59	C7
Donenbay	86	D2
Doneraile	59	E8
Donetsk	79	F6
Dongan *Heilongjiang, China*	88	E2
Dongan *Hunan, China*	93	M3
Dongara	112	C4
Dongbolhai Shan	93	G2
Dongchuan	93	K3
Dongfang	93	L5
Dongfanghong	88	D2
Donggala	91	F6
Dong Hoi	93	L5
Dongjingcheng	88	B3
Dongliu	87	M5
Dongluk	86	F4
Dongning	88	C3
Dongola	102	F4
Dongping	87	M4
Dongshan	87	N5
Dongsheng	87	K4
Dongtai	87	N5
Donguena	106	B6
Dong Ujimqin Qi	87	M2
Dongxi Lian Dao	87	M5
Donington	53	G2
Doniphan	124	E8
Donji Vakuf	72	D3
Donna	62	E3
Donner Pass	122	D8
Donnington	52	E2
Dooagh	58	B5
Doon	57	D5
Doonbeg	59	C7
Doonerak, Mount	118	F2
Doon, Loch	57	D5
Doorin Point	58	F3
Dor	95	R6
Dorada, Costa	67	G2
Dora, Lake	112	E3
Dora Riparia	68	A3
Dorbiljin	86	E2
Dorchester	52	E4
Dorchester, Cape	120	L4
Dordogne	65	C6
Dordrecht	64	F3
Dore	65	E6
Dore Lake	119	P5
Dore, Mont	65	E6
Dorgali	69	B5
Dori	104	E3
Dorking	53	G3
Dormo, Ras	96	F10
Dornbirn	68	B2
Dornie	56	C3
Dornoch	56	D3
Dornoch Firth	56	D3
Dorofeyevskaya	84	C2
Dorohoi	73	J2
Dorotea	62	G4
Dorovitsa	78	H4
Dorset	52	E4
Dortdivan	76	E2
Dortmund	70	B3
Dortyol	77	G4
Doruokha	84	J2
Dorutay	77	L3
Dosatuy	85	K7
Dosso	101	F6
Dossor	79	J6
Dothan	129	K5
Douai	64	E3
Douala	105	G5
Douarnenez	64	A4
Double Mountain Fork	127	M4
Doubs	65	F5
Doubtful Sound	115	A6
Doubtless Bay	115	D1
Doue-la-Fontaine	65	C5
Douentza	100	E5
Douglas *South Africa*	108	D5
Douglas *Isle of Man, U.K.*	54	D2
Douglas *Strathclyde, U.K.*	57	E5
Douglas *Arizona, U.S.A.*	127	H5
Douglas *Georgia, U.S.A.*	129	L5
Douglas *Wyoming, U.S.A.*	123	M6
Doullens	64	E3
Doulus Head	59	B9
Doume	105	H5
Doune	57	D4
Dourada, Serra	137	H6
Dourados *Brazil*	138	E3
Dourados *Brazil*	138	F4
Dourados, Serra dos	138	F4
Douro	66	B2
Dove	55	H3
Dove Dale	55	H3
Dover *U.K.*	53	J3
Dover *Delaware, U.S.A.*	125	N7
Dover *New Hampshire, U.S.A.*	125	Q5
Dover *Ohio, U.S.A.*	125	K6
Dover-Foxcroft	125	R4
Dover, Strait of	53	J4
Dovrefjell	62	C5
Dowa	107	F5
Dowlatabad *Afghanistan*	95	R5
Dowlatabad *Afghanistan*	95	S3
Dowlatabad *Iran*	95	N7
Dowlat Yar	92	C2
Down	58	L4
Downham Market	53	H2
Downpatrick	58	L4
Downpatrick Head	58	D4
Downs, The	53	J3
Downton	53	F4
Dow Rud	94	J5
Dowshi	92	C1
Dozen	89	D7
Draa, Oued	100	D3
Drac	65	F6
Dracevo	73	F5
Drachten	64	G2
Dragalina	73	J3
Dragasani	73	H3
Dragoman	73	G4
Dragonera, Isla	67	H3
Dragon's Mouth	133	S9
Dragsfjard	63	K6
Draguignan	65	G7
Dra, Hamada du	100	D3
Drake	123	P4
Drakensberg	108	E6
Drake Passage	141	V7
Drama	75	H2
Drammen	63	H1
Drangedal	63	C7
Draperstown	58	J3
Dras	92	E2
Drau	68	E2
Drava	72	E3
Dravograd	72	C2
Drawa	70	F2
Drawsko, Jezioro	71	G2
Drayton Valley	119	N5
Dren	73	G4
Drenewydd	52	D2
Dresden	70	E3
Dresvyanka	78	K2
Dreux	64	D4
Drin	75	F2
Drin i zi	74	E1
Drobak	63	H7
Drobin	71	H2
Drogheda	58	K5
Drogichin	71	L2
Drogobych	79	C6
Drohiczyn	71	K2
Droichead Atha	58	K5
Droichead Nua	59	J6
Droitwich	53	E2
Drokiya	73	J1
Drome	65	F6
Dromedary, Cape	113	L6
Dromore	58	K4
Dronfield	55	H3
Dronne	65	D6
Dronning Maud Land	141	Z5
Dropt	65	D6
Drovyanaya	84	A2
Drumcollogher	59	E8
Drumheller	122	H2
Drummond	122	H4
Drummond Islands	124	J3
Drummond Range	113	K3
Drummondville	125	P4
Drummore	54	E2
Drumochter, Pass of	57	D4
Drumshanbo	58	F4
Druridge Bay	55	H1
Druskininkai	71	K1
Druzhba *Kazakhstan*	86	E2
Druzhba *Russia*	71	J1
Druzhina	85	R3
Drvar	72	D3
Drweca	71	H2
Dry	112	G2
Dry Bay *Canada*	121	N6
Dry Bay *U.S.A.*	118	H4
Dryden	124	D2
Drysdale, River	112	F2
Dschang	105	H4
Duab	94	J4
Dualo	91	G6
Duarte, Pico	133	M5
Duba	96	B3
Dubai	97	M4
Dubawnt Lake	119	Q3
Dubayy	97	M4
Dubbagh, Jabal Ad	96	B3
Dubbo	113	K5
Dubenskiy	79	K5
Dublin *Ireland*	59	K6
Dublin *Ireland*	59	K6
Dublin *U.S.A.*	129	L4
Dublin Bay	59	K6
Dubna	78	F4
Dubno	79	D5
Du Bois	125	L6
Dubois *Idaho, U.S.A.*	122	H5
Dubois *Wyoming, U.S.A.*	123	K6
Dubossary	79	D6
Dubreka	104	C4
Dubrovitsa	71	M3
Dubrovka *Russia*	79	E5
Dubrovka *Russia*	79	G6
Dubrovnik	72	E4
Dubrovskoye	84	J5
Dubuque	124	E5
Duchang	87	M6
Duchesne *U.S.A.*	123	J7
Duchesne *U.S.A.*	123	J7
Duchess	113	H3
Ducie Island	143	J5
Duck	129	J3
Ducklington	53	F3
Duck Mountain	119	Q5
Duddington	53	G2
Dudinka	84	D3
Dudley	53	E2
Duenas	66	D2
Duero	66	D2
Duffield	53	F2
Duff Islands	114	N6
Dufftown	56	E3
Dufton	55	G2
Duga Zapadnaya, Mys	85	R5
Dughaill, Loch	56	C3
Dugi Otok	72	C3
Duisburg	70	B3
Dukambiya	96	C9
Dukat	73	G4
Duk Fadiat	102	F6
Duk Faiwil	102	F6
Dukhan	97	K4
Duki Bolen	85	P6
Dukla	71	J4
Dukou	93	K3
Dulan	93	J1
Duldurga	85	J6
Duleek	58	K5
Dulga-Kuyuel	84	J4
Dulgalakh	85	N3
Dullingham	53	H2
Dull Lake	118	C3
Dulnain	56	E3
Dulovo	73	J4
Duluth	124	D3
Duma	77	G6
Dumaguete	91	G4
Dumai	90	C5
Dumaran	91	F3
Dumas *Arkansas, U.S.A.*	128	G3
Dumas *Texas, U.S.A.*	127	M3
Dumbarton	57	D5
Dumbea	114	X17
Dumbier	71	H4
Dumfries	55	F1
Dumfries and Galloway	57	E5
Dumitresti	73	J3
Dumka	93	G4
Dumlu	77	J2
Dumlupinar	76	C3
Dumoine	125	M3
Dumont d'Urville	141	K5
Dumont d'Urville Sea	141	J6
Dumyat	103	F1
Duna	72	E2
Dunaj	71	H5
Dunajec	71	J3
Dunany Point	58	K5
Dunarea	73	J3
Dunaujvaros	72	E2
Dunav	73	H4
Dunay *Moldavia*	73	K3
Dunay *Russia*	88	D4
Dunayevtsy	73	J1
Dunay, Ostrov	85	L2
Dunbar *Australia*	113	J2
Dunbar *U.K.*	57	F4
Dunblane	57	E4
Dunboyne	59	K6
Duncan *Canada*	122	C3
Duncan *U.S.A.*	128	D3
Duncan Passage	93	H6
Duncansby Head	56	E2
Dunchurch	53	F2
Dundaga	63	K8
Dundalk *Ireland*	58	K4
Dundalk *U.S.A.*	125	M7
Dundalk Bay	58	K5
Dundas	120	M2
Dundas, Lake	112	E5
Dundas Peninsula	120	D3
Dundas Strait	112	G1
Dun Dealgan	58	K4
Dundee *South Africa*	108	F5
Dundee *U.K.*	57	F4
Dundonald	57	D5
Dundonnell	56	C3
Dundrennan	54	F2
Dundrod	58	K3
Dundrum	58	L4
Dundrum Bay	58	L4
Dundwa Range	92	F3
Dunecht	57	F3
Dunedin *New Zealand*	115	C6
Dunedin *U.S.A.*	129	L6
Dunfanaghy	58	G2
Dunfermline	57	E4
Dungannon	58	J3
Dungarpur	92	D4
Dungarvan	59	G8
Dungarvan Harbour	59	G8
Dungeness	53	H4
Dungiven	58	J3
Dungloe	58	F3
Dungu	107	E2
Dungun	90	C5
Dunholme	55	J3
Dunhua	88	B4
Dunhuang	86	F3
Dunkeld	113	J6
Dunkerque	64	E3
Dunkirk	125	L5
Dunkur	103	G5
Dunkwa	104	E4
Dun Laoghaire	59	K6
Dunlavin	59	J6
Dunleer	58	K5
Dunmanus Bay	59	C9
Dunmanway	59	D9
Dunmore Town	132	J2
Dunmurry	58	K3
Dunnet Bay	56	E2
Dunnet Head	56	E2
Dunoon	57	D5
Dunragit	54	E2
Duns	57	F4
Dunseith	123	P3
Dunsford	52	D4
Dunstable	53	G3
Dunstan Mountains	115	B6
Dunster	52	D3
Duntelchaig, Loch	56	D3
Duntroon	115	C6
Dunvegan	56	B3
Dunvegan Head	56	B3
Dupang Ling	93	M3
Dupree	123	P5
Duque de York, Isla	139	A10
Du Quoin	124	F7
Duragan	76	F2
Durance	65	F7
Durand, Recif	114	Y17
Durango *Mexico*	130	G5
Durango *U.S.A.*	127	J2
Durankulak	73	K4
Durant	128	D3
Durazno	138	E6
Durazzo	74	E2
Durban	108	F6
Durcal	66	E4
Durdevac	72	D2
Durelj	87	J4
Duren	70	B3
Durg	92	F4
Durgapur *Bangladesh*	93	H3
Durgapur *India*	93	G4
Durham *U.K.*	55	H2
Durham *U.K.*	55	H2

Name	Page	Grid
Durham *U.S.A.*	129	N2
Durisdeer	57	E5
Durma	96	H4
Durmitor	72	E4
Durness	56	D2
Durness, Kyle of	56	D2
Durres	74	E2
Dursey Head	59	B9
Dursey Island	59	B9
Dursley	52	E3
Dursunbey	76	C3
D'Urville Island	115	D4
Dury Voe	56	B1
Dushak	95	Q3
Dushan	93	L3
Dushanbe	86	B4
Dushanzi	86	G4
Duskotna	73	J4
Dusseldorf	70	B3
Dutch Harbor	118	Ae9
Dutovo	78	K3
Duvan	78	K4
Duyun	93	L3
Duzce	76	D2
Duzkoy	77	H2
Dvinskaya Guba	78	F3
Dvorets	84	F5
Dwarka	92	C4
Dyadino	84	H5
Dyatkovo	79	E5
Dyatlovo	71	L2
Dybvad	63	D8
Dyce	56	F3
Dyer, Cape	120	P4
Dyersburg	128	H2
Dyfed	52	C3
Dyfi	52	D2
Dyje	71	G4
Dykh Tau	79	G7
Dynow	71	K4
Dyrnesvagen	62	B5
Dyulino	73	J4
Dzamin Uud	109	J2
Dzaoudzi	109	J2
Dzavhan Gol	86	G2
Dzaygil Hid	•86	H2
Dzerzhinsk *Belorussia*	78	D5
Dzerzhinsk *Russia*	78	G4
Dzhalal-Abad	86	C3
Dzhalinda	85	L6
Dzhambeyty	79	J5
Dzhambul *Kazakhstan*	86	C2
Dzhambul *Kazakhstan*	86	C3
Dzhambul *Kazakhstan*	79	J6
Dzhamm	85	N2
Dzhankoy	79	E6
Dzhebel *Bulgaria*	73	H5
Dzhebel *Turkmenistan*	95	M2
Dzhelinde	84	J2
Dzhezkazgan	80	H5
Dzhirgatal	86	C4
Dzhizak	86	B3
Dzhugdzhur, Khrebet	85	P5
Dzhulfa	94	G2
Dzhungarskiy Alatau, Khrebet	86	E2
Dzhurin	79	D6
Dzhusaly	86	A2
Dzialdowo	71	J2
Dzialoszyn	71	H3
Dzilam de Bravo	131	Q7
Dzungarian Basin	86	F2
Dzuunbayan	87	L3
Dzuunbulag	87	M2

E

Name	Page	Grid
Eagle *Newfoundland, Canada*	121	Q7
Eagle *Yukon, Canada*	118	H2
Eagle *U.S.A.*	118	G3
Eagle Lake *Canada*	124	D2
Eagle Lake *U.S.A.*	122	D7
Eagle, Mount	59	B8
Eagle Pass	127	M6
Eagle Point	114	C4
Eaglesham	57	D5
Eagles Hill	59	B9
Eaglestone Reef	111	S4
Ealing	53	G3
Earby	55	G3
Earlsferry	57	F4
Earl Shilton	53	F2
Earlston	57	F4
Earl Stonham	53	J2
Earn	57	E4
Earn, Loch	57	D4
Earp	126	E3
Easingwold	55	H2
East Anglian Heights	53	H2
Eastbourne	53	H4
East Brent	52	E3
East Bridgford	53	G2
East Cape	115	G2
East China Sea	87	P6
East Cleddau	52	C3
East Dean	53	H4
East Dereham	53	H2
Easter Island	143	K5
Eastern Ghats	92	E6
Eastern Ross	56	D3
East Falkland	139	E10
East Grinstead	53	G3
East Haddon	53	F2
East Hoathly	53	H4

Name	Page	Grid
East Ilsley	53	F3
East Indies	142	H12
East Kilbride	57	D5
East Lake Tarbert	56	B3
Eastleigh	53	F4
East Linton	57	F4
East Loch Roag	56	B2
East London	108	E6
Eastmain *Canada*	121	L7
Eastmain *Canada*	121	M7
Eastmain-Opinaca, Reservoir	121	L7
Eastman	129	L4
East Midlands Airport	53	F2
East Millnocket	125	R4
Eastoft	55	J3
Easton *U.K.*	52	E4
Easton *U.S.A.*	125	N6
East Point *Prince Edward Island, Canada*	121	P8
East Point *Quebec, Canada*	121	P8
Eastport	125	S4
East Retford	55	J3
Eastry	53	J3
East Saint Louis	124	E7
East Siberian Sea	85	T2
East Sussex	53	H3
East Tavaputs Plateau	123	K8
Eastville	55	K3
East Wittering	53	G4
Eastwood	55	H3
Eatonton	129	L4
Eau Claire	124	E4
Ebbw Vale	52	D3
Ebe-Basa	85	M4
Ebebiyin	105	H5
Ebeltoft	63	D8
Eber Golu	76	D3
Ebersberg	70	D4
Eberswalde	70	E2
Ebinur Hu	86	E3
Eboli	69	E5
Ebolowa	105	H5
Ebrach	70	D4
Ebro	66	G2
Ecclefechan	57	E5
Eccles	55	G3
Eccleshall	52	E2
Eccleston	55	G3
Eceabat	76	B2
Echeng	93	M2
Echigo-sammyaku	89	G7
Echo Bay *Ontario, Canada*	124	H3
Echo Bay *NW. Territories, Canada*	119	M2
Echternach	64	G4
Echuca	113	J6
Ecija	66	D4
Eckernforde	70	C1
Eclipse Sound	120	L3
Ecmiadzin	77	L2
Ecuador	136	B4
Ed	103	H5
Ed	63	H7
Edah Wagga	112	D4
Edam	64	F2
Eday	56	F1
Ed Damazin	103	F5
Ed Damer	96	A8
Ed Debba	102	F4
Ed-Deffa	102	E1
Edderton	56	D3
Eddrachillis Bay	56	C2
Ed Dueim	103	F5
Ede *Netherlands*	64	F2
Ede *Nigeria*	105	F4
Edea	105	H5
Edehon Lake	119	R3
Edel Land	112	C4
Eden *Australia*	113	K6
Eden *Cumbria, U.K.*	55	G2
Eden *Kent, U.K.*	53	H3
Eden *U.S.A.*	123	K6
Edenderry	59	H6
Edgecumbe	115	F2
Edgeley	123	Q4
Edgell Island	121	P5
Edgemont	123	N6
Edgeoya	80	D2
Edgeworthstown	58	G5
Edhessa	75	G2
Edievale	115	B6
Edinburg	128	D7
Edinburgh	57	E5
Edirne	76	B2
Edisto	129	M4
Edith River	112	G1
Edjeleh	101	G3
Edland	63	B7
Edmond	128	D3
Edmonds	122	C4
Edmonton	119	N5
Edmunston	125	R3
Edolo	68	C2
Edremit	76	B3
Edremit Korfezi	76	B3
Edson	119	M5
Edward, Lake	107	E3
Edwardson, Cape	115	B7
Edwards Plateau	127	M5
Edzhen	85	P4
Eeklo	64	E3
Eel	122	B7
Efate	114	U12

Name	Page	Grid
Eferding	68	E1
Eflani	76	E2
Efyrnwy, Llyn	52	D2
Ega	63	D8
Egadi, Isole	69	D7
Egersund	63	B7
Egerton, Mount	112	D3
Eggan	105	G4
Egg Lagoon	113	J6
Egglescliffe	55	H2
Eggum	62	E2
Egham	53	G3
Eghol	114	H6
Egilsstadir	62	X12
Egiyn Gol	86	J1
Eglinton	58	H2
Eglinton Island	120	C2
Egmount, Mount	115	E3
Egremont	55	F2
Egridir	76	D4
Egridir Golu	76	D3
Egvekinot	85	Y3
Egypt	102	E2
Ehingen	70	C4
Eibar	66	E1
Eidem	62	D4
Eidfjord	63	B6
Eidi	62	Z14
Eidsvold	113	L4
Eidsvoll	63	D6
Eifel	70	B3
Eigg	57	C4
Eigg, Sound of	57	B4
Eight Degree Channel	92	D7
Eighty Mile Beach	112	E2
Eilerts de Haan Geb	137	F3
Eil, Loch	57	C4
Eilsleben	70	D2
Einbeck	70	C3
Eindhoven	64	F3
Eiriksjokull	62	U12
Eirunepe	136	D5
Eisenach	70	D3
Eisenhuttenstadt	70	F2
Eisenkappel	68	E2
Eishort, Lake	57	C3
Eisleben	70	D3
Eitorf	70	B3
Ejea de los Caballeros	67	F1
Ejido Insurgentes	130	D5
Ejin Horo Qi	87	K4
Ejin Qi	86	J3
Ejutla	131	L9
Ekenas	63	K6
Eket	105	G5
Eketahuna	115	E4
Ekhinadhes	75	F3
Ekhinos	75	H2
Ekibastuz	84	B6
Ekimchan	85	N6
Ekonda	84	G3
Eksjo	63	F8
Ekwan	121	K7
El Affroun	67	H4
Elafonisos	75	G4
El Araiche	100	D1
El Arco	126	F7
El Arish	103	F1
Elasson	75	G3
Elat	94	B7
Elazig	77	H3
El Azraq	94	C6
El Bahri, Borg	67	H4
El Balyana	103	F2
Elban	85	P6
El Banco	136	C2
El Barco de Avila	66	D2
El Barco de Valdeorras	66	C1
Elbasan	74	E2
El Bayadh	100	F2
Elbe	70	C2
Elbert, Mount	123	L8
Elberton	129	L3
Elbeuf	64	D4
Elbeyli	77	G4
Elbing	71	H1
Elbistan	77	G3
Elblag	71	H1
Elbrus	79	G7
El Burgo de Osma	66	E2
El Cajon	126	D4
El Callao	136	E2
El Campo	128	D6
El Carmen *Bolivia*	138	E3
El Carmen *Bolivia*	136	E6
El Centro	126	E4
El Cerro	138	D3
El Chaparro	136	D2
Elche	67	F3
Elche de la Sierra	67	F3
Eldikan	85	P4
Eldivan	76	E2
El Djazair	101	F1
El Djouf	100	D4
Eldon	124	D7
El Dorado *Arkansas, U.S.A.*	128	F4
El Dorado *Kansas, U.S.A.*	128	D2
El Dorado *Venezuela*	133	S11
Eldoret	107	G2
Elektrostal	78	F4
Elephant Butte Reservoir	127	J4
Elephant Island	141	W6
Eleskirt	77	K3

Name	Page	Grid
El Eulma	101	G1
Eleuthera	132	J2
Elevsis	75	G3
El Faiyum	102	F2
El Fasher	102	E5
El Fashn	102	F2
El Ferrol	66	B1
El Fuerte	127	H7
Elgepiggen	63	D5
El Geteina	103	F5
Elgin *U.K.*	56	E3
Elgin *Illinois, U.S.A.*	124	F5
Elgin *N. Dakota, U.S.A.*	123	P4
El Giza	102	F1
Elgol	57	B3
Elgon, Mont	107	F2
El Golea	101	F2
El Golfo de Santa Clara	126	E5
El Hawata	96	B10
El Hodna, Chott	67	J5
El Homra	102	F5
El Hosh	103	F5
El Huecu	139	B7
Elikon	75	G3
Elisabethville	107	E5
Eliseu Martins	137	J5
Elista	79	G6
Elizabeth *Australia*	113	H5
Elizabeth *U.S.A.*	125	N6
Elizabeth City	129	P2
Elizabeth Reef	113	M4
Elizabethton	129	L2
Elizabethtown	124	H8
Elizondo	67	F1
El Jadida	100	D2
El Jafr	94	C6
El Jebelein	103	F5
El Jerid, Chott	101	G2
Elk	122	G3
Elk	71	K2
El Kala	69	B7
El Kamlin	103	F5
Elk City	128	C3
El Khalil	94	B6
El Kharga	102	F2
Elkhart	124	H6
El Khartum	103	F4
Elkhorn	123	Q6
Elkhotovo	79	G7
Elkhovo	73	J4
Elkin	129	M2
Elkins	125	L7
Elko	122	G7
El Koran	103	H6
El Korima, Oued	100	E2
El Lagowa	102	E5
Elland	55	H3
Ellef Ringnes Island	120	F2
Ellen	55	F2
Ellendale *Australia*	112	E2
Ellendale *U.S.A.*	123	Q5
Ellen, Mount	122	J8
Ellensburg	122	D4
Ellesmere	52	E2
Ellesmere Island	120	K2
Ellesmere, Lake	115	D5
Ellesmere Port	55	G3
Ellice	119	Q2
Ellington	114	R8
Elliot	108	E6
Elliot Lake	124	J3
Elliot, Mount	113	K2
Elliston	113	H5
El Llano	132	H10
Ellon	56	F3
Ellsworth	125	R4
Ellsworth Land	141	U4
Ellwangen	70	D4
Elmadag	76	E3
Elma Dagi	76	E3
El Mahalla El Kubra	102	F1
Elmali	76	C4
El Manaqil	103	F5
El Mansura	102	F1
El Mesellemiya	103	F5
El Milk	102	E4
El Minya	102	F2
Elmira	125	M5
Elmore	113	J6
Elmshorn	70	C2
El Muglad	102	E5
El Nido	91	F3
El Obeid	102	F5
El Odaiya	102	E5
Elorza	136	D2
El Oued	101	G2
Eloy	126	G4
El Palmito	127	K8
El Pardo	66	E2
El Paso *Illinois, U.S.A.*	124	F6
El Paso *Texas, U.S.A.*	127	J5
Elphin	56	C2
El Porvenir	127	K5
El Potosi	128	B8
El Progreso	132	D7
El Puente del Arzobispo	66	D3
El Qahira	102	F1
El Qasr	102	E2
El Qunaytirah	94	B5
El Real	132	G2
El Reno	128	D3
El Ronquillo	66	C4
El Rosario	126	E5
El Sahuaro	126	F5

Name	Page	Ref
El Salado	139	C9
El Salto	130	G6
El Salvador	132	C8
El Sam'an de Apure	133	N11
El Sauzal	126	D5
Elsham	55	J3
El Socorro	126	F5
Elster	70	E3
Elsterwerda	70	E3
El Sueco	127	J6
El Suweis	103	F2
El Tambo	136	B4
Eltham	115	E3
El Thamad	96	B2
El Tigre	133	Q10
El Tih	96	A2
Eltisley	53	G2
El Tocuyo	133	N10
Elton *U.K.*	53	G2
Elton *Russia*	79	H6
El Tule	131	L9
El Tur	96	A2
Eluru	92	F5
Elvanfoot	57	E5
Elvas	66	C3
Elveden	53	H2
Elverum	63	D6
El Viejo	133	L11
El Vigia	136	C2
Elwy	55	F3
Ely *Cambridgeshire, U.K.*	53	H2
Ely *Mid Glamorgan, U.K.*	52	D3
Ely *Minnesota, U.S.A.*	124	E3
Ely *Nevada, U.S.A.*	126	E1
Elze	70	C2
Ema	63	M7
Emae	114	U12
Emamrud	95	M3
Emam Taqi	95	P4
Eman	63	G8
Emao	114	U12
Emba	79	K6
Embarcacion	138	D4
Embleton	55	H1
Embona	75	J4
Embrun	65	G6
Embu	107	G3
Embu	70	B2
Emden	70	B2
Emerald	113	K3
Emerald Island	120	D2
Emerson	123	R3
Emet	76	C3
Emeti	114	C3
Emi	84	F6
Emigrant Pass	122	F7
Emin	86	E2
Emine, Nos	73	J4
Emirdag	76	D3
Emir Dagi	76	D3
Emita	113	K7
Emmaboda	63	F8
Emmaste	63	K7
Emmen	64	G2
Emory Peak	127	L6
Empalme	126	G7
Empangeni	109	F5
Empedrado	138	E5
Empingham	53	G2
Empoli	68	C4
Emporia *Kansas, U.S.A.*	128	D1
Emporia *Virginia, U.S.A.*	125	M8
Ems	70	B2
Emu	88	B4
Enard Bay	56	C2
Encantada, Cerro Del La	126	E5
Encarnacion	138	E5
Enchi	104	E4
Encinal	128	C6
Encontrados	136	C2
Encounter Bay	113	H6
Endau	90	C5
Ende	91	G7
Endeavour Strait	113	J1
Enderbury Island	111	U2
Enderby Land	141	D5
Endicott Mountains	118	C2
Ene	136	C6
Enez	76	B2
Enfield *Ireland*	59	J6
Enfield *U.K.*	53	G3
Engano, Cabo	133	N5
Engano, Cape	91	G2
Engaru	88	J3
Engels	79	H5
Enggano	90	C7
Engger Us	87	J3
Engineer Group	114	E4
Englehart	125	L3
Englewood	123	M8
English Channel	50	G5
Enguera	67	F3
Enguera, Sierra de	67	F3
Enid	128	D2
Enkhuizen	64	F2
Enkoping	63	G7
Enna	69	E7
Ennadai Lake	119	Q3
En Nahud	102	E5
Ennedi	102	D4
Ennell, Lough	59	H6
Ennerdale Water	55	F2
Enning	123	N5
Ennis *Ireland*	59	E7
Ennis *U.S.A.*	128	D4
Enniscorthy	59	J7
Enniskillen	58	G4
Ennistymon	59	D7
Enns	68	E1
Enonkoski	62	N5
Enontekio	62	K2
Enrekang	91	F6
Enschede	64	G2
Ensenada	126	D5
Enshi	93	L2
Enstone	53	F3
Entebbe	107	F2
Enterprise	129	K5
Entinas, Punta de las	66	E4
Entraygues	65	E6
Entrecasteaux, Recifs d'	111	N5
Enugu	105	G4
Enurmino	118	A2
Enz	70	C4
Eo	66	C1
Eolie	69	E6
Epano Fellos	75	H4
Epanomi	75	G2
Epernay	64	E4
Ephrata	122	E4
Epi	114	U12
Epinal	64	G4
Epping	53	H3
Eppynt, Mynydd	52	D2
Epsi	77	J4
Epsom	53	G3
Eqlid	95	L6
Equatorial Guinea	105	G5
Equeipa	136	E2
Erap	114	D3
Erbaa	77	G2
Erba, Jebel	96	C6
Ercek	77	K3
Ercis	77	K3
Ercsi	72	E2
Erdek	76	B2
Erdemli	76	F4
Erdenet	87	J2
Erdre	65	C5
Erechim	138	F5
Ereenstav	87	M2
Eregli *Turkey*	76	D2
Eregli *Turkey*	76	F4
Erek Dagi	77	K3
Erenhot	87	L3
Erentepe	77	K3
Eresma	66	D2
Eressos	75	H3
Erfelek	76	F2
Erfurt	70	D3
Ergani	77	H3
Ergene	76	B2
Ergli	63	L8
Ergun He	85	K6
Ergun Zuoqi	87	N1
Eriboll, Loch	56	D2
Ericht, Loch	57	D4
Ericiyas Dagi	76	F3
Erie	125	K5
Erie, Lake	125	K5
Erikousa	74	E3
Erimanthos	75	F4
Erimo-misaki	88	J5
Eriskay	57	A3
Erkelenz	70	B3
Erkilet	76	F3
Erkowit	96	C7
Erlandson Lake	121	N6
Erlangen	70	D4
Erldunda	113	G4
Erme	52	D4
Ermelo	108	F5
Ermenak	76	E4
Ernakulam	92	E7
Erne	58	H5
Erne, Lower Lough	58	G4
Erne, Upper Lough	58	G4
Erode	92	E6
Eromanga	113	J4
Er Rachidia	100	E2
Er Rahad	102	F5
Errego	109	G3
Errigal	58	F2
Erris Head	58	B4
Errochty, Loch	57	D4
Errogie	56	D3
Erromango	114	U13
Erseke	75	F2
Erskine	124	C3
Ertai	86	G2
Eruh	77	K4
Erwigol	86	F3
Eryuan	93	J3
Erzen	74	E2
Erzgebirge	70	E3
Erzin	84	F6
Erzincan	77	H3
Erzurum	77	J3
Esa-Ala	114	E3
Esan-misaki	88	H5
Esashi *Japan*	88	H5
Esashi *Japan*	88	J3
Esbjerg	63	C9
Esbo	63	N6
Escalona	66	D2
Escambia	129	J5
Escanaba	124	G4
Escarpe, Cape	114	X16
Escocesa, Bahia de	133	N5
Escondido *Brazil*	138	J3
Escondido *U.S.A.*	126	D4
Escrick	55	H3
Escuintla	132	B7
Ese-Khayya	85	N3
Esemer	77	K3
Esen	76	C4
Esendere	77	L4
Esfahan	95	K5
Esfarayen, Reshteh ye	95	N3
Eshan	93	K4
Esha Ness	56	A1
Esh Sheikh, Jbel	77	G6
Esino	68	D4
Esk	57	E5
Esk	57	E5
Eske, Lough	58	F3
Eskifjordur	62	Y12
Eskilstuna	63	G7
Eskimalatya	77	H3
Eskimo Lakes	118	J2
Eskimo Point	119	S3
Eskipazar	76	E2
Eskishir	76	D3
Esla	66	D1
Eslamabad-e Gharb	94	H4
Eslam Qaleh	95	Q4
Esme	76	C3
Esmeralda, Isla	139	A9
Esmeraldas	136	B3
Espalion	65	E6
Espanola *Canada*	125	K3
Espanola *U.S.A.*	127	J3
Espanola, Isla	136	A7
Espenberg, Cape	118	C2
Esperance	112	E5
Esperance Bay	112	E5
Esperanza *Antarctic*	141	W6
Esperanza *Argentina*	139	B10
Esperanza *Argentina*	138	D6
Espiel	66	D3
Espinhaco, Serra da	138	H3
Espinho	66	B2
Espinosa de los Monteros	66	E1
Espirito Santo	138	H3
Espiritu Santo	114	T11
Espiritu Santo, Cape	91	H3
Espiritu Santo, Isla	130	D5
Espiye	77	H2
Espoo	63	N6
Esposende	66	B2
Espot	67	G1
Espungabera	109	F4
Esquel	139	B8
Es Sahra en Nubiya	96	B6
Essaouira	100	D2
Es Semara	100	C3
Essen	70	B3
Essex	53	H3
Essex, Punta	136	A7
Esslingen	70	C4
Esso	85	T5
Estacado, Llanos	127	L4
Estados, Isla de los	139	D10
Estahbanat	95	M7
Estancia	138	K6
Estcourt	108	E5
Este	68	C3
Esteli	132	D8
Estella	67	E1
Estepona	66	D4
Este, Punta del	139	F6
Esterhazy	123	N2
Esternay	64	E4
Estes Park	123	M7
Estevan	123	N3
Estherville	124	C5
Eston	55	H2
Estonia	63	L7
Estrela, Sierra da	66	C2
Estrella, Punta	126	E5
Estremadura	66	B3
Estremoz	66	C3
Estrondo, Serra do	137	H5
Esztergom	72	E2
Etah	92	E3
Etain	64	F4
Etampes	64	E4
Etaples	64	D3
Etawah	92	E3
Ethiopia	103	G6
Etive, Loch	57	C4
Etna, Monte	69	E7
Eton	53	G3
Etosha Pan	108	C3
Etretat	64	D4
Ettington	53	F2
Ettlingen	70	C4
Ettrick	57	E5
Ettrick Forest	57	E5
Etwall	53	F2
Eu	64	D3
Euboea	75	H3
Euclid	125	K6
Euclides da Cunha	137	K6
Eufaula	129	K5
Eufaula Lake	128	E3
Eugene	122	C5
Eugenia, Punta	126	E7
Eunice	128	F5
Euphrates	94	G6
Eupora	128	H4
Eure	64	D4
Eureka *California, U.S.A.*	122	B7
Eureka *Montana, U.S.A.*	122	G3
Eureka *Nevada, U.S.A.*	126	D1
Eureka Sound	120	J2
Europa, Ile de l	109	H4
Europa, Picos de	66	D1
Europa Point	66	D4
Eutaw	129	J4
Evans, Lake	121	L7
Evans, Mount	123	M8
Evans Strait	120	K5
Evanston *Illinois, U.S.A.*	124	G5
Evanston *Wyoming, U.S.A.*	122	J7
Evansville	124	G7
Evaux-les-Bains	65	E5
Evaz	95	L8
Evenlode	53	F3
Everard, Cape	113	K6
Everard, Lake	113	G5
Everest, Mount	92	G3
Everett	122	C4
Everett Mountains	120	N5
Everglades, The	129	M7
Evesham	53	F2
Evesham, Vale of	53	F2
Evigheds Fjord	120	R4
Evisa	69	B4
Evje	63	B7
Evora	66	C3
Evreux	64	D4
Evropos	75	G2
Evros	75	J2
Evrotas	75	G4
Evvoia	75	H3
Evvoikos Kolpos	75	G3
Ewasse	114	E3
Ewe, Loch	56	C3
Ewes	57	E5
Exbourne	52	D4
Exe	52	D4
Exeter	52	D4
Exford	52	D3
Exmoor	52	D3
Exmouth	52	D4
Exmouth Gulf	112	C3
Exo Hora	75	F4
Expedition Range	113	K3
Exploits	121	Q8
Exton	52	D3
Extremadura	66	C3
Exuma Sound	132	J2
Eyakit-Terde	85	J3
Eyam	55	H3
Eyasi, Lake	107	F3
Eyemouth	57	F4
Eye Peninsula	56	B2
Eyjafjallajokull	62	U13
Eyjafjordur	62	V11
Eyl	103	J6
Eynesil	77	H2
Eynsham	53	F3
Eyre	112	F5
Eyre Creek	113	H4
Eyre Mountains	115	B6
Eyre North, Lake	113	H4
Eyre Peninsula	113	H5
Eyre South, Lake	113	H4
Eysturoy	62	Z14
Eyvanaki	95	L4
Ezequil Ramos Mexia, Embalse	139	C7
Ezine	76	B3

F

Name	Page	Ref
Faber Lake	119	M3
Faborg	63	D9
Fabriano	68	D4
Facatativa	136	C3
Facundo	139	C9
Fada	102	D4
Fada NGourma	104	F3
Faddeya, Zaliv	84	H2
Faddeyevskiy, Ostrov	85	Q1
Faenza	68	C3
Faeros	62	Z14
Fafen Shet	103	H6
Fagaras	73	H3
Fagersta	63	F6
Faget	73	G3
Fagnano, Lago	139	C10
Fagnes	64	F3
Faguibine, Lac	100	E5
Fagurholsmyri	62	W13
Fahraj	95	P7
Fairbanks	118	F3
Fairborn	124	J7
Fairfield	126	A1
Fair Isle	56	A2
Fairlie	115	C6
Fairlight *Australia*	113	J2
Fairlight *U.K.*	53	H4
Fairmont *Minnesota, U.S.A.*	124	C5
Fairmont *W. Virginia, U.S.A.*	125	K7
Fair Ness	120	M5
Fairview	128	C2
Fairweather, Mount	118	H4
Faisalabad	92	D2
Faith	123	N5
Faither, The	56	A1
Faizabad	92	F3
Fajr, Wadi	96	D2
Fakaofo	111	U3

Name	Page	Grid
Fakenham	53	H2
Fakfak	91	J6
Fakse Bugt	63	E9
Faku	87	N3
Fal	52	C4
Falaise	64	C4
Falam	93	H4
Falavarjan	95	K5
Falcarragh	58	F2
Falcone, Capo del	69	B5
Falcon Lake	128	C7
Falfurrias	128	C7
Falkenberg	63	E8
Falkenburg	70	E3
Falkensee	70	E3
Falkirk	57	E4
Falkland	57	E4
Falkland Islands	139	E10
Falkonera	75	G4
Falkoping	63	E7
Fall Line Hills	129	J4
Fallon	126	C1
Fall River	125	Q6
Fall River Pass	123	M7
Falls City	124	C6
Falmouth	52	B4
Falmouth Bay	52	B4
Falsa Chipana, Punta	139	B4
False Bay	108	C6
False Pass	118	Af9
False Pera Head	113	J1
Falset	67	G2
Falster	63	E9
Falsterbo	63	E9
Falterona, Monte	68	C4
Falticeni	73	J2
Falun	63	F6
Famatina, Sierra de	138	C5
Fanad Head	58	G2
Fandriana	109	J4
Fangak	102	F6
Fangcheng	93	M2
Fangdou Shan	93	L2
Fangshan	87	M4
Fang Xian	93	M2
Fangzheng	88	B3
Fannich, Loch	56	D3
Fannuj	95	P8
Fano	63	C9
Fano	68	D4
Fanquier	122	E3
Fan Si Pan	93	K4
Faraday	141	V5
Faraday, Cape	120	L2
Faradje	107	E2
Farafangana	109	J4
Farah	95	R5
Farah Rud	95	R5
Faraid Head	56	D2
Farallon, Punta	130	G8
Faranah	104	C3
Farasan, Jazair	96	E8
Farcau	71	L5
Fareham	53	F4
Farewell, Cape	115	D4
Farewell Spit	115	D4
Far Falls	123	T2
Fargo	123	R4
Faridpur	93	G4
Farigh, Wadi al	101	K2
Farila	63	F6
Fariman	95	P4
Faringdon	53	F3
Farjestaden	63	G8
Farmington Maine, U.S.A.	125	Q4
Farmington Missouri, U.S.A.	124	E8
Farmington New Mexico, U.S.A.	127	H2
Farnborough	53	G3
Farnham	53	G3
Farnworth	55	G3
Faro	63	H8
Faro Brazil	137	F4
Faro Portugal	66	C4
Farosund	63	H8
Farquhar Islands	82	D8
Farrai	75	F3
Farranfore	59	C8
Farrar	56	D3
Farrashband	95	L7
Farsala	75	G3
Farsi	95	R5
Farsund	63	B7
Fartak, Ra's	97	L9
Farvel, Kap	116	Q3
Fasa	95	L7
Fasad	97	L7
Fasano	69	F5
Faske Bugt	70	E1
Fastov	79	D5
Fatehabad	92	E3
Fatehgarh	92	E3
Fatehpur Rajasthan, India	92	D3
Fatehpur Uttar Pradesh, India	92	F3
Fatezh	79	F5
Fatick	104	B3
Fatima	66	B3
Fatmomakke	62	F4
Fatsa	77	G2
Fatuna	111	T4
Faurei	73	J3
Fauro Vaghena	114	H5
Fausing	63	D8
Fauske	62	F3
Faux Cap	109	J5
Faversham	53	H3
Fawley	53	F4
Fawr, Fforest	52	D3
Faxafloi	62	T12
Faxalven	62	G5
Faya-Largeau	102	C2
Fayetteville Arkansas, U.S.A.	128	E2
Fayetteville N. Carolina, U.S.A.	129	N3
Fayetteville Tennessee, U.S.A.	129	J3
Faylaka	97	J2
Fazilka	92	D2
Fderik	100	C4
Feale	59	D8
Fear, Cape	129	P4
Feather	122	D8
Featherston	115	E4
Fecamp	64	D4
Fedorovka	84	Ad6
Fedulki	84	Ae4
Feeagh, Lough	58	C5
Fegu	87	L4
Fehmarn	70	D1
Fehmer Boelt	70	D1
Feijo	136	C5
Feilding	115	E4
Feira de Santana	137	K6
Feistritz	68	E2
Fei Xian	87	M4
Feke	77	F4
Feklistova, Ostrov	85	P5
Felahiye	77	F3
Felanitx	67	H3
Feldbach	68	E2
Feldberg	68	A2
Feldkirch	68	B2
Feldkirchen	68	E2
Felipe Carrillo Puerto	131	Q8
Felix, Cape	120	G4
Felixstowe	53	J3
Felling	55	H2
Feltre	68	C2
Femer Balt	63	D9
Femund	63	D5
Fener Burun	77	H2
Fengcheng	87	M6
Fengdu	93	L3
Fenggang	93	L3
Fengjie	93	L2
Fengning	87	M3
Fengshan	93	L4
Fengtai	93	N2
Fengxian	93	N3
Fengzhen	87	L3
Fen He	87	L4
Feni Island	114	E2
Fenoarivo Atsinanana	109	J3
Fens, The	53	H2
Fenxi	87	L4
Fenyang	87	L4
Fenyi	93	M3
Feodosiya	79	F6
Feolin Ferry	57	B5
Ferbane	59	G6
Ferdows	95	P4
Fergana	86	B3
Fergus Falls	124	B3
Fergusson Island	114	E3
Ferkessedougou	104	D4
Fermanagh	58	G4
Fermo	68	D4
Fermoy	59	F8
Fernandina Beach	129	M5
Fernandina, Isla	136	A7
Fernando de Noronha, Isla	48	E5
Ferness	56	E3
Fernie	122	G3
Ferns	59	K7
Ferrai	75	J2
Ferrans	59	J6
Ferrara	68	C3
Ferrat, Cap	67	F5
Ferreira do Alentejo	66	B3
Ferrenafe	136	B5
Ferriday	128	G5
Ferrol, Peninsula de	136	B5
Ferto	68	F2
Fes	100	D2
Fessenden	123	Q4
Fetesti	73	J3
Fethaland, Point of	56	A1
Fethiye	76	C4
Fethiye Korfezi	76	C4
Fetisovo	79	J7
Fetlar	56	B1
Fetsund	63	D7
Fetzara El Hadjar	69	A7
Feurs	65	F6
Fevralskoye	85	N6
Feyzabad	92	D1
Ffestiniog	52	D2
Fianarantsoa	109	J4
Fiandberg	62	G4
Fichtel-gebirge	70	D3
Ficksburg	108	E5
Fidenza	68	C3
Fier	74	D2
Fife Ness	57	F4
Figeac	65	E6
Figline Valdarno	68	C4
Figueira da Foz	66	B2
Figueira de Castelo Rodrigo	66	C2
Figueres	67	H1
Figuig	100	E2
Figuiro dos Vinhos	66	B3
Fiji	114	Q8
Filadelfia	138	D4
Filby	53	J2
Filchner Ice Shelf	141	X3
Filey	55	J2
Filey Bay	55	J2
Filiasi	73	G3
Filiatra	75	F4
Filipow	71	K1
Filipstad	63	F7
Fillmore California, U.S.A.	126	C3
Fillmore Utah, U.S.A.	126	F1
Fimi	106	C3
Finale Emilia	68	C3
Final, Punta	126	E6
Findhorn	56	E3
Findik	77	G3
Findikli	77	J2
Findikpinari	76	F4
Findlay	124	J6
Finike	76	D4
Finisterre, Cabo	66	B1
Finke Australia	113	G4
Finke Australia	113	H4
Finland	63	L6
Finland, Gulf of	63	L7
Finnmark	62	L1
Finnmarksvidda	62	K2
Finnsnes	62	M2
Finschhafen	114	D3
Finsteraarhorn	68	B2
Finstown	56	E1
Fintona	58	H4
Fionn Loch	56	C3
Fionnphort	57	B4
Firat	77	H3
Firedrake Lake	119	Q3
Firenze	68	C4
Firle Beacon	53	H4
Firozabad	92	E3
Firozpur	92	D2
Firsovo	88	J2
Firuzabad	95	L7
Firuzkuh	95	L4
Fish	108	C4
Fisher, Cape	120	K5
Fishguard	52	C3
Fismes	64	E4
Fitchburg	125	Q5
Fitful Head	56	A2
Fitsitika	109	H4
Fitzgerald	129	L5
Fitz Roy	139	C9
Fitzroy	112	F2
Fitz Roy, Cerro	139	B9
Fitzroy Crossing	112	F2
Fitzwilliam Strait	120	C2
Fiuggi	69	D5
Fiume	72	C3
Fiumicino	69	D5
Fivemiletown	58	H4
Fizi	107	E3
Fjallasen	62	J3
Fladdabister	56	A2
Flagstaff	126	G3
Flakatrask	62	H4
Flamborough	55	J2
Flamborough Head	55	J2
Flaming	70	E3
Flaming Gorge Reservoir	123	K7
Flamingo	129	M8
Flash	55	H3
Flasjon	62	F4
Flathead	122	G3
Flathead Lake	122	G4
Flathead Range	122	G3
Flattery, Cape	122	B3
Fleet	53	G3
Fleetwood	55	F3
Flekkefjord	63	B7
Flen	63	G7
Flensburg	70	C1
Flers	64	C4
Flesberg	63	C7
Fleurance	65	D7
Flims	68	B2
Flinders Island	113	K6
Flinders Reefs	113	K2
Flin Flon	119	Q5
Flint U.K.	55	F3
Flint Georgia, U.S.A.	129	K5
Flint Michigan, U.S.A.	124	J5
Flintham	53	G2
Flisa	63	E6
Flix	67	G2
Fliyos	76	E2
Floka	75	F4
Florac	65	E6
Florence Italy	68	C4
Florence Alabama, U.S.A.	129	J3
Florence Arizona, U.S.A.	126	G4
Florence Colorado, U.S.A.	127	K1
Florence Oregon, U.S.A.	122	B6
Florence S. Carolina, U.S.A.	129	N3
Florencia	136	B3
Florentino Ameghino, Embalse	139	C8
Flores Brazil	137	J5
Flores Guatemala	132	C6
Flores Indonesia	91	G7
Floreshty	79	D6
Flores, Laut	91	F7
Floresta	137	K5
Floriano	137	J5
Florianopolis	138	G5
Florida Uruguay	139	E6
Florida U.S.A.	129	L6
Florida Islands	114	K6
Florida Keys	129	M8
Florida, Straits of	129	N8
Floridia	69	E7
Florina	75	F2
Floro	63	A6
Flotta	56	E2
Flumen	67	F2
Fly	114	C3
Foca	76	B3
Foca	72	E4
Fochabers	56	E3
Focsani	73	J3
Foggia	69	E5
Fogi	91	H6
Fogo	104	L7
Fogo Island	121	R8
Fohr	70	C1
Foinaven	56	D2
Foix	65	D7
Folda	62	F3
Folegandros	75	H4
Foligno	69	D4
Folkestone	53	J3
Folkingham	53	G2
Folkston	129	L5
Follonica	69	C4
Foltesti	73	K3
Fond-du-Lac Canada	119	Q4
Fond du Lac U.S.A.	124	F5
Fonni	69	B5
Fonsagrada	66	C1
Fonseca, Golfo de	132	D8
Fontainebleau	64	E4
Fonte Boa	136	D4
Fonte do Pau-d'Agua	136	F6
Fontenay-le-Comte	65	C5
Font-Romeu	65	E7
Fontur	62	X11
Fonualei	111	U5
Fonyod	72	D2
Foraker, Mount	118	E3
Forbes	113	K5
Forcados	105	G4
Forcalquier	65	F7
Forde	63	A6
Fordham	53	H2
Fordon	71	H2
Ford Ranges	141	Q3
Fordyce	128	F4
Forecariah	104	C4
Foreland Point	52	D3
Forel, Mount	116	R2
Forest Canada	124	K5
Forest U.S.A.	128	H4
Forestier Peninsula	113	K7
Forest Park	129	K4
Forestville	125	R2
Forez, Monts du	65	E6
Forfar	57	F4
Forgandenny	57	E4
Fork	123	K5
Forks	122	B4
Forli	68	D3
Formartin	56	F3
Formby	55	F3
Formby Point	55	F3
Formentera	67	G3
Formentor, Cabo de	67	H3
Formia	69	D5
Formiga	138	G4
Formosa	87	N7
Formosa Argentina	138	E5
Formosa Brazil	138	G3
Formosa do Rio Preto	137	H6
Foroyar	62	Z14
Forres	56	E3
Forrest	112	F5
Forrest City	128	G3
Forsayth	113	J2
Forsnas	62	H3
Forsnes	62	C5
Forssa	63	K6
Forsyth Missouri, U.S.A.	124	D8
Forsyth Montana, U.S.A.	123	L4
Fort Albany	121	K7
Fortaleza Bolivia	136	D5
Fortaleza Brazil	137	K4
Fort Archambault	102	C2
Fort Beaufort	108	E6
Fort Benton	123	J4
Fort Bragg	122	C8
Fort Charlet	101	G4
Fort Chipewyan	119	N4
Fort Collins	123	M7
Fort Coulonge	125	M4
Fort-Dauphin	109	J5
Fort de Polignac	101	G3
Fort Dodge	124	C5
Fortescue	112	D3
Fort Flatters	101	G3
Fort Foureau	105	J3
Fort Frances	124	D2
Fort Franklin	118	L2
Fort Good Hope	118	K2
Forth	57	D4
Fort Hall	107	G3
Fort Hancock	127	K5

Forth, Firth of 57 F4
Fortin Carlos Antonio Lopez 138 E4
Fortin General Mendoza 138 D4
Fortin Gral Eugenio Garay 138 D4
Fortin Infante Rivarola 138 D4
Fortin Juan de Zalazar 138 E4
Fortin Madrejon 138 E4
Fortin Ravelo 138 D3
Fort Jameson 107 F3
Fort Kent 125 R3
Fort Lamy 102 C5
Fort Lauderdale 129 M7
Fort Liard 118 L3
Fort Macleod 122 H3
Fort McMurray 119 N4
Fort McPherson 118 J2
Fort Madison 124 E6
Fort Manning 107 F5
Fort Morgan 123 N7
Fort Myers 129 M7
Fort Nelson 119 L4
Fort Norman 118 K3
Fortore 69 E5
Fort Payne 129 K3
Fort Peck 123 L3
Fort Peck Dam 123 L4
Fort Peck Reservoir 123 L4
Fort Pierce 129 M7
Fort Portal 107 F2
Fort Providence 119 M3
Fort Qu'Appelle 123 N2
Fort Randall 118 Af8
Fort Resolution 119 N3
Fortrose 56 D3
Fort Rosebery 107 E5
Fort Saint James 118 L5
Fort Saint John 119 L4
Fort Scott 124 C8
Fort Severn 120 J6
Fort Shevchenko 79 J7
Fort Simpson 119 L3
Fort Smith *Canada* 119 N3
Fort Smith *U.S.A.* 128 E4
Fort Soufflay 106 B2
Fort Stockton 127 L5
Fort Sumner 127 K3
Fort Trinquet 100 D1
Fortuna 122 B7
Fortune Bay 121 Q8
Fort Valley 129 L4
Fort Vermilion 119 M4
Fort Victoria 108 F4
Fort Walton Beach 129 J5
Fort Wayne 124 H6
Fort William 57 C4
Fort Worth 128 D4
Fort Yukon 118 F2
Forur 95 M8
Foshan 93 M4
Fosheim Peninsula 120 K2
Fosna 62 D5
Fossombrone 68 D4
Fossvellir 62 X12
Foster 113 K6
Fougeres 64 C4
Foula 56 A2
Foula Morie 104 C3
Foulden 57 F4
Foulness Island 53 H3
Foulness Point 53 H3
Foulwind, Cape 115 C4
Foumban 105 H4
Foundiougne 104 B3
Fountainhall 57 F5
Four Mountains, Islands of the 118 Ad9
Fournoi 75 J4
Foveaux Strait 115 B7
Fowey *U.K.* 52 C4
Fowey *U.K.* 52 C4
Fowler 127 K1
Fowler, Point 112 G5
Fowlers Bay 112 G5
Fowman 94 J3
Fox *Canada* 118 K4
Fox *U.S.A.* 124 F6
Foxe Basin 120 L4
Foxe Peninsula 120 L5
Foxford 58 D5
Fox Islands 118 Ae9
Foxton 115 E4
Foyers, Falls of 56 D3
Foyle 58 H3
Foyle, Lough 58 H2
Foynes 59 D7
Foz do Iguacu 138 F5
Fraga 67 G2
Framington 125 Q5
Framlingham 53 J2
Frampol 71 K3
Franca 138 G4
Francais, Recif des 114 V15
France 65 C5
France, Ile de 64 E4
Frances *Australia* 113 J6
Frances *Canada* 118 K3
Franceville 106 B3
Franche Comte 65 G5
Francis Case, Lake 123 Q6
Francisco Escarcega 131 P8
Francistown 108 E4
Francois Lake 118 K5
Frangista 75 F3
Frankfort *Indiana, U.S.A.* 124 G6
Frankfort *Kentucky, U.S.A.* 124 H7
Frankfurt 70 F2
Frankfurt am Main 70 C3
Frankischer Alb 70 D4
Franklin *Indiana, U.S.A.* 124 H7
Franklin *Louisiana, U.S.A.* 128 G6
Franklin *N. Carolina, U.S.A.* 129 L3
Franklin *Pennsylvania, U.S.A.* 125 L6
Franklin *Tennessee, U.S.A.* 129 J3
Franklin Bay 118 K2
Franklin D Roosevelt Lake 122 E3
Franklin, Lake 119 R2
Franklin Mountains 118 K3
Franklin, Point 118 D1
Franklin Strait 120 G3
Frank's Peak 123 K6
Fransta 62 G5
Frantsa-Iosifa, Zemlya 80 G2
Frascati 69 D5
Fraserburg 108 D6
Fraserburgh 56 F3
Fraserdale 125 K2
Fraser Island 113 L4
Fraser, Mount 112 D4
Frasertown 115 F3
Frauenfeld 68 B2
Fray Bentos 138 E6
Frazer 122 D2
Freckleton 55 G3
Fredericia 63 C9
Frederick *Maryland, U.S.A.* 125 M7
Frederick *Oklahoma, U.S.A.* 128 C3
Frederick Reef 110 M6
Fredericksburg 125 M7
Frederick Sound 118 J4
Fredericktown 124 E8
Fredericton 125 S4
Frederikshab 120 S5
Frederikshabs Isblink 120 S5
Frederikshavn 63 D8
Frederiksted 133 Q6
Fredonia 125 L5
Fredrika 62 M4
Fredrikshamn 63 M6
Fredrikstad 63 D7
Freeling, Mount 113 G3
Freeport *Illinois, U.S.A.* 124 F5
Freeport *Texas, U.S.A.* 128 E6
Freeport City 132 H1
Freer 128 C7
Freetown 104 C4
Fregenal de la Sierra 66 C3
Frehel, Cap 64 B4
Freiberg 70 E3
Freiburg 70 B4
Freising 70 D4
Freistadt 68 E1
Frejus 65 G7
Fremantle 112 D5
Fremont *California, U.S.A.* 126 A2
Fremont *Nebraska, U.S.A.* 123 R7
Fremont *Utah, U.S.A.* 122 J8
French 125 K1
French Broad 129 L2
French Guiana 136 G3
Frenchman 123 L3
Frenchpark 58 F5
French Polynesia 143 J5
Frenda 100 F1
Frensham 53 G3
Fresco 137 G5
Freshfield, Mount 122 F2
Freshwater 53 F4
Fresnillo 130 H6
Fresno 126 C2
Freu, Cabo del 67 H3
Frias 138 C5
Fribourg 68 A2
Fridaythorpe 55 J2
Friedrichshafen 70 C5
Friesach 68 E2
Frio 127 N6
Frio, Cabo 138 H4
Friona 127 L3
Frisco 123 L8
Friza, Proliv 85 R7
Frobisher Bay 120 N5
Frobisher Lake 119 P4
Frodsham 55 G3
Frohavet 62 C5
Frolovo 79 G6
Frome *Dorset, U.K.* 52 E4
Frome *Somerset, U.K.* 52 E3
Frome, Lake 113 H5
Fronteira 66 C3
Frontera 131 N8
Front Royal 125 L7
Frosinone 69 D5
Froya 62 C5
Frutal 138 G3
Frydek Mistek 71 H4
Fteri 75 F3
Fuan 87 M6
Fudai 88 H5
Fuding 87 N6
Fudzin 88 E3
Fuengirola 66 D4
Fuente el Fresno 66 E3
Fuente Obejuna 66 D3
Fuentesauco 66 D2
Fuentes de Onoro 66 C2
Fuerte 127 H7
Fuerteventura 100 C3
Fufeng 93 L2
Fuga 91 G2
Fuhai 86 F2
Fujian 87 M6
Fu Jiang 93 L2
Fujin 88 D2
Fujinomiya 89 G8
Fuji-san 89 G8
Fujisawa 89 G8
Fukang 86 F3
Fukaura 88 G5
Fukuchiyama 89 E8
Fukue-shima 89 B9
Fukui 89 F7
Fukuoka *Japan* 89 C9
Fukuoka *Japan* 88 H5
Fukura 88 G6
Fukushima 89 H7
Fukuyama *Japan* 89 C10
Fukuyama *Japan* 89 D8
Fulacunda 104 B3
Fulad Mahalleh 95 L3
Fulaga 114 S9
Fulanga Passage 114 S9
Fulbourn 53 H2
Fulda *W. Germany* 70 C3
Fulda *W. Germany* 70 C3
Fullerton 126 D4
Fullerton, Cape 119 T3
Fulufjallet 63 E6
Fulwood 55 G3
Fumas, de Represa 138 G4
Fumay 64 F4
Fumel 65 D6
Funabashi 89 H8
Funafuti 111 S3
Funasdalen 62 E5
Funauke 89 F11
Funchal 100 B2
Fundao 66 C2
Fundy, Bay of 121 N8
Funing *Jiangsu, China* 87 M5
Funing *Yunnan, China* 93 L4
Funtua 105 G3
Fuqing 87 M6
Furancungo 109 F2
Furano 88 J4
Furg 95 M7
Furmanov 78 G4
Furmanovka 86 C3
Furmanovo 79 H6
Furneaux Group 113 K7
Furstenfeld 68 E2
Furstenwalde 70 F2
Furth 70 D4
Furukawa *Japan* 89 F7
Furukawa *Japan* 88 H6
Fury and Hecla Strait 120 K4
Fushun 87 N3
Fusui 93 L4
Futuna 114 U13
Fuwayrit 97 K3
Fu Xian 93 L1
Fuxin 87 N3
Fuyang 93 N2
Fuyu 87 N2
Fuyuan 88 E1
Fuyun 86 F2
Fuzesabony 72 F2
Fuzhou *Fujian, China* 87 M6
Fuzhou *Jiangxi, China* 87 M6
Fuzhoucheng 87 N4
Fuzuli 94 H2
Fyfield 53 H3
Fyn 63 D9
Fyne, Loch 57 C4
Fyresdal 63 C7
Fyvie 56 F3

G

Gaalkacyo 103 J6
Gabas 65 C7
Gabbac, Raas 103 K6
Gabela 106 B5
Gabes 101 H2
Gabes, Golfe de 101 H2
Gabgaba, Wadi 103 F3
Gabin 71 H2
Gabon 106 B3
Gaborone 108 E4
Gabriel, Mount 59 C9
Gabriel Vera 138 C3
Gabrik 95 P9
Gabrovo 73 H4
Gace 64 D4
Gach Sar 95 K3
Gach Saran 95 K6
Gacko 72 E4
Gadag 92 E5
Gaddede 62 F4
Gador, Sierra de 66 E4
Gadsden 129 K3
Gadwal 92 E5
Gadyach 79 E5
Gaesti 73 H3
Gaeta 69 D5
Gaeta, Golfo di 69 D5
Gafsa 101 G2
Gagarin 78 E4
Gagnoa 104 D4
Gagnon 121 N7
Gagra 79 G7
Gagui 102 C6
Gaibanda 93 G3
Gaidhouronisi 75 H5
Gailey 53 E2
Gaillac 65 D7
Gaillimh 59 D6
Gailtaler Alpen 68 D2
Gainesville *Florida, U.S.A.* 129 L6
Gainesville *Georgia, U.S.A.* 129 L3
Gainesville *Texas, U.S.A.* 128 D4
Gainford 55 H2
Gainsborough 55 J3
Gairdner, Lake 113 H5
Gairloch, Loch 56 C3
Gai Xian 87 N3
Gaktsynka 85 P6
Galana 107 G3
Galand 95 M3
Galanino 84 E5
Galapagos, Islas 136 A7
Galashiels 57 F5
Galati 73 K3
Galatz 73 K3
Galax 125 K8
Galela 91 H5
Galena *Alaska, U.S.A.* 118 D3
Galena *Illinois, U.S.A.* 124 E5
Galena *Kansas, U.S.A.* 124 C8
Galeota Point 136 E1
Galera, Punta de la 139 B7
Galesburg 124 E6
Galeton 125 M6
Galgate 55 G3
Galich *Russia* 78 G4
Galich *Ukraine* 71 L4
Galicia 66 C1
Galilee, Lake 113 K3
Galimyy 85 T4
Gallabat 103 G5
Gallan Head 56 A2
Gallarate 68 B3
Gallatin 129 J2
Galle 92 F7
Gallegos 139 B10
Galley Head 59 E9
Gallinas Mountains 127 J3
Gallinas, Punta 136 C1
Gallipoli *Italy* 69 F5
Gallipoli *Turkey* 76 B2
Gallivare 62 J3
Gallo 67 F2
Gallo 62 F5
Gallo, Capo 69 D6
Galloway 54 E2
Galloway, Mull of 54 E2
Gallup 127 H3
Galmisdale 57 B4
Galtymore Mount 59 F8
Galty Mountains 58 F8
Galveston 128 E6
Galveston Bay 128 E6
Galveston Island 128 E6
Galway *Ireland* 59 D6
Galway *Ireland* 59 E6
Galway Bay 59 D6
Gambell 118 A3
Gambia, The 104 B3
Gambier, Iles 143 J5
Gamboma 106 C3
Gamkunoro, Gunung 91 H5
Gamlakarleby 62 K5
Gamleby 63 G8
Gamshadzai Kuh 95 Q7
Gamvik 62 N1
Ganado 127 H3
Gananoque 125 M4
Ganaveh 95 K7
Gand 64 E3
Gandadiwata, Bukit 91 F6
Gandajika 106 D4
Gandak 92 F3
Gander 121 R8
Gander Lake 121 R8
Gandesa 67 G2
Gandhi Sagar 92 E4
Gandia 67 F3
Ganga 93 G3
Ganga, Mouths of the 93 G4
Gangan 139 C8
Ganganagar 92 D3
Gangara 101 G6
Gangdise Shan 92 F2
Ganges 93 G4
Gangew Taungdan 93 J4
Gangtok 93 G3
Gangu 93 L2
Ganjam 92 G5
Gan Jiang 87 M6
Gannat 65 E5
Gannett Peak 123 K6
Gansu 93 K2
Gantheaume, Cape 113 H6
Gantsevichi 71 M2
Ganyushkino 79 H6
Ganzhou 87 L6
Gao 100 E5
Gaoan 93 N3
Gaohe 93 M4
Gaolan 93 K1
Gaoqing 87 M4
Gaoua 104 E3
Gaoual 104 C3
Gaoyou Hu 87 M5
Gap 65 G6
Gar 92 E2

Name	Page	Grid
Garachine, Punta	132	H10
Gara, Lough	58	F5
Garanhuns	137	K5
Garara	114	D3
Garberville	122	C7
Garboldisham	53	H2
Garbosh, Kuh-e	95	K5
Garcas	138	F3
Gard	65	F7
Garda, Lago di	68	C3
Gardelegen	70	D2
Garden City	127	M2
Garden Grove	126	C4
Gardez	92	C2
Gardhiki	75	F3
Gardiner	123	J5
Gardnerville	126	C1
Gardno, Jezioro	71	G1
Garelochhead	57	D4
Gareloi Island	118	Ac9
Garessio	68	B3
Garforth	55	H3
Gargalianoi	75	F4
Gargunnock	57	D4
Garies	108	C6
Garissa	107	G3
Garland	128	D4
Garmish-Partenkirchen	70	D5
Garmsar	95	L4
Garnet Bay	120	L4
Garnett	128	E1
Garonne	65	C6
Garoua	105	H4
Garrison Dam	123	P4
Garron Point	58	L2
Garrovillas	66	C3
Garry Lake	119	R2
Garry, Loch	57	D3
Garstang	55	G3
Gartempe	65	D5
Gartocharn	57	D4
Garton Lough	58	G3
Garton-on-the-Wolds	55	J2
Garut	90	D7
Garvagh	58	J3
Garve	56	D3
Garvie Mountains	115	B6
Garwa	92	F4
Garwolin	71	J3
Gary	124	G6
Gar Zangbo	92	F2
Garze	93	J2
Garzon	136	B3
Gasan Kuli	95	L3
Gascogne	65	D7
Gascogne, Golfe de	65	C7
Gasconade	124	D8
Gascoyne	112	C3
Gascuna, Golfo de	67	F1
Gasht	95	Q8
Gashua	105	H3
Gask	95	P5
Gasmata	114	E3
Gaspar, Selat	90	D6
Gaspe	121	P8
Gaspe, Cape	121	P8
Gaspe Peninsula	121	N8
Gastonia	129	M3
Gaston, Lake	129	N2
Gastouni	75	F4
Gastre	139	C8
Gata, Cabo de	66	E4
Gatas, Akra	76	E5
Gata, Sierra de	66	C2
Gatchina	63	P7
Gatehouse of Fleet	54	E2
Gateshead	55	H2
Gateshead Island	119	Q1
Gatineau	125	N3
Gatooma	108	E3
Gatruyeh	95	M7
Gatun Lake	132	H10
Gatvand	94	J5
Gatwick	53	G3
Gaud-i-Zureh	95	R7
Gauer Lake	119	R4
Gauhati	93	H3
Gauja	63	L8
Gauldalen	62	D5
Gausta	63	C7
Gavater	95	Q9
Gavbus, Kuh-e	95	L8
Gavdhopoula	75	G5
Gavdhos	75	H5
Gaviao	66	C3
Gav Koshi	95	N7
Gavle	63	G6
Gavleborg	63	G6
Gavrilov-Yam	78	F4
Gawler	113	H5
Gawler Ranges	113	H5
Gaxun Nur	86	J3
Gaya	92	G4
Gaya La	92	F3
Gaydon	53	F2
Gayndah	113	L4
Gaysin	73	K1
Gayvoron	79	D6
Gaza	94	B6
Gazelle Peninsula	114	E2
Gazelle, Recif de la	114	W16
Gaziantep	77	G4
Gazimur	85	K6
Gazimurskiy Zavod	85	K6
Gazipasa	76	E4
Gbarnga	104	D4
Gboko	105	G4
Gdansk	71	H1
Gdov	63	M7
Geary	56	B3
Gebeit	96	C7
Gebze	76	C2
Gecitli	77	K4
Gedaref	103	G5
Gediz *Turkey*	76	B3
Gediz *Turkey*	76	C3
Gedney Hill	53	G2
Gedser	70	D1
Gee	64	F3
Geelong	113	J6
Geelvink Channel	112	C4
Geeveston	113	K7
Gegyai	92	F2
Geikie	119	Q4
Geilo	63	C6
Geita	107	F3
Geitlandsjokull	62	U12
Gejiu	93	K4
Geka, Mys	85	X4
Gela	69	E7
Geladi	103	J6
Gelendost	76	D3
Gelendzhik	79	F7
Gelibolu	76	B2
Gelibolu Yarimadasi	75	J2
Gelligaer	52	D3
Gelnhausen	70	C3
Gelsenkirchen	70	B3
Gemena	106	C2
Gemerek	77	G3
Gemlik	76	C2
Gemlik Korfezi	75	K2
Gemona del Friuli	68	D2
Gemund	70	B3
Genale Wenz	103	H6
Genc	77	J3
Geneina	102	D5
General Acha	139	D7
General Alvear	139	C7
General Bernardo O'Higgins	141	W6
General Conesa	139	D8
General La Madrid	139	D7
General Lavalle	139	E7
General Madariaga	139	E7
General Paz	139	E7
General Paz, Lago	139	B8
General Pico	139	D7
General Roca	139	C7
General Sam Martin	141	V5
General Santos	91	H4
General Villegas	139	D7
Geneseo	125	M5
Genessee	125	L5
Geneva *Switzerland*	68	A2
Geneva *U.S.A.*	125	M5
Geneva, Lake of	68	A2
Geneve	68	A2
Gen He	87	N1
Genichesk	79	E6
Genil	66	D4
Gennargentu, Monti del	69	B6
Genoa *Australia*	113	K6
Genoa *Italy*	68	B3
Genova	68	B3
Genova, Golfo di	68	B3
Genovesa, Isla	136	B7
Genriyetty, Ostrov	81	S2
Gent	64	E3
Genteng	90	D7
Genyem	91	L6
Geographe Bay	112	D5
Geographe Channel	112	C3
Geokchay	79	H7
George *Canada*	121	N6
George *South Africa*	108	D6
Georgeham	52	C3
George Island	139	E10
George, Lake	129	M6
George Sound	115	A6
Georgetown *Australia*	113	H5
George Town *Australia*	113	K7
Georgetown *Gambia*	104	C3
Georgetown *Grand Cayman, U.K.*	132	G5
Georgetown *Guyana*	136	F2
George Town *Malaysia*	90	C3
Georgetown *U.S.A.*	129	N4
George V Land	141	K4
George VI Sound	141	V4
Georgia	77	K1
Georgia	129	K4
Georgian Bay	125	K4
Georgia, Strait of	122	C3
Georgina	113	H3
Georgina Bay	121	K5
Georgiu-Dezh	79	F5
Georgiyevka	86	E2
Georgiyevsk	79	G7
Georg von Neumayer	141	Z4
Gera	70	E3
Geral de Goias, Serra	137	H6
Geraldine	115	C6
Geraldton *Australia*	112	C4
Geraldton *U.S.A.*	124	G2
Gerardmer	64	G4
Gerasimovka	84	A5
Gercus	77	J4
Gerede *Turkey*	76	E2
Gerede *Turkey*	76	E2
Gereshk	92	B2
Gergal	66	E4
Gerger	77	H4
Gerik	90	C4
Geris	76	D4
Gerlachovsky	71	J4
Germany	70	C3
Germencik	76	B4
Germi	94	J2
Germiston	108	E5
Gerona	67	H2
Gerrards Cross	53	G3
Gerze	76	F2
Geseke	70	C3
Geta	63	G6
Getafe	66	E2
Gettysburg *Pennsylvania, U.S.A.*	125	M7
Gettysburg *S. Dakota, U.S.A.*	123	Q5
Geumapang	90	B5
Gevan	95	N8
Gevas	77	K3
Geyik Dagi	76	E4
Geyik Daglari	76	E4
Geyve	76	D2
Gezi	77	F3
Ghadamis	101	G2
Ghaghara	92	F3
Ghana	104	E4
Ghanzi	108	D4
Gharah, Wadi	97	L8
Gharbi, Al Hajar al	97	N4
Gharbiya, Es Sahra el	103	E2
Ghardaia	101	F2
Ghardimaou	69	B7
Gharrat, Shatt al	94	H6
Gharyan	101	H2
Ghat	101	H3
Ghatampur	92	F3
Ghatere	114	J5
Ghayl Ba Wazir	97	J9
Ghayl Bin Yumayn	97	J9
Ghazaouet	100	E1
Ghaziabad	92	E3
Ghazipur	92	F3
Ghazni	92	C2
Gheorgheni	73	H2
Ghimes-Faget	73	J2
Ghisonaccia	69	B4
Ghisoni	69	B4
Ghubbah	97	P10
Ghubeish	102	E5
Ghudaf, Wadi al	94	E5
Ghurian	95	Q4
Giant's Causeway Head	58	J2
Giarre	69	E7
Gibostad	62	H2
Gibraltar	66	D4
Gibraltar Point	55	K3
Gibraltar, Strait of	66	D5
Gibson Desert	112	E3
Gichgeniyn Nuruu	86	H2
Gidole	103	G6
Gien	65	E5
Giesecke Isfjord	120	Q3
Giessen	70	C3
Gifatin	96	A3
Gifford Creek	112	D3
Gifhorn	70	D2
Gifu	89	F8
Giganta, Sierra de la	130	D5
Gigha Island	57	C5
Gigha, Sound of	57	C5
Giglio, Isola di	69	C4
Gijon	66	D1
Gijunabena Islands	114	J5
Gila	126	F4
Gila Bend	126	F4
Gilan Garb	94	G4
Gilbert	113	J2
Gilbert Islands	111	R2
Gilbert, Mount	122	B2
Gilbues	137	H5
Gile	109	G3
Gilford	58	K4
Gilgandra	113	K5
Gilgit	92	D1
Gillam	119	S4
Gillen, Mount	113	G3
Gillespie Point	115	B5
Gillette	123	M5
Gillian Lake	120	L4
Gillingham	53	H3
Gill, Lough	58	F4
Gilroy	126	B2
Giluwe, Mount	114	C3
Gimli	123	R2
Gimo	63	H6
Gimone	65	D7
Ginda	96	D9
Gingin	112	D5
Ginir	103	H6
Gioia del Colle	69	F5
Gioia, Golfo di	69	E6
Giona	75	G3
Girardot	136	C3
Girdle Ness	57	F3
Giresun	77	H2
Girga	103	F2
Girgir, Cape	114	C2
Giridih	92	G4
Girifalco	69	F6
Gironde	65	C6
Girvan	57	D5
Gisborne	115	G3
Gisenye	107	E3
Gislaved	63	E8
Gisors	64	D4
Gitega	107	E3
Giurgeni	73	J3
Giurgiu	73	H4
Givet	64	F3
Givors	65	F6
Gizhiginskaya Guba	85	T4
Gizol	114	H6
Gizycko	71	J1
Gjesvar	62	L1
Gjirokaster	75	F2
Gjoa Haven	120	G4
Gjovik	63	D6
Glace Bay	121	Q8
Glacier Bay	118	H4
Glacier Peak	122	D3
Gladstone *Australia*	113	L3
Gladstone *U.S.A.*	124	G4
Glama	63	D6
Glamis	57	E4
Glamoc	72	D3
Glarus	68	B2
Glasdrumman	58	L4
Glasgow *U.K.*	57	D5
Glasgow *Kentucky, U.S.A.*	124	H8
Glasgow *Montana, U.S.A.*	123	L3
Glas Maol	57	E4
Glass	56	D3
Glass, Loch	56	D3
Glastonbury	52	E3
Glatz	71	G3
Glauchau	70	E3
Glazov	78	J4
Gleiwitz	71	H3
Glen Affric	56	D3
Glenan, Iles de	65	B5
Glenavy	115	C6
Glen Cannich	56	D3
Glen Canyon	126	G2
Glen Canyon Dam	126	G2
Glencarse	57	E4
Glen Coe	57	D4
Glencoe	108	F5
Glen Cove	125	P6
Glendale *Arizona, U.S.A.*	126	F4
Glendale *California, U.S.A.*	126	C3
Glendive	123	M4
Glenelg *Australia*	113	J6
Glenelg *U.K.*	56	C3
Glen Esk	57	F4
Glenfinnan	57	C4
Glengad Head	58	H2
Glen Garry *Highland, U.K.*	57	C3
Glen Garry *Tayside, U.K.*	57	D4
Glen Innes	113	L4
Glen Mor	57	D3
Glen Moriston	57	D3
Glennallen	118	F3
Glen Orrin	56	D3
Glenrothes	57	E4
Glens Falls	125	P5
Glenshee	57	E4
Glentham	55	J3
Glenwood	128	F3
Glenwood Springs	123	L8
Glin	59	D7
Glina	72	D3
Glittertind	63	C6
Gliwice	71	H3
Gllave	74	E2
Globe	126	G4
Glockner, Gross	68	D2
Glogau	70	G3
Glogow	70	G3
Glomach, Falls of	56	C3
Glomfjord	62	E3
Glommerstrask	62	H4
Glossop	55	H3
Glottof, Mount	118	E4
Gloucester *Australia*	113	L5
Gloucester *Papua New Guinea*	114	D3
Gloucester *U.K.*	52	E3
Gloucester *U.S.A.*	125	Q5
Gloucestershire	52	E3
Gloup	56	A1
Glover Reef	132	D6
Glowno	71	H3
Glubczyce	71	G3
Glubinnoye	88	E2
Glubokoye *Belorussia*	63	M9
Glubokoye *Kazakhstan*	84	C6
Gluckstadt	70	C2
Glukhov	79	E5
Glyadyanskoye	84	Ae6
Glybokaya	73	H1
Glyder Fawr	54	E3
Gmelinka	79	H5
Gmund	68	D2
Gmunden	68	D2
Gnalta	113	J5
Gnarp	63	G5
Gniezno	71	G2
Gnoien	70	E2
Gnosall	52	E2
Goa	92	D5
Goalpara	93	H3
Goatfell	57	C5

Goba 103 H6
Gobabis 108 C4
Gobi 87 K3
Gobo 89 E9
Gochas 108 C4
Godafoss 62 W12
Godalming 53 G3
Godavari 92 F5
Godbout 125 S2
Goderich 125 K5
Godhavn 120 R4
Godhra 92 D4
Godollo 72 E2
Gods 119 S4
Godshill 53 F4
Gods Lake 119 S5
Godthab 120 R5
Godwin Austen 92 E1
Goeland, Lac au 121 L8
Goes 64 E3
Gogama 125 K3
Goginan 52 D2
Gogland, Ostrov 63 M6
Gogolin 71 H3
Goiana 137 L5
Goiania 138 G3
Goias *Brazil* 138 F3
Goias *Brazil* 137 H6
Gojome 88 H6
Gokceada 76 A2
Gokcekaya Baraji 76 D2
Gokdere 77 G2
Gokirmak 76 F2
Gokova Korfezi 76 B4
Goksu *Turkey* 76 E4
Goksu *Turkey* 77 F4
Goksun 77 G3
Goktas 77 J2
Goktepe 76 E4
Gol 63 C6
Golaghat 93 H3
Golam Head 59 C6
Golashkerd 95 N8
Golbasi *Turkey* 76 E3
Golbasi *Turkey* 77 G4
Golcar 55 H3
Golchikha 84 C2
Golconda 122 F7
Golcuk 76 C2
Golcuk Daglari 76 B3
Goldap 71 K1
Gold Coast 113 L4
Golden 122 F2
Golden Bay 115 D4
Goldendale 122 D5
Golden Hinde 122 B3
Goldsboro 129 P3
Goldsworthy 112 D3
Gole 77 K2
Golebert 77 K2
Goleniow 70 F2
Golfito 132 F10
Golfo Aranci 69 B5
Golgeli Daglari 76 C4
Golhisar 76 C4
Golija Planina 72 F4
Golkoy 77 G2
Golmarmara 76 B3
Golmud 93 H1
Golo 69 B4
Golova 76 D4
Golovanevsk 73 L1
Golovnino 88 K4
Golpayegan 95 K5
Golpazari 76 D2
Goma 107 E3
Gombe 105 H3
Gombi 105 H3
Gomel 79 E5
Gomera 100 B3
Gomez Palacio 127 L8
Gomishan 95 M3
Gonaives 133 L5
Gonam *Russia* 85 M5
Gonam *Russia* 85 N5
Gonave, Golfe de la 133 L5
Gonave, Ile de la 133 L5
Gonbad-e Kavus 95 M3
Gonda 92 F3
Gondal 92 D4
Gonder 103 G5
Gondia 92 F4
Gonen *Turkey* 76 B2
Gonen *Turkey* 76 B3
Gongbogyamda 93 H3
Gongolo 105 H3
Gongpoquan 86 H3
Goniadz 71 K2
Gonumillo 139 C8
Gonzales *California, U.S.A.* 126 B2
Gonzales *Texas, U.S.A.* 128 D6
Gonzales Chaves 139 D7
Goob Weyn 107 H3
Goodenough, Cape 141 J5
Goodenough Island 114 E3
Good Hope, Cape of 108 C6
Gooding 122 G6
Goodland 123 P8
Goole 55 J3
Goolgowi 113 K5
Goomen 113 L4
Goondiwindi 113 L4
Goose Bay 121 P7
Goose Creek 129 M4
Goose Lake 122 D7
Goplo, Jezioro 71 H2
Goppingen 70 C4
Gora Kalwaria 71 J3
Gorakhpur 92 F3
Gorazde 72 E4
Gorda, Punta 138 B3
Gordes 76 C3
Gordonsville 125 L7
Gore 115 B7
Gore 103 G6
Gorele 77 H2
Goresbridge 59 J7
Gorey *Ireland* 59 K7
Gorey *U.K.* 53 M7
Gorgan 95 M3
Gorgan, Rud-e 95 M3
Gorgona, Isola di 68 B4
Gorgoram 105 H3
Gori 77 L1
Gorice 75 F2
Gorinchem 64 F3
Goris 94 H2
Gorizia 68 D3
Gorka 78 H3
Gorkha 92 F3
Gorki *Belorussia* 78 E5
Gorki *Russia* 84 Ae3
Gorki *Russia* 78 H4
Gorkiy 78 G4
Gorkovskoye Vodokhranilishche 78 G4
Gorlev 63 D9
Gorlice 71 J4
Gorlitz 70 F3
Gorlovka 79 F6
Gornji Milanovac 72 F3
Gornji Vakuf 72 D4
Gorno-Altaysk 84 D6
Gornozavodsk 88 H2
Gornyak 84 C6
Gornyy *Russia* 79 H5
Gornyy *Russia* 85 P6
Gorodenka 73 H1
Gorodets 78 G4
Gorodok 71 K4
Gorodovikovsk 79 G6
Goroka 114 D3
Gorokhov 71 L3
Gorong, Kepulauan 91 J6
Gorongoza 109 F3
Gorontalo 91 G5
Goroshikha 84 D3
Gorran Haven 52 C4
Gorseinon 52 C3
Gort 59 E6
Gortaclare 58 H3
Gortahork 58 F2
Gorumna Island 59 C6
Goryn 79 D5
Gorzow Wielkopolski 70 F2
Goschen Strait 114 E4
Gosforth 55 H1
Goshogawara 88 H5
Gospic 72 C3
Gosport 53 F4
Gostivar 73 F5
Gota 62 Z14
Gota Kanal 63 G7
Gotaland 63 E8
Goteborg 63 H8
Goteborg Och Bohus 63 D7
Gotene 63 E7
Gotha 70 D3
Gothenburg 63 D8
Gotland 63 H8
Goto-retto 89 B9
Gotse Delchev 73 G5
Gotska Sandon 63 H7
Gotsu 89 D8
Gottingen 70 C3
Gottwaldov 71 G4
Gouda 64 F2
Goudhurst 53 H3
Gough Island 48 F6
Gouin, Reservoir 125 N2
Goulais 124 J3
Goulburn 113 K5
Goulburn Islands 113 G1
Goundam 100 E5
Gourdon 65 D6
Goure 101 H6
Gourma-Rharous 100 E5
Gournay 64 D4
Gourock 57 D5
Govena, Mys 85 V5
Goverla 71 L4
Governador Valadares 138 H3
Governor's Harbour 132 J2
Govind Pant Sagar 92 F4
Govorovo 85 M2
Gowanbridge 115 D4
Gowanda 125 L5
Gower 52 C3
Gowna, Lough 58 G5
Goya 138 E5
Goynucek 77 F2
Goynuk *Turkey* 76 D2
Goynuk *Turkey* 77 J3
Goz Beida 102 D5
Gozne 76 F4
Gozo 74 C4
Goz Regeb 96 B8
Graaff Reinet 108 D6
Gracac 72 C3
Gradaus, Serra dos 137 G5
Grado *Italy* 68 D3
Grado *Spain* 66 C1
Gradoli 69 C4
Gradsko 73 F5
Grafham Water 53 G2
Grafton *Australia* 113 L4
Grafton *N. Dakota, U.S.A.* 123 R3
Grafton *W. Virginia, U.S.A.* 125 K7
Grafton, Islas 139 B10
Graham 128 C4
Graham Island *British Columbia, Canada* 118 J5
Graham Island *NW. Territories, Canada* 120 H2
Graham Land 141 V5
Grahamstown 108 E6
Graie, Alpi 68 A3
Graiguenamanagh 59 J7
Grain 53 H3
Grajau 137 H4
Grajewo 71 K2
Grampian 56 E3
Grampian Mountains 57 D4
Grampound 52 C4
Gramsh 75 F2
Gran 137 F3
Granada *Nicaragua* 132 E9
Granada *Spain* 66 E4
Granard 58 H5
Gran Bajo 139 C9
Granby *Canada* 125 P4
Granby *U.S.A.* 123 L7
Gran Canaria 100 B3
Gran Chaco 138 D4
Grand *Canada* 125 K5
Grand *Michigan, U.S.A.* 124 H5
Grand *Missouri, U.S.A.* 124 C6
Grand *S. Dakota, U.S.A.* 123 P5
Grand Bahama 132 H1
Grand Bois, Coteau de 124 C3
Grand Canal *China* 87 M5
Grand Canal *Ireland* 59 H6
Grand Canyon *U.S.A.* 126 F2
Grand Canyon *U.S.A.* 126 F2
Grand Cayman 132 G5
Grand Coulee 122 E4
Grand Coulee Dam 122 E4
Grande *Brazil* 138 G4
Grande *Mexico* 131 L9
Grande *Nicaragua* 132 E8
Grande, Bahia 139 C10
Grande Cache 119 M5
Grande, Cienaga 133 K10
Grande Comore 109 H2
Grande Miquelon 121 Q8
Grande O'Guapay 138 D3
Grande Prairie 119 M4
Grande, Punta 137 G3
Grande, Rio 127 M6
Grande Ronde 122 F5
Gran Desierto 126 E5
Grandes Rocques 53 M7
Grand Falls *New Brunswick, Canada* 125 S3
Grand Falls *Newfoundland, Canada* 121 Q8
Grand Forks 123 R4
Grand Island 123 Q7
Grand Isle 128 H6
Grand Junction 127 H1
Grand Lahou 104 E4
Grand Lake *New Brunswick, Canada* 128 G6
Grand Lake *Newfoundland, Canada* 121 Q8
Grand Lake *U.S.A.* 125 S3
Grand Lake O' the Cherokees 128 E2
Grand-Lieu, Lac de 65 C5
Grand Manan Island 125 S4
Grand Marais *Michigan, U.S.A.* 124 H3
Grand Marais *Minnesota, U.S.A.* 124 E3
Grand-Mere 125 P3
Grandola 66 B3
Grand Popo 105 F4
Grand Prairie 128 D4
Grand Rapids *Canada* 119 R5
Grand Rapids *Michigan, U.S.A.* 124 H5
Grand Rapids *Minnesota, U.S.A.* 124 D3
Grandrieu 65 E6
Grand Saint Bernard, Col du 68 A3
Grand Santi 137 G3
Graney, Lough 59 E7
Grangemouth 57 E4
Grange-over-Sands 55 G2
Grangesberg 63 F6
Grangeville 122 F5
Granite Peak 123 K5
Granitola, Capo 69 D7
Granna 63 F7
Granollers 67 H2
Gran Pajonal 136 C6
Gran Paradiso 68 A3
Grantham 53 G2
Grant Island 141 R4
Grant, Mount 122 E8
Grantown-on-Spey 56 E3
Grants 127 J3
Grantshouse 57 F4
Grants Pass 122 C6
Granville 64 C4
Granville Lake 119 Q4
Grasby 55 J3
Gras, Lac de 119 N3
Grasmere 55 F2
Graso 63 H6
Grasse 65 G7
Grassrange 123 K4
Grass Valley 122 D8
Grassy 113 J7
Grassy Knob 125 K7
Gratens 65 D7
Graus 67 G1
Gravatai 138 F5
Gravdal 62 E2
Gravelines 64 E3
Grave, Pointe de 65 C6
Gravesend 53 H3
Gravois, Pointe-a- 133 L5
Gray 65 F5
Grayling 124 H4
Grays 53 H3
Grays Harbor 122 B4
Graz 68 E2
Great Abaco 132 J1
Great Artesian Basin 113 J4
Great Astrolabe Reef 114 R9
Great Australian Bight 112 F5
Great Ayton 55 H2
Great Baddow 53 H3
Great Bahama Bank 132 H2
Great Bardfield 53 H3
Great Barrier Island 115 E2
Great Barrier Reef 113 K2
Great Basin 122 F7
Great Bear Lake 119 L2
Great Bend 127 N1
Great Blasket Island 59 A8
Great Budworth 55 G3
Great Cumbrae 57 D5
Great Dividing Range 113 K3
Great Driffield 55 J2
Great Dunmow 53 H3
Greater Antarctica 141 D2
Greater Antilles 132 G4
Greater Khingan Range 87 N2
Greater London 53 G3
Greater Manchester 55 G3
Great Exuma Island 132 K3
Great Falls 122 J4
Great Fish 108 E6
Great Gable 55 F2
Great Guana Cay 132 J2
Great Harwood 55 G3
Great Inagua 133 L4
Great Indian Desert 92 D3
Great Island 59 F9
Great Karas Berg 108 C5
Great Karoo 108 D6
Great Lakes 143 L3
Great Longton 55 H2
Great Malvern 52 E2
Great Mercury Island 115 E2
Great Nicobar 93 H7
Great North East Channel 114 C3
Great Ormes Head 54 F3
Great Ouse 53 H2
Great Papuan Plateau 114 C3
Great Plains 123 J2
Great Ruaha 107 G4
Great Sacandaga Lake 125 N5
Great Salt Lake 122 H7
Great Salt Lake Desert 122 H7
Great Sand Hills 123 K2
Great Sandy Desert 112 E3
Great Sankey 55 G3
Great Sea Reef 114 R8
Great Sitkin Island 118 Ac9
Great Slave Lake 119 N2
Great Smeaton 55 H2
Great Stour 53 J3
Great Sugar Loaf 59 K6
Great Torrington 52 C4
Great Victoria Desert 112 F4
Great Wall of China, The 87 L4
Great Whernside 55 H2
Great Witley 52 E2
Great Yarmouth 53 J2
Great Yeldham 53 H2
Great Zab 94 F3
Gredos, Sierra de 66 D2
Greece 75 F3
Greeley 123 M7
Greely Fjord 120 K1
Green *Kentucky, U.S.A.* 124 G8
Green *Wyoming, U.S.A.* 123 J6
Green Bay *U.S.A.* 124 G4
Green Bay *U.S.A.* 124 G4
Green Bell, Ostrov 80 H1
Greenbrier 125 K8
Greencastle 58 K4
Greeneville 129 L2
Greenfield 125 P5
Green Hammerton 55 H2
Greenhead 55 G2
Green Island 115 C6
Greenisland 58 L3
Green Islands 114 E2
Greenland 116 Q1
Greenlaw 57 F4
Greenlough 112 D4
Greenlowther 57 D5
Green Mountains 125 P5

Greenock	57	D5	Guadalcanal *Solomon Is.*	114	J6	Guillestre	65	G6	Gyangze	93	G3
Green River *Papua New Guinea*	114	C2	Guadalcanal *Spain*	66	D3	Guimaraes	66	B2	Gyaring Hu	93	J2
Green River *Utah, U.S.A.*	127	G1	Guadalete	66	D4	Guinea	104	C3	Gydanskaya Guba	84	B2
Green River *Wyoming, U.S.A.*	123	K7	Guadalimar	66	E3	Guinea Bissau	104	C3	Gydanskiy Poluostrov	84	B2
Greensboro	129	N2	Guadalmez	66	D3	Guinea, Gulf of	105	F5	Gydnia	71	H1
Greensburg	125	L6	Guadalope	67	F2	Guines	132	F3	Gympie	113	L4
Greenstone Point	56	C3	Guadalquivir	66	D4	Guingamp	64	B4	Gynymskaya	85	N5
Green Valley	126	G5	Guadalupe *Mexico*	128	B8	Guiratinga	138	F3	Gyongyos	72	E2
Greenville *Liberia*	104	D4	Guadalupe *Mexico*	127	J5	Guiria	136	E1	Gyonk	72	E2
Greenville *Alabama, U.S.A.*	129	J5	Guadalupe *Spain*	66	D3	Guisanbourg	137	G3	Gyor	72	D2
Greenville *Mississippi, U.S.A.*	128	G4	Guadalupe *Texas, U.S.A.*	128	D6	Guisborough	55	H2	Gypsumville	123	Q2
Greenville *N. Carolina, U.S.A.*	129	P3	Guadalupe Mountains	127	K5	Guise	64	E4	Gyueshevo	73	G4
Greenville *S. Carolina, U.S.A.*	129	L3	Guadalupe, Sierra de	66	D3	Guiseley	55	H3	Gyula	73	F2
Greenville *Texas, U.S.A.*	128	D4	Guadalupe Victoria	130	G5	Guiting Power	53	F3			
Greenwood *Mississippi, U.S.A.*	128	G4	Guadarrama *Spain*	66	D2	Guiuan	91	H3	**H**		
Greenwood *S. Carolina, U.S.A.*	129	L3	Guadarrama *Spain*	66	D2	Guixi	87	M6			
Greers Ferry Lake	128	F3	Guadarrama, Sierra de	66	E2	Gui Xian	93	L4	Haabunga	62	W12
Gregorio	136	C5	Guadeloupe	133	S6	Guiyang	93	L3	Haapai Group	111	U5
Gregory, Lake	113	H4	Guadeloupe Passage	133	S6	Guizhou	93	L3	Haapajarvi	62	L5
Gregory Range	113	J2	Guadelupe	126	D4	Gujarat	92	D4	Haapamaki	63	L5
Greian Head	57	A3	Guadiana	66	C4	Gujranwala	92	D2	Haapsalu	63	K7
Greifswald	70	E1	Guadiana, Bahia de	132	E3	Gujrat	92	D2	Haardt	70	B4
Grein	68	E1	Guadiana Menor	66	E4	Gulbarga	92	E5	Haarlem	64	F2
Greipstad	62	H2	Guadix	66	E4	Gulbene	63	M8	Haast *New Zealand*	115	B5
Greiz	70	E3	Guafo, Isla	139	B8	Gulcayir	76	D3	Haast *New Zealand*	115	B5
Gremikha	78	F2	Guainia	136	D3	Gulcha	86	C3	Haast Passage	115	B6
Gremyachinsk	78	K4	Guaiquinima, Cerro	136	E2	Gulfport	128	H5	Hab	92	C3
Grena	63	D8	Guajira, Peninsula de	136	C1	Gulian	87	N1	Habawnah, Wadi	96	G8
Grenada	133	S8	Gualachulian	57	C4	Gullane	57	F4	Habban	96	H9
Grenada *U.S.A.*	128	H4	Gualaquiza	136	B4	Gullfoss	62	V12	Habbaniyah	94	F5
Grenadines, The	133	S8	Gualeguay *Argentina*	138	E6	Gull Lake	123	K2	Habbaniyah, Hawr al	94	F5
Grenen	63	D8	Gualeguay *Argentina*	138	E6	Gullspang	63	F7	Haberli	77	J4
Grenfell	123	N2	Gualeguaychu	138	E6	Gulluk	76	B4	Habirag	87	M3
Grenivik	62	V12	Guam	83	N5	Gulnar	76	E4	Haboro	88	H3
Grenoble	65	F6	Guama	137	H4	Gulpinar	76	B3	Hachenburg	70	B3
Grenville, Cape	113	J1	Guamblin, Isla	139	A8	Gulsehir	76	F3	Hachijo-jima	89	G9
Gresford	55	G3	Guampi, Sierra de	136	D2	Gulyantsi	73	H4	Hachiman	89	F8
Gresham	122	C5	Guamuchil	130	E5	Gumbaz	95	R6	Hachinohe	88	H5
Gresik	90	E7	Gua Musang	90	C5	Gummi	105	G3	Hachioji	89	G8
Greta	55	H1	Guanare *Venezuela*	136	D2	Gumushacikoy	76	F2	Hacibektas	76	F3
Gretna	55	F2	Guanare *Venezuela*	136	D2	Gumushane	77	H2	Hacihalil Dagi	77	K2
Grevena	75	F2	Guanay, Sierra	136	D2	Guna	92	E4	Haciomer	77	J3
Greybull	123	K5	Guandi	88	B4	Gundagi	113	K6	Hackas	62	F5
Grey Island	121	Q7	Guangan	93	L2	Gundogmus	76	E4	Hadan, Harrat	96	E6
Grey Mare's Tail	57	E5	Guangdong	93	M4	Gunedidalem	91	H6	Hadarah	96	E7
Greymouth	115	C5	Guanghua	93	M2	Guney	76	C3	Hadarba, Ras	96	C5
Grey Range	113	J4	Guangnan	93	L4	Guneydogutoroslar	77	H3	Haddenham	53	H2
Greysteel	58	H2	Guangning	93	M4	Gungu	106	C4	Haddington	57	F5
Greystones	59	K6	Guangping	87	M4	Gunnedah	113	L5	Hadd, Ra's al	97	P5
Greytown	115	E4	Guangxi	93	L4	Gunning	113	K5	Hadejia	105	G3
Griefswald Bodden	70	E1	Guangyuan	93	L2	Gunnison *Colorado, U.S.A.*	127	J1	Hadera	94	B5
Griffin	129	K4	Guangze	87	M6	Gunnison *Colorado, U.S.A.*	123	K8	Haderslev	63	E9
Griffith	113	K5	Guangzhou	93	M4	Gunnison *Utah, U.S.A*	126	G1	Hadhalil, Al	96	G2
Griffith Island	120	G3	Guanhaes	138	H3	Guntakal	92	E5	Hadhramawt	97	J9
Grigoriopol	73	K2	Guanipa	133	R10	Guntersville	129	J3	Hadiboh	97	P10
Grimailov	71	M4	Guanoca	136	E1	Guntersville Lake	129	J3	Hadim	76	E4
Grim, Cape	113	J7	Guantanamo	133	K4	Guntur	92	F5	Hadleigh	53	H2
Grimsby	55	J3	Guan Xian	93	K2	Gunungsitoli	90	B5	Hadley Bay	119	P1
Grimsey	62	W11	Guapi	136	B3	Gunungsugih	90	D6	Hadong	93	L4
Grimshaw	119	M4	Guapiles	132	F9	Gunzenhausen	70	D4	Hadrian's Wall	57	F5
Grimstad	63	C7	Guapore	136	E6	Gurban Obo	87	L3	Hadsund	63	D8
Grindavik	62	T13	Guaqui	138	C3	Gurbulak	77	L3	Haeju	87	P4
Grindsted	63	C9	Guarabira	137	K5	Gurdim	95	Q9	Hafar al Batin	96	H2
Gringley on the Hill	55	J3	Guarapuava	138	F5	Gurdzhaani	79	H7	Hafik	77	G3
Grinnell	124	D6	Guara, Sierra de	67	F1	Gure	76	C3	Hafit	97	M5
Grinnell Peninsula	120	G2	Guarda *Portugal*	66	C2	Gurgaon	92	E3	Hafnarfjordur	62	U12
Grintavec	68	E2	Guarda *Portugal*	66	C2	Gurgei, Jebel	102	D5	Hafratindur	62	U12
Gris-Nez, Cap	64	D3	Guardo	66	D1	Gurghiului, Muntii	73	H2	Haft Gel	94	J6
Griva	78	J3	Guarenas	136	D1	Gurgueia	137	J5	Haftqala	95	R4
Grmec Planina	72	D3	Guaribas, Cachoeira	137	G4	Gur I Topit	75	F2	Hag Abdullah	103	F5
Grobming	68	D2	Guarico	136	D2	Gurpinar	77	K3	Hagemeister Island	118	A3
Grodekovo	88	C3	Guasave	130	E5	Gurue	109	G3	Hagen	70	B3
Grodno	71	K2	Guasdualito	136	C2	Gurun	77	G3	Hagen, Mount	114	C3
Groix, Ile de	65	B5	Guasipati	136	E2	Gurupa	137	G4	Hagerstown	125	M7
Grombalia	69	C7	Guastalla	68	C3	Gurupa, Ilha Grande do	137	G4	Hagfors	63	E6
Grong	62	E4	Guatemala	132	B7	Gurupi	137	H4	Haggenas	62	F5
Groningen *Netherlands*	64	G2	Guatemala	132	B7	Gurupi, Serra do	137	H4	Hagi	89	C8
Groningen *Suriname*	137	F2	Guaviare	136	D3	Guruzala	92	E5	Ha Giang	93	K4
Groot	108	D6	Guaxupe	138	G4	Guryev	79	J6	Hagimas	73	H2
Groote Eylandt	113	H1	Guayaquil	136	B4	Gusau	105	G3	Hagley	53	E2
Grootfontein	108	C3	Guayaquil, Golfo de	136	A4	Gusev	71	K1	Hagondange	64	G4
Grossa, Ponta	137	H3	Guaymas	126	G7	Gusinoozersk	84	H6	Hags Head	59	D7
Grosseto	69	C4	Guazacapan	132	B7	Gus-Khrustalnyy	78	G4	Hague, Cap de la	64	C4
Grossevichi	88	G1	Guba	103	G5	Gustrow	70	E2	Haguenau	64	G4
Gros Ventre Mountains	123	J6	Guba Dolgaya	84	Ac2	Gusyatin	73	J1	Haian	93	M4
Grottaglie	69	F5	Gubakha	78	K4	Gutcher	56	A1	Haibei	88	A2
Groundhog	124	J2	Gubbio	68	D4	Guthrie *Oklahoma, U.S.A.*	128	D3	Haicheng	87	N3
Grove	53	J3	Gubdor	78	K3	Guthrie *Texas, U.S.A.*	127	M4	Hai Duong	93	L4
Grove City	125	K6	Guben	70	F3	Gutian	87	M6	Haifa	94	B5
Grove Hill	129	J5	Gucuk	77	G3	Guttenberg	124	E5	Haifeng	87	M7
Grover City	126	B3	Gudar, Sierra de	67	F2	Guvem	76	E2	Haikang	93	M4
Groznyy	79	H7	Gudbrandsdalen	63	D6	Guyana	136	F2	Haikou	93	M5
Grudovo	73	J4	Gudena	63	C8	Guyenne	65	D6	Hail	96	E3
Grudziadz	71	H2	Gudur	92	E6	Guymon	127	M2	Hailar	87	M2
Gruinard Bay	56	C3	Gudvangen	62	B6	Guyuan	93	L1	Hailar He	87	M2
Gruinart, Loch	57	B5	Guekedou	104	C4	Guzelbag	76	D4	Hailsham	53	H4
Grums	63	E7	Guelma	101	G1	Guzeloluk	76	F4	Hailun	88	A2
Grunaw	108	C5	Guelph	125	K5	Guzelsu	77	K3	Hailuoto *Finland*	62	L4
Grunberg	70	F3	Guereda	102	D5	Guzelyurt	76	F3	Hailuoto *Finland*	63	L2
Grund	62	U12	Gueret	65	D5	Guzman, Laguna de	127	J5	Hainan Dao	93	M5
Grundarfjordur	62	T12	Guernsey *U.K.*	53	M7	Gvardeysk	71	J1	Haines	118	H4
Grundy	124	J8	Guernsey *U.S.A.*	123	M6	Gvardeyskoye	73	J1	Haines City	129	M6
Gruznovka	84	H5	Guerrero Negro	126	E6	Gwa	93	H5	Haiphong	93	L4
Gryazi	79	F5	Gugu	73	G3	Gwabegar	113	K5	Haiti	133	L5
Gryazovets	78	G4	Guhakolak, Tanjung	90	D7	Gwadar	92	B3	Haivare	114	C3
Gryfice	70	F2	Guia	138	E3	Gwalior	92	E3	Haiya	96	C7
Gryfino	70	F2	Guide	93	K1	Gwanda	108	E4	Hajarah, Al	96	F2
Guabito	136	A2	Guider	105	H4	Gweebarra Bay	58	F3	Hajduboszormeny	73	F2
Guacanayabo, Golfo de	132	J4	Guidong	93	M3	Gwelo	108	E3	Hajdunanas	73	F2
Guadajoz	66	D4	Guiglo	104	D4	Gwent	52	E3	Hajiki-saki	89	G6
Guadalajara *Mexico*	130	H7	Gui Jiang	93	M4	Gweru	108	E3	Hajipur	92	G3
Guadalajara *Spain*	66	E2	Guildford	53	G3	Gwoza	105	H3	Hajjah	96	F9
			Guildtown	57	E4	Gwydir,	113	K4	Hajjiabad	95	M7
			Guilin	93	M3	Gwynedd	52	D2			

Name	Page	Ref	Name	Page	Ref	Name	Page	Ref	Name	Page	Ref	Name	Page	Ref
Hajmah	97	N7	Hamra , Al Hammadah al	101	H3	Harrison	128	F2	Hawng Luk	93	J4
Hajr, Wadi	97	J9	Hamrange	63	G6	Harrison Bay	118	E1	Hawra	97	J9
Hakataramea	115	C6	Hamrin, Jebel	77	L5	Harrisonburg	125	L7	Hawran, Wadi	94	E5
Hakkari	77	K4	Hamun-i Mashkel	92	B3	Harrison, Cape	121	Q7	Hawsker	55	J2
Hakkas	62	J3	Hamur	77	K3	Harrison Lake	122	D3	Hawthorne	126	C1
Hakkibey	76	F4	Hanahan	114	E3	Harrisonville	124	C7	Haxby	55	H2
Hakodate	88	H5	Hanak	77	K2	Harris Ridge	140	A1	Hay *New South Wales,*		
Haku-san	89	F7	Hanalei	126	R9	Harris, Sound of	56	A3	*Australia*	113	J5
Hala	92	C3	Hanamaki	88	H6	Harrogate	55	H3	Hay *Northern Territory,*		
Halab	94	C3	Hancheng	93	M1	Harrow	53	G3	*Australia*	113	H3
Halaban	96	G5	Hancock	125	L7	Harsit	77	H2	Hay *Canada*	119	M3
Halabja	94	G4	Handa	89	F8	Harstad	62	G2	Hayden	123	L7
Halaib	103	G3	Handan	87	L4	Harsvik	62	D4	Hayes	119	R4
Halat Ammar	96	C2	Handeni	107	G4	Hart	118	H2	Hayes Halvo	120	N2
Halaveden	63	F7	Handlova	71	H4	Hartbees	108	D5	Hayes, Mount	118	F3
Halawa *Hawaii, U.S.A.*	126	S10	Hanford	126	C2	Hartberg	68	E2	Hayjan	96	G8
Halawa *Hawaii, U.S.A.*	126	T10	Hangang	87	P4	Harteigen	63	B6	Hayl	97	N4
Halba	77	G5	Hangayn Nuruu	86	H2	Hartford	125	P6	Hayl, Wadi al	77	H5
Halberstadt	70	D3	Hanggin Houqi	87	K3	Harthill	57	E5	Haymana	76	B2
Halcon, Mount	91	G3	Hanggin Qi	87	K4	Hartkjolen	62	E4	Hayrabolu	76	B2
Halden	63	D7	Hango	63	K7	Hartland	52	C4	Hay River	119	M3
Haldensleben	70	D2	Hangzhou	87	N5	Hartland Point	52	C3	Hays	96	F10
Halesowen	53	E2	Hangzhou Wan	87	N5	Hartlepool	55	H2	Hays	123	Q8
Halesworth	53	J2	Hanhongor	87	J3	Hartley	127	L3	Haywards Heath	53	G4
Halfeti	77	G4	Hani	77	J3	Hartola	63	M6	Hazaran, Kuh-e	95	N7
Halfin, Wadi	97	N6	Hanifah, Wadi	96	H4	Hartsville	129	M3	Hazard	124	J8
Halfmoon Bay	115	B7	Hanish al Kabir	96	F10	Hartwell Reservoir	129	L3	Hazar Golu	77	H3
Halfway	119	L4	Haniyah, Al	94	H7	Hartz	108	E5	Hazaribag	92	G4
Hali	96	E7	Han Jiang	87	M7	Harut	97	L8	Hazaribagh Range	92	F4
Haliburton Highlands	125	L4	Hanko	63	K7	Harvey *Australia*	112	D5	Hazar Masjed, Kuh-e	95	P3
Halifax *Canada*	121	P9	Hanksville	126	G1	Harvey *U.S.A.*	124	G6	Hazel Grove	55	G3
Halifax *U.K.*	55	H3	Hanna	122	H2	Harwich	53	J3	Hazelton *Canada*	118	K4
Halifax Bay	113	K2	Hannah Bay	121	L7	Haryana	92	E3	Hazelton *U.S.A.*	125	N6
Halikarnassos	76	B4	Hannibal	124	E7	Harz	70	D3	Hazen Bay	118	B3
Halileh, Ra's-e	95	K7	Hann, Mount	112	F2	Hasan Dagi	76	F3	Hazlehurst	128	G5
Halin	88	B3	Hannover	70	C2	Hashish, Ghubbat	97	P6	Hazro	77	J3
Halisah	77	G4	Hano-bukten	63	F9	Haskoy	77	K2	Headcorn	53	H3
Halitpasa	76	B3	Hanoi	93	L4	Haslemere	53	G3	Head of Bight	112	G5
Halkapinar	76	F4	Hanover *Canada*	125	K4	Haslingden	55	G3	Healdsburg	126	A1
Halkett, Cape	118	E1	Hanover *South Africa*	108	D6	Hassa	77	G4	Healesville	113	K6
Halla	62	G5	Hanover *U.S.A.*	125	P5	Hassan	92	E6	Heanor	55	H3
Halladale	56	E2	Hanover, Isla	139	B10	Hassankeyf	77	J4	Heard Islands	142	D6
Hallanca	136	B5	Hanpan, Cape	114	E2	Hassela	63	L5	Hearst	124	J2
Halland	63	E8	Han Pijesak	72	E3	Hassi Habadra	101	F3	Hearst Island	141	V5
Hallandsas	63	E8	Han Shui	93	M2	Hassleholm	63	E8	Heart	123	P4
Halle	70	C3	Hanson Bay	115	F6	Hastings *Australia*	113	K7	Heathfield	53	H4
Hallefors	63	F7	Hanstholm	63	C8	Hastings *New Zealand*	115	F3	Heathrow	53	G3
Hallen	62	F5	Hantay	86	J2	Hastings *U.K.*	53	H4	Hebbronville	128	C7
Halley	141	Y3	Hanyuan	93	K3	Hastings *Michigan, U.S.A.*	124	H5	Hebden Bridge	55	G3
Hallingdal	63	C6	Hanzhong	93	L2	Hastings *Nebraska, U.S.A.*	123	Q7	Hebei	87	M4
Hallingskarvet	63	B6	Haparanda	62	L4	Hastveda	63	E8	Hebel	113	K4
Hall Peninsula	120	N5	Happisburgh	53	J2	Hasvik	62	K1	Heber City	122	J7
Halls Creek	112	F2	Hapsu	88	B5	Haswell	55	H2	Hebi	87	L4
Hallstavik	63	H6	Hapur	92	E3	Hatanbulag	87	K3	Hebrides, Sea of the	57	A4
Hallum	64	F2	Haql	96	B2	Hatchie	128	H3	Hebron *Canada*	121	P6
Halmahera	91	H5	Hara	87	K2	Hatfield *Hertfordshire, U.K.*	53	G3	Hebron *Israel*	94	B6
Halmahera, Laut	91	H6	Harad *Saudi Arabia*	97	J4	Hatfield *S. Yorkshire, U.K.*	55	H3	Hebron *N. Dakota, U.S.A.*	123	N4
Halmstad	63	E8	Harad *Yemen*	96	F8	Hatfield Peverel	53	H3	Hebron *Nebraska, U.S.A.*	123	R7
Hals	63	D8	Harads	62	J3	Hatgal	86	J1	Hecate Strait	118	J5
Halsinge-skogen	63	F6	Haramachi	89	H7	Hathras	92	E3	Hechi	93	L4
Halsingland	63	G6	Harare	108	F3	Hatibah, Ra's	96	D6	Hechuan	93	L2
Halstead	53	H3	Harasis, Jiddat al	97	N7	Ha Tien	93	K6	Heckington	53	G2
Halton Lea Gate	55	G2	Harbin	87	P2	Ha Tinh	93	L5	Hecla and Griper Bay	120	D2
Halul	97	L4	Harbiye	77	G4	Hatip	76	E4	Hector, Mount	115	E4
Ham *France*	64	E4	Harbour Breton	121	Q8	Hat Island	120	G4	Hede	62	E5
Ham *U.K.*	56	A2	Harby	53	G2	Hato	136	A2	Hedland, Port	112	D3
Hamada	89	D8	Hardangerfjord	63	B6	Hatohudo	91	H7	Hedmark	63	D6
Hamad, Al	94	D6	Hardanger-Jokulen	63	B6	Hatskiy	84	D5	Heerenveen	64	F2
Hamadan	94	J4	Hardangervidda	63	B6	Hatteras, Cape	129	Q3	Heerlen	64	F3
Hamah	94	C4	Hardin	123	L5	Hattiesburg	128	H5	Hefa	94	B5
Hamam	77	G4	Hardoi	92	F3	Hatton	56	G3	Hefei	87	M5
Hamamatsu	89	F8	Hardy	128	G2	Hattras Passage	93	J6	Hefeng	93	M3
Hamar	63	D6	Hare Bay	121	Q7	Hatunsaray	76	E4	Hegang	87	Q2
Hamata, Gebel	96	B4	Harer	103	H6	Hatuoto	91	H6	Hegura-jima	89	F7
Hama-Tombetsu	88	J3	Harewood	55	H3	Haugesund	63	A7	Heiban	102	F5
Hambantota	92	F7	Hargeysa	103	H6	Haughton	53	E2	Heide	70	C1
Hambleton	55	G3	Hargigo	96	D9	Hauhui	114	K6	Heidelberg	70	C4
Hamburg *U.S.A.*	124	C6	Har Hu	93	J1	Haukivesi	62	N5	Heidharhorn	62	U12
Hamburg *W. Germany*	70	D2	Harib	96	G9	Haukivuori	63	M5	Heighington	55	H2
Hamdaman, Dasht-i	95	Q4	Haridwar	92	E3	Hauraha	114	K7	Heilbron	108	E5
Hamd, Wadi al	96	C4	Harihari	115	C5	Hauraki Gulf	115	E2	Heilbronn	70	C4
Hame	63	L6	Harima-nada	89	E8	Haut Atlas	100	D2	Heiligenhafen	70	D1
Hameln	70	C2	Harim, Jambal Al	97	N4	Hauts Plateaux	100	E2	Heiligenstadt	70	D3
Hamhung	87	P4	Hari-Rud	95	S4	Havana	124	E6	Heilong Jiang *China*	88	B2
Hami	86	F3	Harjedalen	62	E5	Havant	53	F4	Heilongjiang *China*	88	D1
Hamilton	113	H3	Harlan	124	C6	Havasu, Lake	126	F3	Heimaey	62	U13
Hamilton *Bermuda*	117	N5	Harlem	123	K3	Havasu, Lake	126	E3	Heimdal	62	D5
Hamilton *Canada*	125	L5	Harleston	53	J2	Havel	70	D2	Heinavesi	62	N5
Hamilton *New Zealand*	115	E2	Harlingen	64	F2	Havelock North	115	F3	Heinola	63	M6
Hamilton *U.K.*	57	D5	Harlow	53	H3	Haverfordwest	52	C2	Heinze Islands	93	J6
Hamilton *Alabama, U.S.A.*	129	J3	Harlowton	123	K4	Haverhill *U.K.*	53	H2	Hejing	86	F3
Hamilton *Montana, U.S.A.*	122	G4	Harmancik	76	C3	Haverhill *U.S.A.*	125	Q5	Hekimhan	77	G3
Hamilton *Ohio, U.S.A.*	124	H7	Harmil	96	E8	Havoysund	62	L1	Hel	71	H1
Hamilton Inlet	121	Q7	Harney Basin	122	D6	Havran	76	B3	Helagsfjallet	62	E5
Hamim, Wadi al	101	K2	Harney Lake	122	E6	Havre	123	K3	Helena *Arkansas, U.S.A.*	128	G3
Hamina	63	M6	Harnosand	62	G5	Havre-Saint-Pierre	121	P7	Helena *Montana, U.S.A.*	122	J4
Hamitabat	76	D4	Haro	66	E1	Havsa	76	B2	Helen Island	91	J5
Hamm	70	B2	Haro, Cabo	126	G7	Havza	77	F2	Helensburgh	57	D4
Hammar, Hawr al	94	H6	Haroldswick	56	A1	Hawaii *U.S.A.*	126	R10	Helensville	115	E2
Hammarstrand	62	G5	Harpanahalli	92	E6	Hawaii *U.S.A.*	126	T11	Helgoland	70	B1
Hammeenlinna	63	L6	Harpenden	53	G3	Hawaya, Lake	97	J6	Helgolander Bucht	70	B1
Hammerdal	62	F5	Harper	104	D5	Hawea, Lake	115	B6	Heli	88	C2
Hammerfest	62	K1	Harper Passage	115	C5	Hawera	115	E3	Heligenblut	68	D2
Hammersley Range	112	D3	Harpstedt	70	C2	Hawes	55	G2	Helleh	95	K7
Hammond *Indiana, U.S.A.*	124	G6	Harrah, Ad	94	D6	Haweswater Reservoir	55	G2	Hellin	67	F3
Hammond *Louisiana, U.S.A.*	128	G5	Harran	77	H4	Hawick	57	F5	Hell's Mouth	52	C2
Hammond *Montana, U.S.A.*	123	M5	Harray, Loch of	56	E1	Hawke	121	Q7	Hell-Ville	109	J7
Hamnavoe	56	A1	Harricanaw	125	M2	Hawke Bay	115	F3	Helmand	95	R6
Hampden	115	C6	Harrietsham	53	H3	Hawke, Cape	113	L5	Helmond	64	F3
Hampshire	53	F3	Harrington	55	F2	Hawkesbury	125	N4	Helmsdale *U.K.*	56	E2
Hampshire Downs	53	F3	Harris	56	B3	Hawkhurst	53	H3	Helmsdale *U.K.*	56	E2
Hampton *Arkansas, U.S.A.*	128	F4	Harrisburg *Illinois, U.S.A.*	124	F8	Hawkinge	53	J3	Helong	88	B4
Hampton *S. Carolina, U.S.A.*	129	M4	Harrisburg *Pennsylvania, U.S.A.*	125	M6	Hawknest Point	133	K2	Hel, Polwysep	71	H1
Hampton *Virginia, U.S.A.*	125	M8	Harrismith	108	E5	Hawnby	55	H2	Helsingborg	63	E8

Name	Page	Grid
Helsingfors	63	L6
Helsingor	63	E8
Helsinki	63	K6
Helston	52	B4
Helvecia	137	K7
Helvellyn	55	F2
Hemel Hempstead	53	G3
Hempstead	128	D5
Hemsworth	55	H3
Henan	93	M2
Henares	66	E2
Henashi-zaki	88	G5
Henbury	113	G3
Hendek	76	D2
Henderson *Kentucky, U.S.A.*	124	G8
Henderson *N. Carolina, U.S.A.*	129	N2
Henderson *Nevada, U.S.A.*	126	E3
Henderson *Texas, U.S.A.*	128	E4
Hendersonville	129	L3
Hendorabi	95	L8
Hendota	124	F6
Hendrik Verwoerd Dam	108	E6
Hengdaohezi	88	B3
Hengduan Shan	93	J3
Hengelo	64	G2
Hengshan *Hunan, China*	93	M3
Hengshan *Shanxi, China*	87	K4
Hengshui	87	M4
Heng Xian	93	L4
Hengyang	93	M3
Henley-on-Thames	53	G3
Hennebont	65	B5
Henqam	95	M8
Henrietta Maria, Cape	121	K6
Henryetta	128	E3
Henry Ice Rise	141	W2
Henry Mountains	126	G1
Henry Point	112	D5
Henslow, Cape	114	K6
Hentiyn Nuruu	87	K2
Henty	113	K6
Henzada	93	J5
Heppner	122	E5
Hepu	93	L4
Hequ	87	L4
Heradsfloi	62	X12
Herat	95	R4
Herault	65	E7
Herbertville	115	F4
Herby	71	H3
Heredia	132	E9
Hereford *U.K.*	52	E2
Hereford *U.S.A.*	127	L3
Hereford and Worcester	52	E2
Hereke	76	C2
Heretaniwha Point	115	B5
Herford	70	C2
Herington	123	R8
Herisau	68	B2
Herlen Gol	87	L2
Herm	53	M7
Hermanas	127	M7
Herma Ness	56	B1
Hermanus	108	C6
Hermel	94	C4
Hermiston	122	E5
Hermitage	53	F3
Hermitage Bay	121	Q8
Hermit Islands	114	D2
Hermon, Mount	77	G6
Hermosillo	126	G6
Hernad	73	F1
Herne	70	B3
Herne Bay	53	J3
Herning	63	C8
Herrera del Duque	66	D3
Herriard	53	F3
Herrick	113	K7
Herroro, Punta	131	R8
Hersbruck	70	D4
Herschel Island	118	H2
Hertford	53	G3
Hertfordshire	53	G3
Hervey Bay	113	L3
Herzberg	70	D3
Hesdin	64	E3
Hessfjord	62	M2
Hesteyri	63	T11
Hestra	63	E8
Heswall	55	F3
Hethersett	53	J2
Hetton-le-Hole	55	H2
Heuru	114	K7
Heversham	55	G2
Hexham	55	G2
He Xian *Anhui, China*	87	M5
He Xian *Guangxi, China*	93	M4
Heydalir	62	X12
Heysham	55	G2
Heyuan	87	L7
Heywood	55	G3
Heze	93	N1
Hialeah	129	M8
Hibak, Al	97	L6
Hibaldstow	55	J3
Hibbing	124	D3
Hibernia Reef	110	F4
Hickory	129	M3
Hicks Cays	132	C6
Hico	128	C4
Hidaka-sammyaku	88	J4
Hidalgo del Parral	127	K7
Hiddensee	70	E1
Hidrolandia	138	G3
Hieflau	68	E2
Hienghene	114	W16
Hierro	100	B3
Higashi-suido	89	B8
Higham Ferrers	53	G2
Highampton	52	C4
Highbury	113	J2
Highclere	53	F3
High Force	55	G2
High Hesket	55	G2
Highland	56	C3
Highland Park	124	G5
High Level	119	M4
High Point	129	N3
High River	122	H2
High Street	55	G2
High Wycombe	53	G3
Higuera de Zaragozao	127	H8
Higuey	133	N5
Hiiumaa	63	K7
Hijar	67	F2
Hijaz	96	E6
Hikman, Barr al	97	P6
Hikone	89	F8
Hikurangi	115	E1
Hildesheim	70	C2
Hill City	123	Q8
Hillingdon	53	G3
Hillington	53	H2
Hill Island Lake	119	N3
Hillsboro *N. Dakota, U.S.A.*	123	R4
Hillsboro *Ohio, U.S.A.*	124	J7
Hillsboro *Texas, U.S.A.*	128	D5
Hillsborough	58	K4
Hilo	126	T11
Hilpsford Point	55	F2
Hilton Head Island	129	M4
Hilvan	77	H4
Hilversum	64	F2
Hima	96	G7
Himachal Pradesh	92	E2
Himalaya	92	E3
Himare	74	E2
Himatnagar	92	D4
Himeji	89	E8
Himmerland	63	C8
Himmetdede	76	F3
Hims	94	C4
Hinche	133	L5
Hinchinbrook Island	118	F3
Hinckley	53	F2
Hinderwell	55	J2
Hindhead	53	G3
Hindley	55	G3
Hindmarsh, Lake	113	J6
Hindon	53	E3
Hindubagh	92	C2
Hindu Kush	92	D1
Hindupur	92	E6
Hinganghat	92	E4
Hingoli	92	E5
Hinis	77	J3
Hinnoya	62	F2
Hinojosa del Duque	66	D3
Hintlesham	53	J2
Hinton	119	M5
Hinzir Burun	77	F4
Hirado-shima	89	B9
Hirakud Reservoir	92	F4
Hirara	89	G11
Hiratsuka	89	G8
Hirfanli Baraji	76	E3
Hirlau	73	J2
Hiroo	88	J4
Hirosaki	88	H5
Hiroshima	89	D8
Hirschberg	70	F3
Hirsova	73	J3
Hirtshals	63	C8
Hirwaun	52	D3
Hisar	92	E3
Hisma	96	C2
Hissjon	62	J5
Hit	94	F5
Hitachi	89	H7
Hitchin	53	G3
Hitoyoshi	89	C9
Hitra	62	C5
Hiu	114	T10
Hiuchi-nada	89	D8
Hiz	53	G2
Hizan	77	K3
Hjalmaren	63	G7
Hjalmer Lake	119	P3
Hjelmeland	63	B7
Hjorring	63	C8
Ho	104	F4
Hoa Binh	93	L4
Hobara	89	H7
Hobart	113	K7
Hobbs	127	L4
Hoboksar	86	F2
Hobro	63	C8
Hobyo	103	J6
Hocalar	76	C3
Hochalm Spitze	68	D2
Ho Chi Minh	93	L6
Hochstadt	70	D4
Hockley	53	H3
Hockley Heath	53	F2
Hodal	92	E3
Hodder	55	G3
Hoddesdon	53	G3
Hodge Beck	55	H2
Hodmezovasarhely	72	F2
Hodna, Monts du	67	J5
Hodnet	52	E2
Hodonin	71	G4
Hoea	126	T10
Hoeryong	88	B4
Hof	70	D3
Hofdakaupstadur	62	U12
Hofmeyr	108	E6
Hofn *Iceland*	62	T11
Hofn *Iceland*	62	X12
Hofors	63	G6
Hofsjokull	62	V12
Hofu	89	C8
Hoganas	63	E8
Hoggar	101	G4
Hogsby	63	G8
Hogsty Reef	133	L4
Hohe Rhon	70	C3
Hohe Tauern	68	D2
Hohhot	87	L3
Hoh Xil Shan	92	G1
Hoi An	93	L5
Hoima	107	F2
Hokensas	63	F7
Hokianga Harbour	115	D1
Hokitika	115	C5
Hokkaido	88	H3
Hokksund	63	C7
Hokota	89	H7
Hokou	93	K4
Hokuno	89	F8
Holarfjall	62	V12
Holbeach	53	H2
Holborn Head	56	E2
Holbrook	127	G3
Holdenville	128	D3
Holderness	55	J3
Holdrege	123	Q7
Holguin	132	J4
Holic	71	G4
Holitna	118	D3
Holjes	63	E6
Hollabrunn	68	F1
Holland	124	G5
Hollandstoun	56	F1
Hollis	128	C3
Hollywood	129	M7
Holm	62	E4
Holman Island	119	M1
Holmavik	62	U12
Holme-on-Spalding-Moor	55	J3
Holmes Chapel	55	G3
Holmes Reef	113	K2
Holmfirth	55	H3
Holms O	120	Q3
Holmsund	62	J5
Holoin Gun	86	J3
Holstebro	63	C8
Holsteinsborg	120	R4
Holsworthy	52	C4
Holt	53	J2
Holton *Canada*	121	Q7
Holton *U.S.A.*	124	C7
Holy Cross	118	D3
Holyhead	54	E3
Holyhead Bay	55	E3
Holy Island *Gwynedd, U.K.*	54	E3
Holy Island *Northumberland, U.K.*	55	H1
Holy Island *Strathclyde, U.K.*	57	C5
Holyoke *Colorado, U.S.A.*	123	N7
Holyoke *Massachusetts, U.S.A.*	125	P5
Holywell	55	F3
Holywood *Dumfries and Galloway, U.K.*	57	E5
Holywood *Down, U.K.*	58	L3
Homalin	93	H4
Hombre Muerto, Salar de	138	C5
Home Bay	120	N4
Home Hill	113	K2
Home Point	115	E1
Homer	128	F4
Homer Tunnel	115	A6
Hommelvik	62	D5
Hommersak	63	D6
Homoine	109	G4
Homs	77	G5
Honavar	92	D6
Honaz Dagi	76	C4
Hon Chong	93	K6
Hondo *Mexico*	131	Q8
Hondo *U.S.A.*	128	C6
Honduras	132	C7
Honduras, Golfo de	132	C6
Honefoss	63	D6
Honesdale	125	N6
Honey Lake	122	D7
Hong Kong	87	L7
Hongliuyuan	86	H3
Hongo	86	G2
Hongor *Mongolia*	87	L2
Hongor *Mongolia*	87	L2
Hongshui He	93	L4
Hong, Song	93	K4
Hongsong	87	P4
Hongued Strait	121	P8
Hongxing Sichang	86	F3
Hongze	87	M5
Hongze Hu	87	M5
Honiara	114	J6
Honingham	53	J2
Honiton	52	D4
Honjo	88	G6
Hon Khoai	93	K7
Honningsvag	62	L1
Honohina	126	T11
Honokaa	126	T10
Honolulu	126	S10
Honshu	89	E7
Hood	119	N2
Hood Canal	122	C4
Hood Island	136	A7
Hood, Mount	122	D5
Hood Point	114	D4
Hood River	122	D5
Hoogeveen	64	G2
Hooghly	93	G4
Hook	53	G3
Hooker	127	M2
Hook Head	59	J8
Hook Norton	53	F3
Hooper, Cape	120	N4
Hoor	63	E9
Hoorn	64	F2
Hoover Dam	126	E2
Hopa	77	J2
Hope *Canada*	122	D3
Hope *U.K.*	55	H3
Hope *U.S.A.*	128	F4
Hopedale	121	P6
Hopelchen	131	Q8
Hope, Loch	56	D2
Hopen	80	D2
Hope Pass	115	C5
Hope, Point	118	B2
Hopes Advance, Cape	121	N5
Hopetown	108	D5
Hopewell	125	M8
Hopkins Lake	112	F3
Hopkinsville	124	G8
Hoquiam	122	C4
Horasan	77	K2
Horby	63	E9
Hordaland	63	B6
Horezu	73	G3
Horley	53	G3
Horlick Mountains	141	R1
Hormoz	95	N8
Hormuz, Strait of	97	N3
Horn *Austria*	68	E1
Horn *Iceland*	62	T11
Hornavan	62	G3
Horn, Cape	139	C10
Horncastle	55	J3
Horndal	63	G6
Horndean	53	F4
Hornefors	62	H5
Hornepayne	124	H2
Horn Head	58	G2
Horn, Iles de	111	T4
Horningsham	52	E3
Horn Mountains	119	L3
Hornos, Cabo de	139	C11
Hornsea	55	J3
Horovice	70	E4
Horqin Youyi Qianqi	87	N2
Horqin Zuoyi Houqi	87	N3
Horqueta	138	E4
Horsehoe Bend	122	F6
Horsens	63	C9
Horsey	53	J2
Horsforth	55	H3
Horsham *Australia*	113	J6
Horsham *U.K.*	53	G4
Horsham Saint Faith	53	J2
Horsley	53	G3
Horsovsky Tyn	70	E4
Horten	63	D7
Horton	118	L2
Horwich	55	G3
Hosaina	103	G6
Hosap	77	K3
Hose Mountains	90	E5
Hoseynabad	94	H4
Hoshangabad	92	E4
Hoshiarpur	92	E2
Hospet	92	E5
Hospitalet	67	H2
Hossegor	65	C7
Hoste, Isla	139	C11
Hotamis	76	E4
Hotan	92	F1
Hotazel	108	D5
Hoti	91	J6
Hoting	62	G4
Hot Springs *Arkansas, U.S.A.*	128	F3
Hot Springs *S. Dakota, U.S.A.*	123	N6
Hottah Lake	119	M2
Hotte, Massif de la	133	K5
Houailou	114	W16
Houdan	64	D4
Houghton	124	F3
Houghton-le-Spring	55	H2
Houlton	125	S3
Houma *China*	93	M1
Houma *U.S.A.*	128	G6
Houmt Souk	101	H2
Hounde	104	E3
Hounslow	53	G3
Houston *Mississippi, U.S.A.*	128	H4
Houston *Texas, U.S.A.*	128	E6
Houtman Rocks	112	C4
Hova	63	F7
Hovd	86	G2
Hovd Gol	86	G2
Hove	53	G4
Hoveyzeh	94	J6

Name	Page	Ref
Hovingham	55	J2
Hovlya	79	G6
Hovsgol	87	K3
Hovsgol Nuur	86	J1
Howa	102	E4
Howakil	96	E9
Howard City	124	H5
Howard Lake	119	P3
Howden Moor	55	H3
Howden Reservoir	55	H3
Howe, Cape	113	K6
Howe of the Mearns	57	F4
Howitt, Mount	113	K6
Howland Island	111	T1
Howrah	93	G4
Hoxtolgay	86	F2
Hoxud	86	F3
Hoy	56	E2
Hoyanger	63	B6
Hoyerswerda	70	F3
Hoylake	55	F3
Hoyos	66	C2
Hoy Sound	56	E2
Hradeckralove	70	F3
Hron	71	H4
Hrubieszow	71	K3
Hsin-cheng	87	N7
Hsin-chu	87	N7
Hsipaw	93	J4
Huab	108	B4
Huacho	136	B6
Huachuan	88	C2
Huacrachuco	136	B5
Huade	87	L3
Huadian	87	P3
Huaibei	93	N2
Huaide	87	N3
Huai He	93	M2
Huaihua	93	M3
Huaiji	93	M4
Huainan	87	M5
Huairou	87	M3
Huaiyin	87	M5
Huajuapan de Leon	131	L9
Huallaga	136	B5
Huallanca	136	B5
Huama	88	C2
Huamachuco	136	B5
Huambo	106	C5
Huampusirpi	132	E7
Huanan	88	C2
Huancane	138	C3
Huancavelica	136	B6
Huancayo	136	B6
Huangehuan	93	N2
Huang Hai	87	N4
Huang He	87	L4
Huanghua	87	M4
Huangling	93	L1
Huangpi	93	M2
Huangshi	93	M2
Huang Xian	87	N4
Huangyan	87	N6
Huangyuan	93	K1
Huanren	87	P3
Huanta	136	C6
Huanuco	136	B5
Huan Xian	93	L1
Huanzo, Cordillera	136	C6
Huara	138	C3
Huaral	136	B6
Huaraz	136	B5
Huarmey	136	B6
Huascaran, Nevado	136	B5
Huatabampo	127	H7
Huayin	93	M2
Huayuan	93	L3
Hubei	93	M2
Hubli	92	E5
Hucknall	55	H3
Huddersfield	55	H3
Hudiksvall	63	G6
Hudson Florida, U.S.A.	129	L6
Hudson New York, U.S.A.	125	P5
Hudson New York, U.S.A.	125	P5
Hudson Bay	116	L3
Hudson, Cape	141	L5
Hudson Land	120	X3
Hudson Strait	120	M5
Hue	93	L5
Huebra	66	C2
Huedin	73	G2
Huehuento, Cerro	130	G5
Huehuetenango	132	B7
Huelgoat	64	B4
Huelva Spain	66	C4
Huelva Spain	66	C4
Huercal Overa	67	F4
Huesca	67	F1
Huescar	66	E4
Huetamo	131	J8
Huete	66	E2
Hufrah, Al	96	D2
Hughenden	113	J3
Hugh Town	52	K5
Hugo	128	E4
Hugo Reservoir	128	E3
Hugoton	127	M2
Huhehot	87	L3
Huiarau Range	115	F3
Huichapan	131	K7
Huicholes, Sierra de los	130	G6
Huichon	87	P3
Huila, Nevado del	136	B3
Huimin	87	M4
Huisne	65	D4
Huitong	93	L3
Huittinen	63	K6
Huixtla	131	N10
Huize	93	K3
Huizhou	87	L7
Huj, Al	96	D2
Huka Falls	115	E3
Hukou	87	M6
Hula	114	D4
Hulan He	88	A2
Hulayfah	96	E4
Huld	87	K3
Hulin	88	D3
Hull Canada	125	N4
Hull U.K.	55	J3
Hultsfred	63	F8
Hulun	87	M2
Hulun Nur	87	M2
Huma	87	P1
Humahuaca	138	B4
Humaita	136	E5
Humarklo	62	X12
Humaya	130	F5
Humber	55	J3
Humber, Mouth of the	55	K3
Humberside	55	J3
Humboldt Canada	123	H4
Humboldt Nevada, U.S.A.	122	E7
Humboldt Tennessee, U.S.A.	128	H3
Humboldt, Mount	114	X16
Humbolt Gletscher	120	P2
Humedan	95	P9
Humphreys Peak	126	G3
Humpolec	70	F4
Hunafloi	62	U12
Hunan	93	M3
Hunchun	88	C4
Hunfeld	70	C3
Hungary	72	D2
Hungerford	53	F3
Hunghae	89	B7
Hungnam	87	P4
Hungry Hill	59	C9
Hunjiang	87	P3
Huns Mountains	108	C5
Hunsruck	70	B4
Hunstanton	53	H2
Hunsur	92	E6
Hunte	70	C2
Hunter	113	L5
Hunter, Cape	120	M3
Hunter Islands	113	J7
Huntingdon U.K.	53	G2
Huntingdon U.S.A.	125	M6
Huntington Indiana, U.S.A.	124	H6
Huntington W. Virginia, U.S.A.	124	J7
Huntington Beach	126	C4
Huntley	52	E3
Huntly New Zealand	115	E2
Huntly U.K.	56	F3
Huntsville Canada	125	L4
Huntsville Alabama, U.S.A.	129	J3
Huntsville Texas, U.S.A.	128	E5
Huolongmen	87	P2
Huon Gulf	114	D3
Huon Peninsula	114	D3
Hurd, Cape	125	K4
Hurdiyo	103	K5
Hure Qi	87	N3
Hurghada	103	F2
Hurimta	87	K2
Hurliness	56	E2
Hurn	53	F4
Huron	123	Q5
Huron, Lake	124	J4
Hurricane	126	F2
Hurrungane	63	B6
Hurunui	115	D5
Husavik Denmark	62	Z14
Husavik Iceland	62	W11
Husbands Bosworth	53	F2
Husbondliden	62	H4
Hushan	88	C3
Hushinish	56	A3
Husi	73	K2
Huskvarna	63	F8
Husn Al Abr	96	H8
Husum Sweden	62	H5
Husum W. Germany	70	C1
Hutag	86	J2
Hutaym, Harrat	96	E3
Hutchinson Kansas, U.S.A.	128	D1
Hutchinson Minnesota, U.S.A.	124	C4
Hutou	88	D2
Huttenberg	68	E2
Huttoft	55	K3
Hutton, Mount	113	K4
Hutubi	86	F3
Huwar	97	K4
Huxley, Mount	115	B6
Huyuk	76	D4
Huzhou	87	N5
Hvallatur	62	S12
Hvammstangi	62	U12
Hvar	72	D4
Hveragerdi	62	U13
Hvita	62	U12
Hwange	108	E3
Hwlffordd	52	C2
Hyannis Massachusetts, U.S.A.	125	Q6
Hyannis Nebraska, U.S.A.	123	P7
Hyargas Nuur	86	G2
Hyde New Zealand	115	C6
Hyde U.K.	55	G3
Hyderabad India	92	E5
Hyderabad Pakistan	92	C3
Hyeres	65	G7
Hyeres, Iles d'	65	G7
Hyesan	88	B5
Hyltebruk	63	E8
Hyndman Peak	122	G6
Hynish Bay	57	B4
Hyrynsalmi	62	N4
Hythe Hampshire, U.K.	53	F4
Hythe Kent, U.K.	53	J3
Hyuga	89	C9
Hyvinkaa	63	L6

I

Name	Page	Ref
Iaco	136	D5
Iacobeni	73	H2
Ialomita	73	J3
Iapala	109	G2
Iar Connaught	59	D6
Iasi	73	J2
Ib	78	J3
Iba	91	F2
Ibadan	105	F4
Ibague	136	B3
Ibarra	136	B3
Ibb	96	G10
Ibi	105	G4
Ibiapaba, Serra da	137	J4
Ibiza Spain	67	G3
Ibiza Spain	67	G3
Ibn Suaydan, Ramlat	97	M6
Ibo	109	H2
Ibonma	91	J6
Ibotirama	138	J6
Ibra	97	P5
Ibra, Wadi	102	D5
Ibri	97	N5
Ibriktepe	76	B2
Ibsley	53	F4
Ibusuki	89	C10
Ica	136	B6
Ica	136	D4
Icabaru	136	E3
Icana Brazil	136	D3
Icana Brazil	136	D3
Icel	76	F4
Iceland	62	V12
Ichalkaranji	92	D5
Ichchapuram	92	F5
Ichera	84	H5
Ichilo	138	D3
Ichinomiya	89	F8
Ichinoseki	88	H6
Ichnya	79	E5
Ichoa	138	C3
Icy Bay	118	G4
Icy Cape	118	C1
Icy Strait	118	H4
Idabel	128	E4
Idah	105	G4
Idaho	122	G5
Idaho Falls	122	H6
Idanha-a-Nova	66	C3
Idar-Oberstein	70	B4
Ider	86	H2
Idfu	103	F3
Idhi Oros	75	H5
Idhra	75	G4
Idil	77	J4
Idiofa	106	C3
Idiouia	67	G5
Idlib	94	C4
Idre	63	E6
Idrigill Point	56	B3
Ieper	64	E3
Ierapetra	75	H5
Ierissos	75	G2
Iesi	68	D4
Ifanadiana	109	J4
Ife	105	F4
Iforas, Adrar des	100	F5
Igara Parana	136	C4
Igarape Miri	137	H4
Igarka	84	D3
Igdir	76	E2
Igdir	77	L3
Igdir Dagi	77	H2
Iggesund	63	G6
Iglesia	139	C6
Iglesias	69	B6
Igloolik	120	K4
Igluligarjuk	119	S3
Ignace	124	C2
Igneada	76	B2
Igneada Burun	76	C2
Igoumenitsa	75	F3
Igra	78	J4
Iguala	131	K8
Igualada	67	G2
Iguape	138	G4
Iguatu	137	K5
Iguazu, Cataratas del	138	F5
Iguazu Falls	138	F5
Iguidi, Erg	100	D3
Iheya-retto	89	H10
Ih-Hayrhaan	87	K2
Ihlara	76	F3
Ihosy	109	J4
Ihsaniye	76	D3
Iida	89	F8
Iide-san	89	G7
Iisalmi	62	M5
Ijebu Ode	105	F4
IJmuiden	64	F2
IJssel	64	F2
IJsselmeer	64	F2
Ijzer	64	E3
Ik	78	J4
Ika	84	H5
Ikaalinen	63	K6
Ikaria	75	J4
Ikast	63	C8
Iked	89	D8
Ikeda	88	J4
Ikela	106	D3
Iki-shima	89	B9
Ikizce	76	E3
Ikizdere	77	J2
Ikom	105	G4
Ikomba	107	F4
Ikongo	109	J4
Ikpikpuk	118	E1
Ikuno	89	E8
Ila	105	F4
Ilagan	91	G2
Ilam	94	H5
Ilanskiy	84	F5
Ilaro	105	F4
Ilawa	71	H2
Ilbenge	85	L4
Ileanda	73	G2
Ilebo	106	D3
Ilek	79	J5
Ilesha	105	F4
Ilfracombe	52	C3
Ilgaz	76	E2
Ilgaz Daglari	76	F2
Ilgin	76	D3
Ilheus	137	K6
Ili	86	D3
Ilia	73	G3
Iliamna Lake	118	D4
Ilic	77	H3
Iligan	91	G4
Ilikurangi	115	G2
Ilinskiy	88	J1
Ilintsy	73	K1
Iliodhromia	75	G3
Iliomar	91	H7
Ilja	71	M1
Ilkeston	53	F2
Ilkley	55	H3
Ilkley Moor	55	H3
Illampu, Nevado de	138	C3
Illapel	138	B6
Illbille, Mount	112	G4
Iller	70	D4
Illescas	66	E2
Illimani, Nevado	138	C3
Illinois U.S.A.	124	E6
Illinois U.S.A.	124	E6
Illizi	101	G3
Illo	105	F3
Illote, Punta	136	A4
Ilm	70	D3
Ilmen , Ozero	78	E4
Ilminster	52	E4
Iloilo	91	G3
Ilorin	105	F4
Ilpyrskiy	85	U5
Ilsin-dong	88	B5
Ilwaki	91	H7
Ilych	78	K3
Ilza	71	J3
Ilzanka	71	J3
Ima	85	K5
Imabari	89	D8
Imamoglu	77	F4
Iman	88	E3
Imandra, Ozero	62	Q3
Imari	89	B9
Imataca, Serrania de	136	E2
Imatra	63	N6
Imese	106	C2
Imishli	94	J2
Immenstadt	70	D5
Immingham	55	J3
Imola	68	C3
Imotski	72	D4
Imperatriz	137	H5
Imperia	68	A4
Imperial	123	P7
Imperieuse Reef	112	D2
Impfondo	106	C2
Imphal	93	H4
Imrali	76	C2
Imst	68	C2
Imundsen Gulf	118	L1
Imuris	126	G5
Ina	89	F8
Inagh	59	D7
Inakona	114	K6
In Amenas	101	G3
Inangahua Junction	115	C4
Inanwatan	91	J6
Inapari	136	D6
Inari	62	M2
Inarijarvi	62	M2
Inawashiro-ko	89	H7
Inca	67	H3
Incebel Daglari	77	G3
Ince Burun	76	F1

Incekum Burun	76	E4
Incesu	76	F3
Inchard, Loch	56	C2
Inchon	87	P4
Inchope	109	F3
Indalsalven	62	G5
Inda Silase	96	D9
Indefatigable Island	136	A7
Independence *California, U.S.A.*	126	C2
Independence *Kansas, U.S.A.*	128	E2
Independence *Missouri, U.S.A.*	124	C7
Independence Mountains	122	F7
Inderborskiy	79	J6
India	92	E4
Indiana *Pennsylvania, U.S.A.*	125	L6
Indiana *U.S.A.*	124	G6
Indianapolis	124	G7
Indian Ocean	142	D5
Indianola	128	G4
Indian Springs	126	E2
Indiga	78	H2
Indigirka	85	R2
Indispensable Reefs	111	P4
Indispensable Strait	114	K6
Indonesia	90	D6
Indore	92	E4
Indragiri	90	C6
Indramayu	90	D7
Indrapura	90	D6
Indravati	92	F5
Indre	65	D5
Indre Arna	63	A6
Indura	71	K2
Indus	92	C4
Indus, Mouths of the	92	C4
Inebolu	76	E2
Inece	76	B2
Inecik	76	B2
Inegol	76	C2
In Ekker	101	G4
Ineu	73	F2
Infiernillo, Presa del	130	J8
Ingatestone	53	H3
Ingersoll	125	K5
Inggen	87	J3
Ingham *Australia*	113	K2
Ingham *U.K.*	53	H2
Ingida	84	Aa3
Ingleborough	55	G2
Inglefield Land	120	M2
Ingleton	55	G2
Inglewood	115	E3
Ingoda	85	J6
Ingoldmells	55	K3
Ingolfshofdi	62	W13
Ingolstadt	70	D4
Ingraj Bazar	93	G3
Ingul	79	E6
Ingulets	79	E6
Inguri	77	J1
Inhambane	109	G4
Inhambupe	137	K6
Inharrime	109	G4
Inhassoro	109	G4
Inhumas	138	G3
Inini	137	G3
Inirida	136	D3
Inishark	58	B5
Inishbofin *Donegal, Ireland*	58	F2
Inishbofin *Galway, Ireland*	58	B5
Inishcrone	58	D4
Inisheer	59	C6
Inishkea North	58	B4
Inishkea South	58	B4
Inishmaan	59	C6
Inishmore	59	C6
Inishmurry	58	E4
Inishnabro	59	A8
Inishowen Head	58	J2
Inishowen Peninsula	58	H2
Inishtooskert	59	A8
Inishtrahull	58	H2
Inishturk	58	B5
Inishvickillane	59	A8
Inkberrow	53	F2
Inkisi	106	C4
Inle, Lake	93	J4
Inndyr	62	F3
Inner Hebrides	57	B4
Innerleithen	57	E5
Inner Mongolian Autonomous Region	87	L3
Inner Sound	56	C3
Innisfail	113	K2
Innokentevskiy	88	H1
Innoko	118	D3
Innsbruck	68	C2
Inongo	106	C3
Inowroclaw	71	H2
In Salah	101	F3
Insein	93	J5
Inskip	55	G3
Insko	70	F2
Insterburg	63	J9
Instow	52	C3
Insty	78	G2
Inta	78	L2
Intepe	76	B2
Interlaken	68	A2
International Falls	124	D2
Interview	93	H6
Intletovy	84	B4
Intra Coastal Waterway	128	D6

Inubo-saki	89	H8
Inugsulik Bay	120	Q3
Inukjuak	121	L6
Inuvik *Canada*	118	J2
Inuvik *Canada*	118	K2
Inver	57	E4
Inveraray	57	C4
Inverbervie	57	F4
Invercargill	115	B7
Inverell	113	L4
Invergarry	57	D3
Invergordon	56	D3
Inverkeithing	57	E4
Inverkeithny	56	F3
Invermoriston	56	D3
Inverness *Canada*	121	P8
Inverness *U.K.*	56	D3
Inverurie	56	F3
Investigator Channel	93	J6
Investigator Strait	113	H6
Inya *Russia*	84	D6
Inya *Russia*	85	R4
Inza	78	H5
Inzer	78	K5
Inzia	106	C3
Ioannina	75	F3
Ioinianisia	75	J5
Iokanga	78	F2
Iola	128	E2
Iolotan	95	R3
Iona	57	B4
Ion Corvin	73	J3
Ionesti	73	H3
Ionian Islands	74	E3
Ionian Sea	74	D3
Ionioi Nisoi	74	E3
Ios	75	H4
Iova	62	P2
Iowa *U.S.A.*	124	D5
Iowa *U.S.A.*	124	D5
Iowa City	124	E6
Iowa Falls	124	D5
Ipameri	138	G3
Ipatinga	138	H3
Ipel	71	H4
Ipiales	136	B3
Ipira	137	K6
Ipoh	90	C5
Ipora	138	F3
Ippy	102	D6
Ipsala	76	B2
Ipswich *Australia*	113	L4
Ipswich *U.K.*	53	J2
Ipu	137	J4
Ipupiara	137	J6
Iqualuit	120	N5
Iquique	138	B4
Iquitos	136	C4
Irabu-jima	89	G11
Iracoubo	137	G2
Iraklia	75	H4
Iraklion	75	H5
Iran	95	K5
Iran, Pegunungan	90	F5
Iranshahr	95	Q8
Irapuato	131	J7
Iraq	94	E5
Irbeyskoye	84	F5
Irbid	94	B5
Irbit	84	Ad5
Irece	137	J6
Ireland, Republic of	59	D6
Ireland's Eye	59	K6
Irfon	52	D2
Irgiz	51	V6
Irharen	100	F4
Irharhar	101	G3
Irhezer Wan Agades	101	G5
Irhil MGoun	100	D2
Iri	87	P4
Irian Jaya	91	K6
Iringa	107	G4
Iriomote	87	N7
Iriomote-jima	89	F11
Iriona	132	E7
Iriri	137	G4
Irish Sea	54	E3
Irkineyevo	84	F5
Irkutsk	84	G6
Irkutskaya Oblast	84	H5
Iron Bottom Sound	114	J6
Iron Bridge	52	E2
Irondequoit	125	M5
Iron Knob	113	H5
Iron Mountain	124	G4
Iron Mountains	58	G4
Iron River	124	F3
Ironwood	124	E3
Iroquois Falls	125	K2
Irosin	91	G3
Iro-zaki	89	G8
Irqah	96	H10
Irrawaddy	93	J5
Irrawaddy, Mouths of the	93	H5
Irthing	57	F5
Irthington	55	G2
Irthlingborough	53	G2
Irtysh	84	A6
Irtyshskoye	84	B6
Irumu	107	G2
Irun	67	F1
Irvine	57	D5
Irvinestown	58	G4
Irving	128	D4

Isa	105	G3
Isaac, River	113	K3
Isabela, Cabo	133	M5
Isabela, Isla	136	A7
Isabela, Cordillera	132	E8
Isabella Lake	126	C3
Isachsen	120	F2
Isachsen Peninsula	120	E2
Isafjardarjup	62	T11
Isafjordur	62	T11
Isahaya	89	C9
Isangi	106	D2
Isar	70	E4
Ischia, Isola d	69	D5
Ise	89	F8
Iseo	68	C3
Iseo, Lago d	68	C3
Isere	65	F6
Isernia	69	E5
Isesaki	89	G7
Iset	84	Ad5
Ise-wan	89	F8
Iseyin	105	F4
Isherton	136	F3
Ishigaki	89	G11
Ishigaki-shima	89	G11
Ishikari	88	H4
Ishikari-wan	88	H4
Ishim *Russia*	84	Ae5
Ishim *Russia*	84	Ae5
Ishimbay	78	K5
Ishinomaki	88	H6
Ishioka	89	H7
Ishpeming	124	G3
Isikli	76	C3
Isikli Baraji	76	C3
Isilkul	84	A6
Isiolo	107	G2
Isiro	107	E2
Iskenderun	77	G4
Iskenderun Korfezi	77	F4
Iskilip	76	F2
Iskininskiy	79	J6
Iskur	73	H4
Iskut	118	J4
Isla	56	F3
Islahiye	77	G4
Islamabad	92	D2
Island Lagoon	113	H5
Island Lake	119	S5
Islands, Bay of *Canada*	121	Q8
Islands, Bay of *New Zealand*	115	D1
Islas Columbretes	67	G3
Islay	57	B5
Islay, Sound of	57	B5
Isle *France*	65	D6
Isle *U.K.*	52	E4
Isle of Whithorn	54	E2
Isleornsay	57	C3
Ismailiya	103	F1
Ismetpasa	76	E2
Isna	103	F2
Isohara	89	H7
Iso Syote	62	M4
Isparta	76	D4
Ispir	77	J2
Israel	94	B6
Issano	136	F2
Issaquah	122	C4
Issimu	91	G5
Issoire	65	E6
Issoudun	65	D5
Issyk-kul , Ozero	86	D3
Istanbul	76	C2
Istiaia	75	G3
Istra	72	B3
Istranca Daglari	75	J2
Istres	65	F7
Itab	97	K9
Itabaiana *Paraiba, Brazil*	137	K5
Itabaiana *Sergipe, Brazil*	137	K6
Itaberaba	138	J6
Itaberai	138	G3
Itabuna	137	K6
Itacaiunas	137	H5
Itacoa	136	C5
Itacoatiara	136	F4
Itaituba	137	F4
Itajai	138	G5
Itajuba	138	G4
Italy	68	C3
Itambe, Pico de	138	H3
Itampolo	109	H4
Itanagar	93	H3
Itany	137	G3
Itaobim	138	H3
Itapecuru Mirim	137	J4
Itaperuna	138	H4
Itapetinga	138	H3
Itapetininga	138	G4
Itapeva	138	G4
Itapicuru	137	K6
Itapipoca	137	K4
Itaqui	138	E5
Itbayat	91	G1
Itchen	53	F3
Itea	75	G3
Itenex	136	E6
Ithaca *Greece*	75	F3
Ithaca *U.S.A.*	125	M5
Ithaki	75	F3
Ithon	52	D2
Ito	89	G8
Itoigawa	89	F7

Itumbiara	138	G3
Iturama	138	G3
Iturup, Ostrov	85	R8
Ituverava	138	G4
Ituxi	136	D5
Itzehoe	70	C2
Iultin	85	Y3
Ivakoany, Massif de l	109	J4
Ivalo	62	M2
Ivangrad	72	E4
Ivanhoe	121	K8
Ivanic Grad	72	D3
Ivano-Frankovsk	71	L4
Ivanovka	79	J5
Ivanovo *Belorussia*	71	L2
Ivanovo *Russia*	78	G4
Ivdel	84	Ad4
Ivenets	71	M2
Iveragh Peninsula	59	B9
Ivigtut	120	S5
Ivinhema	138	F4
Iviza	67	G3
Ivory Coast	104	D4
Ivrea	68	A3
Ivujivik	120	L5
Ivybridge	52	D4
Iwafune	89	G6
Iwahai	88	H4
Iwaki *Japan*	89	H7
Iwaki *Japan*	88	H5
Iwaki-san	88	H5
Iwakuni	89	D8
Iwamizawa	88	H4
Iwate	88	H6
Iwo	105	F4
Ixopo	108	F6
Ixtlan	130	G7
Iya	84	G6
Iyal Bakhit	102	E5
Iyo-nada	89	D9
Izabal, Laguna de	132	C7
Izbica	71	K3
Izhevsk	78	J4
Izhma *Russia*	78	J3
Izhma *Russia*	78	J3
Izki	97	N5
Izmail	79	D6
Izmir	76	B3
Izmir Korfezi	75	J3
Izmit	76	C2
Iznik	76	C2
Iznik Golu	76	C2
Izra	94	C5
Iztochni Rodopi	73	H5
Izucar de Matamoros	131	K8
Izumo	89	D8
Izvestiy Ts.I.K., Ostrova	84	C1
Izvestkovyy	88	C1
Izvoru Muntelui, Lacul	73	J2
Izyum	79	F6

J

Jabal az Zannah	97	L4
Jabalon	66	E3
Jabalpur	92	E4
Jabbarah Fara	96	E7
Jabbul, Sabkhat al	94	C4
Jablah	94	B4
Jablanica	75	F2
Jablonec	70	F3
Jablonica	71	G4
Jaboatao	137	J5
Jaboticabal	138	G4
Jaburu	136	E5
Jaca	67	F1
Jacarei	138	G4
Jacaretinga	136	F5
Jachymov	70	E3
Jacksboro	128	C4
Jackson *Alabama, U.S.A.*	129	J5
Jackson *Michigan, U.S.A.*	124	H5
Jackson *Minnesota, U.S.A.*	124	C5
Jackson *Mississippi, U.S.A.*	128	G4
Jackson *Ohio, U.S.A.*	124	J7
Jackson *Tennessee, U.S.A.*	128	H3
Jackson *Wyoming, U.S.A.*	123	J6
Jackson Bay	115	B5
Jackson Head	115	B5
Jackson Lake	123	J6
Jackson Prairie	128	H4
Jacksonville *Arkansas, U.S.A.*	128	H3
Jacksonville *Florida, U.S.A.*	129	M5
Jacksonville *Illinois, U.S.A.*	124	E7
Jacksonville *N. Carolina, U.S.A.*	129	P3
Jacksonville *Texas, U.S.A.*	128	E5
Jacmel	133	L5
Jacobabad	92	C3
Jacobina	137	J6
Jacques-Cartier Passage	121	P8
Jacui	138	F5
Jacunda	137	G4
Jaddi, Ras	92	B3
Jade Busen	70	C2
Jadow	71	J2
Jaen	136	B5
Jaen	66	E4
Jaffna	92	E7
Jafurah, Al	97	K4
Jagdalpur	92	F5
Jagdaqi	87	N1
Jagersfontein	108	E5

Name	Page	Grid
Jagin	95	P9
Jagin, Ra's	95	P9
Jagst	70	C4
Jagtial	92	E5
Jaguarao	138	F6
Jaguariaiva	138	G4
Jaguaribe *Brazil*	137	K5
Jaguaribe *Brazil*	137	K5
Jague	138	C5
Jahmah	94	G7
Jahrom	95	L7
Jaicos	137	J5
Jailolo	91	H5
Jailolo, Selat	91	H5
Jaipur	92	E3
Jaisalmer	92	D3
Jajarm	95	N3
Jajce	72	D3
Jajpur	92	G4
Jakarta	90	D7
Jakhau	92	C4
Jakobstad	62	K5
Jakupica	73	F5
Jalaid Qi	87	N2
Jalalabad	92	D2
Jalalpur Pirwala	92	D3
Jalapa *Mexico*	131	L8
Jalapa *Mexico*	131	N9
Jalasjarvi	62	K5
Jalgaon	92	E4
Jalingo	105	H4
Jalna	92	E5
Jalon	67	F2
Jalor	92	D3
Jalostotitlan	130	H7
Jalpa	130	H7
Jalpaiguri	93	G3
Jalpan	131	K7
Jalu	101	K2
Jam	95	Q4
Jamaica	132	J5
Jamaica Channel	133	K5
Jamalpur *Bangladesh*	93	G4
Jamalpur *India*	92	G3
Jamanxim	137	F5
Jamari	136	E5
Jambi	90	C6
James	123	R6
James Bay	121	K7
James Island	136	A7
James Ross, Cape	120	D3
James Ross Island	141	W6
James Ross Strait	120	G4
Jamestown *South Africa*	108	E6
Jamestown *N. Dakota, U.S.A.*	123	Q4
Jamestown *New York, U.S.A.*	125	L5
Jamjo	63	F8
Jamkhandi	92	E5
Jamkhed	92	E5
Jammerbugten	63	C8
Jammu	92	D2
Jammu and Kashmir	92	E2
Jamnagar	92	D4
Jampur	92	D3
Jamsa	63	L6
Jamshedpur	92	G4
Jamtland	62	F5
Jamuna	93	G3
Janda, Laguna de la	66	D4
Jandaq	95	M4
Jandiatuba	136	D4
Janesville	124	F5
Janjira	92	D5
Jan Mayen	48	F2
Jannatabad	95	Q4
Janos	127	H5
Januaria	138	H3
Janubiyah, Al Badiyah al	94	H6
Jaora	92	E4
Japan	89	G7
Japan, Sea of	88	D6
Japan Trench	142	F3
Japaratuba	137	K6
Japura	136	D4
Jarabulus	94	D3
Jaragua	138	G3
Jaraguari	138	F4
Jarama	66	E2
Jarandilla	66	D2
Jarash	94	B5
Jardee	112	D5
Jardines de la Reina	132	H4
Jari	137	G5
Jarir, Wadi al	96	F4
Jarna	63	G7
Jarnac	65	C6
Jaromer	70	F3
Jaroslaw	71	K3
Jarpen	62	E5
Jarrow	55	H2
Jarruhi	94	J6
Jartai	87	K4
Jarvso	63	G6
Jashpurnagar	92	F4
Jask	95	N9
Jasper *Canada*	119	M5
Jasper *Alabama, U.S.A.*	129	J4
Jasper *Florida, U.S.A.*	129	L5
Jasper *Texas, U.S.A.*	128	F5
Jassy	73	J2
Jastrebarsko	72	C3
Jastrowie	71	G2
Jastrzebie-Zdroj	71	H4
Jaszbereny	72	E2
Jatai	138	F3
Jatapu	136	F4
Jath	92	E5
Jativa	67	F3
Jatoba	137	G6
Jau	136	E4
Jau	138	G4
Jauaperi	136	E4
Jauja	136	B6
Jaunpur	92	F3
Java	90	E7
Java Trench	142	E5
Javier, Isla	139	B9
Javor	72	E3
Javorniky	71	H4
Jawa	90	D7
Jawa, Laut	90	E7
Jawb, Al	97	K5
Jawhar	107	J2
Jawor	71	G3
Jayanca	136	B5
Jaya, Puncak	91	K6
Jayapura	91	L6
Jayawijaya, Pegunungan	91	K6
Jayena	66	E4
Jaypur	92	F5
Jayrud	94	C5
Jazirah, Al	94	E4
Jaz Murian, Hamun-e	95	P8
Jebal Barez, Kuh-e	95	P7
Jebba	105	F4
Jebel, Bahr el	102	F6
Jech Doab	92	D2
Jedburgh	57	F5
Jedeida	69	B7
Jefferson	122	H5
Jefferson City *Missouri, U.S.A.*	124	D7
Jefferson City *Tennessee, U.S.A.*	129	L2
Jefferson, Mount *Nevada, U.S.A.*	122	F8
Jefferson, Mount *Oregon, U.S.A.*	122	D5
Jef Jef el Kebir	102	D3
Jehile Puzak	95	Q6
Jekabpils	63	L8
Jeldesa	103	H6
Jelenia Gora	70	F3
Jelgava	63	K8
Jelow Gir	94	H5
Jemaja	90	D5
Jember	90	E7
Jeminay	86	F2
Jemnice	70	F4
Jena	70	D3
Jendouba	69	B7
Jenin	94	B5
Jenkins	124	J8
Jennings	128	F5
Jenny Lind Island	119	Q2
Jens Munk Island	120	L4
Jequie	137	J6
Jequitinhonha *Brazil*	138	H3
Jequitinhonha *Brazil*	138	H3
Jerada	100	E2
Jerba, Ile de	101	H2
Jeremie	133	K5
Jeremoabo	137	K6
Jerevan	77	L2
Jerez	130	H6
Jerez de la Frontera	66	C4
Jericho *Australia*	113	K3
Jericho *Israel*	94	B6
Jerome	122	G6
Jersey	53	M7
Jersey City	125	N6
Jerseyville	124	E7
Jerusalem	94	B6
Jervis Inlet	122	C2
Jeseniky	71	G3
Jessheim	63	D6
Jessore	92	G4
Jesup	129	M5
Jevnaker	63	D6
Jezerce	74	E1
Jeziorak, Jezioro	71	H2
Jeznas	71	L1
Jezzine	94	B5
Jhang Maghiana	92	D2
Jhansi	92	E3
Jhelum *Pakistan*	92	D2
Jhelum *Pakistan*	92	D2
Jialing Jiang	93	L2
Jiamusi	88	C2
Jian	93	N3
Jianchuan	93	J3
Jiande	87	M6
Jiange	93	L2
Jiangjin	93	L3
Jiangjunmiao	86	F3
Jiangmen	93	M4
Jiangsu	87	M5
Jiangxi	93	M3
Jianning	87	M6
Jianou	87	M6
Jianquanzi	86	H3
Jianshi	93	L2
Jiaohe	87	P3
Jiaoling	87	M7
Jiaozuo	93	M1
Jia Xian	87	L4
Jiaxing	87	N5
Jiayin	88	C1
Jiayuguan	86	H4
Jiboia	136	D3
Jibou	73	G2
Jibsh, Ra's	97	P6
Jicatuyo	132	C7
Jiddah	96	D6
Jidong	88	C3
Jiekkevarre	62	H2
Jieknaffo	62	G3
Jiesavrre	62	L2
Jihlava *Czechoslovakia*	70	F4
Jihlava *Czechoslovakia*	71	G4
Jijel	101	G1
Jijia	73	J2
Jijiga	103	H6
Jijihu	86	F3
Jilava	73	J3
Jilin *China*	87	P3
Jilin *China*	87	P3
Jiloca	67	F2
Jilove	70	F4
Jima	103	G6
Jimba Jimba	112	D4
Jimena de la Frontera	66	D4
Jimenez	127	M6
Jimenez *Mexico*	128	C8
Jimenez *Mexico*	127	K7
Jimo	87	N4
Jinan	87	M4
Jincheng	93	M1
Jingbian	87	K4
Jingchuan	93	L1
Jingdezhen	87	M6
Jinghai	87	M4
Jinghe	86	E3
Jinghong	93	K4
Jingle	87	L4
Jingmen	93	M2
Jingpo	88	B3
Jingpo Hu	88	B4
Jingtai	93	K1
Jingxi	93	L4
Jing Xian	93	L3
Jinhua	87	M6
Jining *Nei Mongol Zizhiqu, China*	87	L3
Jining *Shandong, China*	87	M4
Jinja	107	F2
Jinkou	87	N4
Jinning	93	K4
Jinotepe	132	D9
Jinsha Jiang	93	J3
Jinta	86	H4
Jinxi	87	N3
Jin Xian	87	N4
Jinzhou	87	N3
Jinzhou Wan	87	N4
Jiparana	136	E5
Jipijapa	136	A4
Jiquilpan	130	H8
Jirriiban	103	J6
Jirueque	66	E2
Jirwan	97	K5
Jishou	93	L3
Jisr ash Shughur	94	C4
Jiu	73	G3
Jiujiang	93	N3
Jiuling Shan	93	M3
Jiutai	87	P3
Jiwa , Al	97	M5
Jiwani	92	B3
Jiwani, Ras	92	B4
Jixi *Anhui, China*	87	M5
Jixi *Heilongjiang, China*	87	Q2
Jixian	88	C2
Jizan	96	F8
Jizl, Wadi	96	C3
Jiz, Wadi al	97	K8
Joao Pessoa	137	L5
Joaquin V. Gonzalez	138	D5
Joban	89	H7
Jodar	66	E4
Jodhpur	92	D3
Joensuu	62	N5
Joetsu	89	G7
Jofane	109	F4
Joffre, Mount	122	G2
Jogeva	63	M7
Joghatay	95	N3
Johannesburg	108	E5
John Day *U.S.A.*	122	D5
John Day *U.S.A.*	122	E5
John H. Kerr Reservoir	129	N2
John O'Groats	56	E2
Johnshaven	57	F4
Johnson City	129	L2
Johnston *U.K.*	52	B3
Johnston *U.S.A.*	129	M4
Johnstone	57	D5
Johnston Lakes, The	112	E5
Johnstown	125	L6
Johor Baharu	90	C5
Joigny	65	E5
Joinville *Brazil*	138	G5
Joinville *France*	64	F4
Joinville Island	141	W6
Jokkmokk	62	H3
Jokulbunga	62	T11
Jokulsa a Bru	62	X12
Jokulsa-a Fjollum	62	W12
Jolfa	94	G2
Joliet	124	G6
Joliette	125	P3
Jolo *Philippines*	91	G4
Jolo *Philippines*	91	G4
Jonava	63	N9
Jonesboro	128	G3
Jones Sound	120	J2
Jonglei Canal	102	F6
Joniskis	63	K8
Jonkoping *Sweden*	63	F8
Jonkoping *Sweden*	63	F8
Jonquiere	125	Q2
Jonzac	65	C6
Joplin	124	C8
Jordan	94	B6
Jordan	94	B5
Jordan *U.S.A.*	123	L4
Jordanow	71	H4
Jordan Valley	122	F6
Jorhat	93	H3
Jorn	62	J4
Jorong	90	E6
Jorpeland	63	B7
Jos	105	G3
Jose de San Martin	139	B8
Joseph Bonaparte Gulf	112	F1
Joseph, Lac	121	N7
Josselin	65	B5
Jos Sodarso, Pulau	91	K7
Jostedalsbreen	63	B6
Jotunheimen	63	C6
Jounie	94	B5
Joutsa	63	M6
Joyces Country	59	C5
J. Percy Priest Lake	129	J2
Juan Aldama	130	H5
Juan de Fuca Strait	122	B3
Juan de Nova	109	H3
Juan Fernandez, Islas de	135	A6
Juanjui	136	B5
Juarez, Sierra	126	D4
Juazeiro	137	J5
Juazeiro do Norte	137	K5
Juba	103	F7
Jubany	141	W6
Jubba	107	H2
Juby, Cap	100	C3
Jucar	67	F3
Juchitan	131	M9
Judenburg	68	E2
Juigalpa	132	E8
Juist	70	B2
Juiz de Fora	138	H4
Juklegga	63	E6
Julia	136	D4
Juliaca	138	B3
Julia Creek	113	J3
Julianehab	116	Q2
Julijske Alpe	72	B2
Julio de Castilhos	138	F5
Jullundur	92	E2
Jumilla	67	F3
Jumla	92	F3
Junagadh	92	D4
Junction	127	N5
Junction City	123	R8
Jundiai	138	G4
Juneau	118	J4
Junee	113	K5
Jungfrau	68	A2
Junggar Pendi	86	F2
Junin	139	D6
Junin de los Andes	139	B7
Junosuando	62	K3
Junsele	62	G5
Jun Xian	93	M2
Jura *France*	65	G5
Jura *U.K.*	57	C5
Jura, Sound of	57	C5
Juratishki	71	L1
Juriti	137	F4
Jurua *Brazil*	136	D4
Jurua *Brazil*	136	D4
Juruena	136	F6
Jussey	65	F5
Jutai *Brazil*	136	D4
Jutai *Brazil*	136	D5
Juterbog	70	E3
Juticalpa	132	D7
Jutland	63	C8
Juuka	62	N5
Juva	63	M6
Juventud, Isla de la	132	F4
Ju Xian	87	M4
Juymand	95	P4
Juyom	95	M7
Juzna Morava	73	F4
Jylland	63	C8
Jyvaskyla	62	L5

K

Name	Page	Grid
Kaala-Gomen	114	W16
Kaamanen	62	M2
Kaavi	62	N5
Kaba	104	C4
Kabaena	91	G7
Kabala	104	C4
Kabale	107	E3
Kabalega Falls	107	F2
Kabalo	106	E4
Kabambare	107	E3
Kabara	114	S9
Kabba	105	G4
Kabinatagami	124	H1
Kabinda	106	D4
Kabirkuh	94	H5
Kabompo	106	D5
Kabongo	106	E4
Kabud Gonbad	95	P3

Name	Page	Grid
Kabul *Afghanistan*	92	C2
Kabuli	114	D2
Kaburuang	91	H5
Kabwe	107	E5
Kabyrdak	84	A5
Kachchh, Gulf of	92	C4
Kachchh, Rann of	92	C4
Kachemak Bay	118	E4
Kachikattsy	85	M4
Kachug	84	H6
Kackar Dagi	77	J2
Kadali	85	J5
Kadan Kyun	93	J6
Kadavu	114	R9
Kadavu Passage	114	R9
Kadena	89	H10
Kadhimain	94	G5
Kadikoy	76	B2
Kadina	113	H5
Kadinhani	76	E3
Kadiri	92	E6
Kadirli	77	G4
Kadoma	108	E3
Kadrifakovo	73	G5
Kadugli	102	E5
Kaduna *Nigeria*	105	G3
Kaduna *Nigeria*	105	G4
Kadzherom	78	K3
Kaedi	100	C5
Kaena Point	126	R10
Kaeo	115	D1
Kaesong	87	P4
Kafan	94	H2
Kafanchan	105	G4
Kaffrine	104	B3
Kafirevs, Akra	75	H3
Kafue *Zambia*	106	E6
Kafue *Zambia*	107	E6
Kafue Dam	108	E3
Kaga Bandoro	102	C6
Kagizman	77	K2
Kagmar	102	F5
Kagoshima	89	C10
Kagoshima-wan	89	C10
Kagul	79	D6
Kahama	107	F3
Kahan	92	C3
Kahayan	90	E6
Kahnuj	95	N8
Kahoku	89	H6
Kahoolawe	126	S10
Kahramanmaras	77	G4
Kahta	77	H4
Kahuku	126	R10
Kahurak	95	P7
Kahurangi Point	115	D4
Kaiama	105	F4
Kaiapoi	115	D5
Kaibab Plateau	126	F2
Kai Besar	114	A3
Kaifeng	93	M2
Kaihu	115	D1
Kai Kecil	114	A3
Kai, Kepulauan	91	J7
Kaikohe	115	D1
Kaikoura	115	D5
Kaikoura Range	115	D5
Kailahun	104	C4
Kailu	87	N3
Kailua *U.S.A.*	126	S10
Kaimana	91	J6
Kaimanawa Mountains	115	F3
Kaimur Range	92	F4
Kainantu	114	D3
Kainji Reservoir	105	F3
Kaipara Harbour	115	E2
Kaiping	93	M4
Kairouan	101	H1
Kairuku	114	D3
Kaiserslautern	70	B4
Kaisiadorys	71	L1
Kaitaia	115	D1
Kaitangata	115	B7
Kaiteur Falls	136	F3
Kaitumalven	62	J3
Kaiwaka	115	E2
Kaiwi Channel	126	S10
Kaiyuan *Liaoning, China*	87	N3
Kaiyuan *Yunnan, China*	93	K4
Kaiyuh Mountains	118	D3
Kajaani	62	M4
Kajo Kaji	102	F7
Kaka	103	F3
Kakabeka Falls	124	F2
Kakamari	107	F2
Kakamas	108	D5
Kakamega	107	F2
Kakapotahi	115	C5
Kake	89	D8
Kakhovskoye Vodokhranilishche	79	E5
Kaki	95	K7
Kakinada	92	F5
Kakisa Lake	119	M3
Kakogawa	89	E8
Kaktovik	118	G1
Kalabagh	92	D2
Kalabahi	91	G7
Kalabaka	75	F3
Kalabakan	91	F5
Kalabo	106	D6
Kalach	79	G5
Kalachinsk	84	A5
Kalach-Na-Donu	79	G6
Kaladar	125	M4
Ka Lae	126	T11
Kalahari	108	D4
Kalai-Khumb	86	C4
Kalajoki *Finland*	62	K4
Kalajoki *Finland*	62	L5
Kalakan	85	K5
Kalamai	75	G4
Kalamata	75	G4
Kalamazoo *U.S.A.*	124	H5
Kalamazoo *U.S.A.*	124	H5
Kalao	91	G7
Kalaotoa	91	G7
Kalapana	126	T11
Kalar	85	K5
Kalarash	73	K2
Kalarne	62	G5
Kalat	92	C3
Kalaupapa	126	S10
Kalavardha	75	J4
Kalavrita	75	G3
Kalb, Ra's	97	J9
Kalce	72	C3
Kaldakvisl	62	V12
Kaldungborg	63	D9
Kale *Turkey*	76	C4
Kale *Turkey*	76	C4
Kale *Turkey*	77	H2
Kalecik	76	E2
Kalemie	107	E4
Kal-e-Shur	95	P4
Kalety	71	H3
Kalevala	62	P4
Kalewa	93	H4
Kaleybar	94	H2
Kalfafell	62	W13
Kalgoorlie	112	E5
Kaliakra, Nos	73	K4
Kalianda	90	D7
Kalima	106	E3
Kalimantan	90	E5
Kalimnos *Greece*	75	J4
Kalimnos *Greece*	75	J4
Kalinin	78	F4
Kalininabad	86	B4
Kaliningrad	71	J1
Kalinino	78	K4
Kalininsk	79	G5
Kalinkovichi	79	D5
Kalinovka	79	D6
Kalis	103	J6
Kali Sindh	92	E4
Kalispell	122	G3
Kalisz *Poland*	70	F2
Kalisz *Poland*	71	H3
Kaliua	107	F4
Kalix	62	K4
Kalixalven	62	K3
Kalkan	76	C4
Kalkandere	77	J2
Kall	62	E5
Kallavesi	62	M5
Kalloni	75	J3
Kallsjon	62	E5
Kalmar *Sweden*	63	G8
Kalmar *Sweden*	63	G8
Kalmarsund	63	G8
Kalmykovo	79	J6
Kalni	93	H4
Kalomo	106	E6
Kalon	75	G2
Kalpeni	92	D6
Kalpi	92	E3
Kalpin	86	D3
Kal-Shur, Rud-e	95	P3
Kaluga	78	F5
Kaluku	91	F6
Kalush	79	C6
Kalutara	92	E7
Kalvarija	71	K1
Kalya	78	K3
Kalyan	92	D5
Kalyazin	78	F4
Kama	84	Ad4
Kamaishi	88	H6
Kamalia	92	D2
Kaman	76	E3
Kamaran	96	F9
Kamaria Falls	136	F2
Kamativi	108	E3
Kambalda	112	E5
Kambarka	78	J4
Kambia	104	C4
Kamchatka *Russia*	85	T5
Kamchatka Oblast	85	U5
Kamchiya	73	J4
Kamen	63	N9
Kamenets Podolskiy	73	J1
Kamen, Gora	84	F3
Kamenjak, Rt	72	B3
Kamenka *Kazakhstan*	79	J5
Kamenka *Moldavia*	73	K1
Kamenka *Russia*	84	F5
Kamenka *Russia*	79	G5
Kamenka *Russia*	78	G2
Kamen Kashirskiy	79	D5
Kamen-na-Obi	84	C4
Kamennyy, Mys	85	S1
Kamen Rybolov	88	C3
Kamensk-Shakhtinskiy	79	G6
Kamensk-Uralskiy	84	Ad5
Kamenyuki	71	K2
Kamenz	70	F3
Kames	57	C5
Kameshkovo	78	G4
Kamienna Gora	70	F3
Kamien Pombrski	70	F2
Kamiensk	71	H3
Kamilukuak Lake	119	Q3
Kamina	106	E4
Kaminak Lake	119	R3
Kaminuriak Lake	119	R3
Kamishak Bay	118	E4
Kamisli	76	F4
Kamkaly	86	C3
Kamla	93	G3
Kamloops	122	D2
Kamloops Lake	122	D2
Kammenoye, Ozero	62	P4
Kamnik	72	C2
Kamo *Japan*	88	G6
Kamo *Armenia*	77	L2
Kamp	68	E1
Kampala	107	F2
Kampar	90	C5
Kampen	64	F2
Kamphaeng Phet	93	J5
Kampot	93	K6
Kamsack	123	P2
Kamskiy	78	J3
Kamskoye Vodokhranilishche	78	K4
Kamyaran	94	H4
Kamyshin	79	H5
Kamzar	97	N3
Kan	84	E5
Kana	84	H4
Kanab	126	F2
Kanab Creek	126	F2
Kanab Plateau	126	F2
Kanaga Island	118	Ac9
Kanairiktok	121	P7
Kananda	84	G4
Kananga	106	D4
Kanash	78	H4
Kanastraion, Akra	75	G3
Kanawha	124	K7
Kanazawa	89	F7
Kanchanaburi	93	J6
Kanchenjunga	93	G3
Kanchipuram	92	E6
Kandahar	92	C2
Kandalaksha	62	Q3
Kandalakshskaya Guba	78	E2
Kandang	90	B5
Kandangan	90	F6
Kandanos	75	G5
Kandat	84	D5
Kandi	105	F3
Kandira	76	D2
Kandrian	114	D3
Kandukur	92	E5
Kandy	92	F7
Kane	125	L6
Kane Basin	120	M2
Kaneohe	126	S10
Kanevskaya	79	F6
Kangal	77	G3
Kangalassy	85	M4
Kangan	95	L8
Kangar	90	C4
Kangaroo Island	113	H6
Kangavar	94	H4
Kangaz	73	K2
Kangding	93	K2
Kangean	90	F7
Kangerdtuk	120	R3
Kanggye	87	P3
Kangiqsualujjuaq	121	N6
Kangiqsujuaq	121	M5
Kangirsuk	121	N5
Kangnung	89	B7
Kangping	87	N3
Kangri Karpo Pass	93	J3
Kani	93	H4
Kaniama	106	D4
Kanibadam	86	B3
Kaniet Islands	114	D2
Kanigigsualujak	121	L7
Kanin Nos	78	G2
Kanin Nos, Mys	78	G2
Kanin, Poluostrov	78	G2
Kanjiza	72	F2
Kankaanpaa	63	K6
Kankakee	124	G6
Kankan	104	D3
Kanker	92	F4
Kanmaw Kyun	93	J6
Kannapolis	129	M3
Kannonkoski	62	L5
Kannoura	89	E9
Kannus	62	N4
Kano	105	G3
Kanoya	89	C10
Kanpur	92	F3
Kansas	123	P8
Kansas City *Kansas, U.S.A.*	124	C7
Kansas City *Missouri, U.S.A.*	124	C7
Kansk	84	F5
Kansong	88	B6
Kant	86	D3
Kantemirovka	79	F6
Kanthi	93	G4
Kanton Island	111	U2
Kanturk	59	E8
Kanuku Mountains	136	F3
Kanye	108	E5
Kao	111	T5
Kao-hsiung	87	N7
Kaokoveld	108	B3
Kaolack	104	B3
Kaoma	106	D5
Kapanga	106	D4
Kapchagayskoye Vodokhranilishche	86	D3
Kapellskar	63	H7
Kapidagi Yarimadasi	76	B2
Kapiri Mposhi	107	E5
Kapit	90	E5
Kapiti Island	115	E4
Kaplan	128	F5
Kaplice	70	F4
Kapoeta	103	F7
Kaposvar	72	D2
Kapsan	88	B5
Kapsukas	71	K1
Kaptanpasa	77	J2
Kapuae	90	E6
Kapuas	90	D6
Kapuas Hulu, Pegunungan	90	E5
Kapudzhukh	94	H2
Kapuskasing *Canada*	124	J2
Kapuskasing *Canada*	124	J2
Kapustin Yar	79	H6
Kara *Togo*	104	F4
Kara *Turkey*	77	J3
Kara *Russia*	84	Ae3
Kara Balta	86	C3
Karabas *Kazakhstan*	86	C2
Karabas *Kazakhstan*	86	D2
Karabekaul	95	S2
Karabiga	76	B2
Kara-Bogaz-Gol	79	J7
Kara-Bogaz-Gol, Proliv	79	J2
Kara-Bogaz-Gol, Zaliv	79	J2
Karabuk	76	E2
Karabulak *China*	86	D3
Karabulak *Kazakhstan*	86	E2
Karaburun	76	B3
Karacabey	76	C2
Karacadag	77	H4
Karacakoy	76	C2
Karacali Dagi	77	H4
Karacasu	76	C4
Karacay	77	G4
Karachev	79	E5
Karacheyevsk	79	G7
Karachi	92	C4
Karad	92	D5
Karadeniz Bogazi	76	C2
Karadilli	76	D3
Karagach	84	A5
Karaganda	86	C2
Karagayly	86	D2
Karagel	95	L2
Karaginskiy, Ostrov	85	U5
Karagiye, Vpadina	79	J7
Karahalli	76	C3
Karaidel	78	K4
Karaikal	92	E6
Karaikkudi	92	E6
Karaisali	76	F4
Karaj	95	K4
Karak	94	B6
Kara Kala	95	N2
Karakax He	92	E1
Karakecili	76	E3
Karakelong	91	H5
Karakocan	77	J3
Karakoram	92	E1
Karakuduk	84	B6
Karakul	86	C4
Kara Kul, Ozero	86	C4
Karakumskiy Kanal	95	R3
Karakurt	77	K2
Karaman	76	E4
Karamay	86	E2
Karamea	115	D4
Karamea Bight	115	C4
Karamursel	76	C2
Karand	94	H4
Karanja	92	E4
Karanlik	76	F3
Karanlik Burun	76	B3
Karapelit	73	J4
Karapinar	76	E4
Karasburg	108	C5
Kara Sea	84	A2
Karashoky	84	A6
Karasjok	62	L2
Karasu *Turkey*	76	D2
Karasu *Kazakhstan*	84	A6
Karasu *Kazakhstan*	84	A6
Karasuk	84	B6
Karatal	86	D2
Karatas	76	F4
Kara Tau	86	C3
Karatau, Khrebet *Kazakhstan*	86	B3
Karatau, Khrebet *Kazakhstan*	79	J7
Karatobe	79	J6
Karaton	79	J6
Karatsu	89	B9
Karaudanawa	136	F3
Karauli	92	E3
Karaulkeldy	79	K6
Karavas	75	G4
Karawang	90	D7
Karayazi	77	K3
Karbala	94	G5
Karbole	63	F6
Karcag	73	F2

Name	Page	Ref
Kardhamila	75	J3
Kardhitsa	75	F3
Kardla	63	K7
Karesuando	62	K2
Kargasok	84	C5
Kargat	84	C5
Kargi *Turkey*	76	D4
Kargi *Turkey*	76	F2
Kargopol	78	F3
Kariba	108	E3
Kariba, Lake	108	E3
Karibib	108	C4
Kaributo	88	H4
Karigasniemi	62	L2
Karikari, Cape	115	D1
Karima	103	F4
Karimata, Kepulauan	90	D6
Karimata, Selat	90	D6
Karimganj	93	H4
Karimnagar	92	E5
Karimunjawa, Kepulauan	90	E7
Karin	103	J5
Karistos	75	H3
Kariz	95	Q4
Karkaralinsk	86	D2
Karkaralong, Kepulauan	91	H5
Karkar Island	114	D2
Karkas, Kuh-e	95	L5
Karkkila	63	L6
Karlino	70	F1
Karliova	77	J3
Karl-Marx-Stadt	70	E3
Karlobag	72	C3
Karlovac	72	C3
Karlovo	73	H4
Karlovy Vary	70	E3
Karlsborg	63	F7
Karlskoga	63	F7
Karlskrona	63	F8
Karlsruhe	70	C4
Karlstad *Sweden*	63	F7
Karlstad *U.S.A.*	124	B2
Karlstadt	70	C4
Karmanovka	79	J6
Karmoy	63	A7
Karnafuli Reservoir	93	H4
Karnal	92	E3
Karnali	92	F3
Karnataka	92	E6
Karnobat	73	J4
Karonie	112	E5
Karora	103	G4
Karossa, Tanjung	91	F7
Karousadhes	74	E3
Karoy	86	D2
Karpathos *Greece*	75	J5
Karpathos *Greece*	75	J5
Karpathos Straits	75	J5
Karpathou, Stenon	75	J5
Karpenision	75	F3
Karpinsk	84	Ad5
Karpogory	78	G3
Karratha	112	D3
Karrats Fjord	120	R3
Karree Berge	108	D6
Kars *Turkey*	77	K2
Kars *Turkey*	77	K2
Karsakpay	86	B2
Karsamaki	62	L5
Karsanti	76	F4
Karshi *Kazakhstan*	79	J7
Karshi *Uzbekistan*	80	H6
Karsiyaka	76	B3
Karskoye More	84	A2
Karsun	78	H5
Kartal	76	C2
Kartayel	78	J3
Kartuni	133	T11
Kartuzy	71	H1
Karufa	91	J6
Karun	94	J6
Karvina	71	H4
Karwar	92	D6
Karym	84	Ae4
Karymskoye	85	J6
Kas	76	C4
Kasai	106	C3
Kasaji	106	D5
Kasama	107	F5
Kasane	108	E3
Kasanga	107	F4
Kasangulu	106	C3
Kasaragod	92	D6
Kasar, Ras	96	D7
Kasba Lake	119	Q3
Kasba Tadla	100	D2
Kasempa	106	E5
Kasese	107	F2
Kashaf	95	Q3
Kashan	95	K5
Kashary	79	G6
Kashgar	86	D4
Kashi	86	D4
Kashima	89	C9
Kashin	78	F4
Kashipur	92	E3
Kashira	78	F5
Kashiwazaki	89	G7
Kashkanteniz	86	C2
Kashkarantsy	78	F2
Kashmar	95	P4
Kasimov	78	G5
Kasin	92	D2
Kasiruta	91	H6
Kaskinen	62	J5
Kasko	62	J5
Kas Kong	93	K6
Kasli	84	Ad5
Kasmere Lake	119	Q4
Kasongo	106	E3
Kasongo-Lunda	106	C4
Kasos	75	J5
Kasos, Stenon	75	J5
Kaspiyskiy	79	H6
Kassala	103	G4
Kassandra	75	G2
Kassel	70	C3
Kasserine	101	G1
Kastamonu	76	E2
Kastaneai	75	J2
Kastelli	75	G5
Kastellorizon	76	C4
Kastoria	75	F2
Kastorias, Limni	75	F2
Kastornoye	79	F5
Kastron	75	H3
Kasulu	107	F3
Kasumi	89	E8
Kasumiga-ura	89	H7
Kasungu	107	F5
Kata	84	G5
Kataba	106	E6
Katagum	105	H3
Katahdin, Mount	125	R4
Katako Kombe	106	D3
Katanning	112	D5
Katastari	75	F4
Katav Ivanovsk	78	K5
Katchall	93	H7
Katen	88	F2
Katerini	75	G2
Katha	93	J4
Katherina, Gebel	103	F2
Katherine	112	G1
Kathmandu	92	G3
Kati	100	D6
Katihar	93	G3
Katikati	115	E2
Katiola	104	D4
Katla	62	V13
Katlabukh, Ozero	73	K3
Katmai Volcano	118	E4
Kato Nevrokopion	75	G2
Katoomba	113	L5
Kato Stavros	75	G2
Katowice	71	H3
Katrineholm	63	G7
Katrine, Loch	57	D4
Katsina	105	G3
Katsina Ala	105	G4
Katsuura	89	H8
Katsuyama	89	F7
Kattavia	75	J5
Kattegat	63	D8
Kauai	126	R9
Kauai Channel	126	R10
Kauhajoki	62	K5
Kauiki Head	126	S10
Kaujuitok	120	H3
Kaulakahi Channel	126	Q9
Kaunakakai	126	S10
Kaunas	71	K1
Kaura Namoda	105	G3
Kaushany	73	K2
Kautokeino	62	K2
Kavacha	85	V4
Kavaje	74	E2
Kavak	77	G2
Kavaklidere	76	C4
Kavalerovo	88	E3
Kavali	92	E6
Kavalla	75	H2
Kavar	95	L7
Kavarna	73	K4
Kavgamis	77	H4
Kavieng	114	E2
Kavir, Dasht-e	95	M4
Kavir-e Namak	95	N4
Kavungo	106	D5
Kavusshap Daglari	77	K3
Kaw	137	G3
Kawagoe	89	G8
Kawaguchi	89	G8
Kawaihae	126	T10
Kawakawa	115	E1
Kawambwa	107	E4
Kawardha	92	F4
Kawasaki	89	G8
Kawerau	115	F3
Kawhia	115	E3
Kawhia Harbour	115	E3
Kawimbe	107	F4
Kawkareik	93	J5
Kawthaung	93	J7
Kayak Island	118	G4
Kayan	91	F5
Kaydak, Sor	79	J7
Kaye, Cape	120	H3
Kayenta	127	G2
Kayes	100	C6
Kaymaz	76	D3
Kaynar	86	D2
Kaynarca	76	D2
Kayseri	76	F3
Kayuagung	90	C6
Kazachinskoye	84	H5
Kazachye	85	P2
Kazakh	77	L2
Kazakhskiy Melkosopochnik	86	C2
Kazakhskiy Zaliv	79	J2
Kazakhstan	79	J6
Kazan	78	H4
Kazan *Turkey*	76	E2
Kazan	119	R3
Kazandzhik	95	M2
Kazan Lake	119	R3
Kazanluk	73	H4
Kazan-retto	83	N4
Kazatin	79	D6
Kazbek	77	L1
Kazerun	95	K7
Kazgorodok	84	Ae6
Kazhim	78	J3
Kazi Magomed	94	J1
Kazim Karabekir	76	E4
Kaztalovka	79	H6
Kazumba	106	D4
Kazy	95	N2
Kazym	84	Ae4
Kazymskaya	84	Ae4
Kazymskiy Mys	84	Ae4
Kea *Greece*	75	H4
Kea *Greece*	75	H4
Keady	58	J4
Keal, Loch na	57	B4
Kearny	126	G4
Keaukaha	126	T11
Keban	77	H3
Keban Baraji	77	H3
Kebemer	104	B2
Kebezen	84	D6
Kebnekaise	62	H3
Kebock Head	56	B2
Kebri Dehar	103	H6
Kech a Terara	103	G6
Kechika	118	K4
Keciborlu	76	D4
Kecil, Kai	91	J7
Kecskemet	72	E2
Kedainiai	63	K9
Kedgwick	125	S3
Kediri	90	E7
Kedong	87	P2
Kedougou	104	C3
Kedva	78	J3
Keel	58	B5
Keelby	55	J3
Keele	118	K3
Keele Peak	118	J3
Keeler	126	D2
Keene	125	P5
Keeper Hill	59	F7
Keetmanshoop	108	C3
Keewatin *NW. Territories, Canada*	119	R3
Keewatin *Ontario, Canada*	124	C2
Kefallinia	75	F3
Kefamenanu	91	G7
Kefken	76	D2
Keflavik	62	T12
Keglo Bay	121	N6
Kegulta	79	G6
Kehsi Mansam	93	J4
Keighley	55	H3
Keitele *Kaskisuomi, Finland*	62	L5
Keitele *Kuopio, Finland*	62	M5
Keith	56	F3
Keith Arm	119	L2
Keiyasi	114	Q8
Kekertaluk Island	120	N4
Keketa	114	C3
Kel	85	M3
Kelang	90	C5
Keld	55	G2
Keles	76	C3
Kelibia	101	H1
Kelkit *Turkey*	77	G2
Kelkit *Turkey*	77	H2
Keller Lake	119	L3
Kellett, Cape	118	K1
Kellog	84	D4
Kellogg	122	F4
Kelloselka	62	N3
Kells	58	J5
Kelme	63	K9
Kelmentsy	73	J1
Kelo	102	C6
Kelolokan	91	F5
Kelowna	122	E3
Kelsey Bay	122	B2
Kelso *New Zealand*	115	B6
Kelso *U.K.*	57	F5
Keluang	90	C5
Kelvedon	53	H3
Kelvin	78	E3
Kem	78	E3
Kemah	77	H3
Kemaliye	77	H3
Kemalpasa	77	J2
Kemalpasar	76	B3
Kemano	122	B2
Kemer *Turkey*	76	C4
Kemer *Turkey*	76	C4
Kemer *Turkey*	76	D2
Kemerovo	84	D5
Kemi	62	L4
Kemijarvi *Finland*	62	L3
Kemijarvi *Finland*	62	M3
Kemijoki	62	L3
Kemmerer	123	J7
Kempen	64	F3
Kempendyayi	85	K4
Kemp, Lake	127	N4
Kemps Bay	132	H2
Kempsey	113	L5
Kempten	70	D5
Kempt, Lac	125	N3
Kempton	113	K7
Ken	92	F3
Kenadsa	100	E2
Kenai	118	E3
Kenai Mountains	118	E4
Kenai Peninsula	118	F3
Kendal	55	G2
Kendall, Cape	120	J5
Kendari	91	G6
Kendawangan	90	E6
Kendraparha	92	G4
Kendyrliki	86	F2
Kenema	104	C4
Kenete Karavastas	74	E2
Kenge	106	C3
Kengtung	93	J4
Kenhardt	108	D5
Kenilworth	53	F2
Kenitra	100	D2
Keniut	85	X4
Kenli	87	M4
Kenmare *Ireland*	59	C9
Kenmare *Ireland*	59	C9
Kenmore	57	D4
Kennacraig	57	C5
Kennebec	125	R4
Kenner	128	G5
Kennet	53	F3
Kennewick	122	E4
Kenninghall	53	J2
Kenn Reef	113	M3
Kenogami	121	K7
Keno Hill	118	H3
Kenora	124	C2
Kenosha	124	G5
Kent *U.K.*	53	H3
Kent *U.S.A.*	127	K5
Kentau	86	B3
Kentford	53	H2
Kentmere	55	G2
Kent Peninsula	119	P2
Kentucky *U.S.A.*	124	G8
Kentucky *U.S.A.*	124	H8
Kentucky Lake	124	F8
Kentwood	128	G5
Kenya	107	G2
Keokea	126	S10
Keokuk	124	E6
Keos	75	H4
Kepi	91	K7
Kepno	71	G3
Keppel Bay	113	L3
Kepsut	76	C3
Kerala	92	E6
Kerama-retto	89	H10
Keravat	114	E2
Kerch	79	F6
Kerchenskiy Proliv	79	F6
Kerema	114	D3
Keremeos	122	E3
Keren	103	G4
Kerguelen, Ile	142	D6
Keri	75	F4
Kericho	107	G3
Kerinci, Gunung	90	C6
Keriya He	92	F1
Kerki	95	S3
Kerkinitis, Limni	75	G2
Kerkira *Greece*	74	E3
Kerkira *Greece*	74	E3
Kerma	102	F4
Kermadec Islands	111	T8
Kermadec Trench	143	H6
Kerman	95	N6
Kerman Desert	95	P7
Kermen	73	J4
Kermit	127	L5
Kern	126	C2
Keros	78	J3
Kerpineny	73	K2
Kerrera	57	C4
Kerrville	127	N5
Kerry	59	C8
Kerry Head	59	C8
Kerrykeel	58	G2
Keruh	90	C4
Kerulen	87	L2
Kesalahti	63	N6
Kesan	76	B2
Kesap	77	H2
Kesennuma	88	H6
Keshvar	94	J5
Keskin	76	E3
Keski-Suomi	62	K5
Keskozero	78	E3
Keswick	55	F2
Keszthely	72	D2
Ket	84	D5
Keta	104	F4
Keta, Ozero	84	E3
Ketapang	90	D6
Ketchikan	118	J4
Kete	104	E3
Ketmen, Khrebet	86	E3
Ketoy, Ostrov	85	S7
Ketrzyn	71	J1
Kettering	53	G2
Kettle Ness	55	J2
Kettle River Range	122	E3
Kettlewell	55	G2

Name	Ref	Grid
Kettusoja	62	N3
Keurus-selka	63	L5
Keushki	84	Ae4
Kew	133	M4
Kewanee	124	F6
Keweenaw	124	G3
Keweenaw Bay	124	G3
Keweenaw Point	124	G3
Keyano	121	M7
Keyaygyr	86	D3
Keyi	86	E3
Key Largo	129	M8
Key, Lough	58	F4
Keynsham	52	E3
Key West	129	M8
Keyworth	53	F2
Kez	78	J4
Kezhma	84	G5
Khabarovo	84	Ad3
Khabarovsk	88	E1
Khabarovsk Kray	85	P6
Khabur	94	E4
Khadki	92	D5
Khairagarh	92	F4
Khairpur *Pakistan*	92	C3
Khairpur *Pakistan*	92	D3
Khakhar	85	P5
Khalafabad	94	J6
Khalili	95	L8
Khalkhal	94	J3
Khalki	75	J4
Khalkis	75	G3
Khalmer-Yu	84	Ad3
Khalturin	78	H4
Khamar Daban, Khrebet	84	G6
Khambhat	92	D4
Khambhat, Gulf of	92	D4
Khamili	75	J5
Khamir	96	F8
Khamis Mushayt	96	F7
Kham Keut	93	L5
Khammam	92	F5
Khamra	85	J4
Khanabad	92	C1
Khan al Baghdadi	94	F5
Khanaqin	94	G4
Khanda	84	H6
Khandela	92	E3
Khandra	75	J5
Khandwa	92	E4
Khandyga	85	P4
Khangokurt	84	Ad4
Khanh Hoa	93	L6
Khanh Hung	93	L7
Khani	85	L5
Khania	75	H5
Khaniadhana	92	E4
Khanion Kolpos	75	G5
Khanka, Ozero	88	D3
Khanpur	92	D3
Khan Shaykhun	94	C4
Khantau	86	C3
Khantayka	84	D3
Khantayskoye, Ozero	84	E3
Khanty-Mansiysk	84	Ae4
Khan Yunis	94	B6
Kharabali	79	H6
Kharagpur	93	G4
Kharalakh	85	L3
Kharan	95	N7
Kharanaq	95	M5
Kharaulakhskiy Khrebet	85	M2
Kharbur	77	J5
Kharga, El Wahat el	102	F3
Kharg Island	97	K2
Kharitah, Shiqqat al	96	H8
Khark	97	K2
Kharkov	79	F6
Kharku	97	K2
Khar Kuh	95	L6
Kharlovka	78	F2
Kharsawan	92	G4
Kharstan	85	Q2
Khartoum	103	F4
Khartoum North	103	F4
Kharutayuvam	78	K2
Khasalakh	85	M2
Khasan	88	C4
Khasavyurt	79	H7
Khash	95	Q7
Khash	95	R6
Khash, Dasht-i-	92	B2
Khashm el Girba	96	B9
Khash Rud	95	R6
Khashuri	77	K2
Khasi Hills	93	H3
Khaskovo	73	H5
Khatanga *Russia*	84	G2
Khatanga *Russia*	84	G2
Khatangskiy Zaliv	84	H2
Khatayakha	78	K2
Khatyrka	85	X4
Khaybar, Harrat	96	E4
Khaypudyrskaya Guba	78	K2
Khayran, Ra's al	97	P5
Khaysardakh	85	M4
Khe Bo	93	K5
Kheisia	77	J5
Khemis Miliana	67	H4
Khemisset	100	D2
Khenchela	101	G1
Khenifra	100	D2
Kherrata	67	J4
Khersan	95	K6
Kherson	79	E6
Khe Sanh	93	L5
Kheta	84	G2
Khiitola	63	N6
Khilok	85	J6
Khios *Greece*	75	H3
Khios *Greece*	75	J3
Khirbat Isriyah	77	G5
Khiva	80	H5
Khlebarovo	73	J4
Khmelnik	79	D6
Khmelnitskiy	79	D6
Khodzhakala	95	N2
Kholm *Afghanistan*	92	C1
Kholm *Russia*	78	E4
Kholmogory	78	G3
Kholmsk	88	J2
Khomas Highland	108	C4
Khomeyn	95	K5
Khomeynishahr	95	K5
Khong	93	L6
Khongkhoyuku	85	N4
Khonj	95	L8
Khoper	79	G5
Khor *Russia*	88	E2
Khor *Russia*	88	E2
Khora Sfakion	75	H5
Khorat, Cao Nguyen	93	K5
Khordha	92	G4
Khordogoy	85	K4
Khoreyver	78	K2
Khorgo	84	J2
Khorinsk	84	H6
Khorod	79	E6
Khorol	88	C3
Khorovaya	84	A3
Khorramabad *Iran*	94	J5
Khorramabad *Iran*	95	N4
Khorramshahr	94	J6
Khosf	95	P5
Khosheutovo	79	H6
Khosk	95	R4
Khosrowabad	94	J6
Khotin	73	J1
Khouribga	100	D2
Khoyniki	79	D5
Khristiana	75	H4
Khroma	85	Q2
Khuff	96	G4
Khulna	93	G4
Khulo	77	K2
Khunjerab Pass	92	E1
Khunsar	95	K5
Khunti	92	G4
Khur	95	P4
Khurays	97	J4
Khurja	92	E3
Khuryan Munjan, Jazair	97	N8
Khust	79	C6
Khutu Datta	85	Q7
Khuzdar	92	C3
Khvaf	95	Q4
Khvalynsk	79	H5
Khvor	95	M5
Khvormuj	95	K7
Khvoy	94	G2
Khvoynaya	78	E4
Khwaja Muhammad, Koh-i-	92	D1
Khyber Pass	92	D2
Khyrov	71	K4
Kiamba	91	G4
Kiantajarvi	62	N4
Kiaton	75	G3
Kiberg	62	P1
Kibombo	106	E3
Kibondo	107	F3
Kibwezi	107	G3
Kibworth Harcourt	53	G2
Kicevo	73	F5
Kicking Horse Pass	119	M5
Kidal	100	F5
Kidan, Al	97	M5
Kidderminster	52	E2
Kidnappers, Cape	115	F3
Kidsgrove	55	G3
Kidwelly	52	C3
Kidyut, Wadi	97	K8
Kiel	70	D1
Kielce	71	J3
Kielder	57	F5
Kielder Forest	57	F5
Kielder Water	57	F5
Kieler Bucht	70	D1
Kieta	114	F3
Kiev	79	E5
Kiffa	100	C5
Kifissos	75	G3
Kifri	94	G4
Kigali	107	F3
Kigi	77	J3
Kiglapait, Cape	121	P6
Kigoma	107	E3
Kiholo	126	T11
Kii-sanchi	89	E9
Kii-suido	89	E9
Kikai-jima	89	B11
Kikiakki	84	C4
Kikinda	72	F3
Kikladhes	75	H4
Kikonai	88	H5
Kikori	114	C3
Kikwit	106	C3
Kil	63	E7
Kilafors	63	G6
Kilakh	97	K5
Kilauea	126	R9
Kilauea Crater	126	T11
Kilbasan	76	E4
Kilbeggan	59	H6
Kilberry	58	J5
Kilbirnie	57	D5
Kilbrannan Sound	57	C5
Kilbride *Ireland*	59	K7
Kilbride *U.K.*	57	A3
Kilbuck Mountains	118	D3
Kilchu	88	B5
Kilcock	59	J6
Kilcolgan	59	E6
Kilcormac	59	G6
Kilcoy	113	L4
Kilcullen	59	J6
Kildare *Ireland*	59	J6
Kildare *Ireland*	59	J6
Kildin, Ostrov	62	R2
Kildinstroy	62	Q2
Kilfinnane	59	F8
Kilgore	128	E4
Kilham	57	F5
Kilickaya	77	J2
Kilifi	107	G3
Kilimanjaro	107	G3
Kilinailau Islands	114	F2
Kilis	77	G4
Kiliya	79	D6
Kilkee	59	C7
Kilkeel	58	L4
Kilkelly	58	E5
Kilkenny *Ireland*	59	H7
Kilkenny *Ireland*	59	H7
Kilkhampton	52	C4
Kilkieran Bay	59	C6
Killadysert	59	D7
Killala	58	D4
Killala Bay	58	D4
Killaloe	59	F7
Killarney	59	C8
Killashandra	58	G4
Killeen	128	D5
Killenaule	59	G7
Killiecrankie	57	E4
Killiecrankie, Pass of	57	E4
Killin	57	D4
Killinek Island	121	P5
Killini	75	G4
Killorglin	59	C8
Killybegs	58	F3
Killylea	58	J4
Kilmacthomas	59	H8
Kilmallock	59	E8
Kilmaluag	56	B3
Kilmarnock	57	D5
Kilmaurs	57	D5
Kilmelford	57	C4
Kilmez	78	J4
Kilmurry	59	D7
Kilnsea	55	K3
Kiloran	57	B4
Kilosa	107	G4
Kilpisjarvi	62	J2
Kilrea	58	J3
Kilrush	59	D7
Kilsyth	57	D5
Kiltan	92	D6
Kilwa Masoko	107	G4
Kilwinning	57	F4
Kilyos	76	C2
Kimba	113	H5
Kimbe Bay	114	E3
Kimberley *Canada*	122	G3
Kimberley *South Africa*	108	D5
Kimberley Plateau	112	F2
Kimi	75	H3
Kimito	63	K6
Kimmeridge	53	E4
Kimolos	75	H4
Kimry	78	H4
Kimvula	106	C4
Kimzha	78	G2
Kinabalu, Gunung	90	F4
Kinbasket Lake	122	F2
Kinbrace	56	E2
Kincardine *Canada*	125	K4
Kincardine *U.K.*	57	E4
Kindat	93	H4
Kinder	128	F5
Kinder Scout	55	H3
Kindersley	123	K2
Kindia	104	C3
Kindu	106	E3
Kinel	79	J5
Kinel-Cherkasy	78	J5
Kineshma	78	G4
Kingaroy	113	L4
Kingarth	57	C5
King Christian Island	120	F2
King City	126	B2
King George Island	141	W6
King George Sound	112	D5
Kinghorn	57	E4
Kingisepp	63	M7
Kingiseppa	63	K7
King Island	113	J6
King, Lake	112	D5
King Leopold Ranges	112	F2
Kingman	126	E3
Kingoonya	113	H5
Kings	126	B2
King Salmon	118	D4
Kingsbarns	57	F4
Kingsbridge	52	D4
King's Bromley	53	F2
Kingsclere	53	F3
Kingscote	113	H6
Kingscourt	58	J5
Kingsford	124	F4
Kingsley	55	H3
King's Lynn	53	H2
Kingsmill Group	111	R2
King Sound	112	E2
Kings Peak	123	J7
Kingsport	129	L2
Kingston *Australia*	113	H6
Kingston *Canada*	125	M4
Kingston *Jamaica*	132	J5
Kingston *New Zealand*	115	B6
Kingston *U.S.A.*	125	P6
Kingston Bagpuize	53	F3
Kingston-upon-Hull	55	J3
Kingston-upon-Thames	53	G3
Kingstown	133	S8
Kingsville	128	D7
Kingswood	52	E3
Kington	52	D2
Kingussie	57	D3
King William Island	120	G3
King William's Town	108	E6
Kiniama	107	E5
Kinik	76	B3
Kinloch	57	B3
Kinlochewe	56	C3
Kinloch Hourn	57	C3
Kinna	63	E8
Kinnaird Head	56	F3
Kinnegad	59	H6
Kinnerley	52	E2
Kinnert, Yam	94	B5
Kinoosao	119	Q4
Kinross	57	E4
Kinsale	59	E9
Kinsalebeg	59	G9
Kinsarvik	63	B6
Kinshasa	106	C3
Kinsley	127	N2
Kinston	129	P3
Kintampo	104	E4
Kintore	56	F3
Kintyre	57	C5
Kintyre, Mull of	57	C5
Kinuachdrachd	57	C4
Kiparissia	75	F4
Kiparissiakos Kolpos	75	F4
Kipawa, Lac	125	L3
Kipengere Range	107	F4
Kipili	107	F4
Kipini	107	H3
Kipnuk	118	C4
Kipseli	75	G3
Kirakira	114	K7
Kiraz	76	C3
Kirazli	76	B2
Kirbasi	76	D2
Kirbey	84	H3
Kircubbin	58	L4
Kirec	76	C3
Kirenga	84	H5
Kirenis	76	C4
Kirensk	84	H5
Kirgizskiy Khrebet	86	C3
Kirgiz Step	79	J6
Kiri	106	C3
Kiribati	111	S2
Kirik	77	J2
Kirikhan	77	G4
Kirikkale	76	E3
Kirillo	78	F4
Kirin	87	P3
Kirinyaga	107	G3
Kirka	76	D3
Kirkagac	76	B3
Kirk Bulag Dag	94	H3
Kirkburton	55	H3
Kirkby	55	G3
Kirkby in Ashfield	55	H3
Kirkby Lonsdale	55	G2
Kirkby Stephen	55	G2
Kirkcaldy	57	E4
Kirkcambeck	57	F5
Kirkcolm	54	D2
Kirkcudbright	54	E2
Kirkcudbright Bay	54	E2
Kirkenes	62	P2
Kirkestinden	62	H1
Kirkheaton	57	G5
Kirkintilloch	57	D5
Kirkland Lake	125	K2
Kirk Langley	53	F2
Kirklareli	76	B2
Kirklington	55	J3
Kirk Michael	54	E2
Kirkoswald	55	G2
Kirk Smeaton	55	H3
Kirksville	124	D6
Kirkton	57	F4
Kirkton of Culsalmond	56	F3
Kirkton of Largo	57	F4
Kirkuk	94	G4
Kirkwall	56	F2
Kirkwhelpington	57	G5
Kirkwood	108	E6
Kirlangic Burun	76	D4
Kirmir	76	E2
Kirov *Russia*	78	E5

Name	Page	Grid
Kirov *Russia*	78	H4
Kirova	86	D2
Kirovabad	79	H7
Kirovakan	77	L2
Kirovgrad	79	E6
Kirovo-Chepetsk	78	H4
Kirovsk *Russia*	62	Q3
Kirovsk *Turkmenistan*	95	Q3
Kirovskiy	88	D3
Kirriemuir	57	F4
Kirs	78	J4
Kirsanov	79	G5
Kirsehir	76	F3
Kirtgecit	77	K3
Kirthar Range	92	C3
Kirtlington	53	F3
Kirton	55	J3
Kiruna	62	J3
Kiryu	89	G7
Kisa	63	F8
Kisamou, Kolpos	75	G5
Kisangani	106	E2
Kisar	91	H7
Kisarazu	89	G8
Kiselevsk	84	D6
Kishanganj	93	G3
Kishangarh	92	D3
Kishb, Harrat	96	E5
Kishika-zaki	89	C10
Kishinev	79	D6
Kishiwada	89	E8
Kishorganj	93	H4
Kishorn, Loch	56	C3
Kisii	107	F3
Kiska Island	118	Ab9
Kiskunfelegyhaza	72	E2
Kiskunhalas	72	E2
Kislovodsk	79	G7
Kismaayo	107	H3
Kiso-Fukushima	89	F8
Kiso-sammyaku	89	F8
Kispest	72	E2
Kissidougou	104	C4
Kissimmee	129	M7
Kisumu	107	F3
Kita	100	D6
Kitajaur	62	J3
Kitakami *Japan*	88	H6
Kitakami *Japan*	88	H6
Kitakami-sanmyaku	88	J3
Kita-kyushu	89	C9
Kitale	107	G2
Kitami	88	J4
Kitami-sammyaku	88	H6
Kitangari	107	G5
Kitay, Ozero	73	K3
Kit Carson	127	L1
Kitchener	125	K5
Kitee	62	P5
Kitgum	107	F2
Kithira *Greece*	75	G4
Kithira *Greece*	75	G4
Kithnos *Greece*	75	H4
Kithnos *Greece*	75	H4
Kitikmeot	119	N1
Kitimat	118	K5
Kitinen	62	M3
Kitkiojoki	62	K3
Kitsuki	89	C9
Kittanning	125	L6
Kittila	62	L3
Kitui	107	G3
Kitunda	107	F4
Kitwe	107	E5
Kitzbuhel	68	D2
Kitzbuheler Alpen	68	D2
Kitzingen	70	D4
Kivalo	62	L3
Kivijarvi	62	L5
Kivu, Lake	107	E3
Kiyev	79	E5
Kiyevka	88	D4
Kiyevskoye Vodokhranilishche	79	E5
Kiyikoy	76	C2
Kizel	78	K4
Kizema	78	H3
Kizilagac	77	J3
Kizilcaboluk	76	C4
Kizilcadag	76	C4
Kizilhisar	76	C4
Kizilirmak	76	E2
Kizil Irmak	77	F2
Kizilkaya	76	D4
Kiziloren	76	E4
Kiziltepe	77	J4
Kizlyar	79	H7
Kizyl-Arvat	95	N2
Kizyl-Atrek	95	M3
Kizyl Ayak	95	S3
Kizyl-Su	95	L2
Kjollefjord	62	M1
Kjopsvick	62	L2
Kladanj	72	E3
Kladno	70	F3
Kladovo	73	G3
Klagenfurt	68	E2
Klaipeda	63	L9
Klamath *U.S.A.*	122	B7
Klamath *U.S.A.*	122	C7
Klamath Falls	122	D6
Klamath Mountains	122	C6
Klamono	91	J6
Klaralven	63	J6
Klatovy	70	E4
Klekovaca	72	D3
Klenak	72	E3
Klerksdorp	108	E5
Klichka	85	K7
Klimovichi	79	E5
Klin	78	F4
Klinovec	70	E3
Klintsovka	79	H5
Klintsy	79	E5
Klisura	73	H4
Kljuc	72	D3
Klobuck	71	H3
Klodzka *Poland*	71	G3
Klodzko *Poland*	71	G3
Klos	75	F2
Klosterneuberg	68	F1
Klosters	68	B2
Klrovskiy	79	H6
Kluane	118	H3
Kluane Lake	118	H3
Kluczbork	71	H3
Klyevka	84	A6
Klyuchevskaya Sopka	85	U5
Klyuchi	85	U5
Klyukvinka	84	D5
Kmagta	114	J6
Kmanjab	108	B3
K2, Mount	92	E1
Knapdale	57	C5
Knaresborough	55	H2
Knife	123	N4
Knight Island	118	F3
Knighton	52	D2
Knin	72	D3
Knjazevac	73	G4
Knockadoon Head	59	G9
Knockalla Mount	58	G2
Knockanaffrin	59	G8
Knockaunapeebra	59	G8
Knocklayd	58	K2
Knockmealdown Mountains	59	G8
Knocknaskagh	59	F8
Knottingley	55	H3
Knox, Cape	118	J5
Knoxville *Iowa, U.S.A.*	124	D6
Knoxville *Tennessee, U.S.A.*	129	L3
Knoydart	57	C3
Knud Rasmussen Land	120	P2
Knutholstind	63	C6
Knutsford	55	G3
Knyazhaya Guba	62	Q3
Knyazhevo	78	G4
Knysna	108	D6
Knyszyn	71	K2
Koba	90	D6
Kobarid	72	B2
Kobayashi	89	C10
Kobberminebugt	120	R5
Kobelyaki	79	E6
Kobenhavn	63	E9
Koblenz	70	B3
Kobowre, Pegunungan	91	K6
Kobrin	71	L2
Kobroor	91	J7
Kobuk	118	D2
Kobuleti	77	J2
Kobya	85	M4
Koca *Turkey*	76	B3
Koca *Turkey*	76	C3
Koca *Turkey*	76	E2
Kocapinar	77	K3
Kocarli	76	B4
Koceljevo	72	E3
Koch Bihar	93	G3
Kochechum	84	G3
Kochegarovo	85	K5
Kocher	70	C4
Kochi	89	D9
Koch Island	120	L4
Kochkorka	86	D3
Koch Peak	122	J5
Kochumdek	84	E4
Koden	71	K3
Kodiak	118	E4
Kodiak Island	118	E4
Kodima	78	G3
Kodinar	92	D4
Kodok	103	F6
Kodomari	88	H5
Kodyma	73	L2
Kofcaz	76	B2
Koffiefontein	108	D5
Koflach	68	E2
Koforidua	104	E4
Kofu	89	G8
Koge	63	E9
Kogilnik	73	K2
Ko, Gora	88	F2
Kohat	92	D2
Kohima	93	H3
Koh-i Qaisar	95	S5
Kohtla-Jarve	63	M7
Koide	89	G7
Koi Sanjaq	94	G3
Koitere	62	P5
Koivu	62	L3
Koje	89	B8
Kojonup	112	D5
Kokand	86	B3
Kokas	91	J6
Kokchetav	84	Ae6
Kokemaenjoki	63	K6
Kokenau	91	K6
Kokkola	62	K5
Koko	105	G4
Kokoda	114	D3
Kokomo	124	G6
Kokpekty	86	E2
Koksoak	121	N6
Kokstad	108	E6
Koktas	86	C2
Kokubu	89	C10
Kokuora	85	R2
Kokura	89	C9
Kokuy	85	K6
Kok-Yangak	86	C3
Kola	62	Q2
Kolaka	91	G6
Kolar	92	E6
Kolari	62	K3
Kolarovgrad	73	J4
Kolasin	72	E4
Kolay	77	F2
Kolberg	70	F1
Kolbuszowa	71	J3
Kolchugino	78	F4
Kolda	104	C3
Kolding	63	C9
Kole	106	D3
Kolguyev, Ostrov	78	H2
Kolhapur	92	D5
Kolin	70	F3
Kolki	71	L3
Kolkuskull	62	V12
Kollabudur	62	T12
Koln	70	B3
Kolno	71	J2
Koloa	126	R10
Kolobrzeg	70	F1
Kologriv	78	G4
Kolombangara	114	H5
Kolomna	78	F4
Kolono	91	G6
Koloubara	72	F3
Kolozsvar	73	G2
Kolpashevo	84	C5
Kolpino	78	E4
Kolskiy Poluostrov	78	F2
Koltubanovskiy	79	J5
Koluszki	71	H3
Kolva *Russia*	78	K3
Kolva *Russia*	78	K2
Kolwezi	106	E5
Kolyma	85	U3
Kolymskaya Nizmennost	85	T3
Kolymskiy, Khrebet	85	T4
Komadugu Gana	105	H3
Komandorskiye Ostrova	81	T4
Komarno	71	H5
Komarom	72	E2
Komatsu	89	F7
Komering	90	C6
Kommunarsk	79	F6
Komodo	91	F7
Komoe	104	E4
Kom Ombo	103	F3
Komoran	91	K7
Komosomolets, Ostrov	81	L1
Komotini	75	H2
Komovi	74	E1
Kompong Cham	93	L6
Kompong Chhnang	93	K6
Kompong Som	93	K6
Kompong Speu	93	K6
Kompong Sralao	93	L6
Kompong Thom	93	K6
Komrat	79	D6
Komsomolets, Zaliv	79	J6
Komsomolsk	79	E6
Komsomolskiy	79	J6
Komsomolsk-na-Amure	85	P6
Konakovo	78	F4
Koncanica	72	D3
Konch	92	E3
Konda *Indonesia*	91	J6
Konda *Russia*	84	Ae4
Kondagaon	92	F5
Kondinin	112	D5
Kondinskoye	84	Ae5
Kondoa	107	G3
Kondon	85	P6
Kondoponga	78	E3
Konduz	92	C1
Kone	114	W16
Konevo	78	F3
Kong	104	E4
Kongan	89	J10
Kong Christian den X Land	120	W3
Kong Karls Land	80	D2
Kongolo	106	E4
Kongsberg	63	C7
Kongsvinger	63	E6
Kong Wilhelms Land	120	X2
Koniecpol	71	H3
Konigsberg	71	J4
Konigs Wusterhausen	70	E2
Konin	71	H2
Konitsa	75	F2
Koniya	89	B11
Konkamaalv	62	J2
Konkoure	104	C3
Konnern	70	D3
Konnevesi	62	M5
Konosha	78	G3
Konotop	79	E5
Konqi He	86	F3
Konskie	71	J3
Konstantinovka	79	F6
Konstantinovsk	79	G6
Konstanz	68	B2
Kontagora	105	G3
Kontcha	105	H4
Kontiomaki	62	N4
Kontum	93	L6
Kontum, Plateau du	93	L6
Konya	76	E3
Konya Ovasi	76	E3
Konzhakovskiy Kamen, Gora	78	K4
Kootenai	122	G3
Kootenay	122	F3
Kootenay Lake	122	F3
Kopaonik	73	F4
Kopasker	62	W11
Kopavogur	62	U12
Koper	72	B3
Kopervik	63	A7
Kopet Dag, Khrebet	95	N2
Kopeysk	84	Ad5
Koping	63	F7
Kopka	124	F1
Kopmanholmen	62	H5
Koppang	63	D6
Kopparberg *Sweden*	63	F7
Kopparberg *Sweden*	63	F6
Koppi *Russia*	88	G1
Koppi *Russia*	88	H1
Kopru	76	D4
Koprubasi	76	C3
Koprulu	76	E4
Kopruoren	76	C3
Kopychintsy	73	H1
Kor	95	L6
Kora	77	K2
Korab	72	F5
Korahe	103	H6
Koraluk	121	P6
Korana	72	C3
Korba	69	C7
Korbach	70	C3
Korbu, Gunung	90	C5
Korce	75	F2
Korcula	72	D4
Korda	84	F4
Kord Kuv	95	M3
Korea Bay	87	N4
Korea, North	87	P4
Korea, South	87	P4
Korea Strait	89	B8
Korennoye	84	H2
Korenovsk	79	F6
Korf	85	V4
Korforskiy	88	E1
Korgan	77	G2
Korgen	62	E3
Korhogo	104	D4
Korido	91	K6
Korim	91	K6
Korinthiakos Kolpos	75	G3
Korinthos	75	G4
Koriyama	89	H7
Korkinitskiy Zaliv	79	E6
Korkodon	85	T4
Korkuteli	76	D4
Korla	86	F3
Kormakiti, Akra	76	E5
Kornat	72	C4
Koro	114	R8
Korocha	79	F5
Koroglu Daglari	76	E2
Koronia, Limni	75	G2
Koronowo	71	G2
Koros	72	F2
Korosten	79	D5
Korostyshev	79	D5
Korotaikha	78	L2
Korovin Volcano	118	Ad9
Korpilombolo	62	K3
Korsakov	88	J2
Korsnas	62	J5
Korsor	63	D9
Korti	103	F4
Kortrijk	64	E3
Korucu	76	B3
Koryakskaya Sopka	85	U6
Koryanskiy Khrebet	85	Z5
Koryazhma	78	H3
Korzybie	71	G1
Kos *Greece*	75	J4
Kos *Greece*	75	J4
Koschagyl	79	J6
Koscian	71	G2
Koscierzyna	71	G1
Kosciusco, Mount	113	K6
Kosciusko	128	H4
Kose	77	H2
Kos Golu	76	B2
Koshiki-retto	89	B10
Kosice	71	J4
Koski	63	K6
Koslan	78	H3
Koslin	71	G1
Kosma	78	H2
Kosong	88	B6
Kosong-ni	88	B5
Kossou, Lac de	104	D4
Kossovo	71	L2
Kostajnica	72	D3
Kosti	103	F5
Kostino	84	D3
Kostomuksha	62	P4
Kostopol	71	M3
Kostroma *Russia*	78	G4

Kostroma *Russia* 78 G4
Kostrzyn 70 F2
Kosu-dong 89 B8
Kosva 78 K4
Kosyu 78 K2
Kosyuvom 78 K2
Koszalin 71 G1
Kota 92 E3
Kotaagung 90 C7
Kota Baharu 90 C4
Kotabaru *Indonesia* 90 E6
Kotabaru *Indonesia* 90 F6
Kota Belud 90 F4
Kotabumi 90 C5
Kota Kinabalu 90 F4
Kotala 62 N3
Kotamubagu 91 G5
Kota Tinggi 90 C5
Kotel 73 J4
Kotelnich 78 H4
Kotelnikovo 79 G6
Kotelnyy, Ostrov 85 P1
Kotikovo 88 E2
Kotka 63 M6
Kot Kapura 92 D2
Kotlas 78 H3
Kotli 92 D2
Kotlik 118 C3
Koto 85 P7
Kotor 72 E4
Kotovo 79 G5
Kotovsk *Russia* 79 G5
Kotovsk *Ukraine* 79 D6
Kotri 92 C3
Kottagudem 92 F5
Kottayam 92 E7
Kotto 102 D6
Kotuy 84 G2
Kotyuzhany 73 K2
Kotzebue 118 C2
Kotzebue Sound 118 C2
Kouango 102 C6
Koudougou 104 E3
Koufonisi 75 J5
Koukajuak, Great Plain of the 120 M4
Kouki 102 C6
Koumac 114 W16
Koumenzi 86 F3
Koumra 102 C6
Koundara 104 C3
Koungou Mountains 106 B3
Kounradskiy 86 D2
Kourou 137 G2
Kouroussa 104 D3
Kousseri 105 J3
Koutiala 100 D6
Kouvola 63 M6
Kova 84 G5
Kovachevo 73 J4
Kovanlik 77 H2
Kovdor 62 P3
Kovdozero, Ozero 62 Q3
Kovel 71 L3
Kovernino 78 G4
Kovero 62 P5
Kovik Bay 121 L5
Kovno 71 K1
Kovrov 78 G4
Kovylkino 78 G5
Kowalewo 71 H2
Kowloon 87 L7
Koycegiz 76 C4
Koyda 78 G2
Koyuk 118 C3
Koyukuk 118 D3
Koyulhisar 77 G2
Koza 89 E9
Kozakli 76 F3
Kozan 77 F4
Kozani 75 F2
Kozekovo 71 M1
Kozelsk 78 F5
Kozhevnikovo 84 B5
Kozhikode 92 E6
Kozhim 78 K2
Kozhposelok 78 F3
Kozhva 78 K2
Kozlu 76 D2
Kozludere 77 G4
Kozluk 77 J3
Kozmodemyansk 78 H4
Kozu-shima 89 G8
Kpalime 104 F4
Krabi 93 J7
Kragero 63 C7
Kragujevac 73 F3
Krakow 71 H3
Krakowska, Jura 71 H3
Kral Chlmec 71 K4
Kralendijk 133 N8
Kraljevo 72 F4
Kralovvany 71 H4
Kralupy 70 F3
Kramatorsk 79 F6
Kramfors 62 G5
Krania 75 F3
Kranidhion 75 G4
Kranj 72 C2
Kranskop 108 F5
Krasavino 78 H3
Krasino 84 Ab2
Kraskino 88 C4
Krasneno 85 X4
Krasnoarmeyesk 84 Ae6
Krasnoarmeyskiy 85 W3
Krasnoborsk 78 H3
Krasnodar 79 F6
Krasnogorsk 88 J1
Krasnograd 79 F6
Krasnokamsk 78 K4
Krasnokutskoye 84 B6
Krasnolesnyy 79 F5
Krasnorechenskiy 88 E3
Krasnoselkup 84 C3
Krasnoslobodsk 78 G5
Krasnoturinsk 84 Ad5
Krasnoufimsk 78 K4
Krasnousolskiy 78 K5
Krasnovishersk 78 K3
Krasnovodsk 95 L2
Krasnovodskiy Poluostrov 79 J7
Krasnoyarsk 84 E5
Krasnoyarskiy Kray 84 E3
Krasnoye 78 G4
Krasnstaw 71 K3
Krasnyy Chikoy 84 H6
Krasnyye Okny 73 K2
Krasnyy Kholm 79 J5
Krasnyy Kut 79 H5
Krasnyy Luch 79 F6
Krasnyy Yar *Russia* 79 G5
Krasnyy Yar *Russia* 79 H6
Kratie 93 L6
Kraulshavn 120 Q3
Kravanh, Chuor Phnum 93 K6
Krefeld 70 B3
Kremenchug 79 E6
Kremenchugskoye Vodokhranilishche 79 E6
Kremnets 79 D5
Krems 68 E1
Krenitzin Islands 118 Ae9
Kresevo 72 E4
Kresttsy 78 E4
Kresty 84 D2
Krestyakh 85 K4
Krestyanka 84 C2
Kretinga 63 J9
Kribi 105 G5
Krichev 79 E5
Krichim 73 H4
Krieza 75 H3
Krifovon 75 F3
Krilon, Mys 88 J3
Krios, Akra 75 G5
Krishna 92 E5
Krishnagiri 92 E6
Krishnanagar 93 G4
Kristdala 63 G8
Kristel 67 F5
Kristiansand 63 B7
Kristianstad *Sweden* 63 E8
Kristianstad *Sweden* 63 F8
Kristiansund 62 B5
Kristiinankaupunki 63 J5
Kristinestad 63 J5
Kristinovka 73 K1
Kriti 75 H5
Kritikon Pelagos 75 H5
Kriulyany 73 K2
Kriva Palanka 73 G4
Krivoye Ozero 73 L2
Krivoy Rog 79 E6
Krk 72 C3
Krnov 71 G3
Krokodil 108 E4
Krokom 62 F5
Krokong 90 E5
Krokowa 71 H1
Krolevets 79 E5
Kromy 79 F5
Kronach 70 D3
Krononberg 63 F8
Kronshtadt 63 N7
Kroonstad 108 E5
Kropotkin 79 G6
Krosno 71 J4
Krotoszyn 71 G3
Krsko 72 C3
Krugersdorp 108 E5
Krui 90 C7
Kruje 74 E2
Krumbach 70 D4
Krumovgrad 73 H5
Krung Thep 93 K6
Krusenstern, Cape 118 C2
Krusevac 73 F4
Krusevo 73 F5
Krustpils 63 M8
Kruzenshterna, Proliv 85 S7
Kruzof Island 118 H4
Krym 79 E6
Krymsk 79 F7
Krynki 71 K2
Kryry 70 E3
Krzeszowice 71 H3
Ksabi 100 E3
Ksar El Boukhari 101 F1
Ksarel Kebir 100 D2
Ksar es Souk 100 E2
Ksenofontova 78 K3
Ksour Essaf 101 H1
Kstovo 78 G4
Kualakapuas 90 E6
Kuala Kerai 90 C4
Kuala Lipis 90 C5
Kuala Lumpur 90 C5
Kualapembuang 90 E6
Kuala Penyu 90 F4
Kuala Terengganu 90 C4
Kuandian 87 N3
Kuantan 90 C5
Kuba 89 D8
Kuban 79 G6
Kubenskoye Ozero 78 F4
Kubkain 114 C2
Kubokawa 89 D9
Kubonitu, Mount 114 J6
Kubor, Mount 114 C3
Kubrat 73 J4
Kubuang 90 F5
Kucevo 73 F3
Kuching 90 E5
Kuchinoerabu-jima 89 C10
Kuchinotsu 89 C9
Kuchurgan 73 K2
Kucuk 76 B3
Kucukcekmece 76 C2
Kucuk Kuyu 76 B3
Kudat 90 F4
Kudirkos-Naumiestis 71 K1
Kudus 90 E7
Kudymkar 78 J4
Kufi 76 C3
Kufstein 68 D2
Kugaly 86 D3
Kugi 84 Ad4
Kugmallit Bay 118 J2
Kuhdasht 94 H5
Kuh-e Bul 95 L6
Kuh-e Garbosh 95 K5
Kuh Lab, Ra's 95 Q9
Kuhmo 62 N4
Kuhpayeh *Iran* 95 L5
Kuhpayeh *Iran* 95 N6
Kuhran, Kuh-e 95 P8
Kuh, Ra's-al- 95 N9
Kuito 106 C5
Kuji 88 H5
Kuju-san 89 C9
Kukalar, Kuh-e 95 K6
Kukes 75 F1
Kukhomskaya Volya 71 L3
Kukmor 78 J4
Kukpowruk 118 C2
Kukudu 114 H6
Kukup 90 C5
Kukushka 85 M6
Kula *Turkey* 76 C3
Kula *Yugoslavia* 72 E3
Kulagino 79 J6
Kulakshi 79 K6
Kulal, Mont 107 G2
Kulata 73 G5
Kuldiga 63 N8
Kule 108 D4
Kulebaki 78 G4
Kulgera 113 G4
Kulikov 71 L4
Kulinda *Russia* 84 G4
Kulinda *Russia* 84 H4
Kulmac Daglari 77 G3
Kulmbach 70 D3
Kuloy *Russia* 78 G3
Kuloy *Russia* 78 G2
Kulp 77 J3
Kulsary 79 J6
Kultay 79 J6
Kultuk 84 G6
Kulu 76 E3
Kulu Island 118 J4
Kulul 96 E9
Kulunda 84 B6
Kulundinskoye, Ozero 84 B6
Kulyab 86 B4
Kuma 79 H7
Kumagaya 89 G7
Kumakh-Surt 85 M2
Kumamoto 89 C9
Kumano 89 F9
Kumanovo 73 F4
Kumara 115 C5
Kumasi 104 E4
Kumba 105 G5
Kumbakonam 92 E6
Kum-Dag 95 M2
Kumertau 79 K5
Kuminki 62 L4
Kuminskiy 84 Ae5
Kumkuduk 86 F3
Kumluca 76 D4
Kummerower See 70 E2
Kumnyong 87 P5
Kumon Bum 93 J3
Kumru 77 G2
Kumsong 87 P4
Kumta 92 D6
Kumyr 86 C3
Kunas 86 E3
Kunas Chang 86 E3
Kunashir, Ostrov 88 L3
Kundelungu Mountains 107 E5
Kunduz 92 C1
Kungalv 63 H8
Kungar 78 K4
Kunghit Island 118 J5
Kungrad 51 U7
Kungsor 63 G7
Kungu 106 C2
Kunlun Shan 92 F1
Kunmadaras 72 F2
Kunming 93 K4
Kunsan 87 P4
Kununurra 112 F2
Kunu-ri 87 P4
Kuolayarvi 62 N3
Kuopio *Sweden* 62 M5
Kuopio *Sweden* 62 M5
Kupa 72 C3
Kupang 91 G7
Kuparuk 118 E2
Kupino 84 B6
Kupreanof Island 118 J4
Kupreanof Point 118 Ag8
Kupyansk 79 F6
Kuqa 86 E3
Kura 77 L2
Kurashasayskiy 79 K5
Kurashiki 89 D8
Kurayoshi 89 D8
Kurday 86 D3
Kurdzhali 73 H5
Kure 89 D8
Kure 76 E2
Kurecik 77 G3
Kure Daglari 76 F2
Kureyka 84 D3
Kurgan 84 Ae5
Kurganinsk 79 G7
Kurgan-Tyube 86 B4
Kurikka 62 N4
Kurilskiye Ostrova 85 S7
Kuril Trench 142 G3
Kurkcu 76 E4
Kurlek 84 C5
Kurmuk 103 F5
Kurnool 92 E5
Kuroi 89 E8
Kuroiso 89 G7
Kurow 71 K3
Kursk 79 F5
Kursumlija 73 F4
Kursunlu 76 E2
Kurtalan 77 J4
Kurtamysh 84 Ad6
Kurtun 77 H2
Kuru 63 K6
Kurucasile 76 E2
Kuruman *South Africa* 108 D5
Kuruman *South Africa* 108 D5
Kurume 89 C9
Kurunegala 92 F7
Kurzeme 63 K8
Kusadasi 76 B4
Kusadasi Korfezi 76 B4
Kusel 70 B4
Kusey Andolu Daglari 77 H2
Kushchevskaya 79 F6
Kushima 89 C10
Kushimoto 89 E9
Kushiro 88 K4
Kushka *Russia* 85 U4
Kushka *Turkmenistan* 95 R4
Kushka *Turkmenistan* 95 R4
Kushmurun 84 Ad6
Kushtia 93 G4
Kushva 78 K4
Kuskokwim 118 C3
Kuskokwim Bay 118 C4
Kuskokwim Mountains 118 D3
Kusma 92 F3
Kussharo-ko 88 K4
Kustanay 84 Ad6
Kustrin 70 F2
Kuta 105 G4
Kutahya 76 C3
Kutaisi 77 K1
Kutchan 88 H4
Kutima 84 H5
Kut, Ko 93 K6
Kutna Hora 70 F4
Kutno 71 H2
Kutu 106 C3
Kutubdia 93 H4
Kutum 102 D5
Kuujjuaq 121 N6
Kuujjuarapik 121 L6
Kuuli-Mayak 79 J7
Kuusamo 62 N4
Kuvango 106 C5
Kuvet 85 X3
Kuwait 94 H7
Kuwait 97 J2
Kuwana 89 F8
Kuya 78 G2
Kuybyshev *Russia* 84 B5
Kuybyshev *Russia* 79 J5
Kuybyshevskoye Vodokhranilishche 78 H4
Kuyeda 78 K4
Kuygan 86 C2
Kuytun 86 F3
Kuyucak 76 C4
Kuyumba 84 F4
Kuyus 84 D6
Kuzino 78 K4
Kuzitrin 118 C2
Kuzmovka 84 E4
Kuznetsk 79 H5
Kuznetsovo 88 G2
Kuzomen 78 F2
Kuzucubelen 76 F4
Kvaloy 62 H2
Kvaloya 62 K1
Kvalsund 62 L1

Name	Page	Grid
Kvarner	72	C3
Kvarneric	72	C3
Kvichak Bay	118	D4
Kvidinge	63	E8
Kvigtind	62	E4
Kvikkjokk	62	G3
Kvina	63	B7
Kvorning	63	C8
Kwa	106	C3
Kwale	105	G4
Kwamouth	106	C3
Kwangju	87	P4
Kwango	106	C3
Kwanso-ri	88	B5
Kwatisore	91	J6
Kwekwe	108	E3
Kwidzyn	71	H2
Kwilu	106	C3
Kwoka	91	J6
Kyabe	102	C6
Kyaikto	93	J5
Kyakhta	84	H6
Kyaukpyu	93	H5
Kyaukse	93	J4
Kybartai	71	K1
Kychema	78	G2
Kyeburn	115	C6
Kyelang	92	E2
Kyle	57	D5
Kyleakin	56	C3
Kyle of Lochalsh	56	C3
Kylestrome	56	C2
Kymi	63	M6
Kymijoki	63	M6
Kynuna	113	J3
Kyoga, Lake	107	F2
Kyongju	89	B8
Kyoto	89	E8
Kyrdanyy	85	M3
Kyritz	70	E2
Kyrkheden	63	E6
Kyronjoki	62	K5
Kyrosjarvi	63	K6
Kyrta	78	K3
Kyssa	78	H3
Kystyk, Plato	85	L2
Kyuekh-Bulung	84	J3
Kyurdamir	79	H7
Kyushu	89	C9
Kyushu-sanchi	89	C9
Kyustendil	73	G4
Kyyjarvi	62	L5
Kyyvesi	63	M6
Kyzyk	79	J7
Kyzyl	84	E6
Kyzyldyykan	86	B2
Kyzylkoga	79	J6
Kyzyl-Kommuna	86	B2
Kyzylkum	80	H5
Kzyl-Dzhar	86	B2
Kzyl-Orda	86	B3
Kzyltu	84	A6

L

Name	Page	Grid
La Almunia de Dona Godina	67	F2
Laascaanood	103	J6
Laas Dhuure	103	J5
La Asuncion	136	E1
Laayoune	100	C3
La Baie	125	Q2
La Banda	138	D5
La Baneza	66	D1
La Barca	130	H7
Labasa	114	R8
La Baule	65	B5
La Baza, Ozero	84	F2
Labbah, Al	96	E2
Labe	104	C3
Labe	70	F3
Labelle	125	N3
Laberge, Lake	118	H3
Labi	90	E5
Labin	72	C3
Labinsk	79	G7
Labis	90	C5
La Bisbal	67	H2
Labouheyre	65	C6
Laboulaye	139	D6
La Bourboule	65	E6
Labrador	121	P7
Labrador City	121	N7
Labrador Sea	121	Q6
Labrea	136	E5
Labrit	65	C6
Labuha	91	H6
Labuhan	90	D7
Labuhanbajo	91	F7
Labuhanbilik	90	C5
Labytnangi	84	Ae3
Lac	74	E2
La Calzada de Calatrava	66	E3
Lacanau	65	C6
La Carlota	139	D6
La Carolina	66	E3
La Cava	67	G2
Laccadive Islands	92	D6
Laccadive Sea	92	E7
La Ceiba	132	D7
Lacepede Bay	113	H6
La Chaise-Dieu	65	E6
Lacha, Ozero	78	F3
La Charite	65	E5

Name	Page	Grid
La Chartre-sur-le-Loir	65	D5
La Chatre	65	D5
La Chaux-de-Fonds	68	A2
Lachin	94	H2
Lachlan	113	K5
La Chorrera	132	H10
Lachute	125	N4
La Cieneguita	126	G6
La Ciotat	65	F7
Lac la Biche	119	N5
Lac Megantic	125	Q4
La Colorada	126	G6
Laconi	69	B6
Laconia	125	Q5
La Coruna	66	B1
La Croix, Lac	124	D2
La Crosse	124	E5
La Cruz Costa Rica	132	E9
La Cruz Mexico	130	F6
Lacul Razelm	73	K3
Ladakh Range	92	E2
Ladder Hills	56	E3
La Desirade	133	S6
Ladik	77	F2
Ladismith	108	D6
Ladiz	95	Q7
Ladozhskoye Ozero	63	P6
Ladybank	57	E4
Ladybower Reservoir	55	H3
Ladybrand	108	E5
Ladysmith Canada	122	C3
Ladysmith South Africa	108	E5
Ladysmith U.S.A.	124	E4
Ladyzhenka	84	Ae6
Ladyzhinka	79	D6
Lae	93	K5
Laem Ngop	93	K6
La Esmeralda Paraguay	138	D4
La Esmeralda Venezuela	136	D3
La Fayette	129	K3
Lafayette Colorado, U.S.A.	123	M8
Lafayette Indiana, U.S.A.	124	G6
Lafayette Louisiana, U.S.A.	128	F5
La Fe	132	E3
La Ferte-Bernard	64	D4
La-Ferte-Saint-Aubin	65	D5
Laffan, Ra's	97	K4
Lafia	105	G4
Lafiagi	105	G4
La Fleche	65	C5
La Follette	129	K2
La Fria	136	C2
Laft	95	M8
La Fuente de San Esteban	66	C2
La Galite	69	B7
Lagan	63	E8
Lagarfljot	62	X12
Lagen Norway	63	C6
Lagen Norway	63	D6
Laggan	57	D3
Laggan Bay	57	B5
Laggan, Loch	57	D4
Laghouat	101	F2
Lagny	64	E4
Lagonegro	69	E5
Lago Posadas	139	B9
Lagos Nigeria	105	F4
Lagos Portugal	66	B4
Lagos de Moreno	130	J7
La Grande Canada	121	M7
La Grande U.S.A.	122	E5
La Grande 2, Reservoir	121	L7
La Grande 3, Reservoir	121	L7
La Grande 4, Reservoir	121	M7
La Grange Georgia, U.S.A.	129	K4
La Grange Kentucky, U.S.A.	124	H7
La Grange Texas, U.S.A.	128	D6
La Granja	66	D2
La Gran Sabana	136	E2
La Guardia	66	B2
Laguardia	66	E1
La Gudina	66	C1
La Guerche-de-Bretagne	65	C5
Laguna	138	G5
Laguna Grande	139	C9
Lagunillas Bolivia	138	D3
Lagunillas Venezuela	133	M9
Laha	87	N2
La Habana	132	F3
Lahad Datu	91	F4
Lahave	121	P9
Lahij	96	G10
Lahijan	95	J3
Lahn W. Germany	70	C3
Lahn W. Germany	70	C3
Lahore	92	D2
Lahr	70	B4
Lahti	63	L6
Laibach	72	C2
Laibin	93	L4
Lai Chau	93	K4
L'Aigle	64	D4
Laihia	62	J5
Laimbele, Mount	114	T12
Laina	75	J2
Laingsburg	108	D6
Lainioalven	62	K3
Lair	56	C3
Lairg	56	D2
Lais	90	C6
Laitila	63	J6
Laiwui	91	H6
Laixi	87	N4
Laiyang	87	N4

Name	Page	Grid
Laiyuan	87	L4
Laizhou Wan	87	M4
Lajes	138	F5
La Junta	127	L2
Lakatrask	62	J3
Lake Andes	123	Q6
Lakeba	114	S9
Lakeba Passage	114	S9
Lake Cargelligo	113	K5
Lake Charles	128	F5
Lake City Florida, U.S.A.	129	L5
Lake City S. Carolina, U.S.A.	129	N4
Lake District	55	F2
Lake Grace	112	D5
Lake Harbour	120	N5
Lake Havasu City	126	D3
Lake Jackson	128	E6
Lake King	112	D5
Lake Kopiago	114	C3
Lakeland	129	M6
Lake Louise	122	F2
Lake Murray	114	C3
Lakeport	122	C8
Lake Providence	128	G4
Lakeview	122	D6
Lake Wales	129	M7
Lakewood	124	K6
Lakhdaria	67	H4
Lakhpat	92	C4
Lakki	92	D2
Lakonikos Kolpos	75	G4
Laksefjorden	62	M1
Lakselv	62	L1
Lakshadweep	92	D6
Lakuramau	114	E2
Lala Musa	92	D2
Lalaua	109	G2
Laleh Zar, Kuh-e	95	N7
Lalibela	103	G5
La Libertad	132	B6
La Ligua	139	B6
Lalin	66	B1
Lalin	87	P2
Lalin He	88	A3
Lalitpur	92	E4
Lalla Khedidja	67	J4
La Loche	119	P4
La Loupe	64	D4
La Louviere	64	F3
La Luz	132	E8
Lalyo	102	F7
Lamag	91	F4
La Mancha	66	E3
La Manza	136	D6
Lama, Ozero	84	D3
Lamar Colorado, U.S.A.	127	L1
Lamar Missouri, U.S.A.	124	C8
Lamas	136	B5
Lamastre	65	F6
Lambas	114	R8
Lambay Island	59	K6
Lamberhurst	53	H3
Lambert, Cape	114	E2
Lambert Glacier	141	E4
Lamberts Bay	108	C6
Lamb Head	56	F1
Lambia	75	F4
Lambon	114	E2
Lambourn	53	F3
Lamb's Head	59	B9
Lambton, Cape	118	L1
Lame	102	B6
Lamego	66	C2
Lamenu	114	U12
Lameroo	113	J6
Lamia	75	G3
Lammermuir	57	F5
Lammermuir Hills	57	F5
Lammhult	63	F8
Lammi	63	L6
Lamon Bay	91	G3
Lamont California, U.S.A.	126	C3
Lamont Wyoming, U.S.A.	123	L6
La Morita	127	K6
La Moure	123	Q4
Lam Pao Reservoir	93	K5
Lampasas	128	C5
Lampazos de Naranjo	128	B7
Lampedusa	74	B5
Lampeter	52	C2
Lampinou	75	G3
Lampione	74	B5
Lamport	53	G2
Lampsa	62	P4
Lamu	107	H3
Lan	71	M2
Lanai	126	S10
Lanai City	126	S10
Lanark	57	D5
Lanark	55	G3
Lanbi Kyun	93	J6
Lancang	93	K4
Lancashire	55	G3
Lancaster U.K.	55	G2
Lancaster Ohio, U.S.A.	124	J7
Lancaster Pennsylvania, U.S.A.	125	M6
Lancaster S. Carolina, U.S.A.	129	M3
Lancaster Sound	120	J3
Lanciano	69	E4
Lancut	71	K3
Landau	70	C4

Name	Page	Grid
Landeck	68	C2
Lander	123	K6
Landerneau	64	A4
Landes	65	C6
Landi	95	R6
Landor	112	D4
Landrum	129	L3
Landsberg Poland	70	F2
Landsberg Germany	70	D4
Landsborough	113	J3
Land's End	52	B4
Lands End	120	B2
Landshut	70	E4
Landskrona	63	E9
Lanesborough	58	G5
Lanett	129	K4
Langa Co	92	F3
Langadhia	75	F4
Langavat, Loch	56	B2
Langdon	123	Q3
Lange Berg	108	C6
Langebergen	108	D5
Langeland	63	D9
Langelmavesi	63	L6
Langeoog	70	B2
Langesund	63	C7
Langevag	62	B5
Langfang	87	M4
Langfjord	62	B5
Lang Head	56	A1
Langhirano	68	C3
Langholm	57	E5
Langjokull	62	U12
Langkawi	93	J7
Langnau	68	A2
Langness Point	54	E2
Langogne	65	E6
Langon	65	C6
Langoya	62	F2
Langport	52	E3
Langres	65	F5
Langsa	90	B5
Langsele	62	G5
Langsett	55	H3
Lang Son	93	L4
Langtoft	55	J2
Langtrask	62	J4
Languedoc	65	E7
Langwathby	55	G2
Langzhong	93	L2
Lannemezan	65	D7
Lannion	64	B4
Lansing	124	H5
Lansjarv	62	K3
Lanslebourg	65	G6
Lanta, Ko	93	J7
Lanusei	69	B6
Lanvaux, Landes de	65	B5
Lanxi	87	P2
Lanzarote	100	C3
Lanzhou	93	K1
Laoag	91	G2
Laoang	91	H3
Lao Cai	93	K4
Laois	59	H7
Laon	64	E4
La Oroya	136	B6
Laos	90	C2
Laoye Ling	88	B3
Laoyemiao	86	F3
Lapa	138	G5
Lapalisse	65	E5
La Palma Panama	132	H10
La Palma Spain	100	B3
La Palma del Condado	66	C4
La Paragua	136	E2
La Paz Argentina	139	C6
La Paz Argentina	138	E6
La Paz Bolivia	138	C3
La Paz Mexico	130	D5
La Pedrera	136	D4
La Piedad	130	H7
La Place	128	G5
La Plant	123	P5
La Plata	139	E6
La Pocatiere	125	R3
La Pola de Gordon	66	D1
La Porte	124	G6
Lapovo	73	F3
Lappajarvi	62	K5
Lappeenranta	63	N6
Lappi	62	M3
Lapseki	76	B2
Laptev Sea	85	M1
Laptevykh, More	85	M1
Lapua	62	K5
La Puebla	67	H3
La Puntilla	136	A4
La Quiaca	138	C4
L'Aquila	69	D4
Lar	95	M8
Larache	100	D1
Larak	95	N8
La Rambla	66	D4
Laramie	123	M7
Laramie Mountains	123	M6
Laranjal	137	F4
Larantuka	91	G7
Larat Indonesia	114	A3
Larat Indonesia	114	A3
Larba	67	H4
Laredo Spain	66	E1
Laredo U.S.A.	128	C7
La Reole	65	C6

Name	Page	Grid
Largo *U.S.A.*	129	L7
Largo *Venezuela*	133	R10
Largoward	57	F4
Largs	57	D5
Lari	94	H2
Larino	69	E5
La Rioja	138	C5
Larisa	75	G3
Lark	53	H2
Larkana	92	C3
Larkhall	57	F4
Larlomkiny	84	A5
Larne	58	L3
La Robla	66	D1
La Roche	114	Y16
La Roche-Bernard	65	B5
La Rochelle	65	C5
La Roche-sur-Yon	65	C5
La Roda	67	E3
La Romana	133	N5
La Ronge	119	P4
Larrey Point	112	D2
Larsen Ice Shelf	141	V5
Larvik	63	D7
La Salle	124	F6
Las Animas	127	L1
Las Aves, Isla	136	D1
Las Coloradas	139	B7
Las Cruces	127	J4
La Selle	133	M5
La Serena	138	B5
La Seu d'Urgell	67	G1
Las Flores	139	E7
Lasham	53	F3
Lash-e Joveyn	95	Q6
Lashkar	92	E3
Lashkar Gah	92	B2
Las Horquetas	139	B9
La Sila	69	F6
Lasjerd	95	L4
Las Lomitas	138	D4
Las Marismas	66	C4
Las Mercedes	133	P10
Laso	63	D8
La Souterraine	65	D5
Las Palmas	100	B3
La Spezia	68	B3
Las Plumas	139	C8
Lassen Peak	122	D7
Last Mountain Lake	123	M2
Lastoursville	106	B3
Lastovo	72	D4
Las Trincheras	133	Q11
L'Astrolabe, Recifs de	114	W15
Lasva	72	D3
Las Varillas	138	D6
Las Vegas *Nevada, U.S.A.*	126	E2
Las Vegas *New Mexico, U.S.A.*	127	K3
Latacunga	136	B4
Latady Island	141	U4
Latakia	77	F5
Late	111	U5
Latefoss	63	B7
Latgale	63	M8
Latheron	56	E2
La Tina	136	B4
Latina	69	D5
Latoritsa	71	K4
La Tour-du-Pin	65	F6
Latrobe	113	K7
La Tuque	125	P3
Latur	92	E5
Latvia	63	K8
Lau *Sudan*	102	F6
Lau *Sudan*	102	F6
Laucola	114	S8
Lauder	57	F4
Lauderdale	57	F5
Lauenberg	70	D2
Laughlan Islands	114	E3
Lau Group	114	S8
Launceston *Australia*	113	K7
Launceston *U.K.*	52	C4
Launglon Bok Islands	93	J6
La Union *Bolivia*	138	D3
La Union *Chile*	139	B8
La Union *Colombia*	136	B3
La Union *El Salvador*	132	D8
La Union *Mexico*	131	Q9
La Union *Spain*	67	F4
Laupheim	70	C4
Laura	113	J2
La Urbana	133	P11
Laurel *Mississippi, U.S.A.*	128	H5
Laurel *Montana, U.S.A.*	123	K5
Laurencekirk	57	F4
Laurentian Scarp	125	M3
Laurentien, Plateau	121	M7
Laurenzana	69	E5
Lauria	69	E5
Laurinburg	129	N3
Lausanne	68	A2
Laut	90	F6
Lautaro	139	B7
Laut Kecil, Kepulauan	90	F6
Lautoka	114	Q8
Laval *Canada*	125	P4
Laval *France*	65	C4
Lavan	95	L8
Lavapie, Punta	139	B7
La Vecilla	66	D1
La Vega	133	M5
La Venturosa	136	D2
Lavernock Point	52	D3
Laverton	112	E4
Lavina	123	K4
Lavon, Lake	128	D4
Lavras	138	H4
Lawas	90	F5
Lawdar	96	G10
Lawksawk	93	J4
Lawqah	96	F2
Lawra	104	E3
Lawrence *New Zealand*	115	B6
Lawrence *Kansas, U.S.A.*	124	C7
Lawrence *Massachusetts, U.S.A.*	125	Q5
Lawrenceburg	129	J3
Lawrenceville	124	G7
Lawton	128	C3
Lawu, Gunung	90	E7
Lawz, Jambal Al	96	B2
Laxay	56	B2
Laxford, Loch	56	C2
Laxo	56	A1
Lay	65	C5
Layar, Tanjung	90	F6
Layla	96	H5
Laysar	94	J3
Lazarevac	72	F3
Lazarev Sea	141	A5
Lazaro Cardenas	130	H8
Lazaro Cardenas, Presa	127	K8
Lazdijai	71	K1
Lazo	88	D4
Lead	123	N5
Leadburn	57	E5
Leaden Roding	53	H3
Leader	123	K2
Leader Water	57	F5
Leaf	121	M6
Leaf Bay	121	N6
Leane, Lough	59	C8
Leatherhead	53	G3
Leavenworth *Kansas, U.S.A.*	124	C7
Leavenworth *Washington, U.S.A.*	122	D4
Leba	71	G1
Lebak	91	G4
Lebane	73	F4
Lebanon	94	B4
Lebanon *Missouri, U.S.A.*	125	P5
Lebanon *Pennsylvania, U.S.A.*	129	J2
Lebanon *Tennessee, U.S.A.*	124	D8
Lebanon *Vermont, U.S.A.*	125	M6
Lebed	84	D4
Lebedin	79	E5
Lebesby	62	M1
Le Blanc	65	D5
Lebombo Mountains	109	F4
Lebork	71	G1
Lebrija	66	C4
Lebsko, Jezioro	71	G1
Lebu	139	B7
Lebyazhye	84	B6
Le Cateau	64	E3
Lecce	69	G5
Lecco	68	B3
Lech *Austria*	68	C2
Lech *Germany*	70	D4
Lechang	93	M3
Lechlade	53	F3
Lechtaler Alpen	68	C2
Leconfield	55	J3
Le Conquet	64	A4
Le Creusot	65	F5
Le Croisic	65	B5
Lectoure	65	D7
Lecumberri	67	F1
Leczna	71	K3
Leczyca	71	H2
Ledbury	52	E2
Ledesma	66	D2
Lediba	106	C3
Ledmozero	62	Q4
Ledong	93	L5
Le Dorat	65	D5
Ledu	93	K1
Ledyanaya, Gora	85	W4
Lee	59	E9
Leech Lake	124	C3
Leeds	55	H3
Leedstown	52	B4
Leek	55	G3
Leemoore	126	C2
Leer	70	B2
Leesburg	129	M6
Leesville	128	F5
Leeuwarden	64	F2
Leeuwin, Cape	112	D5
Leeward Islands	133	R5
Le Faouet	65	B4
Lefroy, Lake	112	E5
Leganes	66	E2
Legaspi	91	G3
Legbourne	55	K3
Leghorn	68	C4
Legnago	68	C3
Legnica	71	G3
Leh	92	E2
Le Havre	64	D4
Leiah	92	D2
Leibnitz	68	E2
Leibo	93	K3
Leicester	53	F2
Leicestershire	53	F2
Leichhardt	113	H2
Leiden	64	F2
Leie	64	E3
Leigh *New Zealand*	115	E2
Leigh *U.K.*	55	G3
Leigh Creek	113	H5
Leighlinbridge	59	J7
Leighton Buzzard	53	G3
Leine	70	C3
Leinster	59	H6
Leinster, Mount	59	J7
Leipzig	70	E3
Leiria	66	B3
Leirvik	63	A7
Leisier, Mount	112	F3
Leiston	53	J2
Leitha	68	F2
Leitrim	58	F4
Leixlip	59	K6
Leiyang	93	M3
Lek	64	F3
Leksand	63	F6
Lekshmozero	78	F3
Leksozero, Ozero	62	P5
Leksvik	62	D5
Lelai, Tanjung	91	H5
Leland	62	E3
Le Lavandou	65	G7
Le Luc	65	G7
Leluova	114	M7
Lelysted	64	F2
Leman, Lac	68	A2
Le Mans	65	D4
Le Mars	124	B5
Lemberg	71	L4
Lemgo	70	C2
Lemmer	64	F2
Lemmon	123	N5
Lemnos	75	H3
Le Mont-Dore	65	E6
Lempa	132	C8
Lemreway	56	C2
Le Murge	69	F5
Lena	85	M2
Lenakel	114	U13
Lene, Lough	58	H5
Lengerich	70	B2
Lengshuijiang	93	M3
Lengua de Vaca, Punta	139	B6
Lenhovda	63	F8
Leninabad	86	B3
Leninakan	77	K2
Lenina, Pik	86	C4
Leningrad	63	N7
Leningradskaya	141	L5
Leninogorsk	78	J5
Leninskiy *Kazakhstan*	78	H4
Leninskiy *Russia*	86	E2
Leninsk-Kuznetskiy	84	D6
Leninskoye *Russia*	88	D2
Leninskoye *Russia*	78	H4
Lenkoran	94	J2
Lennox, Isla	139	C11
Lenoir	129	M3
Lens	64	E3
Lensk	85	J4
Lenti	72	D2
Lentini	69	E7
Lentura	62	N4
Leo	104	E3
Leoben	68	E2
Leominster	52	E2
Leon	130	J7
Leon	127	N5
Leon *Mexico*	132	D8
Leon *Nicaragua*	66	D1
Leon *Spain*	65	C7
Leonard Darwin, Gunung	91	K6
Leonforte	69	E7
Leonidhion	75	G4
Leon, Montanas de	66	C1
Leopoldina	138	H4
Leopoldo Bulhoes	138	G3
Leopoldville	106	C3
Leovo	73	K2
Le Palais	65	B5
Lepaya	63	L8
Lepel	63	N9
Lephepe	108	E4
Leping	87	M6
Lepini, Monti	69	D5
Lepontine, Alpi	68	B2
Lepsy	86	D2
Le Puy	65	E6
Lercara Friddi	69	D7
Lere	102	B6
L'Eree	53	M7
Lereh, Tanjung	91	F6
Lerida	67	G2
Lerma	66	E1
Lermontovka	88	E2
Leros	75	J4
Lerum	63	E8
Lerwick	56	A2
Les	73	F2
Les Andelys	64	D4
Lesbos	75	J3
Les Cayes	133	L5
Les Ecrins	65	G6
Les Escoumins	125	R2
Leshan	93	K3
Leshukonskoye	78	H3
Lesjofors	63	F7
Leskovac	73	F4
Lesnica	72	E3
Lesogorsk	85	Q7
Lesopilnoye	88	E2
Lesosibirsk	84	E5
Lesotho	108	E5
Lesozavodsk	88	D3
Lesparre-Medoc	65	C6
Les Sables-d'Olonne	65	C5
Lesser Antarctica	141	T3
Lesser Antilles	133	Q6
Lesser Slave Lake	119	M4
Lesser Zab	94	F4
L'Estartit	67	H1
Lestijarvi	62	L5
Lesvos	75	J3
L'Etacq	53	M7
Letchworth	53	G3
Lethbridge	122	H3
Leticia	136	D4
Leti, Kepulauan	91	H7
Le Touquet-Paris-Plage	64	D3
Le Treport	64	D3
Letsok-aw Kyun	93	J6
Letterfrack	59	C5
Letterkenny	58	G3
Lettermore	59	C6
Leuchars	57	F4
Leuser, Gunung	90	B5
Leuven	64	F3
Levadhia	75	G3
Levan	74	E2
Levanger	62	D5
Levdym	84	Ae4
Leven	57	F4
Leven, Loch *Highland, U.K.*	57	C4
Leven, Loch *Tayside, U.K.*	57	E4
Leveque, Cape	112	E2
Leverburgh	56	A3
Le Verdon-sur-Mer	65	C6
Leverkusen	70	B3
Levice	71	H4
Le Vigan	65	E7
Levin	115	E4
Levis	125	Q3
Levittown	125	N6
Levka Ori	75	G5
Levkas *Greece*	75	F3
Levkas *Greece*	75	F3
Levkimmi	74	F3
Levkosia	76	E5
Levoca	71	J4
Levozero	78	F2
Lev Tolstoy	79	F5
Levuka	114	R8
Lewannick	52	C4
Lewes	53	H4
Lewis	56	B2
Lewis, Butt of	56	B2
Lewisporte	121	Q8
Lewis Range	122	H3
Lewis Smith Lake	129	J2
Lewiston *U.K.*	56	D3
Lewiston *Maine, U.S.A.*	125	Q4
Lewiston *Montana, U.S.A.*	122	F4
Lewistown	123	K4
Lewisville, Lake	128	D4
Lexington *Kentucky, U.S.A.*	124	E7
Lexington *N. Carolina, U.S.A.*	129	M3
Lexington *Nebraska, U.S.A.*	123	Q7
Lexington *Virginia, U.S.A.*	125	L8
Lexington Park	125	M7
Leyburn	55	H2
Leye	93	L4
Leyland	55	G3
Leysdown-on-Sea	53	H3
Leyson Point	120	K5
Leyte	91	G3
Leyte Gulf	91	H3
Lezha	78	G4
Lezhe	74	E2
Lezno	71	G3
Lgov	79	F5
Lhasa	93	H3
Lhaze	93	G3
Lhokseumawe	90	B4
Liancheng	87	M6
Liangbingtai	88	B4
Liangdang	93	L2
Liangpran, Bukit	90	E5
Liangzhen	87	K4
Lianjiang	93	M4
Lianjiangkou	88	C2
Lian Xian	93	M3
Lianyungang	87	M5
Lianzhushan	88	C3
Liaodun	86	F3
Liao He	87	N3
Liaoning	87	N3
Liaoyang	87	N3
Liaoyuan	87	P3
Liapadhes	74	E3
Liard	119	L3
Liban, Jazair	94	A4
Liban, Jebel	77	F6
Libano	136	B3
Libby	122	G3
Libenge	106	C2
Liberal	127	M2
Liberdale	136	C5
Liberec	70	F3
Liberia	104	D4
Liberia *Costa Rica*	132	E9
Liberty *New York, U.S.A.*	125	N6
Liberty *Texas, U.S.A.*	128	E5
Libobo, Tanjung	91	H6

Name	Page	Ref
Libourne	65	C6
Librazhd	75	F2
Libreville	106	A2
Librilla	67	F4
Libya	101	J3
Libyan Desert	102	E3
Libyan Plateau	102	E1
Licata	69	D7
Lice	77	J3
Lichfield	53	F2
Lichinga	109	G2
Lichtenburg	108	E5
Lichtenfels	70	D3
Lichuan	87	M6
Licking	124	J7
Licosa, Punta	69	E5
Lida	71	L2
Lidao	87	N4
Liddel Water	57	F5
Liddesdale	57	F5
Liden	62	G5
Lidingo	63	H7
Lidkoping	63	E7
Lidzbark Warminski	71	J1
Liebling	73	F3
Liechtenstein	70	C5
Liege	64	F3
Liegnitz	71	G3
Lielope	63	L8
Lienz	68	D2
Liepaja	63	L8
Lier	64	F3
Liestal	68	A2
Liezen	68	E2
Liffey	59	J6
Lifford	58	H3
Lifi Mahuida	139	C8
Lifou	114	X16
Ligger Bay	52	B4
Lighthouse Reef	132	D6
Ligonha	109	G3
Ligui	126	G8
Ligure, Appennino	68	B3
Ligurian Sea	68	B4
Lihir Group	114	E2
Lihou Reefs	113	L2
Lihue	126	R10
Lihula	63	K7
Lijiang	93	K3
Likasi	106	E5
Likhoslavl	78	F4
Liku	90	D5
Likupang	91	H5
L'Ile-Rousse	69	B4
Lille	64	E3
Lille Balt	63	C8
Lillebonne	64	D4
Lillehammer	63	D6
Lillesand	63	C7
Lillestrom	63	H7
Lillhamra	63	F6
Lillhardal	63	F6
Lillholmsjon	62	F5
Lillo	66	E3
Lillviken	62	G3
Lilongwe	107	F5
Liloy	91	G4
Lima Paraguay	138	E4
Lima Peru	136	B6
Lima Portugal	66	B2
Lima Montana, U.S.A.	122	H5
Lima Ohio, U.S.A.	124	H6
Limah	97	N4
Limankoy	76	C2
Limavady	58	J2
Limay	139	C7
Limbang	90	E5
Limbani	136	D6
Limbe Cameroon	105	G5
Limbe Malawi	107	G6
Limburg	70	C3
Limeira	138	G4
Limenaria	75	H2
Limen Vatheos	75	J4
Limerick Ireland	59	E8
Limerick Ireland	59	E7
Limfjorden	63	C8
Limin	75	H2
Limmen Bight	113	H1
Limni	75	G3
Limnos	75	H3
Limoeiro Ceara, Brazil	137	K5
Limoeiro Pernambuco, Brazil	137	K5
Limoges	65	D6
Limon	132	F9
Limon	123	N8
Limousin	65	D6
Limoux	65	E7
Limpopo	109	F4
Linaalv	62	J3
Linah	96	F2
Linapacan Strait	91	F3
Linares Chile	139	B7
Linares Mexico	128	C8
Linares Spain	66	E3
Lincang	93	K4
Lincoln New Zealand	115	D5
Lincoln U.K.	55	J3
Lincoln Illinois, U.S.A.	124	F6
Lincoln Maine, U.S.A.	125	R4
Lincoln Nebraska, U.S.A.	123	R7
Lincoln City	122	B5
Lincoln Sea	140	R2
Lincolnshire	55	J3
Lincolnton	129	M3
Lindau	70	C5
Linde	85	L3
Linden Guyana	136	F2
Linden U.S.A.	129	J3
Linderodsasen	63	E9
Lindesberg	63	F7
Lindi	107	G4
Lindley	108	E5
Lindos	75	K4
Lindsay Canada	125	L4
Lindsay California, U.S.A.	126	C2
Lindsay Montana, U.S.A.	123	M4
Lindu Point	114	S8
Linfen	93	M1
Lingao	93	L5
Lingayen	91	G2
Lingen	70	B2
Lingfield	53	G3
Lingga	90	C6
Lingga, Kepulauan	90	C6
Lingle	123	M6
Lingling	93	M3
Lingshi	87	L4
Lingshui	93	M5
Lingsugur	92	E5
Linguere	104	B2
Ling Xian	93	M3
Lingyuan	87	M3
Lingyun	93	L4
Linhai	87	N6
Linhares	138	H3
Linhe	87	K3
Linh, Ngoc	93	L5
Linkoping	63	F7
Linkou	88	C3
Linlithgow	57	E5
Linnhe, Loch	57	C4
Linosa	74	B5
Linru	93	M2
Lins	138	G4
Linsell	63	E5
Linslade	53	G3
Lintao	93	K1
Linton U.K.	53	H2
Linton U.S.A.	123	P4
Linwu	93	M3
Linxi	87	M3
Linxia	93	K1
Linyi China	87	M4
Linyi China	87	M4
Linz Austria	68	E1
Linz Germany	70	B3
Linze	86	J4
Lion, Golfe du	65	F7
Liouesso	106	C2
Lipa Philippines	91	G3
Lipa Yugoslavia	72	D3
Lipari, Isola	69	E6
Lipari, Isole	69	E6
Lipenska nadrz	70	F4
Lipetsk	79	F5
Lipiany	70	F2
Lipin Bor	78	F3
Liping	93	L3
Lipkany	79	D6
Lipljan	73	F4
Lipnishki	71	L2
Lipno	71	H2
Lippe	70	C3
Lipsoi	75	J4
Lipson	75	F3
Lipu	93	M4
Lipusz	71	G1
Lira	107	F2
Lircay	136	C6
Liri	69	D5
Lisabata	91	H6
Lisala	106	D2
Lisboa	66	B3
Lisbon Portugal	66	B3
Lisbon U.S.A.	123	R4
Lisburn	58	K3
Lisburne, Cape	118	B2
Liscannor Bay	59	D7
Lisdoonvarna	59	D6
Lishi	87	L4
Lishui	87	M6
Lisichansk	79	F6
Lisieux	64	D4
Liskeard	52	C4
L'Isle-Jourdain	65	D7
Lismore Australia	113	L4
Lismore Ireland	59	G8
Lismore U.K.	57	C4
Liss	53	G3
Listowel	59	D8
Lit	62	F5
Litang	93	K3
Litani	137	G3
Litchfield	124	F7
Litherland	55	G3
Lithgow	113	L5
Lithinon, Akra	75	H5
Litos	66	C2
Lithuania	63	K9
Litovko	85	P7
Little	128	E4
Little Abaco	132	J1
Little Aden	96	G10
Little Andaman	93	H6
Little Bahama Bank	132	H1
Little Barrier Island	115	E2
Little Belt Mountains	122	J4
Littleborough	55	G3
Little Bow	122	H2
Little Cayman	132	G5
Little Colorado	126	G3
Little Falls Minnesota, U.S.A.	124	C3
Little Falls New York, U.S.A.	125	N5
Littlefield	127	L4
Littlehampton	53	G4
Little Inagua Island	133	L4
Little Karoo	108	D6
Little Minch, The	56	B3
Little Missouri	123	M5
Little Nicobar	93	H7
Little Ouse	53	H2
Little Pamir	92	D1
Littleport	53	H2
Little Red	128	G3
Little Rock	128	F3
Little Rocky Mountains	123	K3
Little Scarcies	104	C4
Little Sitkin Island	118	Ab9
Little Smoky	119	M5
Little Snake	123	K7
Little South-west Miramichi	125	S3
Little Strickland	55	G2
Littleton Colorado, U.S.A.	123	M8
Littleton New Hampshire, U.S.A.	125	Q4
Little Wabash	124	F7
Little Waltham	53	H3
Liulin	87	L4
Liupan Shan	93	L1
Liuyang	93	M3
Liuzhou	93	L4
Livani	63	M8
Live Oak	129	L5
Livermore	126	B2
Livermore, Mount	127	K5
Liverpool Australia	113	L5
Liverpool U.K.	55	G3
Liverpool Bay Canada	118	K1
Liverpool Bay U.K.	55	F3
Livingston Canada	121	N7
Livingston U.K.	57	E5
Livingston Montana, U.S.A.	123	J5
Livingston Texas, U.S.A.	128	E5
Livingstone	106	E6
Livingstone, Chutes de	106	B4
Livingstone Falls	106	B4
Livingstone Mountains	107	F4
Livingston Island	141	V6
Livingston, Lake	128	E5
Livno	72	D4
Livny	79	F5
Livojoki	62	M4
Livonia	124	J5
Livorno	68	C4
Liwiec	71	J2
Liwonde	107	G6
Li Xian	93	M3
Liyang	87	M5
Lizard	52	B4
Lizardo	137	H5
Lizard Point	52	B4
Ljosavatn	62	W12
Ljubinje	72	E4
Ljubisnja	72	E4
Ljubljana	72	C2
Ljungan	62	G5
Ljungby	63	E8
Ljusdal	63	G6
Ljusnan	63	F5
Llanarmon Dyffryn Ceiriog	52	D2
Llanbadarn Fynydd	52	D2
Llanbedr	52	C2
Llanberis	54	E3
Llanbrynmair	52	D2
Llandeilo	52	D3
Llandovery	52	D3
Llandrindod Wells	52	D2
Llandudno	54	F3
Llanelli	52	C3
Llanerchymedd	54	E3
Llanes	66	D1
Llanfaethlu	54	E3
Llanfair Caereinion	52	D2
Llanfairfechan	54	F3
Llanfair Talhaiarn	55	F3
Llanfyllin	52	D2
Llangefni	55	E3
Llanglydwen	52	C3
Llangollen	52	D2
Llangranog	52	C2
Llangurig	52	D2
Llanidloes	52	D2
Llanilar	52	C2
Llanos	136	D2
Llanquihue, Lago	139	B8
Llanrhystud	52	C2
Llanrwst	54	F3
Llantrisant	52	D3
Llanwenog	52	D2
Llanwrtyd Wells	52	D2
Llawhaden	52	C3
Llerena	66	C3
Lleyn Peninsula	52	C2
Lliria	67	F3
Llivia	67	G1
Llobregat	67	G2
Lloydminster	119	P5
Lluchmayor	67	H3
Llyswen	52	D2
Loa	138	C4
Loanhead	57	E5
Lobatse	108	E5
Lobau	70	F3
Loberia	139	E7
Lobez	70	F2
Lobito	106	B5
Lobos	139	E7
Lobos, Island	126	G7
Locarno	68	B2
Lochaber	57	D4
Lochailort	57	C4
Lochan Fada	56	C3
Loch Ard Forest	57	D4
Lochboisdale	57	A3
Lochearnhead	57	D4
Loches	65	D5
Lochgelly	57	E4
Lochgilphead	57	C3
Lochinver	56	C2
Lochmaben	57	E5
Lochmaddy	56	A3
Lochnagar	57	E4
Lochranza	57	C5
Loch Shin	56	D2
Lochy, Loch	57	D4
Lock	113	H5
Lockerbie	57	E5
Lockhart	128	D6
Lock Haven	125	M6
Lockport	125	L5
Locri	69	F6
Loddekopinge	63	E9
Loddon Australia	113	J6
Loddon U.K.	53	J2
Lodeve	65	E7
Lodeynoye Pole	78	E3
Lodge Grass	123	L5
Lodgepole	123	M7
Lodi Italy	68	B3
Lodi U.S.A.	126	B1
Lodingen	62	F2
Lodja	106	D3
Lodwar	107	G2
Lodz	71	H3
Loeriesfontein	108	C6
Lofoten	62	E2
Loftus	55	J2
Logan	122	J7
Logan, Mount	118	G3
Logansport Indiana, U.S.A.	124	G6
Logansport Louisiana, U.S.A.	128	F5
Loge	106	B4
Logishin	71	M2
Logone	102	C5
Logrono	66	E1
Logrosan	66	D3
Loh	114	T10
Lohardaga	92	F4
Loharu	92	E3
Lohit	93	J3
Lohja	63	L6
Lohtaja	62	K4
Loikaw	93	J5
Loimaa	63	K6
Loimijoki	63	K6
Loing	65	E5
Loi, Phu	93	K4
Loir	65	C5
Loire	65	B5
Loja Ecuador	136	B4
Loja Spain	66	D4
Lokantekojarvi	62	M3
Lokhpodgort	78	M2
Lokhvitsa	79	E5
Lokichokio	107	F2
Lokilalaki, Gunung	91	G6
Lokka	62	M3
Loknya	78	E4
Lokoja	105	G4
Lokshak	85	N6
Lokuru	114	H6
Lol	102	E6
Lola	104	D4
Lolland	63	D9
Lolo	122	G4
Loloda	91	H5
Lolo Pass	122	G4
Lolvavana, Passage	114	U11
Lom Bulgaria	73	G4
Lom Norway	63	C6
Lomami	106	D3
Lomas Coloradas	139	C8
Lomazy	71	K3
Lombarda, Serra	137	G3
Lombe	107	G4
Lombez	65	D7
Lomblen	91	G7
Lombok	90	F7
Lome	104	F4
Lomela	106	D3
Lomir	94	J2
Lomond Hills	57	E4
Lomond, Loch	57	D4
Lomonosov Ridge	140	A1
Lompobattang, Gunung	91	F7
Lompoc	126	B3
Lomza	71	K2
London Canada	125	K5
London U.K.	53	G3
Londonderry U.K.	58	H2
Londonderry U.K.	58	J3
Londonderry, Cape	112	F1
Londonderry, Isla	139	B11
Londoni	114	R8
Londrina	138	F4

Name	Page	Ref
Lone Pine	126	C2
Longa *Angola*	106	C5
Longa *Angola*	106	C6
Longa Island	56	C3
Long Akah	90	E5
Longa, Ostrova de	81	S2
Long Bay	129	N4
Long Beach *California, U.S.A.*	126	C4
Long Beach *New York, U.S.A.*	125	P6
Long Branch	125	P6
Longchang	93	L3
Longchuan	87	M7
Longde	93	L1
Long Eaton	53	F2
Longford *Ireland*	58	G5
Longford *Ireland*	58	G5
Longformacus	57	F5
Longframlington	57	G5
Longhoughton	55	H1
Longhua	87	M3
Longhui	93	M3
Long Island *Bahamas*	133	K3
Long Island *Canada*	121	L7
Long Island *New Zealand*	115	A7
Long Island *Papua New Guinea*	114	D3
Long Island *U.S.A.*	125	P6
Long Island Sound	125	P6
Longjiang	87	N2
Longjing	88	B4
Longlac	124	G2
Long Lake	124	G2
Longli	93	L3
Long, Loch	57	D4
Long Melford	53	H2
Longmen	87	L7
Long Mynd, The	52	E2
Longnan	87	L7
Longnawan	90	E5
Longney	52	E3
Long Point *Canada*	125	K5
Long Point *New Zealand*	115	B7
Long Preston	55	G2
Long Range	121	Q8
Long Range Mountains	121	Q7
Longreach	113	J3
Long Reef	114	E4
Longridge	55	G3
Longshan	93	L3
Longsheng	93	M3
Longs Peak	123	M7
Long Stratton	53	J2
Longton	55	G3
Longtown	57	F5
Longuyon	64	F4
Longview *Texas, U.S.A.*	128	E4
Longview *Washington, U.S.A.*	122	C4
Longwy	64	F4
Longxi	93	K2
Long Xuyen	93	L6
Longyan	87	M6
Longyao	87	L4
Lons-le-Saunier	65	F5
Looe	52	C4
Lookout, Cape	129	P3
Loongana	112	F5
Loop Head	59	C7
Lopatin	79	H7
Lopatino	79	H5
Lopatka	85	T6
Lopatka, Mys	85	T6
Lop Buri	93	K6
Lopevi	114	U12
Lopez, Cap	106	A3
Lop Nur	86	G3
Lopphavet	62	J1
Lopra	62	Z14
Lopydino	78	J3
Lora del Rio	66	D4
Lorain	124	J6
Loralai	92	C2
Lorca	67	F4
Lordegan	95	K6
Lord Howe Island	113	M5
Lordsburg	127	H4
Lore	91	H7
Lorengau	114	D2
Lorentz	91	K7
Lorenzo	136	B3
Loreto *Brazil*	137	H5
Loreto *Colombia*	136	C4
Loreto *Mexico*	126	G7
Lorica	133	K10
Lorient	65	B5
Lorillard	119	S3
Lorinci	72	E2
Lorn	57	C4
Lorne	113	J6
Lorn, Firth of	57	C4
Lorrach	70	B5
Lorraine	64	F4
Los	63	F6
Los Alamos	127	J3
Los Andes	139	B6
Los Angeles *Chile*	139	B7
Los Angeles *U.S.A.*	126	C4
Los Angeles Aqueduct	126	C3
Los Banos	126	B2
Los Blancos	138	D4
Los Filabres, Sierra de	66	E4
Losinj	72	C3
Los Mochis	127	H8
Los Pedraches	66	D3
Los Roques	136	D1
Lossie	56	E3
Lossiemouth	56	E3
Los Teques	136	D1
Los Testigos	133	R9
Lost Trail Pass	122	H5
Lostwithiel	52	C4
Lot	65	D6
Lota	139	B7
Lotfahad	95	P3
Lothian	57	E5
Lotta	62	N2
Lottorp	63	G8
Lo-tung	87	N7
Lotzen	71	J1
Loudeac	64	B4
Loudun	65	D5
Louga	104	B2
Loughborough	53	F2
Loughbrickland	58	K4
Lougheed Island	120	E2
Loughor	52	C3
Loughrea	59	E6
Loughsalt Mount	58	G2
Lough Swilly	58	G2
Louhans	65	F5
Louisa	124	J7
Louisiade Archipelago	114	T10
Louisiana	128	F5
Lou Island	114	D2
Louis Trichardt	108	E4
Louisville *Kentucky, U.S.A.*	124	H7
Louisville *Mississippi, U.S.A.*	128	H4
Loukhi	62	Q3
Loule	66	B4
Loup	123	Q7
Lourdes	65	C7
Louth *Ireland*	58	K5
Louth *U.K.*	55	K1
Louvain	64	F3
Louviers	64	D4
Lovanger	62	J4
Lovat	78	E4
Lovberga	62	F5
Lovech	73	H4
Loveland	123	M7
Lovell	123	K5
Lovere	68	C3
Loviisa	63	M6
Lovington	127	L4
Lovisa	63	M6
Lovnas	62	F4
Lovosice	70	F3
Lovua	106	D5
Low, Cape	120	J5
Lower Arrow Lake	122	E3
Lower Hut	115	E4
Lowestoft	53	J2
Lowicz	71	H2
Lowther Hills	57	E5
Lowther Island	120	G3
Loyal, Loch	56	D2
Loyaute, Iles	114	X16
Loyma	78	H3
Loyne, Loch	57	C3
Lozarevo	73	J4
Lozere, Mont	65	E6
Loznica	72	E3
Lozovaya	79	F6
Lualaba	106	E3
Luan	93	N2
Luanda	106	B4
Luang Prabang	93	K5
Luangwa	107	F5
Luan He	87	M4
Luanjing	87	K4
Luanping	87	M3
Luanshya	107	E5
Luapula	107	E5
Luarca	66	C1
Luashi	106	D5
Luau	106	D5
Lubalo	106	C4
Lubanas Ezers	62	M8
Lubang Islands	91	G3
Lubango	106	B5
Lubartow	71	K3
Lubawa	71	H2
Lubben	70	E3
Lubbock	127	M4
Lubeck	70	D2
Lubefu	106	D3
Lubenka	79	J5
Lubero	107	E3
Lubie, Jezioro	70	F2
Lubien	71	H2
Lublin	71	K3
Lubny	79	E5
Lubosalma	62	P5
Lubsko	70	F3
Lubtheen	70	D2
Lubudi	106	E4
Lubuklinggau	90	C6
Lubumbashi	107	E5
Lubutu	106	E3
Lucan	59	K6
Lucano, Appennino	69	E5
Lucaya	129	N7
Lucca	68	C4
Lucea	132	H5
Lucena *Philippines*	91	G3
Lucena *Spain*	66	D4
Lucena del Cid	67	F2
Lucenec	71	H4
Lucera	69	E5
Lucerne	68	B2
Luchow	70	D2
Luckau	70	E3
Luckenwalde	70	E2
Lucknow	92	F3
Lucon	65	C5
Lucrecia, Cabo	133	K4
Lucusse	106	D5
Luda	87	N4
Ludensheid	70	B3
Luderitz	108	C5
Ludford	55	J3
Ludgvan	52	B4
Ludhiana	92	E2
Ludington	124	G5
Ludlow *U.K.*	52	E2
Ludlow *U.S.A.*	126	D3
Ludogorie	73	J4
Ludus	73	H2
Ludvika	63	F6
Ludwigsburg	70	C4
Ludwigshafen	70	B4
Ludwigslust	70	D2
Ludza	63	M8
Luebo	106	D4
Luena	106	C5
Luepa	136	E2
Lueyang	93	L2
Lufeng	87	M7
Lufkin	128	E5
Luga	63	N7
Luga	68	B2
Lugano	68	B2
Lugano, Lago di	68	B3
Luganville	114	T11
Lugela	109	G3
Lugenda	109	G2
Lugg	52	E2
Lugnaquilla	59	K7
Lugo *Italy*	68	C3
Lugo *Spain*	66	C1
Lugoj	73	F3
Lugovoy	86	C3
Lugton	57	D5
Luiana	106	D6
Luichart, Loch	56	D3
Luik	64	F3
Luimneach	59	E7
Luing	57	D4
Luinne Bheinn	57	C3
Luiro	62	M3
Luiza	106	D4
Lujan	139	C6
Lujiang	87	M5
Lukashkin Yar	84	B4
Lukeville	126	F5
Lukovit	73	H4
Lukovo	72	F5
Lukow	71	K3
Lukoyanov	78	G4
Lukulu	106	D5
Lulea	62	K4
Lulealven	62	J3
Luleburgaz	76	B2
Lulo	106	C4
Lulong	87	M4
Lulonga	106	C2
Luluabourg	106	D4
Lulworth Cove	53	E4
Lumbala Nguimbo	106	D5
Lumberton	129	N3
Lumbovka	78	G2
Lumbrales	66	C2
Lumbreras	66	E1
Lumbres	64	E3
Lumijoki	62	L4
Lumphanan	57	F3
Lumsden	115	B6
Lumut, Tanjung	90	D6
Lunan	93	K4
Lunan Bay	57	F4
Lunayyir, Harrat	96	C4
Lunberger Heide	70	C2
Lund	63	E9
Lundar	123	Q2
Lundazi	107	F5
Lundy	52	C3
Lune	55	G2
Luneburg	70	D2
Lunel	65	F7
Luneville	64	G4
Lungga	114	K6
Lungwebungu	106	D5
Luni	92	D3
Luninets	71	M2
Lunsar	104	C4
Lunsemfwa	107	E5
Luntai	86	E3
Luobei	88	C2
Luobuzhuang	86	F4
Luocheng	93	L4
Luodian	93	L3
Luoding	93	M4
Luo He	93	L1
Luohe	93	M2
Luotian	93	N2
Luoyang	93	M2
Luqu	93	K2
Lure	65	G5
Lurgan	58	K4
Lurio *Mozambique*	109	G2
Lurio *Mozambique*	109	H2
Lusaka	107	E6
Lusambo	106	D3
Lusancay Islands	114	E3
Lushi	93	M2
Lush, Mountain	112	F2
Lushoto	107	G3
Lushui	93	J3
Lusignan	65	D5
Lusk	123	M6
Luspebryggan	62	H3
Lussac-les-Chateaux	65	D5
Lut, Bahrat	94	B6
Lut, Dasht-e	95	P6
Lut-e Zangi Ahmad	95	P7
Luthrie	57	E4
Luton	53	G3
Lutong	90	E5
Lutsk	79	D5
Lutterworth	53	F2
Luukkonen	63	N6
Luuq	107	H2
Luverne	124	B5
Luwingu	107	E5
Luwuk	91	G6
Luxembourg	64	F4
Luxembourg	64	G4
Luxeuil	65	G5
Luxi	93	J4
Luxor	103	F2
Luza *Russia*	78	H3
Luza *Russia*	78	H3
Luzern	68	B2
Luzhou	93	L3
Luziania	138	G3
Luzilandia	137	J4
Luzon	91	G2
Luzon Strait	91	G1
Lvov	71	L4
Lvovka	84	B5
Lwowek	71	G2
Lyadova	73	J1
Lyakhovskiye Ostrova	85	Q2
Lyall, Mount	122	G3
Lyallpur	92	D2
Lyapin	78	L3
Lybster	56	E2
Lyck	71	K2
Lycksele	62	H4
Lydd	53	H4
Lyddan Ice Rise	141	Y4
Lydenburg	108	F5
Lydford	52	C4
Lydney	52	E3
Lyell Range	115	D4
Lyman	123	J7
Lyme Bay	52	D4
Lyme Regis	52	D4
Lymington	53	F4
Lymm	55	G3
Lyna	71	J1
Lynchburg	125	L8
Lynd	113	J2
Lyndon	112	D3
Lyne	57	F5
Lyness	56	E2
Lyngdal	63	B7
Lyngseidet	62	J1
Lynher	52	C4
Lynn	125	Q5
Lynn Canal	118	H4
Lynn Lake	119	Q4
Lynton	52	D3
Lynx Lake	119	P3
Lyon *France*	65	F6
Lyon *U.K.*	57	D4
Lyon Inlet	120	K4
Lyon, Loch	57	D4
Lyonnais, Monts du	65	F6
Lyra Reef	114	E2
Lyskovo	78	H4
Lysva	78	K4
Lytham Saint Annes	55	F3
Lythe	55	J2
Lyttelton	115	D5
Lytton	122	C4
Lyubashevka	73	L2
Lyubcha	71	M2
Lyubertsy	78	F4
Lyubeshov	71	L3
Lyubimets	73	J5
Lyuboml	71	L3
Lyubotin	79	F6
Lyudinovo	79	E5
Lyushcha	71	M2

M

Name	Page	Ref
Maaia	109	H2
Maam Cross	59	C6
Maan	94	B6
Maanqiao	86	F3
Maanselka	62	N5
Maanshan	87	M5
Maarianhamina	63	G6
Maarrat an Numan	94	C4
Maas	64	F3
Maaseik	64	F3
Maasin	91	G3
Maastricht	64	F3
Maba	91	H5
Mabalane	109	F4
Mabar	96	G9
Mablethorpe	55	K3
Macachin	139	D7
McAdam	125	S4

Name	Page	Grid
Macae	138	H4
McAlester	128	E3
McAllen	128	C7
McAllister, Mount	113	K5
MacAlpine Lake	119	Q2
Macapa	137	G3
Macara	136	B4
McArthur	113	H2
Macau	137	K5
Macaubas	138	J6
Macauley Islands	111	T8
McBeth Fjord	120	N4
McBride	119	L5
McCamey	127	L5
McCammon	122	H6
McCarthy	118	G3
Macclesfield	55	G3
McClintock Channel	119	Q1
McClintock Range	112	F2
McClure Strait	120	C3
McComb	128	G5
McCook	123	P7
McCreary	123	Q2
McDermitt	122	F7
Macdonnell Ranges	113	G3
Macduff	56	F3
Maceio	137	K5
Maceio, Punta da	137	K4
Macenta	104	D4
Macerata	68	D4
McGehee	128	G4
Macgillycuddy's Reeks	59	C9
Macha	85	K5
Machachi	136	B4
Machakos	107	G3
Machala	136	B4
Machanga	109	G4
Macharioch	57	C5
Machias	125	S4
Machichaco, Cap	66	E1
Machilipatnam	92	F5
Machiques	136	C2
Machir Bay	57	B5
Machynlleth	52	D2
Macin	73	K3
McIntosh	123	P5
Macka	77	H2
Mackay	113	K3
Mackay, Cape	120	D2
Mackay, Lake	112	F3
MacKay Lake	119	N3
McKean Island	111	U2
McKeesport	125	L6
Mackenzie Australia	113	K3
Mackenzie Canada	118	J2
Mackenzie Bay Antarctic	141	E5
Mackenzie Bay Canada	118	H2
Mackenzie King Island	120	D2
Mackenzie Mountains	118	H3
Mackinac, Straits of	124	H4
McKinley, Mount	118	E3
McKinney	128	D4
Macklin	123	K1
McLaughlin	123	P5
Maclean Strait	120	F2
Maclear	108	E6
McLeod, Lake	112	C3
Macmillan	118	J3
McMillan, Lake	127	K4
McMinnville Oregon, U.S.A.	122	C5
McMinnville Tennessee, U.S.A.	129	K3
McMurdo	141	M3
Macomb	124	E6
Macomer	69	B5
Macon	65	F5
Macon Georgia, U.S.A.	129	L4
Macon Missouri, U.S.A.	124	D7
Macossa	109	F3
McPherson	128	D1
Macquarie	113	K5
Macquarie Harbour	113	K7
Macquarie Island	141	L8
McRae	129	L4
Macroom	59	E9
McTavish Arm	119	M2
Macuspana	131	N9
Macuzari, Presa	127	H7
McVicar Arm	119	L2
Mad	122	C7
Madaba	94	B6
Madade	109	F4
Madagascar	109	J3
Madang	101	G6
Madaoua	101	G6
Madaripur	93	H4
Madawaska	125	M4
Maddalena, Isola di	69	B5
Maddaloni	69	E5
Maddy, Loch	56	A3
Madeira Brazil	136	E5
Madeira Portugal	100	B2
Madelia	124	C5
Maden Turkey	77	H3
Maden Turkey	77	J2
Madera Mexico	127	H6
Madera U.S.A.	126	B2
Madetkoski	62	M3
Madhubani	92	G3
Madhya Pradesh	92	E4
Madidi	136	D6
Madinat ash Shab	96	G10
Madingo-Kayes	106	B3
Madingou	106	B3
Madin Jadid	77	H5
Madison Indiana, U.S.A.	124	H7
Madison Montana, U.S.A.	122	J5
Madison Nebraska, U.S.A.	123	R7
Madison S. Dakota, U.S.A.	123	R5
Madison Wisconsin, U.S.A.	124	F5
Madisonville Kentucky, U.S.A.	124	G8
Madisonville Texas, U.S.A.	128	E5
Madiun	90	E7
Mado Gashi	107	G2
Madoi	93	J2
Madona	63	M8
Madrakah, Ra's	97	N7
Madras India	92	F6
Madras U.S.A.	122	D5
Madre de Dios	136	D6
Madre de Dios, Isla	139	A10
Madre, Laguna Mexico	128	D8
Madre, Laguna U.S.A.	128	D7
Madre Occidental, Sierra	127	H6
Madre Oriental, Sierra	127	L7
Madre, Sierra	91	G2
Madrid	66	E2
Madridejos	66	E3
Madrigalejo	66	D3
Madrona, Sierra	66	D3
Madura Australia	112	F5
Madura Indonesia	90	E7
Madurai	92	E7
Madura, Selat	90	E7
Madzharovo	73	H5
Maebashi	89	G7
Maerus	73	H3
Maesteg	52	D3
Maestra, Sierra	132	J4
Maevatanana	109	J3
Maewo	114	U11
Mafa	91	H5
Mafeteng	108	E5
Mafia Island	107	G4
Mafikeng	108	E5
Mafra	66	B3
Mafraq	94	C5
Maga	114	S8
Magadan	85	S5
Magadan Oblast	85	V3
Magadi	107	G3
Magallanes, Estrecho de	139	B10
Magangue	136	C2
Magara	76	E4
Magarida	114	D4
Magburaka	104	C4
Magdagachi	85	M6
Magdalena Bolivia	136	E6
Magdalena Colombia	136	C2
Magdalena Mexico	126	F7
Magdalena Mexico	126	G5
Magdalena Mexico	130	H7
Magdalena, Isla	130	C5
Magdalena, Llano de la	130	D5
Magdalen Islands	121	P8
Magda Plateau	120	K3
Magdeburg	70	D2
Magdelena	127	J3
Magee, Island	58	L3
Magelang	90	E7
Magellan, Strait of	139	B10
Magenta, Lake	112	D5
Mageroya	62	L1
Maggiore, Lago	68	B3
Maghagha	102	F2
Maghera	58	J3
Magherafelt	58	J3
Magheramorne	58	L3
Magilligan Point	58	J2
Magina	66	E4
Maglic	72	E4
Maglie	69	G5
Magnolia	128	F4
Magoe	109	F3
Magog	125	P4
Magpie	121	P7
Magro	67	F3
Magude	109	F5
Maguse Lake	119	R3
Maguse Point	119	S3
Magwe	93	H4
Mahabad	94	G3
Mahabe	109	J3
Mahabharat Range	92	G3
Mahabo	109	H4
Mahaddayweyne	107	J2
Mahadeo Hills	92	E4
Mahagi	107	F2
Mahajanga	109	J3
Mahakam	90	F5
Mahalapye	108	E4
Mahallat	95	K5
Mahanadi	92	F4
Mahanoy City	125	M6
Mahao	88	A4
Maharashtra	92	D4
Maharlu, Daryacheh-ye	95	L7
Maha Sarakham	93	K5
Mahavavy	109	J3
Mahbubnagar	92	E5
Mahdah	97	M4
Mahdia Guyana	136	F2
Mahdia Tunisia	101	H1
Mahe	92	E6
Mahebourg	109	L7
Mahenge	107	G4
Mahesana	92	D4
Mahi	92	D4
Mahia Peninsula	115	G3
Mahmudabad India	92	F3
Mahmudabad Iran	95	L3
Mahmudia	73	K3
Mahmudiye	76	D3
Mahnomen	124	B3
Mahon	67	J3
Mahrah, Al	97	K8
Mahukona	126	T10
Mahuva	92	D4
Maicao	136	C1
Maiche	65	G5
Maicuru	137	G4
Maidenhead	53	G3
Maidi	91	H5
Maidstone	53	H3
Maiduguri	105	H3
Maihar	92	F4
Maijdi	93	H4
Maikala Range	92	F4
Main U.K.	58	K3
Main Germany	70	C4
Main Barrier Range	113	J5
Main Channel	125	K4
Mai-Ndombe, Lac	106	C3
Maine France	64	C4
Maine U.S.A.	125	R4
Maine Soroa	101	H6
Maingkwan	93	J3
Mainland Orkney Is., U.K.	56	E2
Mainland Shetland Is., U.K.	56	A1
Maintirano	109	H3
Mainua	62	M4
Mainz	70	C4
Maio	104	L7
Maipu	139	E7
Maiquetia	133	P9
Maira	68	A3
Maisi, Cabo	133	K4
Maiskhal	93	H4
Maitland New South Wales, Australia	113	L5
Maitland S. Australia, Australia	113	H5
Maiz, Islas del	132	F8
Maizuru	89	E8
Majagual	136	C2
Majene	91	F6
Maji	103	G6
Majiang	93	L3
Majin	87	M6
Majorca	67	H3
Maka Senegal	104	C3
Maka Solomon Is.	114	K6
Makale	91	F6
Makambako	107	F4
Makanza	106	C2
Makarikha	78	K2
Makarova	84	D2
Makarska	72	D4
Makaryev	78	G4
Makassar	91	F7
Makassar, Selat	91	F6
Makat	79	J6
Makatini Flats	109	F5
Makay, Massif du	109	J4
Makeni	104	C4
Makenu	126	S10
Makeyevka	79	F6
Makhachkala	79	H7
Makharadze	77	K2
Makhmur	94	F4
Makhyah, Wadi	97	J8
Maki	91	J6
Makinsk	84	A6
Makkah	96	D6
Makkovik	121	Q6
Makkovik, Cape	121	Q6
Makogai	114	R8
Makokou	106	B2
Makondi Plateau	107	G5
Makov	71	H4
Makra	75	H4
Makrai	92	E4
Makran	92	B3
Makri	75	H2
Makronisi	75	H4
Maksatikha	78	F4
Maksim	78	K3
Maksimovka	88	F2
Makteir	100	C4
Maku	94	G2
Makurazaki	89	C10
Makurdi	105	G4
Makushin Volcano	118	Ae9
Mala	62	M4
Malabang	91	G4
Malabar Coast	92	D6
Malabo	105	G5
Malacca, Strait of	90	C5
Malacky	71	G4
Mala Fatra	71	H4
Malaga Colombia	136	C2
Malaga Spain	66	D4
Malagarasi	107	F4
Malahide	59	K6
Malaita	114	K6
Malakal	103	F6
Malakanagiri	92	F5
Malakand	92	D2
Malakula	114	T12
Malang	90	E7
Malanje	106	C4
Malao	114	T11
Mala, Punta	136	B2
Malaren	63	G7
Malargue	139	C7
Malartic	125	L2
Malaspina	139	C8
Malaspina Glacier	118	G4
Malatya	77	H3
Malatya Daglari	77	H3
Malavate	137	G3
Malavi	94	H5
Malawi	107	F5
Malawi, Lake	107	F5
Malaybalay	91	H4
Malayer	94	J4
Malay Peninsula	90	C5
Malaysia	90	D5
Malazgirt	77	K3
Malbork	71	H1
Malchin Germany	70	E2
Malchin Mongolia	86	G2
Malcolm's Point	57	B4
Malden	124	F8
Maldives	82	F6
Maldon	53	H3
Maldonado	139	F6
Maldonado, Punta	131	K9
Male	82	F6
Malea, Akra	75	G4
Malegaon	92	D4
Male Karpaty	71	G4
Malema	109	G2
Malemba-Nkulu	106	E4
Maleme	75	G5
Maler Kotla	92	E2
Malesherbes	64	E4
Maleta	84	H6
Malevangga	114	H5
Malgobek	79	G7
Malgomaj	62	G4
Malhat	77	K5
Malheur	122	F6
Malheur, Lake	122	E6
Mali	100	E5
Mali Hka	93	J3
Mali Kanal	72	E3
Mali Kyun	93	J6
Malimba, Mont	107	E4
Malin Ireland	58	H2
Malin Ukraine	79	D5
Malin Beg	58	E3
Malindi	107	H3
Malin Head	58	H2
Malin More	58	E3
Malka	85	T6
Malkachan	85	S5
Malkapur	92	E4
Malkara	76	B2
Malkinia	71	K2
Malko Turnovo	73	J5
Mallaig	57	C4
Mallawi	102	F2
Mallorca	67	H3
Mallow	59	E8
Mallwyd	52	D2
Malm	62	D4
Malmberget	62	J3
Malmedy	64	G3
Malmesbury South Africa	108	C6
Malmesbury U.K.	53	E3
Malmo	63	E9
Malmohus	63	E9
Malmyzh	78	J4
Malo	114	T11
Malolo	114	Q8
Malone	125	N4
Malorita	71	L3
Malo Strait	114	T11
Maloy	62	A6
Maloyaroslavets	78	F4
Malozemelskaya Tundra	84	Ab3
Malpartida de Caceres	66	C3
Malpas	55	G3
Malpelo, Isla	134	A2
Malta	74	C5
Malta U.S.A.	123	L3
Malta Channel	74	C4
Maltahohe	108	C4
Maltby	55	H3
Maltepe	76	C2
Malton	55	J2
Malu	73	J3
Maluku	91	H6
Maluku, Laut	91	H5
Malung	63	E6
Maluu	114	K6
Malvan	92	D5
Malvern	128	F3
Malvern Hills	52	E2
Malvinas, Islas	139	E10
Malykay	85	K4
Malyy Anyuy	85	U3
Malyy Lyakhovskiy, Ostrov	85	Q2
Malyy Taymyr, Ostrov	81	M2
Malyy Yenisey	84	F6
Mama	85	J5
Mamankhalinka	79	J6
Mamanuca Group	114	Q8
Mamaru	137	F4
Mambasa	107	E2
Mamberamo	114	B2
Mamburao	91	G3
Mamers	64	D4
Mamfe	105	G4
Mamlyutka	84	Ae6

Mamonovo 71 H1
Mamore 138 D3
Mamore Forest 57 D4
Mamoria 136 D5
Mamou 104 C3
Mampong 104 E4
Mamry, Jezioro 71 J1
Mamuju 91 F6
Man *India* 92 F3
Man *Ivory Coast* 104 D4
Mana 63 C7
Mana *Fr. Guiana* 137 G3
Mana *U.S.A.* 126 R9
Manacapuru 136 E4
Manacapuru, Lago de 136 E4
Manacor 67 H3
Manadir, Al 97 M5
Manado 91 G5
Managua 132 D8
Managua, Laguna de 132 D8
Manakara 109 J4
Manakhah 96 F9
Manambolo 109 H3
Manam Island 114 D2
Mananara *Madagascar* 109 J4
Mananara *Madagascar* 109 J3
Mananjary 109 J4
Manantavadi 92 E6
Manaoba 114 K6
Manapire 136 D2
Manapouri 115 A6
Manapouri, Lake 115 A6
Manas 93 H3
Manau 114 D3
Manaus 136 F4
Manavgat 76 D4
Manbij 94 C3
Mancha Real 66 E4
Manchester *U.K.* 55 G3
Manchester *Connecticut, U.S.A.* 125 P6
Manchester *Kentucky, U.S.A.* 124 J8
Manchester *New Hampshire, U.S.A.* 125 Q5
Manchester *Tennessee, U.S.A.* 129 J3
Mancora 136 A4
Mand 95 K7
Mandab, Bab el 103 H5
Mandal *Afghanistan* 95 Q5
Mandal *Norway* 63 B7
Mandala, Puncak 91 L6
Mandalay 93 J4
Mandalgovi 87 K2
Mandali 94 G5
Mandal-Ovoo 87 J3
Mandan 123 P4
Mandaon 91 G3
Mandar, Teluk 91 F6
Mandasawu, Poco 91 G7
Mandav Hills 92 D4
Mandeville 132 J5
Mandi 92 E2
Mandiore, Lago 138 E3
Mandla 92 F4
Mandoudhion 75 G3
Mandurah 112 D5
Manduria 69 F5
Mandvi 92 C4
Mandya 92 E6
Manea 53 H2
Manevichi 71 L3
Manfredonia 69 E5
Manfredonia, Golfo di 69 F5
Manga 138 J6
Mangakino 115 E3
Mangalia 73 K4
Mangalore 92 D6
Mangaon 92 D5
Mangapehi 115 E3
Manggautu 114 J7
Mangin Range 93 J4
Mangkalihat, Tanjung 91 F5
Manglares, Punta 136 B3
Mangochi 107 G5
Mangoky 109 H4
Mangole 91 H6
Mangonui 115 D1
Mangoro 109 J3
Mangotsfield 52 E3
Mangral 92 D4
Manguari 136 D4
Mangueira, Lagoa 138 F6
Mangui 87 N1
Manguinha, Pontal do 137 K6
Mangut 85 J7
Mangyshlak 79 J7
Mangyshlak, Poluostrov 79 J7
Mangyshlakskiy Zaliv 79 J7
Manhan 86 G2
Manhattan 123 R8
Manhica 109 F5
Manicore 136 E5
Manicouagan 121 N7
Manicouagan, Reservoir 121 N7
Manifah 97 J3
Manika, Plateau de la 106 E4
Manila 91 G3
Manipa, Selat 91 H6
Manipur 93 H4
Manisa 76 B3
Man, Isle of 54 E2
Manistee *U.S.A.* 124 G4
Manistee *U.S.A.* 124 H4
Manistique 124 G4
Manitoba 119 R4
Manitoba, Lake 123 Q2
Manitou Falls 123 T2
Manitou Island 124 G4
Manitoulin 124 J4
Manitowoc 124 G4
Maniwaki 125 N3
Manizales 136 B2
Manja 109 H4
Manjra 92 E5
Mankato 124 C4
Mankono 104 D4
Mankovka 73 L1
Manna 90 C6
Mannar 92 E7
Mannar, Gulf of 92 E7
Mannheim 70 C4
Manning, Cape 120 B2
Manning Strait 114 J5
Manningtree 53 J3
Mannu 69 B6
Manoa Abuna 136 D5
Manokwari 91 J6
Manolas 75 F3
Manonga 107 F3
Manono 107 E4
Manorbier 52 C3
Manorcunningham 58 G3
Manorhamilton 58 F4
Manoron 93 J6
Manosque 65 F7
Manouane, Reservoir 121 M7
Mano-wan 89 G7
Manpojin 87 P3
Manra 111 U2
Manresa 67 G2
Mansa 107 E5
Mansehra 92 D2
Mansel Island 120 L5
Mansfield *U.K.* 55 H3
Mansfield *Louisiana, U.S.A.* 128 F5
Mansfield *Ohio, U.S.A.* 124 J6
Mansfield *Pennsylvania, U.S.A.* 125 M6
Mansfield Woodhouse 55 H3
Mansle 65 D6
Manson Creek 118 L4
Mansoura 67 J4
Manston 53 J3
Mansurlu 77 F4
Manta 136 A4
Mantalingajan, Mount 91 F4
Mantaro 136 B6
Mantecal 136 D2
Mantes 64 D4
Mantiqueira, Serra da 138 G4
Mantova 68 C3
Mantsala 63 L6
Mantta 63 L5
Mantua 68 C3
Mantyharju 63 M6
Manua 111 V4
Manuel 131 K6
Manui 91 G6
Manu Island 114 C2
Manujan 95 N8
Manukau 115 E2
Manukau Harbour 115 E2
Manulla 58 D5
Manus Islands 114 D2
Manya 78 L3
Manyas 76 B2
Manych Gudilo, Ozero 79 G6
Manyoni 107 F4
Manzanares 66 E3
Manzanillo *Cuba* 132 J4
Manzanillo *Mexico* 130 G8
Manzanillo, Punta 136 B2
Manzariyeh 95 K4
Manzhouli 87 M2
Manzini 109 F5
Manzya 84 F5
Mao 102 C5
Maoershan 88 A3
Maoke, Pegunungan 91 K6
Maoming 93 M4
Mapai 109 F4
Mapam Yumco 92 F2
Mapire 133 Q11
Maple Creek 123 K3
Mappi *Indonesia* 91 K7
Mappi *Indonesia* 91 K7
Maprik 114 C2
Mapuera 136 F4
Maputo 109 F5
Maqdam, Ras 96 C7
Maqna 96 B2
Maqueda 66 D2
Maquinchao 139 C8
Maraba 137 H5
Maracaibo 136 C1
Maracaibo, Lago de 136 C2
Maraca, Ilha de 137 G3
Maracay 136 D1
Maradah 101 J3
Maradi 101 G6
Maragheh 94 H3
Marajo, Baia de 137 H4
Marajo, Ilha de 137 H4
Maralal 107 G2
Maramasike 114 K6
Maramba 106 E6
Maran 90 C5
Marand 94 G2
Maranguape 137 K4
Maranhao 137 H5
Maranhao Grande, Cachoeira 137 F4
Maran, Koh-i- 92 C3
Maranon 136 C4
Marans 65 C5
Marari 136 D5
Marasesti 73 J3
Marassume 137 H4
Marateca 66 B3
Marathokambos 75 J4
Marathon *Canada* 124 G2
Marathon *Florida, U.S.A.* 129 M8
Marathon *Texas, U.S.A.* 127 L5
Marau 90 E6
Marau Point 115 G3
Maravovo 114 J6
Marbella 66 D4
Marble Bar 112 D3
Marble Canyon 126 G2
Marburg 70 C3
Marcelino 136 D4
March 53 H2
Marche *Belgium* 64 F3
Marche *France* 65 D5
Marchena 66 D4
Marchena, Isla 136 A7
Mar Chiquita, Lago 138 D6
Marcigny 65 F5
Marcus Baker, Mount 118 F3
Marcus Island 83 P4
Mardan 92 D2
Mar del Plata 139 E7
Mardin 77 J4
Mare 114 Y16
Mareeba 113 K2
Maree, Loch 56 C3
Mareeq 103 J7
Mareuil 65 D6
Margai Caka 92 G1
Marganets 79 E6
Margaret, Cape 120 H3
Margaret River 112 F2
Margarita, Isla de 136 E1
Margaritovo 88 E4
Margate 53 J3
Margeride, Monts de la 65 E6
Margita 73 F3
Margo, Dasht-i 95 R6
Marguerite 121 N7
Marguerite Bay 141 V5
Mari 114 C3
Maria Elena 138 C4
Maria, Golfo de Ana 132 H4
Maria Madre, Isla 130 F7
Maria Magdalena, Isla 130 F7
Marianas Islands 83 N5
Marianas Trench 142 F4
Marian Lake 119 M3
Marianna *Arkansas, U.S.A.* 128 G3
Marianna *Florida, U.S.A.* 129 K5
Marianske Lazne 70 E4
Marias 122 J3
Marias, Islas 130 F7
Mariato, Punta 132 G11
Maria van Diemen, Cape 115 D1
Mariazell 68 E2
Marib 96 G9
Maribor 72 C2
Maridi 102 E7
Marie Byrd Land 141 S3
Marie Galante 133 S7
Mariehamn 63 H6
Marienbad 70 E4
Marienburg 71 H1
Mariental 108 C4
Marienwerder 71 H2
Mariestad 63 E7
Marietta *Georgia, U.S.A.* 129 K4
Marietta *Ohio, U.S.A.* 125 K7
Marigot 133 S7
Mariinsk 84 D5
Marina di Carrara 68 C3
Marina di Leuca 69 G6
Marina di Monasterace 69 F6
Marinette 124 G4
Maringa 106 D2
Maringa 138 F4
Marion *Illinois, U.S.A.* 124 F8
Marion *Indiana, U.S.A.* 124 H6
Marion *Ohio, U.S.A.* 124 J6
Marion *S. Carolina, U.S.A.* 129 N3
Marion *Virginia, U.S.A.* 125 K8
Marion, Lake 129 M4
Marion Reefs 113 L2
Maripa 136 D2
Marisa 91 G5
Mariscal Estigarribia 138 D4
Maritimes, Alpes 65 G6
Maritsa 73 H4
Marivan 94 H4
Marjamaa 63 L7
Marjayoun 94 B5
Marka 96 E7
Marka 107 H2
Markam 93 J3
Market Deeping 53 G2
Market Drayton 52 E2
Market Harborough 53 G2
Markethill 58 J4
Market Rasen 55 J3
Market Weighton 55 J3
Markha 85 K4
Markham 114 D3
Marlborough *Australia* 113 K3
Marlborough *Guyana* 136 F2
Marlborough *U.K.* 53 F3
Marlin 128 D5
Marlinton 125 K7
Marlow 53 G3
Marmagao 92 D5
Marmande 65 D6
Marmara *Turkey* 76 B2
Marmara *Turkey* 76 B2
Marmara Denizi 76 C2
Marmaraereglisi 76 B2
Marmara Golu 76 C3
Marmara, Sea of 76 C2
Marmaris 76 C4
Marmblada 68 C2
Marmelos 136 E5
Marne 64 E4
Maro 102 C3
Maroantsetra 109 J3
Marolambo 109 J4
Marondera 109 F3
Maroni 137 G3
Maros 91 F6
Marotiri Islands 115 E1
Maroua 105 H3
Marovoay 109 J3
Marowyne 137 G3
Marple 55 G3
Marquette 124 G3
Marquise 64 D3
Marquises, Iles 143 J5
Marra, Jebel 102 D5
Marrakech 100 D2
Marrakesh 100 D2
Marrak Point 120 R5
Marrawah 113 J7
Marree 113 H4
Marresale 84 Ae3
Marrupa 109 G2
Marsa Alam 96 B4
Marsabit 107 G2
Marsala 69 D7
Marsden *Australia* 113 K5
Marsden *U.K.* 55 H3
Marseille 65 F7
Mar, Serra do 138 G5
Marsfjallet 62 G3
Marshall *Minnesota, U.S.A.* 124 C4
Marshall *Missouri, U.S.A.* 124 D7
Marshall *Texas, U.S.A.* 128 E4
Marshall Bennett Islands 114 E3
Marshall Islands 143 G4
Marshalltown 124 D5
Marshchapel 55 K3
Marshfield 124 E4
Marsh Island 128 G6
Marske-by-the-Sea 55 H2
Marsta 63 G7
Martaban 93 J5
Martaban, Gulf of 93 J5
Martapura 90 E6
Martes, Sierra 67 F3
Marthaguy 113 K5
Martha's Vineyard 125 Q6
Martigny 68 A2
Martigues 65 F7
Martin *Poland* 71 H4
Martin *Spain* 67 F2
Martin *S. Dakota, U.S.A.* 123 P6
Martin *Tennessee, U.S.A.* 128 H2
Martinavas 53 N6
Martinborough 115 E4
Martinique 133 S7
Martinique Passage 133 S7
Martin Lake 129 K4
Martin Point 118 G1
Martinsberg 68 E1
Martinsville 125 L8
Martock 52 E4
Marton *New Zealand* 115 E4
Marton *U.K.* 55 J3
Martorell 67 G2
Martos 66 E4
Martre, Lac La 119 M3
Martuk 79 K5
Martuni 79 H7
Martyn 78 K2
Martze 136 D4
Marudi 90 E5
Marugame 89 D8
Marum, Mount 114 U12
Marunga 114 E2
Marungu 107 E4
Marv Dasht 95 L7
Marvejols 65 E6
Marvine, Mount 122 J8
Marwar 92 D3
Mary 95 Q3
Maryborough 113 L4
Maryevka 84 Ae6
Maryland 125 M7
Maryport 55 F2
Mary, Puy 65 E6
Marystown 121 Q8
Marysville *California, U.S.A.* 126 B1
Marysville *Kansas, U.S.A.* 123 R8
Maryvale 113 L4
Maryville *Missouri, U.S.A.* 124 C6
Maryville *Tennessee, U.S.A.* 129 L3
Marzo, Cabo 132 J11
Masagua 132 B7
Masai Steppe 107 G3
Masaka 107 F3

Name	Page	Ref
Masally	94	J2
Masan	89	B8
Masasi	107	G5
Masaya	132	D8
Masbate *Philippines*	91	G3
Masbate *Philippines*	91	G3
Mascara	100	F1
Mascarene Islands	109	L7
Masela	91	H7
Maseru	108	E5
Mashabih	96	C4
Masham	55	H2
Mashan *Guangxi, China*	93	L4
Mashan *Heilongjiang, China*	88	C3
Mashhad	95	P3
Mashike	88	H4
Mashiz	95	N7
Mashkid	95	R8
Masi	62	K2
Masilah, Wadi al	97	J9
Masi-Manimba	106	C3
Masindi	107	F2
Masirah	97	P6
Masirah, Khalij	97	N7
Masirah, Khawr al	97	P6
Masiri	95	K6
Masisi	107	E3
Masjed Soleyman	94	J6
Mask, Lough	58	D5
Maskutan	95	P8
Maslen Nos	73	J4
Masoala, Cap	109	K3
Mason Bay	115	A7
Mason City	124	D5
Ma, Song	93	K4
Masqat	97	P5
Massa	68	C3
Massachusetts	125	P5
Massachusetts Bay	125	Q5
Massakori	102	C5
Massa Marittima	68	C4
Massangena	109	F4
Massape	84	Ad4
Massenya	102	C5
Massigui	100	D6
Massillon	124	K6
Massinga	109	G4
Massingir	109	F4
Masteksay	79	H6
Masterton	115	E4
Mastikho, Akra	75	J3
Mastuj	92	D1
Masturah	96	D5
Masuda	89	C8
Masulch	94	J3
Masurai, Bukit	90	C6
Masvingo	108	F4
Masyaf	94	C4
Mat	74	F2
Mataboor	91	K6
Mataca	109	G2
Matachel	66	C3
Matad	87	M2
Matadi	106	B4
Matafome	66	B3
Matagalpa	132	E8
Matagami *Ontario, Canada*	125	M2
Matagami *Quebec, Canada*	125	M2
Matagami, Lac	125	M1
Matagorda Bay	128	D6
Matagorda Island	128	D6
Matakana Island	115	F2
Matakaoa Point	115	G2
Matala	106	C5
Matale	92	F7
Matam	104	C2
Matamata	115	E2
Matamoros *Mexico*	128	D8
Matamoros *Mexico*	127	L8
Matane	125	S2
Mata Negra	136	E2
Matanzas	132	G3
Matapan, Cape	75	G4
Matapedia	125	S2
Matara	92	F7
Mataram	90	F7
Matarani	138	B3
Mataranka	112	G1
Mataro	67	H2
Matata	115	F2
Matatiele	108	E6
Mataura *New Zealand*	115	B6
Mataura *New Zealand*	115	B7
Matawai	115	F3
Matay	86	D2
Matcha	86	B4
Matehuala	131	J6
Matera	69	F5
Mateszalka	73	G2
Mateur	101	G1
Matfors	62	G5
Matheson	125	K2
Mathis	128	D6
Mathry	52	B3
Mathura	92	E3
Mati	91	H4
Matlock	55	H3
Mato, Cerro	133	Q11
Mato Grosso	136	F6
Mato Grosso do Sul	138	E3
Mato Grosso, Planalto do	138	E3
Matra	72	E2
Matrah	97	P5
Matrosovo	71	J1
Matruh	102	E1
Matsubara	89	J10
Matsue	89	D8
Ma-tsu Lieh-tao	87	M6
Matsumae	88	H5
Matsumoto	89	F7
Matsusaka	89	F8
Matsuyama	89	D9
Mattagami	121	K8
Mattancheri	92	E7
Mattawa	125	L3
Matterhorn *Switzerland*	68	A3
Matterhorn *U.S.A.*	122	G7
Matthews Peak	107	G2
Matthew Town	133	L4
Matti, Sabkhat	97	K10
Mattoon	124	F7
Matty Island	120	G3
Matua, Ostrov	85	S7
Matuku	114	R9
Maturin	136	E2
Matyushkinskaya	84	B5
Mau	92	F3
Maua	109	G2
Maubara	91	H7
Maubeuge	64	E3
Maubin	93	J5
Maubourguet	65	D7
Mauchline	57	D5
Maud	56	F3
Maues	136	F4
Mauganj	92	F4
Maui	126	S10
Maula	62	L4
Maule	139	B7
Mauleon-Licharre	65	C7
Maumere	91	G7
Maumtrasna	58	C5
Maumturk Mountains	59	C5
Maun	108	D4
Mauna Kea	126	T11
Mauna Loa	126	T11
Maungmagan Islands	93	J6
Maunoir, Lac	118	L2
Maures	65	G7
Mauriac	65	E6
Maurice, Lake	112	G4
Mauritania	100	C5
Mauritius	109	L7
Mauron	64	B4
Mauston	124	E5
Mautern	68	E2
Mavinga	106	D6
Mawbray	55	F2
Mawhai Point	115	G3
Mawlaik	93	H4
Mawson	141	E5
Maxaila	109	F4
Maxmo	62	K5
Maya	85	N5
Mayaguana Island	133	L3
Mayaguana Passage	133	L3
Mayaguez	133	P5
Mayak *China*	86	F2
Mayak *Russia*	71	H1
Mayak *Russia*	79	K5
Mayamey	95	M3
Mayas, Montanas	132	C6
Maybole	57	D5
May, Cape	125	N7
Maychew	96	D10
Maydh	103	J5
Mayenne *France*	64	C4
Mayenne *France*	65	C5
Mayero	84	G3
Mayfaah	97	H9
Mayfield *U.K.*	53	H3
Mayfield *U.S.A.*	124	F8
May, Isle of	57	F4
Maykop	79	G7
Maykor	78	K4
Maymakan *Russia*	85	N5
Maymakan *Russia*	85	P5
Maymyo	93	J4
Mayn	85	W4
Maynooth	59	J6
Mayo *Argentina*	139	B9
Mayo *Canada*	118	H3
Mayo *Ireland*	58	D5
Mayo *Mexico*	130	E4
Mayor Island	115	F2
Mayor, Pic	67	H3
Mayotte	109	J2
May Pen	132	J6
Mayraira Point	91	G2
Mayrata	75	F3
Maysville	124	J7
Mayumba	106	A3
Mayuram	92	E6
Mayville	123	R4
Mayyun Island	96	F10
Mazalat	73	H4
Mazamari	136	C6
Mazamet	65	E7
Mazar	92	E1
Mazar-e Sharif	92	C1
Mazarete	67	E2
Mazarredo	139	C9
Mazarron	67	F4
Mazarsu	86	C3
Mazaruni	136	F2
Mazatenango	132	B7
Mazatlan	130	F6
Mazdaj	95	K5
Mazeikiai	63	K8
Mazgirt	77	H3
Mazhur, Irq al	96	G3
Mazidagi	77	J4
Mazinan	95	N3
Mazirbe	63	K8
Mazury	71	J2
Mbabane	108	F5
Mbaiki	102	C7
Mbala	107	F4
Mbalavu	114	S8
Mbale	107	F2
Mbalmayo	105	H5
Mbalo	114	K6
Mbandaka	106	C2
MBanza Congo	106	B4
Mbanza-Ngungu	106	B4
Mbarara	107	F3
Mbengwi	105	G4
Mbeya	107	F4
Mbouda	105	H4
Mbour	104	B3
Mbout	100	C5
Mbuji-Mayi	106	D4
Mchinji	107	F5
MClintock	119	S4
Meade *Alaska, U.S.A.*	118	D1
Meade *Kansas, U.S.A.*	127	M2
Meadie, Loch	56	D2
Mead, Lake	126	E2
Meadow Lake	119	P5
Meadville	125	K6
Mealhada	66	B2
Meana	95	Q3
Meath	58	J5
Meaux	64	E4
Mebula	91	G7
Mecca	96	D6
Mechelen	64	F3
Mecheria	100	E2
Mechigmen	118	A2
Mechigmen Zaliv	118	A2
Mecidie	76	B2
Mecitozu	76	F2
Mecklenburger Bucht	70	D1
Mecsek	72	E2
Mecufi	109	H2
Mecula	109	G2
Medak	92	E5
Medan	90	B5
Medanos	139	D7
Medanosa, Punta	139	C9
Medea	101	F1
Medellin	136	B2
Medelpad	62	G5
Medenine	101	H2
Mederdra	100	B5
Medford	122	C6
Medgidia	73	K3
Medicine Bow Mountains	123	L7
Medicine Bow Peak	123	L7
Medicine Hat	123	J3
Medicine Lodge	127	N2
Medina *Saudi Arabia*	96	D4
Medina *N. Dakota, U.S.A.*	123	Q4
Medina *New York, U.S.A.*	125	L5
Medinaceli	66	E2
Medina del Campo	66	D2
Medina de Rioseco	66	D2
Medina Sidonia	66	D4
Medina Terminal Canal	125	L5
Medinipur	93	G4
Mediterranean Sea	98	D3
Medjerda, Monts de la	69	B7
Medkovets	73	G4
Mednyy, Ostrov	81	T4
Medoc	65	C6
Medole	68	C3
Medvezhl, Ostrova	85	U2
Medvezhyegorsk	78	E3
Medvyeditsa	78	F4
Medway	53	H3
Medyn	78	F5
Medynskiy Zavorot, Poluostrov	78	K2
Meeberrie	112	D4
Meechkyn, Kosa	85	Y3
Meekatharra	112	D4
Meeker	123	L7
Meerut	92	E3
Meeteetse	123	K5
Mega	91	J6
Megalo Khorio	75	J4
Megalopolis	75	G4
Megara	75	G3
Megeve	65	G6
Megget Reservoir	57	E5
Meghalaya	93	H3
Megion	84	B4
Megisti	76	C4
Megra *Russia*	78	F3
Megra *Russia*	78	G2
Mehamn	62	M1
Mehndawal	92	F3
Mehran	94	H5
Meig	56	D3
Meighen Island	120	G2
Meiktila	93	J4
Meiningen	70	D3
Meira	66	C1
Meissen	70	E3
Mei Xian	87	M7
Mejez El Bab	69	B7
Mejillones	138	B4
Mekambo	106	B2
Mekele	103	G5
Meknes	100	D2
Mekong	93	L6
Mekong, Mouths of the	93	L7
Mela	62	U12
Melaka	90	C5
Melambes	75	H5
Melanesia	142	F4
Melawi	90	E6
Melbourne *Australia*	113	J6
Melbourne *U.S.A.*	129	M6
Melbourne Island	119	Q2
Melbu	62	F2
Melchor Muzquiz	127	M7
Melenki	78	G4
Meleuz	78	K5
Melfi *Chad*	102	C5
Melfi *Italy*	69	E5
Melfort	119	Q5
Melgaco	137	G4
Melhus	62	D4
Melilla	100	E1
Melipilla	139	B6
Melita	123	P3
Melito di Porto Salvo	69	E7
Melitopol	79	F6
Melk	68	E1
Melksham	53	E3
Mellegue, Oued	101	G1
Mellerud	63	E7
Melle-sur-Bretonne	65	C5
Melling	55	G2
Mellish Reef	113	M2
Mellte	52	D3
Melnik	70	F3
Melo	138	F6
Melolo	91	G7
Melozitna	118	E2
Melrhir, Chott	101	G2
Melrose	124	C4
Melsungen	70	C3
Meltaus	62	L3
Melton Mowbray	53	G2
Melun	64	E4
Melut	103	F5
Melvern Lake	124	C7
Melville	123	N2
Melville Bugt	120	P2
Melville, Cape	113	J1
Melville Hills	118	L2
Melville Island *Australia*	112	G1
Melville Island *Canada*	120	D2
Melville, Kap	120	P2
Melville, Lake	121	Q7
Melville Peninsula	120	K4
Melvin, Lough	58	F4
Melykut	72	E2
Melyuveyem	85	W4
Memba	109	H2
Memberamo	91	K6
Memboro	91	F7
Memel	63	L9
Memmingen	70	D4
Mempawah	90	D5
Memphis *Tennessee, U.S.A.*	128	H3
Memphis *Texas, U.S.A.*	127	M3
Mena	128	E3
Menai Bridge	55	E3
Menaka	101	F5
Mendawai	90	E6
Mende	65	E6
Mendi	114	C3
Mendip Hills	52	E3
Mendocino, Cape	122	B7
Mendoza	138	C6
Menemen	76	B3
Menen	64	E3
Menfi	69	D7
Mengcheng	93	N2
Mengcun	87	M4
Mengen	76	E2
Mengene Dagi	77	L3
Menggala	90	D6
Menghai	93	K4
Mengjiagang	88	C2
Mengjiawan	87	K4
Mengla	93	K4
Mengshan	93	M4
Mengyin	87	M4
Meniet	101	F3
Menihek, Lac	121	N7
Meningie	113	H6
Menkya	78	L3
Menominee *U.S.A.*	124	G4
Menominee *U.S.A.*	124	G4
Menomonee Falls	124	F5
Menongue	106	C5
Menorca	67	J3
Mentawai, Kepulauan	90	B6
Mentawai, Selat	90	B6
Mentok	90	D6
Menton	68	A4
Mentor	125	K6
Menyamya	114	D3
Menzel Bourguiba	69	B7
Meon	53	F4
Meppel	64	G2
Meppen	70	B2
Mequinenza	67	G2
Merabellou, Kolpos	75	H5
Merak	90	D7
Merano	68	C2

Merauke 91 L7
Mercan Dagi 77 H3
Mercato Saraceno 68 D4
Merced 126 B2
Mercedario, Cerro 138 B6
Mercedes *Argentina* 139 C6
Mercedes *Argentina* 139 E6
Mercedes *Argentina* 138 E5
Mercedes *Uruguay* 138 E6
Mercimek 77 F4
Mercimekkale 77 J3
Mercurea 73 G3
Mercury Bay 115 E2
Mercy, Cape 120 P5
Mere 52 E3
Meredith, Cape 139 D10
Meredoua 100 F3
Mere Lava 114 U11
Mereworth 53 H3
Mergenovo 79 J6
Mergui 93 J6
Mergui Archipelago 93 J6
Meribah 113 J5
Meric 76 B2
Merida *Mexico* 131 Q7
Merida *Spain* 66 C3
Merida *Venezuela* 136 C2
Merida, Cordillera de 136 C2
Meriden 125 P6
Meridian 128 H4
Merig 114 T11
Merir 91 J5
Meriruma 137 G3
Merkys 63 L9
Mermaid Reef 112 D2
Merowe 103 F4
Merredin 112 D5
Merrick 57 D5
Merrill 124 F4
Merrillville 124 G6
Merrimack 125 Q5
Merritt 122 D2
Merritt Island 129 M6
Merriwa 113 L5
Mersa Fatma 96 E9
Mersea Island 53 H3
Merseburg 70 D3
Merse, The 57 F5
Mersey 55 G3
Merseyside 55 G3
Mersin 76 F4
Mersing 90 C5
Mersrags 63 K8
Merthyr Tydfil 52 D3
Mertola 66 C4
Mertvyy Kultuk, Sor 79 J6
Mertz Glacier 141 K5
Merzifon 76 F2
Merzig 70 B4
Mesa 126 G4
Mesaras, Kolpos 75 H5
Meschede 70 C3
Meselefors 62 G4
Meshik 118 D4
Meshraer Req 102 E6
Mesolongion 75 F3
Messina *Italy* 69 E6
Messina *South Africa* 108 F4
Messina, Stretto di 69 E6
Messingham 55 J3
Messini 75 F4
Messiniakos Kolpos 75 F4
Messo 84 B3
Messoyakha 84 B3
Mesta 75 H2
Mestiya 77 K1
Mestre 68 D3
Mesudiye 77 G2
Meta 136 D2
Metan 138 D5
Metapan 132 C7
Metaponto 69 F5
Metema 103 G5
Meteran 114 E2
Methven *New Zealand* 115 C5
Methven *U.K.* 57 E4
Methwin, Mount 112 E4
Metkovic 72 D4
Metlika 72 C3
Metropolis 124 F8
Metsovon 75 F3
Metu 103 G6
Metz 64 G4
Meulaboh 90 B5
Meureudu 90 B4
Meurthe 64 G4
Meuse 64 F3
Mexborough 55 H3
Mexia 128 D5
Mexicali 126 E4
Mexico 130 H6
Mexico *U.S.A.* 124 E7
Mexico City 131 K8
Mexico, Gulf of 117 K6
Meydancik 77 K2
Meydan e Gel 95 M7
Meydani, Ra's e 95 P9
Meymaneh 94 S4
Meymeh 95 K5
Meynypilgyno 85 X4
Meyrueis 65 E6
Mezdra 73 G4
Mezen *Russia* 78 G2
Mezen *Russia* 78 H2
Mezenc, Mont 65 F6
Mezenskaya Guba 78 G2
Mezenskiy 84 F2
Mezhdurechensk 84 D6
Mezhdusharskiy, Ostrov 80 G2
Mezhgorye 71 K4
Mezotur 72 F2
Mezquital 130 G6
Mezzana 68 C2
Mhangura 108 F3
Mhow 92 E4
Miahuatlan 131 L9
Miajadas 66 D3
Miami *Arizona, U.S.A.* 126 G4
Miami *Florida, U.S.A.* 129 M8
Miami *Ohio, U.S.A.* 124 H7
Miami Beach 129 M8
Mianabad 95 N3
Miandowab 94 H3
Mianeh 94 H3
Miang, Pou 93 K5
Mianwali 92 D2
Mianyang 93 K2
Miarinarivo *Madagascar* 109 J3
Miarinarivo *Madagascar* 109 J3
Miass 84 Ad5
Miastko 71 G1
Micang Shan 93 L2
Michalovce 71 J4
Michelson, Mount 118 G2
Michigan 124 H5
Michigan City 124 G6
Michigan, Lake 124 G5
Michipicoten 124 H3
Michipicoten Island 124 H3
Michurinsk 79 G5
Mickle Fell 55 G2
Mickleton 53 F2
Micronesia 142 F4
Micurin 73 J4
Middelburg *Netherlands* 64 E3
Middelburg *South Africa* 108 E5
Middelburg *South Africa* 108 E6
Middle Andaman 93 H6
Middle Barton 53 F3
Middlebury 125 P4
Middlefart 63 C9
Middlemarch 115 C6
Middlesboro 124 J8
Middlesbrough 55 H2
Middleton *Greater Manchester, U.K.* 55 G3
Middleton *Strathclyde, U.K.* 57 B4
Middleton Cheney 53 F2
Middle Tongue 55 G2
Middleton-on-the-Wolds 55 J3
Middleton Reef 113 M4
Middletown *U.K.* 52 D2
Middletown *New York, U.S.A.* 125 N6
Middletown *Ohio, U.S.A.* 124 H7
Middlewich 55 G3
Mid Glamorgan 52 D3
Midhurst 53 G4
Midi 96 F8
Midland *Canada* 125 L4
Midland *Michigan, U.S.A.* 124 H5
Midland *Texas, U.S.A.* 127 M5
Midleton 59 F9
Midongy Atsimo 109 J4
Midsomer Norton 52 E3
Midwest 123 L6
Midwest City 128 D3
Midyan 96 B3
Midyat 77 J4
Mid Yell 56 A1
Midzor 73 G4
Miechow 71 J3
Miedwie, Jezioro 70 F2
Miedzyrzecz 70 F2
Mielec 71 J3
Miena 113 K7
Mieres 66 D1
Mieso 103 H6
Mieszkowice 70 F2
Miford Sound 115 A6
Mighan 95 P6
Miguel Aleman, Presa 131 L8
Miguel Alves 137 J4
Miguel Hidalgo, Presa 127 H7
Mihaliccik 76 D3
Mihara 89 D8
Miharu 89 H7
Mihrad, Al 97 L6
Miida 96 E9
Mijares 67 F2
Mikha Tskhakaya 77 J1
Mikhaylova 84 D1
Mikhaylovgrad 73 G4
Mikhaylov Island 141 F6
Mikhaylovka *Russia* 88 C4
Mikhaylovka *Russia* 79 G5
Mikindani 107 G5
Mikkeli *Finland* 63 M6
Mikkeli *Finland* 63 M6
Mikolajki 71 J2
Mikonos 75 H4
Mikri Prespa, Limni 75 F2
Mikulov 71 G4
Mikun 78 J3
Mikuni 89 F7
Mikuni-sammyaku 89 G7
Mikura-jima 89 G9
Milaca 124 D4
Milagro 136 B4
Milan *Italy* 68 B3
Milan *U.S.A.* 128 H3
Milano 68 B3
Milas 76 B4
Milazzo 69 E6
Milbank 123 R5
Mildenhall 53 H2
Mildurra 113 J5
Mile 93 K4
Mileh Tharthar 94 F5
Miles 113 L4
Miles City 123 M4
Milford *U.K.* 58 G2
Milford *U.S.A.* 125 N7
Milford Haven 52 B3
Milford Sound 115 A6
Milgun 112 D4
Milh, Bahr al 94 F5
Miliana 101 F1
Miliane, Oued 69 C7
Milk 123 L3
Millas 65 E7
Millau 65 E6
Milledgeville 129 L4
Mille Lacs, Lac des 124 E2
Mille Lacs Lake 124 D3
Miller 123 Q5
Millerovo 79 G6
Millers Flat 115 B6
Millford 58 J4
Millington 128 H3
Mill Island *Antarctic* 141 G5
Mill Island *Canada* 120 L5
Millisle 58 L3
Millnocket 125 R4
Millom 55 F2
Millport 57 D5
Mills Lake 119 M3
Milltown 58 K2
Milltown Malbay 59 D7
Millville 125 N7
Millwood Lake 128 F4
Milngavie 57 D5
Milogradovo 88 E4
Milolii 126 T11
Milos *Greece* 75 H4
Milos *Greece* 75 H4
Milowka 71 H4
Milparinka 113 J4
Milpillas 131 K9
Milton *New Zealand* 115 B7
Milton *Florida, U.S.A.* 129 J5
Milton *Pennsylvania, U.S.A.* 125 M6
Milton Abbot 52 C4
Milton Ernest 53 G2
Milton Keynes 53 G2
Miluo 93 M3
Milwaukee 124 G5
Mimizan 65 C6
Mimon 70 F3
Mina Abd Allah 97 J2
Minab 95 N8
Mina de San Domingos 66 C4
Minahassa Peninsula 91 G5
Minamata 89 C9
Minas *Indonesia* 90 C5
Minas *Uruguay* 139 E6
Mina Saud 97 J2
Minas Gerais 138 G3
Minas, Sierra de las 132 C7
Minatitlan 131 M8
Minbu 93 H4
Minch, The 56 C2
Mincio 68 C3
Mindanao 91 G4
Mindelo 104 L7
Minden *U.S.A.* 128 F4
Minden *Germany* 70 C2
Mindoro 91 G3
Mindoro Strait 91 G3
Mindra 73 G3
Minehead 52 D3
Mine Head 59 G9
Mineola 128 E4
Mineral Wells 128 C4
Minerva Reefs 111 T6
Minervino Murge 69 F5
Minfeng 92 F1
Mingechaur 79 H7
Mingela 113 K2
Minglanilla 67 F3
Mingshui *Gansu, China* 86 H3
Mingshui *Heilongjiang, China* 87 P2
Mingulay 57 A4
Minicoy 92 D7
Minigwal 112 E4
Min Jiang 93 K3
Minle 86 J4
Minna 105 G4
Minneapolis 124 D4
Minnedosa 123 Q2
Minnesota *U.S.A.* 124 C3
Minnesota *U.S.A.* 124 C4
Minnitaki Lake 124 E1
Mino 66 B1
Minorca 67 J3
Minot 123 P3
Minsk 78 D5
Minsk Mazowiecki 71 J2
Minsterley 52 E2
Mintlaw 56 F3
Minto 125 S3
Minto Inlet 119 M1
Minto, Lac 121 L6
Minturn 123 L8
Minusinsk 84 E6
Minwakh 97 J8
Min Xian 93 K2
Minyar 78 K4
Miquelon 125 M2
Mira *Italy* 68 D3
Mira *Portugal* 66 B4
Mirabad 95 Q6
Miracema do Norte 137 H5
Miraflores 136 C2
Miraj 92 D5
Miramichi Bay 121 N8
Miramont 65 D6
Miram Shah 92 D2
Miranda *Brazil* 138 E4
Miranda *Brazil* 138 E4
Miranda de Ebro 66 E1
Miranda do Douro 66 C2
Mirande 65 D7
Mirandela 66 C2
Mirandola 68 C3
Mirapinima 136 E4
Miravci 73 G5
Mirbat, Ra's 97 M8
Mirbut 97 M8
Mirear Island 96 B5
Mirebeau 65 D5
Mirgorod 79 E6
Miri 90 E5
Miri Hills 93 H3
Mirimire 136 D1
Mirim, Lagoa 138 F6
Mirjaveh 95 Q7
Mirnyy *Antarctic* 141 G5
Mirnyy *Russia* 85 J4
Mironovo 84 H5
Mirpur Khas 92 C3
Mirriam Vale 113 L3
Mirtoan Sea 75 G4
Mirtoon Pelagos 75 G4
Miryang 89 B8
Mirzapur 92 F3
Misgar 92 D1
Mishan 88 C3
Mi-shima 89 C8
Mishkino 78 K4
Misima Island 114 T10
Miskolc 73 F1
Misool 91 J6
Misratah 101 J2
Missinaibi 121 K7
Mission *Canada* 122 C3
Mission *U.S.A.* 123 P6
Mission Viejo 126 D4
Mississauga 125 L5
Mississippi *U.S.A.* 128 G4
Mississippi *U.S.A.* 128 G5
Mississippi Delta 128 H6
Missoula 122 G4
Missouri *U.S.A.* 124 D7
Missouri *U.S.A.* 124 E7
Missouri, Coteau de 123 P4
Mistassibi 121 M8
Mistassini *Canada* 125 P2
Mistassini *Canada* 125 P2
Mistassini, Lac 121 M7
Mistelbach 68 F1
Mistretta 69 E7
Mitatib 96 C9
Mitchell *Australia* 113 J2
Mitchell *Australia* 113 K4
Mitchell *U.S.A.* 123 Q6
Mitchell, Mount 129 L3
Mitchelstown 59 F8
Mithankot 92 D3
Mithimna 75 J3
Mitilini 75 J3
Mito 89 H7
Mitre 111 R4
Mitrofanovskaya 78 K3
Mitsio, Nosy 109 J2
Mitsiwa 103 G4
Mitsiwa Channel 96 D9
Mittelland Kanal 70 B2
Mittelmark 70 E2
Mitumba, Chaine des 107 E4
Mitwaba 107 E4
Mitzic 106 B2
Mixteco 131 K8
Miyah, Wadi al 77 H5
Miyake-jima 89 G8
Miyake-shoto 89 G11
Miyako 88 H6
Miyako-jima 89 G11
Miyakonojo 89 C10
Miyaly 79 J6
Miyazaki 89 C10
Miyazu 89 E8
Miyoshi 89 D8
Mizdah 101 H2
Mizen Head *Cork, Ireland* 59 C10
Mizen Head *Wicklow, Ireland* 59 K7
Mizhi 87 L4
Mizil 73 J3
Mizoram 93 H4
Mizpe Ramon 94 B6
Mjolby 63 F7
Mjosa 63 D6
Mlada Boleslav 70 F3
Mladenovac 72 F3
Mlawa 71 J2
Mljet 72 D4
Moa *Cuba* 133 K4

Name	Page	Grid
Moa *Indonesia*	91	H7
Moab	127	H1
Moa Island	114	C4
Moala	114	R9
Moate	59	G6
Moatize	109	F3
Moba	107	E4
Mobaye	102	D7
Mobayi-Mbongo	106	D2
Moberly	124	D7
Mobile	129	H5
Mobile Bay	129	H5
Mobridge	123	P5
Mobutu Sese Seko, Lake	107	F2
Moca	114	S9
Mocajuba	137	G4
Mocambique	109	H3
Mocamedes	106	B6
Mocha, Isla	139	B7
Mochudi	108	E4
Mocimboa da Praia	109	H2
Moctexuma	127	H6
Moctezuma	131	K7
Mocuba	109	G3
Modder	108	E5
Modena *Italy*	68	C3
Modena *U.S.A.*	126	F2
Modesto	126	B2
Modica	69	E7
Modigliana	68	C3
Modling	68	F1
Modowi	91	J6
Moe	113	K6
Moelv	63	D6
Moengo	137	G2
Moffat	57	E5
Moffat Peak	115	B6
Mogadishu	107	J2
Mogadouro	66	C2
Mogdy	85	N6
Mogilev	78	E5
Mogilev-Podolskiy	79	D6
Mogi-Mirim	138	G4
Mogincual	109	H3
Moglice	75	F2
Mogocha	85	L6
Mogoi	91	J6
Mogok	93	J4
Mogollon Plateau	126	G3
Mogotoyevo, Ozero	85	R2
Mogoyn	86	H2
Mogoytuy	85	J6
Moguer	66	C4
Mohacs	72	E2
Mohaka	115	F3
Mohall	123	P3
Mohammadabad	95	Q6
Mohammadia	100	F1
Mohawk	125	N5
Moheli	109	H2
Mohill	58	G5
Mohoro	107	G4
Moi	63	B7
Moidart	57	C4
Moimenta da Beira	66	C2
Moindou	114	W16
Mointy	86	C2
Mo i Rana	62	F3
Moisie	121	N7
Moissac	65	D6
Moissala	102	C6
Mojave	126	C3
Mojave Desert	126	D3
Moji	89	C9
Mojones, Cerro	138	C5
Moju	137	H4
Mokai	115	E3
Mokelumne	122	D8
Moknine	101	H1
Mokohinau Island	115	E1
Mokokchung	93	H3
Mokolo	105	H3
Mokpo	87	P5
Mokra Gora	72	F4
Molaoi	75	G4
Molat	72	C3
Mold	55	F3
Moldavia	73	J2
Molde	62	B5
Moldova	73	J2
Moldova Noua	73	F3
Moldoveanu	73	H3
Moldovita	73	H2
Mole *Devon, U.K.*	52	D4
Mole *Surrey, U.K.*	53	G3
Molepolole	108	E4
Molfetta	69	F5
Molina de Aragon	67	F2
Molina de Segura	67	F3
Moline	124	E6
Molkom	63	E7
Mollakendi	77	H3
Mollaosman	77	K3
Mollendo	138	B3
Molln	71	M1
Molnlycke	63	E8
Molodechno	71	M1
Molodezhnaya	141	D5
Molodo *Russia*	85	L3
Molodo *Russia*	85	L3
Mologa	78	F4
Molokai	126	S10
Moloma	78	H4
Molotov	78	K4
Moloundou	105	J5
Molsheim	64	G4
Molson Lake	119	R5
Moluccas	91	H6
Moma *Mozambique*	109	R3
Moma *Russia*	85	Q3
Mombasa	107	R3
Mombetsu	88	J3
Momboyo	106	C3
Momi, Ra's	97	P9
Momol	71	L2
Mompos	136	C2
Mon	63	E9
Monach Islands	56	A3
Monach, Sound of	56	A3
Monaco	65	G7
Monadhliath Mountains	57	D3
Monaghan	58	J4
Monahans	127	L5
Mona, Isla	133	P5
Mona Passage	133	N5
Monarch Mount	118	K5
Monarch Pass	123	L8
Monar, Loch	56	C3
Monashe Mountains	122	E2
Monasterevin	59	H6
Monastir *Albania*	73	F5
Monastir *Italy*	69	B6
Monastir *Tunisia*	101	H1
Monastyriska	73	H1
Monatele	105	H5
Moncalieri	68	A3
Moncao	66	B1
Monchdorf	68	E1
Monchegorsk	62	Q3
Monchique	66	B4
Monclova	127	M7
Moncontour	64	B4
Moncton	121	P8
Mondego	66	C2
Mondonedo	66	C1
Mondovi	68	A3
Mondragone	69	D5
Mondsee	68	D2
Monemvasia	75	G4
Moneron, Ostrov	88	H2
Monesterio	66	C3
Moneymore	58	J3
Monfalcone	68	D3
Monforte	66	C3
Monforte de Lemos	66	C1
Monga	106	D2
Mongala	106	D2
Mongalla	103	F6
Mong Cai	93	L4
Mongga	114	H5
Mongge	91	J6
Mong Hang	93	J4
Monghyr	92	G3
Mong Lin	93	K4
Mongo	102	C5
Mongolia	86	G2
Mongororo	102	D5
Mongu	106	D6
Monhhaan	87	L2
Moniaive	57	E5
Monifieth	57	F4
Moniquira	136	C2
Monitor Range	122	F8
Monkira	113	J3
Monkland	52	E2
Monkoto	106	D3
Monmouth *U.K.*	52	E3
Monmouth *U.S.A.*	124	E6
Monnow	52	E3
Mono	105	F4
Mono Lake	126	C2
Monolithos	75	J4
Monopoli	69	F5
Monovar	67	F3
Monreal del Campo	67	F2
Monreale	69	D6
Monroe *Georgia, U.S.A.*	129	L4
Monroe *Louisiana, U.S.A.*	128	F4
Monroe *Michigan, U.S.A.*	124	J6
Monroe *N. Carolina, U.S.A.*	129	M3
Monroe *Wisconsin, U.S.A.*	124	F5
Monrovia	104	C4
Mons	64	E3
Monsaras, Ponta da	138	J3
Monselice	68	C3
Monserrat	67	F3
Montaigu	65	C5
Montalban	67	F2
Montalbo	66	E3
Montalcino	68	C4
Montalto	69	E6
Montalvo	136	B4
Montamarta	66	D2
Montana	122	K4
Montanchez	66	C3
Montanita	136	B3
Montargis	65	E5
Montauban	65	D6
Montauk Point	125	Q6
Montbard	65	F5
Montbeliard	65	G5
Montblanch	67	G2
Montbrison	65	F6
Montceau-les-Mines	65	F5
Montcornet	64	F4
Mont-de-Marsan	65	C7
Montdidier	64	E4
Monte Alegre	137	G4
Monte Azul	138	H3
Monte Bello	136	B5
Montebello	125	N4
Monte Carlo	68	A4
Monte Caseros	139	E6
Montecatini Terme	68	C4
Monte Cristi	133	M5
Montecristo, Isola di	69	C4
Montego Bay	132	J5
Montelimar	65	F6
Montemaggiore Belsito	69	D7
Montemorelos	128	C8
Montemor-o-Novo	66	B3
Montepuez	109	G2
Montepulciano	68	C4
Monte Quemado	138	D5
Montereau-faut-Yonne	64	E4
Monterey	126	B2
Monterey Bay	126	B2
Monteria	136	B2
Montero	138	D3
Monterotondo	69	D4
Monterrey	128	B8
Monte Santu, Capo di	69	B5
Montes Claros	138	E3
Montevideo *Uruguay*	139	E6
Montevideo *U.S.A.*	124	C4
Monte Vista	127	J2
Montezuma Peak	127	J2
Montfort-sur-Meu	64	B4
Montgomery *U.K.*	52	D2
Montgomery *U.S.A.*	129	J4
Montguyon	65	C6
Monti	69	B5
Monticello *Arkansas, U.S.A.*	128	G4
Monticello *Florida, U.S.A.*	129	L5
Monticello *New York, U.S.A.*	125	N6
Monticello *Utah, U.S.A.*	127	H2
Montiel, Campo de	66	E3
Montignac	65	D6
Montilla	66	D4
Mont-Joli	125	R2
Mont Laurier	125	N3
Montlucon	65	E5
Montmagny	125	Q3
Montmedy	64	F4
Montmirail	64	E4
Montmorillon	65	D5
Monto	113	L3
Montoro	66	D4
Montpelier	122	J6
Montpelier *France*	65	E7
Montpellier *U.S.A.*	125	P4
Montraux	68	A2
Montreal	124	H3
Montreal	125	P4
Montreal Lake	119	P5
Montreal River Harbour	124	H3
Montrose *U.K.*	57	F4
Montrose *U.S.A.*	127	J1
Mont Saint-Michel	64	C4
Montseny	67	H2
Montserrat	133	R6
Mont Wright	121	N7
Monywa	93	J4
Monza	68	B3
Monzon	67	G2
Moonie	113	K4
Moopna	112	F5
Moora	112	D5
Mooraberree	113	J4
Moorcroft	123	M5
Moore, Lake	112	D4
Moorfoot Hills	57	E5
Moorhead	124	B3
Moorlands	113	H6
Moorlinch	52	E3
Moose	121	K7
Moosehead Lake	125	R4
Moose Jaw	123	M2
Moose Lake *Canada*	119	Q5
Moose Lake *U.S.A.*	124	D3
Moose Mountain Creek	123	N2
Moosonee	121	K7
Mopeia Velha	109	G3
Mopti	100	E6
Moqor	92	C2
Moquequa	138	B3
Mora *Cameroon*	105	H3
Mora *Portugal*	66	B3
Mora *Sweden*	63	F6
Moradabad	92	E3
Moradal, Sierra do	66	C3
Mora de Rubielos	67	F2
Morafenobe	109	H3
Morag	71	H2
Morales	132	C7
Moramanga	109	J3
Moran	123	J6
Morant Cays	132	K6
Morant Point	132	J6
Moratuwa	92	E7
Morava *Czechoslovakia*	71	G4
Morava *Yugoslavia*	73	F3
Moraveh Tappeh	95	M3
Morawa	112	D4
Moray Firth	56	E3
Morbi	92	D4
Mor Budejovice	70	F4
Morbylanga	63	G8
Morden	123	Q3
Mordogan	76	B3
Mordovo	79	G5
Moreau	122	N5
Morebattle	57	F5
Morecambe	55	G2
Morecambe Bay	55	E2
Moreda	66	E4
Moree	113	K4
Morehead *Papua New Guinea*	114	C3
Morehead *U.S.A.*	124	J7
Morehead City	129	P3
Morelia	131	J8
Morella	67	F2
More, Loch *U.K.*	56	D2
More, Loch *U.K.*	56	E2
Morena, Sierra	66	D3
Moreno	126	G6
Moreno, Bahia	138	B4
More og Romsdal	62	C5
Moresby Island	118	J5
Mores Island	132	J1
Moreton Bay	113	L4
Moreton-in-Marsh	53	F3
Moreton Island	113	L4
Morez	65	G5
Morgan City	128	G6
Morganton	129	M3
Morgantown	125	L7
Morgongava	63	G7
Mori *China*	86	F3
Mori *Japan*	88	H4
Moriarty	127	K3
Morioka	88	H6
Morlaix	64	B4
Morley	55	H3
Morlunda	63	F8
Mormanno	69	F6
Mornington, Isla	139	A9
Mornington Island	113	H2
Morobe	114	D3
Morocco	100	D2
Morogoro	107	G4
Moro Gulf	91	G4
Morokovo	85	W3
Moroleon	131	J7
Morombe	109	H4
Moron	132	H3
Moron *Mongolia*	86	J2
Moron *Mongolia*	87	L2
Moronade, Cerro des	130	G7
Morondava	109	H4
Moron de la Frontera	66	D4
Moroni	109	H2
Moron Us He	93	H2
Morotai	91	H5
Moroto	107	F2
Morozovsk	79	G6
Morpara	137	J6
Morpeth	55	H1
Morrilton	128	F3
Morrinhos	138	G3
Morrinsville	115	E2
Morris *Canada*	123	R3
Morris *U.S.A.*	124	C4
Morris Jesup, Kap	140	Q2
Morris, Mount	112	G4
Morristown	129	L2
Morro Bay	126	B3
Morro do Chapeu	137	J6
Morro, Punta	139	B5
Morros, Punta	131	P8
Morrosquillo, Golfo de	133	K10
Mors	63	C8
Morshansk	79	G5
Mortagne	64	D4
Mortain	64	C4
Mortara	68	B3
Morteau	65	G5
Morte Bay	52	C3
Mortes	137	G6
Morton *U.K.*	53	G2
Morton *U.S.A.*	122	C4
Morundah	113	K5
Morven *Australia*	113	K4
Morven *U.K.*	57	E3
Morvern	57	C4
Morwell	113	K6
Mosakula	63	L7
Mosby	63	B7
Moscow *U.S.A.*	122	F4
Moscow *Russia*	78	F4
Mosedale	55	F2
Mosel	70	B4
Moselle	64	G4
Moses Lake	122	E4
Moseyevo	78	H2
Mosgiel	115	C6
Mosha	78	G3
Moshchnyy, Ostrov	63	M6
Moshi	107	G4
Mosjoen	62	E4
Moskenesoya	62	E3
Moskosel	62	H4
Moskva	78	F4
Mosonmagyarovar	72	D2
Mosquera	136	B3
Mosquitia	132	E7
Mosquito Lake	119	Q3
Mosquitos, Costa de	132	F8
Mosquitos, Golfo de los	132	G10
Moss	63	D7
Mossaka	106	C3
Mossburn	115	B6
Mosselbaai	108	D6
Mossley	58	L3
Mossman	113	K2
Mossoro	137	K5

Name	Page	Grid
Most	70	E3
Mosta	74	C5
Mostaganem	100	F1
Mostar	72	D4
Mostiska	71	K4
Mosty	71	L2
Mostyn	55	F3
Mosul	77	K4
Mosulpo	87	P5
Mota	103	G5
Mota	114	T10
Mota del Cuervo	66	E3
Motala	63	F7
Mota Lava	114	T10
Motegi	89	H7
Motherwell	57	E5
Motihari	92	F3
Motilla del Palancar	67	F3
Motovskiy Zaliv	62	G2
Motril	66	E4
Motueka *New Zealand*	115	D4
Motueka *New Zealand*	115	D4
Motupiko Blenheim	115	D4
Motykleyka	85	R5
Moudhros	75	H3
Moudjeria	100	C5
Mouka	102	D6
Mould Bay	120	C2
Moulins	65	E5
Moulmein	93	J5
Moulouya, Oued	100	E2
Moulton	55	H2
Moultrie	129	L5
Moultrie, Lake	129	M4
Mounda, Akra	75	F3
Mound City	124	C6
Moundou	102	C6
Moung	93	K6
Mountain	118	K2
Mountain Ash	52	D3
Mountain Home *Arkansas, U.S.A.*	128	F2
Mountain Home *Idaho, U.S.A.*	122	G6
Mountain Village	118	C3
Mount Airy	129	M2
Mount Ararat	77	L3
Mount Bellew	59	E6
Mount Desert Island	125	R4
Mount Doreen	112	G3
Mount Douglas	113	K3
Mount Elba	113	H5
Mount Gambier	113	J6
Mount Hagen	114	C3
Mount Isa	113	H3
Mount Magnet	112	D4
Mountmellick	59	H6
Mount Pleasant *Iowa, U.S.A.*	124	E6
Mount Pleasant *Michigan, U.S.A.*	124	H5
Mount Pleasant *Texas, U.S.A.*	128	E4
Mount Pleasant *Utah, U.S.A.*	126	G1
Mountrath	59	H6
Mount's Bay	52	B4
Mount Shasta	122	C7
Mount Thule	120	L3
Mount Vernon *Alabama, U.S.A.*	129	H5
Mount Vernon *Illinois, U.S.A.*	124	F7
Mount Vernon *Indiana, U.S.A.*	124	G8
Mount Vernon *Ohio, U.S.A.*	124	J6
Mount Vernon *Washington, U.S.A.*	122	C3
Moura *Brazil*	136	E4
Moura *Portugal*	66	C3
Mourdi, Depression du	102	D4
Mourne Mountains	58	K4
Moussoro	102	C5
Moutong	91	G5
Movas	127	H6
Moville	58	H4
Moy	58	D4
Moyale	107	G2
Moyamba	104	C4
Moyen Atlas	100	E2
Moygashel	58	J4
Moyo *Indonesia*	91	F7
Moyo *Uganda*	106	F2
Moyobamba	136	B5
Moyu	92	E1
Mozambique	109	G3
Mozambique Channel	109	H3
Mozhaysk	78	F4
Mozhga	78	J4
Mozyr	79	D5
Mpanda	107	F4
Mpe	106	B3
Mpika	107	F5
Mporokoso	107	F4
Mpraeso	104	E4
Mrakovo	79	K5
M.R. Gomez, Presa	127	N7
Mrkonjic Grad	72	D3
Msaken	101	H1
MSila	67	J5
Msta	78	E4
Mstislav	78	E5
Mtsensk	79	F5
Mtwara	107	G5
Mualo	109	G2
Muang Chiang Rai	93	J5
Muang Khon Kaen	93	K5
Muang Lampang	93	J5
Muang Lamphun	93	J5
Muang Loei	93	K5
Muang Nan	93	K5
Muang Phayao	93	J5
Muang Phetchabun	93	K5
Muang Phichit	93	K5
Muang Phitsanulok	93	K5
Muang Phrae	93	K5
Muanza	109	F3
Muar	90	C5
Muara	90	E4
Muarabungo	90	D6
Muaraenim	90	D6
Muaralesan	91	F5
Muarasiberut	90	B6
Muarasigep	90	B6
Muarasipongi	90	B5
Muaratebo	90	D6
Muarateweh	90	E6
Mubende	107	F2
Mubi	105	H3
Mubrani	91	J6
Mucajai	136	E3
Muchinga Escarpment	107	F5
Much Wenlock	52	E2
Muck	57	B4
Muckanagh Lough	59	E7
Muckish Mount	58	G2
Muckle Roe	56	A1
Muckross Head	58	E3
Muconda	106	D5
Mucuim	136	E5
Mucur	76	F3
Mudanjiang	88	B3
Mudan Jiang	88	B3
Mudanya	76	C2
Mudayy	97	L8
Muddy Gap Pass	123	L6
Mudgee	113	K5
Mudurnu	76	D2
Mueda	109	G2
Muelas	66	D2
Mueo	114	W16
Mufulira	107	E5
Mufu Shan	93	M3
Muganskaya Step	94	J2
Mughar	95	L5
Mughshin	97	M7
Mugi	89	E9
Mugia	66	B1
Mugila, Monts	107	E4
Mugla	76	C4
Muhammad Qol	103	G3
Muhammad, Ras	103	F2
Muhaywir	77	J7
Muhldorf	70	E4
Muhlhausen	70	D3
Muhu	63	K7
Mui Bai Bung	93	K7
Muick	57	E3
Muirkirk	57	D5
Muite	109	G2
Mukachevo	79	C6
Mukah	90	E5
Mukawa	88	H4
Mukawwar	96	C6
Mukdahan	93	K5
Mukden	87	N3
Mukhen	88	F1
Mukhor-Konduy	85	J6
Mukomuko	90	D6
Mukur	79	J6
Mula	67	F3
Mulaly	86	D2
Mulan	88	B3
Mulanay	91	G3
Mulayit Taung	93	J5
Mulchatna	118	D3
Mulchen	139	B7
Mulde	70	E3
Muleshoe	127	L3
Mulga Downs	112	D3
Mulgrave	121	P8
Mulgrave Island	114	C4
Mulhacen	66	E4
Mulheim	70	B3
Mulhouse	65	G5
Muligort	84	Ad4
Muling *China*	88	C3
Muling *China*	88	C3
Muling He	88	D3
Mull	57	C4
Mullaghanattin	59	C9
Mullaghanish	59	D9
Mullaghareirk Mountains	59	D8
Mullaghcleevaun	59	K6
Mullaghmore	58	J3
Muller, Pegunungan	90	E5
Mullet, The	58	B4
Mullewa	112	D4
Mull Head *U.K.*	56	F7
Mull Head *U.K.*	56	F1
Mullinavat	59	H8
Mullingar	59	H5
Mullsjo	63	E8
Mull, Sound of	57	C4
Mulobezi	106	E6
Mulrany	58	C5
Multan	92	D2
Multanovy	84	A4
Multia	62	L5
Mulymya	84	Ad4
Mumbles, The	52	C5
Mumbwa	106	E6
Mumra	79	H6
Muna *Indonesia*	91	G7
Muna *Russia*	85	L3
Munayly	79	J6
Munchberg	70	D3
Munchen	70	D4
Munchengladbach	70	B3
Muncie	124	H6
Munda	114	H6
Mundesley	53	J2
Mundford	53	H2
Mundo	67	F3
Mundo Novo	138	D6
Mungbere	107	E2
Munich	70	D4
Muniesa	67	F2
Munkfors	63	E7
Mun, Mae Nam	93	K5
Munoz Gamero, Peninsula de	139	B10
Munster	70	B3
Munster	59	D8
Munsterland	70	B3
Muntenia	73	J3
Muntinlupa	91	G3
Munzur Daglari	77	H3
Muong Khoua	93	K4
Muong Ou Tay	93	K4
Muong Sing	93	K4
Muonio	62	K3
Muoniojoki	62	K3
Muqdisho	107	J2
Muqshin, Wadi	97	M7
Mur	68	E2
Mura	72	D2
Muradiye *Turkey*	76	B3
Muradiye *Turkey*	77	K3
Murallon, Cerro	139	B9
Muranga	107	G3
Murashi	78	H4
Murat *France*	65	E6
Murat *Turkey*	77	J3
Muratbasi	77	K3
Murat Dagi	76	C3
Muratli	76	B2
Muraysah, Ras al	101	K2
Murban	97	L5
Murcheh Khvort	95	K5
Murchison *Australia*	112	C4
Murchison *Canada*	120	H4
Murchison *New Zealand*	115	D4
Murchison Sund	120	M2
Murcia *Spain*	67	F4
Murcia *Spain*	67	F3
Murdo	123	P6
Murdochville	125	T2
Murefte	76	B2
Mures	73	F2
Muret	65	D7
Murfreesboro *N. Carolina, U.S.A.*	129	P2
Murfreesboro *Tennessee, U.S.A.*	129	J3
Murgab *Tajikistan*	86	C4
Murgab *Turkmenistan*	95	R3
Muri	95	N3
Muriae	138	H4
Muriege	106	D4
Muritz See	70	E2
Murmansk	78	E2
Murmanskaya Oblast	62	P2
Murmansk Bereg	78	F2
Murmashi	62	Q2
Murnau	70	D5
Murom	78	G4
Muromtsevo	84	B5
Muroran	88	H4
Muros	66	B1
Muroto-zaki	89	E9
Murphy	129	L3
Murra Murra	113	K4
Murray *Australia*	113	H5
Murray *Kentucky, U.S.A.*	124	F8
Murray *Utah, U.S.A.*	122	J7
Murray Bridge	110	J9
Murray Harbour	121	P8
Murray, Lake *Papua New Guinea*	114	C3
Murray, Lake *U.S.A.*	129	M3
Murraysburg	108	D6
Murree	92	D2
Murrumbidgee	113	K5
Mursal	77	H3
Mursala	90	B5
Murud	90	F5
Murukta	84	G3
Murupara	115	F3
Murwara	92	F4
Murwillumbah	113	L4
Murz	68	E2
Murzuq	101	H3
Murzuq, Idhan	101	H4
Murzzuschlag	68	E2
Mus	77	J3
Musala	73	G4
Musallam, Wadi	97	N5
Musan	88	B4
Musandam Peninsula	97	N3
Musayid	97	K4
Muscat	97	P5
Musgrave Ranges	112	G4
Mushash al Hadi	97	J3
Musheramore	59	D8
Mushie	106	C3
Musi	90	C6
Musian	94	H5
Muskegon *U.S.A.*	124	G5
Muskegon *U.S.A.*	124	H5
Muskingum	124	K7
Muskogee	128	E3
Musmar	103	G4
Musoma	107	F3
Mussau	114	D2
Musselburgh	57	E5
Musselshell	123	K4
Mussende	106	C5
Musserra	106	B4
Mussidan	65	D6
Mussuma	106	D5
Mussy	65	F5
Mustafakemalpasa	76	C2
Mustang	92	F3
Mustang Draw	127	L4
Musters, Lago	139	C9
Mustvee	63	M7
Musu-dan	88	B5
Muswellbrook	113	L5
Mut *Egypt*	102	E2
Mut *Turkey*	76	E4
Muta Ponta do	137	K6
Mutarara	109	G3
Mutare	109	F3
Mutki	77	J3
Mutnyy Materik	78	K2
Mutoko	109	F3
Mutoray	84	G4
Mutsu-wan	88	H5
Muurame	63	L5
Muurola	62	L3
Muwaffaq	97	M7
Muxima	106	B4
Muya	85	J5
Muyunkum, Peski	86	C3
Muzaffarabad	92	D2
Muzaffargarh	92	D2
Muzaffarnagar	92	E3
Muzaffarpur	92	G3
Muzon, Cape	118	J5
Muz Tagh Ata Range	92	E1
Mvuma	108	F3
Mwaniwowo	114	L7
Mwanza	107	F3
Mwaya	107	F4
Mweelrea	58	C5
Mwene Ditu	106	D4
Mwenezi *Zimbabwe*	108	F4
Mwenezi *Zimbabwe*	108	F4
Mwenga	107	E3
Mweru, Lake	107	E4
Mweru Wantipa, Lake	107	E4
Mwinilunga	106	D5
Myakit	85	S4
Myanaung	93	J5
Myaundzha	85	R4
Myaungmya	93	H5
Myeik Kyunzu	93	J6
Myingyan	93	J4
Myinmu	93	J4
Myitkyina	93	J3
Myitnge	93	J4
Myittha	93	J4
Myla	78	J2
Mymensingh	93	H4
Myre	62	F2
Myri	62	W12
Myrtle Beach	129	N4
Myrviken	62	F5
Mysen	63	H7
Mysliborz	70	F2
Mysore	92	E6
Mys Shmidta	85	Y3
My Tho	93	L6
Mytishchi	78	F4
Mzab	101	F2
Mze	70	E4
Mzuzu	107	F5

N

Name	Page	Grid
Naalehu	126	T11
Naantali	63	K6
Naas	59	J6
Nabao	66	B3
Nabavatu	114	R8
Naberezhnyye	78	J4
Nabeul	101	H1
Nabire	91	K6
Nablus	94	B5
Nabouwalu	114	R8
Naburn	55	H3
Nacala-a-Velha	109	H2
Nacaome	132	D8
Nachiki	85	T6
Nachvak Fjord	121	P6
Nacogdoches	128	E5
Nacozari de Garcia	127	H5
Nadachi	89	G7
Nadezhdinskoye	88	D1
Nadezhnyy, Mys	85	S2
Nadi	114	Q8
Nadiad	92	D4
Nadlac	72	F2
Nador	100	E1
Naduri	114	R8
Nadvornaya	71	L4
Nadym	84	A3
Naft-e Safid	94	J6
Nafud, An	96	E2
Nafy	96	F4
Naga	91	G3
Nagagami	124	H2

Name	Page	Ref.
Nagahama	89	D9
Naga Hills	93	H3
Nagai	89	G6
Nagaland	93	H3
Nagano	89	G7
Nagaoka	89	G7
Nagappattinam	92	E6
Nagarjuna Sagar	92	E5
Nagasaki	89	B9
Nagashima	89	F8
Nagato	89	C8
Nagaur	92	D3
Nagercoil	92	E7
Nagishot	103	F7
Nagles Mountains	59	F8
Nagornyy	85	L5
Nagorsk	78	J4
Nagoya	89	F8
Nagpur	92	E4
Nagqu	93	H2
Nags Head	129	Q3
Nagykanizsa	72	D2
Nagykata	72	E2
Nagykoros	72	E2
Naha	89	H10
Nahariya	94	B5
Nahavand	94	J4
Nahe	70	B4
Nahoi, Cap	114	T11
Nahuel Huapi, Lago	139	B8
Naikliu	91	G7
Nailsea	52	E3
Nailsworth	52	E3
Naiman Qi	87	N3
Nain	95	L5
Nain	121	P6
Naini Tal	92	E3
Nairai	114	R8
Nairn	56	E3
Nairobi	107	G3
Najafabad	95	K5
Najd	96	E4
Najibabad	92	E3
Najin	88	C4
N Ajjer, Tassili	101	G3
Najran	96	G8
Najran, Wadi	96	G8
Nakadori-shima	89	B9
Nakajo	89	G6
Nakamura	89	D9
Nakano	89	G7
Nakano-shima	89	B11
Nakatay	84	Ad5
Nakatsu	89	C9
Nakatsugawa	89	F8
Nakfa	103	G4
Nakhichevan	77	L3
Nakhl Egypt	96	A2
Nakhl Oman	97	N5
Nakhodka Russia	84	B3
Nakhodka Russia	88	D4
Nakhon Pathom	93	J6
Nakhon Phanom	93	K5
Nakhon Ratchasima	93	K6
Nakhon Sawan	93	K5
Nakhon Si Thammarat	93	J7
Nakina	121	J7
Nakiri	89	F8
Naknek Lake	118	D4
Nakskov	63	F9
Naktong	87	P4
Nakuru	107	G3
Nakusp	122	F2
Nalchik	79	G7
Nalgonda	92	E5
Nallamala Hills	92	E5
Nallihan	76	D2
Nalut	101	H2
Namaa, Tanjung	91	H6
Namacunde	106	C6
Namacurra	109	G3
Namak, Daryacheh-ye	95	K4
Namaki	95	M6
Namakzar	95	Q5
Namakzar, Daryacheh-ye	95	Q5
Namangan	86	C3
Namapa	109	G2
Namaponda	109	G3
Namarroi	109	G3
Namasagali	107	F2
Namatanai	114	E2
Nambour	113	L4
Nam Can	93	K7
Nam Co	93	H2
Nam Dinh	93	L4
Nametil	109	G3
Namib Desert	108	B4
Namibe	106	B6
Namibia	108	C4
Namlea	91	H6
Namoi	113	L5
Namosi Peak	114	R8
Nampa	122	F6
Nampula	109	G3
Namse La	92	F3
Namsen	62	E4
Namsos	62	D4
Namti	93	J3
Namtok	93	J5
Namuka-i-Lau	114	S9
Namuli	109	G3
Namur	64	F3
Namutoni	108	C3
Namwala	106	C6
Nana Barya	102	C6
Nanaimo	122	C3
Nanam	88	B5
Nanao	89	F7
Nancha	88	B2
Nanchang	87	M6
Nanchong	93	L2
Nancowry	93	H7
Nancy	64	G4
Nanda Devi	92	E2
Nandan	93	L3
Nanded	92	E5
Nandurbar	92	D4
Nandyal	92	E5
Nanfeng	87	M6
Nanga Eboko	105	H5
Nangahpinoh	90	E6
Nanga Parbat	92	D1
Nangatayap	90	E6
Nangong	87	M4
Nan Hai	83	K5
Nanjing	87	M5
Nanking	87	M5
Nan, Mae Nam	93	K5
Nanning	93	L4
Nanortalik	116	Q2
Nanpan Jiang	93	K4
Nanpara	92	F3
Nanpi	87	M4
Nanping	87	M6
Nansei-shoto	89	H10
Nansen Sound	120	H1
Nanshan Islands	90	E4
Nansha Qundao	90	E4
Nantais, Lac	121	M5
Nantes	65	C5
Nantong	87	N5
Nantua	65	F5
Nantucket Island	125	Q6
Nantucket Sound	125	Q6
Nantwich	55	G3
Nant-y-moch Reservoir	52	D2
Nanuku Passage	114	S8
Nanuku Reef	114	S8
Nanumanga	111	S3
Nanumea	111	S3
Nanusa, Kepulauan	91	H5
Nanyang	93	M2
Nanyuki	107	G2
Nao, Cabo de la	67	G3
Naococane, Lake	121	M7
Naousa	75	G2
Napa	126	A1
Napabalana	91	G6
Napalkovo	84	A2
Napas	84	C5
Nape	93	L5
Napier	115	F3
Naples Italy	69	E5
Naples U.S.A.	129	M7
Napo	136	C4
Napoleon	124	H6
Napoletano, Appennino	69	E5
Napoli	69	E5
Napoli, Golfo di	69	E5
Naqadeh	94	G3
Nar	53	H2
Nara Japan	89	E8
Nara Mali	100	D5
Nara Pakistan	92	C4
Naracoorte	113	J6
Naran	87	L2
Narasapur	92	F5
Narat	86	E3
Narathiwat	93	K7
Narayanganj	93	H4
Narberth	52	C3
Narbonne	65	E7
Narborough Island	136	A7
Narcea	66	C1
Nardin	95	M3
Narew Poland	71	J2
Narew Poland	71	K2
Narince	77	H4
Narken	62	K3
Narkher	92	E4
Narli	77	G4
Narmada	92	E4
Narman	77	J2
Narnaul	92	E3
Narodnaya, Gora	84	Ad3
Naro-Fominsk	78	F4
Narowal	92	D2
Narpes	62	J5
Narrabri	113	K5
Narrandera	113	K5
Narrogin	112	D5
Narromine	113	K5
Narsimhapur	92	E4
Narsinghgarh	92	E4
Nart	87	M3
Nartabu	91	J6
Naruko	88	H6
Narva	63	N7
Narvik	62	G2
Naryan Mar	78	J2
Narymskiy Khrebet	86	E2
Naryn Russia	84	F6
Naryn Kirghizia	86	C3
Naryn Kirghizia	86	D3
Nasarawa	105	G4
Naseby	115	C6
Nashua	125	Q5
Nashville	129	J2
Nasice	72	E3
Nasielsk	71	J2
Nasijarvi	63	K6
Nasik	92	D5
Nasir	103	F6
Nasir, Buhayrat	103	F3
Nasorolevu	114	R8
Nasrabad	95	K4
Nass	118	K4
Nassau	129	P8
Nasser, Lake	103	F3
Nassjo	63	F8
Nastapoka Islands	121	L6
Nastved	63	D9
Nata	108	E4
Natagaima	136	B3
Natal Brazil	137	K5
Natal Indonesia	90	B5
Natanz	95	K5
Natara	85	L3
Natashquan	121	P7
Natchez	128	G5
Natchitoches	128	F5
Natewa Bay	114	R8
National City	126	D4
Natitingou	105	F3
Natividade	137	H6
Natori	89	H6
Natron, Lake	107	G3
Nattavaara	62	J3
Natuna Besar	90	D5
Natuna, Kepulauan	90	D5
Naturaliste, Cape	112	D5
Naturaliste Channel	112	C4
Nauen	70	E2
Naueyi Akmyane	63	K8
Naujoji Vilnia	71	L1
Naul	58	K5
Naumburg	70	D3
Naungpale	93	J5
Nauru	111	Q2
Naurzum	84	Ad6
Nausori	114	R9
Nautanwa	92	F3
Nautla	131	L7
Nauzad	95	S5
Navadwip	93	G4
Navahermosa	66	D3
Naval	91	G3
Navalcarnero	66	D2
Navalmoral de la Mata	66	D3
Navalpino	66	D3
Navan	58	J5
Navarin, Mys	85	X4
Navarino, Isla	139	C11
Navarra	67	F1
Navars	67	G2
Navasota	128	D5
Navassa Island	133	K5
Navax Point	52	B4
Navenby	55	J3
Naver, Loch	56	D2
Navia Spain	66	C1
Navia Spain	66	C1
Naviti	114	Q8
Navlya	79	E5
Navojoa	127	H7
Navolato	130	F5
Navpaktos	75	F3
Navplion	75	G4
Navrongo	104	E3
Navsari	92	D4
Navua	114	R9
Nawabshah	92	C3
Nawada	92	G4
Nawah	92	C2
Nawasif, Harrat	96	F6
Naws, Ra's	97	M8
Nawton	55	J2
Naxos Greece	75	H4
Naxos Greece	75	H4
Nayagarh	92	G4
Nayau	114	S8
Nay Band	95	L8
Nay Band	95	N5
Nayoro	88	J3
Nazare	137	K6
Nazareth Israel	94	B5
Nazareth Peru	136	B5
Nazarovo	84	E5
Nazas	130	G5
Nazca	136	C6
Naze	89	B11
Nazerat	94	B5
Naze, The	53	J3
Nazik	94	G2
Nazik Golu	77	K3
Nazilli	76	C4
Nazmiye	77	H3
Nazwa	97	N5
Nazyvayevsk	84	A5
Ncheu	107	F5
Ndalatando	106	B4
Ndele	102	D6
Ndeni	114	N7
Ndjamena	102	C5
Ndjote	106	B3
Ndola	107	E5
Nea	62	D5
Nea Filippias	75	F3
Neagh, Lough	58	K3
Neah Bay	122	B3
Neale, Lake	112	G3
Nea Moudhania	75	G2
Neapolis Greece	75	F2
Neapolis Greece	75	H5
Nea Psara	75	G3
Near Islands	118	Aa9
Neath	52	D3
Nebine	113	K4
Nebit Dag	95	M2
Neblina, Pico da	136	D3
Nebraska	123	N7
Nebraska City	124	C6
Nebrodi, Monti	69	E7
Nechako	118	L5
Nechi	133	K11
Neckar	70	C4
Necochea	139	E7
Nedong	93	H3
Nedstrand	63	A7
Needles Canada	122	E3
Needles U.S.A.	126	E3
Needles Point	115	E2
Needles, The	53	F4
Neepawa	123	Q2
Neergaard Lake	120	L3
Nefedovo	84	A5
Nefta	101	G2
Neftechala	94	J2
Neftegorsk	79	J5
Neftekamsk	78	J4
Nefyn	52	C2
Nefza	69	B7
Negele	103	G6
Negev	94	B6
Negoiu	73	H3
Negombo	92	E7
Negotin	73	G3
Negrais, Cape	93	H5
Negra, Punta	136	A5
Negritos	136	A4
Negro Argentina	139	C7
Negro Amazonas, Brazil	136	E4
Negro Santa Catarina, Brazil	138	F5
Negro Uruguay	138	F6
Negros	91	G3
Negru Voda	73	K4
Nehavand	94	J4
Nehbandan	95	Q6
Nehe	87	N2
Nehoiasu	73	J3
Neijiang	93	K3
Nei Mongol Zizhiqu	87	L3
Neisse Poland	70	F3
Neisse Poland	71	G3
Neiteyugansk	84	A4
Neiva	136	B3
Neixiang	93	M2
Nekemte	103	G6
Neksikan	85	R4
Nekso	63	H9
Nelidovo	78	E4
Neligh	123	Q6
Nelkan	85	P5
Nellore	92	E6
Nelma	88	G2
Nelson Canada	122	F3
Nelson New Zealand	115	D4
Nelson U.K.	55	G3
Nelson, Cape Australia	113	J6
Nelson, Cape Papua New Guinea	114	D3
Nelson Lagoon	118	Af8
Nelspruit	108	F5
Nema	100	D5
Neman	78	C4
Neman	71	K1
Nemira	73	J2
Nemirov	73	K1
Nemiscau	121	L7
Nemours	64	E4
Nemun	63	J9
Nemuro	88	K4
Nemuro-kaikyo	88	K4
Nemuy	85	P5
Nenagh	59	F7
Nenana	118	F3
Nene	53	G2
Nen Jiang	87	P1
Nenjiang	87	P2
Nenthead	55	G2
Neokhorion	75	F3
Neon Karlovasi	75	J4
Neosho Kansas, U.S.A.	124	C7
Neosho Missouri, U.S.A.	124	C8
Nepa Russia	84	H5
Nepa Russia	84	H5
Nepal	92	F3
Nephi	126	G1
Nephin Beg Range	58	C4
Nera	69	D4
Nerac	65	D6
Nerchinsk	85	K6
Neretva	72	D4
Neriquinha	106	D6
Neris	63	L9
Nermete, Punta	136	A5
Neryuktey-l-y	85	K4
Neryuvom	84	Ad3
Nes	63	C6
Nesbyen	63	C6
Neskaupstadur	62	Y12
Nesna	62	E3
Nesscliffe	52	E2
Ness, Loch	56	D3
Nesterov Russia	71	K3
Nesterov Ukraine	71	K1

Nesterovo 84 H6
Neston 55 F3
Nestos 75 H2
Nesvizh 71 M2
Netanya 94 B5
Netherlands 64 F2
Neto 69 F6
Nettilling Lake 120 M4
Nettleham 55 J3
Netzahualcoyotl, Presa 131 N9
Neubrandenburg 70 E2
Neuchatel 68 A2
Neuchatel, Lac de 68 A2
Neufchateau *Belgium* 64 F4
Neufchateau *France* 64 F4
Neufchatel 64 D4
Neufelden 68 D1
Neumunster 70 C1
Neunkirchen *Austria* 68 F2
Neunkirchen *Germany* 70 B4
Neuquen *Argentina* 139 C7
Neuquen *Argentina* 139 C7
Neuruppin 70 E2
Neuse 129 P3
Neusiedler See 68 F2
Neuss 70 B3
Neustadt 70 C5
Neustettin 71 G2
Neustrelitz 70 E2
Neu-Ulm 70 D4
Nevada *Missouri, U.S.A.* 124 C8
Nevada *U.S.A.* 122 F8
Nevada, Sierra *Argentina* 138 C5
Nevada, Sierra *Spain* 66 E4
Nevada, Sierra *U.S.A.* 126 C2
Nevado, Cerro 139 C7
Nevado, Sierra del 139 C7
Nevel 78 E4
Nevelsk 88 H2
Nevers 65 E5
Neve, Sierra da 106 B5
Nevesinje 72 E4
Nevezis 63 L9
Nevinnomyssk 79 G7
Nevis, Loch 57 C4
Nevsehir 76 F3
Nevyansk 84 Ad5
New 125 K8
New Abbey 55 F2
New Albany 124 H7
New Alresford 53 F3
Newark *New Jersey, U.S.A.* 125 N6
Newark *Ohio, U.S.A.* 124 J6
Newark-on-Trent 55 J3
New Bedford 125 Q6
New Bedford River 53 H2
New Bern 129 P3
Newberry 129 M3
Newbiggin 55 G2
Newbiggin-by-the-Sea 55 H1
Newbigging 57 E5
New Braunfels 128 C6
Newbridge 59 J6
New Britain 114 E3
New Brunswick *Canada* 121 N8
New Brunswick *U.S.A.* 125 N6
Newbuildings 58 H3
Newburgh *U.K.* 57 E4
Newburgh *U.S.A.* 125 N6
Newbury 53 F3
New Bussa 105 F4
Newby Bridge 55 G2
New Castle 125 K6
Newcastle *Australia* 113 L5
Newcastle *South Africa* 108 E5
Newcastle *U.K.* 58 L4
Newcastle *Indiana, U.S.A.* 124 H7
Newcastle *Wyoming, U.S.A.* 123 M6
Newcastle Emlyn 52 C2
Newcastleton 57 F5
Newcastle-under-Lyme 55 G3
Newcastle-upon-Tyne 55 H2
Newcastle Waters 113 G2
Newcastle West 59 D8
Newchurch 52 D2
New Cumnock 57 D5
Newdegate 112 D5
New Delhi 92 E3
Newell, Lake 122 J2
New England Range 113 L5
Newenham, Cape 118 C4
Newfoundland *Canada* 121 P6
Newfoundland *Canada* 121 Q8
New Galloway 57 D5
New Georgia 114 H6
New Georgia Island 114 H6
New Glasgow 121 P8
New Guinea 114 C2
New Halfa 96 B9
New Hampshire 125 Q5
New Hampton 124 D5
New Hanover 114 E2
Newhaven 53 H4
New Haven 125 P6
New Iberia 128 G5
Newick 53 H4
New Ireland 114 E2
New Jersey 125 N6
New Kandla 92 D4
New Liskeard 125 L3
New London 125 P6
Newman, Mount 112 D3
New Market 125 L7
Newmarket *Ireland* 59 D8
Newmarket *U.K.* 53 H2
Newmarket-on-Fergus 59 E7
New Martinsville 125 K7
New Meadows 122 F5
New Mexico 127 J3
Newmill 57 F5
Newmilns 57 D5
New Milton 53 F4
Newnan 129 K4
New Orleans 128 G5
New Philadelphia 125 K6
New Pitsligo 56 F3
New Plymouth 115 E3
Newport *Ireland* 58 C5
Newport *Dyfed, U.K.* 52 C2
Newport *Essex, U.K.* 53 H3
Newport *Gwent, U.K.* 52 E3
Newport *Isle of Wight, U.K.* 53 F4
Newport *Shropshire, U.K.* 52 E2
Newport *Arkansas, U.S.A.* 128 G3
Newport *Kentucky, U.S.A.* 124 H7
Newport *Rhode Island, U.S.A.* 125 Q6
Newport *Tennessee, U.S.A.* 129 L3
Newport *Vermont, U.S.A.* 125 P4
Newport News 125 M8
Newport Pagnell 53 G2
New Providence 132 J2
Newquay 52 B4
New Quay 52 C2
New Richmond 125 T2
New Romney 53 H4
New Ross 59 J8
Newry 58 K4
Newry Canal 58 K4
New Smyrna Beach 129 M6
New South Wales 113 K5
Newton *Dumfries and Galloway, U.K.* 57 E5
Newton *Lancashire, U.K.* 55 G3
Newton *Iowa, U.S.A.* 124 D6
Newton *Kansas, U.S.A.* 128 D1
Newton *Mississippi, U.S.A.* 128 H4
Newton Abbot 52 D4
Newton Aycliffe 55 H2
Newtonferry 56 A3
Newton Flotman 53 J2
Newtongrange 57 E5
Newtonmore 57 D3
Newton on Trent 55 J3
Newton Poppleford 52 D4
Newton Stewart 54 E2
Newtown 52 D2
New Town 123 N4
Newtownabbey 58 L3
Newtownards 58 L3
Newtownbreda 58 L3
Newtownbutler 58 H4
Newtown-Crommelin 58 K3
Newtowncunningham 58 G3
Newtownmountkennedy 59 K6
Newtownstewart 58 H3
New Ulm 124 C4
New York *U.S.A.* 125 M5
New York *U.S.A.* 125 P6
New York Erie Canal 125 M5
New Zealand 115 B3
Nexpa 130 H8
Neya 78 G4
Neybasteh 95 Q5
Neyland 52 C3
Neyriz 95 M7
Neyshabur 95 P3
Nezhin 79 E5
Ngabe 106 C3
Ngabordamlu, Tanjung 91 J7
Ngadda 105 H3
Ngangla Ringco 92 F2
Nganglong Kangri 92 F2
Ngangze Co 93 G2
Ngaoundere 105 H4
Ngaruawahia 115 E2
Ngaruroro 115 F3
Ngau 114 R9
Ngauruhoe 115 E3
Ngatokae 114 J6
Nggela Pile 114 K6
Nggela Sule 114 K6
Nggele Levu 114 S8
Ngoila 105 H5
Ngong 107 G3
Ngoring Hu 93 J2
Ngorongoro Crater 107 G3
NGouri 102 C5
Ngozi 107 E3
Nguigmi 101 H6
Ngulu Atoll 91 K4
Nguna 114 U12
Ngunju, Tanjung 91 G8
Nguru 105 H3
Nhamunda 136 F4
Nha Trang 93 L6
Nhill 113 J6
Niafounke 100 E5
Niagara 124 G4
Niagara Falls 125 L5
Niah 90 E5
Niamey 101 F6
Niangara 107 E2
Nias 90 B5
Nibe 63 C8
Nicaj Shale 74 E1
Nicaragua 132 D8
Nicaragua, Lago de 132 E9
Nicastro 69 F6
Nice 65 G7
Nichicun, Lake 121 M7
Nichinan 89 C10
Nicholas, Cape 120 G3
Nicholas Channel 132 G3
Nicholls Town 132 H2
Nicholl's Town 129 P8
Nicholson 113 H2
Nickol Bay 112 D3
Nicobar Islands 93 H7
Nicosia *Cyprus* 76 E5
Nicosia *Italy* 69 E7
Nicotera 69 E6
Nicoya, Golfo de 132 E10
Nicoya, Peninsula de 132 E10
Nida 71 J3
Nidd 55 H3
Nidzica 71 J2
Niebull 70 C1
Niederbronn 64 G4
Niedere Tauern 68 D2
Niefang 105 H5
Niemisel 62 J3
Nienburg 70 C2
Nieuw Amsterdam 137 F2
Nieuw Nickerie 137 F2
Nieuwpoort 64 E3
Nigde 76 F4
Niger 105 G4
Niger 101 G5
Nigeria 105 G4
Nigg 56 D3
Niigata 89 G7
Niihama 89 D9
Niihau 126 Q10
Nii-jima 89 G8
Niimi 89 D8
Nijar 66 E4
Nijmegan 64 F3
Nikaria 75 J4
Nikel 62 P2
Nikitas 75 G2
Nikki 105 F4
Nikolaev 71 K4
Nikolayev 79 E6
Nikolayevka 84 Ae6
Nikolayevsk-na-Amure 85 Q6
Nikolsk *Russia* 79 H5
Nikolsk *Russia* 78 H4
Nikolskiy 86 B2
Nikopol 79 E6
Niksar 77 G2
Nikshahr 95 Q8
Niksic 72 E4
Nikulino 84 D4
Nikumarora 111 U2
Nil 103 F2
Nila 91 H7
Nilgiri Hills 92 E6
Nil, Nahren 103 F2
Nilsia 62 N5
Nimach 92 D4
Nimba Mountains 104 D4
Nimes 65 F7
Nimmitabel 113 K6
Nimule 103 F6
Nina Bang Lake 120 L3
Nine Degree Channel 92 D7
Ninety Mile Beach 115 D1
Ninfas, Punta 139 D8
Ninfield 53 H4
Ningan 88 B3
Ningbo 87 N6
Ningde 87 M6
Ningdu 87 M6
Ningguo 87 M5
Ninghe 87 M4
Ninghua 87 M6
Ningjing Shan 93 J2
Ningqiang 93 L2
Ningshan 93 L2
Ningwu 87 L4
Ningxia 93 L1
Ningyang 87 M4
Ninh Hoa 93 L6
Ninigo Group 114 C2
Ninnis Glacier 141 K5
Ninyako Vogumma 84 B2
Nioaque 138 E4
Niobrara 123 P6
Niono 100 D6
Nioro du Sahel 100 D5
Niort 65 C5
Nios 75 H4
Nipigon 124 F2
Nipigon, Lake 124 F2
Nipisiguit 125 S3
Nipissing, Lac 125 L3
Niquelandia 137 H6
Nir 94 H2
Nirmal 92 E5
Nirmal Range 92 E5
Nis 73 F4
Nisa 66 C3
Nisab 96 H9
Nisava 73 G4
Nishinoyama 89 E8
Nishi-suido 89 B8
Nisiros 75 J4
Nisling 118 H3
Nisporeny 73 K2
Nissan 63 E8
Nisum Bredning 63 C8
Nitchequon 121 M7
Niteroi 138 H4
Nith 57 E5
Nithsdale 57 E5
Nitra 71 H4
Niuafoou 111 T5
Niuatoputapu 111 U5
Niue 111 V5
Niulakita 111 S4
Niulan Jiang 93 K3
Niutao 111 S3
Nivelles 64 F3
Nivernais 65 E5
Nivshera 78 J3
Niwbwrch 54 E3
Nizamabad 92 E5
Nizhneangarsk 84 H5
Nizhneimbatskoye 84 D4
Nizhnekamsk 78 J4
Nizhnekamsko Vodokhranilishche 78 J4
Nizhneudinsk 84 F6
Nizhnevartovsk 84 B4
Nizhneye Bugayevo 84 Ab3
Nizhniy Lomov 79 G5
Nizhniy Yenangsk 78 H4
Nizhnyaya Bugayevo 78 J2
Nizhnyaya Chulym 84 B6
Nizhnyaya Omka 84 A5
Nizhnyaya Salda 84 Ad5
Nizhnyaya Shakhtama 85 K6
Nizhnyaya Tunguska 84 H5
Nizhnyaya Tura 78 K4
Nizhnyaya Voch 78 J3
Nizip 77 G4
Nizke Tatry 71 H4
Nizmennyy, Mys 88 E4
Njombe 107 F4
Njoroveto 114 H5
Njurundabommen 63 L5
Nkambe 105 H4
Nkayi 108 E3
Nkhotakota 107 F5
Nkongsamba 105 G5
Nmai Hka 93 J3
Noasca 68 A3
Noatak 118 C2
Nobeoka 89 C9
Nobres 137 F6
Nocera 69 E5
Nogales *Mexico* 126 G5
Nogales *U.S.A.* 126 G5
Nogata 89 C9
Nogent-le-Rotrou 64 D4
Nogent-sur-Seine 64 E4
Noginsk 78 F4
Noginskiy 84 E4
Nogoa 113 K3
Nogoya 138 E6
Noheji 88 H5
Noire 93 K4
Noire, Montagnes 64 B4
Noirmoutier 65 B5
Noirmoutier, Ile de 65 B5
Nok Kundi 92 B3
Nola *Central African Republic* 102 C7
Nola *Italy* 69 E5
Nolinsk 78 H4
Nomad 114 C3
Noma-misaki 89 C10
Nome 118 B3
Nomuka 111 U6
Nonburg 78 J2
Nonda 113 J3
Nondugl 114 C3
Nongan 87 P3
Nong Khai 93 K5
Nongoma 109 F5
Nonouti 111 R2
Nonthaburi 93 K6
Nontron 65 D6
Nookta Island 122 A3
Nootka Sound 122 A3
Nora 103 H4
Noranda 125 L2
Nordaustlandet 140 L2
Nordborg 63 E9
Nord Cap 62 T11
Norddepil 62 Z14
Norden 70 B2
Nordenham 70 C2
Nordenshelda, Arkhipelag 84 F1
Norderney 70 B2
Nordfjord 62 A6
Nordfjordeid 62 A6
Nordfold 62 F3
Nord-Friesische Inseln 63 C9
Nordhausen 70 D3
Nordhorn 70 B2
Nordkapp 62 L1
Nordkinn-halvoya 62 M1
Nord Kvaloy 62 H1
Nordland 63 E4
Nordmaling 62 H5
Nordostsee Kanal 70 C2
Nordoyar 62 Z14
Nordre Isortoq 120 R4
Nordre Strmfjord 120 R4
Nordstrand 70 C1
Nordurfjordur 62 U11
Nordvik 84 J2
Nordvik, Mys 84 J2
Nore 59 H8
Norfolk *U.K.* 53 H2
Norfolk *Nebraska, U.S.A.* 123 R6

Norfolk *Virginia, U.S.A.* **125** M8
Norfolk Island **111** Q7
Norfolk Lake **128** F2
Norheimsund **63** B6
Nori **84** A3
Norilsk **84** D3
Norlat **78** J5
Norman *Australia* **113** J2
Norman *U.S.A.* **128** D3
Normanby **113** J1
Normanby Island **114** E3
Normandes, Iles **64** B4
Normandie **64** D4
Normandie, Collines de **64** C4
Normanton *Australia* **113** J2
Normanton *U.K.* **55** H3
Norman Wells **118** K2
Nornalup **112** D5
Norra Storfjallet **62** F4
Norrbotten **62** M3
Norresundby **63** C8
Norrfjarden **62** J4
Norristown **125** N6
Norrkoping **63** L7
Norrland **62** F5
Norrtalje **63** H7
Norseman **112** E5
Norsjo **62** M4
Norsk **85** N6
Norsup **114** T12
Norte, Punta *Argentina* **139** D8
Norte, Punta *Argentina* **139** E7
Norte, Serra do **136** F6
Northallerton **55** H2
Northam **112** D5
Northampton *U.K.* **53** G2
Northampton *U.S.A.* **125** P5
Northamptonshire **53** G2
North Andaman **93** H6
North Arm **119** N3
North Astrolabe Reef **114** R9
North Battleford **119** P5
North Bay *Canada* **125** L3
North Bay *Ireland* **59** K8
North Bend **122** B6
North Berwick **57** F4
North Canadian **128** C3
North, Cape **121** P8
North Cape *New Zealand* **115** D1
North Cape *Norway* **62** L1
North Cape *U.S.A.* **118** A3
North Carolina **129** M3
North Cave **55** J3
North Channel *Canada* **124** J3
North Channel *U.K.* **58** L2
Northchapel **53** G3
North Charlton **55** H1
Northcliffe **112** D5
North Dakota **123** P4
North Dorset Downs **52** E4
North Downs **53** H3
Northeast Cape **118** B3
Northeast Providence Channel **132** J2
North Elmham **53** H2
Northern Ireland **58** H3
Northern Sporades **75** H3
Northern Territory **112** G3
North Esk **57** F4
Northfield **124** D4
North Flinders Range **113** H5
North Foreland **53** J3
North Geomagnetic Pole **140** S3
North Henik Lake **119** R3
North Korea **87** P4
North Kyme **55** J3
North Lakhimpur **93** H3
Northleach **53** F3
North Magnetic Pole **140** U3
North Miami Beach **129** M8
North Platte *U.S.A.* **123** N7
North Platte *U.S.A.* **123** P7
North Point *Canada* **121** P8
North Point *U.S.A.* **124** J4
North Pole **140** A1
North River **119** S4
North Roe **56** A1
North Ronaldsay **56** F1
North Ronaldsay Firth **56** F1
North Saskatchewan **119** P5
North Sea **50** H4
North Sentinel **93** H6
North Shields **55** H1
North Shoshone Peak **122** F8
North Sound **59** C6
North Sound, The **56** F1
North Stradbroke Island **113** L4
North Taranaki Bight **115** E3
North Tawton **52** D4
North Thoresby **55** J3
North Tolsta **56** B2
North Tonawanda **125** L5
North Twin Island **121** K7
North Tyne **57** F5
North Uist **56** A3
Northumberland **57** F5
Northumberland Islands **113** L3
Northumberland O **120** M2
Northumberland Strait **121** P8
Northwall **56** F1
North Walsham **53** J2
Northway Junction **118** G3
Northwest Cape **118** A3
North West Cape **112** C3
North West Highlands **56** C3
Northwest Providence Channel **132** H1
Northwest Territories **119** Q2
Northwich **55** G3
North York **125** L5
North Yorkshire **55** H2
Norton *U.K.* **55** J2
Norton *U.S.A.* **123** Q8
Norton Bay **118** C3
Norton Sound **118** C3
Norvegia, Cape **141** Z4
Norwalk **124** J6
Norway **63** C6
Norway House **119** R5
Norwegian Bay **120** H2
Norwegian Sea **62** A3
Norwich *U.K.* **53** J2
Norwich *U.S.A.* **125** Q6
Noshiro **88** G5
Noshul **78** H3
Nosok **84** C2
Nosop **108** D5
Nosovshchina **78** F3
Nosratabad **95** P7
Nossen **70** E3
Noss Head **56** E2
Noss, Island of **56** A2
Nosy-Varika **109** J4
Notec **71** G2
Noto **69** E7
Notodden **63** C7
Noto-hanto **89** F7
Notre Dame Bay **121** Q8
Notre Dame Mountains **121** N8
Nottingham **53** F2
Nottingham Island **120** L5
Nottinghamshire **55** H3
Notukeu Creek **123** L3
Nouadhibou **100** B4
Nouadhibou, Ras **100** B4
Nouakchott **100** B5
Noukloof Mountains **108** C4
Noumea **114** X17
Noup Head **56** E1
Noupoort **108** D6
Nouvelle-Caledonie **114** W16
Nouvelle Caledonie **114** W16
Nouvelle-France, Cap de **120** M5
Novabad **86** C4
Nova Bana **71** H4
Nova Cruz **137** K5
Nova Era **138** H3
Nova Friburgo **138** H4
Nova Iguacu **138** H4
Nova Lima **138** H4
Nova Mambone **109** G4
Novara **68** B3
Nova Remanso **137** J5
Nova Scotia **121** P8
Nova Sento Se **137** J5
Nova Sofala **109** F4
Nova Vanduzi **109** F3
Nova Varos **72** E4
Novaya Kakhovka **79** E6
Novaya Katysh **84** Ae5
Novaya Kazanka **79** H6
Novaya Novatka **84** G5
Novaya Odessa **79** E6
Novaya Sibir , Ostrov **85** R1
Novaya Tevriz **84** B5
Novaya Vodolaga **79** F6
Novaya Zemlya **84** Ab2
Novayo Ushitsa **73** J1
Nove Mesto **70** G4
Nove Zamky **71** H4
Novgorod **78** E4
Novgorod Serverskiy **79** E5
Novigrad **72** C3
Novikovo **88** J2
Novi Ligure **68** B3
Novi Pazar **72** F4
Novi Sad **72** E3
Novo Acre **137** J6
Novoaleksandrovsk **79** G6
Novoalekseyevka **79** K5
Novoanninskiy **79** G5
Novoarchangelsk **73** L1
Novo Aripuana **136** E5
Novobogatinskoye **79** J6
Novocheboksarsh **78** H4
Novocherkassk **79** G6
Novodolinka **84** A6
Novodvinsk **78** G3
Novograd-Volynskiy **79** D5
Novogrudok **71** L2
Novo Hamburgo **138** F5
Novoilinovka **85** P6
Novokazalinsk **86** A2
Novokhopersk **79** G5
Novokiyevskiy Uval **85** M6
Novokocherdyk **84** Ad6
Novokuybyshevsk **79** H5
Novokuznetsk **84** D6
Novolazareyskaya **141** A4
Novoletovye **84** G2
Novo Milosevo **72** F3
Novomitino **84** Ae5
Novomoskovsk *Russia* **78** F5
Novomoskovsk *Ukraine* **79** F6
Novopavlovka **84** H6
Novopokrovskaya **79** G6
Novopolotsk **63** N9
Novo Redondo **106** B5
Novo-Rokrovka **88** E3
Novoromanovo **84** C6
Novorossiysk **79** F7
Novorzhev **63** N8
Novo Sagres **91** H7
Novo Sergeyevka **79** J5
Novoshakhtinsk **79** F6
Novosibirsk **84** C4
Novosibirskiye Ostrova **85** Q1
Novospasskoye **79** H5
Novoukrainka **79** E6
Novo Uzensk **79** H5
Novo-Vyatsk **78** H4
Novoyeniseysk **84** E5
Novozhilovskaya **78** J3
Novozybkov **79** E5
Novska **72** D3
Novy Jicin **71** G4
Novyy **84** H2
Novyy Bor **78** J2
Novyy Bug **79** E6
Novyy Oskol **79** F5
Novyy Port **84** A3
Novyy Uzen **79** J7
Nowbaran **95** J4
Nowe **71** H2
Nowen Hill **59** D9
Nowgong **93** H3
Nowitna **118** E3
Nowograd **70** F2
Nowogrod **71** J2
Nowra **113** L5
Now Shahr **95** K3
Nowshera **92** D2
Nowy Sacz **71** J4
Nowy Targ **71** J4
Noyon *France* **64** E4
Noyon *Mongolia* **86** J3
Nozay **65** C5
Nsanje **107** G6
Nsukka **105** G4
Nsuta **104** E4
Ntem **105** H5
Ntwetwe Pan **108** E4
Nuba, Lake **102** F3
Nuba Mountains **102** F5
Nubian Desert **103** F3
Nubiya **102** E4
Nubiya, Es Sahra en **103** F3
Nudo Coropuna **136** C7
Nueces **128** C6
Nueltin Lake **119** R3
Nueva Florida **133** N10
Nueva Rosita **127** M7
Nueva San Salvador **132** C8
Nueve de Julio **139** D7
Nuevitas **132** J4
Nuevo, Bajo **132** H7
Nuevo Casas Grandes **127** J5
Nuevo Churumuco **130** J8
Nuevo Laredo **128** C7
Nugaruba Islands **114** E2
Nugget Point **115** B7
Nugrus, Gebel **96** B4
Nuhaka **115** F3
Nuh, Ra's **95** R9
Nui **111** S3
Nuits-Saint-Georges **65** F5
Nu Jiang **93** J3
Nukhayb **94** F5
Nukiki **114** H5
Nukualofa **111** T6
Nukufetau **111** S3
Nukuhu **114** D3
Nukulaelae **111** S3
Nukumanu Islands **111** N2
Nukunau **111** S2
Nukunono **111** U3
Nukus **51** U7
Nullarbor **112** G5
Nullarbor Plain **112** F5
Numan **105** H4
Numata **89** G7
Numazu **89** G8
Numedal **63** C6
Numfor **114** B2
Numto **84** A4
Nuneaton **53** F2
Nunivak Islands **116** C2
Nunligran **85** Y4
Nunney **52** E3
Nuomin He **87** N2
Nuoro **69** B5
Nupani **114** M7
Nuqdah, Ra's an **97** P6
Nuqrah **96** E4
Nur **95** K3
Nura **86** C2
Nurabad **95** K6
Nur Daglari **77** G4
Nure **68** B3
Nurek **86** B4
Nurhak **77** G4
Nurhak Dagi **77** G3
Nuristan **92** D1
Nurmes **62** N5
Nurnberg **70** D4
Nurri **69** B6
Nurzec **71** K2
Nusaybin **77** J4
Nusayriyah, Jebel al **77** G5
Nushagak Bay **118** D4
Nu Shan **93** J3
Nushki **92** C3
Nutak **121** P6
Nuugaatsiaq **120** R3
Nuuk **120** R5
Nuupas **62** M3
Nuwara **92** F7
Nuweveldreeks **108** D6
Nuyakuk, Lake **118** D4
Nuyts, Point **112** D6
Nuzayzah **77** H5
Nyahururu **107** G2
Nyainqentanglha Shan **92** G3
Nyaksimvol **84** Ad4
Nyala **102** D5
Nyamboyto **84** C3
Nyandoma **78** G3
Nyang **93** H3
Nyanza **107** E3
Nyasa, Lake **107** F5
Nyashabozh **78** J2
Nyaungu **93** H4
Nyayba **85** N2
Nyborg **63** D9
Nybster **56** E2
Nyeri **107** G3
Nyerol **103** F6
Nyima **93** G2
Nyirbator **73** G2
Nyiregyhaza **73** F2
Nyiru, Mont **107** G2
Nykarleby **62** N4
Nykobing *Denmark* **63** C8
Nykobing *Denmark* **63** D9
Nykoping **63** G7
Nylstroom **108** E4
Nymagee **113** K5
Nymburk **70** F3
Nynashamn **63** G7
Nyngan **113** K5
Nyong **105** H5
Nyons **65** F6
Nyrany **70** E4
Nyrud **62** N2
Nysa **71** G3
Nysh **85** Q6
Nyshott **63** N6
Nystad **63** J6
Nytva **78** K4
Nyuk, Ozero **62** P4
Nyuksenitsa **78** G3
Nyunzu **107** E4
Nyurba **85** K4
Nyurolskiy **84** B5
Nyuya **85** J4
Nyvrovo **85** Q6
Nzambi **106** B3
Nzega **107** F3
Nzerekore **104** D4
Nzeto **106** B4
Nzo **104** D4

O

Oadby **53** F2
Oahe Dam **123** P5
Oahe, Lake **123** P5
Oahu **126** S10
Oakdale **126** B2
Oakengates **52** E2
Oakes **123** Q4
Oakford **52** D4
Oakham **53** G2
Oak Hill **125** K8
Oakington **53** H2
Oakland *California, U.S.A.* **126** A2
Oakland *Nebraska, U.S.A.* **123** R7
Oak Lawn **124** G6
Oakley **123** P8
Oakover **112** E3
Oakridge **122** C6
Oak Ridge **129** K2
Oak Valley **125** N7
Oamaru **115** C6
Oa, Mull of **57** B5
Oates Land **141** L4
Oa, The **57** B5
Oatlands **113** K7
Oaxaca **131** L9
Ob **84** Ae3
Oban **57** D4
Oberammergau **70** D5
Oberhausen **70** B3
Oberlin **123** P8
Obidos *Brazil* **137** F4
Obidos *Portugal* **66** B3
Obihiro **88** J4
Obi, Kepulauan **91** H6
Obilnoye **79** G6
Obion **128** H2
Obninsk **78** F4
Obo **102** E6
Obock **103** H5
Obok-tong **88** B5
Oborniki **71** G2
Oboyan **79** F5
Obozerskiy **78** G3
Obregon, Presa **127** H6
Obruk **76** E3
Obryvistoye **85** Q7
Observatoire, Caye de l' **111** N6
Obskaya Guba **84** A3
Obuasi **104** E4
Ocala **129** L6
Ocana *Colombia* **136** C2

Name	Page	Ref
Ocana *Spain*	66	E3
Occidental, Cordillera *Colombia*	136	B3
Occidental, Cordillera *Peru*	136	B6
Occidental, Grand Erg	100	F2
Oceanside	126	D4
Ocejon, Pic	66	E2
Ochamchire	77	J1
Ochil Hills	57	E4
Ochiltree	57	D5
Ock	53	F3
Ockelbo	63	G6
Ocmulgee	129	L5
Ocna Mures	73	G2
Oconee	129	L4
Ocotlan	130	H7
Ocracoke Island	129	Q3
Ocreza	66	C3
Ocsa	72	E2
Oda	89	D8
Oda	104	E4
Odadhraun	62	W12
Odaejin	88	B5
Oda, Jebel	103	G3
Odate	88	H5
Odawara	89	G8
Odda	63	B6
Odemira	66	B4
Odemis	76	B3
Odendaalsrus	108	E5
Odense	63	D9
Oder	70	F2
Oderhaff	70	F2
Oderzo	68	D3
Odeshog	63	F7
Odessa *U.S.A.*	127	L5
Odessa *Ukraine*	79	E6
Odesskoye	84	A6
Odienne	104	D4
Odmarden	63	L6
Odorheiu Secuiesc	73	H2
Odra	70	F2
Odzaci	72	E3
Oeiras	137	J5
Oekussi	91	G7
Oelrichs	123	N6
Oena, Wadi	103	F2
Oenpelli Mission	113	G1
Of	77	J2
Ofanto	69	E5
Offaly	59	G6
Offenbach	70	C3
Offenburg	70	B4
Offord D'Arcy	53	G2
Ofidhousa	75	J4
Ofotfjord	62	G2
Ofunato	88	H6
Oga	88	G6
Ogaden	103	H6
Ogaki	89	F8
Ogasawara-shoto	83	N4
Ogbomosho	105	F4
Ogden	122	J7
Ogdensburg	125	N4
Ogea	114	S9
Ogeechee	129	M4
Ogho	114	H5
Ogi	89	G7
Ogilvie Mountains	118	H3
Oginskiy, Kanal	71	L2
Ogle Point	120	G4
Oglethorpe, Mount	129	K3
Oglio	68	C3
Ognon	65	F5
Ogoamas, Gunung	91	G5
Ogoja	105	G4
Ogoki	121	J7
Ogooue	106	B3
Ogoron	85	M6
Ogosta	73	G4
Ograzden	73	G5
Ogre	63	L8
Ogurchinskiy, Ostrov	79	J8
Oguz	77	H3
Oguzeli	77	G4
Ogwashi-Uku	105	G4
Ohai	115	A6
Ohakune	115	E3
Ohata	88	H5
Ohau, Lake	115	B6
O'Higgins, Lago	139	B9
Ohingaiti	115	E3
Ohio *Kentucky, U.S.A.*	124	F8
Ohio *U.S.A.*	124	J6
Ohre	70	D2
Ohre	70	E3
Ohrid	73	F5
Ohridska Jezero	72	F5
Ohura	115	E3
Oiapoque *Brazil*	137	G3
Oiapoque *Brazil*	137	G3
Oikiqtaluk	120	L3
Oil City	125	L6
Oise	64	E4
Oita	89	C9
Oituz, Pasul	73	J2
Oiwake	88	H4
Ojinaga	127	K6
Ojo de Agua	138	D5
Ojos del Salado	138	C5
Oka *Russia*	78	G4
Oka *Russia*	84	G6
Okaba	114	B3
Okahandja	108	C4
Okahukura	115	E3
Okaihau	115	D1
Okanagan Lake	122	E3
Okanogan *U.S.A.*	122	E3
Okanogan *U.S.A.*	122	E3
Okara	92	D2
Okarem	95	M2
Okaukuejo	108	C3
Okavango	108	D3
Okavango Delta	108	D3
Okaya	89	G7
Okayama	89	D8
Okazaki	89	F8
Okeechobee, Lake	129	M7
Okehampton	52	C4
Okene	105	G4
Oketo	88	J4
Okha	85	Q6
Okhota	85	Q5
Okhotsk	85	Q5
Okhotskoye More	85	R5
Okhotsk, Sea of	85	R5
Okigwi	105	G4
Okinawa	89	H10
Okinawa-shoto	89	H10
Okinoerabu-shima	89	J10
Oki-shoto	89	D7
Okitipupa	105	F4
Oklahoma	127	N3
Oklahoma City	128	D3
Oklya	71	L3
Okmulgee	128	D3
Okondja	106	B3
Okoppe	88	J3
Oko, Wadi	103	G3
Oksfjord	62	K1
Oksino	78	J2
Okstindan	62	F3
Oktyabrskiy *Russia*	78	G3
Oktyabrskiy *Russia*	78	J5
Oktyabrskiy *Russia*	85	T6
Oktyabrskoye	79	K5
Oktyabrskoy Revolyutsii, Ostrov	81	L2
Oku	89	J10
Okulovka	78	E4
Okurchan	85	S5
Okushiri-to	88	G4
Okwa	108	D4
Olafsfjordur	62	V11
Olafsvik	62	T12
Oland	63	G8
Olanga	62	P3
Olathe	124	C7
Olavarria	139	D7
Olbia	69	B5
Old Bedford River	53	H2
Oldcastle	58	H5
Old Crow	118	H2
Old Deer	56	F3
Oldenburg *Germany*	70	C2
Oldenburg *Germany*	70	D1
Oldham	55	G3
Old Head of Kinsale	59	E9
Old Hickory Lake	129	J2
Oldman	122	H3
Old Man of Coniston	55	F2
Old Man of Hoy	56	E2
Oldmeldrum	56	F3
Old Nene	53	H2
Old Post Point	121	P8
Olds	122	G2
Old Tongy	113	K4
Old Town	125	R4
Old Wives Lake	123	L2
Olean	125	L5
Olekma	85	L5
Olekminsk	85	L4
Olekmo-charskoye Nagorye	85	L5
Olema	78	H3
Olen	63	A7
Olenegorsk	62	Q2
Olenek	85	L2
Olenekskiy Zaliv	85	N2
Oleniy, Ostrov	84	B2
Oleron, Ile d'	65	C6
Olesko	71	L4
Olesnica	71	G3
Olevsk	79	D5
Olevugha	114	K6
Olfjellet	62	F3
Olga	88	E4
Olgiy	86	G2
Olgopol	73	K1
Olhava	62	L4
Oliana	67	G1
Olib	72	C3
Olifants *Namibia*	108	C4
Olifants *South Africa*	108	C6
Olifants *South Africa*	108	F4
Olimbos *Greece*	75	G2
Olimbos *Greece*	75	J5
Olinda	137	L5
Olio	113	J3
Olite	67	F1
Oliva	138	D6
Olivares, Cerro del	138	C5
Olivia	124	C4
Olkhovka	79	G6
Ollague	138	C4
Ollague, Volcan	138	C4
Ollerton	55	H3
Ollila	62	M2
Olmedo	66	D2
Olmos	136	B5
Olney	124	F7
Olofstrom	63	F8
Olom	85	N3
Olomouc	71	G4
Olonets	78	E3
Olongapo	91	G3
Oloron-Sainte-Marie	65	C7
Olot	67	H1
Olovo	72	E3
Olovyannaya	85	K6
Olpe	70	B3
Olsztyn	71	J2
Olsztynek	71	J2
Olt	73	H3
Olten	68	A2
Oltet	73	G3
Oltu *Turkey*	77	J2
Oltu *Turkey*	77	K2
Oltul	73	H3
Olu Deniz	76	C4
Olur	77	K2
Olvera	66	D4
Olympia	122	C4
Olympus *Cyprus*	76	E5
Olympus *Greece*	75	G2
Olympus, Mount	122	C4
Olyutorskiy, Mys	85	W5
Oma *Russia*	78	H2
Oma *Russia*	78	H2
Omachi	89	F7
Omae-zaki	89	G8
Omagari	88	H6
Omagh	58	H3
Omaha	124	C6
Omak	122	E3
Omakau	115	B6
Oman	97	M7
Oman, Gulf of	97	P4
Omarama	115	B6
Omaruru	108	C4
Oma-saki	88	H5
Ombrone	69	C4
Omchali	79	J7
Omdurman	103	F4
Omeath	58	K4
Omeleut	85	W4
Omeo	113	K6
Omerli Baraji	76	C2
Ometepe, Isla de	132	E9
Om Hajer	96	C9
Ominato	88	H5
Omineca Mountains	118	K4
Omis	72	D4
Omitlan	131	K9
Omiya	89	G8
Ommaney, Cape	118	J4
Ommanney Bay	120	F3
Omnogovi	86	G2
Omodeo, Lago	69	B5
Omolon	85	T3
Omoloy *Russia*	84	H5
Omoloy *Russia*	85	N2
Omono	88	H6
Omoto	88	H6
Omo Wenz	103	G6
Omsk	84	A6
Omsukchan	85	T4
Omu	88	J3
Omulevka	85	S4
Omulew	71	J2
Omura	89	B9
Omuramba Eiseb	108	C4
Omuramba Omatako	108	C4
Omurtag	73	J4
Omuta	89	C9
Omutinskiy	84	Ae5
Omutninsk	78	J4
Onalaska	124	E5
Onan	85	J6
Oncocua	106	B6
Ondaroa	66	E1
Ondava	71	J4
Ondjiva	106	C6
Ondo	105	F4
Ondorhaan	87	L2
Ondorkara	86	F2
Ondozero	78	E3
Ondverdarnes	62	S12
Oneata	114	S9
Onega *Russia*	78	F3
Onega *Russia*	78	F3
One Hundred Mile House	122	D2
Oneida Lake	125	N5
O'Neill	123	Q6
Onekotan, Ostrov	85	S7
Oneonta	125	N5
Onezhskaya Guba	78	F3
Onezhskiy Poluostrov	78	F3
Onezhskoye, Ozero	78	F3
Ongerup	112	D5
Ongole	92	F5
Ongon	87	L2
Ongt Gol	86	J3
Onguday	84	D6
Onich	57	C4
Oni-i-Lau	111	T6
Onilahy	109	H4
Onitsha	105	G4
Onjuul	87	K2
Onkivesi	62	M5
Ono	89	F8
Ono *Fiji*	114	R9
Ono *Japan*	89	H7
Onotoa	111	S2
Onslow	112	D3
Onslow Bay	129	P3
Onsong	88	B4
Ontario *Canada*	121	H7
Ontario *California, U.S.A*	126	D3
Ontario *Oregon, U.S.A.*	122	F6
Ontario, Lake	125	M5
Onteniente	67	F3
Ontong Java Atoll	111	N3
Oodnadatta	113	H4
Oolagah Lake	128	E2
Ooldea	112	G5
Oostelijk-Flevoland	64	F2
Oostende	64	E3
Oosterschelde	64	E3
Ootsa Lake	118	K5
Opala	106	D3
Opanake	92	F7
Oparino	78	H4
Opatow	71	J3
Opava	71	G4
Opawica	125	N2
Opelika	129	K4
Opelousas	128	F5
Opheim	123	L3
Ophir, Gunung	90	B5
Opiscoteo, Lake	121	N7
Opobo	105	G5
Opochka	63	N8
Opole	71	G3
Opornyy	79	J6
Oporto	66	B2
Opotiki	115	F3
Opp	129	J5
Oppdal	62	C5
Oppeln	71	G3
Oppland	63	C6
Opua	115	E1
Opunake	115	D3
Oradea	73	F2
Orafajokull	62	W12
Orai	92	E3
Oran	138	D4
Oran	100	E1
Orange *Australia*	113	K5
Orange *France*	65	F6
Orange *Namibia*	108	C5
Orange *U.S.A.*	128	F5
Orangeburg	129	M4
Orange, Cabo	137	G3
Orangeville	125	K4
Orange Walk	132	C5
Oranienburg	70	E2
Oranje	108	D5
Oranje Gebergte	137	F3
Oranjemund	108	C5
Oranjestad	136	C1
Oranmore	59	E6
Oras	91	H3
Oravita	73	F3
Oravska nadrz	71	H4
Orawia	115	A7
Orbec	64	D4
Orbetello	69	C4
Orbigo	66	D1
Orbost	113	K6
Orbyhus	63	G6
Orcadas	141	X6
Orcera	66	E3
Orchila, Isla	136	D1
Orchowo	71	G2
Orco	68	A3
Ord	112	F2
Orderville	126	F2
Ord, Mountain	112	F2
Ordu	77	G2
Orduna	66	E1
Ordzhonikidze	77	L1
Ore	57	E4
Orealven	62	H4
Orebro *Sweden*	63	F7
Orebro *Sweden*	63	F7
Oregon	122	D6
Oregon City	122	C5
Orekhovo Zuyevo	78	F4
Orel	79	F5
Orem	122	J7
Oren	76	B4
Orenburg	79	K5
Orencik	76	C3
Orense	66	C1
Orestias	75	J2
Oreti	115	B6
Orford Ness	53	J2
Organ Peak	127	J4
Orgaz	66	E3
Orgeyev	79	D6
Orgiva	66	E4
Orgon Tal	87	L3
Orhaneli	76	C3
Orhangazi	76	C2
Orhon Gol	87	K2
Oriental, Cordillera *Colombia*	136	C2
Oriental, Cordillera *Peru*	136	B5
Oriental, Grand Erg	101	G2
Orihuela	67	F3
Orinoco	136	E2
Oriomo	114	C3
Oris	68	C2
Orissa	92	F4
Oristano	69	B6
Oristano, Golfo di	69	B6

Name	Page	Grid
Orivesi *Hame, Finland*	63	L6
Orivesi *Pohjois-karjala, Finland*	62	N5
Oriximina	137	F4
Orizaba	131	L8
Orizare	73	J4
Orje	63	D7
Orjen	72	E4
Orkanger	62	C5
Orkelljunga	63	E8
Orkla	62	C5
Orkney	56	E1
Orkney Islands	56	F1
Orla	71	G3
Orlando	129	M6
Orleanais	65	D5
Orleans	65	D5
Ormara	92	B3
Ormara, Ras	92	B3
Ormoc	91	G3
Ormond Island	120	K4
Ormos	75	H4
Ormskirk	55	G3
Ornain	64	F4
Orne	64	C4
Ornskoldsvik	62	H5
Oro	130	G4
Orobi, Alpi	68	B3
Orocue	136	C3
Orofino	122	F4
Oromocto	125	S4
Oron	85	K5
Orona	111	U2
Oronsay	57	B5
Oronsay, Passage of	57	B5
Orontes	77	G5
Oropesa	66	D3
Oroqen Zizhiqi	87	N1
Oroquieta	91	G4
Orosei, Golfo di	69	B5
Oroshaza	72	F2
Orotukan	85	S4
Oroville *California, U.S.A.*	122	D8
Oroville *Washington, U.S.A.*	122	E3
Oroville, Lake	122	D8
Orrin Reservoir	56	D3
Orsa	63	F6
Orsa Finnmark	63	F6
Orsaro, Monte	68	C3
Orsha	78	E5
Orsta	62	B5
Orta	76	E2
Ortabag	77	K4
Ortaca	76	C4
Ortakoy *Turkey*	76	F2
Ortakoy *Turkey*	76	F3
Ortatoroslar	76	F4
Ortega	136	B3
Ortegal, Cabo	66	C1
Ortelsburg	71	J2
Orthez	65	C7
Ortigueira	66	C1
Ortiz	133	P10
Ortles	68	C2
Ortona	69	E4
Orto-Tokoy	86	D3
Orumiyeh	77	L4
Orumiyeh, Daryacheh-ye	94	G3
Oruro	138	C3
Orvieto	69	D4
Orwell	53	J3
Oryakhovo	73	G4
Os	62	D5
Osa	78	K4
Osage	124	D7
Osaka *Japan*	89	E8
Osaka *Japan*	89	F8
Osaka-wan	89	E8
Osa, Peninsula de	132	F10
Osceola *Arkansas, U.S.A.*	128	H3
Osceola *Iowa, U.S.A.*	124	D6
Osh	86	B3
Oshamambe	88	H4
Oshawa	125	L5
O-shima	89	G8
Oshkosh	124	F4
Oshkurya	84	Ac3
Oshmarino	84	C2
Oshmyanskaya Vozvyshennost	71	M1
Oshmyany	71	L1
Oshnoviyeh	94	G3
Oshogbo	105	F4
Oshtoran Kuh	94	J5
Oshtorinan	94	J4
Oshwe	106	C3
Osijek	72	E3
Osimo	68	D4
Osinniki	84	D6
Osipovichi	79	D5
Oskaloosa	124	D6
Oskamull	57	B4
Oskara, Mys	84	F1
Oskarshamn	63	G8
Oskarstrom	63	E8
Oskoba	84	G4
Oskol	79	F5
Oslo *Norway*	63	D7
Oslo *Norway*	63	D7
Oslob	91	G4
Oslofjorden	63	H7
Osmanabad	92	E5
Osmancik	76	F2
Osmaneli	76	C2
Osmaniye	77	G4
Osmington	52	E4
Osmino	63	N7
Osmo	63	G7
Osnabruck	70	C2
Osogovska Planina	73	G4
Osorno *Chile*	139	B8
Osorno *Spain*	66	D1
Osoyro	63	A6
Osprey Reef	113	K1
Oss	64	F3
Ossa	75	G3
Ossa, Mount	110	L10
Ossett	55	H3
Ossian, Loch	57	D4
Ossokmanuan Lake	121	P7
Ostashkov	78	E4
Ostavall	62	F5
Ostby	63	E6
Oste	70	C2
Osterburken	70	C4
Osterdalalven	63	E6
Osterdalen	63	D5
Ostergotland	63	F7
Osterode	71	H2
Ostfold	63	D7
Ost Friesische Inseln	70	B2
Ostfriesland	70	B2
Osthammar	63	H6
Ostiglia	68	C3
Ostra	68	D4
Ostrava	71	H4
Ostroda	71	H2
Ostrog	79	D5
Ostrogozhsk	79	F5
Ostroleka	71	J2
Ostrov	63	N8
Ostrovnoy, Mys	88	D4
Ostrow	71	G3
Ostrowiec	71	J3
Ostrow Mazowiecki	71	J2
Ostuni	69	F5
Osum	75	F2
Osum	73	H4
Osumi-kaikyo	89	C10
Osumi-shoto	89	C10
Osuna	66	D4
OsVan	78	K2
Oswaldtwistle	55	G3
Oswego	125	M5
Oswestry	52	D2
Otaki	115	E4
Otaru	88	H4
Otava	70	E4
Otavi	108	C3
Otawara	89	G7
Otchinjau	106	B6
Otelec	73	F3
Otelu Rosu	73	G3
Otematata	115	C6
Othe, Foret d'	65	E4
Othonoi	74	E3
Othris	75	G3
Oti	104	F4
Otira	115	C5
Otis	123	N7
Otish, Monts	121	M7
Otjiwarongo	108	C4
Otley	55	H3
Otlukbeli Daglari	77	J2
Otnes	63	D6
Otocac	72	C3
Otorohanga	115	E3
Otoskwin	121	H7
Otra	63	B7
Otranto	69	G5
Otranto, Capo d	69	G5
Otranto, Strait of	74	E2
Otsu	89	E8
Otsu	89	H7
Otta *Norway*	63	C6
Otta *Norway*	63	C6
Ottawa *Canada*	125	L3
Ottawa *Canada*	125	N4
Ottawa Islands	121	K6
Otter	52	D4
Otterburn	57	F5
Otter Rapids	125	K1
Otterup	63	D9
Ottery	52	C4
Ottery Saint Mary	52	D4
Ottumwa	124	D6
Oturkpo	105	G4
Otway, Bahia	139	B10
Otway, Cape	113	J6
Otway, Seno	139	B10
Otwock	71	J2
Otynya	71	L4
Otztaler Alpen	68	C2
Ouachita	128	F4
Ouachita, Lake	128	F3
Ouachita Mountains	128	E3
Ouadda	102	D6
Ouagadougou	104	E3
Ouahigouya	104	E3
Oualata	100	D5
Oua-n Ahaggar, Tassili	101	G4
Ouanda Djaile	102	D6
Ouarane	100	D4
Ouargla	101	G2
Ouarra	102	E6
Ouarsenis, Massif de l'	67	G5
Ouarzazate	100	D2
Ouatoais	125	M4
Oubangui	106	C3
Oudenaarde	64	E3
Oude Rijn	64	F2
Oudtshoorn	108	D6
Oued Zem	100	D2
Oueme	105	F4
Ouen	114	X17
Ouessant, Ile d'	64	A4
Ouesso	106	C2
Ouezzane	100	D2
Oughterard	59	D6
Oughter, Lough	58	H4
Ouidah	105	F4
Oujda	100	E2
Oulainen	62	L4
Oulmes	100	D2
Oulu *Finland*	62	L4
Oulu *Finland*	62	M4
Oulujarvi	62	M4
Oulujoki	62	M4
Oulx	68	A3
Oum Chalouba	102	D4
Oum El Bouaghi	101	G1
Oum er Rbia, Oued	100	D2
Ou, Nam	93	K4
Ounasjoki	62	L3
Oundle	53	G2
Ounianga Kebir	102	D4
Oupu	87	P1
Ouricuri	137	J5
Ourinhos	138	G4
Ouro Preto	138	H4
Ourthe	64	F3
Ouse *Australia*	113	K7
Ouse *U.K.*	55	H3
Oust	65	B5
Outardes, Reservoir	121	N7
Outer Hebrides	56	A3
Outokumpu	62	N5
Out Skerries	56	B1
Outwell	53	H2
Ouvea	114	X16
Ouyen	113	J6
Ovacik *Turkey*	77	H4
Ovacik *Turkey*	77	J2
Ovada	68	B3
Ovalau Batiki	114	R8
Ovalle	138	B6
Ovau	114	H5
Ovejo	66	D3
Oven	115	X17
Overbister	56	F1
Overbygd	62	H2
Overkalix	62	K3
Overnas	62	G3
Overtornea	62	K3
Oviedo	66	D1
Ovinishche	78	F4
Ovre Ardal	63	B6
Ovruch	79	D5
Owahanga	115	F4
Owaka	115	B7
Owando	106	C3
Owase	89	F8
Owatonna	124	D4
Owbeh	95	R4
Owel, Lough	58	H5
Owenbeg	58	E4
Owenkillew	58	H3
Owenmore	58	C4
Owens	126	C2
Owensboro	124	G8
Owens Lake	126	D2
Owen Sound	125	K4
Owen Stanley Range	114	D3
Owerri	105	G4
Owo	105	G4
Owosso	124	H5
Owyhee *Nevada, U.S.A.*	122	F7
Owyhee *Oregon, U.S.A.*	122	F6
Oxbow	123	N3
Oxelosund	63	G7
Oxenholme	55	G2
Oxenhope	55	H3
Oxford *New Zealand*	115	D5
Oxford *U.K.*	53	F3
Oxford *U.S.A.*	128	H3
Oxfordshire	53	F3
Ox Mountains	58	E4
Oxnard	126	C3
Oxton	55	H3
Oyaca	76	E3
Oyali	77	J4
Oyapock	137	G3
Oyem	106	B2
Oykel	56	D3
Oykel Bridge	56	D3
Oymyakon	85	Q4
Oyo	105	F4
Ozalp	77	L3
Ozamiz	91	G4
Ozark Plateau	124	D8
Ozarks, Lake of the	124	D7
Ozd	72	F1
Ozernovskiy	85	T6
Ozernoye	84	A5
Ozersk	71	K1
Ozhogina	85	R3
Ozieri	69	B5
Ozinki	79	H5
Ozona	127	M5
Ozora	72	E2
Ozyurt	76	F3

P

Name	Page	Grid
Paama	114	U12
Paarl	108	C6
Pabbay *U.K.*	56	A3
Pabbay *U.K.*	57	A4
Pabellon de Arteaga	130	H6
Pabjanice	71	H3
Pabna	92	G4
Pabrade	63	L9
Pacaas Novos, Serra dos	136	E6
Pacaraima, Sierra	136	E3
Pacasmayo	136	B5
Pachino	69	E7
Pachora	92	E4
Pachuca	131	K7
Pacifica	126	A2
Pacific Ocean	87	P7
Pacific Ocean, North	143	H3
Pacific Ocean, South	143	J5
Pacitan	90	E7
Packwood	122	D4
Padang *Indonesia*	90	C6
Padang *Indonesia*	90	C5
Padangpanjang	90	D6
Padangsidimpuan	90	B5
Padasjoki	63	L6
Padauiri	136	E3
Paderborn	70	C3
Pades	73	G3
Padiham	55	G3
Padilla *Bolivia*	138	D3
Padilla *Mexico*	131	K5
Padina	73	J3
Padje-Ianta	62	G3
Padloping Island	120	P4
Padova	68	C3
Padrao, Pointa do	106	B4
Padron	66	B1
Padstow	52	C4
Padstow Bay	52	C4
Padua	68	C3
Paducah *Kentucky, U.S.A.*	124	F8
Paducah *Texas, U.S.A.*	127	M4
Padunskoye More	62	P2
Paekariki	115	E4
Paengnyong-do	87	N4
Paeroa	115	E2
Pag *Yugoslavia*	72	C3
Pag *Yugoslavia*	72	C3
Pagadian	91	G4
Pagasitikos Kolpos	75	G3
Pagatan	90	F6
Page	126	G2
Pagosa Springs	127	J2
Pagwa River	124	H2
Pagwi	114	C2
Pahala	126	T11
Pahang	90	C5
Pahia Point	115	A7
Pahiatua	115	E4
Pahlavi Dezh	95	M3
Pahoa	126	T11
Pahokee	129	M7
Pahra Kariz	95	Q4
Paia	126	S10
Paide	63	L7
Paignton	52	D4
Paijanne	63	L6
Pailolo Chan	126	S10
Paimpol	64	B4
Painswick	53	E3
Painted Desert	126	G2
Paisley	57	D5
Paita	136	A5
Paita	114	X17
Paittasjarvi	62	K2
Pajala	62	K3
Pakaraima Mountains	136	E2
Pakistan	92	C3
Pak Lay	93	K5
Pakokku	93	H4
Pakpattan	92	D2
Pakrac	72	D3
Paks	72	E2
Pakse	93	L5
Pala	102	B6
Palabuhanratu	90	D7
Palafrugell	67	H2
Palagruza	72	D4
Palaiokastron	75	J5
Palaiokhora	75	G5
Pala Laharha	92	G4
Palamos	67	H2
Palana	85	T5
Palanan Point	91	G2
Palanga	63	J9
Palangan, Kuh-e	95	Q6
Palangkaraya	90	E6
Palanpur	92	D4
Palapye	108	E4
Palar	92	E6
Palata	69	E5
Palatka *U.S.A.*	129	M6
Palatka *Russia*	85	S4
Palau	69	B5
Palau Islands	91	J4
Palawan	91	F4
Palawan Passage	91	F4
Palayankottai	92	E7
Palazzola Acreide	69	E7
Paldiski	63	L7
Palembang	90	C6

Name	Page	Grid
Palena, Lago	139	B8
Palencia	66	D1
Palermo	69	D6
Palestine	128	E5
Paletwa	93	H4
Palghat	92	E6
Palgrave Point	108	B4
Palhoca	138	G5
Pali	92	D3
Palisade	127	H1
Palit, Kep i	74	E2
Palkane	63	L6
Palk Strait	92	E7
Pallaresa	67	G1
Pallas Green	59	F7
Pallasovka	79	H5
Pallastunturi	62	K2
Palliser Bay	115	E4
Palliser, Cape	115	E4
Palma *Mozambique*	109	H2
Palma *Spain*	67	H3
Palma, Baia de	67	H3
Palma del Rio	66	D4
Pal Malmal	114	E3
Palmanova	68	D3
Palmares	137	K5
Palmar, Punta del	139	F6
Palmas	138	G5
Palmas, Cape	104	D5
Palmas, Golfo di	69	B6
Palma Soriano	132	J4
Palmatkina	85	V4
Palmeira	138	F5
Palmeiras	137	J6
Palmer *Antarctic*	141	V6
Palmer *U.S.A.*	118	F3
Palmer Land	141	V4
Palmerston	115	C6
Palmerston Island	111	W5
Palmerston North	115	E4
Palm Harbor	129	L6
Palmi	69	E6
Palmira	136	B3
Palm Springs	126	D4
Palmyra	94	D4
Palmyras Point	92	G4
Palo de las Letras	136	B2
Palomar, Mount	126	D4
Palopo	91	G6
Palos, Cabo de	67	F4
Palpetu, Tanjung	91	H6
Palu *Indonesia*	91	F6
Palu *Indonesia*	91	F6
Palu *Turkey*	77	H3
Palyavaam	85	W3
Pama	104	F3
Pamban	92	E7
Pamekasan	90	E7
Pameungpeuk	90	D7
Pamiers	65	D7
Pamisos	75	F4
Pamlico Sound	129	P3
Pampa	127	M3
Pampachiri	136	C6
Pampas *Argentina*	139	D7
Pampas *Peru*	136	C6
Pampilhosa da Serra	66	C2
Pamplona *Colombia*	136	C2
Pamplona *Spain*	67	F1
Pana	124	F7
Panaca	126	E2
Panagyurishte	73	H4
Panaji	92	D5
Panama	132	G10
Panama	132	H10
Panama, Bahia de	132	H10
Panama Canal	136	B2
Panama City	129	K5
Panama, Golfo de	136	B2
Panandak	95	K4
Panaro	68	C3
Panay	91	G3
Pancevo	72	F3
Panda	109	F4
Pandan *Philippines*	91	G3
Pandan *Philippines*	91	G3
Pandany	78	E3
Pandharpur	92	E5
Pando	139	E6
Pandunskoye More	78	E2
Panevezys	63	N9
Panfilov	86	E3
Pangalanes, Canal des	109	J4
Pangani	107	G4
Panggoe	114	H5
Pangi	106	E3
Pangkalanbuun	90	E6
Pangkalpinang	90	D6
Pangnirtung	120	N4
Pangong Tso	92	E2
Pangrango, Gunung	90	D7
Pangtara	93	J4
Pangururar	90	B5
Pangutaran Group	91	G4
Panhandle	127	M3
Paniai, Danau	114	B2
Panie, Mount	114	W16
Panipat	92	E3
Panjim	92	D5
Panna	92	F4
Panovo	84	G5
Pant *Essex, U.K.*	53	H3
Pant *Shropshire, U.K.*	52	D2
Pantar	91	G7
Pantelleria, Isola di	69	D7
Pantones	66	E3
Panuco *Mexico*	131	K6
Panuco *Mexico*	131	K6
Pan Xian	93	K3
Panyam	105	G4
Pao-de-Acucar	137	K5
Paola	69	F6
Paoua	102	C6
Papa	72	D2
Papakura	115	E2
Papantla	131	L7
Paparoa	115	E2
Paparoa Range	115	C5
Papa Stour	56	A1
Papatoetoe	115	E2
Papa Westray	56	F1
Papenburg	70	B2
Papigochic	127	J6
Papisoi, Tanjung	114	A2
Paps of Jura	57	B5
Paps, The	59	D8
Papua, Gulf of	114	C3
Papua New Guinea	114	C2
Papuk	72	D3
Papun	93	J5
Para	137	G4
Paracas, Peninsula	136	B6
Paracatu *Brazil*	138	G3
Paracatu *Brazil*	138	G3
Paracin	73	F4
Paradubice	70	F3
Paragould	128	G2
Paragua	136	E6
Paragua	136	E2
Paraguacu	137	J6
Paraguai	136	F7
Paraguana, Peninsula de	133	M8
Paraguari	138	E5
Paraguay	138	E4
Paraguay	138	E4
Paraiba	138	H4
Paraiba	137	K5
Parajuru	137	K4
Parakou	105	F4
Paralakhemundi	92	F5
Paralkot	92	F5
Paramaribo	137	F2
Paramillo	136	B2
Paramirim	137	J6
Paramonga	136	B6
Paramushir, Ostrov	85	T6
Parana	138	D6
Parana	137	H6
Paranagua	138	G5
Paranaiba *Maranhao, Brazil*	137	J4
Paranaiba *Mato Grosso do Sul, Brazil*	138	F3
Paranaiba *Minas Gerais, Brazil*	138	G3
Paranaidji	137	H5
Paranapanema	138	F4
Paranapiacaba, Serra	138	G4
Paranatinga	137	F6
Parangipettai	92	E6
Paraparaum	115	E4
Parapola	75	G4
Parauna	138	F3
Parbati	92	E4
Parbhani	92	E5
Parcel Islands	93	M5
Parchim	70	D2
Pardo	138	F4
Parecis, Serra dos	136	F6
Pareditas	139	C6
Pare Mountains	107	G3
Parengarenga Harbour	115	D1
Parepare	91	F6
Paria, Golfo de	133	R9
Pariaguan	136	E2
Paria, Peninsula de	133	R9
Paricutin, Volcan el	130	H8
Parigi	91	G6
Parikkala	63	N6
Parima, Serra	136	E3
Parintins	137	F4
Paris *France*	64	E4
Paris *Kentucky, U.S.A.*	124	H7
Paris *Tennessee, U.S.A.*	129	H2
Paris *Texas, U.S.A.*	128	E4
Parkano	63	K5
Parker	126	E3
Parkersburg	125	K7
Parkes	113	K5
Parkgate	57	E5
Park Range	123	L7
Parksville	122	B3
Parma *Italy*	68	C3
Parma *U.S.A.*	125	K6
Parnaiba	137	J4
Parnamirim	137	K5
Parnassos	75	G3
Parnassus	115	D5
Parnis	75	G3
Parnon Oros	75	G4
Parnu	63	L7
Parnu	63	L7
Paro	93	G3
Paropamisus	95	R4
Paros *Greece*	75	H4
Paros *Greece*	75	H4
Parowan	126	F2
Parral	139	B7
Parras	127	L8
Parrett	52	E3
Parrsboro	121	P8
Parry Bay	120	K4
Parry Islands	120	C2
Parry, Kap	120	M2
Parry Peninsula	118	L2
Parry Sound	125	L4
Parseta	71	G2
Parshino	85	J5
Parsons	128	E2
Partabpur	92	F4
Parthenay	65	C5
Partizansk	88	D4
Parton	57	D5
Partry Mountains	58	C5
Paru	137	G4
Parys	108	E5
Pasa Barris	137	K6
Pasadena *California, U.S.A.*	126	C3
Pasadena *Texas, U.S.A.*	128	E6
Pasado, Cabo	136	A4
Pascagoula *U.S.A.*	128	H5
Pascagoula *U.S.A.*	128	H5
Pascani	73	J2
Pasco	122	E4
Pascua, Isla de	143	K5
Pasewalk	70	F2
Pashiya	78	K4
Pashkovo	88	C1
Pasig	91	G3
Pasinler	77	J3
Pasirpangarayan	90	C5
Paslek	71	H1
Pasley, Cape	112	E5
Pasmajarvi	62	L3
Pasman	72	C4
Pasni	92	B3
Paso de los Indios	139	C8
Paso de los Libres	138	E5
Paso de los Toros	138	E6
Paso Real	131	M9
Paso Rio Mayo	139	B9
Paso Robles	126	B3
Pasquia Hills	119	Q5
Passage East	59	J8
Passage West	59	F9
Passamaquoddy Bay	125	S4
Passau	70	E4
Passero, Capo	69	E7
Passo Fundo	138	F5
Passos	138	G4
Pastaza	136	B4
Pas, The	119	Q5
Pasto	136	B3
Pastol Bay	118	C3
Pastos Bons	137	J5
Pastrana	66	E2
Pasuruan	90	E7
Patache, Punta de	138	B4
Patagonia	139	C9
Patan *India*	92	D4
Patan *Nepal*	92	G3
Patani	91	H5
Patea	115	E3
Pateley Bridge	55	H2
Paterno	69	E7
Paterson	125	N6
Pathankot	92	E2
Pathfinder Reservoir	123	L6
Pathhead	57	F4
Patiala	92	E2
Patkai Bum	93	J3
Patman, Lake	128	E4
Patmos	75	J4
Patna	92	G3
Patnagarh	92	F4
Patnos	77	K3
Patomskoye Nagorye	85	J4
Patos	137	K5
Patos de Minas	138	G3
Patos, Lagoa dos	138	F6
Patquia	138	C6
Patrai	75	F3
Patras	75	F3
Patrasuy	78	L3
Patricio Lynch, Isla	139	A9
Patrington	55	J3
Patrocinio	138	G3
Pattani	93	K7
Patterdale	55	G2
Patti	69	E6
Patu	137	K5
Patuca	132	E7
Patuca, Punta	132	E7
Patzcuaro	130	J8
Patzcuaro, Laguna	130	J8
Pau	65	C7
Pau d'Arco	137	H5
Pau dos Ferros	137	K5
Pau, Gave de	65	C7
Pauini *Brazil*	136	D5
Pauini *Brazil*	136	D5
Paulilatino	69	B5
Paulista	137	K5
Paulistana	137	J5
Pauls Valley	128	D3
Paungde	93	J5
Pauni	92	E4
Pauri	92	E2
Pauto	136	C2
Pavarandocito	136	B2
Paveh	94	H4
Pavia	68	B3
Pavilosta	63	J8
Pavlikeni	73	H4
Pavlodar	84	B6
Pavlof Volcano	118	Af8
Pavlograd	79	F6
Pavlovo	78	G4
Pavlovsk	79	G5
Pavlovskaya	79	F6
Pavullo nel Frigano	68	C3
Pavuvu	114	J6
Pawan	90	E6
Paxoi	75	F3
Paxton	57	F4
Payakumbuh	90	D6
Payette *U.S.A.*	122	F5
Payette *U.S.A.*	122	F5
Payne, Lake	121	M6
Paynes Find	112	D4
Paysandu	138	E6
Payun, Volcan	139	C7
Pazanan	95	J6
Pazar	77	J2
Pazarbasi Burun	76	D2
Pazarcik	77	G4
Pazardzhik	73	H4
Pazaroren	77	G3
Pazaryeri	76	C2
Paz, Bahia de la	130	D5
Pazin	72	B3
Pcim	71	H4
Peabody Bugt	120	N2
Peace *Canada*	119	N4
Peace *U.S.A.*	129	M7
Peacehaven	53	M4
Peace River	119	M4
Peaima Falls	136	E2
Pea Island	129	Q3
Peak Hill	112	D4
Peale, Mount	123	K8
Pearl	128	H5
Pearl City	126	R10
Pearl Harbor	126	R10
Pearsall	128	C6
Peary Channel	120	F2
Pease	127	N3
Pebane	109	G3
Pec	72	F4
Pechenezhin	71	L4
Pechenga	62	P2
Pechora	78	J2
Pechorskaya Guba	78	J2
Pechorskoye More	78	J2
Pechory	63	M8
Pecos *U.S.A.*	127	L5
Pecos *U.S.A.*	127	L5
Pecos Plains	127	K4
Pecs	72	E2
Pedasi	132	G11
Pededze	63	M8
Pedernales	133	M5
Pedo La	92	F3
Pedorovka	79	J5
Pedra Azul	138	H3
Pedregal	132	F10
Pedreiras	137	J4
Pedro Afonso	137	H5
Pedro Cays	132	J6
Pedro Juan Caballero	138	E4
Pedro Luro	139	D7
Peebles	57	E5
Pee Dee	129	N3
Peel *Canada*	118	J2
Peel *U.K.*	54	E2
Peel Sound	120	G3
Peene	70	E2
Pegasus Bay	115	D5
Pegnitz *Germany*	70	D4
Pegnitz *Germany*	70	D4
Pegu	93	J5
Pegu Yoma	93	J5
Pegwell Bay	53	J3
Pegysh	78	J3
Pehlivankoy	76	B2
Pehuajo	139	D7
Peine	70	D2
Peipus, Lake	63	M7
Peixe	137	H6
Pei Xian	93	N2
Pekalongan	90	D7
Pekan	90	C5
Pekanbaru	90	C5
Pekin	124	F6
Peking	87	M4
Pekkala	62	M3
Pelabuanratu, Teluk	90	D7
Pelabuhan Kelang	90	C5
Pelagie, Isole	74	B5
Pelagos	75	H3
Pelat, Mont	65	G6
Peleaga	73	G3
Peleduy	85	J5
Pelee Island	124	J6
Peleng	91	G6
Peljesac	72	D4
Pelkosenniemi	62	M3
Pella	124	D6
Pellegrini	139	D7
Pello	62	L3
Pellworm	70	C1
Pelly	118	J3
Pelly Bay	120	J4
Pelly Mountains	118	J3
Peloponnisos	75	G4
Pelotas	138	F5

Name	Page	Grid
Pelplin	71	H2
Pelym	78	L3
Pemali, Tanjung	91	G6
Pematangsiantar	90	B5
Pemba	109	H2
Pemba Island	107	G4
Pemberton	122	C2
Pembina	119	M5
Pembroke *Canada*	125	M4
Pembroke *U.K.*	52	C3
Pembroke Dock	52	C3
Pena de Francia, Sierra da	66	C2
Penafiel	66	B2
Penafiel	66	D2
Penala	113	J6
Penalara, Pic de	66	E2
Penamacor	66	C2
Penapolis	138	F4
Penaranda de Bracamonte	66	D2
Penarroya	67	C2
Penarroya-Pueblonuevo	66	D3
Penarth	52	D3
Penas, Cabode	66	C1
Penasco, Puerto	126	F5
Pena, Sierra de la	67	F1
Pencader	52	C3
Pencaitland	57	F5
Pendalofon	75	F2
Pendembu	104	C4
Pendine	52	C3
Pendleton	122	E5
Pend Oreille Lake	122	F4
Pendra	92	F4
Penedo	138	K6
Penfro	52	C3
Penganga	92	E5
Pengkou	87	M6
Pengze	87	M5
Peniche	66	B3
Penicuik	57	E5
Peniscola	67	G2
Penistone	55	H3
Penitentes, Serra do	137	H5
Penmaenmawr	54	F3
Penmarch, Pointe de	65	A5
Penne	69	D4
Penner	92	E6
Penneshaw	113	H6
Pennine, Alpi	68	A2
Pennines	55	G2
Pennsylvania	125	L6
Penny Highlands	120	N4
Peno	78	E4
Penobscot	125	R4
Penobscot Bay	125	R4
Penonome	132	G10
Penrith	55	G2
Penryn	52	B4
Pensacola	129	J5
Pensamiento	136	E6
Pentecost Island	114	U11
Pentire Head	52	C4
Pentland Firth	56	E2
Pentland Hills	57	E5
Pen-y-ghent	55	G2
Penza	79	H5
Penzance	52	B4
Penzhina	85	V4
Penzhinskaya Guba	85	U4
Peoria	124	F6
Peqin	74	E2
Perak	90	C5
Perama	75	F3
Percival Lakes	112	E3
Perdido, Monte	67	G1
Peregrebnoye	84	Ae4
Pereira	136	B3
Perelazovskiy	79	G6
Perello	67	G2
Peremyshlyany	71	L4
Perenjori	112	D4
PereslavlZalesskiy	78	F4
Perevolotskiy	79	J5
Pereyaslavka	88	E2
Pergamino	139	D6
Pergamum	76	B3
Perhojoki	62	K5
Peri	77	J3
Peribonca	121	M8
Peribonca	125	Q2
Perigueux	65	D6
Perija, Sierra de	136	C2
Perim	96	F10
Peris	73	J3
Peristrema	76	F3
Perito Moreno	139	B9
Peritoro	137	J4
Perlas, Punta de	132	F8
Perlez	72	F3
Perm	78	K4
Pernambuca	137	K5
Pernik	73	G4
Peronne	64	E4
Perote	131	L8
Perote, Cofre de	131	L8
Perouse Strait, La	88	J3
Perpignan	65	E7
Perran Bay	52	B4
Perranporth	52	B4
Perros-Guirec	64	B4
Perry *Canada*	119	Q2
Perry *Florida, U.S.A.*	129	L5
Perry *Oklahoma, U.S.A.*	128	D2
Perryton	127	M2
Perryville *Alaska, U.S.A.*	118	D4
Perryville *Missouri, U.S.A.*	124	F8
Persembe	77	G2
Perseverancia	136	E6
Persian Gulf	97	K3
Pertek	77	H3
Perth *Australia*	112	D5
Perth *Canada*	125	M4
Perth *U.K.*	57	E4
Perth-Andover	125	S3
Pertominsk	78	F3
Pertugskiy	78	H4
Pertuis Breton	65	C5
Peru	136	B5
Peru *Illinois, U.S.A.*	124	F6
Peru *Indiana, U.S.A.*	124	G6
Peru-Chile Trench	143	L5
Perugia	68	D4
Perushtitsa	73	H4
Pervari	77	K4
Pervomaskiy	79	K5
Pervomaysk *Russia*	78	G5
Pervomaysk *Ukraine*	79	E6
Pervouralsk	84	Ac5
Pesaro	68	D4
Pescara	69	E4
Peschanyy, Mys	79	J7
Pesha	78	H2
Peshanjan	95	Q5
Peshawar	92	D2
Peshkopi	75	F2
Peski *Belorussia*	71	L2
Peski *Kazakhstan*	84	Ae6
Pesqueira *Brazil*	137	K5
Pesqueria *Mexico*	127	N8
Pestovo	78	F4
Petah Tiqwa	94	B5
Petajavesi	62	L5
Petalcalco, Bahia	130	H9
Petalioi	75	H4
Petalion, Kolpos	75	H4
Petaluma	126	A1
Petatlan	131	J9
Petauke	107	F5
Peterborough *Australia*	113	H5
Peterborough *Canada*	125	L4
Peterborough *U.K.*	53	G2
Peterhead	56	G3
Peterlee	55	H2
Petermann Ranges	112	F3
Peter Pond Lake	119	P4
Petersburg *Alaska, U.S.A.*	118	J4
Petersburg *Virginia, U.S.A.*	125	M8
Petersfield	53	G3
Peterstow	52	E3
Petite Kabylie	67	J4
Petite Miquelon	121	Q8
Petit Mecatina, Riviere du	121	P7
Petitot	119	L4
Petkula	62	M3
Peto	131	Q7
Petoskey	124	H4
Petra Velikogo, Zaliv	88	C4
Petre Bay	115	F6
Petrila	73	G3
Petrodvorets	63	N7
Petrolandia	137	K5
Petrolina *Amazonas, Brazil*	136	D4
Petrolina *Pernambuco, Brazil*	137	J5
Petropavlovsk	84	Ae6
Petropavlovsk-Kamchatskiy	85	T6
Petropolis	138	H4
Petrovac	72	E4
Petrovsk	79	H5
Petrovskoye	78	K5
Petrovsk-Zabaykalskiy	84	H6
Petrozavodsk	78	E3
Petsamo	62	P2
Petterli	55	G2
Petukhovo	84	Ae5
Petworth	53	G4
Peureula	90	B5
Pevek	85	W3
Pewsey, Vale of	52	F3
Peza	78	H2
Pezenas	65	E7
Pezinok	71	G4
Pezmog	78	J3
Pfaffenhofen	70	D4
Pfarrkirchen	70	E4
Pforzheim	70	C4
Phalaborwa	108	F4
Phalodi	92	D3
Phaltan	92	D5
Phangan, Ko	93	K6
Phangnga	93	J7
Phan Rang	93	L6
Phan Thiet	93	L6
Phatthalung	93	K7
Phenix City	129	K4
Phet Buri	93	J6
Phetchabun, Thiu Khao	93	K5
Philadelphia *Mississippi, U.S.A.*	128	H4
Philadelphia *Pennsylvania, U.S.A.*	125	N6
Philip	123	J3
Philip Island	111	Q7
Philippeville	64	F3
Philippines	91	G2
Philippine Sea	91	G1
Philipstown	108	D6
Phillipsburg	123	Q8
Philpots Island	120	L2
Phnom Penh	93	K6
Phoenix	126	F4
Phoenix Islands	111	U2
Phong Saly	93	K4
Phong Tho	93	K4
Phu Cuong	93	L6
Phu Dien Chau	93	L5
Phuket	93	J7
Phuket, Ko	93	J7
Phulabani	92	F4
Phu Ly	93	L4
Phuoc Le	93	L6
Phu Tho	93	L4
Phyajoki	62	L4
Piacenza	68	B3
Piana	69	B4
Pianosa, Isola	69	C4
Piatra Neamt	73	J2
Piaui	137	J5
Piaui, Serra do	137	J5
Piave	68	D3
Piaya	90	F7
Piazza Armerina	69	E7
Pibor	103	F6
Pibor Post	103	F6
Pic	124	G2
Picardie	64	E4
Picayune	128	H5
Pichilemu	139	B6
Pickering	55	J2
Pickering, Vale of	55	J2
Pickle Lake	121	J7
Pico	69	D5
Picos	137	J5
Pico Truncado	139	C9
Picton	115	E4
Picun-Leufu	139	C7
Pidalion, Akra	76	F5
Pidurutalagala	92	F7
Piedecuesta	136	C2
Piedrabuena	66	D3
Piedrahita	66	D2
Piedralaves	66	D2
Piedras Negras	127	M6
Piedra Sola	138	E6
Pielavesi	62	M5
Pielinen	62	N5
Pierowall	56	F1
Pierre	123	P5
Pietarsaari	62	K5
Pietermaritzburg	108	F5
Pietersburg	108	E4
Pietrosu	73	H2
Pieve di Cadore	68	D2
Pigadhia	75	J5
Piggott	128	G2
Pihtipudas	62	L5
Pijijiapan	131	N10
Pikes Peak	123	M8
Pikeville	124	J8
Pikhtovka	84	C5
Pila	71	G2
Pilar	138	E5
Pilaya	138	D4
Pilcanieyu	139	B8
Pilcomayo	138	D4
Pili	75	J4
Pilibhit	92	E3
Pilica	71	H3
Pilion	75	G3
Pilos	75	F4
Pilot Point	118	D4
Pilsen	70	E4
Pimenta Bueno	136	E6
Pimentel	137	G4
Pina	67	F2
Pinang *Malaysia*	90	C4
Pinang *Malaysia*	90	C4
Pinarbasi *Turkey*	76	E2
Pinarbasi *Turkey*	77	G3
Pinar del Rio	132	F3
Pinarhisar	76	B2
Pinawa	123	S2
Pincher Creek	122	H3
Pindare	137	H4
Pindhos Oros	75	F3
Pindi Gheb	92	D2
Pine Bluff	128	F3
Pine Bluffs	123	M7
Pine City	124	D4
Pine Creek	112	G1
Pine Creek Lake	128	E3
Pinedale	123	K6
Pine Falls	119	R5
Pinega *Russia*	78	G3
Pinega *Russia*	78	G3
Pine Island Bay	141	T4
Pine Pass	119	L5
Pine Point	119	N3
Pine Ridge	123	N6
Pinerolo	68	A3
Pines, Lake O' the	128	E4
Pinetop-Lakeside	127	H3
Pineville	124	J8
Pingbian	93	K4
Pingdingshan	93	M2
Pingelly	112	D5
Pingeyri	62	T12
Pingguo	93	L4
Pingjiang	93	M3
Ping, Mae Nam	93	J5
Pingquan	93	L1
Pingtan Dao	87	M6
Ping-tung	87	N7
Pingwu	93	K2
Pingxiang *Guangxi, China*	93	L4
Pingxiang *Jiangxi, China*	93	M3
Pingyang	87	N6
Pingyao	87	L4
Pingyi	87	M4
Pingyin	87	M4
Pinhao	66	C2
Pinhel	66	C2
Pini	90	B5
Pinios *Greece*	75	F4
Pinios *Greece*	75	F3
Pinnes, Akra	75	H2
Pinos, Point	126	B2
Pinotepa Nacional	131	L9
Pinrang	91	F6
Pins, Ile des	114	X17
Pinsk	71	M2
Pintados	138	C4
Pinta, Isla	136	A7
Pinto	138	D5
Pinyug	78	H3
Pioche	126	E2
Piombino	69	C4
Pioner, Ostrov	81	L2
Pionerskiy *Russia*	84	Ad4
Pionerskiy *Russia*	71	J1
Piotrkow Trybunalski	71	H3
Piove di Sacco	68	D3
Piperi	75	H3
Pipestone	124	B5
Pipmudcan, Reservoir	125	Q2
Piracicaba	138	G4
Piracuruca	137	J4
Piraeus	75	G4
Pirahmet	77	H2
Piraievs	75	G4
Piranhas *Amazonas, Brazil*	136	E5
Piranhas *Sergipe, Brazil*	137	K5
Piranshahr	77	L4
Pirapora	138	H3
Pirara	136	F3
Pirgos *Greece*	75	F4
Pirgos *Greece*	75	H5
Pirimapun	114	B3
Pirineos	67	F1
Pirin Planina	73	G5
Piripiri	137	J4
Pirmasens	70	B4
Pirna	70	E3
Piro do Rio	138	G3
Pirot	73	G4
Pir Panjal Range	92	D2
Piru	91	H6
Piryatin	79	E5
Piryi	75	H3
Pisa	68	C4
Pisco	136	B6
Piscopi	75	J4
Pisek	70	F4
Pishan	92	E1
Pishin	95	Q8
Pishin-Lora	92	C3
Pistayarvi, Ozero	62	P4
Pisticci	69	F5
Pistilfjordur	62	X11
Pistoia	68	C4
Pisuerga	66	D1
Pit	122	D7
Pita	104	C3
Pitanga	138	E4
Pitcairn Island	143	J5
Pitea	62	J4
Pitealven	62	H4
Pitesti	73	H3
Pithiviers	64	E4
Pitkyaranta	78	E3
Pitlochry	57	E4
Pitlyar	84	Ae3
Pitt Island *Canada*	118	K5
Pitt Island *New Zealand*	115	F7
Pittsburg	124	C8
Pittsburgh	125	K6
Pittsfield	124	E7
Pitt Strait	115	F7
Piui	138	G4
Piura	136	A5
Pjorsa	62	N2
Pjorsa	62	V12
Placentia Bay	121	Q8
Placer	91	G3
Placerville	126	B1
Placido do Castro	136	D6
Plackovica	73	G5
Plainview	127	M3
Plaka	75	H2
Plakenska Planina	73	F5
Plampang	91	F7
Plana	70	E4
Planeta Rica	133	K10
Plankinton	123	Q6
Plant City	129	L7
Plaquemine	128	G5
Plasencia	66	C2
Plastun	88	F3
Platani	69	D7
Plata, Rio de la	139	E6
Plati	75	G2
Plato	136	C2
Platte	123	R7
Platteville	124	E5
Plattling	70	E4
Plattsburgh	125	P4
Plattsmouth	124	C6

Plauen	**70**	E3
Plav	**72**	E4
Playa Azul	**130**	H8
Pleasanton	**128**	C6
Pleihari	**90**	E6
Pleiku	**93**	L6
Plenty, Bay of	**115**	F2
Plentywood	**123**	M3
Plesetsk	**78**	G3
Plessisville	**125**	Q3
Pleszew	**71**	G3
Pletipi Lake	**121**	M7
Pleven	**73**	H4
Plitra	**75**	G4
Pljevlja	**72**	E4
Plock	**71**	H2
Plockenstein	**70**	E4
Ploermel	**65**	B5
Ploiesti	**73**	J3
Plomb du Cantal	**65**	E6
Plombieres	**65**	G5
Ploner See	**70**	D1
Plonsk	**71**	J2
Ploty	**70**	F2
Plovdiv	**73**	H4
Plumpton	**55**	G2
Plym	**52**	C4
Plymouth *Devon, U.K.*	**52**	C4
Plymouth *Monserrat, U.K.*	**133**	R6
Plymouth *Indiana, U.S.A.*	**124**	G6
Plymouth *New Hampshire, U.S.A.*	**125**	Q5
Plymouth Sound	**52**	C4
Plynlimon	**52**	D2
Plyussa *Russia*	**63**	N7
Plyussa *Russia*	**63**	N7
Plzen	**70**	E4
Pniewy	**71**	G2
Po *Burkina Faso*	**104**	E3
Po *Italy*	**68**	C3
Pobeda, Gora	**85**	R3
Pobedy, Pik	**86**	D3
Pobiedziska	**71**	G2
Pobla de Segur	**67**	G1
Pocatello	**122**	H6
Pocatky	**70**	F4
Pochep	**79**	E5
Pochinok	**78**	E5
Pochutla	**131**	L10
Pocomoke City	**125**	N7
Pocone	**138**	E3
Pocos de Caldas	**138**	G4
Podcherye	**78**	K3
Po della Pila, Bocche del	**68**	D3
Podgorica	**72**	E4
Podgornoye	**84**	C5
Podkamennaya Tunguska	**84**	E4
Podlaska, Nizina	**71**	K2
Podolsk	**78**	F4
Podor	**104**	C2
Podporozhye	**78**	E3
Pofadder	**108**	C5
Poggibonsi	**68**	C4
Pohang	**89**	B7
Pohjois-Karjala	**62**	N5
Pohorela	**71**	J4
Pohorje	**72**	C2
Poiana Teiului	**73**	J2
Poinsett, Cape	**141**	H5
Pointe-a-Pitre	**133**	S6
Pointe-Noire	**106**	B3
Point Etienne	**100**	B4
Point Fortin	**133**	S9
Point Hope	**118**	B2
Point Lake	**119**	N2
Point Pleasant	**124**	J7
Poipet	**93**	K6
Poitiers	**65**	D5
Poitou	**65**	C5
Poix	**64**	D4
Pokataroo	**113**	K4
Pokhara	**92**	F3
Pokka	**62**	L2
Pokrovka *Kirghizia*	**86**	D3
Pokrovka *Russia*	**88**	C4
Pokrovsk	**85**	M4
Pokrovskoye	**84**	Ae5
Polacca Wash	**126**	G3
Pola de Laviana	**66**	D1
Polan	**95**	Q9
Polana	**71**	H4
Poland	**71**	G2
Polar Plateau	**141**	A1
Polati	**76**	E3
Pole Khatun	**95**	Q3
Pol-e Safid	**95**	L3
Polesie Lubelskie	**71**	K3
Polessk	**71**	J1
Polesye	**79**	D5
Polgar	**73**	F2
Poliaigos	**75**	H4
Policastro, Golfo di	**69**	E6
Poligny	**65**	F5
Poligus	**84**	E4
Polikastron	**75**	G2
Polikhnitos	**75**	J3
Polillo Islands	**91**	G3
Polis	**76**	E5
Polisan, Tanjung	**91**	H5
Politovo	**78**	H3
Poliyiros	**75**	G2
Polkyko	**84**	F2
Pollachi	**92**	E6
Pollino, Monte	**69**	F6
Polmak	**62**	N2
Polmont	**57**	E5
Polna	**63**	N7
Polnovat	**84**	Ae4
Polonnoye	**79**	D5
Polotsk	**63**	N9
Polperro	**52**	C4
Polski Trumbesh	**73**	H4
Poltava	**79**	E6
Poltavka	**84**	A6
Poltsamaa	**63**	L7
Polunochnoye	**84**	Ad4
Poluostrov Shirokostan	**85**	P2
Poluy	**84**	Ae3
Polyanovo	**84**	Ae4
Polyarnik	**85**	Y3
Polyarnyy	**62**	Q2
Polynesia	**143**	H4
Polyuc	**131**	Q8
Pombal *Para, Brazil*	**137**	G4
Pombal *Paraiba, Brazil*	**137**	K5
Pombal *Portugal*	**66**	B3
Pomerania	**70**	E2
Pomona	**126**	D3
Pomorskie, Pojezierze	**70**	F2
Pomorskiy Proliv	**78**	H2
Pompano Beach	**129**	M7
Pompeyevka	**88**	C1
Pomyt	**84**	Ae4
Ponca City	**128**	D2
Ponce	**133**	P5
Ponce de Leon Bay	**129**	M8
Poncheville, Lac	**125**	M1
Pondicherry	**92**	E6
Pond Inlet	**120**	L3
Pondo	**114**	E2
Ponerihouen	**114**	W16
Ponferrada	**66**	C1
Pongoma	**78**	E2
Ponnaiyar	**92**	E6
Ponnani	**92**	E6
Pono	**114**	A3
Ponomarevka	**78**	J5
Ponoy *Russia*	**78**	F2
Ponoy *Russia*	**78**	G2
Pons	**65**	C6
Pont	**57**	G5
Ponta de Pedras	**137**	G4
Ponta Grossa	**138**	F5
Pont-a-Mousson	**64**	G4
Ponta Pora	**138**	E4
Pontardulais	**52**	C3
Pontarlier	**65**	G5
Pontchartrain, Lake	**128**	G5
Ponte de Barca	**66**	B2
Ponte de Pedra	**137**	F6
Pontedera	**68**	C4
Ponte de Sor	**66**	B3
Pontefract	**55**	H3
Ponteland	**55**	H1
Ponte Nova	**138**	H4
Ponterwyd	**52**	D2
Pontevedra	**66**	B1
Ponthierville	**106**	E3
Pontiac	**124**	J5
Pontianak	**90**	D6
Pontivy	**64**	B4
Pont-l'Abbe	**65**	A5
Pontoetoe	**137**	F3
Pontois	**64**	E4
Pontremoli	**68**	B3
Pontrilas	**52**	E3
Ponts	**67**	G2
Pontypool	**52**	D3
Pontypridd	**52**	D3
Ponziane, Isole	**69**	D5
Poole	**53**	F4
Poole Bay	**53**	F4
Poolewe	**56**	C3
Pooley Bridge	**55**	G2
Poona	**92**	D5
Poopo, Lago	**138**	C3
Poor Knights Islands	**115**	E1
Popayan	**136**	B3
Popigay *Russia*	**84**	H2
Popigay *Russia*	**84**	J2
Poplar Bluff	**124**	E8
Poplarville	**128**	H5
Popocatepetl, Volcan	**131**	K8
Popokabaka	**106**	C4
Popoli	**69**	D4
Popomanaseu, Mount	**114**	K6
Popondetta	**114**	D3
Porbandar	**92**	C4
Porcher Island	**118**	J5
Porcuna	**66**	D4
Porcupine	**118**	G2
Pordenone	**68**	D3
Pordim	**73**	H4
Pore	**136**	C2
Porec	**72**	B3
Pori	**63**	J6
Porirua	**115**	E4
Porjus	**62**	H3
Porkhov	**63**	N8
Porlakshofn	**62**	U13
Porlamar	**136**	E1
Porlock	**52**	D3
Porlock Bay	**52**	D3
Pornic	**65**	B5
Porog *Russia*	**78**	F3
Porog *Russia*	**78**	K3
Poronaysk	**85**	Q7
Poros *Greece*	**75**	G4
Poros *Greece*	**75**	G4
Porosozero	**78**	E3
Porozhsk	**78**	J3
Porozovo	**71**	L2
Porpoise Bay	**141**	J5
Porrentury	**68**	A2
Porsangen	**62**	L1
Porsanger-halvoya	**62**	L1
Porsgrunm	**63**	C7
porshofn	**62**	X11
Porsuk	**76**	D3
Porsuk Baraji	**76**	D3
Porsyakha	**84**	A3
Portachuelo	**138**	D3
Portadown	**58**	K4
Portaferry	**58**	L4
Portage	**124**	F5
Portage la Prairie	**119**	R5
Portal	**123**	N3
Port Alberni	**122**	B3
Port Albert	**113**	K6
Portalegre	**66**	C3
Portales	**127**	L3
Port Alfred	**108**	E6
Port Alice	**122**	A2
Port Angeles	**122**	C3
Port Antonio	**132**	J5
Portarlington	**59**	H6
Port Arthur *Australia*	**113**	K7
Port Arthur *U.S.A.*	**128**	F6
Port Askaig	**57**	B5
Port Augusta	**113**	H5
Port-au-Prince	**133**	L5
Port Austin	**124**	J4
Portavogie	**58**	M4
Port-Berge	**109**	J3
Port Blair	**93**	H6
Portboil	**53**	N7
Port Burwell	**121**	P5
Port Cartier	**121**	N7
Port Chalmers	**115**	C6
Port Charlotte	**129**	L7
Port Clarence	**118**	B2
Port Clinton	**124**	J6
Port Coquitlam	**122**	C3
Port Darwin	**139**	E10
Port-de-Paix	**133**	L5
Port Dickson	**90**	C5
Portel	**66**	C3
Port Elgin	**125**	K4
Port Elizabeth	**108**	E6
Port Ellen	**57**	C5
Port Erin	**54**	E2
Porterville	**126**	C2
Port-Eynon	**52**	C3
Port Francqui	**106**	D3
Port Gentil	**106**	A3
Port Glasgow	**57**	F4
Port Harcourt	**105**	G5
Port Hardy	**118**	K5
Porthcawl	**52**	D3
Port Heiden	**118**	D4
Port Herald	**107**	G6
Porthleven	**52**	B4
Porthmadog	**52**	C2
Porth Neigwl	**52**	C2
Port Huron	**124**	J5
Port Il'ich	**94**	J2
Portimao	**66**	B4
Port Isaac	**52**	C4
Port Isaac Bay	**52**	C4
Portishead	**52**	E3
Port Jackson	**113**	L5
Port Jervis	**125**	N6
Port Kaituma	**136**	F2
Port Kembla	**113**	L5
Port Kenney	**113**	G5
Portknockie	**56**	F3
Port Lairge	**59**	H8
Portland *Australia*	**113**	J6
Portland *New Zealand*	**115**	E1
Portland *Indiana, U.S.A.*	**124**	H6
Portland *Maine, U.S.A.*	**125**	Q5
Portland *Oregon, U.S.A.*	**122**	C5
Portland Bay	**113**	J6
Portland, Bill of	**52**	E4
Portland, Cape	**113**	K7
Portland, Isle of	**52**	E4
Portland Point	**132**	J6
Portland Promontory	**121**	L6
Port Laoise	**59**	H6
Port Lavaca	**128**	D6
Port-Leucate	**65**	E7
Port Lincoln	**113**	H5
Portlock Reefs	**114**	C3
Port Loko	**104**	C4
Port Louis	**109**	L7
Port McArthur	**113**	H2
Port Macquarie	**113**	L5
Port Menier	**121**	P8
Port Moresby	**114**	D3
Portnacroish	**57**	C4
Portnahaven	**57**	B5
Port Nelson	**119**	S4
Port Nolloth	**108**	C5
Portnyagino, Ozero	**84**	H2
Porto	**66**	B2
Porto Alegre	**138**	F4
Porto Alexandre	**106**	B6
Porto Amboim	**106**	B5
Porto Camargo	**138**	F4
Porto d'Ascoli	**69**	D4
Porto dos Gauchos	**137**	F6
Porto Esperanca	**138**	E3
Porto Esperidiao	**138**	E3
Portoferraio	**69**	C4
Port-of-Spain	**136**	E1
Porto Grande	**137**	G3
Portogruaro	**68**	D3
Porto Lucena	**138**	F5
Portom	**62**	J5
Portomaggiore	**68**	C3
Porto Nacional	**138**	H6
Porto Novo *Benin*	**105**	F4
Porto Novo *Cape Verde*	**104**	L7
Port Orford	**122**	B6
Porto San Stefano	**69**	C4
Porto Sao Jose	**138**	F4
Porto Seguro	**137**	K7
Porto Socompa	**138**	C4
Porto Tolle	**68**	D3
Porto Torres	**69**	B5
Porto-Vecchio	**69**	B5
Porto Velho	**136**	E5
Portoviejo	**136**	A4
Portpatrick	**54**	D2
Port Pegasus	**115**	A7
Port Phillip Bay	**113**	J6
Port Pirie	**113**	H5
Portraine	**59**	K6
Portreath	**52**	B4
Portree	**56**	B3
Portrush	**58**	J2
Port Said	**103**	F1
Port Saint Joe	**129**	K6
Port Saint Johns	**108**	E6
Port-Saint-Louis	**65**	F7
Port Sandwich	**114**	T12
Port Saunders	**121**	Q7
Port Shepstone	**108**	F6
Portskerra	**56**	E2
Portsmouth *U.K.*	**53**	F4
Portsmouth *New Hampshire, U.S.A.*	**125**	Q5
Portsmouth *Ohio, U.S.A.*	**124**	J7
Portsmouth *Virginia, U.S.A.*	**125**	M8
Portsoy	**56**	F3
Port Stephens	**113**	L5
Portstewart	**58**	J2
Port Sudan	**103**	G4
Port Talbot	**52**	D3
Porttipahdan tekojarvi	**62**	M2
Port Townsend	**122**	C3
Portugal	**66**	B3
Portuguesa	**136**	D2
Portumna	**59**	F6
Port Washington	**124**	G5
Port William	**54**	E2
Porvenir *Bolivia*	**136**	D6
Porvenir *Chile*	**139**	B10
Porvoo	**63**	L6
Posadas	**138**	E5
Posen	**71**	G2
Poshekhonye Volodarsk	**78**	F4
Posht-e Badam	**95**	M5
Poso	**91**	G6
Posof	**77**	K2
Post	**127**	M4
Postavy	**63**	M9
Poste Weygand	**100**	F4
Postmasburg	**108**	D5
Postojna	**72**	C3
Posusje	**72**	D4
Posyet	**88**	C4
Potamia	**75**	F4
Potamos	**75**	G4
Potapovo	**84**	D3
Potchefstroom	**108**	E5
Poteau	**128**	E3
Potenza	**69**	E5
Potes	**66**	D1
Potgietersrus	**108**	E4
Poti	**77**	J1
Potiskum	**105**	H3
Potlogi	**73**	H3
Potnarvin	**114**	U13
Potomac	**125**	M7
Potosi	**138**	C3
Potsdam *U.S.A.*	**125**	N4
Potsdam *Germany*	**70**	E2
Pott	**114**	V15
Potters Bar	**53**	G3
Pottstown	**125**	N6
Pottsville	**125**	M6
Pouebo	**114**	W16
Poughkeepsie	**125**	P6
Poulaphouca Reservoir	**59**	J6
Poulter	**55**	H3
Poulton-le-Fylde	**55**	G3
Poundstock	**52**	C4
Pouso Alegre	**138**	G4
Pouzauges	**65**	C5
Povenets	**78**	E3
Poverty Bay	**115**	G3
Povorino	**79**	G5
Povungnituk	**121**	L6
Povungnituk Bay	**121**	L6
Powder	**123**	M5
Powell	**123**	K5
Powell, Lake	**126**	F2
Powell River	**122**	B3
Power Head	**59**	F9
Powys	**52**	D2
Poya	**114**	W16
Poyang Hu	**87**	M6
Poyraz	**77**	H3
Poysdorf	**68**	F1
Poytya	**63**	K6

Pozanti	**76**	F4
Pozarevac	**73**	F3
Poza Rica	**131**	L7
Pozharskoye	**88**	E2
Poznan	**71**	G2
Pozoblanco	**66**	D3
Pozohondo	**67**	F3
Pozzuoli	**69**	E5
Prabumulih	**90**	D6
Prachin Buri	**93**	K6
Prachuap Khiri Khan	**93**	J6
Praded	**71**	G3
Pradelles	**65**	E6
Prades	**65**	E7
Prague	**70**	F3
Praha	**70**	F3
Prahova	**73**	H3
Praia	**104**	L7
Prainha *Amazonas, Brazil*	**136**	E5
Prainha *Para, Brazil*	**137**	G4
Prairie Dog Town Fork	**127**	L3
Prairie du Chien	**124**	E5
Prairies, Coteau des	**124**	C5
Prairie Village	**124**	C7
Prapat	**90**	B5
Prasonisi, Akra	**75**	J5
Prasto	**63**	E9
Prata	**138**	G3
Prato	**68**	C4
Pratt	**127**	N2
Pravets	**73**	G4
Pravia	**66**	C1
Predazzo	**68**	C2
Predcal	**73**	H3
Predeal, Pasul	**73**	H3
Predivinsk	**84**	E5
Predlitz	**68**	D2
Premer	**113**	K5
Premuda	**72**	C3
Prenai	**71**	K1
Prentice	**124**	E4
Prenzlau	**70**	E2
Preobrazhenka	**84**	H5
Preparis	**93**	H6
Preparis North Channel	**93**	H5
Preparis South Channel	**93**	H6
Prerov	**71**	G4
Prescot	**55**	G3
Prescott *Arizona, U.S.A.*	**126**	F3
Prescott *Arkansas, U.S.A.*	**128**	F4
Prescott Island	**120**	G3
Preseli, Mynydd	**52**	C3
Preservation Inlet	**115**	A7
Presevo	**73**	F4
Presho	**123**	Q6
Presidencia Roque Saenz Pena	**138**	D5
Presidente Dutra	**137**	J4
Presidente Epitacio	**138**	F4
Presidente Prudente	**138**	E4
Presidio	**127**	K6
Preslav	**73**	J4
Presnovka	**84**	Ae6
Presov	**71**	J4
Prespansko Jezero	**75**	F2
Presque Isle	**125**	S3
Pressburg	**71**	G4
Prestatyn	**55**	F3
Presteigne	**52**	D2
Preston *U.K.*	**55**	G3
Preston *Minnesota, U.S.A.*	**124**	D5
Preston *Missouri, U.S.A.*	**124**	D8
Prestonburg	**124**	J8
Prestonpans	**57**	F5
Prestwick	**57**	F4
Pretoria	**108**	E5
Preveza	**75**	F3
Prey Veng	**93**	L6
Pribilof Islands	**118**	Ad8
Pribinic	**72**	D3
Pribram	**70**	F4
Price	**126**	G1
Price, Cape	**93**	H6
Prichard	**129**	H5
Priego	**66**	E2
Priego de Cordoba	**66**	D4
Prieska	**108**	D5
Priest Lake	**122**	F3
Priest River	**122**	F3
Prievidza	**71**	H4
Prignitz	**70**	D2
Prijedor	**72**	D3
Prikaspiyskaya Nizmennost	**79**	J6
Prilep	**73**	F5
Priluki *Russia*	**78**	G3
Priluki *Ukraine*	**79**	E5
Primavera	**141**	V6
Primorsk *Azerbaijan*	**79**	H7
Primorsk *Ukraine*	**79**	F6
Primorsk *Russia*	**79**	H6
Primorsk *Russia*	**63**	N6
Primorskiy Kray	**88**	E3
Primorsko	**73**	J4
Primorsko-Akhtarsk	**79**	F6
Primrose Lake	**119**	P5
Prince Albert *Canada*	**119**	P5
Prince Albert *South Africa*	**108**	D6
Prince Albert Peninsula	**119**	N1
Prince Albert Road	**108**	D6
Prince Albert Sound	**119**	N1
Prince Alfred, Cape	**120**	B3
Prince Charles Island	**120**	L4
Prince Charles Mountains	**141**	E4
Prince Edward Island	**121**	P8
Prince Edward Islands	**142**	C6
Prince George	**119**	L5
Prince Gustav Adolph Sea	**120**	E2
Prince of Wales, Cape *Canada*	**121**	M5
Prince of Wales, Cape *U.S.A.*	**118**	B2
Prince of Wales Island *Australia*	**114**	C4
Prince of Wales Island *Canada*	**120**	G3
Prince of Wales Island *U.S.A.*	**118**	J4
Prince of Wales Strait	**119**	M1
Prince Patrick Island	**120**	B2
Prince Regent Inlet	**120**	H3
Prince Rupert	**118**	J5
Princes Risborough	**53**	G3
Princess Astrid Coast	**141**	A4
Princess Charlotte Bay	**113**	J1
Princess Elizabeth Land	**141**	F4
Princess Marie Bay	**120**	L2
Princethorpe	**53**	F2
Princeton *Canada*	**122**	D3
Princeton *Illinois, U.S.A.*	**124**	F6
Princeton *Kentucky, U.S.A.*	**124**	G8
Princeton *Missouri, U.S.A.*	**124**	D6
Princeton *W. Virginia, U.S.A.*	**125**	K8
Prince William Sound	**118**	F3
Principe	**105**	G5
Prineville	**122**	D5
Prins Karls Forland	**80**	C2
Prinzapolca	**132**	E8
Priozersk	**63**	P6
Pripet Marshes	**79**	D5
Pripyat	**71**	M2
Pristina	**73**	F4
Pritzwalk	**70**	E2
Privas	**65**	F6
Privolzhskaya Vozvyshennost	**79**	H5
Prizzi	**69**	D7
Prnjavor	**72**	D3
Probolinggo	**90**	E7
Proddatur	**92**	E6
Progreso	**131**	Q7
Prokhladnyy	**79**	G7
Prokletije	**74**	E1
Prokopyevsk	**84**	D6
Prokuplje	**73**	F4
Proletarsk	**79**	G6
Prome	**93**	J5
Proprad	**71**	J4
Propria	**137**	K6
Propriano	**69**	B5
Prorva	**79**	J6
Prosna	**71**	G3
Prospect	**122**	C6
Prosperous	**59**	J6
Prostejov	**71**	G4
Provence	**65**	G7
Providence *Seychelles*	**82**	D7
Providence *U.S.A.*	**125**	Q6
Providence, Cape *Canada*	**120**	D3
Providence, Cape *New Zealand*	**115**	A7
Providencia	**136**	B4
Providencia, Isla de	**132**	G8
Provideniya	**81**	V3
Provincetown	**125**	Q5
Provins	**64**	E4
Provo	**122**	J7
Prudhoe	**55**	H2
Prudhoe Bay	**118**	F1
Prum	**70**	B3
Pruszkow	**71**	J2
Prut	**73**	K2
Prutul	**73**	J2
Pruzhany	**71**	L2
Pryazha	**78**	E3
Prydz Bay	**141**	F5
Pryor	**128**	E2
Przechlewo	**71**	G2
Przemysl	**71**	K4
Przeworsk	**71**	K3
Przhevalsk	**86**	D3
Przysucha	**71**	J3
Psakhna	**75**	G3
Psara	**75**	H3
Pskov	**63**	Q8
Pskovskoye, Ozero	**63**	M7
Ptolemals	**75**	F2
Ptuj	**72**	C2
Puan	**87**	P4
Pucallpa	**136**	C5
Pucarani	**138**	C3
Pudai	**95**	R6
Pudasjarvi	**62**	M4
Puddletown	**52**	E4
Pudnya	**63**	N8
Pudozh	**78**	F3
Pudsey	**55**	H3
Puduchcheri	**92**	E6
Pudukkottai	**92**	E6
Puebla	**131**	K8
Puebla de Don Rodrigo	**66**	D3
Puebla de Sanabria	**66**	C1
Puebla de Trives	**66**	C1
Pueblo	**127**	K1
Pueblo Hundido	**138**	B5
Pueblo Nuevo	**136**	D1
Puelen	**139**	C7
Puente Alto	**139**	C6
Puerto Acosta	**138**	C3
Puerto Aisen	**139**	B9
Puerto Asis	**136**	B3
Puerto Ayacucho	**136**	D2
Puerto Ayora	**136**	A7
Puerto Barrios	**132**	C7
Puerto Cabello	**136**	D1
Puerto Cabezas	**132**	F7
Puerto Carreno	**136**	D2
Puerto Casado	**138**	E4
Puerto Coig	**139**	C10
Puerto Cortes *Costa Rica*	**132**	F10
Puerto Cortes *Honduras*	**132**	D7
Puerto Cumarebo	**136**	D1
Puerto del Rosario	**100**	C3
Puerto de Pollensa	**67**	H3
Puerto Deseado	**139**	C9
Puerto Escondido	**131**	L10
Puerto Estrella	**136**	C1
Puerto Eten	**136**	B5
Puerto Guarani	**138**	E4
Puerto Juarez	**131**	R7
Puerto La Cruz	**136**	E1
Puerto-Lapice	**66**	E3
Puerto Leguizamo	**136**	C4
Puerto Libertad	**126**	F6
Puertollano	**66**	D3
Puerto Lobos	**139**	C8
Puerto Madryn	**139**	C8
Puerto Maldonado	**136**	D6
Puerto Merazan	**132**	D8
Puerto Montt	**139**	B8
Puerto Natales	**139**	B10
Puerto Ordaz	**133**	R10
Puerto Paez	**136**	D2
Puerto Penasco	**126**	F5
Puerto Pico	**138**	E5
Puerto Plata	**133**	M5
Puerto Portillo	**136**	C5
Puerto Princesa	**91**	F4
Puerto Rey	**132**	J10
Puerto Rico *Bolivia*	**136**	D6
Puerto Rico *U.S.A.*	**133**	P5
Puerto Rico Trench	**133**	P5
Puerto San Antonio Oeste	**139**	C8
Puerto Santa Cruz	**139**	C10
Puerto Sastre	**138**	E4
Puerto Siles	**136**	D6
Puerto Suarez	**138**	E3
Puerto Tejado	**136**	B3
Puerto Vallarta	**130**	G7
Puerto Varas	**139**	B8
Puerto Villazon	**136**	E6
Puesto Arturo	**136**	C4
Pueyrredan, Lago	**139**	B9
Pugachev	**79**	H5
Pugachevo	**88**	J1
Pugal	**92**	D3
Puger	**90**	E7
Puget-Theniers	**65**	G7
Pui	**73**	G3
Puigcerda	**67**	G1
Pujehun	**104**	C4
Pukaki, Lake	**115**	C6
Pukchong	**88**	B5
Puke	**74**	E1
Pukekohe	**115**	E2
Pukeuri	**115**	C6
Puksa	**78**	F3
Pula	**72**	B3
Pular, Cerro	**138**	C4
Pulaski *New York, U.S.A.*	**125**	M5
Pulaski *Tennessee, U.S.A.*	**129**	J3
Pulaski *Virginia, U.S.A.*	**125**	K8
Pulau Jos Sodarso	**114**	B3
Pulaupunjung	**90**	D6
Pulborough	**53**	G4
Pu-li	**87**	N7
Pulicat Lake	**92**	F6
Pulkkila	**62**	L4
Pullman	**122**	F4
Pulo Anna	**91**	J5
Pulog, Mount	**91**	G2
Pulonga	**78**	G2
Pulpito, Punta	**126**	G7
Pultusk	**71**	J2
Pulumur	**77**	H3
Pumasillo, Cerro	**136**	C6
Pumsaint	**52**	D2
Puna, Isla	**136**	A4
Punakha	**93**	G3
Pune	**92**	D5
Pungsan	**88**	B5
Punjab	**92**	E2
Puno	**138**	B3
Punta Alta	**139**	D7
Punta Arenas	**139**	B10
Punta, Cerro de	**133**	P5
Punta de Diaz	**138**	B5
Punta Delgada	**139**	D8
Punta Delgado	**139**	C10
Punta Gorda	**132**	C6
Punta Prieta	**126**	E6
Puntarenas	**132**	E9
Punta Saavedra	**139**	B7
Punto Fijo	**136**	C1
Puolanka	**62**	M4
Puquio	**136**	C6
Puquios	**138**	C5
Pur	**84**	B3
Pura	**84**	D2
Purari	**114**	D3
Purbeck, Isle of	**53**	E4
Purchena	**66**	E4
Purdy Islands	**114**	D2
Purepero	**130**	J8
Puri	**92**	G5
Purnia	**93**	G3
Pursat	**93**	K6
Purtuniq	**120**	M5
Puruliya	**92**	G4
Purus	**136**	E4
Puruvesi	**63**	N6
Purwakarta	**90**	D7
Purwokert	**90**	D7
Puryong	**88**	B4
Pusa	**63**	M8
Pusan	**89**	B8
Pushkino	**94**	J2
Pushlakhta	**78**	F3
Pusht-i-Rud	**95**	R6
Pustoshka	**63**	N8
Putao	**93**	J3
Putaruru	**115**	E3
Putian	**87**	M6
Putila	**71**	L5
Puting, Tanjung	**90**	E6
Putnok	**72**	F1
Putorana, Gory	**84**	F3
Putorino	**115**	F3
Puttalam	**92**	E7
Puttgarden	**70**	D1
Putumayo	**136**	C4
Putusibau	**90**	E5
Puulavesi	**63**	M6
Puuwai	**126**	Q10
Pu Xian	**93**	M1
Puyko	**84**	Ae3
Puyo	**136**	B4
Puzla	**78**	J3
Pweto	**107**	E4
Pwllheli	**52**	C2
Pyaozero, Ozero	**62**	P3
Pyapon	**93**	J5
Pyasina	**84**	D2
Pyasinado	**84**	B3
Pyasino, Ozero	**84**	D3
Pyatigorsk	**79**	G7
Pygmalion Point	**93**	H7
Pyhajarvi *Finland*	**62**	L5
Pyhajarvi *Finland*	**62**	L5
Pyhajarvi *Turku-Pori, Finland*	**63**	K6
Pyhajoki	**62**	L4
Pyhaselka	**62**	N5
Pyinmana	**93**	J5
Pylkaram	**84**	C4
Pyonggok-tong	**89**	B7
Pyonghae-ri	**89**	B7
Pyongyang	**87**	P4
Pyramid Lake	**122**	E7
Pyrenees	**65**	D7
Pyrzyce	**70**	F2
Pytalovo	**63**	M8

Q

Qaamiyat, Al	**97**	J7
Qabr Hud	**97**	J8
Qadimah	**96**	D5
Qadub	**97**	P10
Qaemshahr	**95**	L3
Qagan Tolgoi	**87**	K4
Qaidam Pendi	**93**	H1
Qaidam Shan	**93**	J1
Qaisar	**94**	S4
Qala Adras Kand	**95**	R5
Qalaen Nahl	**96**	B10
Qalamat ar Rakabah	**97**	L6
Qalamat Faris	**97**	K6
Qalansiyah	**97**	P10
Qalat	**92**	C2
Qalat Bishah	**96**	F6
Qalat Salih	**94**	H6
Qalat Sukkar	**94**	H6
Qala Vali	**95**	R4
Qaleh-ye Now	**95**	R4
Qamar, Ghubbat al	**97**	L8
Qamar, Jabal al	**97**	L8
Qaminis	**101**	K2
Qamsar	**95**	K5
Qandala	**103**	J5
Qapqal	**86**	E3
Qarabagh	**95**	Q4
Qara, Jabal al	**97**	M8
Qaratshuk	**94**	F3
Qardho	**103**	J6
Qareh Aqaj	**94**	H3
Qareh Su	**94**	H2
Qareh Su	**94**	H5
Qarqan He	**86**	F4
Qarqi	**86**	F3
Qaryat al Ulya	**97**	H3
Qasab	**77**	K4
Qasa Murg	**95**	S4
Qasr Amij	**77**	J6
Qasr-e-Qand	**95**	Q8
Qasr-e-Shirin	**94**	G4
Qatabah	**96**	G10
Qatah	**77**	J5
Qatana	**94**	C5
Qatar	**97**	K4
Qatrana	**94**	C6
Qattara Depression	**102**	E2
Qattara, Munkhafed el	**102**	E2
Qayen	**95**	P5
Qazvin	**95**	K3
Qeisum	**96**	A3
Qena	**103**	F2
Qeshm *Iran*	**95**	N8
Qeshm *Iran*	**95**	N8
Qeydar	**94**	J3
Qeys	**95**	L8
Qezel Owzan	**94**	J3
Qeziot	**94**	B6
Qianan	**87**	N2
Qianjiang	**93**	L3

Name	Page	Grid
Qianwei	87	N3
Qianxi	93	L3
Qianxinan	93	K3
Qiaowan	86	H3
Qidong *Hunan, China*	93	M3
Qidong *Jiangsu, China*	87	N5
Qiemo	92	G1
Qihe	87	M4
Qihreg	87	L3
Qijiaojing	86	F3
Qikou	87	M4
Qila Ladgasht	92	B3
Qila Saifullah	92	C2
Qilian Shan	86	H4
Qinab, Wadi	97	J8
Qingan	88	A2
Qingdao	87	N4
Qinggang	87	P2
Qinghai	93	J2
Qinghai Hu	93	K1
Qinghai Nanshan	93	J1
Qinghe	88	B2
Qing Xian	87	M4
Qingyang	93	L1
Qingyuan *Liaoning, China*	87	N3
Qingyuan *Zhejiang, China*	87	M6
Qinhuangdao	87	M4
Qin Ling	93	L2
Qinshui	93	M1
Qin Xian	87	L4
Qinyuan	87	L4
Qinzhou	93	L4
Qionglai	93	K2
Qionglai Shan	93	K2
Qiongzhong	93	L5
Qiongzhou Haixia	93	L4
Qiqihar	87	N2
Qir	95	L7
Qishn	97	K9
Qishran	96	E6
Qitai	86	F3
Qitaihe	87	Q2
Qitbit, Wadi	97	M7
Qixing He	88	D2
Qixingpao	88	C2
Qiyang	93	M3
Qizil Bulak	95	Q4
Qojur	94	H3
Qolleh-ye Damavand	95	L4
Qom	95	K4
Qomisheh	95	K5
Qomolangma Feng	92	G3
Qornetes Saouda	94	B4
Qorveh	94	H4
Qotbabad	95	N8
Qotur *Iran*	77	L3
Qotur *Iran*	77	L3
Quaidabad	92	D2
Quairading	112	D5
Quakenbruck	70	B2
Quanah	127	N3
Quang Ngai	93	L5
Quang Tri	93	L5
Quang Yen	93	L4
Quan Long	93	L7
Quannan	87	L7
Quan Phu Quoc	93	K6
Quantock Hills	52	D3
Quanzhou *Fujian, China*	87	M7
Quanzhou *Guangxi, China*	93	M3
Qu'Appelle	123	N2
Quaqtaq	121	N5
Quarai *Brazil*	138	E6
Quarai *Brazil*	138	E6
Quartu San Elena	69	B6
Quartzsite	126	E4
Quatsino Sound	122	A2
Quayti	97	J9
Quchan	95	P3
Qudaym	77	H5
Queanbeyan	113	K6
Quebec *Canada*	121	L7
Quebec *Canada*	125	Q3
Quedal, Cabo de	139	B8
Queen Bess, Mount	122	B2
Queen, Cape	120	L5
Queen Charlotte Islands	118	J5
Queen Charlotte Sound	118	K5
Queen Charlotte Strait	118	K5
Queen Elizabeth Islands	120	G2
Queen Mary Land	141	G4
Queen Maud Gulf	119	Q2
Queen Maud Land	141	A4
Queen Maud Mountains	141	N1
Queensbury	55	H3
Queens Channel	112	F1
Queensferry *Clwyd, U.K.*	55	F3
Queensferry *Lothian, U.K.*	57	E5
Queensland	113	J3
Queenstown *Australia*	113	K7
Queenstown *New Zealand*	115	B6
Queenstown *South Africa*	108	E6
Queija, Sierra de	66	C1
Queimadas	137	K6
Quela	106	C4
Quelimane	109	G3
Quelpart Island	87	P5
Quemado	127	H3
Quembo	106	C5
Quepos	132	E10
Que Que	108	E3
Queretaro	131	J7
Queshan	93	M2
Quesnel	119	L5
Quesnel Lake	119	L5
Quetena	138	C4
Quetta	92	C2
Quettehou	64	C4
Quevedo	136	B4
Quezaltenango	132	B7
Quezon City	91	G3
Quibala	106	B5
Quibaxi	106	B4
Quibdo	136	B2
Quiberon	65	B5
Quiberon, Baie de	65	B5
Quilengues	106	B5
Quillabamba	136	C6
Quillacollo	138	C3
Quillagua	138	C4
Quillan	65	E7
Quill Lakes	123	M2
Quillota	139	B6
Quilon	92	E7
Quilpie	113	J4
Quimbele	106	C4
Quimper	64	A4
Quimperle	65	B5
Quinag	56	C2
Quince Mil	136	C6
Quincy *California, U.S.A.*	122	D8
Quincy *Illinois, U.S.A.*	124	E7
Quincy *Massachusetts, U.S.A.*	125	Q5
Quines	139	C6
Qui Nhon	93	L6
Quintanar de la Orden	66	E3
Quintero	139	B6
Quipungo	106	B5
Quiroga	66	C1
Quissanga	109	H2
Quita Sueno Bank	132	G7
Quito	136	B4
Quixada	137	K4
Qu Jiang	93	L2
Qujing	93	K3
Qulban Layyah	94	H7
Qumarleb	93	J2
Qumbu	108	E6
Qunayfidhah, Nafud	96	G4
Quoin Point	108	C6
Quorn	113	H5
Quorndon	53	F2
Quru Gol Pass	94	G2
Qus	103	F2
Quseir	103	F2
Qutiabad	94	J4
Qutu	96	E7
Quzhou	87	M6

R

Name	Page	Grid
Raab *Austria*	68	E2
Raab *Hungary*	72	D2
Raahe	62	L4
Raakkyla	62	N5
Raanes Peninsula	120	J2
Raanujarvi	62	L3
Raasay	56	B3
Raasay, Sound of	56	B3
Rab	72	C3
Raba	72	D2
Raba *Indonesia*	91	F7
Raba *Poland*	71	H4
Rabastens	65	D7
Rabat *Morocco*	100	D2
Rabat *Turkey*	77	J2
Rabaul	114	E2
Rabi	114	S8
Rabigh	96	D5
Rabor	95	N7
Rabyanah, Ramlat	101	K4
Race, Cape	121	R8
Rach Gia	93	L6
Raciborz	71	H3
Racine	124	G5
Rackwick	56	E2
Racoon	124	C5
Racoon Mountains	129	J3
Rada	96	G9
Radauti	73	H2
Radcliff	124	H8
Radde	88	C1
Radekhov	71	L3
Radford	125	K8
Radisson	121	L7
Radna	73	F2
Radnice	70	E4
Radnor Forest	52	D2
Radom	71	J3
Radomsko	71	H3
Radomyshl	79	D5
Radovis	73	G5
Radstadt	68	D2
Radstock	52	E3
Radstock, Cape	113	G5
Radzyn Podlaski	71	K3
Rae	119	M2
Rae Bareli	92	F3
Rae Isthmus	120	J4
Raetihi	115	E3
Rafaela	138	D6
Rafai	102	D6
Rafalovka	71	L3
Rafha	96	F2
Rafsanjan	95	M6
Raga	102	E6
Ragged Cays	133	K3
Raghtin More	58	H2
Raglan Harbour	115	E2
Ragusa *Italy*	69	E7
Ragusa *Yugoslavia*	72	E4
Rahad	96	B10
Rahat, Harrat	96	E5
Rahimyar Khan	92	D3
Rahuri	92	D5
Raichur	92	E5
Raigarh *Madhya Pradesh, India*	92	F4
Raigarh *Orissa, India*	92	F5
Rainbow City	129	J4
Rainham	53	H3
Rainier, Mount	122	D4
Rainy	124	C2
Rainy Lake	124	D2
Raippaluoto	62	J5
Raipur	92	F4
Raisduoddarhaldde	62	J2
Raistakka	62	N3
Rajada	137	J5
Rajahmundry	92	F5
Rajang	90	E5
Rajanpur	92	D3
Rajapalaiyam	92	E7
Rajapur	92	D5
Rajasthan	92	D3
Rajasthan Canal	92	D3
Rajgarh	92	E4
Rajgrod	71	K2
Rajkot	92	D4
Rajmahal Hills	93	G4
Raj Nandgaon	92	F4
Rajpipla	92	D4
Rajshahi	92	G4
Rakaia	115	C5
Rakan, Ra's	97	K3
Rakbah, Sahl	96	E5
Raketskjutfalt	62	J2
Rakhes	75	G3
Rakhov	79	C6
Rakhovo	71	L4
Rakitnoye	88	E3
Rakkestad	63	D7
Rakops	108	D4
Rakov	71	M2
Rakusha	79	J6
Rakvere	63	M7
Raleigh	129	N3
Rama	132	E8
Ramallah	94	B6
Ramasaig	56	B3
Rambi	114	S8
Rambouillet	64	D4
Rambutyo Island	114	D2
Ramdurg	92	E5
Rameco	139	D7
Rame Head	52	C4
Rameswaram	92	E7
Ramgarh	92	F4
Ramhormoz	95	J6
Ram, Jambal	96	B2
Ramor, Lough	58	H5
Ramos	130	G5
Ramos Island	114	K6
Rampart	118	E2
Rampur	92	E3
Ramree	93	H5
Ramsbottom	55	G3
Ramsele	62	G5
Ramsey *Cambridgeshire, U.K.*	53	G2
Ramsey *Essex, U.K.*	53	J3
Ramsey *Isle of Man, U.K.*	54	E2
Ramsey Bay	54	E2
Ramsey Island	52	B3
Ramsgate	53	J3
Ramsjo	63	F5
Ramtha	94	C5
Ramu	114	C3
Ramvik	62	G5
Ranau	90	F4
Rancagua	139	J6
Rance	64	B4
Rancha Cordova	126	B1
Ranchi	92	G4
Rancho California	126	D4
Randalstown	58	K3
Randazzo	69	E7
Randers	63	D8
Randolph	123	R6
Randsfjord	63	D6
Ranea	62	K4
Ranfurly	115	C6
Rangas, Tanjung	91	F6
Rangiora	115	D5
Rangitaiki	115	F3
Rangitata	115	C5
Rangkasbitung	90	D7
Rangkul	86	C4
Rangoon	93	J5
Rangpur	93	G3
Rangsang	90	C5
Ranibennur	92	E6
Raniganj	93	G4
Ranken	113	H3
Rankin Inlet *Canada*	119	S3
Rankin Inlet *Canada*	119	S3
Rankins Springs	113	K5
Rannoch Moor	57	D4
Rannoch, Loch	57	D4
Ranon	114	U12
Ranongga	114	H5
Ransiki	91	J6
Ranskill	55	H3
Rantau *Kalimantan, Indonesia*	90	F6
Rantau *Sumatera, Indonesia*	90	C5
Rantauprapat	90	B5
Rantoul	124	F6
Ranya	94	G3
Raohe	88	D2
Raon-l'Etape	64	G4
Raoul	111	T7
Rapallo	68	B3
Raper, Cape	120	N4
Rapid City	123	N5
Rapla	63	L7
Rapli	92	F3
Rapness	56	F1
Rappahannock	125	M7
Rapperswil	68	B2
Rapsani	75	G3
Rapulo	136	D6
Rapur	92	E6
Ras al Ayn	77	J4
Ras al Khafji	97	J2
Ra's al Khaymah	97	M4
Rasa, Punta	139	D8
Ras Dashen	96	D10
Raseiniai	63	K9
Ras el Ma	100	E5
Ras en Naqb	94	B6
Rashad	102	F5
Rasharkin	58	K3
Rashid	102	F1
Rasht	95	J3
Rask	95	Q8
Raska	72	F4
Raso, Cabo	139	C8
Rason, Lake	112	E4
Rasshua, Ostrov	85	S7
Rasskazovo	79	G5
Rassokha	84	H2
Rastenburg	71	J1
Rastigaissa	62	M1
Rasul	95	M8
Ratangarh	92	D3
Rat Buri	93	J6
Rathangan	59	J6
Rathcoole	59	K6
Rathdowney	59	G7
Rathdrum	59	K7
Rathen	56	F3
Rathenow	70	E2
Rathfriland	58	K4
Rathkeale	59	E7
Rathlin Island	58	K2
Rathlin Sound	58	K2
Rathluirc	59	E8
Rathmore	59	D8
Rathnew	59	K7
Rathoath	59	K5
Ratibor	71	H3
Ratisbon	70	E4
Rat Islands	118	Ab9
Ratlam	92	E4
Ratnagiri	92	D5
Ratnapura	92	F7
Ratno	79	C5
Raton	127	K2
Ratta	84	C4
Rattray	57	E4
Rattray Head	56	G3
Rattvik	63	F6
Ratzeburg	70	D2
Ratz, Mount	118	J4
Rauch	139	E7
Rauchua	85	V3
Raudales	131	N9
Raudhatain	97	H2
Raufarhofn	62	X11
Raufoss	63	D6
Raukumara Range	115	F3
Raul Leoni, Represa	133	R11
Rauma	63	J6
Raung, Gunung	90	F7
Raurkela	92	F4
Rausu	88	K3
Ravansar	94	H4
Ravar	95	N6
Rava Russkaya	79	C5
Ravenglass	55	F2
Ravenna	68	D3
Ravenscar	55	J2
Ravensthorpe	112	E5
Ravenstonedale	55	G2
Ravenswood	125	K7
Ravensworth	55	H2
Ravi	92	D2
Ravno	72	E3
Rawa	93	J3
Rawah	77	J5
Rawaki	111	U2
Rawalpindi	92	D2
Rawandiz	94	G3
Rawcliffe	55	J3
Rawdah	77	J5
Rawicz	71	G3
Rawlinna	112	F5
Rawlins	123	L7
Rawmarsh	55	H3
Rawson	139	C8
Rawtenstall	55	G3
Ray	53	F3
Rayachoti	92	E6
Rayadurg	92	E6
Rayagarha	92	F5
Rayakoski	62	N2
Ray, Cape	121	Q8

Raychikhinsk 85 M7
Rayen 95 N7
Rayeskiy 78 J5
Rayleigh 53 H3
Raymondville 128 D7
Ray Mountains 118 E2
Raysut 97 L8
Razan 94 J5
Razan 94 J4
Razdelnaya 79 E6
Razdolnoye 88 C4
Razgrad 73 J4
Razmak 92 C2
Raznas Ezers 63 M8
Raz, Pointe du 64 A4
Reading *U.K.* 53 G3
Reading *U.S.A.* 125 N6
Realico 139 D7
Rea, Lough 59 E6
Rearsby 53 F2
Reawick 56 A2
Reay 56 E2
Rebecca, Lake 112 E5
Rebi 91 J7
Reboly 62 P5
Rebrikha 84 C6
Rebrovo 73 G4
Rebun-to 88 H3
Recanati 68 D4
Recea 73 G3
Recherche, Archipelago of the 112 E5
Rechitsa 79 E5
Rechna Doab 92 D2
Recife 137 L5
Recklinghausen 70 B3
Recknitz 70 E2
Reconquista 138 E5
Recreio 136 F5
Red *Canada* 123 R2
Red *U.S.A.* 128 F5
Redalen 63 D6
Red Bay 121 Q7
Redbird 123 M6
Red Bluff 122 C7
Red Bluff Lake 127 L5
Redcar 55 H2
Redcliffe 113 L4
Red Cloud 123 Q7
Red Deer *Canada* 122 G2
Red Deer *Canada* 122 H1
Red Deer *Canada* 123 J2
Red Deer *Saskatchewan, Canada* 119 Q5
Redding 122 C7
Redditch 53 F2
Redencao 137 J5
Redfield 123 Q5
Redhakhol 92 F4
Redhill 53 G3
Red Hills 127 N2
Red Lake *Canada* 123 S2
Red Lake *Canada* 123 T2
Red Lake *U.S.A.* 124 C3
Red Lake *U.S.A.* 123 R4
Red Lodge 123 K5
Redmond 122 D5
Redon 65 B5
Redondela 66 B1
Redondo 66 C3
Red Rock 124 F2
Redruth 52 B4
Red Sea 103 G3
Red Tank 113 K5
Red Wharf Bay 54 E3
Red Wing 124 D4
Redwood City 126 A2
Reed City 124 H5
Reedsport 122 B6
Ree, Lough 58 G5
Reetton 115 C5
Refahiye 77 H3
Refresco 138 C5
Rega 70 F2
Regen 70 E4
Regensburg 70 E4
Reggane 100 F3
Reggio di Calabria 69 E6
Reggio nell Amelia 68 C3
Regina *Brazil* 137 G3
Regina *Canada* 123 M2
Reguengos de Monsaraz 66 C3
Rehna 70 D2
Rehoboth 108 C4
Rehoboth Beach 125 N7
Rehovot 94 B6
Reidh, Rubha 56 C3
Reidsville 129 N2
Reiff 56 C2
Reigate 53 G3
Reighton 55 J2
Re, Ile de 65 C5
Reims 64 F4
Reina Adelaida, Archipielago de la 139 B10
Reindeer Lake 119 Q4
Reine 62 E3
Reinga, Cape 115 D1
Reinheimen 62 B5
Reinosa 66 D1
Reitz 108 E5
Relizane 100 F1
Remada 101 H2
Rembang 90 E7
Remeshk 95 P8
Remiremont 65 G4
Remontnoye 79 G6
Remoulins 65 F7
Remscheid 70 B3
Rena *Norway* 63 D6
Rena *Norway* 63 D6
Renaix 64 E3
Renard Islands 114 E4
Rendova Island 114 H6
Rendsburg 70 C1
Renfrew *Canada* 125 M4
Renfrew *U.K.* 57 D5
Rengat 90 D6
Rengo 139 B6
Renish Point 56 B3
Renk 103 F5
Renmark 113 J5
Renmin 87 P2
Rennell Island 114 K7
Rennes 64 C4
Reno *Italy* 68 C3
Reno *U.S.A.* 122 E8
Reo 91 G7
Repetek 95 R2
Repolovo 84 Ae4
Republican 123 R7
Repulse Bay *Australia* 113 K3
Repulse Bay *Canada* 120 J4
Requena *Peru* 136 C5
Requena *Spain* 67 F3
Rere 114 K6
Resadiye *Turkey* 76 B4
Resadiye *Turkey* 77 G2
Resen 73 F5
Resia, Passo de 68 C2
Resistencia 138 E5
Resita 73 F3
Resolution Island *Canada* 121 P5
Resolution Island *New Zealand* 115 A6
Resolution Lake 121 P6
Restigouche 125 S3
Retalhuleu 132 B7
Rethel 64 F4
Rethimnon 75 H5
Retiche, Alpi 68 C2
Retsag 72 E2
Retuerta de Bullaque 66 D3
Reunion 109 L7
Reus 67 G2
Reuss 68 B2
Reut 73 J2
Reutlingen 70 C4
Revel 65 D7
Revelstoke 122 E2
Reventador, Volcan 136 B4
Revillagigedo Island 118 J5
Revillagigedo, Islas 130 D8
Rewa 92 F4
Rewari 92 E3
Rexburg 122 J6
Reyes, Point 122 C9
Reyhanli 77 G4
Rey, Isla del 132 H10
Reykjaheidi 62 W12
Reykjahhd 62 W12
Reykjanesta 62 T13
Reykjavik 62 U12
Reynivellir *Iceland* 62 U12
Reynivellir *Iceland* 62 W12
Reynosa 128 C7
Rezekne 63 M8
Rhatikon Pratigau 68 B2
Rhayader 52 D2
Rheda-Wiedenbruck 70 C3
Rhee 53 G2
Rhein 70 B3
Rheine 70 B2
Rhewl 55 F3
Rhiconich 56 D2
Rhine 64 G4
Rhinelander 124 F4
Rhino Camp 107 F2
Rhir, Cap 100 D2
Rho 68 B3
Rhode Island 125 Q6
Rhodes 75 J4
Rhodopi Planina 73 G4
Rhondda 52 D3
Rhone 65 F7
Rhoose 52 D3
Rhosneigr 55 E3
Rhuddlan 55 F3
Rhum 57 B3
Rhum, Sound of 57 B4
Rhydaman 52 C3
Rhyl 55 F3
Rhynie 56 F3
Riachao do Jacuipe 138 K6
Riacho de Santana 138 J6
Riano 66 D1
Riansares 66 E3
Riau, Kepulauan 90 C5
Riaza 66 E2
Ribadeo 66 C1
Ribadesella 66 D1
Ribas do Rio Pardo 138 F4
Ribat 95 R5
Ribatejo 66 B3
Ribble 55 G2
Ribe 63 C9
Ribeirao Preto 138 G4
Ribeiro do Pombal 137 K6
Riberac 65 D6
Riberalta 136 D6
Ribnica 72 C3
Ribnitz-Damgarten 70 E1
Riccall 55 H3
Rice Lake *Canada* 125 L4
Rice Lake *U.S.A.* 124 E4
Richard Collinson Inlet 119 N1
Richards Island 118 H2
Richardson 128 D4
Richardson Mountains 118 H2
Richelieu 125 P4
Richfield 126 F1
Richland 122 E4
Richlands 125 K8
Richmond *Australia* 113 J3
Richmond *New Zealand* 115 D4
Richmond *South Africa* 108 D6
Richmond *Greater London, U.K.* 53 G3
Richmond *North Yorkshire, U.K.* 55 H2
Richmond *Indiana, U.S.A.* 124 H7
Richmond *Kentucky, U.S.A.* 124 H8
Richmond *Virginia, U.S.A.* 125 M8
Richmond Range 115 D4
Rickmansworth 53 G3
Ricla 67 F2
Ricobayo, Embalse de 66 D2
Ridgecrest 126 D3
Ridgeland 129 M4
Ridgway 125 L6
Riding Mountain 123 P2
Ridsdale 57 F5
Ried 68 D1
Rienza 68 C2
Riesa 70 E3
Riesco, Isla 139 B10
Rietfontein 108 D4
Rieti 69 D4
Rifle 123 L8
Rifstangi 62 W11
Riga 63 L8
Riga, Gulf of 63 K8
Rigan 95 P7
Rigistan 92 B2
Rigolet 121 Q7
Rihab, Ar 94 G6
Rihand 92 F4
Riiser-Larsen Sea 141 B5
Rijeka 72 C3
Rika 71 K4
Rika, Wadi al 96 G5
Rimah, Wadi al 96 E3
Rimal, Ar 97 L6
Rimavska Sobota 71 J4
Rimbo 63 H7
Rimini 68 D3
Rimna 73 J3
Rimnicu Sarat 73 J3
Rimnicu Vilcea 73 H3
Rimouski 125 R2
Rinca 91 F7
Rinchinlhumbe 86 H1
Ringe 63 D9
Ringebu 63 D6
Ringgold Isles 114 S8
Ringkobing 63 C8
Ringkobing Fjord 63 C9
Ringmer 53 H4
Ringselet 62 L3
Ringvassoy 62 H2
Ringwood 53 F4
Rinia 75 H4
Rinjani, Gunung 90 F7
Rinns Point 57 B5
Riobamba 136 B4
Rio Branco *Brazil* 136 D5
Rio Branco *Uruguay* 138 F6
Rio Bravo 128 D8
Rio Bueno 139 B8
Rio Caribe 136 E1
Rio Claro 136 E1
Rio Colorado 139 D7
Rio Cuarto 138 D6
Rio de Janeiro *Brazil* 138 H4
Rio de Janeiro *Brazil* 138 H4
Rio de Oro, Baie de 100 B4
Rio Gallegos 139 C10
Rio Grande *Argentina* 139 C10
Rio Grande *Brazil* 138 F6
Rio Grande *U.S.A.* 130 H6
Rio Grande City 128 C7
Rio Grande de Santiago 130 G7
Rio Grande do Norte 137 K5
Rio Grande do Sul 138 F5
Riohacha 136 C1
Rio Hato 132 G10
Rio Lagartos 131 Q7
Riom 65 E6
Riom-es-Montagnes 65 E6
Rio Mulatos 138 C3
Rionegro 136 C2
Rio Negro *Brazil* 138 G5
Rio Negro *Spain* 66 C1
Rio Negro, Embalse del 138 E6
Rio Negro, Pantanal do 138 E3
Rioni 77 J1
Rio Pardo de Minas 138 H3
Rio Primero 138 D6
Rio Sao Goncalo 138 H4
Riosucio *Colombia* 136 B2
Riosucio *Colombia* 136 B2
Rio Verde 138 F3
Ripley *Ohio, U.S.A.* 124 J7
Ripley *Tennessee, U.S.A.* 128 H3
Ripley *W. Virginia, U.S.A.* 125 K7
Ripoll 67 H1
Ripon 55 H2
Ripponden 55 H3
Risca 52 D3
Rishiri-to 88 H3
Rishon le Zion 94 B6
Risle 64 D4
Risor 63 C7
Risoyhamn 62 F2
Ritchie's Archipelago 93 H6
Ritter, Mount 122 E9
Ritzville 122 E4
Riva 68 C3
Rivas 132 E9
Rivera 138 E6
River Falls 124 D4
Riverina 113 K5
Riversdale 108 D6
Riverside 126 D4
Riverton *Australia* 113 H5
Riverton *Canada* 123 R2
Riverton *New Zealand* 115 B7
Riverton *U.S.A.* 123 K6
Riviere-du-Loup 125 R3
Rivoli 68 A3
Riwaka 115 D4
Riwoqe 93 J2
Riyan 97 J9
Rize 77 J2
Rizhskiy Zaliv 63 K8
Rizokarpaso 76 F5
Rjukan 63 C7
Rjuven 63 B7
Roa 66 E2
Road Town 133 Q5
Roan Fell 57 F5
Roanne 65 F5
Roanoke *N. Carolina, U.S.A.* 129 P2
Roanoke *U.S.A.* 125 L8
Roanoke *U.S.A.* 125 L8
Roanoke Rapids 129 P2
Roan Plateau 123 K8
Robat 95 R6
Robat Karim 95 K4
Robat Thand 95 Q7
Robel 70 E2
Robert Brown, Cape 120 K4
Roberton 57 E5
Robertsbridge 53 H4
Robertsfors 62 J4
Robert S. Kerr Reservoir 128 E3
Robertson Range 112 E3
Robertsport 104 C4
Roberval 125 P2
Robinson 124 G7
Robinson Ranges 112 D4
Robleda 66 C2
Robledollano 66 D3
Robles La Paz 136 C1
Roblin 123 P2
Robore 138 E3
Rob Roy Island 114 H5
Robson, Mount 119 M5
Roca, Cabo da 66 B3
Roca Partida, Isla 130 C8
Roca Partida, Punta 131 M8
Roccella Ionica 69 F6
Rocha 139 F6
Rocha da Gale, Barragem 66 C4
Rochdale 55 G3
Rochechouart 65 D6
Rochefort 65 C6
Rochelle 124 F6
Rochester *Kent, U.K.* 53 H3
Rochester *Northumberland, U.K.* 57 F5
Rochester *New Hamshire, U.S.A.* 125 Q5
Rochester *New York, U.S.A.* 125 M5
Rochester *Winconsin, U.S.A.* 124 D4
Rochford 53 H3
Rochfortbridge 59 H6
Rock 124 F5
Rockefeller Plateau 141 R3
Rock Falls 124 F6
Rockford 124 F5
Rockglen 123 L3
Rockhampton 113 L3
Rockingham *Australia* 112 D5
Rockingham *U.S.A.* 129 N3
Rockingham Bay 113 K2
Rock Island 124 E6
Rockland *Maine, U.S.A.* 125 R4
Rockland *Michigan, U.S.A.* 124 F3
Rock Springs *Montana, U.S.A.* 123 L4
Rock Springs *Wyoming, U.S.A.* 123 K7
Rockwood 125 R4
Rocky Ford 127 L1
Rocky Mount 129 P3
Rocky Mountain House 119 N5
Rocky Mountains 116 G3
Rocroi 64 F4
Rodberg 63 C6
Rodby 63 D9
Rodeby 63 F8
Rodel 56 B3
Roden 52 E2
Rodez 65 E6
Rodhos *Greece* 75 J4
Rodhos *Greece* 75 K4
Rodi Garganico 69 E5
Roding 53 H3
Rodinga 113 G3

Rodna 73 H2
Rodnei, Muntii 73 H2
Rodney, Cape *New Zealand* 115 E2
Rodney, Cape *U.S.A.* 118 B3
Rodonit, Kep i 74 E2
Rodosto 76 B2
Roebuck Bay 112 E2
Roermond 64 F3
Roeselare 64 E3
Roes Welcome Sound 120 J5
Rogachev 79 E5
Rogaland 63 B7
Rogatin 71 L4
Rogers 128 E2
Rogers, Mount 125 K8
Roggeveld Berge 108 D6
Rogliano 68 B4
Rognan 62 F3
Rogozno 71 G2
Rohri 92 C3
Rohtak 92 E3
Rois Bheinn 57 C3
Rojas 139 D6
Rojo, Cabo *Mexico* 131 L7
Rojo, Cabo *U.S.A.* 133 P6
Rokan 90 C5
Rokel 104 C4
Rokiskis 63 L9
Rolla 124 E8
Rolleston 113 K3
Roma *Australia* 113 K4
Roma *Italy* 69 D5
Roma *Sweden* 63 H8
Romain, Cape 129 N4
Romaine 121 P7
Romaldkirk 55 G2
Roman 73 J2
Romang 91 H7
Romania 73 G3
Romano, Cape 129 M8
Romanovka 85 J6
Romans-sur-Isere 65 F6
Romanzof, Cape 118 B3
Romao 136 E4
Romblon 91 G3
Rome *Italy* 69 D5
Rome *U.S.A.* 129 K3
Romerike 63 D6
Romilly 64 E4
Romney 125 L7
Romny 79 E5
Romo 63 C9
Romorantin 65 D5
Romsey 53 F4
Rona 56 C3
Ronay 56 A3
Roncador, Cayos 132 G8
Roncador, Serra do 137 G6
Ronco 68 D3
Ronda *India* 92 E1
Ronda *Spain* 66 D4
Rondane 63 C6
Ronda, Sierra de 66 D4
Ronde 63 D8
Rondeslottet 63 C6
Rondonia *Brazil* 136 E6
Rondonia *Brazil* 136 E6
Rondonopolis 138 F3
Ronge, Lac La 119 Q4
Rong Jiang 93 L4
Rong, Kas 93 K6
Rongshui 93 L3
Rong Xian 93 M4
Ronne 63 H9
Ronneby 63 F8
Ronne Entrance 141 U4
Ronne Ice Shelf 141 V3
Ronse 64 E3
Roodepoort 108 E5
Roof Butte 127 H2
Roosendaal 64 F3
Roosevelt 136 E5
Roosevelt Island 141 P3
Roosevelt, Mount 118 K4
Ropcha 78 J3
Roper 113 G1
Ropi 62 J2
Roquefort 65 C6
Rora Head 56 E2
Roraima 136 E3
Roraima, Mount 136 E2
Roros 62 D5
Rorvik 62 D4
Rosa, Cap 69 B7
Rosalia, Punta 126 E6
Rosa, Monte 68 A3
Rosario 137 J4
Rosario *Argentina* 138 D6
Rosario *Mexico* 130 G6
Rosario *Mexico* 127 H7
Rosario de la Frontera 138 D5
Rosarito 126 F6
Roscoe 127 M4
Roscommon *Ireland* 58 F5
Roscommon *Ireland* 58 F5
Roscrea 59 G7
Roseau 133 S7
Roseberth 113 H4
Rosebery 113 K7
Rosebud 122 H2
Roseburg 122 C6
Rosedale Abbey 55 J2
Rosehearty 56 F3
Rose Island 111 V4
Rosenburg 128 E6
Rosenheim 70 E5
Rose Point 118 J5
Roses 67 H1
Roses, Golfo de 67 H1
Roseto d'Abruzzi 69 D4
Rosetown 123 K2
Rosetta 102 F1
Roshkhvar 95 P4
Rosiori de Vede 73 H3
Rositsa 73 H4
Roskilde 63 E9
Roslavl 78 E5
Ross *New Zealand* 115 C5
Ross *U.K.* 57 G5
Rossall Point 55 F3
Rossano 69 F6
Rossan Point 58 E3
Rosscarbery Bay 59 D9
Ross Dependency 141 P7
Rossel Island 114 E4
Rosses Bay 58 F2
Rosses Point 58 E4
Rosses, The 58 F3
Ross Ice Shelf 141 N2
Rossington 55 H3
Ross Island 141 M3
Rosslare Harbour 59 K8
Ross-on-Wye 52 E3
Rossosh 79 F5
Ross River 118 J3
Ross Sea 141 N3
Rost 62 E3
Rostaq 95 L8
Rostock 70 E1
Rostonsolka 62 J2
Rostov 78 F4
Rostov-na-Donu 79 F6
Rostrevor 58 K4
Roswell *Georgia, U.S.A.* 129 K3
Roswell *New Mexico, U.S.A.* 127 K4
Rotemo 63 B7
Rotenburg 70 C2
Rothaargebirge 70 C3
Rothbury 57 G5
Rothbury Forest 57 G5
Rother *Kent, U.K.* 53 H3
Rother *W. Sussex, U.K.* 53 G4
Rothera 141 V5
Rotherham 55 H3
Rothesay 57 C5
Rothiesholm 56 F1
Rothwell *Northamptonshire, U.K.* 53 G2
Rothwell *W. Yorkshire, U.K.* 55 H3
Roti 91 G8
Rotja, Punta 67 G3
Roto 113 K5
Rotondella 69 F5
Rotorua 115 F3
Rottenberg 70 C3
Rottenburg *Germany* 70 C4
Rottenburg *Germany* 70 E4
Rotterdam 64 F3
Rottweil 70 C4
Rotuma 111 S4
Rotz 70 E4
Roubaix 64 E3
Rouen 64 D4
Rouge 93 K4
Rouillac 65 C6
Round Hill Head 113 L3
Roundup 123 K4
Roura 137 G3
Rousay 56 E1
Roussillon 65 E7
Rouxville 108 E6
Rouyn 125 L2
Rovaniemi 62 L3
Rovdino 78 G3
Rovereto 68 C3
Rovieng 93 L6
Rovigo 68 C3
Rovinj 72 B3
Rovno 79 D5
Rovnoye 79 H5
Rowan 94 J4
Rowlands Gill 55 H2
Rowley Island 120 L4
Rowley Shoals 112 D2
Roxas 91 G3
Roxboro 129 N2
Roxburgh 115 B6
Roxo, Cape 104 B3
Roxton 53 G2
Roy 123 K4
Royal Canal 59 J6
Royale, Isle 124 F3
Royal Geographical Society Islands 119 Q2
Royal Leamington Spa 53 F2
Royan 65 C6
Roy Hill 112 D3
Royston *Hertfordshire, U.K.* 53 G2
Royston *S. Yorkshire, U.K.* 55 H3
Royton 55 G3
Rozan 71 J2
Rozden 73 F5
Rozel Bay 53 M7
Rozewie 71 H1
Rozhishche 71 L3
Roznava 71 J4
Roztocze 71 K3
Rtishchevo 79 G5
Ruahine Range 115 F3
Ruapehu 115 E3
Ruapuke Island 115 B7
Ruawai 115 E2
Rubeho Mountains 107 G4
Rubio 133 L11
Rubtsovsk 84 C6
Ruby Dome 122 G7
Ruby Lake 122 G7
Ruby Mountains 122 G7
Rucheng 93 M3
Ruchi 78 G2
Rudan 95 N8
Ruda Slaska 71 H3
Rudbar 94 J3
Rudbar 95 R6
Rudkobing 63 D9
Rudnaya 88 K3
Rudnaya Pristan 88 E3
Rudnichnyy 78 J4
Rudnik 71 K3
Rudnitsa 73 K1
Rudnya 78 E5
Rudnyy *Kazakhstan* 84 Ad6
Rudnyy *Russia* 88 E3
Rudolfa, Ostrov 80 G1
Rudolf, Lake 107 G2
Rudolstadt 70 D3
Rudozem 73 H5
Rud Sar 95 K3
Rufaa 103 F5
Ruffec 65 D5
Rufiji 107 G4
Rufino 139 D6
Rugby *U.K.* 53 G2
Rugby *U.S.A.* 123 Q3
Rugen 70 E1
Rugozero 78 E3
Ruhengeri 107 E3
Ruhimaki 63 L6
Ruhnu 63 K8
Ruhr 70 B3
Ruijin 87 M6
Rujiena 63 L8
Rujmayn, Jbel Abu 77 H5
Rukumkot 92 F3
Rukwa, Lake 107 F4
Rul Dadnah 97 N4
Ruma 72 E3
Rumah 96 H4
Rumaylah, Uruq ar 96 H6
Rumbek 102 E6
Rum Cay 133 K3
Rumford 125 Q4
Rummelsburg 71 G1
Rumoi 88 H4
Runanga 115 C5
Runaway, Cape 115 F2
Runcorn 55 G3
Runde 108 F4
Rundu 108 C3
Running Water Creek 127 L3
Ruokolahti 63 N6
Ruoqiang 86 F4
Ruo Shui 86 J3
Rupat 90 C5
Rupea 73 H2
Rupert *Canada* 121 L7
Rupert *U.S.A.* 122 H6
Rupert Bay 121 L7
Rupununi 136 F3
Rurrenabaque 136 D6
Rusanovo 84 Ac2
Ruse 73 J4
Rush 59 K5
Rushden 53 G2
Rusk 128 E5
Ruskington 55 J3
Russas 137 K4
Russel, Cape 120 C2
Russell *Canada* 123 P2
Russell *New Zealand* 115 E1
Russell *U.S.A.* 123 Q8
Russell Island 120 G3
Russell Islands 114 J6
Russell Range 112 E5
Russell Springs 124 H8
Russellville *Alabama, U.S.A.* 129 J3
Russellville *Kentucky, U.S.A.* 124 G8
Russia 49 J3
Russian 122 C8
Russkaya 141 Q4
Russkaya Techa 84 Ad5
Russkiy-Kamlak 84 D6
Russkiy, Ostrov *Russia* 88 C4
Russkiy, Ostrov *Russia* 84 F1
Russkiy Zavorot, Poluostrov 78 J2
Rustavi 77 L2
Rustenburg 108 E5
Ruston 128 F4
Rutana 107 E3
Rute 66 D4
Ruteng 91 G7
Ruth 126 E1
Ruthin 55 F3
Rutigliano 69 F5
Rutland *India* 93 H6
Rutland *U.S.A.* 125 P5
Rutland Water 53 G2
Rutog 92 E2
Rutqa, Wadi 77 J6
Rutshuru 107 E3
Ruvuma 107 G5
Ruzayevka 84 Ae6
Ruzomberok 71 H4
Rwanda 107 E3
Ryan, Loch 54 D2
Ryazan 78 F5
Ryazhsk 79 G5
Rybachiy, Poluostrov 78 E2
Rybachye 86 D3
Rybachye 86 F2
Rybinsk 78 F4
Rybinskoye Vodokhranilishche 78 F4
Rybnik 71 H3
Rybnitsa 73 K2
Rybnoye 84 E5
Ryd 63 F8
Rydaholm 63 F8
Ryde 53 F4
Rydet 63 E8
Rye *E. Sussex, U.K.* 53 H4
Rye *N. Yorkshire, U.K.* 55 H2
Rye Bay 53 H4
Rylsk 79 E5
Ryn Peski 79 H6
Ryotsu 89 G6
Rypin 71 H2
Ryukyu Islands 87 P6
Rzeszow 71 J3
Rzhev 78 E4

S

Saadatabad 95 L6
Saale 70 D3
Saalfeld 70 D3
Saar 70 B4
Saarbrucken 70 B4
Saarburg 70 B4
Saare 63 K8
Saaremaa 63 K7
Saarijarvi 62 L5
Saarikoski 62 J2
Saariselka 62 N2
Saarlouis 70 B4
Saatly 94 J2
Saba 133 R6
Sab Abar 94 C5
Sabac 72 E3
Sabadell 67 H2
Sabah 91 F4
Sabalana, Kepulauan 91 F7
Sabalan, Kuhhaye 94 H2
Sabana, Archipielago de 132 G3
Sabana de la Mar 133 N5
Sabanalarga 136 C1
Sabang *Sulawesi, Indonesia* 91 F5
Sabang *Sumatera, Indonesia* 90 B4
Sabanozu 76 E2
Sabarmati 92 D4
Sabatyn, Ramlat as 96 H9
Sabaya, Jabal 96 E7
Saberi, Hamun-e 95 Q6
Sabha 101 H3
Sabi 109 F4
Sabie 109 F5
Sabinal, Cayo 132 J4
Sabinas *Mexico* 127 M7
Sabinas *Mexico* 127 M7
Sabinas Hidalgo 128 B7
Sabine 128 F5
Sabine Peninsula 120 E2
Sabini, Monti 69 D4
Sabirabad 94 J1
Sabkhat al Jabbul 77 G5
Sable, Cape *Canada* 121 N9
Sable, Cape *U.S.A.* 129 M8
Sable Island 121 Q9
Sable Island Bank 121 P9
Sable-sur-Sarthe 65 C5
Saboia 66 B4
Sabon Birni 105 G3
Sabor 66 C2
Sabres 65 C6
Sabrina Coast 141 H5
Sabugal 66 C2
Sabulu 91 G6
Sæby 63 D8
Sabya 96 F8
Sabzevar 95 N3
Sabzvaran 95 N7
Sacaca 138 C3
Sacco 69 D5
Sacedon 66 E2
Sacel 73 H2
Sachigo 119 S5
Sachs Harbour 118 L1
Saco 123 L3
Sacramento *U.S.A.* 126 B1
Sacramento *U.S.A.* 122 D8
Sacramento Mountains 127 K4
Sacramento Valley 122 C8
Sadaba 67 F1
Sadabad 95 K7
Sadad 77 G5
Sadah 96 F8
Sada-misaki 89 D9
Sadani 107 G4
Sadarak 77 L3
Sadd al Aswan 103 F3
Sa Dec 93 L6
Sadgora 73 H1
Sadh 97 M8
Sadid 77 K5
Sadiya 93 J3

Sadiyah, Hawr as 94 H5
Sado 66 B3
Sado-shima 89 G6
Saeki 89 C9
Safa 94 C5
Safaga 96 B3
Safarabad 94 H2
Safarikovo 71 J4
Safed Khirs 92 D1
Saffaniyah, Ra's as 97 J3
Saffle 63 E7
Safford 127 H4
Saffron Walden 53 H2
Safi 100 D2
Safidabeh 95 Q6
Safid Kuh 95 R4
Safid Rud 95 J3
Safonovo 78 E4
Safranbolu 76 E2
Safwan 94 H6
Saga *China* 92 G3
Saga *Japan* 89 C9
Sagami-nada 89 G8
Sagamoso 133 L11
Saganthit Kyun 93 J6
Sagar *Karnataka, India* 92 D6
Sagar *Madhya Pradesh, India* 92 E4
Saggart 59 K6
Saginaw 124 J5
Saginaw Bay 124 J5
Sagiz *Kazakhstan* 79 J6
Sagiz *Kazakhstan* 79 J6
Sagiz *Kazakhstan* 79 J6
Sagkaya 77 F4
Saglek Bay 121 P6
Sagone, Golfe de 69 B4
Sagres 66 B4
Saguache 127 J1
Sagua la Grande 132 G3
Saguenay 121 M8
Sagunto 67 F3
Sahagun 66 D1
Sahand, Kuh-e 94 H3
Sahara 98 C4
Saharanpur 92 E3
Sahin 76 B2
Sahiwal *Pakistan* 92 D2
Sahiwal *Pakistan* 92 D2
Sahm 97 N4
Sahra al Hijarah 94 G6
Sahuaripa 127 H6
Sahuayo 130 H7
Sa Huynh 93 L6
Sahy 71 H4
Saibai Island 114 C3
Saicla 94 B5
Saida *Algeria* 100 F2
Saida *Lebanon* 76 F6
Saidabad 95 M7
Saidapet 92 F6
Saidor 114 D3
Saidpur 93 G3
Saigon 93 L6
Saijo 89 D9
Saimaa 63 M6
Saimbeyli 77 G3
Saindak 95 Q7
Saindezh 94 H3
Saint Abb's Head 57 B5
Saint-Affrique 65 E7
Saint-Agathe-des-Monts 125 N3
Saint Agnes *U.K.* 52 B4
Saint Agnes *U.K.* 52 K5
Saint-Agreve 65 F6
Saint Albans *U.K.* 53 G3
Saint Albans *Vermont, U.S.A.* 125 P4
Saint Albans *W. Virginia, U.S.A.* 124 K7
Saint Alban's Head 53 E4
Saint Aldhelm's 53 E4
Saint-Amand-Montrond 65 E5
Saint-Ambroix 65 F6
Saint Andre, Cap 109 H3
Saint Andrew 53 M7
Saint Andrews *New Zealand* 115 C6
Saint Andrews *U.K.* 57 F4
Saint Andrews Bay 57 F4
Saint-Anne-des-Monts 125 S2
Saint Annes 53 M6
Saint Ann's Bay 132 J5
Saint Ann's Head 52 B3
Saint Anthony *Canada* 121 Q7
Saint Anthony *U.S.A.* 122 J6
Saint Arnaud 115 D4
Saint Asaph 55 F3
Saint Aubin 53 M7
Saint Augustin 121 Q7
Saint Augustine 129 M6
Saint Augustin Saguenay 121 Q7
Saint Austell 52 C4
Saint Austell Bay 52 C4
Saint Bees 55 F2
Saint Bees Head 55 F2
Saint Benoit 109 L7
Saint Blazey 52 C4
Saint Brides 52 B3
Saint Brides Bay 52 B3
Saint-Brieuc 64 B4
Saint-Calais 65 D5
Saint Catherines 125 L5
Saint Catherines Island 129 M5
Saint Catherine's Point 53 F4
Saint-Cere 65 D6
Saint-Chamond 65 F6
Saint Charles 124 E7
Saint Clair, Lake 124 J5
Saint-Claude 65 F5
Saint Clears 52 C3
Saint Cloud *Florida, U.S.A.* 129 M6
Saint Cloud *Minnesota, U.S.A.* 124 C4
Saint Columb Major 52 C4
Saint Croix *Canada* 125 S4
Saint Croix *Minnesota, U.S.A.* 124 D4
Saint Croix *U.S.A.* 133 Q6
Saint Croix Falls 124 D4
Saint David's 52 B3
Saint David's Head 52 B3
Saint-Denis 64 E4
Saint Denis 109 L7
Sainte-Foy-la-Grande 65 D6
Saint Elias, Mount 118 G3
Saint Elias Mountains 118 H3
Sainte-Marie 109 J3
Sainte-Marie-aux-Mines 64 G4
Sainte Marie, Cap 109 J5
Sainte-Maxime 65 G7
Sainte-Menehould 64 F4
Sainte Nazaire 65 B5
Saintes 65 C6
Saintes, Iles des 133 S7
Saintes-Maries-de-la-Mer 65 F7
Saint Etienne 65 F6
Saint Eustatius 133 R6
Saint-Fargeau 65 E5
Saintfield 58 L4
Saint Finan's Bay 59 B9
Saint-Florent, Golfe de 69 B4
Saint-Florentin 65 E4
Saint-Flour 65 E6
Saint Francis *Canada* 125 P4
Saint Francis *Arkansas, U.S.A.* 128 G3
Saint Francis *Kansas, U.S.A.* 123 P8
Saint Francis, Cape 108 D6
Saint Gallen 68 B2
Saint-Gaudens 65 D7
Saint George *Australia* 113 K4
Saint George *U.S.A.* 126 F2
Saint George, Cape *Canada* 121 Q8
Saint George, Cape *Papua New Guinea* 114 E2
Saint George Head 113 L6
Saint George Island *Alaska, U.S.A.* 118 Ae8
Saint George Island *Florida, U.S.A.* 129 K6
Saint Georges 125 Q3
Saint George's 133 S8
Saint Georges Bay 121 Q8
Saint George's Channel *Papua New Guinea* 114 E2
Saint George's Channel *U.K.* 52 B3
Saint-Germain 64 D4
Saint-Gildas-de-Rhuys 65 B5
Saint-Gilles-Croix-de-Vie 65 C5
Saint-Girons 65 D7
Saint Gotthard Pass 68 B2
Saint Govan's Head 52 C3
Saint Helena 99 C8
Saint Helena Bay 108 C6
Saint Helens *Australia* 113 K7
Saint Helens *U.K.* 55 G3
Saint Helens, Mount 122 C4
Saint Helens Point 113 K7
Saint Helier 53 M4
Saint Ignace 124 H4
Saint Ignatius 122 G4
Saint Ives *Cambridgeshire, U.K.* 53 G2
Saint Ives *Cornwall, U.K.* 52 B4
Saint Ives Bay 52 B4
Saint James, Cape 118 J5
Saint-Jean-d'Angely 65 C6
Saint-Jean-de-Luz 65 C7
Saint-Jean-de-Maurienne 65 G6
Saint-Jean-de-Monts 65 B5
Saint-Jean, Lac 125 P2
Saint-Jean-Pied-de-Port 65 C7
Saint-Jean-Sur-Richelieu 125 P4
Saint Jerome 125 P4
Saint John *Canada* 121 N8
Saint John *Canada* 121 N8
Saint John *U.K.* 53 M7
Saint John *U.S.A.* 133 Q5
Saint John Bay 121 Q7
Saint John's *Antigua* 133 S6
Saint Johns *Canada* 121 R8
Saint Johns *Arizona, U.S.A.* 127 H3
Saint Johns *Florida, U.S.A.* 129 M6
Saint Johns *Michigan, U.S.A.* 124 H5
Saint Johnsbury 125 Q4
Saint John's Point *Ireland* 58 F3
Saint John's Point *U.K.* 58 L4
Saint Joseph *Arkansas, U.S.A.* 128 G5
Saint Joseph *Missouri, U.S.A.* 124 C7
Saint Joseph Island 128 D7
Saint-Junien 65 D6
Saint Just 52 B4
Saint Keverne 52 B4
Saint Kitts-Nevis 133 R6
Saint Laurent 137 G2
Saint Lawrence *Australia* 113 K3
Saint Lawrence *Canada* 121 N8
Saint Lawrence *Canada* 121 Q8
Saint Lawrence, Gulf of 121 P8
Saint Lawrence Island 118 B3
Saint Lawrence Seaway 125 N4
Saint Leonard 125 S3
Saint-Leonard-de-Noblat 65 D6
Saint Lewis 121 Q7
Saint Lo 64 C4
Saint Louis *Minnesota, U.S.A.* 124 D3
Saint Louis *Missouri, U.S.A.* 124 E7
Saint Louis *Senegal* 104 B2
Saint Lucia 133 S6
Saint Lucia, Cape 109 F5
Saint Lucia Channel 133 S7
Saint Lucia, Lake 109 F5
Saint Magnus Bay 56 A1
Saint-Maixent-l'Ecole 65 C5
Saint Malo 64 B4
Saint-Malo, Golfe de 64 C4
Saint Marc 133 L5
Saint-Marcellin 65 F6
Saint Margaret's-at-Cliffe 53 J3
Saint Maries 122 F4
Saint Martin *France* 133 R5
Saint Martin *U.K.* 53 M7
Saint Martin, Lake 123 Q2
Saint Martin's 52 L5
Saint-Martin-Vesubie 65 G6
Saint Mary Peak 113 H5
Saint Marys *Australia* 113 K7
Saint Mary's *Cornwall, U.K.* 52 L5
Saint Mary's *Orkney Islands, U.K.* 56 F2
Saint Marys *Florida, U.S.A.* 129 M5
Saint Marys *Pennsylvania, U.S.A.* 125 L6
Saint Mary's Loch 57 E5
Saint Matthias Group 114 D2
Saint-Maurice 121 M8
Saint Maurice 125 P3
Saint Mawes 52 B4
Saint-Maximin 65 F7
Saint Michael 118 C3
Saint-Mihiel 64 F4
Saint Monance 57 F4
Saint Moritz 68 B2
Saint Neots 53 G2
Saint Niklaas 64 F3
Saint Ninian's Island 56 A2
Saintogne 65 C6
Saint Omer 64 E3
Saint Pamphile 125 R3
Saint Pascal 125 R3
Saint Paul *Alberta, Canada* 119 N5
Saint Paul *Quebec, Canada* 121 Q7
Saint Paul *Liberia* 104 C4
Saint Paul *Minnesota, U.S.A.* 124 D4
Saint Paul Island 118 Ad8
Saint Peter 124 D4
Saint Peter Port 53 M7
Saint Petersburg *U.S.A.* 129 L7
Saint Petersburg *Russia* 63 N7
Saint Pierre *Canada* 121 Q8
Saint Pierre *France* 109 L7
Saint Pierre Bank 121 Q8
Saint Pol 64 E3
Saint-Pol-de-Leon 64 B4
Saint Polten 68 E1
Saint-Pons 65 E7
Saint-Pourcain 65 E5
Saint Queens Bay 53 M7
Saint-Quentin 64 E4
Saint-Raphael 65 G7
Saint Sampson 53 M7
Saint Sebastian Bay 108 D6
Saint-Seine-l'Abbaye 65 F5
Saint-Sever 65 C7
Saint Simeon 125 R3
Saint Stephen *Canada* 125 S4
Saint Stephen *U.S.A.* 129 N4
Saint Thomas *Canada* 125 K5
Saint Thomas *U.S.A.* 133 Q5
Saint-Tropez 65 G7
Saint-Valery-en-Caux 64 D4
Saint Veit 68 E2
Saint Vincent 133 S6
Saint Vincent, Gulf of 113 H6
Saint Vincent Island 129 K6
Saint Vincent Passage 133 S8
Saint Vith 64 G3
Saint-Yrieix 65 D6
Sajama 138 C3
Sajama, Nevado de 138 C3
Saji-dong 88 B5
Sajir, Ra's 97 L8
Sak 108 D6
Sakai 89 E8
Sakai-Minato 89 D8
Sakakah 96 E2
Sakakawea, Lake 123 P4
Sakami 121 L7
Sakami, Lake 121 L7
Sakania 107 E5
Sakarya *Turkey* 76 D2
Sakarya *Turkey* 76 D2
Sakata 88 G6
Sakete 105 F4
Sakhalin 85 Q6
Sakht-Sar 95 K3
Sakiai 71 K1
Sakmara 79 K5
Sakon Nakhon 93 K5
Sak-shima-shoto 89 G11
Sakti 92 F4
Sal *Cape Verde* 104 L7
Sal *Russia* 79 G6
Sala 63 G7
Salaberry-De-Valleyfield 125 N4
Salaca 63 L8
Salacgriva 63 L8
Sala Consilina 69 E5
Saladillo 139 E7
Salado *Argentina* 139 C6
Salado *Argentina* 138 D5
Salaga 104 E4
Salalah 97 M8
Salama 132 B7
Salamanca *Mexico* 131 J7
Salamanca *Spain* 66 D2
Salamanca *U.S.A.* 125 L5
Salamina 136 B2
Salamis 75 G4
Salamiyah 77 G5
Salard 73 G2
Salas 73 G3
Salas de los Infantes 66 E1
Salat 77 J4
Salavat 78 K5
Salawati 91 J6
Salba 84 E6
Salbris 65 E5
Salcha 118 F3
Salcia 73 H4
Salcombe 52 D4
Salda Golu 76 C4
Saldana 66 D1
Saldanha 108 C6
Saldus 63 K8
Sale 100 D2
Sale *Australia* 113 K6
Sale *U.K.* 55 G3
Salebabu 91 H5
Salekhard 84 Ae3
Salem *India* 92 E6
Salem *Illinois, U.S.A.* 124 F7
Salem *Oregon, U.S.A.* 122 C5
Salemi 69 D7
Salen *Highland, U.K.* 57 C4
Salen *Strathclyde, U.K.* 57 C4
Salernes 65 G7
Salerno 69 E5
Salerno, Golfo di 69 E5
Salford 55 G3
Salgotarjan 72 E1
Salgueiro 137 K5
Salida 127 J1
Salies-de-Bearn 65 C7
Salihli 76 C3
Salima 107 F5
Salina *Kansas, U.S.A.* 123 R8
Salina *Utah, U.S.A.* 126 G1
Salina, Isola 69 E6
Salinas *Ecuador* 136 A4
Salinas *U.S.A.* 126 B2
Salinas *U.S.A.* 126 B2
Salinas, Cabo de 67 H3
Salinas Grandes 138 C4
Salinas O'Lachay, Punta de 136 B6
Salinas, Pampa de la 138 C6
Saline 123 Q8
Salinopolis 137 H4
Salins 65 F5
Salisbury *Maryland, U.S.A.* 125 N7
Salisbury *N. Carolina, U.S.A.* 129 M3
Salisbury *U.K.* 53 F3
Salisbury *Zimbabwe* 108 F3
Salisbury Island 120 L5
Salisbury Plain 52 F3
Saliste 73 G3
Salkhad 94 C5
Salla 62 N3
Sallisaw 128 E3
Sallvit 120 L5
Sallybrook 59 F9
Salmas 77 L3
Salmi 78 E3
Salmon *Canada* 119 L5
Salmon *U.S.A.* 122 F5
Salmon *U.S.A.* 122 H5
Salmon Arm 122 E2
Salmon Falls Creek 122 G6
Salmon River Mountains 122 G5
Salo 68 C3
Salo 63 K6
Salon-de-Provence 65 F7
Saloniki 75 G2
Salonta 73 F2
Salor 66 C3
Sal, Punta 132 D7
Salsacate 139 C6
Salsbruket 62 H4
Salsipuedes, Punta 126 D4
Salsk 79 G6
Salso 69 D7
Salsomaggiore Terme 68 B3
Salt *Jordan* 94 B5
Salt *Kentucky, U.S.A.* 124 H8
Salt *Missouri, U.S.A.* 124 D7
Salt *Oklahoma, U.S.A.* 128 D2
Salta 138 C4
Saltash 52 C4
Saltburn-by-the-Sea 55 J2
Salt Cay 133 M4
Saltcoats 57 D5
Saltfjellet 62 F3
Saltfjord 62 F3
Saltfleet 55 K3
Saltillo 127 M8
Salt Lake City 122 J7
Salto *Italy* 69 D4
Salto *Uruguay* 138 E6
Salto da Divisa 138 G3
Salton Sea 126 E4
Saltpond 104 E4
Saluda *U.S.A.* 129 L3
Saluda *U.S.A.* 129 M3
Salumbar 92 D4

Saluzzo 68 A3
Salvador 137 K6
Salvatierra 131 J7
Salwah 97 K4
Salween 93 J5
Salyany 94 J2
Salyersville 124 J8
Salzach 68 D2
Salzburg 68 D2
Salzgitter 70 D2
Salzwedel 70 D2
Samah 96 G2
Samaipata 138 D3
Samak, Tanjung 90 D6
Samales Group 91 G4
Samana, Bahia de 133 N5
Samana, Cabo 133 N5
Samana Cay 133 L3
Samandag 77 F4
Samani 88 J4
Samanli Daglari 76 D2
Samanskoye 86 C2
Samar 91 H3
Samara 79 J5
Samarga *Russia* 88 G2
Samarga *Russia* 88 G2
Samariapo 136 D2
Samarina 75 F2
Samarinda 91 F6
Samarka 88 E3
Samarkand 86 B4
Samarra 77 K5
Samarskoye 86 F2
Sambah 97 N10
Sambaliung 91 F5
Sambalpur 92 F4
Sambar, Tanjung 90 E6
Sambas 90 D5
Sambava 109 K2
Sambhal 92 E3
Sambhar 92 E3
Sambhar Lake 92 D3
Samboja 91 F6
Sambor 79 C6
Samborombon, Bahia 139 E7
Sambre 64 F3
Samchok 89 B7
Samhan, Jabal 97 M8
Sami 75 F3
Samirah 96 F3
Sam Neua 93 K4
Samoded 78 G3
Samos 75 J4
Samosomo Strait 114 R8
Samothraki *Greece* 74 E3
Samothraki *Greece* 75 H2
Samothraki *Greece* 75 H2
Samoylovka 79 G5
Sampit *Indonesia* 90 E6
Sampit *Indonesia* 90 E6
Sam Rayburn Lake 128 E5
Samre 96 D10
Samrong 93 K6
Samso 63 D9
Samsu 88 A5
Samsun 77 G2
Samtredia 77 K1
Samui, Ko 93 K6
Samut Prakan 93 K6
San *Mali* 100 E6
San *Poland* 71 K3
Sana 72 D3
Sana 96 G9
Sanae 141 Z4
Sanaga 105 H5
San Agustin 136 B3
San Agustin, Cape 91 H4
Sanaigmore 57 B5
Sanak Island 118 Af9
Sanam, As 97 K6
San Ambrosio, Isla 135 B5
Sanana 91 H6
Sanandaj 94 H4
San Andreas 126 B1
San Andres, Isla de 132 G8
San Andres Mountains 127 J4
San Andres Tuxtla 131 M8
San Angelo 127 M5
San Antonio *Chile* 139 B6
San Antonio *New Mexico, U.S.A.* 127 J4
San Antonio *U.S.A.* 128 C6
San Antonio *U.S.A.* 128 D6
San Antonio Abad 67 G3
San Antonio, Cabo 132 E4
San Antonio de Caparo 136 C2
San Antonio de los Cobres 138 C4
San Antonio Nuevo 132 C6
San Antonio, Punta 126 E6
Sanaw 97 K8
San Bartolomeo in Galdo 69 E5
San Benedetto del Tronto 69 D4
San Benedicto, Isla 130 D8
San Benito 128 D7
San Bernardino *Paraguay* 138 E5
San Bernardino *U.S.A.* 126 D3
San Bernardino Mountains 126 D3
San Bernardino Pass 68 B2
San Bernardo *Chile* 139 B6
San Bernardo *Mexico* 127 K7
San Bernardo do Campo 138 G4
San Blas 127 H7
San Blas, Cape 129 K6
San Blas, Punta 136 B2
San Borja 136 D6
San Borjas, Sierra de 126 F6
Sancak 77 J3
San Carlos *Argentina* 139 C6
San Carlos *Chile* 139 B7
San Carlos *Colombia* 136 D3
San Carlos *Nicaragua* 132 E9
San Carlos *Philippines* 91 G3
San Carlos *Philippines* 91 G2
San Carlos *Uruguay* 139 F6
San Carlos *U.S.A.* 126 G4
San Carlos *Venezuela* 136 D2
San Carlos de Bariloche 139 B8
San Carlos de la Rapita 67 G2
San Carlos del Zulia 136 C2
San Carlos Lake 126 G4
Sancerre 65 E5
Sanchakou 86 D4
Sanchor 92 D4
San Clemente 66 E3
San Clemente Island 126 C4
San Cristobal *Argentina* 138 D6
San Cristobal *Bolivia* 138 C4
San Cristobal *Solomon Is.* 114 L7
San Cristobal *Venezuela* 136 C2
San Cristobal, Bahia de 126 E7
San Cristobal de las Casas 131 N9
San Cristobal, Isla 136 A7
Sancti Spiritus 132 H4
Sancy, Puy de 65 E6
Sandagou 88 E4
Sanda Island 57 C5
Sandakan 91 F4
Sandanski 73 G5
Sandaohumiao 87 J4
Sandaotong 88 B3
Sandarne 63 G6
Sandasel 62 V13
Sanday 56 F1
Sanday Sound 56 F1
Sandbach 55 G3
Sandefjord 63 D7
Sanderson 127 L5
Sandhead 54 E2
Sand Hills 123 N6
San Diego 126 D4
San Diego, Cabo 139 C10
Sandikli 76 D3
Sandila 92 F3
Sandnes 63 A7
Sandness 56 A1
Sandnessjoen 62 E3
Sandoa 106 D4
Sandomierz 71 J3
Sandon 53 E2
San Dona di Piave 68 D3
Sandoway 93 H5
Sandown 53 F4
Sandoy 62 Z14
Sandpoint 122 F3
Sandray 57 A4
Sandsele 62 G4
Sandstone *Australia* 112 D4
Sandstone *U.S.A.* 124 D3
Sandusky *U.S.A.* 124 J6
Sandusky *U.S.A.* 124 J6
Sandvig 70 F1
Sandvika 62 E5
Sandviken 63 G6
Sandwich 53 J3
Sandy 53 G2
Sandy Cape 113 L3
Sandy Lake 119 S5
Sandy Point 93 H6
San Esteban, Isla de 126 F6
San Felipe *Chile* 139 B6
San Felipe *Mexico* 126 E5
San Felipe *Mexico* 131 J7
San Felipe *Venezuela* 136 D1
San Felix, Isla 135 A5
San Fermin, Punta 126 E5
San Fernando *Chile* 139 B6
San Fernando *Mexico* 128 C8
San Fernando *Mexico* 128 C8
San Fernando *Philippines* 91 G2
San Fernando *Spain* 66 C4
San Fernando *Trinidad and Tobago* 133 S9
San Fernando de Apure 136 D2
San Fernando de Atabapo 136 D3
Sanford *Florida, U.S.A.* 129 M6
Sanford *Maine, U.S.A.* 125 Q5
Sanford *N. Carolina, U.S.A.* 129 N3
Sanford, Mount 118 G3
San Francisco *Argentina* 138 D6
San Francisco *California, U.S.A.* 126 A2
San Francisco *New Mexico, U.S.A.* 127 H4
San Francisco, Cabo de 136 A3
San Francisco de Assis 138 E5
San Francisco del Oro 127 K7
San Francisco de Macoris 133 M5
San Francisco de Paula, Cabo 139 C9
San Francisco Javier 67 G3
San Francisco, Paso de 138 C5
San Gabriel, Punta 126 F6
Sangan 95 P4
Sangar 85 M4
Sang Bast 95 P3
Sangeang 91 F7
Sanggau 90 E5
Sangha 106 C2
Sangihe 91 H5
Sangihe, Kepulauan 91 H5
San Gil 136 C2
San Giovanni in Fiore 69 F6
Sangkhla Buri 93 J6
Sangli 92 D5
Sangmelima 105 H5
Sangonera 67 F4
San Gorgonio Peak 126 D3
Sangowo 91 H5
Sangre de Cristo Range 127 K1
Sangro 69 E4
Sangue 137 F6
Sanguesa 67 F1
San Guiseppe Iato 69 D7
San Hipolito, Punta 126 F7
Sanibel Island 129 L7
San Ignacio *Bolivia* 138 D3
San Ignacio *Bolivia* 136 D6
San Ignacio *Mexico* 126 F7
San Ignacio *Paraguay* 138 E5
Sanikiluaq 121 L6
San Ildefonso, Cape 91 G2
San Javier 138 D3
Sanjbod 94 J3
Sanjo 89 G7
San Joaquin *Bolivia* 136 E6
San Joaquin *U.S.A.* 126 B2
San Joaquin Valley 126 B2
San Jorge *Colombia* 133 K10
San Jorge *Solomon Is.* 114 J6
San Jorge, Bahia de 126 F5
San Jorge, Golfo de *Argentina* 139 C9
San Jorge, Golfo de *Spain* 67 G2
San Jose *Costa Rica* 132 E10
San Jose *Philippines* 91 G3
San Jose *Spain* 67 E4
San Jose *California, U.S.A.* 126 B2
San Jose *New Mexico, U.S.A.* 127 J3
San Jose de Amacuro 136 E2
San Jose de Buenavista 91 G3
San Jose de Chiquitos 138 D3
San Jose de Gracia 126 F7
San Jose de Jachal 139 C6
San Jose del Cabo 130 E6
San Jose de Mayo 139 E6
San Jose, Isla 130 D5
San Juan 131 M8
San Juan *Argentina* 138 C6
San Juan *Argentina* 138 C6
San Juan *Dominican Republic* 133 M5
San Juan *Mexico* 127 N8
San Juan *Nicaragua* 132 E8
San Juan *Peru* 136 B7
San Juan *Puerto Rico, U.S.A.* 133 P5
San Juan *Utah, U.S.A.* 127 H2
San Juan Bautista 67 G3
San Juan Bautista, Cabo 126 F6
San Juan del Norte 132 F9
San Juan del Norte, Bahia de 132 F9
San Juan de los Morros 136 D2
San Juan del Rio 131 K7
San Juanico, Punta 126 F7
San Juan Islands 122 C3
San Juan Mountains 127 J2
San Julian 139 C9
Sankt Blasjon 62 F4
Sankuru 106 D3
San Lazaro, Cabo 130 C5
San Lazaro, Sierra de 130 E6
San Lorenzo 136 D6
San Lorenzo, Cabo 136 A4
San Lorenzo, Cerro 139 B9
San Lorenzo de El Escorial 66 D2
San Lorenzo de la Parrilla 66 E3
San Lorenzo, Isla 126 F6
Sanlucar de Barrameda 66 C4
Sanlucar la Mayor 66 C4
San Lucas *Bolivia* 138 C4
San Lucas *Mexico* 130 E6
San Lucas, Cabo 130 E6
San Luis 132 C6
San Luis *Argentina* 139 C6
San Luis *Venezuela* 133 N9
San Luis Obispo 126 B3
San Luis Potosi 131 J6
San Luis Rio Colorado 126 E4
Sanluri 69 B6
San Manuel 126 G4
San Marco, Capo 69 B6
San Marcos *Mexico* 131 K9
San Marcos *U.S.A.* 128 D6
San Marcos, Island 126 F7
San Marino 68 D4
San Marino 68 D4
San Martin *Bolivia* 136 E6
San Martin *Colombia* 136 C3
San Martin de Valdeiglesias 66 D2
San Martin, Lago 139 B9
San Mateo 136 E2
San Matias 138 E3
San Matias, Golfo 139 D8
Sanmenxia 93 M2
San Miguel *Bolivia* 138 D3
San Miguel *Bolivia* 138 D3
San Miguel *El Salvador* 132 C8
San Miguel de Allende 131 J7
San Miguel de Tucuman 138 C5
San Miguel do Araguaia 137 G6
San Miguel Island 126 B3
San Miguelito 132 H10
Sanming 87 M6
Sannicandro Garganico 69 E5
San Nicolas 138 D6
San Nicolas, Bahia de 136 B7
San Nicolas Island 126 C4
Sannikova, Proliv 85 Q2
Sanok 71 K4
San Pablo 91 G3
San Pablo, Cabo 139 C10
San Pablo de Loreto 136 C4
San Pablo, Punta 126 E7
San Pedro 104 D5
San Pedro *Argentina* 139 E6
San Pedro *Mexico* 130 D6
San Pedro *Paraguay* 138 E4
San Pedro *U.S.A.* 126 G4
San Pedro Channel 126 C4
San Pedro de las Colonias 127 L8
San Pedro de Lloc 136 B5
San Pedro Martir, Sierra 126 E5
San Pedro, Punta 138 B5
San Pedros 130 G6
San Pedros de Macoris 133 N5
San Pedro, Sierra de 66 C3
San Pedro Sula 132 C7
San Pietro, Isola di 69 B6
Sanquhar 57 E5
San Quintin, Bahia de 126 E5
San Rafael *Argentina* 139 C6
San Rafael *Colombia* 136 C1
San Rafael *U.S.A.* 126 A2
San Remo 68 A4
San Salvador *Bahamas* 133 K2
San Salvador *El Salvador* 132 C8
San Salvador de Jujuy 138 C4
San Salvador, Isla 136 A7
San Sebastian 67 F1
San Sebastian Bahia de 139 C10
San Sebastiao, Ponta 109 G4
Sansepolcro 68 D4
San Severo 69 E5
San Silvestre 133 M10
Sanski Most 72 D3
Santa Ana *Bolivia* 136 D6
Santa Ana *El Salvador* 132 C7
Santa Ana *Mexico* 126 G5
Santa Ana *U.S.A.* 126 D4
Santa Ana Island 114 L7
Santa Barbara 126 C3
Santa Barbara *Honduras* 132 C7
Santa Barbara *Mexico* 127 K7
Santa Barbara Channel 126 B3
Santa Catalina, Gulf of 126 D4
Santa Catalina, Isla 130 D5
Santa Catalina Island 126 C4
Santa Catarina 138 F5
Santa Catarina, Ilha 138 G5
Santa Clara 132 H3
Santa Coloma de Farnes 67 H2
Santa Coloma de Gramanet 67 H2
Santa Comba Dao 66 B2
Santa Comba de Rossas 66 C2
Santa Cruz *Argentina* 139 B10
Santa Cruz *Bolivia* 138 D3
Santa Cruz *U.S.A.* 126 A2
Santa Cruz de la Palma 100 B3
Santa Cruz de Moya 67 F3
Santa Cruz de Tenerife 100 B3
Santa Cruz do Sul 138 F5
Santa Cruz, Isla *Ecuador* 136 A7
Santa Cruz, Isla *Mexico* 130 D5
Santa Cruz Island 126 C3
Santa Cruz Islands 114 N7
Santa Elena 136 E3
Santa Elena, Cabo 132 E9
Santa Eulalia del Rio 67 G3
Santafe 66 E4
Santa Fe *Argentina* 138 D6
Santa Fe *Panama* 132 G10
Santa Fe *U.S.A.* 127 K3
Sant Agata di Militello 69 E6
Santai *Sichuan, China* 93 L2
Santai *Xinjiang Uygur Zizhiqu, China* 86 E3
Santa Ines, Isla 139 B10
Santa Isabel *Argentina* 139 C7
Santa Isabel *Equatorial Guinea* 105 G5
Santa Isabel *Solomon Is.* 114 J5
Santa Lucia 139 E6
Santa Lucia Range 126 B2
Santa Luzia 137 K5
Santa Margarita, Isla 130 D5
Santa Maria *Brazil* 138 F5
Santa Maria *Mexico* 127 J6
Santa Maria *Mexico* 127 K8
Santa Maria *U.S.A.* 126 B3
Santa Maria *Vanuatu* 114 T11
Santa Maria *Venezuela* 133 P11
Santa Maria, Cabo de *Mozambique* 109 F5
Santa Maria, Cabo de *Portugal* 66 C4
Santa Maria di Leuca, Capo 69 G6
Santa Maria, Isla 136 A7
Santa Maria, Laguna de 127 J5
Santa Marta 136 C1
Santa Marta, Cabo de 106 B5
Santa Marta Grande, Cabo de 138 G5
Santa Maura 75 F3
Santa Monica 126 C3
Santan 91 F6
Santana 137 J6
Santana do Ipanema 137 K5
Santana do Livramento 138 E6
Santander *Colombia* 136 B3
Santander *Spain* 66 E1
Sant Antioco 69 B6
Santarem *Brazil* 137 G4
Santarem *Spain* 66 B3

Santaren Channel **132** H3
Santa Rita **136** C1
Santa Rosa *Argentina* **139** C6
Santa Rosa *Argentina* **139** D7
Santa Rosa *Bolivia* **136** D6
Santa Rosa *Brazil* **138** F5
Santa Rosa *California, U.S.A.* **126** A1
Santa Rosa *New Mexico, U.S.A.* **127** K3
Santa Rosa de Cabal **136** B3
Santa Rosa de Copan **132** C7
Santa Rosa Island **126** B4
Santa Rosalia **126** F7
Santa Rosa Range **122** F7
Santa Teresa Gallura **69** B5
Santa Vitoria do Palmar **139** F6
Santa Ynez **126** B3
Santee **129** M4
Santerno **68** C3
Sant Eufemia, Golfo di **69** F6
Santhia **68** B3
Santiago *Brazil* **138** F5
Santiago *Chile* **139** B6
Santiago *Dominican Republic* **133** M5
Santiago *Panama* **132** G10
Santiago *Peru* **136** B4
Santiago, Cerro **132** G10
Santiago de Chuco **136** B5
Santiago de Compostela **66** B1
Santiago de Cuba **133** K4
Santiago del Estero **138** D5
Santiago do Cacem **66** B3
Santiago Ixcuintla **130** G7
Santiago Papasquiaro **130** G5
San Tiburcio **130** J5
Santo Amaro **137** K6
Santo Andre **138** G4
Santo Angelo **138** F5
Santo Antao **104** L7
Santo Antonio do Ica **136** D4
Santo Domingo *Dominican Republic* **133** N5
Santo Domingo *Mexico* **126** E5
Santo Domingo de la Calzada **66** E1
Santo Domingo de los Colorados **136** B4
Santorini **75** H4
Santos **138** G4
Santos Dumont *Amazonas, Brazil* **136** D5
Santos Dumont *Minas Gerais, Brazil* **138** H4
Santo Tomas **126** D5
Santo Tome **138** E5
San Valentin, Cerro **139** B9
San Vicente de la Barquera **66** D1
San Vicente del Caguan **136** C3
San Vincent **132** C8
San Vincente **91** G2
San Vito, Capo **69** D6
Sanyati **108** E3
Sanyshand **87** L3
Sao Borja **138** E5
Sao Bras de Alportel **66** C4
Sao Carlos *Rondonia, Brazil* **136** E5
Sao Carlos *Sao Paulo, Brazil* **138** G4
Sao Domingos **137** H6
Sao Felix **137** G5
Sao Francisco *Acre, Brazil* **136** D6
Sao Francisco *Bahia, Brazil* **137** K5
Sao Francisco do Sul **138** G5
Sao Francisco, Ilha de **138** G5
Sao Joao del Rei **138** H4
Sao Joao do Araguaia **137** H5
Sao Joao do Piaui **137** J5
Sao Joao, Ilhas de **137** H4
Sao Jose **136** D4
Sao Jose do Gurupi **137** H4
Sao Jose do Rio Preto **138** G4
Sao Jose dos Campos **138** G4
Sao Leopoldo **138** F5
Sao Lourenco **138** E3
Sao Luis **137** J4
Sao Manuel **136** F5
Sao Marcos **138** G3
Sao Marcos, Baia de **137** J4
Sao Maria da Boa Vista **137** K5
Sao Mateus **138** K7
Sao Miguel dos Campos **137** K5
Sao Miguel do Tapuio **137** J5
Saona, Isla **133** N5
Saone **65** F5
Sao Nicolau **104** L7
Sao Paulo *Brazil* **138** G4
Sao Paulo *Brazil* **138** G4
Sao Paulo de Olivenca **136** D4
Sao Pedro do Sul **66** B2
Sao Raimundo Nonato **137** J5
Sao Romao **138** G3
Sao Roque, Cabo de **137** K5
Sao Sebastiao do Paraiso **138** G4
Sao Tiago **104** L7
Sao Tome **105** G5
Sao Tome **105** G5
Sao Tome and Principe **105** G5
Sao Tome, Cabo de **138** H4
Saouda, Qornet es **77** G5
Saoura, Oued **100** E2
Sao Vicente **138** G4
Sao Vicente, Cabo de **66** B4
Sao Vincente **104** L7
Sapai **75** H2
Sapanca **76** D2
Sapanca Golu **76** D2
Sape **91** F7
Sapele **105** G4
Sapientza **75** F4
Saposoa **136** B5
Sapporo **88** H4
Sapri **69** E5
Sapulut **90** F5
Saqqez **94** H3
Sarab **94** H3
Sara Buri **93** K6
Saragossa **67** F2
Saraguro **136** B4
Sarajevo **72** E4
Sarakhs **95** Q3
Sarakli **75** G2
Saraktash **79** K5
Saralzhin **79** J6
Saranac Lake **125** P4
Sarande **74** E3
Saran, Gunung **90** E6
Saranpaul **84** Ad4
Saransk **78** H5
Sarapul **78** J4
Sarapul'skoye **88** F1
Sarasota **129** L7
Sarata **73** K2
Saratoga **126** A2
Saratoga Springs **125** P5
Saratov **79** H5
Saravan **95** R8
Saravane **93** L5
Sarawak **90** E5
Saray *Turkey* **76** B2
Saray *Turkey* **77** L3
Saraychik **79** J6
Saraykent **76** F3
Saraykoy *Turkey* **76** C4
Saraykoy *Turkey* **76** F3
Sarayonu **76** E3
Sarbaz **95** Q8
Sarbisheh **95** P5
Sarcham **94** J3
Sarda **92** F3
Sardarshahr **92** D3
Sardegna **69** B5
Sardinia **69** B5
Sardis Lake **128** H3
Sareks **62** G3
Sar-e Pol **92** C1
Sar-e Yazd **95** M6
Sargans **68** B2
Sargodha **92** D2
Sarh **102** C6
Sari **95** L3
Saria **75** J5
Sarickaya **76** D2
Sarigol **76** C3
Sarikamis **77** K2
Sarikaya **76** F3
Sarinay **86** C4
Sarine **68** A2
Sarioglan **77** F3
Sarisu **77** K3
Sariwon **87** P4
Sariyar Baraji **76** D2
Sariz **77** G3
Sark **53** M7
Sarkikaraagac **76** D3
Sarkisla **77** G3
Sarkoy **76** B2
Sarlat-la-Caneda **65** D6
Sarmi **91** K6
Sarmiento **139** C9
Sarna **63** E6
Sarneh **94** H5
Sarnen **68** B2
Sarnia **124** J5
Sarny **79** D5
Saronikos Kolpos **75** G4
Saronno **68** B3
Saros Korfezi **76** B2
Sarowbi **92** C2
Sar Planina **72** F5
Sarpsborg **63** H7
Sarralbe **64** G4
Sarre **64** G4
Sarrebourg **64** G4
Sarria **66** C1
Sarshive **94** H4
Sartang **85** N3
Sartatovskoye Vodokhranilishche **79** H5
Sartene **69** B5
Sarthe **65** C5
Sartu **87** N2
Saruhanli **76** B3
Sarvabad **94** H4
Sarvar **72** D2
Sarvestan **95** L7
Sarviz **72** E2
Sarych, Mys **79** E7
Sary-Ishikotrau, Peski **86** D2
Sary Ozek **86** D3
Sary-Shagan **86** C2
Sary-Tash **86** C4
Sarzana **68** B3
Sasamungga **114** H5
Sasaram **92** F4
Sasd **72** E2
Sasebo **89** B9
Saskatchewan *Canada* **119** P5
Saskatchewan *Canada* **119** Q5
Saskatoon **123** L1
Saskylakh **84** J2
Sasovo **78** G5
Sassandra *Ivory Coast* **104** D4
Sassandra *Ivory Coast* **104** D5
Sassari **69** B5
Sassnitz **70** E1
Sasstown **104** D5
Sassuolo **68** C3
Sas-Tobe **86** C3
Sasyk, Ozero **73** K3
Satadougou **100** C6
Satara **92** D5
Sater **63** F6
Satley **55** H2
Satmala Range **92** E5
Satna **92** F4
Satoraljaujhely **71** J4
Satpura Range **92** E4
Sattahip **93** K6
Satu Mare **73** G2
Satun **93** K7
Satyga **84** Ad5
Sauceda **127** M8
Saucillo **127** K6
Sauda **63** B7
Saudarkrokur **62** V12
Saudi Arabia **96** F3
Sauerland **70** B3
Saugeen **124** K4
Sauk City **124** F5
Saulieu **65** F5
Sault Sainte Marie *Canada* **124** H3
Sault Sainte Marie *U.S.A.* **124** H3
Saumarez Reef **113** L3
Saumlakki **91** J7
Saumur **65** C5
Saunders, Cape **115** C6
Saundersfoot **52** C3
Saurimo **106** D4
Sava **72** E3
Savaii **111** U4
Savalou **105** F4
Savannah *Tennessee, U.S.A.* **129** H3
Savannah *U.S.A.* **129** M4
Savannah *U.S.A.* **129** M4
Savannakhet **93** K5
Savant Lake **124** E1
Savantvadi **92** D5
Savanur **92** E6
Savar **62** J5
Savastepe **76** B3
Save **105** F4
Save *France* **65** D7
Save *Mozambique* **109** F4
Saveh **95** K4
Saveni **73** J2
Saverne **64** G4
Savinja **72** C2
Savirsin **73** G2
Savitaipale **63** M6
Savnik **72** E4
Savoie **65** G6
Savona **68** B3
Savo Nggatokae **114** J6
Savonlinna **63** N6
Savsat **77** K2
Savsjo **63** F8
Savukoski **62** N3
Savur **77** J4
Savusavu **114** R8
Savusavu Bay **114** R8
Sawab, Wasi as **77** J5
Sawadah, As **96** G5
Sawara **88** H4
Sawatch Mountains **123** L8
Sawbridgeworth **53** H3
Sawel **58** H3
Sawqirah, Ghubbat **97** N7
Sawqirah, Ra's **97** N7
Sawston **53** H2
Sawtooth Mountains *Idaho, U.S.A.* **122** G5
Sawtooth Mountains *Minnesota, U.S.A.* **124** E3
Sawtry **53** G2
Sawu **91** G8
Sawu, Laut **91** G7
Saxby Downs **113** J3
Saxmundham **53** J2
Saxthorpe **53** J2
Sayak **86** D2
Saydy **85** N3
Sayhan-Ovoo **87** J2
Sayhut **97** K9
Saylac **103** H5
Sayula **130** H8
Sayulita **130** G7
Sayun **97** J9
Say-Utes **79** J7
Sazan **74** E2
Sazava **70** F4
Sazin **92** D1
Scafell Pikes **55** G2
Scalasaig **57** B4
Scalby **55** J2
Scalea **69** E6
Scalloway **56** A2
Scalpay **56** C3
Scamblesby **55** J3
Scammon Bay **118** B3
Scapa Flow **56** E2
Scaraben **56** E2
Scaramia, Capo **69** E7
Scarba **57** C4
Scarborough *Canada* **125** L5
Scarborough *Trinidad and Tobago* **133** S9
Scarborough *U.K.* **55** J2
Scarinish **57** B4
Scarp **56** A2
Scarpanto **75** J5
Scarpe **64** E3
Scarriff **59** E7
Schaal See **70** D2
Schaffhausen **68** B2
Scharhorn **70** C2
Schefferville **121** N7
Scheibbs **68** E1
Scheitling **68** E2
Schelde **64** E3
Schenectady **125** P5
Schiedam **64** F3
Schiehallion **57** D4
Schiermonnikoog **64** G2
Schio **68** C3
Schitu Duca **73** J2
Schlei **70** C1
Schleiz **70** D3
Schleswig **70** C1
Schneidemuhl **71** G2
Schoningen **70** D2
Schonsee **70** E4
Schouten Islands **114** C2
Schouwen **64** E3
Schreiber **124** G2
Schwabische Alb **70** C4
Schwandorf **70** E4
Schwaner, Pegunungan **90** E6
Schwarmstedt **70** C2
Schwarze Elser **70** E3
Schwarzwald **70** C5
Schwaz **68** C2
Schwedt **70** F2
Schweinfurt **70** D3
Schwerin **70** D2
Schweriner See **70** D2
Schwieloch See **70** F2
Schwyz **68** B2
Sciacca **69** D7
Scilly, Isles of **52** L5
Scioto **124** J7
Sckuls **68** C2
Scobey **123** M3
Sconser **56** B3
Score Head **56** A1
Scoresby, Cape **120** H3
Scotia Ridge **139** F10
Scotia Sea **139** F1
Scott Base **141** M3
Scottburgh **108** F6
Scott, Cape **118** K5
Scott City **127** M1
Scott Glacier **141** P1
Scott Lake **119** P4
Scott Reef **112** E1
Scottsbluff **123** N7
Scottsboro **129** J3
Scottsdale **126** G4
Scourie **56** C2
Scrabster **56** E2
Scranton **125** N6
Screeb **59** C6
Scridain, Loch **57** B4
Scunthorpe **55** J3
Scuol **68** C2
Scurrival Point **57** A3
Scutari **74** E1
Seaford *U.K.* **53** H4
Seaford *U.S.A.* **125** N7
Seaforth, Loch **56** B3
Seaham **55** H2
Seahorse Point **120** K5
Seahouses **55** H1
Seal **119** R4
Sea Lake **113** J6
Seal, Cape **108** D6
Seal Cape **118** D4
Seamer **55** J2
Searcy **128** G3
Searles Lake **126** D3
Seascale **55** F2
Seaside **122** C5
Seathwaite **55** F2
Seaton **52** D4
Seaton Sluice **55** H1
Seattle **122** C4
Sebago Lake **125** Q5
Sebangka **90** C5
Sebastian Vizcaino, Bahia de **126** E6
Sebderat **103** G4
Seben **76** D2
Sebenico **72** C4
Sebes **73** G3
Sebesului, Muntii **73** G3
Sebezh **63** N8
Sebinkarahisar **77** H2
Sebring **129** M7
Sebta **66** D5
Sebuku **90** F6
Secchia **68** C3
Sechura, Bahia de **136** A5
Sechura, Desierto de **136** A5
Secretary Island **115** A6
Secunderabad **92** E5
Seda **66** C3
Sedalia **124** D7
Sedan **64** F4
Sedano **66** E1
Sedbergh **55** G2

Name	Pg	Ref
Sedden, Kap	120	Q2
Seddonville	115	C4
Sedeh	95	P5
Sedgefield	55	H2
Sedona	126	G3
Seduva	63	K9
Seefeld	68	C2
Seefin	59	E8
Sees	64	D4
Sefaatli	76	F3
Sefadu	104	C4
Seferihisar	76	B3
Sefrou	100	E2
Sefton, Mount	115	C5
Segamat	90	C5
Segbwema	104	C4
Segea	91	H5
Segendy	79	J7
Segeneyti	96	D9
Seget	91	J6
Segezha	78	E3
Seghe	114	H6
Segid	96	F8
Segorbe	67	F3
Segou	100	D6
Segovia *Honduras*	132	E7
Segovia *Spain*	66	D2
Segozero, Ozero	78	E3
Segre	65	C5
Segre	67	G2
Seguam Island	118	Ad9
Seguela	104	D4
Segula Island	118	Ab9
Segura *Portugal*	66	C3
Segura *Spain*	67	F3
Segurra, Sierra de	66	E4
Sehwan	92	C3
Seia	66	C2
Seil	57	D4
Seiland	62	K1
Seiling	128	C2
Seille *France*	65	F5
Seille *France*	64	G4
Seinajoki	62	N4
Seine	64	D4
Seine, Baie de la	64	C4
Seini	73	G2
Sekondi Takoradi	104	E4
Se Kong	93	L6
Sekota	103	G5
Selaru	91	J7
Selatan	90	C6
Selatan, Tanjung	90	E6
Selawik Lake	118	C2
Selayar	91	G7
Selayar, Selat	91	G7
Selby *U.K.*	55	H3
Selby *U.S.A.*	123	P5
Selcuk	76	B4
Selde	63	C8
Selebi-Phikwe	108	E4
Selemdzha	85	N6
Selendi	76	C3
Selenduma	84	H6
Selenge	87	J2
Selenge Moron	87	K2
Selennyakh	85	Q3
Selenter See	70	D1
Selestat	64	G4
Seletyteniz, Ozero	84	A6
Selfoss	62	U13
Selgon	85	P7
Selibabi	100	C5
Seligman	126	F3
Selijord	63	C7
Selim	77	K2
Selimiye	76	B4
Selizharovo	78	E4
Seljaland	62	V13
Selkirk *Canada*	123	R2
Selkirk *U.K.*	57	F5
Selkirk Mountains	122	F2
Sellafirth	56	A1
Selma	129	J4
Selseleh-ye- Pir Shuran	95	Q7
Selsey	53	G4
Selsey Bill	53	G4
Selsviken	62	F5
Selva	138	D5
Selvagens, Ilhas	100	B2
Selvas	136	D5
Selwyn Lake	119	Q3
Selwyn Range	113	J3
Selyatin	71	L5
Seman	74	E2
Semarang	90	E7
Sematan	90	D5
Semau	91	G8
Sembakung	91	F5
Sembe	106	B2
Semdinli	77	L4
Semenov	78	G4
Semenovka	79	E6
Seminoe Reservoir	123	L6
Seminole *Oklahoma, U.S.A.*	128	D3
Seminole *Texas, U.S.A.*	127	L4
Seminole, Lake	129	K5
Semipalatinsk	84	C6
Semirara Islands	91	G3
Semirom	95	K6
Semisopochnoi Island	118	Ab9
Semitau	90	E5
Semiyarka	84	B6
Semnan	95	L4
Semois	64	F4
Semporna	91	F5
Senador Pompeu	137	K5
Sena Madureira	136	D5
Senanga	106	D6
Senatobia	128	H3
Sendai *Japan*	89	C10
Sendai *Japan*	89	H6
Senec	71	G4
Seneca Lake	125	M5
Senegal	104	B2
Senegal	100	C5
Senekal	108	E5
Sengata	91	F5
Sengiley	78	H5
Senhor do Bonfim	137	J6
Senigallia	68	D4
Senirkent	76	D3
Senise	69	F5
Senj	72	C3
Senja	62	H2
Senjahopen	62	L2
Senkaku-shoto	89	F11
Senkaya	77	K2
Senkyabasa	84	J3
Senlin Shan	88	C4
Senlis	64	E4
Sennar	103	F5
Sennen	52	B4
Senno	78	D5
Sennybridge	52	D3
Senquerr	139	C9
Sens	64	E4
Senta	72	F3
Senyurt	77	J4
Seoni	92	E4
Seoul	87	P4
Sepanjang	90	F7
Separation Point	115	D4
Sepidan	95	L6
Sepik	114	C2
Sepolno	71	G2
Sept-Iles	121	N7
Sepulveda	66	E2
Sequeros	66	C2
Sequillo	66	D2
Serafimovich	79	G6
Serakhs	95	Q3
Seram	91	H6
Seram, Laut	91	H6
Serang	90	D7
Serasan, Selat	90	D5
Serba	96	E10
Sercaia	73	H3
Serchio	68	C4
Serdobsk	79	G5
Serdtse Karmen, Mys	118	A2
Sered	71	G4
Seredka	63	N7
Sereflikochisar	76	E3
Serein	65	E5
Seremban	90	C5
Serengeti Plain	107	F3
Serenje	107	F5
Seret	71	L4
Sergach	78	H4
Sergelen	87	K2
Sergeyevka	88	D4
Sergino	84	Ae4
Sergipe	137	K6
Seria	90	E5
Serian	90	E5
Serifos *Greece*	75	H4
Serifos *Greece*	75	H4
Serik	76	D4
Seringapatum Reef	112	E1
Serio	68	B3
Sermata, Kepulauan	91	H7
Sermiligaarsuk	120	S5
Sernovodsk *Russia*	78	J5
Sernovodsk *Russia*	88	K4
Sernur	78	H4
Seroglazovka	79	H6
Serov	84	Ad5
Serpa	66	C4
Serpent's Mouth	136	E2
Serpukhov	78	F5
Serra Bonita	138	G3
Serracapriola	69	E5
Serra do Navio	137	G3
Serrai	75	G2
Serrana Bank	132	G7
Serranilla Bank	132	H7
Serra Talhada	137	K5
Serrat, Cap	69	B7
Serres	65	F6
Serrinha	137	K6
Serta	66	B3
Sertania	137	K5
Serui	91	K6
Seruyan	90	E6
Servia	75	G2
Serxu	93	J2
Se San	93	L6
Sese Island	107	F3
Seshachalam Hills	92	E6
Sesheke	106	D6
Sesia	68	B3
Se Srepok	93	L6
Sessa	106	D5
Sestri Levante	68	B3
Sestroretsk	63	N6
Sesupe	71	K1
Set	93	L5
Setana	88	G4
Sete	65	E7
Sete Lagoas	138	H3
Setermoen	62	H2
Setesdal	63	C7
Setif	101	G1
Seto	89	F8
Settat	100	D2
Settle	55	G2
Setubal	66	B3
Setubal, Baia de	66	B3
Seul, Lac	119	S5
Seumayan	90	B5
Seurre	65	F5
Sevan, Ozero	77	L2
Sevastopol	79	E7
Seven	55	J2
Seven Heads	59	E9
Seven Hogs, The	59	B8
Sevenoaks	53	H3
Seven Sisters	118	K4
Severac-le-Chateau	65	E6
Severn *Canada*	121	J6
Severn *U.K.*	52	E3
Severnaya Dvina	78	G3
Severnaya Sosva	84	Ad4
Severnaya Zemlya	81	M1
Severn, Mouth of the	52	E3
Severnyy	78	H2
Severodonetsk	79	F6
Severodvinsk	78	F3
Severomorsk	62	Q2
Severouralsk	84	Ad4
Severskiy Donets	79	G6
Sevier	122	H8
Sevier Lake	122	H8
Sevilla *Colombia*	136	B3
Sevilla *Spain*	66	D4
Seville	66	D4
Sevola	71	L4
Sevre Nantaise	65	C5
Sevre Niortaise	65	C5
Sevsk	79	E5
Sewa	104	C4
Seward *Alaska, U.S.A.*	118	F3
Seward *Nebraska, U.S.A.*	123	R7
Seward Peninsula	118	C2
Seyah Kuh, Kavir-e	95	L5
Seyakha	84	A2
Seychelles	82	D7
Seydisehir	76	D4
Seydisfjordur	62	Y12
Seyhan	76	F4
Seyitgazi	76	D3
Seym	79	E5
Seymchan	85	S4
Seymour *Australia*	113	K6
Seymour *Indiana, U.S.A.*	124	H7
Seymour *Texas, U.S.A.*	127	N4
Sezanne	64	E4
Sfax	101	H2
Sfintu Gheorghe	73	H3
Sfintu Gheorghe, Bratul	73	K3
s'Gravenhage	64	F2
Sgurr na Lapaich	56	C3
Shaam	97	N4
Shaanxi	93	L2
Shabunda	106	E3
Shadad, Namakzar-e	95	P6
Shadrinsk	84	Ad5
Shadwan	96	A3
Shaftesbury	53	E3
Shagany, Ozero	73	K3
Shagonar	84	E6
Shag Point	115	C6
Shahabad	92	E3
Shahbandar	92	C4
Shahdad	95	N6
Shahdol	92	F4
Shah Fuladi	92	C2
Shahgarh	92	C3
Shahhat	101	K2
Shahjahanpur	92	E3
Shahpur	92	D2
Shahpura *Madhya Pradesh, India*	92	F4
Shahpura *Rajasthan, India*	92	D3
Shahrabad	95	N3
Shahrak	95	S5
Shahr-e Babak	95	M6
Shahr-e Kord	95	K5
Shahr Rey	95	K4
Shah Rud	95	J3
Shajapur	92	E4
Shakhauz	94	G2
Shakhs, Ras	96	E9
Shakhty	79	G6
Shakhunya	78	H4
Shaki	105	H4
Shakotan-misaki	88	H4
Shaktoolik	118	C3
Shalamzar	95	K5
Shaler Mountains	119	N1
Shalfleet	53	F4
Shalkhar, Ozero	79	J5
Shaluli Shan	93	J2
Shama, Ash	94	D6
Shamary	78	K4
Shambe	102	F6
Shamil	95	N8
Shamiyah	94	D4
Sham, Jambal	97	N5
Shammar	96	E3
Shand	95	R6
Shandan	86	J4
Shandong	87	M4
Shangani	108	E3
Shanghang	87	M7
Shangqiu	93	N2
Shangrao	87	M6
Shang Xian	93	L2
Shangzhi	87	P2
Shanklin	53	F4
Shannon *Ireland*	59	E7
Shannon *New Zealand*	115	E4
Shannon, Mouth of the	59	C7
Shantarskiye Ostrova	85	P5
Shantou	87	M7
Shanxi	93	M1
Shan Xian	93	N2
Shanyin	87	L4
Shaoguan	93	M4
Shaowu	87	M6
Shaoxing	87	N6
Shaoyang	93	M3
Shap	55	G2
Shapinsay	56	F1
Shapkina	78	J2
Shaqra	96	G4
Sharanga	78	H4
Sharbithat, Ra's	97	N8
Shari	88	K4
Shari, Buhayrat	77	L5
Shark Bay	112	C4
Sharlauk	95	M2
Sharlyk	79	J5
Sharmah	96	B2
Sharm el Sheikh	96	B3
Sharon	125	K6
Sharon Springs	127	M1
Sharqi, Al Hajar ash	97	P5
Sharqi, Jazair esh	94	C5
Sharqi, Jebel esh	77	G6
Sharqiyah, Ash	97	P5
Sharqiya, Sahra Esh	103	F2
Sharurah	96	H8
Sharwayn, Ra's	97	K9
Sharya	78	H4
Shashe	108	E4
Shashemene	103	G6
Shashi	93	M2
Shasta Lake	122	C7
Shasta, Mount	122	C7
Shatsk	78	G5
Shatura	78	F4
Shaubak	94	B6
Shaunavon	123	K3
Shaw	55	G3
Shawano	124	F4
Shawbury	52	E2
Shawinigan	125	P3
Shawnce	128	D3
Sha Xi	87	M6
Sha Xian	87	M6
Shaybara	96	C4
Shaytanovka	78	K3
Shchara	71	L2
Shchekino	78	F5
Shchelyayur	78	J2
Shcherbakovo	85	U3
Shchigry	79	F5
Shchirets	71	K4
Shchors	79	E5
Shchuchin	71	L2
Shchuchinsk	84	Ad5
Shchuchye	84	Ad5
Shebalino	84	D6
Shebekino	79	F5
Sheberghan	92	C1
Sheboygan	124	G5
Shebshi Mountains	105	H4
Shebunino	88	H2
Sheelin, Lough	58	H1
Sheenjek	118	G2
Sheep Haven	58	G2
Sheep's Head	59	C9
Sheerness	53	H3
Sheffield *Alabama, U.S.A.*	129	J3
Sheffield *Texas, U.S.A.*	127	M5
Sheffield *U.K.*	55	H3
Shegmas	78	H3
Shekhupura	92	D2
Sheki	79	H7
Shelagskiy	85	W2
Shelagskiy, Mys	85	V2
Shelburne	121	N9
Shelburne Bay	113	J1
Shelby *Montana, U.S.A.*	122	J3
Shelby *N. Carolina, U.S.A.*	129	M3
Shelbyville *Indiana, U.S.A.*	124	H7
Shelbyville *Tennessee, U.S.A.*	129	J3
Shelikhova, Zaliv	85	T5
Shelikof Strait	118	E4
Shell Creek Range	122	G8
Shelly	122	H6
Shelton	122	C4
Sheltozero	78	F3
Shemakha	79	H7
Shemonaikha	84	C6
Shenandoah *Iowa, U.S.A.*	124	C6
Shenandoah *Virginia, U.S.A.*	125	L7
Shendam	105	G4
Shendi	103	F4
Shenge	104	C4
Shenkursk	78	G3
Shenton, Mount	112	E4
Shenyang	87	N3
Shepetovka	79	D5

Shepherd Bay	120	H4
Shepherd Islands	114	U12
Shepparton	113	K6
Sheppey, Isle of	53	H3
Shepshed	53	F2
Shepton Mallet	52	E3
Sheragul	84	G6
Sherard, Cape	120	K3
Sherborne	52	E4
Sherbro	104	C4
Sherbro Island	104	C4
Sherbrooke	125	Q4
Sherburne Reef	114	D2
Sherburn in Elmet	55	H3
Shereik	96	A7
Sheridan *Arkansas, U.S.A.*	128	F3
Sheridan *Wyoming, U.S.A.*	123	L5
Sheringham	53	J2
Sherlovaya Gora	85	K6
Sherman	128	D4
's-Hertogenbosch	64	F3
Shetland	56	A1
Shetland Islands	56	A1
Shetpe	79	J7
Shevchenko	79	J7
Shewa Gimira	103	G6
Sheya	85	K4
Sheyang	87	N5
Sheyenne	123	Q4
Shiant Islands	56	B3
Shiant, Sound of	56	B3
Shiashkotan, Ostrov	85	S7
Shibam	97	J9
Shibata	89	G7
Shibecha	88	K4
Shibetsu *Japan*	88	J3
Shibetsu *Japan*	88	K4
Shibin el Kom	102	F1
Shibotsu-jima	88	L4
Shibushi	89	C10
Shickshock Mountains	125	S2
Shiel Bridge	56	C3
Shieldaig	56	C3
Shiel, Loch	57	C4
Shihan, Wadi	97	L8
Shihezi	86	F3
Shiikh	103	J6
Shijiazhuang	87	L4
Shikarpur	92	C3
Shikoku	89	D9
Shikoku-sanchi	89	D9
Shikong	87	K4
Shikotan-to	88	L4
Shikotsu-ko	88	H4
Shildon	55	H2
Shilega	78	G3
Shiliguri	93	G3
Shilka *Russia*	85	K6
Shilka *Russia*	85	L6
Shillingstone	52	E4
Shillong	93	H3
Shilovo	78	G5
Shimabara	89	C9
Shimada	89	G8
Shimanovsk	85	M6
Shimian	93	K3
Shimizu	89	G8
Shimoda	89	G8
Shimoga	92	E6
Shimonoseki	89	C9
Shinano	89	G7
Shinas	97	N4
Shindand	95	R5
Shin Falls	56	D3
Shingu	89	E9
Shinjo	88	H6
Shinness	56	D2
Shinshar	77	G5
Shinyanga	107	F3
Shiogama	89	H6
Shiono-misaki	89	E9
Shiosawa	89	G7
Shiping	93	K4
Shipley	55	H3
Shippensburg	125	M6
Shippigan Island	121	P8
Shipston-on-Stour	53	F2
Shipton	55	H2
Shipton-under-Wychwood	53	F3
Shipunovo	84	C6
Shirakawa	89	H7
Shirane-san *Japan*	89	G8
Shirane-san *Japan*	89	G7
Shiraz	95	L7
Shire	107	F6
Shirebrook	55	H3
Shiretoko-misaki	88	K3
Shiriya-saki	88	H5
Shir Kuh	95	M6
Shirten Holoy Gobi	86	H3
Shirvan	95	N3
Shishaldin Volcano	118	Af9
Shivpuri	92	E3
Shivwits Plateau	126	F2
Shiwan Dashan	93	L4
Shiyan	93	M2
Shizhu	93	L3
Shizugawa	88	H6
Shizuishan	87	K4
Shizuoka	89	G8
Shkoder	74	E1
Shkumbin	74	E2
Shmidta, Ostrov	81	L1
Shobara	89	D8
Shokalskogo, Ostrov	84	A2
Shorapur	92	E5
Shorawak	95	S6
Shoreham-by-Sea	53	G4
Shorkot	92	D2
Shoshone	122	G6
Shoshone Mountains	122	F8
Shoshoni	123	K6
Shostka	79	E5
Shouguang	87	M4
Shouning	87	M6
Showa	141	C5
Showak	96	B9
Shozhma	78	G3
Shpikov	73	K1
Shpola	79	E6
Shrankogl	68	C2
Shreveport	128	F4
Shrewsbury	52	E2
Shrewton	53	F3
Shrigonda	92	D5
Shropshire	52	E2
Shrule	59	D5
Shuab, Ra's	97	P9
Shuanghezhen	87	P3
Shuangliao	87	N3
Shuangyashan	87	Q2
Shubar-Kuduk	79	K6
Shubra el-Khema	102	F1
Shucheng	87	M5
Shuga	84	B6
Shuicheng	93	K3
Shuikou	87	M6
Shujaabad	92	D3
Shulan	87	P3
Shumagin Islands	118	Af9
Shumen	73	J4
Shumerlya	78	H4
Shungnak	118	D2
Shuqrah	96	G10
Shura	77	K4
Shurab	95	K5
Shurab	95	N5
Shusf	95	Q6
Shush	94	J5
Shushenskoye	84	E6
Shushtar	94	J5
Shuswap Lake	122	E2
Shuya	78	G4
Shuya	89	G7
Shwebo	93	J4
Shwegyin	93	J5
Shweli	93	J4
Shyok	92	E2
Siahan Range	92	B3
Siah Koh	95	S5
Sialkot	92	D2
Siargao	91	H4
Siau	91	H5
Siauliai	63	K9
Sibenik	72	C4
Siberut	90	B6
Siberut, Selat	90	B6
Sibi	92	C3
Sibirskaya Nizmennost	84	G2
Sibirtsevo	88	D3
Sibiryakovo, Ostrov	84	B2
Sibiti	106	B3
Sibiu	73	H3
Sibolga	90	B5
Sibsagar	93	H3
Sibsey	55	K3
Sibu	90	E5
Sibut	102	C6
Sibutu	91	F5
Sibutu Passage	91	F5
Sibuyan	91	G3
Sibuyan Sea	91	G3
Sicasica	138	C3
Sichuan	93	K2
Sichuan Pendi	93	L3
Sicie, Cap	65	F7
Sicilia	69	D7
Sicilian Channel	69	C7
Sicily	69	D7
Sicuani	136	C6
Sidatun	88	E3
Sideby	63	J5
Sidheros, Akra	75	J5
Sidhirokastron	75	G2
Sidi Akacha	67	G4
Sidi Barram	102	E1
Sidi Bel Abbes	100	E1
Sidi Ifni	100	C3
Sidi Kacem	100	D2
Sidima	88	E1
Sidlaw Hills	57	E4
Sidmouth	52	D4
Sidmouth, Cape	113	J1
Sidney *Canada*	122	C3
Sidney *Montana, U.S.A.*	123	M4
Sidney *Ohio, U.S.A.*	124	H6
Sidon	94	B5
Sidorovsk	84	C3
Siedlce	71	K2
Siegen	70	C3
Siemiatycze	71	K2
Siem Reap	93	K6
Siena	68	C4
Sieniawa	71	K3
Sierpc	71	H2
Sierra Colorada	139	C8
Sierra Leone	104	C4
Sierra Vista	127	G5
Sierre	68	A2
Sifnos	75	H4
Sifton Pass	118	K4
Sigatoka *Fiji*	114	Q8
Sigatoka *Fiji*	114	Q9
Sigean	65	E7
Sighetu Marmatiei	73	G2
Sighisoara	73	H2
Sigli	90	B4
Siglufjordur	62	V11
Sigmaringen	70	C4
Signy	141	W6
Sigovo	84	D4
Sigtuna	63	G7
Siguenza	66	E2
Siguiri	104	D3
Sigulda	63	L8
Siikajoki	62	L4
Siikavuopio	62	J2
Siilinjarvi	62	M5
Siin	88	E2
Siipyy	63	J5
Siirt	77	J4
Sikar	92	E3
Sikasso	100	D6
Sikeston	124	F8
Sikhote Alin	88	E3
Sikinos	75	H4
Sikkim	93	G3
Sil	66	C1
Sila	97	K4
Silchar	93	H4
Sile	76	C2
Silesia	71	G3
Silgarhi	92	F3
Silifke	76	E4
Siligir	84	J3
Siling Co	93	G2
Silistra	73	J3
Silivri	76	C2
Siljan	63	F6
Silkeborg	63	C8
Sillajhuay	138	C3
Sillan, Lough	58	J4
Sillon de Talbert	64	B4
Siloam Springs	128	E2
Silom	114	E2
Silopi	77	K4
Silovayakha	78	L2
Silsbee	128	E5
Silute	63	J9
Silvan	77	J3
Silver Bay	124	E3
Silver City	127	H4
Silvermines Mountains	59	F7
Silver Spring	125	M7
Silverstone	53	F2
Silverton *U.K.*	52	D4
Silverton *U.S.A.*	127	J2
Simanggang	90	E5
Simard, Lac	125	L3
Simareh Karkheh	94	H5
Simav *Turkey*	76	C3
Simav *Turkey*	76	C2
Simayr	96	E8
Simcoe	125	K5
Simcoe, Lake	125	L4
Simeonovgrad	73	H4
Simeulue	90	B5
Simferopol	79	E7
Simi	75	J4
Simiti	136	C2
Simitli	73	G5
Simla	92	E2
Simleu Silvaniei	73	G2
Simmern	70	B3
Simojarvi	62	M3
Simojoki	62	L4
Simonka	71	J4
Simplicio Mendes	137	J5
Simplon Pass	68	B2
Simpson Bay	119	N2
Simpson Desert	113	H3
Simpson Peninsula	120	J4
Simrishamn	63	F9
Simsor	77	J3
Simushir, Ostrov	85	S7
Sinabang	90	B5
Sinabung	90	B5
Sinac	72	C3
Sinafir	96	B3
Sinaia	73	H3
Sinai Peninsula	103	F2
Sinaloa	130	F4
Sinanaj	74	E2
Sinaxtla	131	L9
Sincan *Turkey*	76	E3
Sincan *Turkey*	77	G3
Since	133	K10
Sincelejo	136	B2
Sinclair's Bay	56	E2
Sind	92	E3
Sinda	88	F1
Sindal	63	D8
Sindangbarang	90	D7
Sindel	73	J4
Sindhuli Garhi	92	G3
Sindirgi	76	C3
Sindominic	73	H2
Sindor	78	J3
Sind Sagar Doab	92	D2
Sinegorye	78	J4
Sinelnikovo	79	F6
Sines	66	B4
Sines, Cabo de	66	B4
Sinetta	62	L3
Sinfra	104	D4
Singa	103	F5
Singapore	90	C5
Singaraja	90	F7
Sing Buri	93	K6
Singida	107	F3
Singitikos, Kolpos	75	G2
Singkang	91	G6
Singkawang	90	D5
Singkep	90	C6
Singleton	53	G4
Singleton, Mount	112	G3
Singosan	87	P4
Siniatsikon	75	F2
Siniscola	69	B5
Sinj	72	D4
Sinjai	91	G7
Sinjajevina	72	E4
Sinjar	77	J4
Sinkat	103	G4
Sinnamary	137	G2
Sinnes	63	B7
Sinni	69	F5
Sinnicolau Mare	72	F2
Sinoe	104	D4
Sinoe, Lacul	73	K3
Sinop	76	F2
Sinpo	88	B5
Sinpung-dong	88	B5
Sintang	90	E5
Sint Maarten	133	R5
Sinton	128	D6
Sintra	66	B3
Sinu	136	B2
Sinuiju	87	N4
Sinyavka	71	M2
Sinyaya	63	N8
Siocon	91	G4
Siofok	72	E2
Sion	68	A2
Sionascaig, Loch	56	C2
Sion Mills	58	H3
Sioule	65	E5
Sioux City	124	B5
Sioux Falls	123	R6
Sioux Lookout	119	S5
Sipalay	91	G4
Siping	87	N3
Sip Song Chau Thai	93	K4
Sipul	114	D3
Sipura	90	B6
Siquia	132	E8
Siquijor	91	G4
Sira *India*	92	E6
Sira *Norway*	63	B7
Sir Abu Nuayr	97	M4
Siracusa	69	E7
Sirajganj	93	G4
Sir Alexander, Mount	119	M5
Siran	77	H2
Sir Bani Yas	97	L4
Sir Edward Pellew Group	113	H2
Siret *Romania*	73	J2
Siret *Romania*	73	J2
Sirhan, Wadi	94	D6
Siri Kit Dam	93	K5
Sirik, Tanjung	90	E5
Sir James McBrien, Mount	118	R3
Sirjan, Kavir-e	95	L6
Sirk	95	N8
Sirna	75	J4
Sirnal	77	K4
Sirohi	92	D4
Siros *Greece*	75	H4
Siros *Greece*	75	H4
Sirri	95	M9
Sirr, Nafud as	96	G4
Sirsa	92	D3
Sir Sanford, Mount	122	F2
Sirsi	92	D6
Sirte	101	J2
Sirte, Gulf of	101	J2
Sirvan	77	K3
Sisak	72	D3
Sisaket	93	K5
Sisophon	93	K6
Sisseton	123	R5
Sissonne	64	E4
Sistan	95	P8
Sistan, Daryacheh-ye-	95	Q6
Sisteron	65	F6
Sistig-Khem	84	F6
Sistranda	62	C5
Sitamau	92	E4
Sitapur	92	F3
Sitges	67	G2
Sithonia	75	G2
Sitia	75	J5
Sitian	86	F3
Sitidgi Lake	118	J2
Sitio da Abadia	138	H6
Sitka	118	H6
Sittang	93	J5
Sittingbourne	53	H3
Sittwe	93	H4
Situbondo	90	E7
Siuri	93	G4
Siuruanjoki	62	M4
Sivas	77	G3
Sivasli	76	C3
Siverek	77	H4
Siverskiy	63	P7

Name	Page	Grid
Sivrice	77	H3
Sivrihisar	76	D3
Sivrihisar Daglari	76	D3
Sivuk	85	Q6
Siwa	102	E2
Siwalik Range	92	F3
Siwan	92	F3
Si Xian	87	M5
Sixmilebridge	59	E7
Sixpenny Handley	53	E4
Siya	78	G3
Siyal Islands	96	C5
Sizin	84	F6
Sjælland	63	D9
Sjorup	63	C8
Skadarsko Jezero	74	E1
Skadovsk	79	E6
Skafta	62	V13
Skagafjordur	62	V12
Skagaflos	62	T12
Skagen	63	D8
Skaggerak	63	C8
Skagit	122	D3
Skagway	118	H4
Skaill	56	F2
Skala-Podolskaya	73	J1
Skanderborg	63	C8
Skanor	63	E9
Skansholm	62	G4
Skantzoura	75	H3
Skara	63	E7
Skaraborg	63	E7
Skarbak	63	C9
Skard	62	V12
Skardu	92	E1
Skarnes	63	D6
Skattkarr	63	E7
Skaudvile	63	K9
Skaulo	62	J3
Skawina	71	H4
Skeena	118	K5
Skeena Mountains	118	K4
Skegness	55	K1
Skeidararsandur	62	W13
Skelda Ness	56	A2
Skelleftea	62	J4
Skelleftealven	62	H4
Skelmersdale	55	G3
Skelton	55	J2
Skerpioenpunt	108	D5
Skerries	58	K5
Skerries, The	54	E3
Skhiza	75	F4
Ski	63	D7
Skiathos	75	G3
Skibbereen	59	D9
Skiddaw	55	F2
Skidegate	118	J5
Skidel	71	L2
Skien	63	C7
Skierniewice	71	J3
Skiftet Kihti	63	J6
Skikda	101	G1
Skipton	55	G3
Skiropoula	75	H3
Skiros *Greece*	75	H3
Skiros *Greece*	75	H3
Skive	63	C8
Skjakerhatten	62	E4
Skjalfandafljot	62	W12
Skjalfandi	62	W11
Skjern	63	C9
Skjervoy	62	J1
Sklad	85	L2
Skoghall	63	E7
Skole	71	K4
Skomer Island	53	B3
Skopelos *Greece*	75	G3
Skopelos *Greece*	75	G3
Skopelos Kaloyeroi	75	H3
Skopin	79	F5
Skopje	73	F4
Skopun	62	Z14
Skorodum	84	A5
Skorovatn	62	E4
Skoruvik	62	X11
Skovde	63	E7
Skovorodino	85	L6
Skowhegan	125	R4
Skreia	63	D6
Skudenshavn	63	D6
Skulgam	62	H2
Skull	59	C9
Skulyany	73	J2
Skuodas	63	J8
Skutec	70	F4
Skutskar	63	G6
Skvira	79	D6
Skwierzyna	70	F2
Skye	56	B3
Skyring, Peninsula	139	B9
Skyring, Seno	139	B10
Slagelse	63	D9
Slagnas	62	H4
Slamannan	57	E5
Slamet, Gunung	90	D7
Slane	58	J5
Slaney	59	J8
Slany	70	F3
Slapin, Loch	57	B3
Slatina	73	H3
Slave	119	N4
Slave Lake	119	N4
Slavgorod *Russia*	84	*B6*
Slavgorod *Ukraine*	79	F6
Slavo	85	Q6
Slavyanka	88	C4
Slavyansk	79	F6
Slavyansk-na-Kubani	79	F6
Slawno	71	G1
Slawoborze	70	F2
Slea	55	J3
Sleaford	53	G2
Sleat, Sound of	57	C3
Sleetmute	118	D3
Sleights	55	J2
Slidell	128	H5
Slieve Anieren	58	G4
Slieveanorra	58	K2
Slieveardagh Hills	59	G7
Slieve Aughty Mountains	59	E6
Slieve Beagh	58	H4
Slieve Bloom Mountains	59	G6
Slieve Callan	58	C4
Slieve Car	58	C4
Slieve Donard	58	L4
Slieve Elva	59	D6
Slieve Gamph	58	E4
Slieve Kimalta	59	F7
Slieve League	58	E3
Slieve Mish Mountains	59	C8
Slieve Miskish	58	C9
Slieve Na Calliagh	58	H5
Slieve Rushen	58	G4
Slieve Snaght	58	H2
Sligo *Ireland*	58	E4
Sligo *Ireland*	58	F4
Sligo Bay	58	E4
Slioch	56	C3
Slipper Island	115	E2
Sliven	73	J4
Slobodchikovo	78	H3
Slobodka	73	K2
Slobodskoy	78	J4
Slobodzeya	73	K2
Slobozia *Romania*	73	H3
Slobozia *Romania*	73	J3
Slonim	71	L2
Slot, The	114	J6
Slough	53	G3
Sluch	79	D5
Slunj	72	C3
Slupsk	71	G1
Slussfors	62	G4
Slutsk	79	D5
Slyne Head	59	B6
Slyudyanka	84	G6
Smaland	63	F8
Smallwood Reservoir	121	P7
Smcanli	76	D3
Smederevo	73	F3
Smela	79	E6
Smethwick	53	E2
Smidovich	88	D1
Smiltene	63	M8
Smirnykh	85	Q7
Smith Arm	118	L2
Smith Bay *Canada*	120	L2
Smith Bay *U.S.A.*	118	E1
Smithfield *N. Carolina, U.S.A.*	129	N3
Smithfield *Utah, U.S.A.*	122	J7
Smith Island	121	L5
Smith Mount Lake	125	L8
Smiths Falls	125	N4
Smith Sound	120	M2
Smithton	113	K7
Smjorfjoll	62	X12
Smoky	119	M4
Smoky Cape	113	L5
Smoky Falls	121	K7
Smoky Hill	123	R8
Smoky Hills	123	Q8
Smola	62	C5
Smolenka	79	H5
Smolensk	78	E5
Smolikas	75	F2
Smolyan	73	H5
Smolyaninovo	88	D4
Smooth Rock Falls	125	K2
Smorgon	71	M1
Smotrich	73	J1
Smyrna	76	B3
Snaefell	54	E2
Snafell	62	X12
Snafellsjokull	62	T12
Snaith	55	H3
Snake	122	E4
Snake Range	122	G8
Snake River Plain	122	H6
Snap Point	132	J3
Snap, The	56	B1
Snares Islands	111	Q11
Snasa	62	E4
Snasavatn	62	E4
Sndre Isortoq	120	R4
Sndre Strmfjord	120	R4
Sndre Sund	120	Q3
Sneek	64	F2
Sneem	59	C9
Snettisham	53	H2
Snezka	70	F3
Sneznik	72	C3
Sniardwy, Jezioro	71	J2
Snina	71	K4
Snizort, Loch	56	B3
Snodland	53	H3
Snohetta	62	C5
Snoqualmie Pass	122	D4
Snoul	93	L6
Snowdon	54	E3
Snowtown	113	H5
Snowville	122	H7
Snowy, Mount	122	G3
Snug Corner	133	L3
Snyatyn	73	H1
Snyder	127	M4
Soalala	109	J3
Soalara	109	H4
Soan Kundo	87	P5
Soa Pan	108	E4
Soar	53	F2
Soa-Siu	91	H5
Soavinandriana	109	J3
Soay	57	B3
Soay Sound	57	B3
Sobat	103	F6
Sobinka	78	F4
Sobopol	85	M3
Sobradinho, Barragem de	137	J5
Sobrado	137	G5
Sobral *Acre, Brazil*	136	C5
Sobral *Ceara, Brazil*	137	J4
Sobv'yevsk	85	K7
Soca	72	B2
Socha	136	C2
Sochi	79	F7
Societe, Iles de la	143	H5
Socorro *Colombia*	136	C2
Socorro *U.S.A.*	127	J4
Socorro, Isla	130	D8
Socotra	97	P10
Soda Lake	126	D3
Sodankyla	62	M3
Soda Springs	122	J6
Soderala	63	G6
Soderhamn	63	G6
Soderkoping	63	G7
Sodermanland	63	G7
Sodertalje	63	G7
Sodra Ratansbyn	62	F5
Soe	91	G7
Soest	70	C3
Sofia *Bulgaria*	73	G4
Sofia *Madagascar*	109	J3
Sofiya	73	G4
Sofiysk	85	P6
Sogamoso *Colombia*	136	C2
Sogamoso *Colombia*	136	C2
Sogndalsfjora	63	B6
Sognefjorden	63	A6
Sogn og Fjordan	63	B6
Sogod	91	G3
Sogut *Turkey*	76	C4
Sogut *Turkey*	76	D2
Sogutlu	76	D2
Sog Xian	93	H2
Sohag	103	F2
Sohano	114	E3
Sohela	92	F4
Sohuksan	87	P5
Soissons	64	E4
Sojat	92	D3
Sojotan Point	91	G4
Sokal	71	L3
Soke	76	B4
Soko Banja	73	F4
Sokode	104	F4
Sokol	78	G4
Sokolo	100	D6
Sokolovka	88	D4
Sokolow Podlaski	71	K2
Sokoto *Nigeria*	105	F3
Sokoto *Nigeria*	105	G3
Sola	71	H4
Solander Island	115	A7
Solapur	92	E5
Sol, Costa del	66	D4
Soledad	133	K9
Soledade	136	D5
Solen	63	D6
Solent, The	52	F4
Solhan	77	J3
Soligorsk	79	D5
Solihull	53	F2
Solikamsk	78	K4
Sollletsk	79	J5
Solimoes	136	E4
Solingen	70	B3
Solleftea	62	G5
Soller	67	H3
Solnechnogorsk	78	F4
Solo	90	E7
Solobkovtsy	73	J1
Solok	90	D6
Solomon	123	Q8
Solomon Islands	114	J5
Solon Springs	124	E3
Solontsovo	85	K6
Solor, Kepulauan	91	G7
Solothurn	68	A2
Solotobe	86	B3
Solovyevsk	85	L6
Solta	72	D4
Soltanabad	95	P3
Soltaniyeh	94	J3
Soltau	70	C2
Soltsy	78	E4
Solvesborg	63	F8
Solway Firth	55	F2
Solwezi	106	E5
Soma	76	B3
Soma	89	H7
Somalia	103	J6
Sombor	72	E3
Sombrerete	130	H6
Sombrero Channel	93	H7
Somerset *Kentucky, U.S.A.*	124	H8
Somerset *Pennsylvania, U.S.A.*	125	L6
Somerset *U.K.*	52	D3
Somerset East	108	E6
Somerset Island	120	H3
Somerton	52	E3
Somerville Reservoir	128	D5
Somes	73	G2
Somes Point	115	F6
Somme	64	D3
Sommerda	70	D3
Somosomo	114	S8
Sompolno	71	H2
Somport, Puerto de	67	F1
Somuncura, Meseta de	139	C8
Son	92	F4
Sonakh	85	P6
Sonapur	92	F4
Sonara	127	M5
Sonderborg	63	C9
Sondre Strmfjord	120	R4
Sondrio	68	B2
Songea	107	G5
Songhua	88	B2
Songhua Jiang	87	P2
Songjin	88	B5
Songkhla	93	K7
Songololo	106	B4
Sonhat	92	F4
Sonid-Youqi	87	L3
Sonid Zuoqi	87	L3
Sonipat	92	E3
Sonkajarvi	62	M5
Sonkovo	78	F4
Son La	93	K4
Sonmiani	92	C3
Sonmiani Bay	92	C3
Sonoita	126	F5
Sonora	126	G6
Sonoran Desert	126	F4
Sonsonate	132	C8
Sonsorol Island	91	J4
Son Tay	93	L4
Sooghemeghat	118	B3
Sopi, Tanjung	91	H5
Sopot	71	H1
Sopron	72	D2
Sopur	92	D2
Sor	66	B3
Sora	69	D5
Sorada	92	F5
Soraker	62	G5
Sorata	138	C3
Sorbas	67	E4
Sore	65	C6
Sorel	125	P3
Sorgun	76	F3
Soria	66	E2
Sorisdale	57	B4
Sorka	78	F4
Sorkh, Kuh-e	95	M5
Sormjole	62	J5
Sorocaba	138	G4
Sorochinsk	79	J5
Soroki	79	D6
Sorong	91	J6
Sorot	63	N7
Soroti	107	F2
Soroya	62	K1
Soroysundet	62	K1
Sorraia	66	B3
Sorrento	69	E5
Sorsele	62	G4
Sorso	69	B5
Sorsogon	91	G3
Sortavala	63	P6
Sortland	62	F2
Sor-Trondelag	62	D6
Sorvagsvatn	62	Z14
Sorvagur	62	Z14
Sorvar	62	K1
Sorvattnet	63	E5
Sos del Rey-Catolico	67	F1
Sosnogorsk	78	J3
Sosnovka	84	H6
Sosnovo	63	P6
Sosnovo-Ozerskoye	85	J6
Sosnowiec	71	H3
Sosunova, Mys	88	G2
Sosva	84	Ad5
Sotik	107	G3
Sotra	63	A6
Sotuelamos	66	E3
Soubre	104	D4
Soudan	113	H3
Souflion	75	J2
Souk Ahras	101	G1
Soumntam	67	J4
Sour	94	B5
Sour al Ghozlane	67	H4
Soure	137	H4
Souris *Manitoba, Canada*	123	P3
Souris *Prince Edward Island, Canada*	121	P8
Sousse	101	H1
South Africa, Republic of	108	D6
Southampton *U.K.*	53	F4
Southampton *U.S.A.*	125	P6
Southampton Island	120	K5
Southampton Water	53	F4

South Andaman **93** H6
South Baldy **127** J4
South Baymouth **124** J4
South Bend *Indiana, U.S.A.* **124** G6
South Bend *Washington, U.S.A.* **122** C4
South Benfleet **53** H3
Southborough **53** H3
South Boston **125** L8
South Canadian **128** D3
South Cape *Fiji* **114** R8
South Cape *U.S.A.* **126** T11
South Carolina **129** M3
South China Sea **87** L7
South Creake **53** H2
South Dakota **123** N5
South Dorset Downs **52** E4
South Downs **53** G4
Southeast Cape **118** B3
South East Cape **113** K6
Southend **119** Q4
Southend-on-Sea **53** H3
Southern Alps **115** C5
Southern Cross **112** D5
Southern Indian Lake **119** R4
Southern Pine Hills **128** H5
Southern Pines **129** N3
Southern Uplands **57** E5
Southery **53** H2
South Esk **57** E4
South Foreland **53** J3
South Forty Foot Drain **53** G2
South Geomagnetic Pole **141** H3
South Georgia **139** J10
South Glamorgan **52** D3
South Harbour **56** A2
South Haven **124** G5
South Hayling **53** G4
South Henik Lake **119** R3
South Hill **125** L8
South Korea **87** P4
South Lake Tahoe **126** C1
South Magnetic Pole **141** K5
Southminster **53** H3
South Molton **52** D3
South Morar **57** C4
South Nahanni **118** K3
South Negril Point **132** H5
South Orkney Islands **141** W4
South Platte **123** N7
South Point **133** K3
South Pole **141** A1
Southport **55** F3
South River **125** L4
South Ronaldsay **56** F2
South Sandwich Islands **141** Y7
South Saskatchewan **123** L2
South Seal **119** R4
South Shields **55** H2
South Sister **122** D5
South Skirlaugh **55** J3
South Sound **59** C6
South Taranaki Bight **115** E3
South Twin Island **121** K7
South Tyne **55** G2
South Uist **56** A3
Southwell **55** J3
Southwest Bay **139** J10
Southwest Cape **115** A7
South West Cape **113** K7
South-west Miramichi **121** N8
Southwold **53** J2
South Woodham Ferrers **53** H3
South Yemen **97** J8
South Yorkshire **55** H3
South Zeal **52** D4
Sovata **73** H2
Sovets **78** H4
Sovetsk **71** J1
Sovetskaya Gavan **88** H1
Soya-Kaikyo **88** J3
Soya-misaki **88** H3
Soyana **78** G2
Soylemez **77** J3
Soyo **106** B4
Sozopol **73** J4
Spa **64** F3
Spain **66** D2
Spalato **72** D4
Spalding **53** G2
Spaldwick **53** G2
Spanish Town **132** J5
Sparkford **52** E3
Sparks **122** E8
Sparta **75** G4
Spartanburg **129** M3
Spartel, Cap **100** D1
Sparti **75** G4
Spartivento, Capo *Italy* **69** B6
Spartivento, Capo *Italy* **69** F7
Sparwood **122** G3
Spas Demensk **78** E5
Spasskaya Guba **78** E3
Spassk Dalniy **88** D3
Spatha, Akra **75** G5
Spean Bridge **57** D4
Spearfish **123** N5
Spence Bay **120** H4
Spencer *Indiana, U.S.A.* **124** G7
Spencer *Iowa, U.S.A.* **124** C5
Spencer *W. Virginia, U.S.A.* **125** K7
Spencer, Cape **113** H6
Spencer Gulf **113** H5
Spences Bridge **122** D2
Spennymoor **55** H2
Spenser Mountains **115** D5
Sperrin Mountains **58** H3
Spessart **70** C3
Spetsai **75** G4
Spey **56** E3
Spey Bay **56** E3
Speyer **70** C4
Spicer Islands **120** L4
Spiddle **59** D6
Spiekeroog **70** B2
Spiez **68** A2
Spili **75** H5
Spilsby **55** K3
Spinazzola **69** F5
Spithead **53** F4
Spitsbergen **80** C2
Spittal **68** D2
Spittal of Glenshee **57** E4
Spjelkavik **62** B5
Split **72** D4
Spokane *U.S.A.* **122** E4
Spokane *U.S.A.* **122** F4
Spoleto **69** D4
Spooner **124** E4
Spornoye **85** S4
Spremberg **70** F3
Spring **124** C8
Springbok **108** C5
Springdale *Canada* **121** Q8
Springdale *U.S.A.* **128** E2
Springer **127** K2
Springerville **127** H3
Springfield *New Zealand* **115** C5
Springfield *Colorado, U.S.A.* **127** L2
Springfield *Illinois, U.S.A.* **124** F7
Springfield *Massachusetts, U.S.A.* **125** P5
Springfield *Missouri, U.S.A.* **124** D8
Springfield *Ohio, U.S.A.* **124** J7
Springfield *Oregon, U.S.A.* **122** C5
Springfield *Tennessee, U.S.A.* **129** J2
Springfield *Vermont, U.S.A.* **125** P5
Springfontein **108** E6
Spring Garden **136** F2
Spring Mountains **126** E2
Springs **108** E5
Springs Junction **115** D5
Spruce Knob **125** L7
Spurn Head **55** K3
Squamish **122** C3
Squillace, Golfo di **69** F6
Srbica **72** F4
Srebrnica **72** E3
Sredhiy **85** S5
Sredinnyy Khrebet **85** U5
Sredna Gora **73** H4
Srednekolymsk **85** S3
Sredne Olekma **85** L5
Sredne Russkaya Vozvyshennost **79** F5
Sredne-Sibirskoye Ploskogorye **84** H3
Sredneye Kuyto, Ozero **62** P4
Sredni Rodopi **73** H5
Sredniy Kalar **85** K5
Sremska Mitrovica **72** E3
Sretensk **85** K6
Sre Umbell **93** K6
Srikakulam **92** F5
Sri Lanka **92** F7
Srinagar **92** D2
Sroda **71** G2
Sroda Slaska **71** G3
Stack, Loch **56** D2
Stade **70** C2
Stadhampton **53** F3
Stadthagen **70** C2
Staffin **56** B3
Stafford **53** E2
Staffordshire **53** F2
Staines **53** G3
Staintondale **55** J2
Stakhanov **79** F6
Stalac **73** F4
Stalham **53** J2
Stalingrad **79** G6
Stalybridge **55** G3
Stamford *Australia* **113** J3
Stamford *Connecticut, U.S.A.* **125** P6
Stamford *New York, U.S.A.* **125** N5
Stamford *Texas, U.S.A.* **127** N4
Stamford *U.K.* **53** G2
Stamford Bridge **55** J3
Stamfordham **57** G5
Stampiky **109** J3
Stamsund **62** E2
Standerton **108** E5
Standish *U.K.* **55** G3
Standish *U.S.A.* **124** J4
Stanford **123** J4
Stanford-le-Hope **53** H3
Stanger **108** F5
Stanhope **55** G2
Stanislav **71** L4
Stanke Dimitrov **73** G4
Stanley *Durham, U.K.* **55** H2
Stanley *Falkland Islands, U.K.* **139** E10
Stanley *U.S.A.* **123** N3
Stanley *Zaire* **107** E2
Stanley Mission **119** Q4
Stanleyville **106** E2
Stann Creek **132** C6
Stanos **75** F3
Stanovoye Nagorye **85** J5
Stanovoy Khrebet **85** L5
Stansted **53** H3
Stanthorpe **113** L4
Stanton **53** H2
Stapleford **53** F3
Stara Planina **73** G4
Staraya Russa **78** E4
Staraya Vorpavla **84** Ae4
Stara Zagora **73** H4
Starcross **52** D4
Stargard **70** F2
Starikovo **85** R2
Starke **129** L6
Starkville **128** H4
Starmyri **62** X12
Starnberg **70** D5
Starnberger See **70** D5
Staroaleyskoye **84** C6
Starobelsk **79** F6
Starodub **79** E5
Starodubskoye **88** J2
Starogard **71** H2
Starokazachye **73** K2
Starokonstantinov **79** D6
Starominskaya **79** F6
Starosielce **71** K2
Start Bay **52** D4
Start Point *Devon, U.K.* **52** D4
Start Point *Orkney Is., U.K.* **56** F1
Stary Sacz **71** J4
Staryy Oskol **79** F5
Staryy Sambor **71** K4
State College **125** M6
Staten Island **139** D10
Statesboro **129** M4
Statesville **129** M3
Staunton *U.K.* **52** E3
Staunton *U.K.* **52** E3
Staunton *U.S.A.* **125** L7
Staunton on Wye **52** E2
Stavanger **63** A7
Staveley *Cumbria, U.K.* **55** G2
Staveley *Derbyshire, U.K.* **55** H3
Staveley *N. Yorkshire, U.K.* **55** H2
Stavelot **64** F3
Stavropol **79** G6
Stavropolskaya Vozvyshennost **79** G6
Stawiski **71** K2
Staxton **55** J2
Steensby Inlet **120** L3
Steensby Peninsula **120** J3
Steens Mountain **122** E6
Steenstrups Glacier **120** Q2
Steeping **55** K3
Steere, Mount **112** D3
Stefanesti **73** J2
Stefansson Island **120** E3
Stege **63** E9
Steigerwald **70** D4
Steinbach **123** R3
Steinhuder Meer **70** C2
Steinkjer **62** D4
Stellenbosch **108** C6
Steller, Mount **118** G3
Stenay **64** F4
Stendal **70** D2
Stenhousemuir **57** E4
Stenness **56** A1
Stenness, Loch of **56** E2
Stentrask **62** H3
Stepan **71** M3
Stepanakert **94** H2
Stephens, Cape **115** D4
Stephenville *Canada* **121** Q8
Stephenville *U.S.A.* **128** C4
Stepnogorsk **84** A6
Stepnyak **84** A6
Sterkstroom **108** E6
Sterlibashevo **78** K5
Sterling *Colorado, U.S.A.* **123** N7
Sterling *Illinois, U.S.A.* **124** F6
Sterling Heights **124** J5
Sterlitamak **78** K5
Steshevskaya **78** F3
Stettin **70** F2
Steubenville **125** K6
Stevenage **53** G3
Stevens Point **124** F4
Stevenston **57** D5
Stewart **118** H3
Stewart Island **115** A7
Stewart Islands **111** P3
Stewarton **57** D5
Stewartstown **58** J3
Steynsburg **108** E6
Steyr **68** E1
St-Gildas, Pointe de **65** B5
Stibb Cross **52** C4
Stickford **55** K3
Stikine **118** J4
Stikine Mountains **118** K4
Stilis **75** G3
Stillwater *Minnesota, U.S.A.* **124** D4
Stillwater *Oklahoma, U.S.A.* **128** D2
Stilo, Punta **69** F6
Stinchar **57** D5
Stip **73** G5
Stirling *Australia* **113** G3
Stirling *U.K.* **57** E4
Stirling Range **112** D5
Stjernoya **62** K1
Stjordal **62** D5
Stockach **70** C5
Stockbridge **53** F3
Stockerau **68** F1
Stockholm *Sweden* **63** H7
Stockholm *Sweden* **63** H7
Stockport **55** G3
Stocksbridge **55** H3
Stockton *California, U.S.A.* **126** B2
Stockton *Kansas, U.S.A.* **123** Q8
Stockton Heath **55** G3
Stockton-on-Tees **55** H2
Stockton Plateau **127** L5
Stode **62** G5
Stoer, Point of **56** C2
Stoke Ferry **53** H2
Stoke-on-Trent **55** G3
Stokesley **55** H2
Stokes Point **113** J7
Stokhod **71** L3
Stokkseyri **62** U13
Stokmarknes **62** F2
Stolbovoy, Ostrov **85** P2
Stolbtsy **71** M2
Stolica **71** J4
Stolin **79** D5
Stolp **71** G1
Stolsheimen **63** B6
Stone **53** E2
Stonehaven **57** F4
Stonehouse *Gloucestershire, U.K.* **52** E3
Stonehouse *Strathclyde, U.K.* **57** E5
Stony **118** D3
Stora **63** C8
Stora Lulevatten **62** H3
Storavan **62** H4
Storby **63** H6
Stord **63** A7
Store Balt **63** D9
Store Heddinge **63** E9
Storen **62** D5
Storjord **62** F3
Storlien **62** E5
Storm Bay **113** K7
Storm Lake **124** C5
Stornoway **56** B2
Storozhevsk **78** J3
Storozhinets **73** H1
Storr, The **56** B3
Storsjon **62** F5
Storslett **62** J2
Storsteinfjellet **62** G2
Stort **53** H3
Storuman *Sweden* **62** G4
Storuman *Sweden* **62** G4
Stosch, Isla **139** A9
Stour *Dorset, U.K.* **53** E4
Stour *Suffolk, U.K.* **53** H3
Stourbridge **53** E2
Stourport-on-Severn **52** E2
Stowmarket **53** J2
Stow-on-the-Wold **53** F3
Stoyba **85** N6
Stozac **72** E4
Strabane **58** H3
Strachur **57** C4
Stradbroke **53** J2
Strait of Belle Isle **121** Q7
Strakonice **70** E4
Stralsund **70** E1
Strand **108** C6
Stranda **62** B5
Strandhill **58** E4
Strangford **58** L4
Strangford Lough **58** L4
Strangnas **63** G7
Stranorlar **58** G3
Stranraer **54** D2
Strasbourg **64** G4
Strasheny **73** K2
Strasswalchen **68** D2
Stratfield Mortimer **53** F3
Stratford *Canada* **125** K5
Stratford *New Zealand* **115** E3
Stratford *U.S.A.* **127** L2
Stratford-upon-Avon **53** F2
Strathaven **57** D5
Strathblane **57** D5
Strathbogie **56** F3
Strath Carron **56** D3
Strathclyde **57** D5
Strath Dearn **56** E3
Strath Earn **57** E4
Strath Halladale **56** E2
Strathmore *Canada* **122** H2
Strathmore *Highland, U.K.* **56** D2
Strathmore *Tayside, U.K.* **57** F4
Strath Naver **56** D2
Strath of Kildonan **56** E2
Strath Oykel **56** D2
Strath Spey **56** E3
Strathy Point **56** D2
Stratos **75** F3
Stratton *U.K.* **52** C4
Stratton *U.S.A.* **125** Q4
Straubing **70** E4
Straumnes **62** T11
Straumsjoen **62** F2
Strausberg **70** E2
Strawberry Mountains **122** E5
Strawberry Reservoir **122** J7
Streaky Bay *Australia* **113** G5
Streaky Bay *Australia* **113** G5
Streator **124** F6

Strehaia	73	G3	Sukhona	78	G3	Suqutra	97	P10	Svrljig	73	G4

Strehaia 73 G3
Strela 70 E4
Strelka-Chunya 84 G4
Stretford 55 G3
Stretton 53 G2
Streymoy 62 Z14
Strezhevoy 84 B4
Strimasund 62 F3
Strimon 75 G2
Strimonikos, Kolpos 75 G2
Strokestown 58 F5
Strolka 84 E5
Stroma 56 E2
Stromboli, Isola 69 E6
Stromness 56 E2
Stromsburg 123 R7
Stromstad 63 D7
Stromsund 62 F5
Stroms Vattudal 62 F4
Strongoli 69 F6
Stronsay 56 F1
Stronsay Firth 56 F1
Strontian 57 C4
Strood 53 H3
Stropkov 71 J4
Stroud 52 E3
Struer 63 C8
Struga 72 F5
Strugi Krasnye 63 N7
Struma 73 G4
Strumble Head 52 B2
Strumica 73 G5
Stryama 73 H4
Stryn 63 B6
Stryy 79 C6
Strzyzow 71 J4
Stuart Florida, U.S.A. 129 M7
Stuart Nebraska, U.S.A. 123 Q6
Stuart Island 118 C3
Stuart Lake 118 L5
Stuart, Mount 122 D4
Stung Treng 93 L6
Stura 68 A3
Sturgeon 125 K3
Sturgeon Bay 124 G4
Sturgeon Falls 125 L3
Sturgeon Lake 124 E1
Sturgis 123 N5
Sturovo 71 H5
Sturry 53 J3
Sturt Desert 113 J4
Sturton by Stow 55 J3
Stutterheim 108 E6
Stuttgart U.S.A. 128 G3
Stuttgart Germany 70 C4
Stykkisholmur 62 T12
Styr 71 L3
Suakin 103 G4
Suakin Archipelago 96 D7
Suavanao 114 J5
Subashi 94 J4
Subay, Irq 96 F6
Subei 86 H4
Subi 90 D5
Subiaco 69 D5
Sublette 127 M2
Subotica 72 E2
Suceava 73 J2
Sucha 71 H4
Suchedniow 71 J3
Suck 59 F6
Sucre 138 C3
Suda 78 F4
Sudan 102 E5
Sudbury Canada 125 K3
Sudbury Derbyshire, U.K. 53 F2
Sudbury Suffolk, U.K. 53 H2
Sudety 70 F3
Sudirman, Pegunungan 91 K6
Sudr 96 A2
Sud, Recif du 114 X17
Suduroy 62 Z14
Sudzha 79 F5
Sue 102 E6
Suess Land 120 W3
Suez 103 F2
Suez Canal 103 F1
Suez, Gulf of 103 F2
Suffolk 53 H2
Sufian 94 G2
Sugarloaf Mount 125 Q4
Sugla Golu 76 D4
Sugoy 85 T4
Suhait 87 J4
Suhar 97 N4
Suhbaatar 87 K1
Suhut 76 D3
Suibin 88 C2
Suichuan 93 M3
Suide 87 L4
Suidong 88 D2
Suifenhe 88 C3
Suifen He 88 C4
Suihua 88 A2
Suileng 88 A2
Suining 93 L2
Suiping 93 M2
Suir 59 G8
Suixi 93 M4
Sui Xian 93 M2
Suizhong 87 N3
Suj 87 K3
Sukabumi 90 D7
Sukhinichi 78 F5

Sukhona 78 G3
Sukhumi 79 G7
Sukkertoppen 120 R5
Sukkertoppen Iskappe 120 R4
Sukkur 92 C3
Sukma 92 F5
Sukon 91 G6
Sukpay 88 F2
Sukpay Datani 88 F2
Suksun 78 K4
Sukumo 89 D9
Sulaiman Range 92 C3
Sula, Kepulauan 91 H6
Sulakyurt 76 E2
Sulawesi 91 G6
Sulawesi, Laut 91 G5
Sulaymaniyah 94 G4
Sulby 54 E2
Sulejow 71 H3
Sulina 73 K3
Sulina, Bratul 73 K3
Sulingen 70 C2
Sulitjelma 62 G3
Sullana 136 A4
Sullivan 124 E7
Sullivan Lake 122 J2
Sullom Voe 56 A1
Sullorsuaq 120 R3
Sully 65 E5
Sulmona 69 D4
Sulphur Oklahoma, U.S.A. 128 D3
Sulphur Texas, U.S.A. 128 E4
Sulphur Springs 128 E4
Sultandagi 76 D3
Sultanhani Turkey 76 E3
Sultanhani Turkey 77 F3
Sultanhisar 76 C4
Sultanpur 92 F3
Sulu Archipelago 91 G4
Suluklu 76 E3
Sulu Sea 91 F4
Suly 84 Ae6
Sulz 70 C4
Sulzberger Bay 141 P3
Sumar 94 G5
Sumarokovo 84 D4
Sumatera 90 C6
Sumba 91 F7
Sumbar 95 H2
Sumbawa 91 F7
Sumbawabesar 91 F7
Sumbawanga 107 F4
Sumbe 106 B5
Sumburgh 56 A2
Sumburgh Head 56 A2
Sumedang 90 D7
Sumenep 90 E7
Sumgait 79 H7
Summan, As Saudi Arabia 96 H3
Summan, As Saudi Arabia 97 J5
Summer Isles 56 C2
Summer Lake 122 D6
Summerside 121 P8
Summit Lake 118 L4
Sumner Lake 127 K3
Sumperk 71 G4
Sumprabum 93 J3
Sumter 129 M4
Sumy 79 E5
Sunamganj 93 H3
Sunart, Loch 57 C4
Sunaynah 97 M5
Sunaysilah 77 J5
Sunbury 125 M6
Sunchon 87 P5
Sun City 126 F4
Sundance 123 M5
Sundargarh 92 F4
Sunda, Selat 90 D7
Sunday Strait 112 E2
Sunde 63 D6
Sunderland 55 H2
Sundiken Daglari 76 D3
Sundsvall 62 G5
Sungaipenuh 90 D6
Sungikai 102 E5
Sungurlu 76 F2
Suning 87 M4
Sunland Park 127 J5
Sunlight Peak 127 J2
Sunndalsora 62 C5
Sunne 63 E7
Sunnyside 122 D4
Sunnyvale 126 A2
Suntar 85 K4
Sun Valley 122 G6
Sunwu 87 P2
Sunyani 104 D4
Suoirman, Pegunungan 114 B2
Suomenlahti Finskij Zaliv 63 L7
Suomussalmi 62 N4
Suo-nada 89 C9
Suonenjoki 62 M5
Suoyarvi 78 E3
Supaul 92 G3
Superior Arizona, U.S.A. 126 G4
Superior Nebraska, U.S.A. 123 Q7
Superior Wisconsin, U.S.A. 124 D3
Superior, Lake 124 G3
Suphan Dagi 77 K3
Supiori 91 K6
Suq ash Shuyukh 94 H6
Suqian 87 M5

Suqutra 97 P10
Sur 97 P5
Sura 78 H4
Surab 92 C3
Surabaya 90 E7
Surahammar 63 G7
Surak 95 P9
Surakarta 90 E7
Suran 95 Q8
Surat Australia 113 K4
Surat India 92 D4
Suratgarh 92 D3
Surat Thani 93 J7
Surduc, Pasul 73 G3
Surendranagar 92 D4
Surgeres 65 C5
Surgut 84 A4
Surigao 91 H4
Surigao Strait 91 H3
Surin 93 K6
Suriname 137 F3
Surmene 77 J2
Surnadalsora 62 C5
Surovikino 79 G6
Surrah, Nafud as 96 G5
Surrey 53 G3
Sur Sari 63 M6
Surt 101 J2
Surt, Khalij 101 J2
Surtsey 62 U13
Suruc 77 H4
Suruga-wan 89 G8
Surulangun 90 D6
Susa Italy 68 A3
Susa Japan 89 C8
Susac 72 D4
Susak 72 C3
Susaki 89 D9
Susami 89 E9
Susangerd 94 J6
Susanville 122 D7
Susehri 77 H2
Susitna 118 E3
Suso 93 J7
Susquehanna 125 M6
Susuka 114 H5
Susurluk 76 C3
Susuz 77 K2
Sutculer 76 D4
Sutherland 108 D6
Sutherlin 122 C6
Sutlej 92 D2
Sutterton 53 G2
Sutton 53 G3
Sutton Bridge 53 H2
Sutton Coldfield 53 F2
Sutton in Ashfield 55 H3
Sutton-on-the-Forest 55 H2
Sutton Scotney 53 F3
Suttor 113 K3
Suttsu 88 H4
Sutwik Island 118 D4
Suva 114 R9
Suvasvesi 62 N5
Suverovo 88 E3
Suvorov Island 111 W4
Suwalki 71 K1
Suwannee 129 L6
Suwanose-jima 89 B11
Suwar 77 J5
Suwayqiyah, Hawr as 94 G5
Suweis, Khalij-as- 103 F2
Suwon 87 P4
Suyevatpaul 78 L3
Suyfun 88 C4
Suzaka 89 G7
Suzhou Anhui, China 93 N2
Suzhou Jiangsu, China 87 N5
Suzu 89 F7
Suzu-misaki 89 F7
Suzun 84 C6
Svalbard 80 C2
Svalyava 71 K4
Svappavaara 62 J3
Svarta 63 F7
Svartisen 62 E3
Svarvolthalvoya 62 M1
Svatovo 79 F6
Svatoy Nos, Mys 85 Q2
Svay Rieng 93 L6
Sveg 63 F5
Svelvik 63 D7
Svencioneliai 63 M9
Svendborg 63 D9
Svenstavik 62 F5
Sventoji 63 N8
Sverdlovsk 84 Ad5
Sverdrup Islands 120 G2
Sverdrup, Ostrov 84 B2
Svetlaya 88 G2
Svetlogorsk 79 D5
Svetlograd 79 G6
Svetlyy 85 K5
Svetogorsk 63 N6
Svilajnac 73 F3
Svilengrad 73 J5
Svir 63 M9
Svirtsa 78 E3
Svishtov 73 H4
Svisloc 71 L2
Svitavy 71 G4
Svobodnyy 85 M6
Svolvar 62 F2

Svrljig 73 G4
Svyatoy Nos, Mys 78 H2
Swadlincote 53 F2
Swaffham 53 H2
Swainby 55 H2
Swain Reefs 113 L3
Swainsboro 129 L4
Swains Island 111 U4
Swakop 108 C4
Swakopmund 108 B4
Swale 55 H2
Swaledale 55 H2
Swale, The 53 H3
Swallow Falls 54 F3
Swallow Island 114 N7
Swanage 53 F4
Swan Hill 113 J6
Swan Islands 132 F6
Swankhalok 93 J5
Swanley 53 H3
Swan Reach 113 H5
Swan River 119 Q5
Swansea 52 D3
Swansea Bay 52 D3
Swanton 125 P4
Swatragh 58 F3
Swaziland 109 F5
Sweden 63 F8
Sweet Home 122 C5
Sweetwater Texas, U.S.A. 127 M4
Sweetwater Wyoming, U.S.A. 123 K6
Swellendam 108 D6
Swidnica 71 G3
Swiebodzin 70 F2
Swietokrzyskie, Gory 71 J3
Swift Current 123 L2
Swinburne, Cape 120 G3
Swindon 53 F3
Swinemunde 70 F2
Swineshead 53 G2
Swinoujscie 70 F2
Swinton Borders, U.K. 57 F5
Swinton S. Yorkshire, U.K. 55 H3
Switzerland 68 A2
Swona 56 E2
Swords 59 K6
Syalakh 85 L3
Syamzha 78 G3
Sybil Point 59 B8
Sychevka 78 E4
Sydney Australia 113 L5
Sydney Canada 121 P8
Sydney Lake 123 S2
Sykehouse 55 H3
Syktyvkar 78 J3
Sylacauga 129 J4
Sylene 63 E5
Sylhet 93 H4
Sylt 70 C1
Sylva 78 K4
Sylvania 129 M4
Sym 84 D4
Synya 78 K2
Synzhera 73 K2
Syracuse Italy 69 E7
Syracuse Kansas, U.S.A. 127 M2
Syracuse New York, U.S.A. 125 M5
Syr-Darya 86 C3
Syrdar-ya 80 H5
Syrdaryn 86 B3
Syria 94 C4
Syriam 93 J5
Sysola 78 J3
Syston 53 F2
Sytomino 84 A4
Syumsi 78 J4
Syutkya 73 G5
Syzran 79 H5
Szarvas 72 F2
Szczecin 70 F2
Szczecinek 71 G2
Szczecinski, Zalew 70 F2
Szczekociny 71 H3
Szczucin 71 J3
Szczuczyn 71 K2
Szczytno 71 J2
Szeged 72 F2
Szeghalom 73 F2
Szekesfehervar 72 E2
Szekszard 72 E2
Szentes 72 F2
Szentgotthard 72 D2
Szolnok 72 F2
Szombathely 72 D2
Szprotawa 70 F3

T

Taal, Lake 91 G3
Tabaqah 94 D4
Tabar Islands 114 E2
Tabarka 69 B7
Tabas Iran 95 N5
Tabas Iran 95 Q5
Tabasara, Serrania de 132 G10
Tabashimo 78 H4
Tabatinga, Serra da 137 J6
Tabiteuea 111 R2
Tablas 91 G3
Tablas, Cabo 138 B6
Table Cape 115 G3
Taboleiro 137 K5
Tabor 70 F4

Name	Page	Ref
Tabora	107	F4
Tabou	104	D5
Tabriz	94	H2
Tabuk	96	C2
Tabuka	89	C9
Tabut	97	L9
Tabwemasana	114	T11
Taby	63	H7
Tacheng	86	F2
Tacloban	91	G3
Tacna *Peru*	138	B3
Tacna *U.S.A.*	126	F4
Tacoma	122	C4
Tacora, Cerro de	138	C3
Tacuarembo	138	E6
Tadcaster	55	H3
Tademait, Plateau du	101	F3
Tadjoura	103	H5
Tadmur	77	H5
Tadoule Lake	119	R4
Tadoussac	125	R2
Tadpatri	92	E6
Tadworth	53	G3
Taegu	89	B8
Taehuksan	87	P5
Taejon	87	P4
Taf	52	C3
Tafahi	111	U5
Tafalla	67	F1
Tafassasset	101	G4
Tafassasset, Tenere du	101	H4
Taff	52	D3
Taff, At	97	M4
Tafila	94	B6
Tafi Viejo	138	C5
Tafresh	95	K4
Taft	95	M6
Taftan, Kuh-e-	95	Q7
Taganrog	79	F6
Taganrogskiy Zaliv	79	F6
Tagbilaran	91	G4
Taghmon	59	J8
Tagliamento	68	D3
Tagolo Point	91	G4
Tagounite	100	D3
Tagu	73	H2
Taguatinga	138	H6
Tagudin	91	G2
Tagula	114	E4
Tagula Island	114	E4
Tagum	91	H4
Tagus	66	C3
Tahan, Gunung	90	C5
Tahat, Mont	101	G4
Ta He	87	N1
Tahe	87	N1
Taheri	95	L8
Tahiryuak Lake	119	N1
Tahiti	143	J5
Tahlab, Dasht-i-	92	B3
Tahlequah	128	E3
Tahoe Lake *Canada*	119	P1
Tahoe, Lake *U.S.A.*	122	E8
Tahoka	127	M4
Tahoua	101	G6
Tahrud	95	N7
Tahta	102	F2
Tahtali Daglari	77	G3
Tahuamanu	136	D6
Tahulandang	91	H5
Taian	87	M4
Taibai Shan	93	L2
Taibus Qi	87	M3
Tai-chung	87	N7
Taier	115	C6
Taieri	115	C6
Taigu	87	L4
Taihape	115	E3
Taihe *Anhui, China*	93	N2
Taihe *Jiangxi, China*	93	M3
Tai Hu	87	N5
Taimba	84	F4
Tain	56	D3
Tai-nan	87	N7
Tainaron, Akra	75	G4
Taining	87	M6
Taipale	62	N5
Tai-pei	87	N6
Taiping	90	C5
Taipingbao	86	J4
Taipinggou	88	C1
Taira	89	H7
Taisei	88	G4
Taisha	89	D8
Taitao, Peninsula de	139	B9
Tai-tung	87	N7
Taivalkoski	62	N4
Taiwan	87	N7
Taiwan Haixia	87	M7
Taiyetos Oros	75	G4
Taiyuan	87	L4
Taiza	89	E8
Taizhou	87	M5
Taizz	96	G10
Tajabad	95	M6
Tajikistan	86	B4
Tajima	89	G7
Tajin-dong	88	B5
Tajito	126	F5
Tajo	66	D3
Tajrish	95	K4
Tajumuclo, Volcan de	132	B7
Tajuna	66	E2
Tak	93	J5
Takab	94	H3
Takada	89	G7
Takaka	115	D4
Takamatsu	89	E8
Takanabe	89	C9
Takaoka	89	F7
Takapuna	115	E2
Takasaki	89	G7
Takatshwane	108	D4
Takaungu	107	G3
Takayama	89	F7
Takefu	89	F8
Takengon	90	B5
Takeo	93	K6
Takestan	95	J3
Takhadid	94	G7
Takhi-i-Suleiman	95	K3
Takhta Bazar	95	R4
Takhtabrod	84	Ae6
Takikawa	88	H4
Takinoue	88	J3
Taklimakan Shamo	92	F1
Taku	118	J4
Takum	105	G4
Takwa	114	K6
Talagang	92	D2
Talamanca, Cordillera de	132	F10
Talangbetutu	90	C6
Talara	136	A4
Talar-i-Band	92	B3
Talas	86	C3
Talasea	114	E3
Talaton	52	D4
Talaud, Kepulauan	91	H5
Talavera de la Reina	66	D3
Talayuelas	67	F3
Talbot Inlet	120	L2
Talca	139	B7
Talcahuano	139	B7
Talcher	92	G4
Taldy-Kurgan	86	D2
Talgarth	52	D3
Taliabu	91	G6
Talihina	128	E3
Tali Post	102	F6
Talisay	91	G3
Talitsa	84	Ad5
Taliwang	91	F7
Talkeetna	118	E3
Talkeetna Mountains	118	F3
Talladega	129	J4
Tall Afar	77	K4
Tallahassee	129	K5
Tallinn	63	L7
Tall Kalakh	77	G5
Tall Kayf	77	K4
Tall Kujik	77	K4
Tallow	59	F8
Tall Tamir	77	J4
Talmenka	84	C6
Talnoye	79	E6
Taloda	92	D4
Talodi	102	F5
Talok	91	F5
Talovka	84	E5
Taloye	85	M4
Talsi	63	K8
Taltal	138	B5
Taltson	119	N3
Talu	114	F3
Taluma	85	L5
Talvik	62	K1
Tama	124	D6
Tamabo Range	90	F5
Tamale	104	E4
Tamames	66	C2
Tamana	111	S2
Tamano	89	D8
Tamanrasset *Algeria*	100	F4
Tamanrasset *Algeria*	101	G4
Tamar *Australia*	113	K7
Tamar *U.K.*	52	C4
Tamar, Alto de	133	K11
Tamatave	109	J3
Tamaulipas, Llanos de	128	C8
Tamazunchale	131	K7
Tambacounda	104	C3
Tambangsawah	90	C6
Tambelan, Kepulauan	90	D5
Tambey	84	A2
Tambo	113	K3
Tambora, Gunung	91	F7
Tamboril	137	J4
Tambov	79	G5
Tambre	66	B1
Tambura	102	E6
Tamchaket	100	C5
Tame	136	C2
Tamega	66	C2
Tamiahua, Laguna de	131	L7
Tamil Nadu	92	E6
Tamis	72	F3
Tamit, Wadi	101	J2
Tammerfors	63	M6
Tammisaari	63	K6
Tampa	129	L7
Tampa Bay	129	L7
Tampere	63	M6
Tampico	131	L6
Tamsagbulag	87	M2
Tamuin	131	K7
Tamworth *Australia*	113	L5
Tamworth *U.K.*	53	F2
Tana *Chile*	138	C3
Tana *Kenya*	107	H3
Tana *Norway*	62	M1
Tanabe	89	E9
Tana bru	62	N2
Tanafjorden	62	N1
Tana Hayk	103	G5
Tanahbala	90	B6
Tanahgrogot	90	F6
Tanahjampea	91	G7
Tanahmasa	90	B6
Tanahmerah	114	C3
Tanah Merah	90	C4
Tanami	112	F3
Tanana	118	E2
Tananarive	109	J3
Tanchon	88	B5
Tandag	91	H4
Tandek	91	F4
Tandil	139	E7
Tando Adam	92	C3
Tandragee	58	K4
Taneatua	115	F3
Tanega-shima	89	C10
Tanen Tong Dan	93	J5
Tanew	71	K3
Tanezrouft	100	E4
Tanf, Jbel al	77	H6
Tanga *Tanzania*	107	G4
Tanga *Russia*	85	J6
Tanga Islands	114	E2
Tanganyika, Lake	107	F4
Tangarare	114	J6
Tanger	100	D1
Tanggula Shan	93	G2
Tanggula Shankou	93	H2
Tangra Yumco	92	G2
Tangshan	87	M4
Tangwang He	88	B2
Tangwanghe	88	B1
Tangyuan	88	B2
Tan Hill	53	F3
Tanhua	62	M3
Taniantaweng Shan	93	J2
Tanimbar, Kepulauan	114	A3
Tanjung	90	F6
Tanjungbalai	90	B5
Tanjungkarang Telukbetung	90	D7
Tanjungpandan	90	D6
Tanjungpura	90	B5
Tanjungredeb	91	F5
Tanjungselor	91	F5
Tankapirtti	62	M2
Tankovo	84	D4
Tankse	92	E2
Tanlovo	84	A3
Tanna	114	U13
Tannu Ola	84	E6
Tannurah, Ra's	97	K3
Tanout	101	G6
Tan-shui	87	N6
Tanta	102	F1
Tan-Tan	100	C3
Tantoyuca	131	K7
Tanumshede	63	D7
Tanzania	107	G4
Taoan	87	N2
Tao He	93	K2
Tao, Ko	93	J6
Taolanaro	109	J5
Taormina	69	E7
Taos	127	K2
Taoudenni	100	E4
Taourirt	100	E2
Tapa	63	L7
Tapachula	131	N10
Tapah	90	C5
Tapajos	137	F4
Tapaktuan	90	B5
Tapan	90	D6
Tapanahoni	137	F3
Tapaua	136	D5
Taperoa	137	K6
Tappahannock	125	M8
Tappi-saki	88	H5
Tapsuy	78	L3
Tapti	92	D4
Tapuaenuku	115	D4
Tapul Group	91	G4
Taqah	97	M8
Taqtaq	94	G4
Taquari	138	E3
Taquari, Pantanal do	138	E3
Tara	84	A5
Tarabulus	101	H2
Taradale	115	F3
Tarakan	91	F5
Tarakli	76	D2
Tarakliya	73	K3
Taramana	91	G7
Taramo-jima	89	G11
Taran	84	A2
Tarancon	66	E2
Taransay	56	A3
Taransay, Sound of	56	A3
Taranto	69	F5
Taranto, Golfo di	69	F5
Tarapoto	136	B5
Tararua Range	115	E4
Tarascon	65	F7
Tarasovo	78	H2
Tarauaca *Brazil*	136	C5
Tarauaca *Brazil*	136	C5
Taravo	69	B5
Tarazona	67	F2
Tarazona de la Mancha	67	F3
Tarbagatay, Khrebet	86	E2
Tarbert *Ireland*	59	D7
Tarbert *Strathclyde, U.K.*	57	C5
Tarbert *Western Isles, U.K.*	56	B3
Tarbes	65	D7
Tarbet	57	D4
Tarbolton	57	D5
Tarboro	129	P3
Tarcaului, Muntii	73	J2
Tarcoola	113	G5
Tardienta	67	F2
Tardoki-yani, Gora	88	L1
Taree	113	L5
Tarendo	62	K3
Tareya	84	E2
Tarfa, Ra's at	96	F8
Tarfa, Wadi el	103	F2
Tarfaya	100	C3
Tarfside	57	F4
Targhee Pass	122	J5
Tarhunah	101	H2
Tarif	97	L4
Tarifa	66	D4
Tarija	138	D4
Tariku	114	B2
Tarim	97	J8
Tarim Basin	86	E3
Tarim He	86	E3
Tarim Pendi	86	E3
Taritatu	114	B2
Tarkasale	84	A3
Tarkastad	108	E6
Tarkhankut, Mys	79	E6
Tarkio	124	C6
Tarkwa	104	E4
Tarlac	91	G2
Tarlak	86	E3
Tarleton	55	G3
Tarma	136	B6
Tarn	65	D7
Tarna	72	F2
Tarnaby	62	F4
Tarnobrzeg	71	J3
Tarnow	71	J4
Tarnsjo	63	G6
Taro	68	B3
Taron	114	E2
Taroom	113	K4
Taroudannt	100	D2
Tarporley	55	G3
Tarragona	67	G2
Tarrasa	67	H2
Tarrega	67	G2
Tarsus	76	F4
Tartagal	138	D4
Tartas	65	C7
Tartu	63	P7
Tartung	90	B5
Tartus	94	B4
Tartus	77	F5
Tarutino	73	K2
Tarzout	67	G4
Tasci	77	F3
Tashakta	86	F2
Tashauz	80	G5
Tashigang	93	H3
Tashk, Daryacheh-ye	95	L7
Tashkent	86	B3
Tashkepri	95	R3
Tashla	79	J5
Tashtagol	84	D6
Tasikmalaya	90	D7
Tasiujaq	121	N6
Taskesken	86	E2
Taskopru	76	F2
Tas-Kumsa	85	N3
Taslicay	77	K3
Tasman Bay	115	D4
Tasmania	113	K7
Tasman Mountains	115	D4
Tasnad	73	G2
Tasova	77	G2
Tas-Tumus	85	N2
Tasty	86	B3
Tasucu	76	E4
Tasuj	77	L3
Tataba	91	G6
Tatabanya	72	E2
Tatarbunary	73	K3
Tatarka	84	B6
Tatarsk	84	B5
Tataurovo	85	J6
Tateyama	89	G8
Tathlina Lake	119	M3
Tathlith	96	F7
Tathlith, Wadi	96	F6
Tatnam, Cape	119	S4
Tatry	71	H4
Tatsinskiy	79	G6
Tatsuno	89	E8
Tatta	92	C4
Tatum	127	L4
Tatvan	77	K3
Tau	111	V4
Tauari	137	F4
Taubate	138	G4
Tauchik	79	J7
Taumarunui	115	E3
Taung-gyi	93	J4
Taungnyo Range	93	J5

Name	Page	Grid
Taunton *U.K.*	52	D3
Taunton *U.S.A.*	125	Q6
Taunus	70	C3
Taupo	115	F3
Taupo, Lake	115	E3
Tauq	94	G4
Tauq	77	L5
Taurage	63	K9
Tauranga	115	F2
Tauroa Point	115	D1
Taurus	76	E4
Tauste	67	F2
Tauu Islands	114	F2
Tavalesh, Kuhha-ye	94	J3
Tavana-i-Tholo	111	T6
Tavas	76	C4
Tavda *Russia*	84	Ad5
Tavda *Russia*	84	Ae5
Taverner Bay	120	M4
Taveuni	114	S8
Tavira	66	C4
Tavistock	52	C4
Tavolara, Isola di	69	B5
Tavoy	93	J6
Tavrichanka	88	C4
Tavsanli	76	C3
Tavua	114	Q8
Tavuna-i-Ra	111	T6
Tavy	52	C4
Taw	52	D4
Tawakoni, Lake	128	E4
Tawau	91	F5
Tawe	52	D3
Taweisha	102	E5
Tawila	96	A3
Tawil, At	96	D2
Tawitawi Group	91	G4
Ta-wu	87	N7
Tawurgha, Sabkhat	101	J2
Taxco	131	K8
Taxkorgan	92	E1
Tay	57	E4
Tayandu, Kepulauan	91	J7
Tayastehus	63	L6
Tayeeglow	107	H2
Tay, Firth of	57	E4
Tayga	84	D5
Tayinloan	57	C5
Tay, Loch	57	D4
Taylor	123	Q7
Taylor Island	119	Q2
Taylor, Mount	127	J3
Taylorville	124	F7
Tayma	96	D3
Taymura	84	F4
Taymyr	84	E3
Taymyr, Ozero	84	G2
Taymyr, Poluostrov	84	F2
Tay Ninh	93	L6
Taynuilt	57	C4
Tayport	57	F4
Tayshet	84	F5
Tayshir	86	H2
Tayside	57	E4
Taysiyah, At	96	F2
Taytay	91	F3
Tayyebad	95	Q4
Taz *Russia*	84	B3
Taz *Russia*	84	C3
Taza	100	E2
Tazin Lake	119	P4
Tazirbu	101	K3
Tbilisi	77	L2
Tchad, Lac	102	B5
Tchibanga	106	B3
Tczew	71	H1
Teaca	73	H2
Te Anau	115	A6
Te Anau, Lake	115	A6
Te Anga	115	E3
Te Aroha	115	E2
Te Awamutu	115	E2
Tebesjuak Lake	119	R3
Tebessa	101	G1
Tebingtinggi *Indonesia*	90	B5
Tebingtinggi *Indonesia*	90	C6
Teboursouk	69	B7
Tecate	126	D4
Techirghiol	73	K3
Tecirli	77	G4
Tecoman	130	H8
Tecuci	73	J3
Tedelkynak	84	C4
Tedzhen	95	Q3
Teeapo, Lake	115	C5
Tees	55	H2
Tees Bay	55	H2
Teesdale	55	H2
Tefe *Brazil*	136	D4
Tefe *Brazil*	136	E4
Tefenni	76	C4
Tegal	90	D7
Tegid, Llyn	52	D2
Tegua	114	T10
Tegucigalpa	132	D7
Tehachapi Mountains	126	C3
Tehachapi Pass	126	C3
Te Haroto	115	F3
Tehek Lake	119	R2
Tehert	119	R2
Tehoru	91	H6
Tehran	95	K4
Tehuacan	131	L8
Tehuantepec *Mexico*	131	M9
Tehuantepec *Mexico*	131	M9
Tehuantepec, Golfo de	131	M10
Teign	52	D4
Teignmouth	52	D4
Tejo	66	C3
Te Karaka	115	F3
Tekes	86	E3
Tekeze	96	C9
Tekin	88	D1
Tekirdag	76	B2
Tekman	77	J3
Te Kopuru	115	D2
Te Kuiti	115	E3
Tela	132	D7
Tel Ali	77	K5
Telavi	77	L2
Tel Aviv-Yafo	94	B5
Telegraph Creek	118	J4
Telekhany	71	L2
Telemark	63	C7
Telemba	85	J6
Telen	139	C7
Telen	90	F5
Teleorman	73	H3
Telescope Peak	126	D2
Teles Pires	136	F5
Telford	52	E2
Teli	84	E6
Telimele	104	C3
Tell City	124	G8
Tellicherry	92	E6
Telposiz, Gora	78	K3
Telsen	139	C8
Telsiai	63	K9
Teluk Anson	90	C5
Telukbatang	90	D6
Telukdalam	90	B5
Tem	84	G5
Tema	104	E4
Temagami, Lake	125	K3
Temascaltepec	131	K8
Tembenchi	84	F4
Tembleque	66	E3
Tembo Aluma	106	C4
Teme	52	E2
Temerin	72	E3
Temerloh	90	C5
Temirtau	86	C2
Temiscamingve, Lac	125	L3
Temnikov	78	G5
Temnyy	85	K6
Tempe	126	G4
Tempio Pausania	69	B5
Temple	128	D5
Templemore	59	G7
Tempoal	131	K7
Tempue	106	C5
Temryuk	79	F6
Temuco	139	B7
Temuka	115	C6
Tena	136	B4
Tenali	92	F5
Tenasserim	93	J6
Tenbury Wells	52	E2
Tenby	52	C3
Tende	68	A3
Ten Degree Channel	93	H7
Tendelti	103	F5
Tendrovskaya Kosa	79	E6
Tenduruk Dagi	77	K3
Tenerife	100	B3
Tenes	100	F1
Tenevo	73	J4
Tengahdai	91	G7
Tengchong	93	J3
Tenggarong	90	F6
Tengiz, Ozero	84	Ae6
Teng, Nam	93	J4
Teng Xian	87	M4
Teniente Rodolfo Marsh	141	W6
Tenkasi	92	E7
Tenke	106	E5
Tenkodogo	104	E3
Tennant Creek	113	G2
Tennessee *U.S.A.*	129	H2
Tennessee *U.S.A.*	129	J2
Tennessee Pass	123	L8
Tenniojoki	62	N3
Tenosique	131	P9
Tensift, Oued	100	D2
Tenterden	53	H3
Tenterfield	113	L4
Teofilo Otoni	138	E3
Teouta	114	X16
Tepasto	62	L2
Tepatitlan	130	H7
Tepebasi	76	E4
Tepecikoren	77	F4
Tepeji	131	K8
Tepelene	74	F2
Tepic	130	G7
Teplice	70	E3
Teplik	73	K1
Tepoca, Cabo	126	F5
Te Puke	115	F2
Ter	67	H2
Tera	66	C2
Teramo	69	D4
Terasa	93	H7
Tercan	77	J3
Teren-Uzyak	86	A2
Teresina	137	J5
Teresita	136	D3
Teresopolis	138	H4
Teriberka	78	F2
Terme	77	G2
Termez	80	H6
Termini Imerese	69	D7
Terminillo	69	D4
Terminos, Laguna de	131	P8
Termoli	69	E4
Ternate	91	H5
Terneuzen	64	E3
Terney	88	F3
Terni	69	D4
Ternopol	79	D6
Terpeniya, Mys	85	Q7
Terpeniya, Zaliv	85	Q7
Terrace	118	K5
Terrace Bay	124	G2
Terracina	69	D5
Terrak	62	E4
Terralba	69	B6
Terre Adelie	141	K7
Terre Haute	124	G7
Terrell	128	D4
Terschelling	64	F2
Terskiy Bereg	78	F2
Teruel	67	F2
Terutao	93	J7
Tervel	73	J4
Tervo	62	M5
Teseney	103	G4
Teshekpuk Lake	118	E1
Teshio	88	H3
Teshio-sammyaku	88	H4
Tesica	73	F4
Tesiyn Gol	86	H2
Teslin *Canada*	118	J3
Teslin *Canada*	118	J3
Tesouro	138	F3
Tessalit	100	F4
Tessaoua	101	G6
Test	53	F3
Testa, Capo	69	B5
Testa del Gargano	69	F5
Tet	65	E7
Tetbury	53	E3
Tete	109	F3
Tetepare	114	H6
Tetere	84	G4
Teterow	70	E2
Tetouan	100	D1
Tetovo	73	F4
Te Tungano	114	K7
Teulada	69	B6
Teulada, Capo	69	B6
Teun	91	H7
Tevere	69	D4
Teverya	94	B5
Teviot	57	F5
Tevriz	84	A5
Te Waewae Bay	115	A7
Te Whanga Lagoon	115	F6
Tewkesbury	53	E3
Tewo	93	K2
Texada Islands	122	B3
Texarkana	128	E4
Texas	127	M5
Texas City	128	E6
Texcoco	131	K8
Texel	64	F2
Texoma, Lake	128	D4
Teykovo	78	G4
Teziutlan	131	L8
Tezpur	93	H3
Tha-anne	119	R3
Thabana Ntlenyana	108	E5
Thabazimbi	108	E4
Thadiq	96	G4
Thai Binh	93	L4
Thailand	93	K5
Thailand, Gulf of	93	K7
Thai Nguyen	93	L4
Thakhek	93	K5
Thal	92	D2
Thalab, Dasht-i	95	Q7
Thal Desert	92	D2
Thale Luang	93	K7
Thamarit	97	M8
Thame	53	G3
Thames *Canada*	124	J5
Thames *New Zealand*	115	E2
Thames *U.K.*	53	H3
Thamud	97	J8
Thane	92	D5
Thanet, Isle of	53	J3
Thanh Hoa	93	L5
Thanjavur	92	E6
Thankerton	57	E5
Thann	65	G5
Thano Bula Khan	92	C3
Tharad	92	D4
Thar Desert	92	D3
Thargomindah	113	J4
Tharrawaddy	93	J5
Tharthar	77	K5
Tharthar, Wadi ath	77	K5
Thasos *Greece*	75	H2
Thasos *Greece*	75	H2
Thatcham	53	F3
Thaton	93	J5
Thaungdut	93	H4
Thayetmyo	93	J5
Thazi	93	J4
Thebes	75	G3
Thedford	123	P7
Thelon	119	Q3
Thenia	67	H4
Theniet El Had	67	H5
Theodore Roosevelt Reservoir	126	G4
Thermaikos Kolpos	75	G2
Thermia	75	H4
Thermon	75	F3
Thermopolis	123	K6
Thessalon	124	J3
Thessaloniki	75	G2
Thetford	53	H2
Thetford Mines	125	Q3
Thiamis	75	F3
Thibodaux	128	G6
Thief River Falls	124	B2
Thiel Mountains	141	U1
Thierache	64	F4
Thiers	65	E6
Thies	104	B3
Thiladummathi Atoll	92	D7
Thimbu	93	G3
Thimphu	93	G3
Thio	114	X16
Thionville	64	G4
Thira *Greece*	75	H4
Thira *Greece*	75	H4
Thirasia	75	H4
Thirsk	55	H2
Thisted	63	C8
Thivai	75	G3
Thiviers	65	D6
Thlewiaza	119	R3
Thohoyandou	108	F4
Thomaston	129	K4
Thomastown	59	H7
Thomasville *Alabama, U.S.A.*	129	J5
Thomasville *Georgia, U.S.A.*	129	L5
Thompson *British Columbia, Canada*	119	L5
Thompson *Manitoba, Canada*	119	R4
Thompson *U.S.A.*	124	C6
Thompson Sound	115	A6
Thomson *Australia*	113	J3
Thomson *U.S.A.*	129	L4
Thonon-les-Bains	65	G5
Thornaby	55	H2
Thornbury	52	E3
Thornby	53	F2
Thorndon	53	J2
Thorne	55	J3
Thorney	53	G2
Thornhill	57	E5
Thornley	55	H2
Thornton	55	F3
Thouars	65	C5
Thouet	65	C5
Thrakikon Pelagos	75	H2
Thrapston	53	G2
Three Forks	122	J5
Three Kings Islands	111	R8
Three Points, Cape	104	E5
Three Rivers *Michigan, U.S.A.*	124	H6
Three Rivers *Texas, U.S.A.*	128	C6
Three Sisters Islands	114	K7
Threshfield	55	G2
Throsell Range	112	E3
Thueyts	65	F6
Thuin	64	F3
Thule	120	N2
Thun	68	A2
Thunder Bay	124	F2
Thunder Mount	118	C2
Thung Song	93	J7
Thuringer Wald	70	D3
Thurles	59	G7
Thurloo Downs	113	J4
Thurnscoe	55	H3
Thursby	55	F2
Thurso *U.K.*	56	E2
Thurso *U.K.*	56	E2
Thurston Island	141	T4
Thusis	68	B2
Thwaites Glacier	141	S3
Tiancang	86	H3
Tianchang	87	M5
Tiandong	93	L4
Tiane	93	L3
Tiangua	137	J4
Tianjin	87	M4
Tianjun	93	J1
Tianqiaoling	88	B4
Tianshui	93	L2
Tianyang	93	L4
Tianzhen	87	L3
Tianzhu	93	K1
Tiaret	100	F1
Tibati	105	H4
Tiber	69	D4
Tiberias	94	B5
Tibesti	102	C3
Tibet, Plateau of	92	F2
Tiboku Falls	136	F2
Tiburon, Isla	126	F6
Tichitt	100	D5
Ticino	68	B3
Ticul	131	Q7
Tidaholm	63	E7
Tidjikdja	100	C5
Tieli	88	B2
Tieling	87	N3
Tien Shan	86	D3
Tien Yen	93	L4

Tierp	63	G6	Tirgu Neamt	73	J2	Tokelau	111	U3	Tonstad	63	B7
Tierra Amarilla	127	J2	Tirgu Ocna	73	J2	Tokiwa	88	J3	Tonya	77	H2
Tierra Blanca	131	L8	Tirich Mir	92	D1	Tokke	63	C7	Tooele	122	H7
Tierra del Fuego, Isla			Tirnava Mare	73	H2	Toklar	77	G3	Toowoomba	113	L4
Grande de	139	C10	Tirnava Mica	73	H2	Tokmak	86	D3	Topeka	124	C7
Tietar	66	D2	Tirnavos	75	G3	Tokolon	84	H5	Toplane	74	E1
Tiete	138	F4	Tirol	68	C2	Tokoro	88	K3	Toplica	73	F4
Tifton	129	L5	Tirpul	95	Q4	Tokoroa	115	E3	Toplita	73	H2
Tifu	91	H6	Tirso	69	B6	Toksun	86	F3	Topocalma, Punta	138	B6
Tiger	122	F3	Tirua Point	115	E3	Tok-to	89	C7	Topola	72	F3
Tigharry	56	A3	Tiruchchirappalli	92	E6	Toktogul	86	C3	Topolcani	73	F5
Tigil *Russia*	85	T5	Tirumangalam	92	E7	Tokuno-shima	89	J10	Topoli	79	J6
Tigil *Russia*	85	T5	Tirunelveli	92	E7	Tokushima	89	E8	Topolkki	63	N6
Tignish	121	P8	Tirupati	92	E6	Tokuyama	89	C8	Topolovgrad	73	J4
Tigre *Peru*	136	B4	Tiruppur	92	E6	Tokyo	89	G8	Topozero, Ozero	62	P4
Tigre *Venezuela*	136	E2	Tiruvannamalai	92	E6	Tolar, Cerro	138	C5	Toppenish	122	D4
Tigres, Baia dos	106	B6	Tisa	72	F3	Tolbonuur	86	G2	Toprakli	76	F3
Tigris	94	H6	Tisisat Falls	103	G5	Tolbukhin	73	J4	Toraka Vestale	109	H3
Tigzerte, Oued	100	D3	Tissa	71	K4	Toledo *Spain*	66	D3	Tora-Khem	84	F6
Tigzirt	67	J4	Tissington	55	H3	Toledo *U.S.A.*	124	J6	Torbali	76	B3
Tihamat ash Sham	96	E7	Tista	93	G3	Toledo Bend Reservoir	128	F5	Torbat-e-Heydariyeh	95	P4
Tihamat Asir	96	F8	Tisza	72	F2	Toledo, Montes de	66	D3	Torbat-e Jam	95	Q4
Tihsimir	77	J3	Tit-Ary	85	M2	Tolentino	68	D4	Tor Bay *Australia*	112	D5
Tijoca	137	H4	Titchfield	53	F4	Toliara	109	H4	Tor Bay *U.K.*	52	D4
Tijuana	126	D4	Titicaca, Lago	138	C3	Tolitoli	91	G5	Tordesillas	66	D2
Tikal	132	C6	Titograd	72	E4	Tolka	84	C4	Tore	56	D3
Tikamgarh	92	E4	Titova Mitrovica	73	F4	Tolmezzo	68	D2	Tore	62	K4
Tikanlik	86	F3	Titovo Uzice	72	E4	Tolmin	72	B2	Torfastadir	62	U12
Tikhoretsk	79	G6	Titovo Velenje	72	C2	Tolochin	78	D5	Torgau	70	E3
Tikhvin	78	E4	Titov Veles	73	F5	Tolosa	67	E1	Torgo	85	K5
Tikitiki	115	G2	Titran	62	C5	Tolo, Teluk	91	G6	Torhout	64	E3
Tikopica	111	Q4	Tittmoning	70	E4	Tolsta Head	56	B2	Torino	68	A3
Tikrit	77	K5	Titu	73	H3	Tolstoye	73	H1	Torkaman	94	H3
Tiksi	85	M2	Titusville	129	M6	Tolstoy, Mys	85	T5	Tormes	66	D2
Tilburg	64	F3	Tiumpan Head	56	B2	Toluca	131	K8	Tornealven	62	K3
Tilbury	53	H3	Tivaouane	104	B2	Toluca, Nevado de	131	K8	Tor Ness	56	E2
Tilemsi, Vallee du	100	F5	Tiveden	63	F7	Tolyatti	79	H5	Torne-trask	62	H2
Till	57	F5	Tiverton	52	D4	Tomah	124	E4	Torngat Mountains	121	P6
Tillaberi	100	F6	Tivoli	69	D5	Tomahawk	124	F4	Tornio	62	L4
Tillanchang	93	H7	Tiwi	97	P5	Tomakomai	88	H4	Toro, Cerro de	138	C5
Tillicoultry	57	E4	Tiyas	77	G5	Tomani	90	F5	Toroiaga	73	H2
Tilomar	91	H7	Tizimin	131	Q7	Tomaniivi	114	R8	Torokina	114	F3
Tilos	75	J4	Tizi Ouzou	101	F1	Tomar *Portugal*	66	B3	Torokszentmiklos	72	F2
Tilsit	71	J1	Tiznit	100	D3	Tomar *Kazakhstan*	86	D2	Toronaios, Kolpos	75	G2
Tilt	57	E4	Tjamotis	62	H3	Tomari	88	J2	Toronto	125	L5
Timanskiy Kryazh	78	H3	Tjornuvik	62	Z14	Tomarza	77	F3	Toropets	78	E4
Timar	77	K3	Tjotta	62	E4	Tomasevo	72	E4	Tororo	107	F2
Timaru	115	C6	Tlaltenango	130	H7	Tomashevka	71	K3	Toros Dagi	76	F4
Timashevsk	79	F6	Tlapa	131	K9	Tomaszow Lubelski	71	K3	Toros Daglari	76	E4
Timbakion	75	H5	Tlapehuala	131	J8	Tomaszow Mazowiecka	71	J3	Torpoint	52	C4
Timbedra	100	D5	Tlaxiaco	131	L9	Tombador, Serra do	136	F6	Torquay	52	D4
Timbo *Guinea*	104	C3	Tlemcen	100	E2	Tombe	103	F6	Torrance	126	C4
Timbo *Liberia*	104	D4	Toad River	118	K4	Tombigbee	129	H5	Torrao	66	B3
Timbuktu	100	E5	Toamasina	109	J3	Tomboco	106	B4	Torre Annunziata	69	E5
Timfristos	75	F3	Tobago	133	S9	Tombouctou	100	E5	Torre Baja	67	F2
Timimoun	100	F3	Toba Kakar Ranges	92	C2	Tombua	106	B6	Torreblanca	67	G2
Timiris, Cap	100	B5	Tobercurry	58	E4	Tomelilla	63	E9	Torrecilla en Cameros	66	E1
Timis	73	G3	Tobermory *Canada*	125	K4	Tomelloso	66	E3	Torre del Greco	69	E5
Timisoara	73	F3	Tobermory *U.K.*	57	B4	Tomini, Teluk	91	G6	Torrelaguna	66	E2
Timkapaul	84	Ad4	Toberonochy	57	C4	Tomioka	89	H7	Torrelavega	66	D1
Timmernabben	63	G8	Tobi	91	J5	Tomkinson Ranges	112	F4	Torremolinos	66	D4
Timmins	125	K2	Tobin Lake	112	F3	Tomma	62	E3	Torrens Creek	113	K3
Timok	73	G3	Tobi-shima	88	G6	Tommot	85	M5	Torrens, Lake	113	H5
Timolin	59	J7	Toboali	90	D6	Tomo	136	D2	Torrente	67	F3
Timor	91	H7	Tobol	84	Ae5	Tomochic	127	J6	Torreon	127	L8
Timor, Laut	91	H7	Tobolsk	84	Ae5	Tompa	84	H5	Torres Island	114	T10
Timoshino	78	F3	Tobseda	78	J2	Tompo	85	P4	Torres Novas	66	B3
Timsher	78	J3	Tobysh	78	J3	Tomsk	84	D5	Torres Strait	114	C4
Tinaca Point	91	H4	Tocache Nuevo	136	B5	Tonbridge	53	H3	Torres Vedras	66	B3
Tinaco	133	N10	Tocantins	137	H4	Tondano	91	G5	Torrevieja	67	F4
Tinahely	59	K7	Toccoa	129	L3	Tonder	70	C1	Torr Head	58	K2
Tinakula	114	M7	Toco	133	S9	Tone	52	E3	Torridge	52	C4
Tindivanam	92	E6	Toconao	138	C4	Tonelagee	59	K6	Torridon, Loch	56	C3
Tindouf	100	D3	Tocopilla	138	B4	Tonga	111	U6	Torrijos	66	D3
Tineo	66	C1	Tocuyo	133	N9	Tonga *Sudan*	102	F6	Torrington *Connecticut, U.S.A.*	125	P6
Tinglev	63	C9	Todeli	91	G6	Tongariro	115	E3	Torrington *Wyoming, U.S.A.*	123	M6
Tingo Maria	136	B5	Todi	68	B2	Tongatapu	111	U6	Torrox	66	E4
Tingsryd	63	F8	Todi	69	D4	Tongatapu Group	111	T6	Torsas	63	F8
Tingvoll	62	C5	Todmorden	55	G3	Tonga Trench	143	H5	Torsby	63	E6
Tinhare, Ilha de	137	K6	Todog	86	E3	Tongcheng	93	M3	Torshavn	62	Z14
Tinogasta	138	C5	Todos os Santos, Baia de	137	K6	Tongchuan	93	L1	Torsken	62	L2
Tinompo	91	G5	Todos Santos *Bolivia*	138	C3	Tongdao	93	L3	Tortkuduk	84	A6
Tinos *Greece*	75	H4	Todos Santos *Mexico*	130	D6	Tonggu	93	M3	Tortola	133	Q5
Tinos *Greece*	75	H4	Todos Santos, Bahia de	126	D5	Tongguan	93	M2	Tortona	68	B3
Tintinara	113	J6	Toe Head *Ireland*	59	D10	Tonghai	93	K4	Tortosa	67	G2
Tinto *Spain*	66	C4	Toe Head *U.K.*	56	A3	Tonghe	88	B2	Tortosa, Cabo de	67	G2
Tinto *U.K.*	57	E5	Toetoes Bay	115	B7	Tonghua	87	P3	Tortue, Ile de la	133	L4
Tinto Hills	57	E5	Tofino	122	B3	Tongjiang	88	D2	Tortuga, Isla	126	G7
Tinwald	115	C5	Toft	56	A1	Tongking, Gulf of	93	L5	Tortuga, Isla la	136	D1
Tiomilaskogen	63	E6	Tofte	63	D7	Tongliao	87	N3	Tortum	77	J2
Tipaza	67	H4	Tofua	111	T5	Tongling	87	M5	Torul	77	H2
Tipitapa	132	D8	Toga	114	T10	Tonglu	87	M6	Torun	71	H2
Tippecanoe	124	G6	Togi	89	F7	Tongnae	89	B8	Tory Island	58	F2
Tipperary *Ireland*	59	F8	Togiak	118	C4	Tongoa	114	U12	Torysa	71	J4
Tipperary *Ireland*	59	G7	Togian, Kepulauan	91	G6	Tongren	93	L3	Tory Sound	58	F2
Tipton	124	H6	Togni	96	B7	Tongtianheyan	93	H2	Torzhok	78	F4
Tiptree	53	H3	Togo	104	F4	Tongue *U.K.*	56	D2	Torzym	70	F2
Tiquicheo	131	J8	Togtoh	87	L3	Tongue *U.S.A.*	123	L5	Tosa-shimizu	89	D9
Tiracambu, Serra do	137	H4	Toguchi	89	H10	Tongue, Kyle of	56	D2	Tosa-wan	89	D9
Tiran	96	B3	Togur	84	C5	Tongue of the Ocean	132	J2	Toscaig	56	C3
Tirana	74	E2	Tohamiyam	103	G4	Tong Xian	87	M4	Tosco-Emiliano, Appennino	68	C3
Tirane	74	E2	Tohatchi	127	H3	Tongxin	93	L1	Tostado	138	D5
Tirano	68	C2	Tohma	77	G3	Tongyu	87	N3	Tosya	76	F2
Tiraspol	79	D6	Toi-misaki	89	C10	Tongzi	93	L3	Totana	67	F4
Tire	76	B3	Tojo	89	D8	Tonichi	127	H6	Totes	64	D4
Tirebolu	77	H2	Tok	118	G3	Tonk	92	E3	Totma	78	G4
Tiree	57	C4	Tokachi	88	J4	Tonkabon	95	K3	Totnes	52	D4
Tirga Mor	56	B3	Tokachi-Dake	88	J4	Tonle Sap	93	K6	Totness	137	F2
Tirgoviste	73	H3	Tokaj	73	F1	Tonneins	65	D6	Totora	138	C3
Tirgu Bujor	73	J3	Tokanui	115	B7	Tonnerre	65	E5	Totota	104	C4
Tirgu Carbunesti	73	G3	Tokar	103	G4	Tono	88	H6	Totoya	114	S9
Tirgu Frumos	73	J2	Tokara-kaikyo	89	C10	Tonopah	126	D2	Totton	53	F4
Tirgu Jiu	73	G3	Tokara-retto	89	B11	Tonosi	132	G11	Tottori	89	E8
Tirgu Mures	73	H2	Tokat	77	G2	Tonsberg	63	D7	Touba	104	D4

Name	Page	Grid
Toubkal, Jebel	100	D2
Tougan	104	E3
Touggourt	101	G2
Touho Ouegoa	114	W16
Toul	64	F4
Toulon	65	F7
Toulouse	65	E7
Toummo	101	H4
Toumodi	104	D4
Toungoo	93	J5
Touraine	65	D5
Tourcoing	64	E3
Tournai	64	E3
Tournon *France*	65	D5
Tournon *France*	65	F6
Tournus	65	F5
Touros	137	K5
Tours	65	D5
Tousside, Pic	102	C3
Touws River	108	D6
Tovarkovskiy	79	F5
Towada	88	H5
Towanda	125	M6
Towcester	53	G2
Tower Island	136	B7
Towie	56	F3
Townsend	122	J4
Townshend Island	113	L3
Townsville	113	K2
Towson	125	M7
Toxkan He	86	D3
Toya-ko	88	H4
Toyama	89	F7
Toyama-wan	89	F7
Toyohashi	89	F8
Toyonaka	89	E8
Toyooka	89	E8
Tozeur	101	G2
Traben-Trarbach	70	B4
Trablous	77	F5
Trabzon	77	H2
Trafalgar, Cabo	66	C4
Traighli	59	C8
Trail	122	F3
Traipu	137	K5
Trakai	71	L1
Trakt	78	J3
Tralee	59	C8
Tralee Bay	59	C8
Trallwng	52	D2
Tram Khnar	93	K6
Tramore	59	H8
Tramore Bay	59	H8
Tranas	63	F7
Trancoso	66	C2
Tranent	57	F4
Trang	93	J7
Trangan	114	A3
Trani	69	F5
Tran Ninh, Cao Nguyen	93	K5
Transantarctic Mountains	141	L2
Transtrand	63	E6
Transylvania	73	G2
Trapani	69	D6
Trappes	64	E4
Trasimeno, Lago	68	D4
Tras os Montes	66	C2
Trat	93	K6
Traverse City	124	H4
Travis, Lake	127	N5
Travnik	72	D3
Trawsfynydd	52	D2
Trawsfynydd, Llyn	52	D2
Treasury Island	114	G5
Trebbia	68	B3
Trebic	70	F4
Trebinje	72	E4
Trebnje	72	C3
Tredegar	52	D3
Treen	52	B4
Treffgarne	52	C3
Tregaron	52	D2
Tregynon	52	D2
Trehorningsjo	62	H5
Treig, Loch	57	D4
Treinta y Tres	138	F6
Trelew	139	C8
Trelleborg	63	E9
Trelleck	52	E3
Tremadog Bay	52	C2
Tremiti, Isole di	69	E4
Tremonton	122	H7
Tremp	67	G1
Trencin	71	H4
Trenque Lauquen	139	D7
Trent	55	J3
Trento	68	C2
Trenton *Canada*	125	M4
Trenton *Missouri, U.S.A.*	124	D6
Trenton *New Jersey, U.S.A.*	125	N6
Tres Arroyos	139	D7
Tres Cerros	139	C9
Tresco	52	L5
Tres Esquinas	136	B3
Treshnish Isles	57	B4
Treskavica	72	E4
Tres Lagoas	138	F4
Tres Lagos	139	B9
Tres Marias, Represa	138	G3
Tres Montes, Peninsula	139	A9
Tres Rios	138	H4
Tresta *U.K.*	56	A1
Tres Virgenes, Volcan Las	126	F7
Tretten	63	D6
Treuchtlingen	70	D4
Treungen	63	C7
Treviglio	68	B3
Treviso	68	D3
Trevose Head	52	B4
Trevoux	65	F6
Treysa	70	C3
Triabunna	113	K7
Trial Bay	113	H1
Triangle	109	F4
Tria Nisia	75	J4
Tribec	71	H4
Triberg	70	C4
Tribulation, Cape	113	K2
Tricase	69	G6
Trichur	92	E6
Trient	68	C2
Trier	70	B4
Trieste	68	D3
Trieste, Golfo di	68	D3
Triglav	68	D2
Trikhonis, Limni	75	F3
Trikkala	75	F3
Trim	59	J5
Trincomalee	92	F7
Trindade	66	C2
Trindade, Ilha da	48	F5
Tringia	75	F3
Trinidad *Bolivia*	136	E6
Trinidad *Cuba*	132	G4
Trinidad *Trinidad and Tobago*	133	S9
Trinidad and Tobago	133	S9
Trinidad, Isla	139	D7
Trinity *California, U.S.A.*	122	C7
Trinity *Texas, U.S.A.*	128	E5
Trinity Bay *Australia*	113	K2
Trinity Bay *Canada*	121	R8
Trionto, Capo	69	F6
Tripoli *Lebanon*	94	B4
Tripoli *Libya*	101	H2
Tripolis	75	G4
Tripura	93	H4
Trischen	70	C1
Tristan da Cunha	48	F6
Triste, Golfo	133	N9
Triunfo	137	K5
Trivandrum	92	E7
Trnava	71	G4
Trobriand Islands	114	E3
Trofors	62	E4
Trogir	72	D4
Troglav	72	D4
Trois Fourches, Cap des	100	E1
Trois-Pistoles	125	R2
Trois Rivieres	125	P3
Troitskiy	84	A6
Troitsko-Pechora	78	K3
Troitsko-Pechorsk	84	Ac4
Troitskoye *Russia*	84	C6
Troitskoye *Ukraine*	73	L2
Trollattan	63	E7
Trolltindane	62	B5
Tromba Grande, Cabo	137	K6
Trombetas	137	F4
Troms	62	H2
Tromsdalen	62	M2
Tromso	62	H2
Tronador, Cerro	139	B8
Trondheim	62	D5
Trondheimsfjorden	62	D5
Tronto	69	D4
Troodos, Mount	76	E5
Troon	57	D5
Tropoje	72	F4
Tropoje	75	F1
Trosh	78	K2
Trossachs, The	57	D4
Trostan	58	K2
Trostyanets	73	K1
Trotus	73	J2
Troun	93	L6
Trout Lake *NW. Territories, Canada*	119	L3
Trout Lake *Ontario, Canada*	119	S5
Trouville	64	D4
Trowbridge	52	E3
Troy *Alabama, U.S.A.*	129	K5
Troy *Montana, U.S.A.*	122	G3
Troy *New York, U.S.A.*	125	P5
Troy *Ohio, U.S.A.*	124	H6
Troyes	64	F4
Trstenik	73	F4
Trubchevsk	79	E5
Truchas Peak	127	K2
Trucial Coast	97	L4
Trujillo *Honduras*	132	E7
Trujillo *Peru*	136	B5
Trujillo *Spain*	66	D3
Trujillo *Venezuela*	136	C2
Trun	73	G4
Truro *Australia*	113	H5
Truro *Canada*	121	P8
Truro *U.K.*	52	B4
Truskmore	58	F4
Truth or Consequences	127	J4
Trutnov	70	F3
Trysil	63	E6
Tsagaanhayrhan	86	H2
Tsangpo	93	H3
Tsaratanana	109	J3
Tsaratanana, Massif du	109	J2
Tsau	108	D4
Tselinograd	84	A6
Tsenhermandal	87	K2
Tsenogora	78	H3
Tsetserleg *Mongolia*	86	H2
Tsetserleg *Mongolia*	86	J2
Tshabong	108	D5
Tshane	108	D4
Tshela	106	B3
Tshikapa	106	D4
Tshimbulu	106	D4
Tsimlyansk	79	G6
Tsimlyanskoye Vodokhranilishche	79	G6
Tsinan	87	M4
Tsinga	75	H2
Tsingtao	87	N4
Tsipa	85	K5
Tsiroanomandidy	109	J3
Tsitondroina	109	J4
Tsitsihar	87	N2
Tskhinvali	77	K1
Tsna	71	M2
Tsogttsetsiy	87	K3
Tsu	89	F8
Tsubata	89	F7
Tsuchiura	89	H7
Tsugaru-kaikyo	88	H5
Tsumeb	108	C3
Tsuruga	89	F8
Tsurugi	89	F7
Tsuruoka	88	G6
Tsushima	89	B8
Tsushima-kaikyo	89	B8
Tsuyama	89	D8
Tsyp Navolok	62	Q2
Tsyurupinsk	79	E6
Tuaheni Point	115	G3
Tuai	115	F3
Tuakau	115	E2
Tual	114	A3
Tuam	59	E5
Tuamotu, Iles	143	J5
Tuangku	90	B5
Tuapse	79	F7
Tuatapere	115	A7
Tuath, Loch	57	B4
Tuba	84	G5
Tuban	90	E7
Tuban, Wadi	96	G10
Tubarao	138	G5
Tubayq, At	96	C2
Tubbataha Reefs	91	F4
Tubingen	70	C4
Tubruq	101	K2
Tucano	138	K6
Tuchola	71	G2
Tucholskie, Bory	71	G2
Tuchow	71	J4
Tucson	126	G4
Tucumcari	127	L3
Tucupare	137	F5
Tucupita	136	E2
Tucurui	137	H4
Tuddenham	53	J2
Tudela	67	F1
Tuela	66	C2
Tufanbeyli	77	G3
Tugela	108	F5
Tugrovskiy	84	Ad4
Tuguegarao	91	G2
Tugur	85	P6
Tukangbesi, Kepulauan	91	G7
Tukituki	115	F3
Tuknyu	107	F4
Tukrah	101	K2
Tuktoyaktuk	118	J2
Tukums	63	K8
Tukuno-shima	87	P6
Tula *Mexico*	131	K6
Tula *Russia*	78	F5
Tulak	95	R3
Tulancingo	131	K7
Tulare Lake	126	C3
Tularosa	127	K4
Tulcan	136	B3
Tulcea	73	K3
Tulchin	73	K1
Tulear	109	H4
Tulik Volcano	118	Ae9
Tulkarm	94	B5
Tullahoma	129	J3
Tullamore	59	H6
Tulle	65	D6
Tullow	59	J7
Tully	113	K2
Tullybrack	58	G4
Tulovo	73	H4
Tulpan	78	K3
Tulsa	128	E2
Tulsk	58	F5
Tulua	136	B3
Tulun	84	G6
Tulungagung	90	E7
Tuma	78	G4
Tumaco	136	B3
Tumaco, Bada de	136	B3
Tumanskiy	85	X4
Tumany	85	T4
Tumbarumba	113	K6
Tumbes	136	A4
Tumd Youqi	87	L3
Tumen *China*	88	B4
Tumen *China*	88	B4
Tumeremo	136	E2
Tumereng	133	S11
Tumkur	92	E6
Tummel Bridge	57	D4
Tummel, Loch	57	E4
Tump	92	B3
Tumpat	90	C4
Tumu	104	E3
Tumucumaque, Serra	137	G3
Tunari, Cerro	138	D3
Tunbal Kubra	95	M8
Tunbridge Wells	53	H3
Tunceli	77	H3
Tunduru	107	G5
Tundzha	73	J4
Tungabhadra	92	E5
Tungozero	62	P4
Tungurahua, Volcan	136	B4
Tunguska	84	E4
Tunguskoye Plato	84	E4
Tuni	92	F5
Tunis	101	H1
Tunis, Golfo di	69	C7
Tunisia	101	G2
Tunja	136	C2
Tunka	84	G6
Tunnsjoen	62	E4
Tunungayualok Island	121	P6
Tunxi	87	M6
Tuo Jiang	93	K3
Tuomioja	62	L4
Tuostakh	85	P3
Tupana	136	E4
Tupanaoca	136	E4
Tupelo	128	H3
Tupinambaranas, Ilha	136	F4
Tupiza	138	C4
Tupos	62	L4
Tupungato, Cerro	139	C6
Tuquan	87	N2
Tuquerres	136	B3
Tura *India*	93	H3
Tura *Russia*	84	Ad5
Tura *Russia*	84	G4
Turabah	96	E6
Turabah, Wadi	96	E6
Turama	84	F4
Turan	84	E6
Turana, Khrebet	85	N6
Turangi	115	E3
Turbaco	136	B1
Turbat	92	B3
Turbo	136	B2
Turda	73	G2
Turek	71	H2
Turfan Depression	86	F3
Turgay	84	A6
Turgen Uul	86	G2
Turgovishte	73	J4
Turgutlu	76	B3
Turhal	77	G2
Turi	63	L7
Turia	67	F3
Turiacu	137	G4
Turiacu	137	G4
Turin	68	A3
Turinsk	84	Ad5
Turiy Rog	88	C3
Turka	71	K4
Turkana, Lake	107	G2
Turkeli	76	F2
Turkestan	86	B3
Turkestan, Bandi-	95	S4
Turkey	76	E3
Turkey Creek	112	F2
Turkmenistan	80	G6
Turkoglu	77	G2
Turks Island	133	M4
Turks Island Passage	133	M4
Turku	63	M6
Turku-Pori	63	K6
Turnagain	118	K4
Turnagain, Cape	115	F4
Turneffe Island	132	D6
Turnhout	64	F3
Turnitz	68	E2
Turnov	70	F3
Turnu Magurele	73	H4
Turnu Rosu, Pasul	73	H3
Turpan	86	F3
Turriff	56	F3
Tursunzade	86	B4
Turta	86	J1
Turtas	84	Ae5
Turtkul	80	H5
Turtle Mountain	123	P3
Turukhansk	84	D3
Turya	71	L3
Tuscaloosa	129	J4
Tuscania	69	C4
Tuscola	127	N4
Tustumena Lake	118	E3
Tutak	77	K3
Tutayev	78	F4
Tuticorin	92	E7
Tutoia	137	J4
Tutonchana	84	E3
Tutonchany	84	E4
Tutrakan	73	J3
Tuttle Creek Lake	123	R8
Tuttlingen	70	C5
Tutuila	115	U4
Tuvalu	111	S3
Tuvuca	114	S8
Tuwayq, Jabal *Saudi Arabia*	96	G4
Tuwayq, Jabal *Saudi Arabia*	96	H5

Name	Page	Grid
Tuxford	55	J3
Tuxpan	130	G7
Tuxpan *Mexico*	130	H8
Tuxpan *Mexico*	131	L7
Tuxtepec	131	L8
Tuxtla Gutierrez	131	N9
Tuy	66	B1
Tuyao	86	F3
Tuyen Quang	93	L4
Tuy Hoa	93	L6
Tuymazy	78	J5
Tuysarkan	94	J4
Tuzantla	131	J8
Tuz Golu	76	E3
Tuz Khurmatu	77	L5
Tuzla	72	E3
Tuzluca	77	K2
Tuzlukcu	76	D3
Tvedestrand	63	C7
Tvoroyri	62	Z14
Tweed	57	F5
Tweedsmuir	57	E5
Tweedsmuir Hills	57	E5
Twelve Pins, The	59	C5
Twentynine Palms	126	E3
Twin Bridges	122	H5
Twin Buttes Reservoir	127	M5
Twin Falls	122	G6
Two Bridges	52	D4
Two Rivers	124	G4
Twrch	52	D2
Twycross	53	F2
Twyford *Berkshire, U.K.*	53	G3
Twyford *Hampshire, U.K.*	53	F3
Twyford *Leicestershire, U.K.*	53	G2
Tyachev	71	K4
Tyana Shan	86	D3
Tyanya	85	K5
Tychany	84	F4
Tychy	71	H3
Tygda	85	M6
Tyler	128	E4
Tyloskog	63	F7
Tym	84	C5
Tymovskoye	85	Q6
Tynda	85	L5
Tyndall, Mount	115	C5
Tyndrum	57	D4
Tyne	55	H2
Tyne and Wear	55	H2
Tynemouth	55	H1
Tynset	62	D5
Tyr	85	P6
Tyre	94	B5
Tyret	84	G6
Tyrma	85	N6
Tyrone *U.K.*	58	H3
Tyrone *U.S.A.*	125	L6
Tyrrhenian Sea	69	D5
Tysnesoy	63	A7
Tyukalinsk	84	A5
Tyulgan	79	K5
Tyuli	84	Ae4
Tyung	85	L4
Tywi	52	C3
Tywyn	52	C2
Tzaneen	108	F4
Tzoumerka	75	F3

U

Name	Page	Grid
Uainambi	136	C3
Uapao, Cape	114	X16
Uapes	136	D4
Uatuma	136	F4
Uaupes	136	D3
Uava	137	K5
Uba	138	H4
Ubaitaba	137	K6
Ube	89	C9
Ubeda	66	E3
Ubekendt O	120	R3
Uberaba	138	J3
Uberaba, Laguna	138	E3
Uberlandia	138	G3
Ubinskoye	84	B5
Ubolratna Reservoir	93	K5
Ubombo	109	F5
Ubon Ratchathani	93	K5
Ubundu	106	E3
Ucayali	136	C4
Ucdam	77	J3
Uch Adzhi	95	R2
Uchami	84	F4
Ucharal	86	F2
Uchiura-wan	88	H4
Uchte	70	C2
Uchur	85	N5
Uckermark	70	E2
Uckfield	53	H4
Ucluelet	122	B3
Uda	85	N6
Udachnyy	84	J3
Udaipur	92	D4
Udayd, Ra's al	97	K4
Udbina	72	C3
Uddevalla	63	D7
Uddjaur	62	G4
Udine	68	D2
Udon Thani	93	K5
Udskoye	85	N6
Udupi	92	D6

Name	Page	Grid
Ueckermunde	70	F2
Ueda	89	G7
Uele *Russia*	84	J2
Uele *Zaire*	106	D2
Uelen	81	V3
Uelkal	85	Y3
Uelzen	70	D2
Ufa *Russia*	78	K4
Ufa *Russia*	78	K5
Ugab	108	B4
Uganda	107	F2
Ugashik Bay	118	D3
Ugashik Lakes	118	D4
Ughelli	105	G4
Ugijar	66	E4
Uglich	78	F4
Ugljane	72	D4
Ugra	78	E5
Ugun	85	M5
Ugurlu	77	J2
Ugurludag	76	F2
Ugut	84	A4
Uherske Hradiste	71	G4
Uhlava	70	E4
Uhrusk	71	K3
Uig	56	B3
Uige	106	C4
Uil *Kazakhstan*	79	J6
Uil *Kazakhstan*	79	J6
Uinskoye	78	K4
Uinta Mountains	122	J7
Uisong	89	B7
Uitenhage	108	E6
Ujiji	107	E3
Uji-shoto	89	B10
Ujjain	92	E4
Ujpest	72	E2
Ujscie	71	G2
Ujung Pandang	91	F7
Uka	85	U5
Ukholovo	79	G5
Ukhta	78	J3
Ukhunku	85	L3
Uki	114	K7
Ukiah	122	C8
Ukmerge	63	L9
Ukraine	79	D6
Ukta	71	J2
Uku	106	B5
Uku-jima	89	B9
Ukuma	106	C5
Ula	76	C4
Ulaangom	86	G2
Ulan Bator	87	K2
Ulan-Erge	79	G6
Ulanhad	87	M3
Ulan-Khol	79	H6
Ulan Tohoi	86	J3
Ulan-Ude	84	H6
Ulan Ula	93	H2
Ulas	77	G3
Ulawa	114	K6
Ulchin	89	B7
Ulcinj	74	E2
Uled Saidan	101	J3
Ulfborg	63	C8
Ulgumdzha	85	K4
Ulhasnagar	92	D5
Uliastay	86	H2
Ulithi Atoll	91	K4
Uljan	72	C3
Uljma	73	F3
Ulla	66	B1
Ullaanbaatar	87	K2
Ullanger	62	H5
Ullapool	56	C3
Ullock	55	F2
Ullswater	55	G2
Ullung-do	89	C7
Ulm	70	C4
Ulog	72	E4
Ulongue	109	F2
Ulricehamn	63	E8
Ulsan	89	B8
Ulsta	56	A1
Ulsteinvik	62	A5
Ulster	58	H3
Ulster Canal	58	H4
Ulubat Golu	76	C2
Ulubey *Turkey*	76	C3
Ulubey *Turkey*	77	F2
Uluborlu	76	D3
Ulucinar	77	F4
Uludag	76	C2
Ulu Dagi	76	C2
Uludere	77	K4
Uluguru Mountains	107	G4
Ulukisla	76	F4
Ulunkhan	85	J6
Ulus	76	E2
Ulva	57	B4
Ulverston	55	F2
Ulyanovsk	78	H5
Ulysses	127	M2
Ulzburg	70	C2
Umala	138	C3
Uman	79	E6
Uman	131	Q7
Umanak Fjord	120	R3
Umari	114	B2
Umarkot	92	C3
Umba	78	E2
Umbertide	68	D4
Umboi Island	114	D3

Name	Page	Grid
Umbro-Marchigiano, Appennino	68	D4
Umea	62	J5
Umealven	62	H4
Umm al Qaywayn	97	M4
Umm as Samim	97	M6
Umm Bel	102	E5
Umm Keddada	102	E5
Umm Lajj	96	C4
Umm Ruwaba	102	F5
Umm Said	97	K4
Umm Urumah	96	C4
Umnak Island	118	Ae9
Umred	92	E4
Umtali	109	F3
Umtata	108	E6
Umzingwani	108	E4
Una *Brazil*	137	K7
Una *Yugoslavia*	72	C3
Unalaska Island	118	Ae9
Unare	133	Q10
Unayzah	96	F3
Uncia	138	C3
Uncompahgre Peak	123	L8
Uncompahgre Plateau	122	K8
Underwood	123	P4
Unecha	79	E5
Uneiuxi	136	D4
Ungava Bay	121	N6
Ungave, Peninsule d'	121	L5
Unggi	88	C4
Uniao dos Palmares	137	K5
Uniao do Vitoria	138	E5
Unije	72	C3
Unimak Island	118	Af9
Unimak Pass	118	Ae9
Unini	136	E4
Union	129	M3
Union City	128	H2
Uniondale	108	D6
Union Springs	129	K4
Uniontown	125	L7
United Arab Emirates	97	L5
United States of America	116	H4
Unity	122	E5
Universales, Montes	67	F2
University Park	127	J4
Unnao	92	F3
Unst	56	B1
Untaek	88	A5
Unye	77	G2
Unzha	78	G4
Uodgan	96	D8
Uoyan	85	J5
Upata	133	R10
Upavon	53	F3
Upemba, Lake	106	E4
Upernavik	120	Q3
Upernavik Isfjord	120	R3
Upington	108	D5
Upolu	111	U4
Upolu Point	126	T10
Upper Arrow Lake	122	F2
Upper Broughton	53	G2
Upper Hutt	115	E4
Upper Klamath Lake	122	D6
Upper Seal Lake	121	M6
Uppingham	53	G2
Uppsala *Sweden*	63	G6
Uppsala *Sweden*	63	L7
Upsala	124	E2
Upstart Bay	113	K2
Uqla Sawab	77	J6
Urad Qianqi	87	K3
Urad Zhongqi	87	K3
Urak	85	Q5
Urakan	84	H5
Urakawa	88	J4
Ural	79	J6
Ural Mountains	78	K3
Uralsk	79	J5
Uralskiy Khrebet	78	K3
Urandangi	113	H3
Urandi	137	J6
Uranium City	119	P4
Uraricoera	136	E3
Urawa	89	G8
Urayirah	97	J4
Urayq, Al	96	D2
Urayq, Nafud al	96	F4
Urbana	124	J6
Urbino	68	D4
Urda	79	H6
Urdzhar	86	E2
Uren	78	H4
Urengoy	84	B3
Ureparapara	114	T10
Ures	126	G6
Urfa	77	H4
Urgal	85	N6
Urgel, Llanos de	67	G2
Urgench	80	G5
Urgup	76	F3
Urho	86	F2
Uritskiy	84	Ae6
Urkan	85	M6
Urla	76	B3
Urlingford	59	G7
Urmi	88	D1
Urosevac	73	F4
Urr Water	57	E5
Ursatyevskaya	86	B3
Uruacu	137	H6
Uruapan	130	H8

Name	Page	Grid
Urubamba	136	C6
Urubu	136	F4
Urucui	137	J5
Urucuia	138	G3
Urucui, Serra do	137	J5
Uruguaiana	138	E5
Uruguay	138	E6
Urumchi	86	F3
Urumqi	86	F3
Urupadi	137	F4
Urup, Ostrov	85	S7
Uruti Point	115	F4
Urville, Tanjung d'	114	B2
Uryupinsk	79	G5
Urzhum	78	H4
Urziceni	73	J3
Usa	78	K2
Usak	76	C3
Usambara Mountains	107	G3
Usedom	70	F1
Ushant	64	A4
Ushitsa	73	J1
Ushtobe	86	D2
Ushuaia	139	C10
Usk *Gwent, U.K.*	52	E3
Usk *Powys, U.K.*	52	D3
Usk Reservoir	52	D3
Uskudar	76	C2
Uslar	70	C3
Usman	79	F5
Usolye	78	K4
Usolye-Sibirskoye	84	G6
Uspenka	84	B6
Ussel	65	E6
Ussuri	88	E2
Ussuriysk	88	C4
Ust-Barguzin	84	H6
Ust-Belaya	85	W3
Ust-Chara	85	L4
UstChizhapka	84	B5
Ustica, Isola di	69	D6
UstIlimsk	84	G5
Ust-Ilimsk Vodokhranilishche	84	J4
Ust-Ilych	84	Ac4
Usti nad Lebem	70	F3
Ustinov	78	J4
Ustka	71	G1
UstKamchatsk	85	U5
Ust-Kamenogorsk	86	E2
Ust-Kamo	84	F4
Ust-Kan	84	E5
Ust-Kara	84	Ad3
Ust-Karenga	85	K6
UstKatav	78	K5
Ust-Kulom	78	J3
Ust-Kut	84	H5
Ust-Kuyga	85	P3
Ust-Labinsk	79	F6
UstLuga	63	N7
Ust-Maya	85	N4
Ust-Mayn	85	W3
Ust-Mil	85	N5
Ust-Muya	85	K5
UstNem	78	J3
Ust-Nera	85	Q4
UstNiman	85	N6
UstOmchug	85	R4
Ust-Ordynskiy	84	G6
Ustovo	73	H5
Ust-Ozernoye	84	D5
UstPenzhino	85	V4
Ust-Pit	84	E5
Ust-Port	84	C3
UstReka	78	H3
UstSara	78	E3
UstTapsuy	78	L3
Ust-Tatta	85	N4
Ust-Tsilma	78	J2
Ust-Tym	84	C5
UstTyrma	85	N6
UstUra	78	G3
UstUsa	78	K2
Ust-Vaga	78	G3
UstVyyskaya	78	H3
UstYuribey	84	Ae3
Ustyurt, Plato	51	T7
Usuki	89	C9
Usulatan	132	C8
Usumacinta	131	P9
Utah	122	H8
Utah Lake	122	J7
Utajarvi	62	M4
Utara	90	C6
Ute Creek	127	L2
Utena	63	N9
Uthal	92	C3
Utiariti	136	F6
Utica	125	N5
Utiel	67	F3
Utikuma Lake	119	M4
Utkholok	85	T5
Utrecht	64	F2
Utrera	66	D4
Utsera	77	K1
Utsjoki	62	M2
Utsonomiya	89	G7
Utta	79	H6
Uttaradit	93	K5
Uttar Pradesh	92	F3
Uttoxeter	53	F2
Uttyakh	85	N3
Utubulak	86	F2
Utukok	118	C2

Name	Page	Grid
Utupua	114	N7
Uuldza	87	L2
Uummannaq	120	R3
Uusikaarlepyy	62	K5
Uusikaupunki	63	J6
Uusimaa	63	L6
Uvac	72	E4
Uvalde	127	N6
Uvarovo	79	G5
Uvea	111	T4
Uvinza	107	F4
Uvira	107	E3
Uvol	114	E3
Uvs Nuur	86	G1
Uwajima	89	D9
Uwayrid, Harrat al	96	C3
Uy	84	Ad6
Uyak	118	E4
Uyandina	85	Q3
Uyeg	78	J2
Uyuni	138	C4
Uyuni, Salar de	138	C4
Uz	71	K4
Uzaym, Nahr al	94	G4
Uzbekistan	86	B3
Uzda	71	M2
Uzen	79	J7
Uzerche	65	D6
Uzes	65	F6
Uzhgorod	79	C6
Uzhok	71	K4
Uzlovaya	78	F5
Uzumlu	76	D4
Uzun	84	D6
Uzundere	77	J2
Uzungol	77	J2
Uzunisa	77	G2
Uzunkopru	76	B2
Uzunkuyu	76	B3

V

Name	Page	Grid
Vaajakoski	62	L5
Vaal	108	E5
Vaala	62	M4
Vaal Dam	108	E5
Vaasa *Finland*	62	J5
Vaasa *Finland*	62	K5
Vacaria	138	F5
Vacha	70	D3
Vache, Ile-a-	133	L5
Vadodara	92	D4
Vadso	62	N1
Vadu	73	K3
Vaduz	68	B2
Vaga	78	G3
Vagar	62	Z14
Vagay *Russia*	84	Ae5
Vagay *Russia*	84	Ae5
Vage	63	A6
Vaghena	114	H5
Vagnharad	63	G7
Vah	71	G5
Vaich, Loch	56	D3
Vainikkala	63	N6
Vaitupu	111	S3
Vakarel	73	G4
Vakfikebir	77	H2
Valaam, Ostrov	63	P6
Valandovo	73	G5
Valcheta	139	C8
Valday *Russia*	78	E4
Valday *Russia*	78	F3
Valdayskaya Vozvyshennost	78	E4
Valdemarsvik	63	G7
Valdepenas	66	E3
Valderaduey	66	D2
Valderrobres	67	G2
Valdes, Peninsula	139	D8
Valdez	118	F3
Valdivia	139	B7
Val-d'Or	125	M2
Valdosta	129	L5
Valdres	63	C6
Valea Lui Mihai	73	G2
Valenca	66	B2
Valenca	138	K6
Valenca do Piaui	137	J5
Valencay	65	D5
Valence	65	F6
Valencia *Spain*	67	F3
Valencia *Venezuela*	136	D1
Valencia de Alcantara	66	C3
Valencia de Don Juan	66	D1
Valencia, Golfo de	67	G3
Valencia Island	59	B9
Valencia, Lago de	133	P9
Valenciennes	64	E3
Valentim, Serra do	137	J5
Valentin	88	E4
Valentine	123	P6
Valenzuela	91	G3
Valera	136	C2
Valga	63	M8
Valiente, Peninsula	132	G10
Valjevo	72	E3
Valkinkay	71	L1
Valladolid *Mexico*	131	Q7
Valladolid *Spain*	66	D2
Vallasana de Mena	66	E1
Vallay	56	A3
Valle de la Pascua	136	D2
Valle de Santiago	131	J7
Valledupar	136	C1
Valle Grande	138	D3
Valle Hermosa	128	D8
Vallejo	126	A1
Vallenar	138	B5
Valletta	74	C5
Valley Falls	122	D6
Valleyview	119	M4
Vallgrund	62	J5
Vallimanca	139	D7
Vallo di Lucania	69	E5
Valls	67	G2
Valmiera	63	L8
Valognes	64	C4
Val-Paradis	125	L2
Valparaiso	129	J5
Valparaiso *Chile*	139	B6
Valparaiso *Mexico*	130	H6
Valpovo	72	E3
Valsjobyn	62	F4
Vals, Tanjung	114	B3
Valtos	56	B2
Valurfossen	63	B6
Valuyki	79	F5
Valverde	100	B3
Valverde de Jucar	66	E3
Valverde del Camino	66	C4
Van	77	K3
Vanajanselka	63	L6
Vanavona	114	H6
Van Buren *Arkansas, U.S.A.*	128	E3
Van Buren *Maine, U.S.A.*	125	S3
Van Canh	93	L6
Vancouver *Canada*	122	C3
Vancouver *U.S.A.*	122	C5
Vancouver Island	122	A2
Vanda	63	N6
Vandalia	124	F7
Vanderhoof	118	L5
Van Diemen, Cape	112	G1
Van Diemen Gulf	112	G1
Vanern	63	E7
Vanersborg	63	E7
Vanga	107	G3
Vangaindrano	109	J4
Van Golu	77	K3
Vangou	88	D4
Vangunu	114	J6
Van Horn	127	K5
Vanikoro Islands	114	N7
Vanimo	114	C2
Vanna	62	H1
Vannas	62	H5
Vannes	65	B5
Van Rees, Pegunungan	114	B2
Vanrhynsdorp	108	C6
Vanrock	113	J2
Vansbro	63	F6
Vanset	77	K4
Vansittart Island	120	K4
Vantaa	63	N6
Vanua Balavu	114	T10
Vanua Lava	114	T10
Vanua Levu	114	R8
Vanua Levu Barrier Reef	114	R8
Vanuatu	114	T12
Vanwyksvlei	108	D6
Vanzevat	84	Ae4
Vapnyarka	73	K1
Varallo	68	B3
Varamin	95	K4
Varanasi	92	F3
Varandey	78	K2
Varangerfjorden	62	P1
Varangerhalvoya	62	N1
Varazdin	72	D2
Varazze	68	B3
Varberg	63	E8
Vardar	73	F5
Varde	63	C9
Vardo	62	P1
Varena	71	L1
Varennes	65	E5
Varese	68	B3
Varfolomeyevka	88	D3
Vargarda	63	E7
Vargas Guerra	136	B4
Varginha	138	G4
Varilla	138	B4
Varkaus	63	L5
Varmland	63	E7
Varmlands-nas	63	E7
Varna	73	J4
Varnamo	63	F8
Varnek	84	Ad3
Varnya	84	A3
Varoy	62	E3
Varto	77	J3
Vartry Reservoir	59	K6
Varzea Grande	137	J5
Varzino	78	F2
Varzuga	78	F2
Varzy	65	E5
Vasa	62	J5
Vascao	66	C3
Vascongadas	66	E1
Vashkovtsy	73	H1
Vasilishki	71	L2
Vasilkov	79	E5
Vasilyevka	79	F6
Vaskha	78	H3
Vaslui	73	J2
Vassdalsegga	63	B7
Vasteras	63	G7
Vasterbotten	62	G4
Vasterdalalven	63	E6
Vastergotland	63	E7
Vasterhaninge	63	H7
Vasternorrland	62	G5
Vastervik	63	G8
Vastmanland	63	G7
Vasto	69	E4
Vasyugan	84	B5
Vatersay	57	A4
Vathi *Greece*	75	F3
Vathi *Greece*	75	J4
Vaticano, Capo	69	E6
Vatilau	114	J6
Vatnajokull	62	W12
Vatneyri	62	A2
Vatoa	111	T5
Vatomandry	109	J3
Vatra Dornei	73	H2
Vattern	63	F7
Vatu-i-Ra Channel	114	R8
Vatulele	114	Q9
Vaughn	127	K3
Vaupes	136	C3
Vavatenina	109	J3
Vavau Group	111	U5
Vavuniya	92	F7
Vaxholm	63	H7
Vaxjo	63	F8
Vayalpad	92	E6
Vaygach	84	Ac2
Vaygach, Ostrov	84	Ac2
Veberod	63	E9
Vebomark	62	J4
Vecht	64	G2
Vechta	70	C2
Vechte	70	B2
Veddige	63	E8
Vega *Norway*	62	D4
Vega *U.S.A.*	127	L3
Vegorritis, Limni	75	F2
Vegreville	119	N5
Veidholmen	62	B5
Veinge	63	E8
Vejen	63	C9
Vejer de la Frontera	66	D4
Vejle	63	C9
Velanidhia	75	G4
Velas, Cabo	132	E9
Velasco, Sierra de	138	C5
Velay, Monts du	65	E6
Velebit Planina	72	C3
Velestinon	75	G3
Velez Malaga	66	D4
Velez Rubio	67	E4
Velhas	138	H3
Velichayevskoye	79	H7
Velika Gorica	72	D3
Velika Kapela	72	C3
Velikaya *Russia*	78	H2
Velikaya *Russia*	85	W4
Velikaya Kema	88	F3
Veliki Kanal	72	E3
Velikiy Bereznyy	71	K4
Velikiye Luki	78	E4
Velikonda Range	92	E6
Veliko Turnovo	73	H4
Veliky Ustyug	78	H3
Velingara	104	C3
Velingrad	73	H4
Velizh	78	E4
Vella Gulf	114	H5
Vella Lavella	114	H5
Velletri	69	D5
Vellore	92	E6
Velsk	78	G3
Velt	78	J2
Velvestad	62	E4
Venado Tuerto	139	D6
Venafro	69	E5
Venaria	68	A3
Venda Nova	66	C2
Vendas Novas	66	B3
Vendome	65	D5
Vendsyssel	63	D8
Venecia	136	D6
Venezia	68	D3
Venezia, Golfo di	68	D3
Venezuela	136	D2
Venezuela Basin	134	C1
Venezuela, Golfo de	136	C1
Vengurla	92	D5
Veniaminof Volcano	118	Ag8
Venlo	64	G3
Venice *U.S.A.*	128	H6
Venkatapuram	92	F5
Vennesla	63	C7
Venta	63	J8
Ventimiglia	68	A4
Ventnor	53	F4
Ventry	59	B8
Ventspils	63	N8
Ventuari	136	D3
Ventura	126	C3
Venus Bay	113	K6
Venustiano Carranza *Mexico*	130	G5
Venustiano Carranza *Mexico*	131	N9
Vera *Argentina*	138	D5
Vera *Spain*	67	F4
Veracruz	131	L8
Veranopolis	138	F5
Veraval	92	D4
Verbania	68	B3
Vercelli	68	B3
Verdalsora	62	D5
Verde *Mexico*	131	L9
Verde *U.S.A.*	126	G3
Verden	70	C2
Verdigris	124	C8
Verdinho, Serra do	138	F3
Verdon	65	G2
Verdun	64	F4
Vereeniging	108	E5
Vereshchagino	78	J4
Verga, Cap	104	C3
Verin	66	C2
Verin Talin	77	K2
Verkhne-Avzyar	78	K5
Verkhnedvinsk	63	M9
Verkhne-Imanskiy	88	E3
Verkhneimbatskoye	84	D4
Verkhne Matur	84	D6
Verkhne Nildino	84	Ad4
Verkhne Skoblino	84	D5
Verkhnetulomskiy	62	P2
Verkhne Tura	78	K4
Verkhnevilyuysk	85	L4
Verkhniy Baskunchak	79	H6
Verkhniy Shar	78	J2
Verkhnyaya Amga	85	M5
Verkhnyaya Inta	78	L2
Verkhnyaya Toyma	78	H3
Verkhoturye	84	Ad5
Verkhovye	79	F5
Verkhoyansk	85	N3
Verkhoyanskiy Khrebet	85	M3
Verkhyaya Nildino	78	L3
Vermilion	119	N5
Vermilion Bay	128	G6
Vermilion Lake	124	D3
Vermillion	123	R6
Vermillion Bay	124	D2
Vermont	125	P5
Vernal	123	K7
Verneuil	64	D4
Vernon *Canada*	122	E2
Vernon *France*	64	D4
Vernon *U.S.A.*	127	N3
Veroia	75	G2
Verona	68	C3
Versailles	64	E4
Vert, Cape	104	B3
Verviers	64	F3
Vervins	64	E4
Veryan Bay	52	C4
Veryuvom	78	L2
Veshenskaya	79	G6
Veslos	63	C8
Veslyana	78	J3
Vesoul	65	G5
Vest-Agder	63	B7
Vesteralen	62	F2
Vestfjorden	62	F2
Vest-Fold	63	D7
Vestre Jakobselv	62	N1
Vestvagoy	62	E2
Vesuvio	69	E5
Vesyegonsk	78	F4
Veszprem	72	D2
Vetekhtina	85	K5
Vetlanda	63	F8
Vetluga *Russia*	78	H4
Vetluga *Russia*	78	H4
Vetluzskiy	78	H4
Vettore, Monte	69	D4
Veun Kham	93	L6
Veurne	64	E3
Vevey	68	A2
Veyatie, Loch	56	C2
Vezelay	65	E5
Vezere	65	D6
Vezirkopru	76	F2
Viacha	138	C3
Viamao	138	F6
Viana	137	J4
Viana do Castelo	66	B2
Viangchan	93	K5
Viareggio	68	C4
Viaur	65	E6
Viborg	63	C8
Vibo Valentia	69	F6
Vicecomodoro Marambio	141	W6
Vicente Guerrero	130	H6
Vicenza	68	C3
Vich	67	H2
Vichada	136	D3
Vichuga	78	G4
Vichy	65	E5
Vicksburg	128	G4
Vico	69	B4
Vicosa	137	K5
Victor Emanuel Range	114	C3
Victor Harbor	113	H6
Victoria *Argentina*	138	D6
Victoria *Northern Territory, Australia*	112	G2
Victoria *Victoria, Australia*	113	J6
Victoria *Cameroon*	105	G5
Victoria *Canada*	122	C3
Victoria *Chile*	139	B7
Victoria *Hong Kong*	90	E1
Victoria *Malaysia*	90	F4
Victoria *Seychelles*	82	D7
Victoria *U.S.A.*	128	D6
Victoria de las Tunas	132	J4
Victoria Falls	108	E3
Victoria Island	119	P1

Name	Page	Ref
Victoria, Lake	107	F3
Victoria Land	141	L4
Victoria, Mount *Burma*	93	H4
Victoria, Mount *Papua New Guinea*	114	D3
Victoria Nile	107	F2
Victoria Peak	118	K5
Victoria Strait	119	Q2
Victoriaville	125	Q3
Victoria West	108	D6
Victorica	139	C7
Victorville	126	D3
Vicuna	138	B6
Vidago	66	C2
Vidalia	129	L4
Vidareidi	62	Z14
Vididalur	62	X12
Vidim	84	G5
Vidimyri	62	V12
Vidin	73	G4
Vidisha	92	E4
Vidivellir	62	X12
Vidomlya	71	K2
Vidsel	62	J4
Viedma	139	D8
Viedma, Lago	139	B9
Viella	67	G1
Vienna *Austria*	68	F1
Vienna *Illinois, U.S.A.*	124	F8
Vienna *Ohio, U.S.A.*	125	K7
Vienne *France*	65	D5
Vienne *France*	65	F6
Vientiane	93	K5
Vieques	133	Q5
Vierwaldstatter See	68	B2
Vierzon	65	E5
Vieste	69	F5
Vietnam	93	L5
Vif	65	F6
Vigan	91	G2
Vigevano	68	B3
Viggiano	69	E5
Vigia	137	G4
Viglio, Monte	69	D5
Vigo	66	B1
Vigrestad	63	A7
Viiala	63	K6
Vijayawada	92	F5
Vijose	74	E2
Vik	62	E4
Vik	62	V13
Vikajarvi	62	M3
Vikersund	63	D7
Vikhorevka	84	G5
Vikna	62	D4
Viksoyri	63	B6
Vila	114	U12
Viladikars	77	K2
Vila Franca	66	B3
Vilaine	65	C5
Vilaller	67	G1
Vilanculos	109	G4
Vila Nova	137	F4
Vila Nova de Famalicao	66	B2
Vila Pouca de Aguiar	66	C2
Vila Real	66	C2
Vila Real de Santo Antonio	66	C4
Vila Velha	138	H4
Vila Velha de Rodao	66	C3
Vila Vicosa	66	C3
Vilcheka, Zemlya	80	H1
Viled	78	H3
Vileyka	71	M1
Vilhelmina	62	G4
Vilhena	136	E6
Viliga-Kushka	85	T4
Viljandi	63	L7
Vilkitskogo, Proliv	81	M2
Vilkovo	73	K3
Villa Abecia	138	C4
Villa Angela	138	D5
Villa Aroma	138	C3
Villa Bella	136	D6
Villa Bens	100	C3
Villablino	66	C1
Villacarrillo	66	E3
Villacastin	66	D2
Villach	68	D2
Villa Cisneros	100	B4
Villa Constitucion	138	D6
Villa de Cura	136	D2
Villadiego	66	D1
Villa Dolores	139	C6
Villafranca del Bierzo	66	C1
Villafranca de los Barros	66	C3
Villafranca del Penedes	67	G2
Villafranca di Verona	68	C3
Villaguay	138	E6
Villa Hayes	138	E6
Villahermosa	131	N9
Villa Huidobro	139	D6
Villa Iris	139	D7
Villajoyosa	67	F3
Villalba	66	C1
Villalon de Campos	66	D1
Villalpando	66	D2
Villa Maria	138	D6
Villamayor de Santiago	66	E3
Villa Montes	138	D4
Villanueva	130	H6
Villanueva de Cordoba	66	D3
Villanueva del Fresno	66	C3
Villanueva de los Castillejos	66	C4
Villanueva de los Infantes	66	E3
Villanueva y Geltru	67	G2
Villaputzu	69	B6
Villarcayo	66	E1
Villarejo	66	E2
Villarrica	138	E5
Villarrobledo	66	E3
Villasandino	66	D1
Villa Union *Argentina*	138	C5
Villa Union *Mexico*	127	M6
Villavicencio	136	C3
Villaviciosa	66	D1
Villazon	138	C4
Villedieu	64	C4
Villefort	65	E6
Villefranche-de-Rouergue	65	E6
Villefranche-sur-Saone	65	F6
Villena	67	F3
Villeneuve-sur-Lot	65	D6
Villeneuve-sur-Yonne	65	E4
Ville Platte	128	F5
Villers-Bocage	64	C4
Villers-Cotterets	64	E4
Villeurbanne	65	F6
Villodrigo	66	D1
Vilna	71	L1
Vilnius	71	L1
Vilnya	71	L1
Vilshofen	70	E4
Vilyuy	85	M4
Vilyuysk	85	L4
Vilyuyskoye Plato	84	H3
Vimmerby	63	F8
Vimperk	70	E4
Vina del Mar	139	B6
Vinaroz	67	G2
Vinas	63	F6
Vincennes	124	G7
Vincennes Bay	141	H5
Vinchina	138	C5
Vindelalven	62	J4
Vindeln	62	H4
Vindhya Range	92	E4
Vineland	125	N7
Vinga	73	F3
Vinh	93	L5
Vinh Loi	93	L7
Vinh Long	93	L6
Vinh Yen	93	L4
Vinica	73	G5
Vinkovci	72	E3
Vinnitsa	79	D6
Vinogradov	71	K4
Vipiteno	68	C2
Vir	72	C3
Virac	91	G3
Viramgam	92	D4
Virandozero	78	F3
Viransehir	77	H4
Virarajendrapet	92	E6
Virden	123	P3
Vire *France*	64	C4
Vire *France*	64	C4
Virfurile	73	G2
Virgenes, Cabo	139	C10
Virgin	126	E2
Virgin Gorda	133	Q5
Virginia *Ireland*	58	H5
Virginia *Minnesota, U.S.A.*	124	D3
Virginia *U.S.A.*	125	L8
Virginia Beach	125	N8
Virginia Falls	118	L3
Virgin Islands	133	Q5
Virmasvesi	62	M5
Virovitica	72	D3
Virrat	63	K5
Virudunagar	92	E7
Vis	72	D4
Visalia	126	C2
Visayan Sea	91	G3
Visby	63	H8
Viscount Melville Sound	120	E3
Visegrad	72	E4
Viseu *Brazil*	137	H4
Viseu *Portugal*	66	C2
Vishakhapatnam	92	F5
Vishera	78	K3
Vishnevets	71	L4
Vislanda	63	F8
Visoko	72	E4
Viso, Monte	68	A3
Vistonis, Limni	75	H2
Vit	73	H4
Vitava	70	F4
Vitebsk	78	E4
Viterbo	69	D4
Viterog Planina	72	D3
Vitiaz Strait	114	C3
Vitichi	138	C4
Vitigudino	66	C2
Viti Levu	114	Q9
Vitim *Russia*	85	J5
Vitim *Russia*	85	J5
Vitina	75	G4
Vitoria	66	E1
Vitoria	138	H4
Vitoria da Conquista	137	J6
Vitoria de Santa Antao	137	K5
Vitre	64	C4
Vitry-le-Francois	64	F4
Vittangi	62	J3
Vittel	64	F4
Vittoria	69	E7
Vittorio Veneto	68	D3
Vivarais, Monts du	65	F6
Viver	67	F3
Vivero	66	C1
Vivi *Russia*	84	F4
Vivi *Russia*	84	F4
Vizcaino, Desierto de	126	F7
Vizcaino, Sierra	126	E7
Vize	76	B2
Vizhas	78	H2
Vizianagaram	92	F5
Vizinga	78	J3
Vizzavona	69	B4
Vladicin Han	73	G4
Vladimir	78	G4
Vladimirets	71	M3
Vladimirovka	79	J5
Vladimir Volynskiy	71	L3
Vladivostok	88	C4
Vlakherna	75	G4
Vlasenica	72	E3
Vlieland	64	F2
Vlissingen	64	E3
Vlore	74	E2
Vodice	72	C4
Vodlozero, Ozero	78	F3
Vogan	105	F4
Voghera	68	B3
Voh	114	W16
Vohemar	109	J2
Vohilava	109	J4
Vohimarina	109	J2
Vohipeno	109	J4
Voi	107	G3
Voiron	65	F6
Vojens	63	C9
Vojmsjon	62	G4
Vojnic	72	C3
Volary	70	E4
Volborg	123	M5
Volchansk	79	F5
Volda	62	B5
Volga	79	H6
Volgodonsk	79	G6
Volgograd	79	G6
Volgogradskoye Vodokhranilishche	79	H6
Volgsele	62	G4
Volissos	75	H3
Volkhov *Russia*	78	E4
Volkhov *Russia*	78	E4
Volklingen	70	B4
Volkovysk	71	L2
Volksrust	108	E5
Volnovakha	79	F6
Volochankao	84	E2
Volochayevka	88	E1
Volochisk	71	M4
Volodskaya	78	G3
Vologda	78	F4
Volokon	84	H5
Volonga	78	H2
Volos	75	G3
Voloshka	78	F3
Volovets	71	K4
Volozhin	71	M1
Volpa	71	L2
Volsk	79	H5
Volta	104	F4
Volta, Lake	104	E4
Volta Redonda	138	H4
Volterra	68	C4
Volteva	78	G3
Volturno	69	E5
Volvi, Limni	75	G2
Volynskaya Vozvyshennost	71	L3
Volynskoje Polesje	71	L3
Volzhskiy	79	G6
Von Martius, Cachoeira	137	G6
Vopnafjordur	62	X12
Voras Oros	75	F2
Vordingborg	63	D9
Voriai Sporadhes	75	H3
Vorkuta	78	L2
Vormsi	62	K7
Voronezh	79	F5
Voronovo	71	L1
Vorontsovo	63	N8
Voronya	78	F2
Voroshilovgrad	79	F6
Voroshno	78	H4
Vortsjarv	63	M7
Voru	63	M8
Vosges	64	G4
Voskresensk	78	F4
Voss *Norway*	63	B6
Voss *Norway*	63	B6
Vostochno-Sibirskoye More	85	T2
Vostochnyy *Russia*	88	D4
Vostochnyy *Russia*	88	J1
Vostock	141	H3
Vostretsovo	88	E1
Votice	70	F4
Votkinsk	78	J4
Votkinskoye Vodokhranilishche	78	K4
Vot Tande	114	T10
Vouga	66	C2
Vouziers	64	F4
Vowchurch	52	E2
Voxnan *Sweden*	63	F6
Voxnan *Sweden*	63	F6
Voynitsa	62	P4
Voy Vozh	78	J3
Voyvozh	78	K3
Voza	114	H5
Vozhayel	78	H3
Vozhega	78	G3
Vozhe, Ozero	78	F3
Voznesensk	79	E6
Voznesenye	78	F3
Vozvyshennost Karabil	95	R3
Vrancei, Muntii	73	J3
Vrangelya, Mys	85	P6
Vrangelya, Ostrov	81	U2
Vranje	73	F4
Vranov	71	J4
Vratsa	73	G4
Vrbas	72	D3
Vrbovsko	72	C3
Vrede	108	E5
Vrhnika	72	C3
Vrindavan	92	E3
Vrlika	72	D4
Vrondadhes	75	J3
Vrsac	73	F3
Vrsacki Kanal	73	F3
Vryburg	108	D5
Vryheid	108	F5
Vucitrn	73	F4
Vukovar	72	E3
Vulavu	114	J6
Vulcan	73	G3
Vulcano, Isola	69	E6
Vung Tau	93	L6
Vunisea	114	R9
Vuokatti	62	N4
Vuollerim	62	J3
Vyartsilya	62	P5
Vyatka	78	J4
Vyatskiye Polyany	78	J4
Vyazemskiy	88	E2
Vyazma	78	E4
Vyazniki	78	G4
Vyborg	63	N6
Vychegda	78	H3
Vydrino	84	F5
Vygoda	73	L2
Vygozero, Ozero	78	F3
Vyhorlat	71	K4
Vyksa	78	G4
Vym	78	J3
Vyrnwy	52	D2
Vyshniy-Volochek	78	E4
Vysokoye	71	K2
Vytegra	78	F3
Vyzhva	71	L3

W

Name	Page	Ref
Wa	104	E3
Waal	64	F3
Waat	103	F6
Wabana	121	R8
Wabasca	119	N4
Wabash	124	G7
Wabe Gestro Wenz	103	H6
Wabe Shabele Wenz	103	H6
Wabigoon Lake	124	D2
Wabowden	119	R4
Wabush	121	N7
Waccasassa Bay	129	L6
Waco	128	D5
Wad Banda	102	E5
Waddan	101	J3
Waddeneilanden	64	F2
Waddenzee	64	F2
Waddesdon	53	G3
Waddington, Mount	118	K5
Wadebridge	52	C4
Wadena	124	C3
Wadi Gimal	96	B4
Wadi Halfa	102	F3
Wad Medani	103	F5
Wadomari	89	J10
Wad Rawa	103	F4
Wafra	97	H2
Wager Bay	120	J4
Wagga Wagga	113	K6
Wagin	112	D5
Wahai	91	H6
Waharoa	115	E2
Wahiawa	126	R10
Wahibah, Ramlat ahl	97	P6
Wahidi	96	H9
Wahoo	123	R7
Wahpeton	123	R4
Waialua	126	R10
Waianae	126	R10
Waiau *New Zealand*	115	A6
Waiau *New zealand*	115	D5
Waiau *New Zealand*	115	D5
Waibeem	91	J6
Waidhofen *Austria*	68	E2
Waidhofen *Austria*	68	E2
Waigeo	91	J6
Waiheke Island	115	E2
Waihi	115	E2
Waikabubak	91	F7
Waikato	115	E3
Waikerie	113	H5
Waikouaiti	115	C6
Wailuku	126	S10
Waimakariri	115	D5
Waimamaku	115	D1
Waimate	115	C6
Wainganga	92	E4

Waingapu 91 G7
Waini Point 136 F2
Wainwright 118 D1
Waiotapu 115 F3
Waiouru 115 E3
Waipa 115 E2
Waipahi 115 B7
Waipara 115 D5
Waipawa 115 F3
Waipiro 115 G3
Waipu 115 E1
Waipukurau 115 F3
Wairau 115 D4
Wairau Valley 115 D4
Wairio 115 B7
Wairoa 115 F3
Waitaki 115 C6
Waitangi 115 F6
Waitara 115 E3
Waitoa 115 E2
Waiuku 115 E2
Wajima 89 F7
Wajir 107 H2
Wakasa-wan 89 E8
Waka, Tanjung 91 H6
Wakatipu, Lake 115 B6
Wakaya 114 R8
Wakayama 89 E8
Wake 89 E8
Wakeeny 123 Q8
Wakefield 55 H3
Wakkanai 88 H3
Wakool *Australia* 113 J6
Wakool *Australia* 113 J6
Waku Kungo 106 C5
Walachia 73 H3
Walade 114 K6
Walagan 87 N1
Walbrzych 71 G3
Walcha 113 L5
Walcheren 64 E3
Walcz 71 G2
Waldenburg 71 G3
Waldon 52 C4
Waldron 128 E3
Waldshut 70 C5
Wales 118 A2
Wales Island 120 J4
Walgett 113 K4
Walikale 107 E3
Walinga 114 D3
Walker 122 E8
Walkeringham 55 J3
Walker Lake 122 E8
Wallace 129 P3
Wallaceburg 124 J5
Wallal Downs 112 E2
Wallasey 55 F3
Walla Walla 122 E4
Walldurn 70 C4
Wallhallow 113 H2
Wallingford 53 F3
Wallis, Iles 111 T4
Wallowa 122 F5
Walls 56 A1
Wallsend 55 H2
Walney, Island of 55 F2
Walpole 114 Y17
Walsall 53 F2
Walsenburg 127 K2
Walsingham, Cape 120 P4
Walsrode 70 C2
Walterboro 129 M4
Walter F. George Reservoir 129 K5
Waltham Abbey 53 H3
Walton 53 G3
Walvis Bay 108 B4
Wama 106 C5
Wamba *Nigeria* 105 G4
Wamba *Zaire* 106 C4
Wami 114 A2
Wana 92 C2
Wanaaring 113 J4
Wanaka 115 B6
Wanaka, Lake 115 B6
Wanapiri 91 K6
Wanapitei 124 K3
Wanda Shan 88 C3
Wandel Sea 140 P2
Wandingzhen 93 J4
Wanganui *New Zealand* 115 E3
Wanganui *New Zealand* 115 E3
Wangaratta 113 K6
Wangary 113 H5
Wangerooge 70 B2
Wangiwangi 91 G7
Wangjiadian 88 C2
Wangkui 87 P2
Wang, Mae Nam 93 J5
Wangqing 88 B4
Wanie-Rukula 106 E2
Wankaner 92 D4
Wankie 108 E3
Wanlaweyn 107 H2
Wanquan 87 L3
Wantage 53 F3
Wanxian 93 L2
Wanyuan 93 L2
Wanzai 93 M3
Wapenamanda 114 C3
Wapsipinicon 124 E5
Warangal 92 E5
Waratah Bay 113 K6
Warboys 53 G2
Warbreccan 113 J3
Warburg 70 C3
Warburton 113 H4
Ward 115 E4
Wardha 92 E4
Ward Hunt, Cape 114 D3
Ward Hunt Strait 114 E3
Ware *Canada* 118 K4
Ware *U.K.* 53 G3
Ware *U.S.A.* 125 P5
Wareham 53 E4
Waren *Germany* 70 E2
Waren *Indonesia* 91 K6
Warka 71 J3
Wark Forest 57 F5
Warkworth 115 E2
Warlingham 53 G3
Warmbad 108 C5
Warminster 53 E3
Warm Springs 126 D1
Warner Robins 129 L4
Warnow 70 D2
Warora 92 E4
Warracknabeal 113 J6
Warrego 113 K5
Warren *Minnesota, U.S.A.* 124 B2
Warren *Ohio, U.S.A.* 125 K6
Warren *Pennsylvania, U.S.A.* 125 L6
Warrenpoint 58 K4
Warrenton *South Africa* 108 D5
Warrenton *U.S.A.* 125 M7
Warri 105 G4
Warrina 113 H4
Warrington *U.K.* 55 G3
Warrington *U.S.A.* 129 J5
Warrior Reefs 114 C3
Warrnambool 113 J6
Warroad 124 C2
Warsaw 71 J2
Warshiikh 107 J2
Warsop 55 H3
Warszawa 71 J2
Warta 71 G2
Waru 91 J6
Warwick *Australia* 113 L4
Warwick *U.K.* 53 F2
Warwick *U.S.A.* 125 Q6
Warwick Channel 113 H1
Warwickshire 53 F2
Wasbister 56 E1
Wasco 126 C3
Wasdale Head 55 F2
Washburn Lake 119 P1
Washim 92 E4
Washington *U.K.* 55 H2
Washington *District of Columbia, U.S.A.* 125 M7
Washington *Georgia, U.S.A.* 129 L4
Washington *Indiana, U.S.A.* 124 G7
Washington *Missouri, U.S.A.* 124 E7
Washington *N.Carolina, U.S.A.* 129 P3
Washington *Pennsylvania, U.S.A.* 125 K6
Washington *U.S.A.* 122 D4
Washington Cape 141 M4
Washington Land 120 N1
Washington, Mount 125 Q4
Wash, The 53 H2
Wasian 91 J6
Wasior 91 J6
Wasisi 91 H6
Waskaganish 121 L7
Waspan 132 E7
Wast Water 55 F2
Watam 114 C2
Watampone 91 G6
Watansoppeng 91 F6
Watchet 52 D3
Waterbeach 53 H2
Waterbury 125 P6
Wateree 129 M3
Waterford *Ireland* 59 G8
Waterford *Ireland* 59 H8
Watergrasshill 59 F8
Waterloo *Belgium* 64 F3
Waterloo *U.S.A.* 124 D5
Waterlooville 53 F4
Waternish 56 B3
Waternish Point 56 B3
Waterside 57 D5
Watertown *New York, U.S.A.* 125 N4
Watertown *S.Dakota, U.S.A.* 123 R5
Watertown *Wisconsin, U.S.A.* 124 F5
Waterville *Ireland* 59 B9
Waterville *U.S.A.* 125 R4
Watford 53 G3
Watford City 123 N4
Watheroo 112 D5
Watkaremoana, Lake 115 F3
Watling Island 133 K2
Watlington 53 F3
Watroa 115 F3
Watsa 107 E2
Watseka 124 G6
Watson 123 M1
Watson Lake 118 K3
Watsonville 126 B2
Watten 56 E2
Watten, Loch 56 E2
Watton 53 H2
Watubela, Kepulauan 91 J6
Wau *Papua New Guinea* 114 D3
Wau *Sudan* 102 E6
Wauchope 113 G3
Waukarlycarly, Lake 112 E3
Waukegan 124 G5
Waurika 128 D3
Wausau 124 F4
Wave Hill 112 G2
Waveney 53 J2
Waverly 125 M5
Wavre 64 F3
Wawa 124 H3
Waxahachie 128 D4
Waya 114 Q8
Wayabula 91 H5
Waycross 129 L5
Way, Lake 112 E4
Waynesboro *Georgia, U.S.A.* 129 L4
Waynesboro *Mississippi, U.S.A.* 128 H5
Waynesboro *Pennsylvania, U.S.A.* 125 M7
Waynesburg 125 K7
Waynesville *Missouri, U.S.A.* 124 D8
Waynesville *Tennessee, U.S.A.* 129 L3
Waynoka 128 C2
Wda 71 H2
We 90 B4
We 114 X16
Weald, The 53 H3
Wear 55 H2
Weardale 55 H2
Weasenham 53 H2
Weatherall Bay 120 E2
Weatherford 128 C3
Weaver 55 G3
Webi Shabeelle 103 J7
Webster 123 R5
Webster City 124 D5
Weda 91 H5
Weddell Sea 141 W4
Wedel 70 C2
Weduar, Tanjung 91 J7
Weeley 53 J3
Weemelah 113 K4
Wegorzewo 71 J1
Wegorzyno 70 F2
Weichang 87 M3
Weiden 70 E4
Weifang 87 M4
Weihai 87 N4
Weihe 88 B3
Wei He 93 L2
Weilu 87 L3
Weimar 70 D3
Weinan 93 L2
Weingarten 70 C5
Weiser 122 F5
Weissenburg 70 D4
Weissenfels 70 D3
Weiss Lake 129 K3
Weitra 68 E1
Weixin 93 K3
Wejherowo 71 H1
Welch 125 K8
Welcome Kop 108 C6
Welda 70 E3
Weldiya 103 G5
Welkom 108 E5
Welland 53 G2
Wellesley Islands 113 H2
Wellingborough 53 G2
Wellington *New Zealand* 115 E4
Wellington *South Africa* 108 C6
Wellington *Shropshire, U.K.* 52 E2
Wellington *Somerset, U.K.* 52 D4
Wellington *Kansas, U.S.A.* 128 D2
Wellington *Texas, U.S.A.* 127 M3
Wellington Channel 120 H2
Wellington, Isla 139 B9
Wells *U.K.* 52 E3
Wells *U.S.A.* 122 G7
Wellsford 115 E2
Wells-next-the-Sea 53 H2
Welney 53 H2
Wels 68 D1
Welshpool 52 D2
Welwyn Garden City 53 G3
Wemindji 121 L7
Wenasaga 123 T2
Wenatchee 122 D4
Wenchang 93 M5
Wenchuan 93 K2
Wendover 122 G7
Wengen 68 A2
Wenling 87 N6
Wenlock Edge 52 E2
Wenshan 93 K4
Wensleydale 55 H2
Wensu 86 E3
Wen Xian 93 K2
Wenzhou 87 N6
Wepener 108 E5
Weri 91 J6
Wernigerode 70 D3
Werra 70 D3
Werris Creek 113 L5
Wertach 70 D4
Weser 70 C2
Weslaco 128 D7
Wessel Islands 113 H1
West Auckland 55 H2
West Bay 128 H6
West Bengal 93 G4
West Branch Susquehanna 125 M6
West Bromwich 53 E2
Westbrook 125 Q5
West Burra 56 A2
Westbury 53 E3
Westbury-sub-Mendip 52 E3
Westby 124 E5
West Calder 57 E5
West End 129 N7
Westerdale 55 J2
Westerham 53 H3
Westerland 70 C1
Western Australia 112 E3
Western Desert 103 E2
Western Ghats 92 D5
Western Isles 56 A3
Westernport 125 L7
Western Ross 56 C3
Western Sahara 100 C4
Western Samoa 111 U4
Westerschelde 64 E3
Westerstede 70 B2
Westerwald 70 B3
West Falkland 139 E10
Westfield *U.K.* 56 E2
Westfield *Massachusetts, U.S.A.* 125 P5
Westfield *New York, U.S.A.* 125 L5
West Frankfort 124 F8
Westgate 55 G2
West Gerinish 56 A3
West Glamorgan 52 D3
West Glen 53 G2
West Harptree 52 E3
West Heslerton 55 J2
West Hoathly 53 G3
West Indies 48 D4
West Kilbride 57 D5
West Kirby 55 F3
West Linton 57 E5
Westlock 119 N5
Westmeath 59 G6
West Memphis 128 G3
West Meon 53 F3
West Mersea 53 H3
West Midlands 53 F2
West Moors 53 F4
Westmoreland 113 H2
Weston 125 K7
Weston-Super-Mare 52 E3
West Palm Beach 129 M7
West Plains 124 E8
West Point *Mississippi, U.S.A.* 128 H4
West Point *Nebraska, U.S.A.* 123 R7
Westport *Ireland* 58 C5
Westport *New Zealand* 115 C4
Westport Quay 58 C5
Westray 56 F1
Westray Firth 56 E1
West Road 118 L5
West Sussex 53 G4
West Tavaputs Plateau 122 J8
West Virginia 125 K7
West Wellow 53 F4
West Wyalong 113 K5
West Yellowstone 122 J5
West Yorkshire 55 H3
Wetar 91 H7
Wetar, Selat 91 H7
Wetaskiwin 119 N5
Wetherby 55 H3
Wewahitchka 129 K5
Wewak 114 C2
Wexford *Ireland* 59 J8
Wexford *Ireland* 59 K8
Wexford Bay 59 K8
Wey 53 G3
Weybridge 53 G3
Weyburn 123 N3
Weyhill 53 F3
Weymouth 52 E4
Weymouth Bay *Australia* 113 J1
Weymouth Bay *U.K.* 52 E4
Whakataki 115 F4
Whakatane 115 F2
Whalsay 56 A1
Whanganui Inlet 115 D4
Whangaparaoa 115 G2
Whangarei 115 E1
Whangaruru Harbour 115 D1
Whaplode 53 G2
Wharanui 115 E4
Wharfe 55 H2
Wharfedale 55 H3
Wharton 128 D6
Whataroa 115 C5
Wheatland 123 M6
Wheatley *Nottinghamshire, U.K.* 55 J3
Wheatley *Oxfordshire, U.K.* 53 F3
Wheeler Peak 122 G8
Wheeling 125 K6
Whernside 55 G2
Whidbey, Point 113 H5
Whitburn *Lothian, U.K.* 57 E5
Whitburn *Tyne and Wear, U.K.* 55 H2
Whitby 55 J2
Whitchurch *Avon, U.K.* 52 E3
Whitchurch *Hampshire, U.K.* 53 F3
Whitchurch *Shropshire, U.K.* 52 E2
White *Canada* 118 G3
White *Arkansas, U.S.A.* 128 G3
White *Indiana, U.S.A.* 124 G7
White *Missouri, U.S.A.* 124 D8
White *S.Dakota, U.S.A.* 123 P6
White *Texas, U.S.A.* 127 M4
Whiteadder Reservoir 57 F5
White Bay 121 Q7
Whitecourt 119 M5

Name	Page	Grid
Whitefish	122	G3
Whitefish Lake	119	P3
Whitefish Point	124	H3
White Gull Lake	121	P6
Whitehall	125	P5
White Handkerchief, Cape	121	P6
Whitehaven	55	F2
Whitehead	58	L3
Whitehorse	118	H3
Whitehorse Hill	53	F3
White Island	115	F2
White, Lake	112	E5
White Lake	128	F6
Whiteman Range	114	E3
White Mountains	118	F2
White Mount Peak	122	E9
Whitemouth	124	B2
Whiten Head	56	D2
Whiteparish	53	F3
White Pass	118	H4
White River	124	H2
White River Plateau	123	L8
White Salmon	122	D5
White Sea	78	F2
White Sulphur Springs	122	J4
White Volta	104	E4
Whitewater	124	F5
Whitewood	123	N2
Whitfield Moor	55	G2
Whithorn	54	E2
Whiting Bay	57	C5
Whitley Bay	55	H1
Whitmore	52	E2
Whitney, Mount	126	C2
Whitney-on-Wye	52	D2
Whitsand Bay	52	C4
Whitstable	53	J3
Whittlesey	53	G2
Whitton	55	J3
Whittonstall	55	H2
Whitworth	55	G3
Wholdaia Lake	119	Q3
Whyalla	113	H5
Wiarton	125	K4
Wiay	56	A3
Wichita	128	D2
Wichita Falls	127	N4
Wichita Mountains	128	C3
Wick U.K.	56	E2
Wick U.K.	56	E2
Wickenburg	126	F4
Wickford	53	H3
Wickham	55	H2
Wickhambrook	53	H2
Wickham, Cape	113	J6
Wicklow Ireland	59	K7
Wicklow Ireland	59	K7
Wicklow Head	59	L7
Wicklow Mountains	59	K6
Widawka	71	H3
Wide Firth	56	E1
Widnes	55	G3
Widyan, Al	94	E6
Wielen	70	G2
Wielun	71	H3
Wien	68	F1
Wiener Neustadt	68	F2
Wieprz	71	K3
Wieren	70	D2
Wiesbaden	70	C3
Wigan	55	G3
Wiggins	128	H5
Wighill	55	H3
Wight, Isle of	53	F4
Wigmore	52	E2
Wigry, Jezioro	71	K1
Wigston	53	F2
Wigton	55	F2
Wigtown	54	E2
Wigtown Bay	54	E2
Wil	68	B2
Wilbur	122	E4
Wilcannia	113	J5
Wild Spitze	68	C2
Wilhelm II Land	141	F4
Wilhelm, Mount	114	D3
Wilhelm-Pieck-Stadt	70	F3
Wilhelmshaven	70	C2
Wilkes-Barre	125	N6
Wilkes Land	141	J4
Wilkhaven	56	E3
Wilkins Sound	120	D2
Willamette	122	B5
Willard	126	G6
Willaumez Peninsula	114	D2
Willemstad	136	D1
Willeroo	112	G2
William, Mount	113	J6
Williams Australia	112	D5
Williams U.S.A.	122	C8
Williamsburg	125	M8
Williams Lake	119	L5
Williamson	124	J8
Williamsport	125	M6
Williamston	129	P3
Willingboro	125	N6
Willington Derbyshire, U.K.	53	F2
Willington Durham, U.K.	55	H2
Willipa Bay	122	B4
Willis Group	110	M5
Williston South Africa	108	D6
Williston Florida, U.S.A.	129	L6
Williston N.Dakota, U.S.A.	123	N3
Williston Lake	118	L4
Williton	52	D3
Willmar	124	C4
Willoughby-on-the-Wolds	53	F2
Willow Bunch	123	M3
Willow Springs	124	E8
Wills, Lake	112	F3
Wilmington Australia	113	H5
Wilmington N.Carolina, U.S.A.	129	P3
Wilmington New Jersey, U.S.A.	125	N7
Wilmot Passage	115	A6
Wilmslow	55	G3
Wilson	129	P3
Wilson's Promontory	113	K6
Wilstedt	70	C2
Wilton	53	F3
Wiltshire	53	F3
Wiluna	112	E4
Wimbleball Lake	52	D3
Wimborne Minster	53	F4
Wincanton	52	E3
Winchcombe	53	F3
Winchelsea	53	H4
Winchester U.K.	53	F3
Winchester Kentucky, U.S.A.	124	H8
Winchester Tennessee, U.S.A.	129	J3
Winchester Virginia, U.S.A.	125	L7
Wind	118	H2
Winder	129	L4
Windermere Canada	122	G2
Windermere U.K.	55	G2
Windermere, Lake	55	G2
Windhoek	108	C4
Windischgarsten	68	E2
Windom	124	C5
Windorah	113	J4
Wind River Range	123	K6
Windrush	53	F3
Windsor Australia	113	L5
Windsor Newfoundland, Canada	121	Q8
Windsor Ontario, Canada	124	J5
Windsor Quebec, Canada	125	Q4
Windsor U.K.	53	G3
Windsor U.S.A.	129	P3
Windsor, Lake	133	L4
Windward Islands	133	S7
Windward Passage	133	K5
Winfield Alabama, U.S.A.	129	J4
Winfield Kansas, U.S.A.	128	D2
Winisk Canada	121	J7
Winisk Canada	121	J6
Winkler	123	R3
Winneba	104	E4
Winnemucca	122	F7
Winnenvicca, Lake	122	E7
Winner	123	Q6
Winnfield	128	F5
Winnibigoshish Lake	124	C3
Winning Pool	112	C3
Winnipeg Canada	123	R3
Winnipeg Canada	123	S2
Winnipeg, Lake	123	R2
Winnipegosis, Lake	119	Q5
Winnipesaukee, Lake	125	Q5
Winnsboro	128	G4
Winona Minnesota, U.S.A.	124	E4
Winona Mississippi, U.S.A.	128	H4
Winschoten	64	G2
Winsford	55	G3
Winslow U.K.	53	G3
Winslow U.S.A.	126	G3
Winslow Reef	111	U2
Winston-Salem	129	M2
Winterbourne Abbas	52	E4
Winter Garden	129	M6
Winterthur	68	B2
Wintinna	113	G4
Winton Australia	113	J3
Winton New Zealand	115	B7
Wiqia	86	C4
Wirksworth	55	H3
Wirraminna	113	H5
Wisbech	53	H2
Wisconsin U.S.A.	124	E5
Wisconsin U.S.A.	124	E4
Wisconsin U.S.A.	124	F4
Wisconsin Rapids	124	F4
Wishaw	57	E5
Wislany, Zalew	71	H1
Wislok	71	K3
Wismar	70	D2
Wissembourg	64	G4
Wistanstow	52	E2
Witbank	108	E5
Witham Essex, U.K.	53	H3
Witham Lincolnshire, U.K.	55	J3
Witheridge	52	D4
Withernsea	55	J3
Withington Gloucestershire, U.K.	53	F3
Withington Hereford and Worcester, U.K.	52	E2
Witney	53	F3
Witten	70	B3
Wittenberg	70	E3
Wittenberge	70	D2
Wittingen	70	D2
Witti Range	90	F5
Wittstock	70	E2
Witu	107	H3
Witu Islands	114	D2
Wkra	71	J2
Wladyslawowo	71	H1
Wloclawek	71	H2
Wlodawa	71	K3
Wloszczowa	71	H3
Wodzislaw	71	J3
Wodzislaw Slaski	71	H3
Woitape	114	D3
Wokam	91	J7
Woken	88	C2
Woking	53	G3
Wokingham	53	G3
Wolds, The	55	J3
Wolf	124	F4
Wolf Point	123	M3
Wolfsberg	68	E2
Wolfsburg	70	D2
Wolf, Volcan	136	A7
Wolin	70	F2
Wollaston, Cape	119	M1
Wollaston, Islas	139	C11
Wollaston Lake	119	Q4
Wollaston Peninsula	119	M2
Wollongong	113	L5
Wologisi Mountains	104	C4
Wolomin	71	J2
Wolstenholme, Cape	120	L5
Wolsztyn	70	G2
Wolverhampton	53	E2
Wolverton	53	G2
Wolviston	55	H2
Wombourne	53	E2
Wombwell	55	H3
Wondoola	113	J2
Wonju	87	P4
Wonosobo	90	D7
Wonsan	87	P4
Wonthagg	110	L9
Wood	123	L3
Woodbourne	115	D4
Woodbridge	53	J2
Woodburn	113	L4
Woodhall Spa	55	J3
Woodland	126	B1
Woodlark Island	114	E3
Woodlark Islands	114	E3
Woodroffe, Mount	112	G4
Woodside	113	K6
Woods, Lake	113	G2
Woods, Lake of the	124	C2
Woods Point	113	K6
Woodstock Australia	113	J3
Woodstock New Brunswick, Canada	125	S3
Woodstock Ontario, Canada	125	K5
Woodstock U.K.	53	F3
Woodville New Zealand	115	E4
Woodville U.S.A.	128	E5
Woodward	128	C2
Woody Head	115	E2
Wooler	57	F5
Woonsocket	125	Q6
Wooramel	112	C4
Woore	52	E2
Wooton Wawen	53	F2
Wootton Bassett	53	F3
Worcester South Africa	108	C6
Worcester U.K.	52	E2
Worcester U.S.A.	125	Q5
Worgl	68	D2
Workington	55	F2
Worksop	55	H3
Worland	123	L5
Worms	70	C4
Worms Head	52	C3
Worth	70	C4
Worthing	53	G4
Wotu	91	G6
Wowoni	91	G6
Wragby	55	J3
Wrangel Island	116	B1
Wrangell	118	J4
Wrangle	55	K3
Wrath, Cape	56	C2
Wray	123	N7
Wreake	53	G2
Wreck Reef	113	M3
Wrecsam	55	G3
Wrexham	55	G3
Wrington	52	E3
Wroclaw	71	G3
Wronki	71	G2
Wrottesley, Cape	120	B3
Wroxham	53	J2
Wrzesnia	71	G2
Wubin	112	D5
Wubu	87	L4
Wuchang	87	P3
Wuchuan	87	L3
Wudayah	96	H8
Wudinna	113	H5
Wudu	93	K2
Wufeng	93	M2
Wugang	93	M3
Wuhai	87	K4
Wuhan	93	M2
Wuhu	87	M5
Wu Jiang	93	L3
Wukari	105	G3
Wuliang Shan	93	K4
Wuliaru	91	J7
Wulin	88	B3
Wumeng Shan	93	K3
Wuning	93	M3
Wunstorf	70	C2
Wuntho	93	J4
Wuping	87	M6
Wuppertal	70	B3
Wurarga	112	D4
Wurmsee	70	D5
Wurno	105	G3
Wurzburg	70	C4
Wurzen	70	E3
Wushi	86	D3
Wutonggou	86	H3
Wuvulu Island	114	C2
Wuxi Jiangsu, China	87	N5
Wuxi Sichuan, China	93	L2
Wuxing	87	N5
Wuxuan	93	L4
Wuyiling	88	B1
Wuying	88	B1
Wuyuan	87	K3
Wuzhi Shan	93	M5
Wuzhou	93	M4
Wye Derbyshire, U.K.	55	H3
Wye Gwent, U.K.	52	E3
Wylye	53	E3
Wymondham	53	J2
Wynard	123	M2
Wynbring	113	G5
Wyndham Australia	112	F2
Wyndham New Zealand	115	B7
Wynne	128	G3
Wyoming	123	K6
Wyoming Peak	122	J6
Wyre	55	G3
Wyre Forest	52	E2
Wyrzysk	71	G2
Wysokie	71	K3
Wyszogrod	71	J2
Wytheville	125	K8

X

Name	Page	Grid
Xaafuun	103	K5
Xaafuun, Raas	103	K5
Xai-Xai	109	F5
Xambioa	137	H5
Xangongo	106	C6
Xanten	70	B3
Xanthi	75	H2
Xapuri	136	D6
Xarardheere	103	J7
Xavantes, Serra dos	137	H6
Xegil	86	D3
Xenia	124	J7
Xiachengzi	88	C3
Xiaguan	93	K3
Xiahe	93	K1
Xiamen	87	M7
Xian	87	L4
Xian	93	L2
Xianfeng	93	L3
Xiangfang	93	M2
Xiang Jiang	93	M3
Xiangquan He	92	F2
Xiangtan	93	M3
Xiangyang	88	A3
Xianning	93	M3
Xian Xian	87	M4
Xianyang	93	L2
Xiaobai	88	B2
Xiao Hinggan Ling	87	P1
Xiaojiahe	88	D2
Xiao Shui	93	M3
Xicotepec	131	L7
Xieng Khouang	93	K5
Xifeng	93	L3
Xigaze	93	G3
Xiji	88	A2
Xi Jiang	93	M4
Xilin Guangxi, China	93	L4
Xilin Heilongjiang, China	88	B2
Xilin Hot	87	M3
Xilokastron	75	G3
Ximiao	86	H3
Xin Barag Youqi	87	M2
Xin Barag Zuoqi	87	M2
Xinchang	87	N6
Xinfeng Guangdong, China	87	L6
Xinfeng Jiangxi, China	87	L7
Xingan	93	M3
Xingcheng	87	N3
Xinglong Hebei, China	87	M3
Xinglong Heilongjiang, China	87	P1
Xinglongzhen	88	A2
Xingtai	87	L4
Xingtang	87	L4
Xingu	137	G4
Xingwen	93	K3
Xingxingxia	86	H3
Xinhua	93	M3
Xining	93	K1
Xinjiang	93	M1
Xinjiang Uygur Zizhiqu	92	F1
Xinjin	87	N4
Xinlin	87	M3
Xinmin	87	P2
Xinpu	87	M5
Xintai	87	M4
Xinwen	87	M4
Xinxiang	93	M1
Xinyang	93	M2
Xinyi Guangdong, China	93	M4
Xinyi Jiangsu, China	87	M5
Xinyi He	87	M5
Xinyuan	86	E3

Name	Page	Ref
Xinzhou	87	L4
Xiqing Shan	93	K2
Xique-Xique	137	J6
Xisha Qundao	93	M5
Xi Ujimqin Qi	87	M3
Xiushan	93	L3
Xixia	93	M2
Xixiang	93	L2
Xizang Gaoyuan	92	F2
Xizang Zizhiqu	92	F2
Xochimilco	131	K8
Xpujil	131	Q8
Xuanwei	93	K3
Xuchang	93	M2
Xuddur	107	H2
Xuefeng Shan	93	M3
Xunke	87	P2
Xuru Co	92	G2
Xushui	87	M4
Xuwen	93	M4
Xuyong	93	L3
Xuzhou	93	N2

Y

Name	Page	Ref
Yaan	93	K2
Yabassi	105	G5
Yablanitsa	73	H4
Yablis	132	F7
Yablonitse, Pereval	71	L4
Yablonov	71	L4
Yablonovyy Khrebet	85	J6
Yabrai Yanchang	86	J4
Yabrud	77	G6
Yabuyanos	136	C4
Yada	84	A3
Yadgir	92	E5
Yadkin	129	M2
Yadua	114	R8
Yaeyama-shoto	89	F11
Yafran	101	H2
Yagan	86	J3
Yagodnoye	85	R4
Yagodnyy	84	Ae5
Yahuma	106	D2
Yahyali	76	F3
Yaizu	89	G8
Yakacik	77	G4
Yakapinar	77	F4
Yakima *U.S.A.*	122	D4
Yakima *U.S.A.*	122	D4
Yako	104	E3
Yakoruda	73	G4
Yakovlevka	88	D3
Yakrik	86	E3
Yaksha	78	K3
Yakumo	88	H4
Yaku-shima	89	C10
Yakutat	118	H4
Yakutsk	85	M4
Yala	93	K7
Yalak	77	G3
Yalcizcam	77	K2
Yalinca	77	K4
Yalinga	102	D6
Yalkubul, Punta	131	Q7
Yallourn	113	K6
Yalong Jiang	93	K3
Yalova	76	C2
Yalpug	73	K2
Yalpug, Ozero	73	K3
Yalta	79	E7
Yaltushkov	73	J1
Yalu	87	P3
Yalu He	87	N2
Yalutorovsk	84	Ae5
Yalvac	76	D3
Yamagata	89	H6
Yamaguchi	89	C8
Yamal, Poluostrov	84	Ae2
Yaman Dagi	77	G3
Yambering	104	C3
Yambio	102	E7
Yambol	73	J4
Yamdena	91	J7
Yamethin	93	J4
Yamgort	78	L3
Yamin, Puncak	91	K6
Yamma Yamma, Lake	113	J4
Yamoussoukro	104	D4
Yampa	123	L7
Yamparaez	138	D3
Yampol	73	K1
Yam, Ramlat	96	G8
Yamsk	85	S5
Yamuna	92	E3
Yamunanagar	92	E2
Yamyshevo	84	B6
Yamzho Yumco	93	H3
Yana	85	P2
Yanam	92	F5
Yanan	93	L1
Yanaul	78	J4
Yanbual Bahr	96	D4
Yancheng	87	N5
Yanchi	87	K4
Yanchuan	87	L4
Yande	114	V16
Yandrakinot	118	A3
Yandun	86	F3
Yangarey	78	L2
Yangchun	93	M4
Yanghe	87	M5
Yangjiang	93	M4
Yangquan	87	L4
Yangshan	93	M4
Yangshuo	93	M4
Yangtze	93	L2
Yangyang	88	B6
Yangzhou	87	M5
Yanina	75	F3
Yanji	88	B4
Yankton	123	R6
Yanqi	86	F3
Yanshou	88	B3
Yantai	87	N4
Yantra	73	H4
Yanxing	88	C2
Yanzhou	87	M4
Yao	102	C5
Yaoquanzi	86	H4
Yaounde	105	H5
Yaoxiaolong	88	A1
Yapen	91	K6
Yapen, Selat	91	K6
Yap Islands	91	K4
Yaprakali	76	E2
Yaqui	127	H6
Yar *U.K.*	53	F4
Yar *Russia*	78	J4
Yaraka	113	J3
Yaransk	78	H4
Yarashev	73	J1
Yardley Hastings	53	G2
Yare	53	J2
Yarenga	78	H3
Yarensk	78	H3
Yariga-take	89	F7
Yarim	96	G9
Yarimca	76	C2
Yaritagua	136	D2
Yarkant He	92	E1
Yarkovo	84	Ae5
Yarlung Zangbo Jiang	93	H3
Yarma	76	E4
Yarmolintsy	73	J1
Yarmouth	121	N9
Yarongo	84	Ae3
Yaroslavl	78	F4
Yarraloola	112	D3
Yarra Yarra Lakes	112	D4
Yarroto	84	A3
Yarrow	57	E5
Yar Sale	84	A3
Yarsomovy	84	A4
Yartsevo *Russia*	84	D4
Yartsevo *Russia*	78	E4
Yarty	52	D4
Yarumal	136	B2
Yary	84	Ae3
Yasawa	114	Q8
Yasawa Group	114	Q8
Yaselda	71	L2
Yashbum	96	H9
Yashiro-jima	89	D9
Yashkul	79	H6
Yasin	92	D1
Yasinya	71	L4
Yasnaya Polyana	88	F3
Yass	113	K5
Yasuj	95	K6
Yasun Burun	77	G2
Yata	136	D6
Yatagan	76	C4
Yate	114	X17
Yates Center	128	E2
Yates Point	115	A6
Yathkyed Lake	119	R3
Yatsushiro	89	C9
Yatta Plateau	107	G3
Yatton	52	E3
Yauri Espinar	136	C6
Yavatmal	92	E4
Yavi, Cerro	136	D2
Yavlenka	84	Ae6
Yavorov	71	K4
Yavr	62	N2
Yavu	77	G3
Yavuzeli	77	G4
Yawatahama	89	D9
Yawng-hwe	93	J4
Yawri Bay	104	C4
Ya Xian	93	L5
Yaxley	53	G2
Yaya	84	D5
Yaygin	77	J3
Yayla	77	J3
Yayladagi	77	G5
Yazd	95	M6
Yazd-e Khvast	95	L6
Yazihan	77	H3
Yazoo City	128	G4
Yazovir Dimitrov	73	H4
Ybbs	68	E1
Ydseram	105	H3
Ye	93	J5
Yealmpton	52	C4
Yecla	67	F3
Yedinka	88	G2
Yedinsty	79	D6
Yedoma *Russia*	78	G3
Yedoma *Russia*	78	J2
Yedondin	85	J6
Yeeda River	112	E2
Yefira	75	G3
Yefremov	79	F5
Yegorova, Mys	88	F3
Yegoryevsk	78	F4
Yei	102	F7
Yeijo, Cerro	136	B4
Yekaterininka	78	L3
Yekaterinoslavka	85	M6
Yekhegnadzor	77	L3
Yelabuga	78	J4
Yelantsy	84	H6
Yelets	79	F5
Yeletskiy	78	L2
Yelizarovo	84	Ae4
Yelizavety, Mys	85	Q6
Yelkenli	77	K3
Yell	56	A1
Yellandu	92	F5
Yellel	67	G5
Yellowhead Pass	119	M5
Yellowknife *Canada*	119	N3
Yellowknife *Canada*	119	N3
Yellow River	87	M4
Yellow Sea	87	N4
Yellowstone	123	M4
Yellowstone Lake	123	J5
Yell Sound	56	A1
Yelnya	78	E5
Yemen, *Republic of*	96	G9
Yemetsk	78	G3
Yemtsa	78	G3
Yen Bai	93	K4
Yendi	104	E4
Yengisar *China*	86	D4
Yengisar *China*	86	E3
Yengue	105	G5
Yenice *Turkey*	76	B3
Yenice *Turkey*	77	F3
Yenice *Turkey*	76	F4
Yeniceoba	76	E3
Yenikem	76	E3
Yenikoy *Turkey*	77	G4
Yenikoy *Turkey*	77	K2
Yenipazar	76	C4
Yenisarbademli	76	D4
Yenisehir	76	C2
Yenisey	84	D3
Yeniseysk	84	E5
Yeniseyskiy Zaliv	84	C2
Yenotayevka	79	H6
Yeoryios	75	G4
Yeovil	52	E4
Yeraliyev	79	J7
Yerbent	95	P2
Yerbogachen	84	H4
Yerema	84	H4
Yerevan	77	L2
Yergeni	79	G6
Yerkoy	76	F3
Yermak	84	B6
Yermaki	84	H5
Yermakovo	84	D3
Yermitsa	78	J2
Yermolayevo	79	K5
Yerofey-Pavlovich	85	L6
Yerolimin	75	G4
Yershov	79	H5
Yerupaja, Cerro	136	B6
Yerushalayim	94	B6
Yesil	77	G2
Yesilcay	76	C2
Yesilgolcuk	76	F3
Yesilhisar	76	F3
Yesilkent	77	G4
Yesilova	76	C4
Yesilova	76	E3
Yesilyurt	77	G3
Yessey	84	G3
Yeste	66	E3
Yeu, Ile d'	65	B5
Yevlakh	79	H7
Yevpatoriya	79	E6
Yevreyskaya Ao	88	D1
Ye Xian	87	M4
Yeysk	79	F6
Y-Fenni	52	D3
Yhu	138	D5
Yian	87	P2
Yiannitsa	75	G2
Yibin	93	K3
Yichang	93	M2
Yicheng	93	M2
Yichun	87	P2
Yidu	93	M2
Yigilca	76	D2
Yilan	88	B2
Yildizeli	77	G3
Yimianpo	88	A3
Yimuhe	87	N1
Yinchuan	87	K4
Yindarlgooda, Lake	112	E5
Yingde	93	M4
Ying He	93	M2
Yingkou	87	N3
Yining	86	E3
Yin Shan	87	K3
Yinxian	87	N6
Yioura *Greece*	75	H4
Yioura *Greece*	75	H3
Yirga Alem	103	G6
Yirol	102	F6
Yishui	87	M4
Yithion	75	G4
Yitong	87	P3
Yi Xian	87	N3
Yixing	87	M5
Yiyang	93	M3
Yliharma	62	N4
Yli-kitka	62	N3
Yli-li	62	L4
Ylitornio	62	K3
Ylivieska	62	L4
Y Llethr	52	C2
Yntaly	86	C2
Yoakum	128	D6
Yogope Yaveo	131	M9
Yogyakarta	90	E7
Yojoa, Laguna de	132	D7
Yokadouma	105	J5
Yokkaichi	89	F8
Yokohama *Japan*	89	G8
Yokohama *Japan*	88	H5
Yokosuka	89	G8
Yokote	88	H6
Yola	105	H4
Yolaina, Cordillera de	132	E9
Yom, Mae Nam	93	J5
Yonabaru	89	H10
Yonago	89	D8
Yonam-dong	88	B5
Yon dok	89	B7
Yonezawa	89	H7
Yong-an	88	B5
Yongan	87	M6
Yongchang	86	J4
Yongchuan	93	L3
Yongdeng	93	K1
Yongfeng	87	M6
Yongfu	93	L4
Yonghe	87	L4
Yonghung	87	P4
Yongju	89	B7
Yongkang	87	N6
Yongren	93	K3
Yongsanpo	87	P4
Yongsheng	93	K3
Yonkers	125	P6
Yonne	65	E5
York *U.K.*	55	H3
York *Nebraska, U.S.A.*	123	R7
York *Pennsylvania, U.S.A.*	125	M7
York, Cape *Australia*	113	J1
York, Cape *Papua New Guinea*	114	C4
Yorke Peninsula	113	H6
Yorketown	113	H6
York Factory	119	S4
York, Kap	120	N2
Yorkshire Moors	55	J2
Yorkshire Wolds	55	J3
Yorkton	123	N2
York, Vale of	55	H2
Yoro	132	D7
Yosemite Valley	126	C2
Yosemite Village	126	C2
Yoshioka	88	H6
Yoshkar-Ola	78	H4
Yosu	87	P5
Yotsukura	89	H7
Youghal	59	G9
Youghal Bay	59	G9
Youhao	88	B2
You Jiang	93	L4
Youkounkoun	104	C3
Young	113	K5
Young, Cape	115	F6
Youngstown	125	K6
Youssoufia	100	D2
You Xian	93	M3
Youyang	93	L3
Yozgat	76	F3
Ypres	64	E3
Yreka	122	C7
Ysabel Channel	114	E2
Ysbyty Ifan	54	F3
Ysgubor-y-coed	52	D2
Yssingeaux	65	F6
Ystad	63	E9
Ythan	56	F3
Ytterbyn	62	K4
Ytterhogdal	63	F5
Yuanjiang	93	K4
Yuan Jiang	93	M3
Yuanling	93	M3
Yuanmou	93	K3
Yuanping	87	L4
Yuba City	126	B1
Yubari	88	H4
Yucatan Channel	132	E4
Yucebag	77	J3
Yuci	87	L4
Yudaokou	87	M3
Yudoma	85	P5
Yudu	87	M6
Yuendumu	112	G3
Yueqing	87	N6
Yuexi	93	N2
Yuexi He	93	K3
Yueyang	93	M3
Yug	78	H3
Yugorskiy Poluostrov	84	Ad3
Yugoslavia	72	D3
Yuhebu	87	K4
Yuhuan	87	N6
Yuilsk	84	Ae4
Yu Jiang	93	L4
Yukon	118	D3
Yukon Delta	118	C3
Yuksekova	77	L4

Name	Page	Grid
Yukta	84	H4
Yukutat Bay	118	H4
Yula	78	G3
Yuli	86	F3
Yulin *Guangxi, China*	93	M4
Yulin *Shaanxi, China*	87	K4
Yuma	126	E4
Yumen	86	H4
Yumenzhen	86	H3
Yumurtalik	77	F4
Yuna	133	N5
Yunak	76	D3
Yunaska Island	118	Ad9
Yuncheng	93	M2
Yungay	136	B5
Yunnan	93	K4
Yunotsu	89	D8
Yunta	113	H5
Yunxiao	87	M7
Yurga	84	C5
Yurgamysh	84	Ad5
Yuribey *Russia*	84	A3
Yuribey *Russia*	84	B2
Yurimaguas	136	B5
Yurla	78	J4
Yurya	78	H4
Yuryevets	78	G4
Yuryev Polskiy	78	F4
Yusef, Bahr	102	F2
Yushan	87	M6
Yushino	78	J2
Yushkozero	62	Q4
Yushu *Jilin, China*	87	P3
Yushu *Qinghai, China*	93	J2
Yushugou	86	F3
Yusta	79	H6
Yusufeli	77	J2
Yutian	92	F1
Yuty	138	E5
Yuxi	93	K4
Yu Xian	87	L4
Yuzha	78	G4
Yuzhno Kamyshovyy Khrebet	88	J2
Yuzhno-Sakhalinsk	88	J2
Yuzhnoye	88	J2
Yuzhnyy Bug	79	E6
Yverdon	68	A2
Yvetot	64	D4

Z

Name	Page	Grid
Zaandam	64	F2
Zabal Saghir, Nahr al	77	K5
Zabaykalsk	85	K7
Zab-e Kuchek	94	G3
Zabid	96	F9
Zabok	72	C2
Zabol	95	Q6
Zaboli	95	Q8
Zabren	71	G4
Zabrze	71	H3
Zaburunye	79	J6
Zacapa	132	C7
Zacapu	130	J8
Zacatecas	130	H6
Zacatecoluca	132	C8
Zacoalco	130	H7
Zadar	72	C3
Zadetkyi Kyun	93	J7
Zafora	75	J4
Zafra	66	C3
Zagan	70	F3
Zagazig	102	F1
Zagorsk	78	F4
Zagreb	72	C3
Zagros, Kuhha-ye	95	K6
Zagubica	73	F3
Zagyva	72	F2
Zahedan	95	Q7
Zahle	77	F6
Zahran	96	F8
Zahrat al Batin	94	F6
Zaindeh	95	L5
Zaire	106	C3
Zaire	106	D3
Zajecar	73	G4
Zakamensk	84	G6
Zakatly	79	H7
Zakharovka	86	C2
Zakhmet	95	R3
Zakho	94	F3
Zakho	77	K4
Zakinthos *Greece*	75	F4
Zakinthos *Greece*	75	F4
Zakros	75	J5
Zala	72	D2
Zalaegerszeg	72	D2
Zalalovo	72	D2
Zalau	73	G2
Zaleshchiki	73	H1
Zalim	96	F5
Zalingei	102	D5
Zamakh	97	H8
Zambales Mountains	91	G2
Zambeze	109	F3
Zambezi	106	D5
Zambia	107	E5
Zamboanga	91	G4
Zambrow	71	K2
Zamora *Ecuador*	136	B4
Zamora *Spain*	66	D2
Zamora de Hidalgo	130	H7
Zamosc	71	K3
Zancara	66	E3
Zanesville	124	K8
Zangezurskiy Khrebet	94	G2
Zanjan	94	J3
Zanjon	138	C6
Zante	75	F4
Zanthus	112	E5
Zanule	78	H3
Zanzibar	107	G4
Zanzibar Island	107	G4
Zaoyang	93	M2
Zaozernyy	84	E5
Zaozhuang	87	M5
Zapadna Morava	72	F3
Zapadnaya Dvina	78	E4
Zapadno Sibirskaya Ravnina	84	Ae4
Zapadnyy Chink Ustyurta	79	J7
Zapadnyy Sayan	84	E6
Zapata	128	C7
Zapata, Peninsula de	132	G3
Zapatosa	136	C2
Zapatoza, Cienaga de	133	L10
Zapiga	138	C3
Zapolyarnyy	62	P2
Zaporozhye	79	F6
Zapotlanejo	130	H7
Zap Suyu	77	K4
Zara *Turkey*	77	G3
Zara *Yugoslavia*	72	C3
Zaragoza *Colombia*	136	C2
Zaragoza *Spain*	67	F2
Zarand *Iran*	95	K4
Zarand *Iran*	95	N6
Zarandului, Muntii	73	G2
Zaranj	95	Q6
Zarasai	63	M9
Zarate	139	E6
Zaraysk	78	F5
Zaraza	136	D2
Zardak	95	P4
Zard Kuh	95	K5
Zaria	105	G3
Zarnesti	73	H3
Zarqa	94	C5
Zarqan	95	L7
Zary	70	F3
Zarzaitine	101	G3
Zarzis	101	H2
Zashchita	84	C6
Zaskar Mountains	92	E2
Zaslavl	71	M1
Zastron	108	E6
Zatec	70	E3
Zatishye	73	K2
Zator	71	H4
Zavitinsk	85	M6
Zavodskoy	84	C6
Zawiercie	71	H3
Zawr, Ra's az	97	J3
Zaysan	86	E2
Zaysan, Ozero	86	E2
Zbarazh	71	L4
Zbaszyn	70	F2
Zborov	71	L4
Zbruch	71	M4
Zdolbunov	71	M3
Zdunska Wola	71	H3
Zebak	92	D1
Zebirget	96	C5
Zeebrugge	64	E3
Zeerust	108	E5
Zefat	94	B5
Zehdernick	70	E2
Zei Badinan	94	F3
Zei Koya	94	F4
Zeitz	70	E3
Zelenoborskiy	62	Q3
Zelenodolsk	78	H4
Zelenogorsk	63	N6
Zelenogradsk	71	J1
Zelenokumsk	79	G7
Zelina	72	D3
Zella Mehlis	70	D3
Zell am See	68	D2
Zelva	71	L2
Zemaitija	63	K9
Zemetchino	79	G5
Zemgale	63	L8
Zemio	102	E6
Zemlya Bunge	85	Q1
Zemmora	67	G5
Zempoala	131	K8
Zempoaltepec	131	M9
Zemun	72	F3
Zenica	72	D3
Zepce	72	E3
Zerbst	70	E3
Zerkow	71	G2
Zermatt	68	A2
Zernograd	79	G6
Zerqan	75	F2
Zestafoni	77	K1
Zetouji	87	N4
Zeya *Russia*	85	M6
Zeya *Russia*	85	M6
Zeysk	85	M6
Zeytinbagi	76	C2
Zeytinlik	77	J2
Zezere	66	C2
Zgierz	71	H3
Zgorzelec	70	F3
Zhabe	71	L4
Zhalanash	84	Ae6
Zhamansor	79	J6
Zhamshi	86	C2
Zhanabas	86	B2
Zhanatas	86	B3
Zhangbei	87	L3
Zhangdian	87	M4
Zhangguangcai Ling	88	B3
Zhangiz-Tobe	86	E2
Zhangjiakou	87	L3
Zhangping	87	M6
Zhangpu	87	M7
Zhangzhou	87	M7
Zhanjiang	93	M4
Zhaoan	87	M7
Zhaoguang	88	A1
Zhaoqing	93	M4
Zhaotong	93	K3
Zhaoxing	88	C2
Zhaoyuan	87	P2
Zharbulak	86	F2
Zharma	86	E2
Zharyk	86	C2
Zhashkov	79	E6
Zhatay	85	M4
Zhaxigang	92	E2
Zhdanov	79	F6
Zhejiang	87	M6
Zhelaniya, Mys	80	H2
Zheldyadyr	84	Ae7
Zheleznodorozhnyy *Russia*	84	G5
Zheleznodorozhnyy *Russia*	71	J1
Zheleznodorozhnyy *Russia*	78	J3
Zheleznogorsk	79	F5
Zhenan	93	L2
Zhengan	93	L3
Zhenglan Qi	87	M3
Zhengzhou	93	M2
Zhenjiang	87	M5
Zhenyuan	93	L3
Zherdevka	79	G5
Zhigalovo	84	H6
Zhigansk	85	L3
Zhijiang	93	L3
Zhilaya Kosa	79	J6
Zhiloy, Ostrov	79	J7
Zhitkovichi	79	D5
Zhitomir	79	D5
Zhlobin	79	E5
Zhmerinka	79	D6
Zhob *Pakistan*	92	C2
Zhob *Pakistan*	92	C2
Zhodino	78	D5
Zhokhova, Ostrov	85	S1
Zholymbet	84	A6
Zhongba	92	F3
Zhongdian	93	J3
Zhongwei	93	L1
Zhong Xian	93	L2
Zhongyaozhan	87	P1
Zhoushan Dao	87	M6
Zhovten	73	L2
Zhucheng	87	M4
Zhukovka	79	E5
Zhulong	87	M4
Zhuozi	87	L3
Zhuxi	93	L2
Zhuzhou	93	M3
Ziama-Mansouria	67	J4
Zibo	87	M4
Zicavo	69	B5
Zidani Most	72	C2
Zidarovo	73	J4
Ziel, Mount	112	G3
Zielona Gora	70	F3
Ziesar	70	E2
Zigazinskiy	78	K5
Zigong	93	K3
Ziguinchor	104	B3
Zihuatanejo	131	J9
Zilair	79	K5
Zile	77	F2
Zilina	71	H4
Zima	84	G6
Zimapan	131	K7
Zimbabwe	108	E3
Zimkan	94	H4
Zimnicea	73	H4
Zimniy Bereg	78	G2
Zimovniki	79	G6
Zinapecuaro	131	J8
Zindajan	95	Q4
Zinder	101	G6
Zinjibar	96	G10
Zipaquira	136	C2
Zirje	72	C4
Zi Shui	93	M3
Zitacuaro	131	J8
Ziyun	93	L3
Zizhong	93	K3
Zlatibor	72	E4
Zlitan	101	H2
Zloczew	71	H3
Zlutice	70	E3
Zmigrod	71	G3
Zmiyevka	79	F5
Znamenka *Russia*	84	B6
Znamenka *Ukraine*	79	E6
Znamenskoye	84	A5
Znin	71	G2
Znojmo	70	G4
Zohreh	95	K6
Zoige	93	K2
Zolochev *Ukraine*	79	F5
Zolochev *Ukraine*	71	L4
Zolotinka	85	L5
Zolotonosha	79	E6
Zolotoy, Mys	88	G2
Zomba	107	G6
Zongo	106	C2
Zonguldak	76	D2
Zongyang	87	M5
Zonza	69	B5
Zorleni	73	J2
Zouar	102	C3
Zouerate	100	C4
Zrenjanin	72	F3
Zubayr, Jazair az	96	F9
Zuenoula	104	D4
Zufaf	96	E8
Zufar	97	M8
Zug	68	B2
Zugdidi	77	J1
Zugspitze	70	D5
Zujar	66	D3
Zula	96	D9
Zulia	133	L10
Zumbo	108	F3
Zumpango	131	K8
Zungeru	105	G4
Zuni	127	H3
Zuni Mountains	127	H3
Zunyi	93	L3
Zuo Jiang	93	L4
Zupanja	72	E3
Zuqqaq	96	E7
Zurich	68	B2
Zurichsee	68	B2
Zuru	105	G3
Zut	72	C4
Zutphen	64	G2
Zuwarah	101	H2
Zuyevka	78	J4
Zvishavane	108	F4
Zvornik	72	E3
Zwedru	104	D4
Zweibrucken	70	B4
Zwettl	68	E1
Zwickau	70	E3
Zwiesel	70	E4
Zwolen	71	J3
Zwolle	64	G2
Zyrardow	71	J2
Zyryanka *Russia*	84	C2
Zyryanka *Russia*	85	S3
Zyryanovsk	86	E2